MW00609916

THE
NEIL GAIMAN
LIBRARY

SNOW, GLASS, APPLES

ART AND ADAPTATION
COLLEEN DORAN

LETTERS
TODD KLEIN

COLOR FLATTING ASSISTANCE
VAL TRULLINGER

COVER
COLLEEN DORAN

THE PROBLEM OF SUSAN AND OTHER STORIES

ADAPTATION AND ART (*THE PROBLEM OF SUSAN, LOCKS*)
P. CRAIG RUSSELL

LETTERS (*THE PROBLEM OF SUSAN, LOCKS*)
GALEN SHOWMAN

ART (*OCTOBER IN THE CHAIR*)
SCOTT HAMPTON

LETTERS (*OCTOBER IN THE CHAIR*)
RICK PARKER

ART (*THE DAY THE SAUCERS CAME*)
PAUL CHADWICK

LETTERS (*THE DAY THE SAUCERS CAME*)
GASPAR SALADINO

COLORS (*THE PROBLEM OF SUSAN, LOCKS*)
LOVERN KINDZIERSKI

COVER
P. CRAIG RUSSELL
WITH LOVERN KINDZIERSKI

ONLY THE END OF THE WORLD AGAIN

ADAPTATION AND LAYOUTS
P. CRAIG RUSSELL

LETTERING
SEAN KONOT

ART
TROY NIXEY

COLORS
MATTHEW HOLLINGSWORTH

COVER
TROY NIXEY WITH MATTHEW HOLLINGSWORTH

CREATURES OF THE NIGHT

ART
MICHAEL ZULLI

LETTERING
TODD KLEIN

COVER
MICHAEL ZULLI

COVER BY
FÁBIO MOON

321

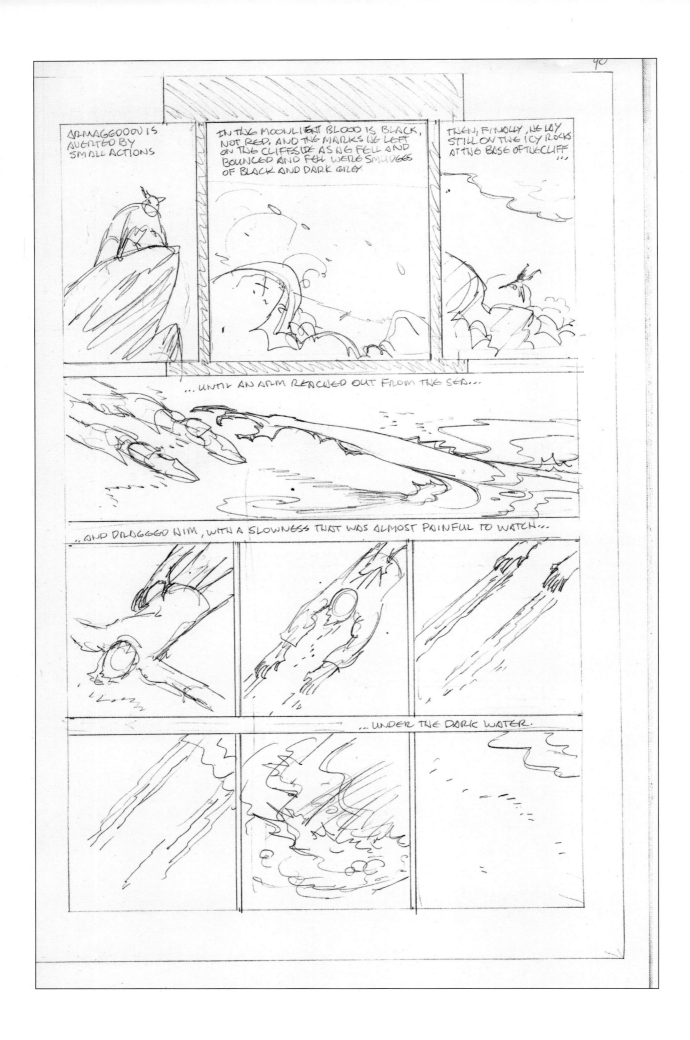

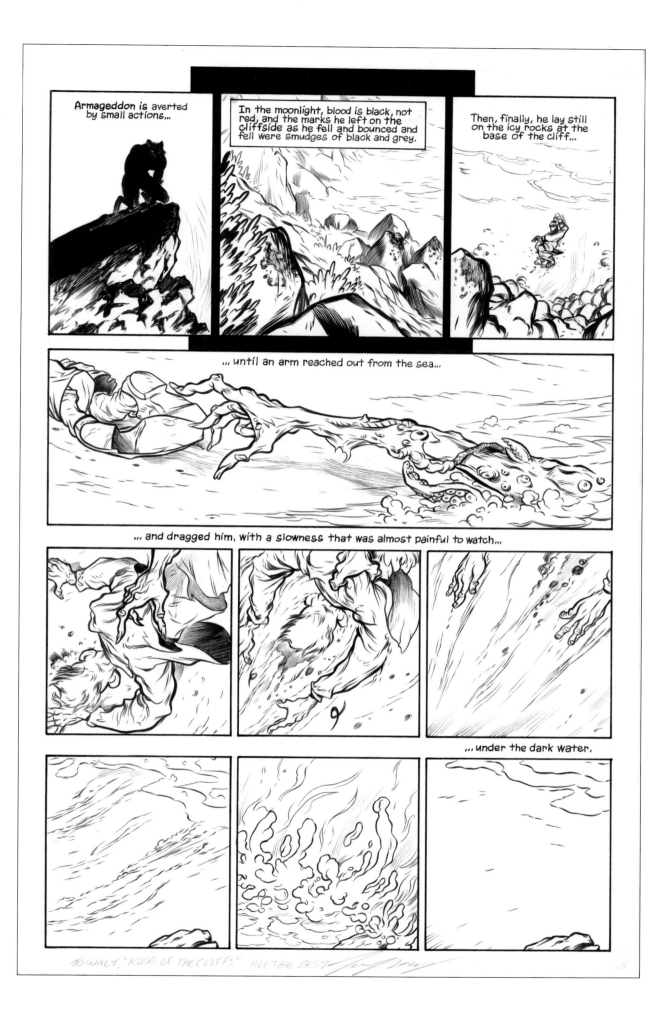

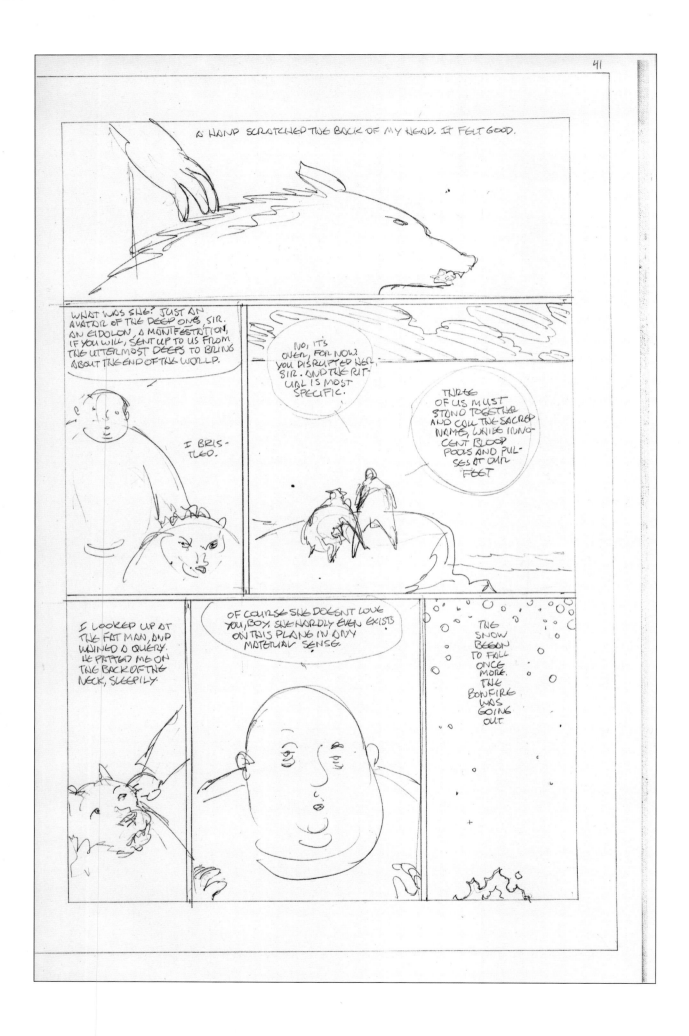

325

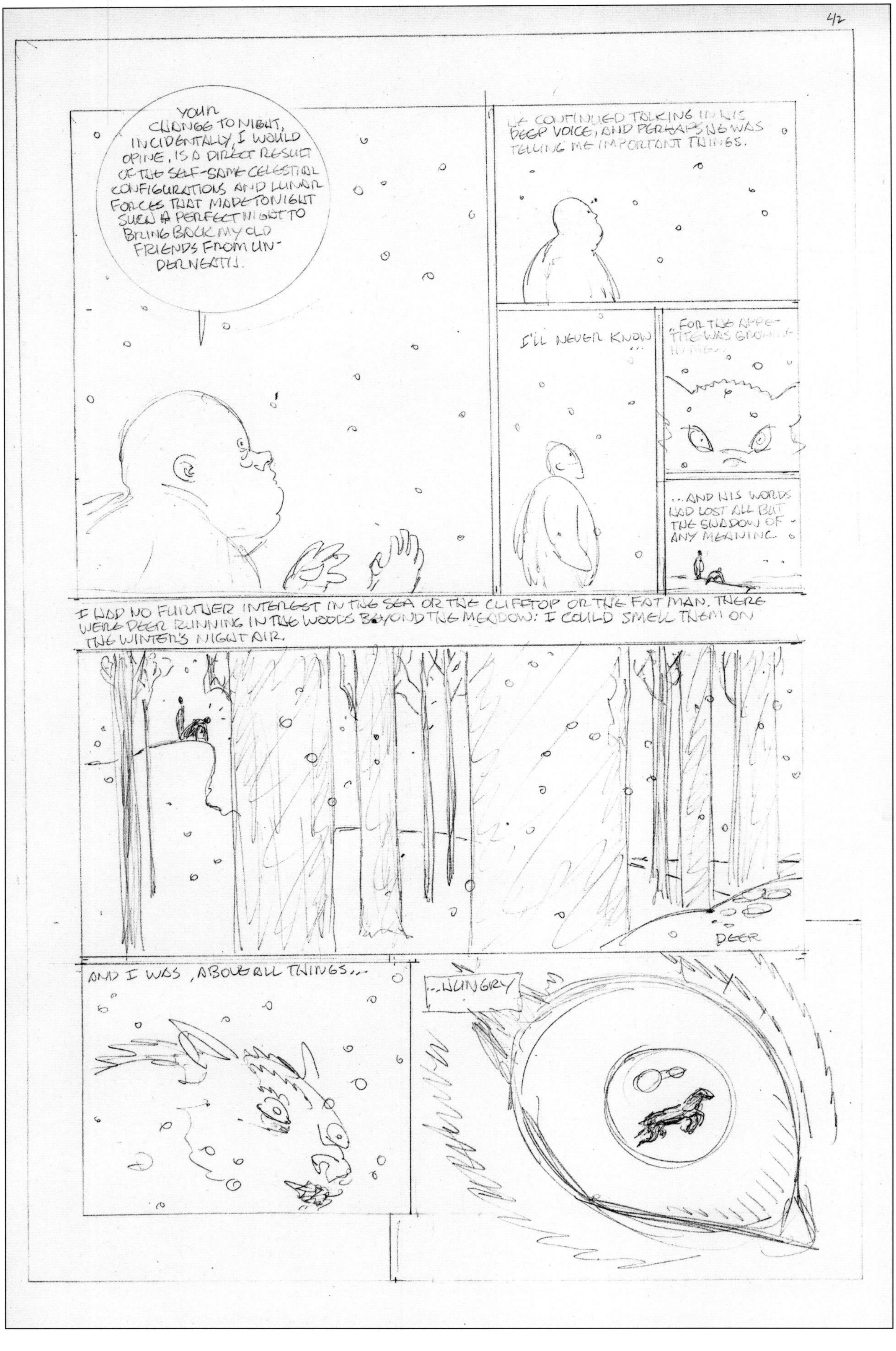
42
YOUR CHANGE TO NIGHT, INCIDENTALLY, I WOULD OPINE, IS A DIRECT RESULT OF THE SELF-SAME CELESTIAL CONFIGURATIONS AND LUNAR FORCES THAT MADE TONIGHT SUCH A PERFECT NIGHT TO BRING BACK MY OLD FRIENDS FROM UNDERNEATH.
HE CONTINUED TALKING IN HIS DEEP VOICE, AND PERHAPS HE WAS TELLING ME IMPORTANT THINGS.
I'LL NEVER KNOW...
...FOR THE APPETITE WAS GROWING IN ME...
...AND HIS WORDS HAD LOST ALL BUT THE SHADOW OF ANY MEANING.
I HAD NO FURTHER INTEREST IN THE SEA OR THE CLIFFTOP OR THE FAT MAN. THERE WERE DEER RUNNING IN THE WOODS BEYOND THE MEADOW: I COULD SMELL THEM ON THE WINTER'S NIGHT AIR.
DEER
AND I WAS, ABOVE ALL THINGS...
...HUNGRY

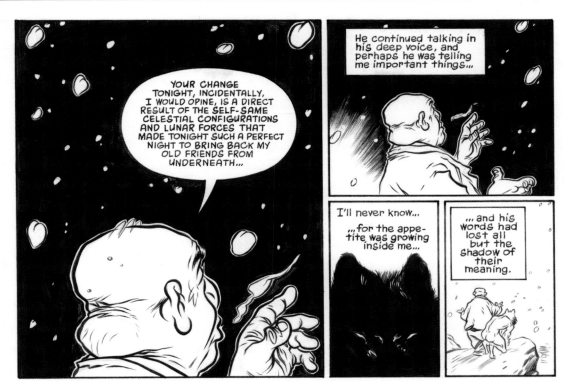

I had no further interest in the sea or the clifftop or the fat man. There were deer running in the woods beyond the meadow: I could smell them on the winter night's air.

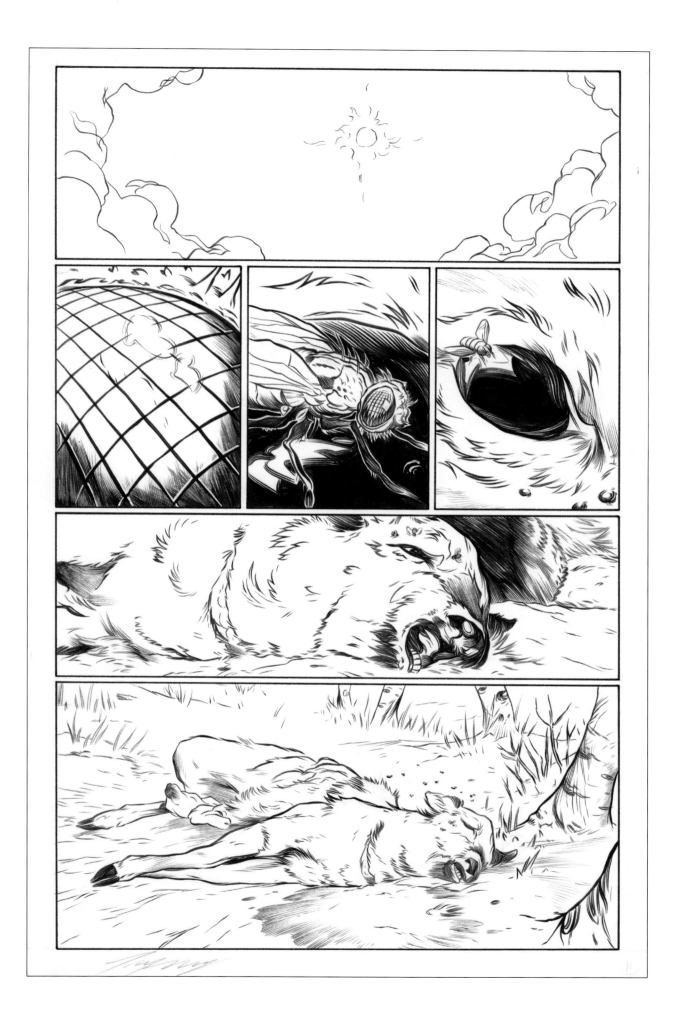

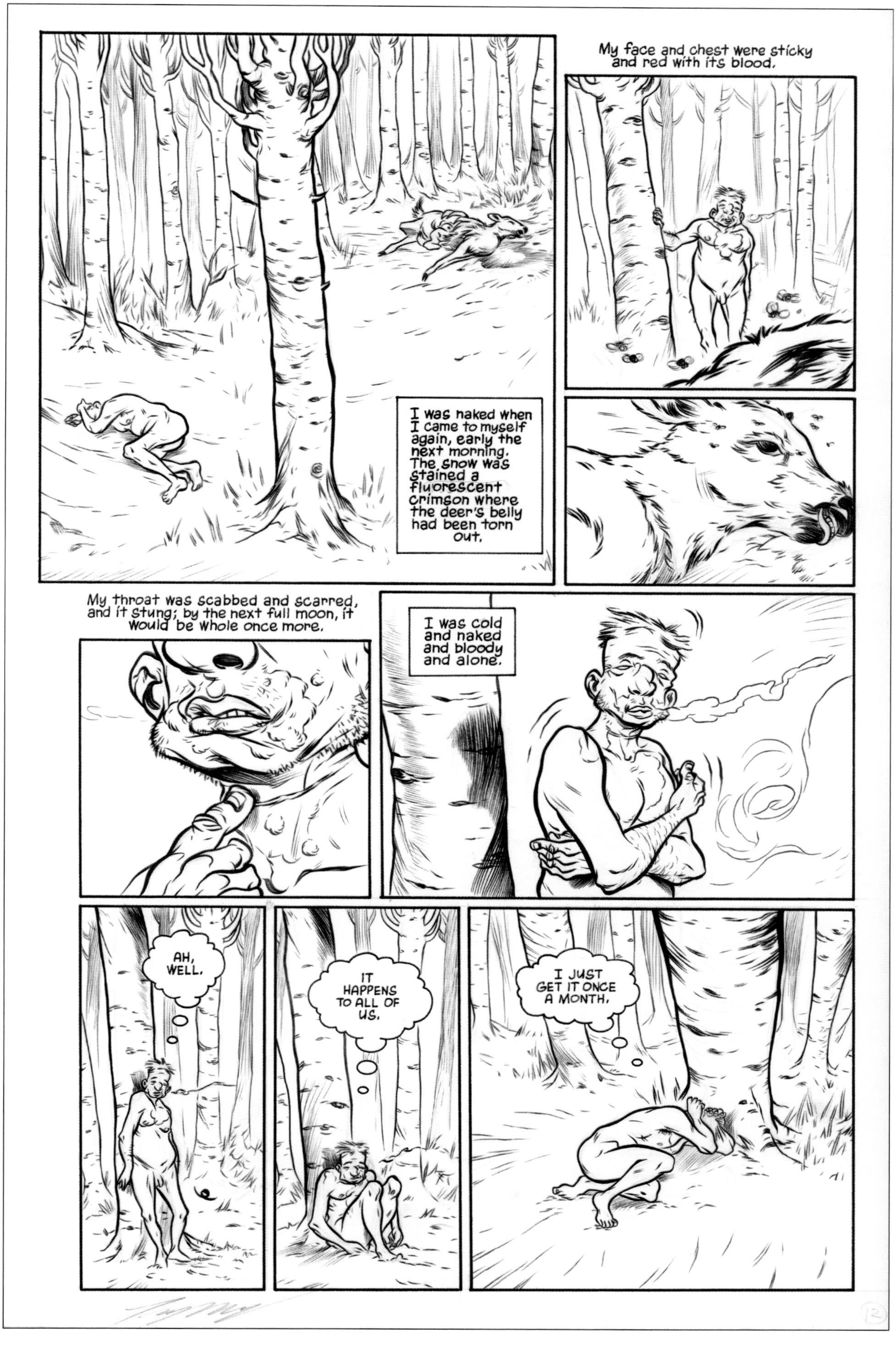
My face and chest were sticky and red with its blood.
I was naked when I came to myself again, early the next morning. The snow was stained a fluorescent crimson where the deer's belly had been torn out.
My throat was scabbed and scarred, and it stung; by the next full moon, it would be whole once more.
I was cold and naked and bloody and alone.
AH, WELL.
IT HAPPENS TO ALL OF US.
I JUST GET IT ONCE A MONTH.

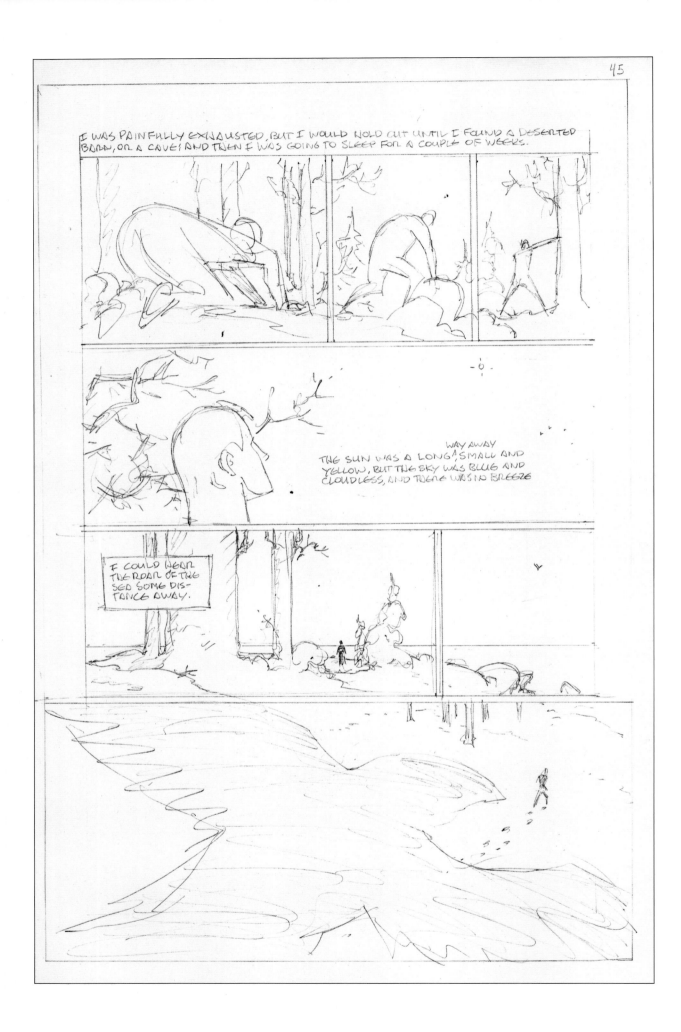

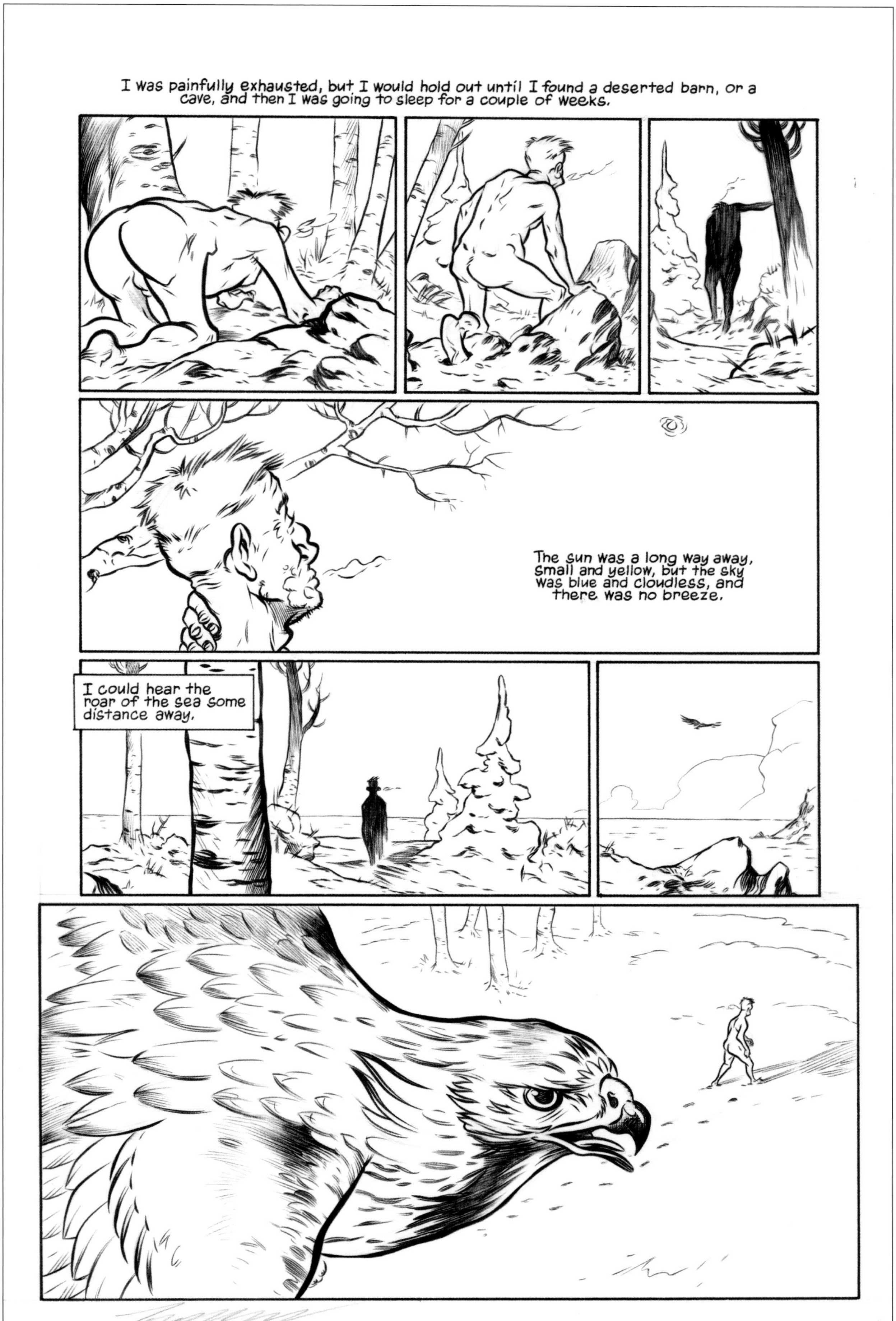
I was painfully exhausted, but I would hold out until I found a deserted barn, or a cave, and then I was going to sleep for a couple of weeks.
The sun was a long way away, small and yellow, but the sky was blue and cloudless, and there was no breeze.
I could hear the roar of the sea some distance away.

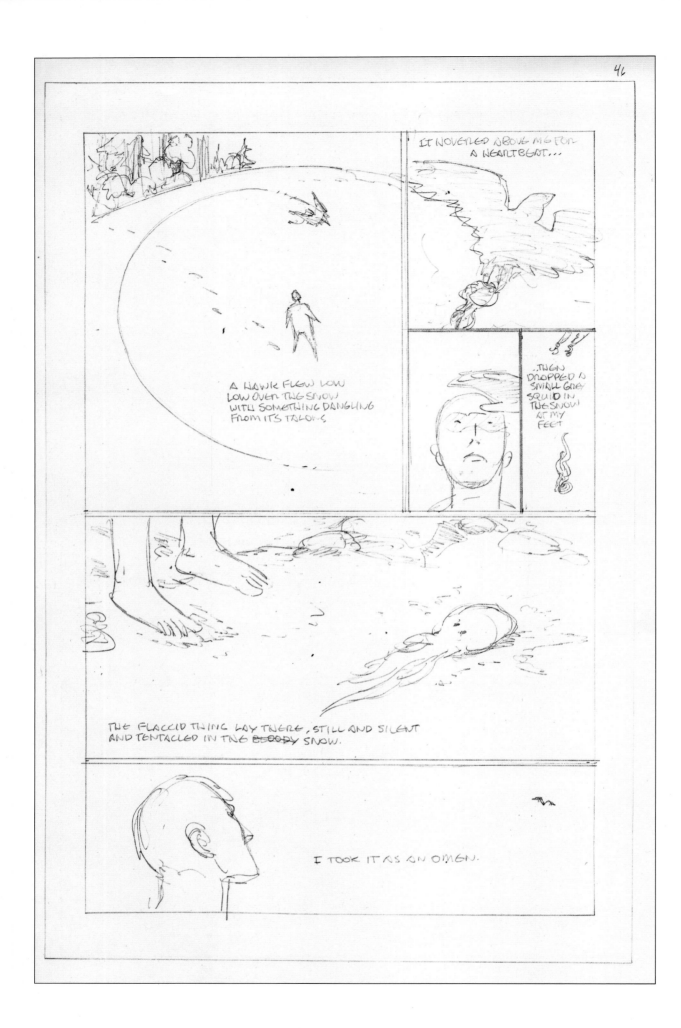

IT HOVERED ABOVE ME FOR A HEARTBEAT...

A HAWK FLEW LOW LOW OVER THE SNOW WITH SOMETHING DANGLING FROM ITS TALONS

...THEN DROPPED A SMALL GREY SQUID IN THE SNOW AT MY FEET

THE FLACCID THING LAY THERE, STILL AND SILENT AND TENTACLED IN THE BLOODY SNOW.

I TOOK IT AS AN OMEN.

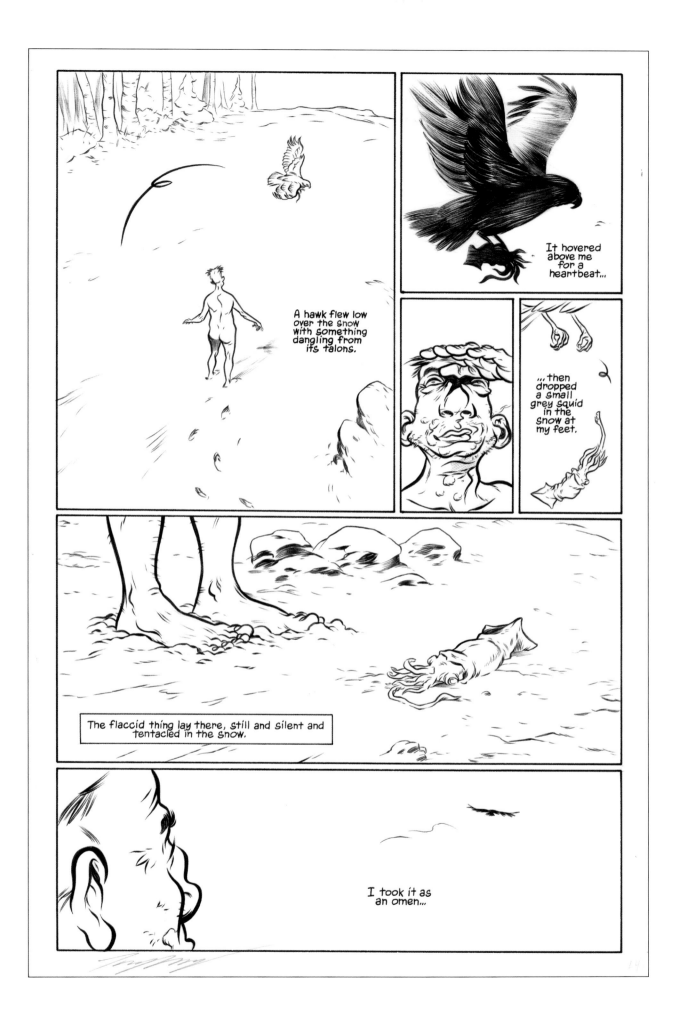

A hawk flew low over the snow with something dangling from its talons.

It hovered above me for a heartbeat...

...then dropped a small grey squid in the snow at my feet.

The flaccid thing lay there, still and silent and tentacled in the snow.

I took it as an omen...

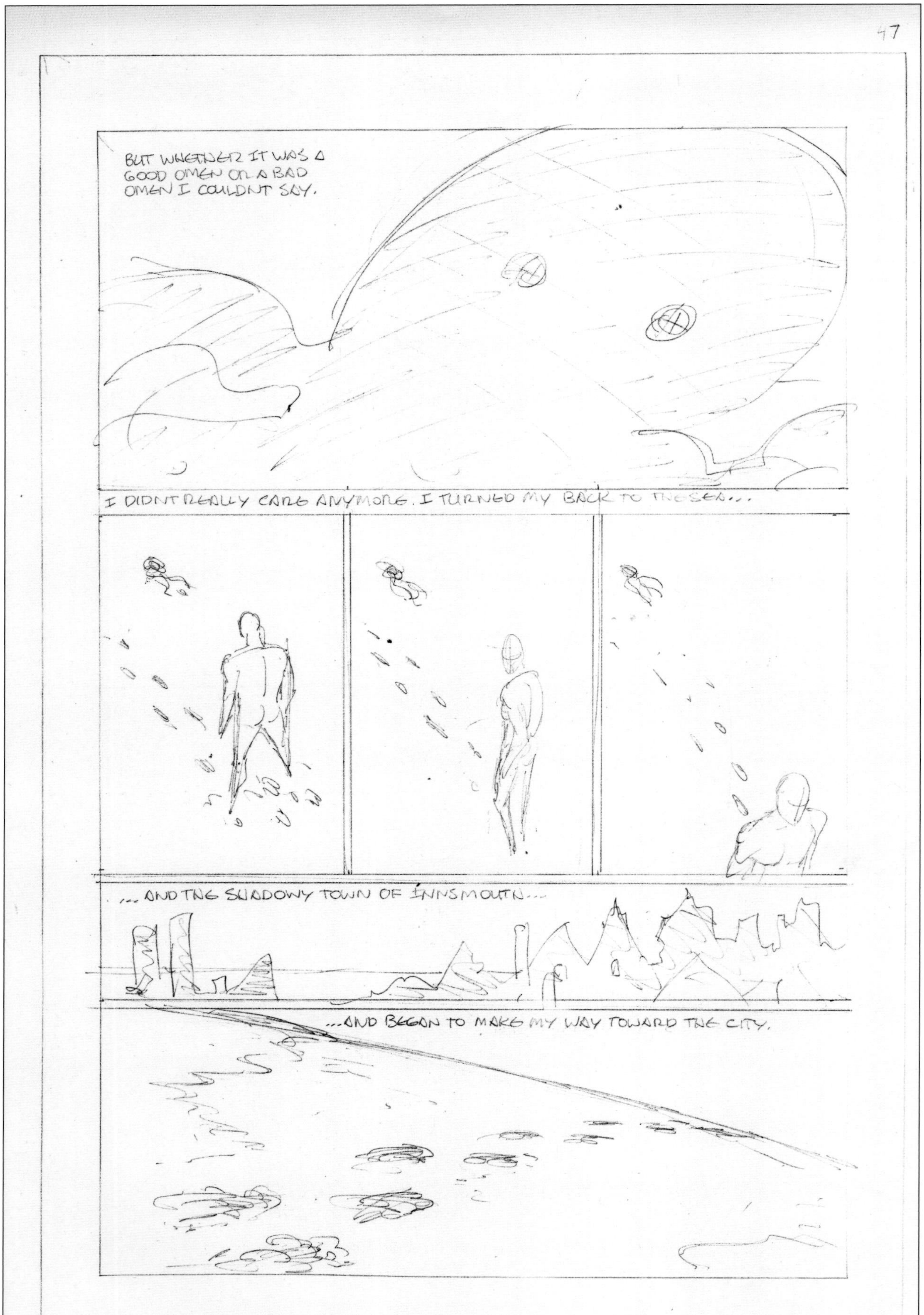
47
BUT WHETHER IT WAS A GOOD OMEN OR A BAD OMEN I COULDNT SAY.
I DIDNT REALLY CARE ANYMORE. I TURNED MY BACK TO THE SEA...
...AND THE SHADOWY TOWN OF INNSMOUTH...
...AND BEGAN TO MAKE MY WAY TOWARD THE CITY.

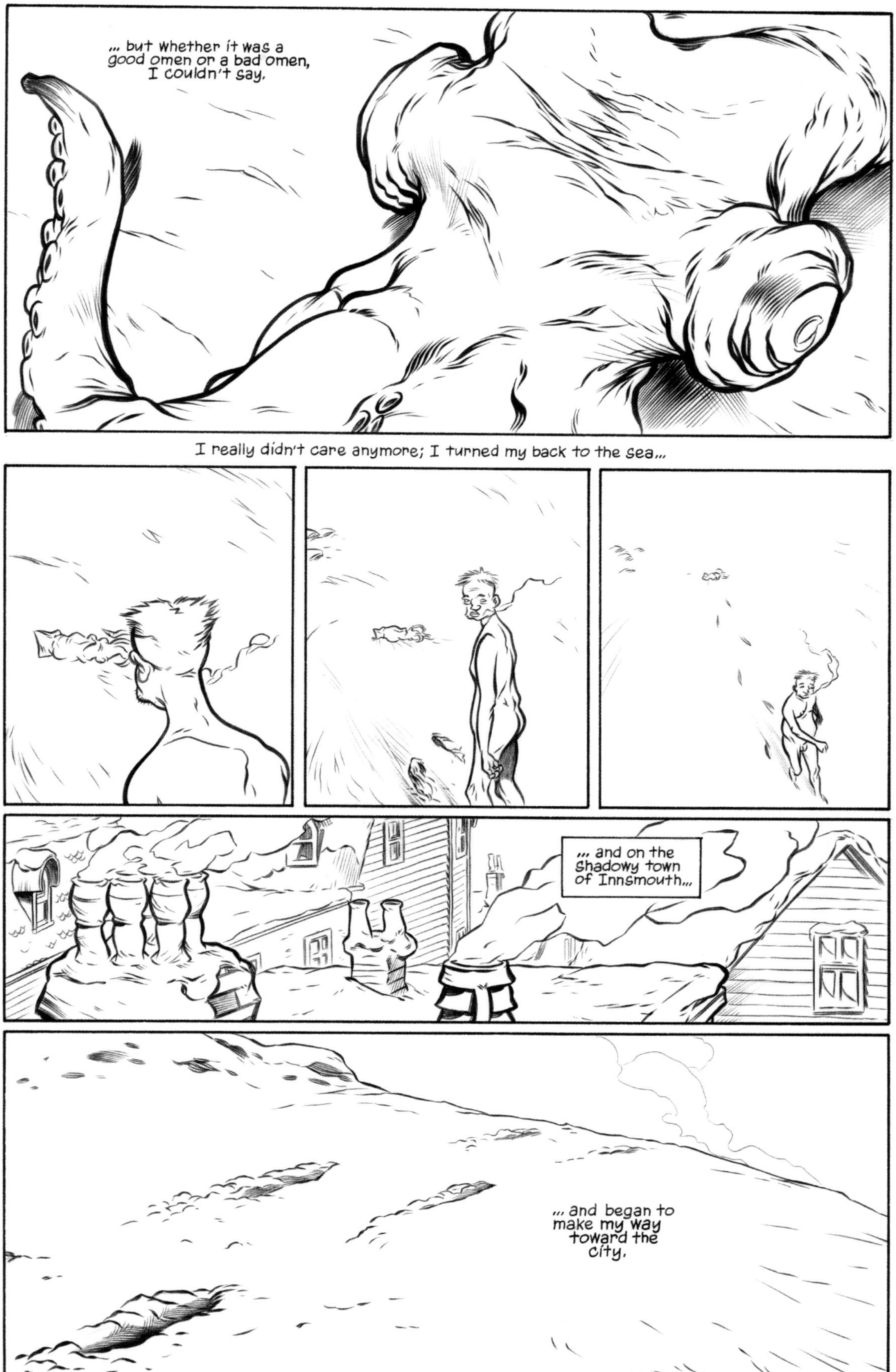
... but whether it was a good omen or a bad omen, I couldn't say.
I really didn't care anymore; I turned my back to the sea...
... and on the shadowy town of Innsmouth...
... and began to make my way toward the city.

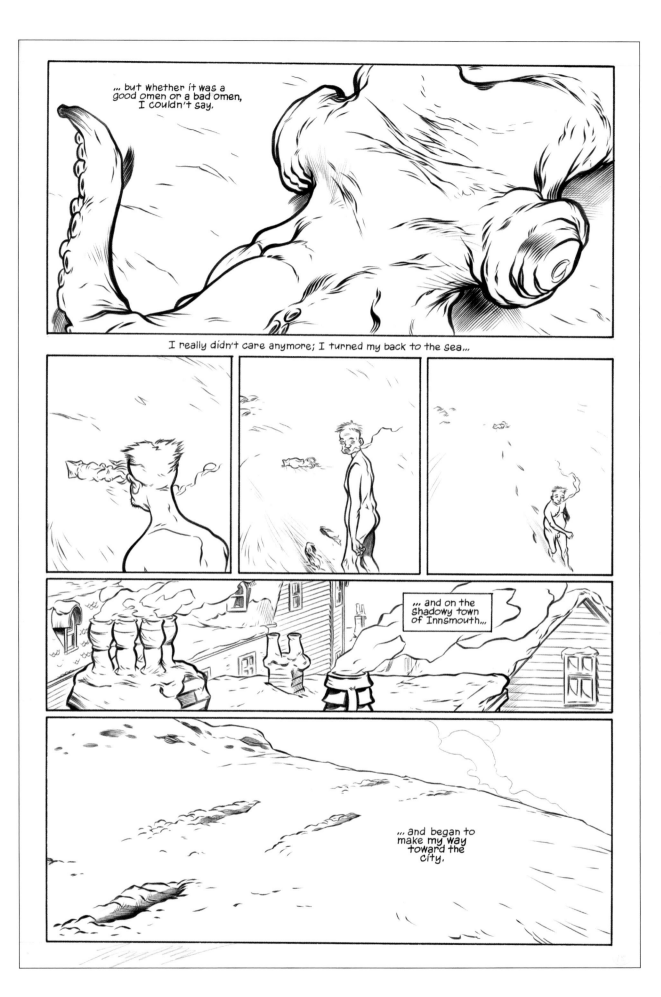

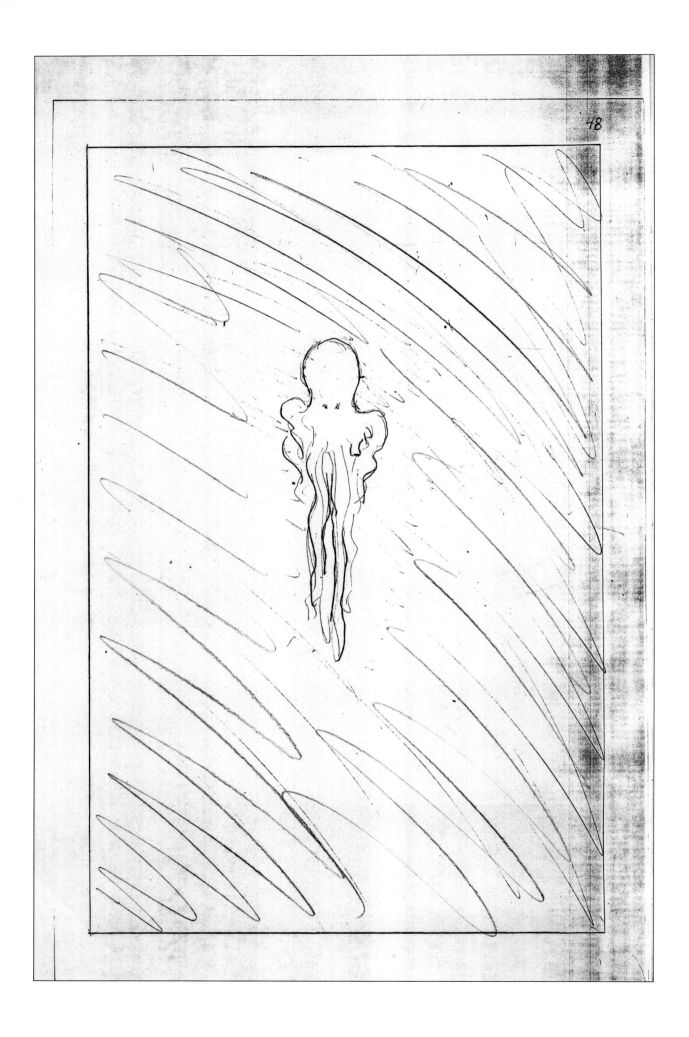

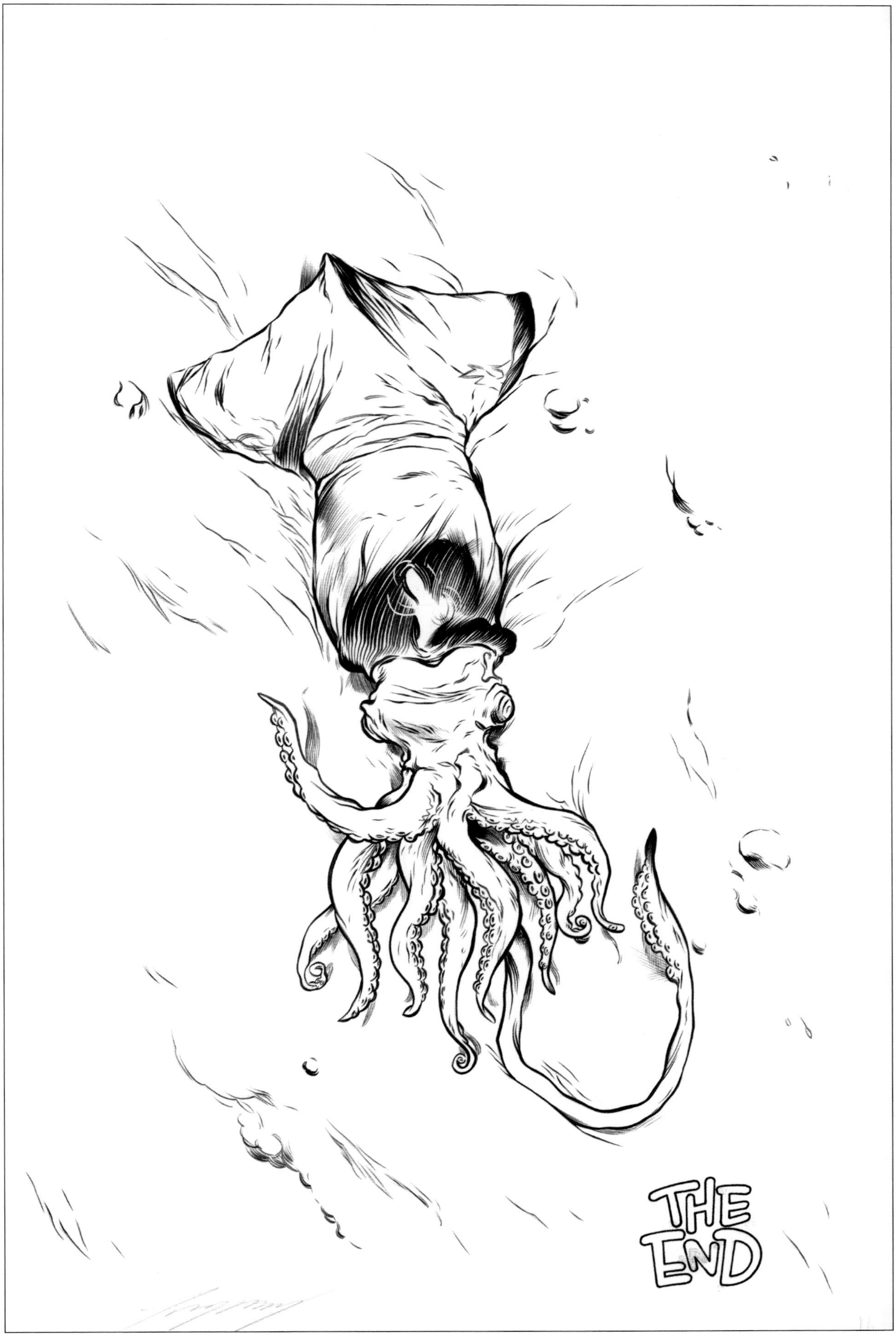
THE END

MORE TITLES FROM

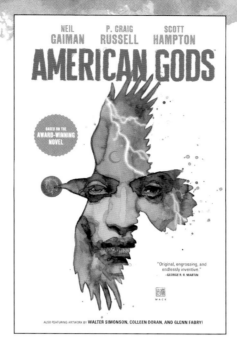

GABRIEL BÁ AND FÁBIO MOON!

"Twin Brazilian artists Fábio Moon and Gabriel Bá have made a huge mark on comics." —*Publishers Weekly*

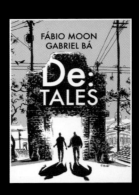

TWO BROTHERS
Fábio Moon Gabriel Bá

THE UMBRELLA ACADEMY
APOCALYPSE SUITE
NETFLIX

FÁBIO MOON
GABRIEL BÁ
De:
TALES

THE UMBRELLA ACADEMY: APOCALYPSE SUITE
Story by Gerard Way
Art by Gabriel Bá
TPB ISBN: 978-1-59307-978-9 | $17.99
Library Edition HC ISBN:
987-1-50671-547-6 | $39.99

THE UMBRELLA ACADEMY: DALLAS
Story by Gerard Way
Art by Gabriel Bá
TPB ISBN: 978-1-59582-345-8 | $17.99
Library Edition HC ISBN:
987-1-50671-548-3 | $39.99

THE UMBRELLA ACADEMY: HOTEL OBLIVION
Story by Gerard Way
Art by Gabriel Bá
TPB ISBN: 978-1-50671-142-3 | $19.99
Library Edition HC ISBN:
978-1-50671-646-6 | $39.99

PIXU: THE MARK OF EVIL
Story and art by Gabriel Bá, Becky Cloonan, Vasilis Lolos, and Fábio Moon
ISBN: 978-1-61655-813-0 | $14.99

B.P.R.D.: VAMPIRE
Story by Mike Mignola, Fábio Moon, and Gabriel Bá
Art by Fábio Moon and Gabriel Bá
ISBN: 978-1-61655-196-4 | $19.99

B.P.R.D.: 1946–1948
Story by Mike Mignola, Joshua Dysart, and John Arcudi
Art by Fábio Moon, Gabriel Bá, Paul Azaceta, and Max Fiumara
ISBN: 978-1-61655-646-4 | $34.99

NEIL GAIMAN'S HOW TO TALK TO GIRLS AT PARTIES
Story by Neil Gaiman
Art by Fábio Moon and Gabriel Bá
ISBN: 978-1-61655-955-7 | $17.99

TWO BROTHERS
Story and art by Gabriel Bá and Fábio Moon
ISBN: 978-1-61655-856-7 | $24.99

DE:TALES
Story and art by Gabriel Bá and Fábio Moon
ISBN: 978-1-59582-557-5 | $19.99

DARK HORSE BOOKS

AVAILABLE AT YOUR LOCAL COMICS SHOP OR BOOKSTORE!

To find a comics shop in your area, visit comicshoplocator.com. For more information or to order direct, visit DarkHorse.com

THE NEIL GAIMAN LIBRARY

• VOLUME 3 •

STORIES AND WORDS BY
NEIL GAIMAN

PUBLISHER
MIKE RICHARDSON

COLLECTION EDITOR
DANIEL CHABON

COLLECTION ASSISTANT EDITOR
CHUCK HOWITT

DESIGNERS
CINDY CACEREZ-SPRAGUE AND PATRICK SATTERFIELD

DIGITAL ART TECHNICIAN
ADAM PRUETT

SNOW, GLASS, APPLES

EDITORIAL
EDITOR DANIEL CHABON
ASSISTANT EDITOR CHUCK HOWITT

THE PROBLEM OF SUSAN AND OTHER STORIES

EDITORIAL
EDITOR DANIEL CHABON
ASSISTANT EDITOR BRETT ISRAEL

ONLY THE END OF THE WORLD AGAIN

EDITORIAL
COLLECTION EDITOR DANIEL CHABON
ORIGINAL SERIES EDITOR BOB SCHRECK
ASSISTANT EDITOR RACHEL ROBERTS

CREATURES OF THE NIGHT

EDITORIAL
SECOND EDITION EDITOR DANIEL CHABON
FIRST EDITION EDITOR DIANA SCHUTZ
SECOND EDITION ASSISTANT EDITOR CARDNER CLARK

SNOW, GLASS, APPLES: WITH RESPECT AND GRATITUDE, THE ARTIST WISHES TO ACKNOWLEDGE HER DEBT TO
HARRY CLARKE (IRISH ARTIST) 1889–1931
THE PROBLEM OF SUSAN AND OTHER STORIES: SPECIAL THANKS TO DIANA SCHUTZ

EXECUTIVE VICE PRESIDENT NEIL HANKERSON · CHIEF FINANCIAL OFFICER TOM WEDDLE · VICE PRESIDENT OF PUBLISHING RANDY STRADLEY · CHIEF BUSINESS DEVELOPMENT OFFICER NICK McWHORTER · CHIEF INFORMATION OFFICER DALE LaFOUNTAIN · VICE PRESIDENT OF MARKETING MATT PARKINSON · VICE PRESIDENT OF PRODUCTION AND SCHEDULING VANESSA TODD-HOLMES · VICE PRESIDENT OF BOOK TRADE AND DIGITAL SALES MARK BERNARDI · GENERAL COUNSEL KEN LIZZI · EDITOR IN CHIEF DAVE MARSHALL · EDITORIAL DIRECTOR DAVEY ESTRADA · SENIOR BOOKS EDITOR CHRIS WARNER · DIRECTOR OF SPECIALTY PROJECTS CARY GRAZZINI · ART DIRECTOR LIA RIBACCHI · DIRECTOR OF DIGITAL ART AND PREPRESS MATT DRYER SENIOR DIRECTOR OF LICENSED PUBLICATIONS MICHAEL GOMBOS · DIRECTOR OF CUSTOM PROGRAMS KARI YADRO · DIRECTOR OF INTERNATIONAL LICENSING KARI TORSON · DIRECTOR OF TRADE SALES SEAN BRICE

This volume collects *Snow, Glass, Apples*, *The Problem of Susan and Other Stories*, *Only the End of the World Again*, and *Creatures of the Night*.

Published by Dark Horse Books
A division of Dark Horse Comics LLC
10956 SE Main Street, Milwaukie, OR 97222

DarkHorse.com
Facebook.com/DarkHorseComics   Twitter.com/DarkHorseComics
To find a comics shop in your area, visit comicshoplocator.com.

First hardcover edition: May 2021
Ebook ISBN 978-1-50671-598-8
Hardcover ISBN 978-1-50671-595-7

10 9 8 7 6 5 4 3 2 1
Printed in China

TABLE OF
CONTENTS

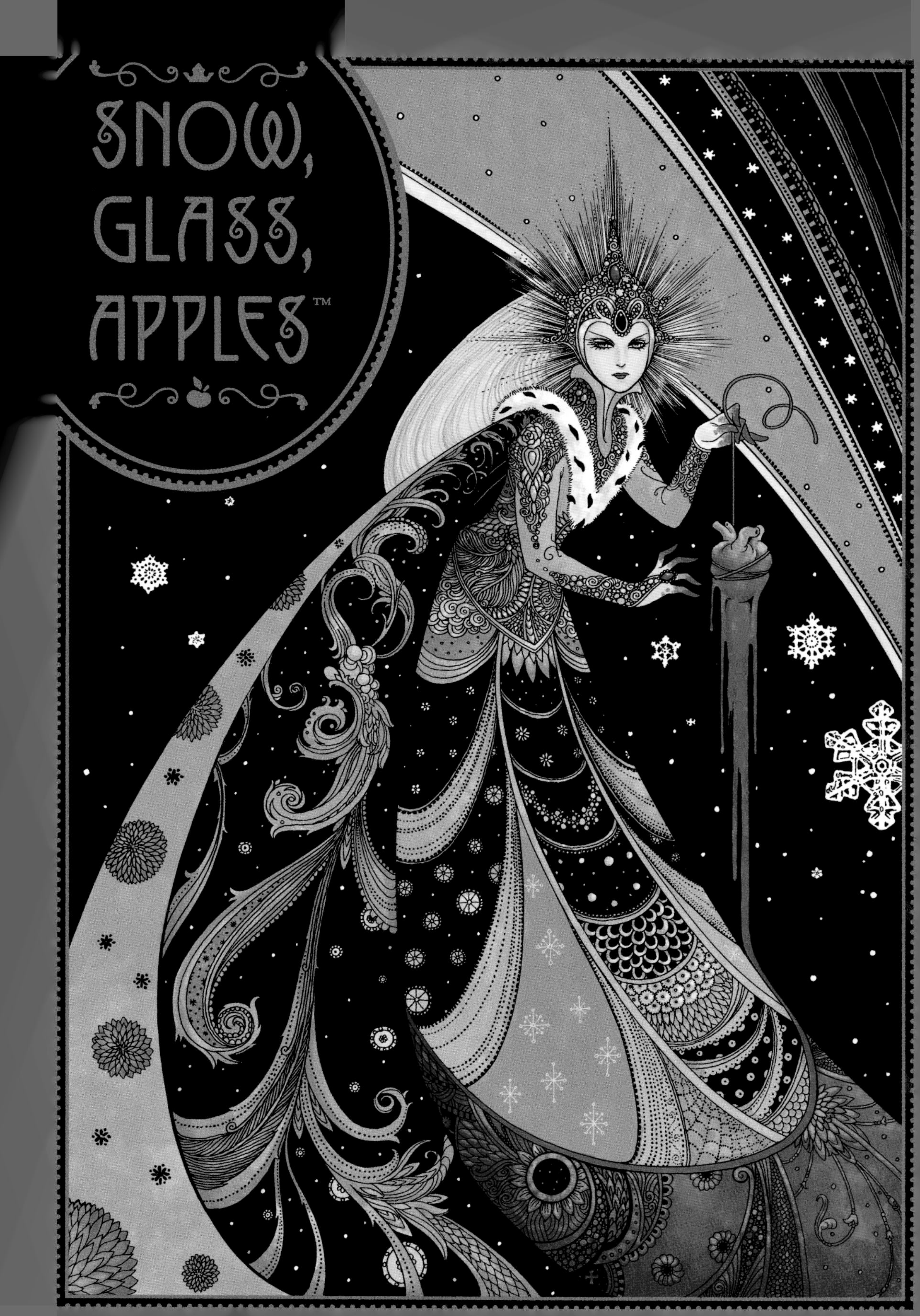
SNOW, GLASS, APPLES™

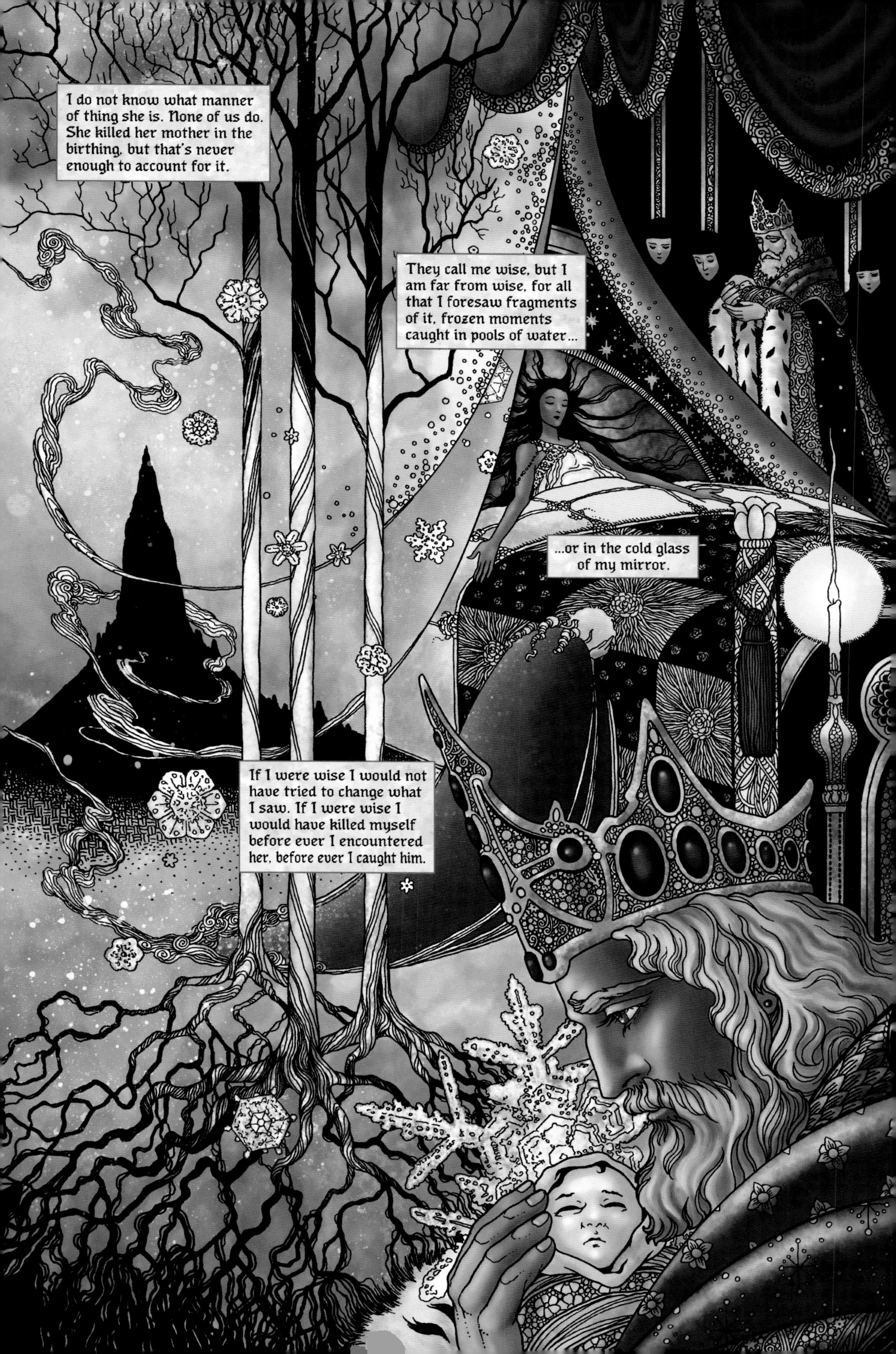
I do not know what manner of thing she is. None of us do. She killed her mother in the birthing, but that's never enough to account for it.
They call me wise, but I am far from wise, for all that I foresaw fragments of it, frozen moments caught in pools of water...
...or in the cold glass of my mirror.
If I were wise I would not have tried to change what I saw. If I were wise I would have killed myself before ever I encountered her, before ever I caught him.

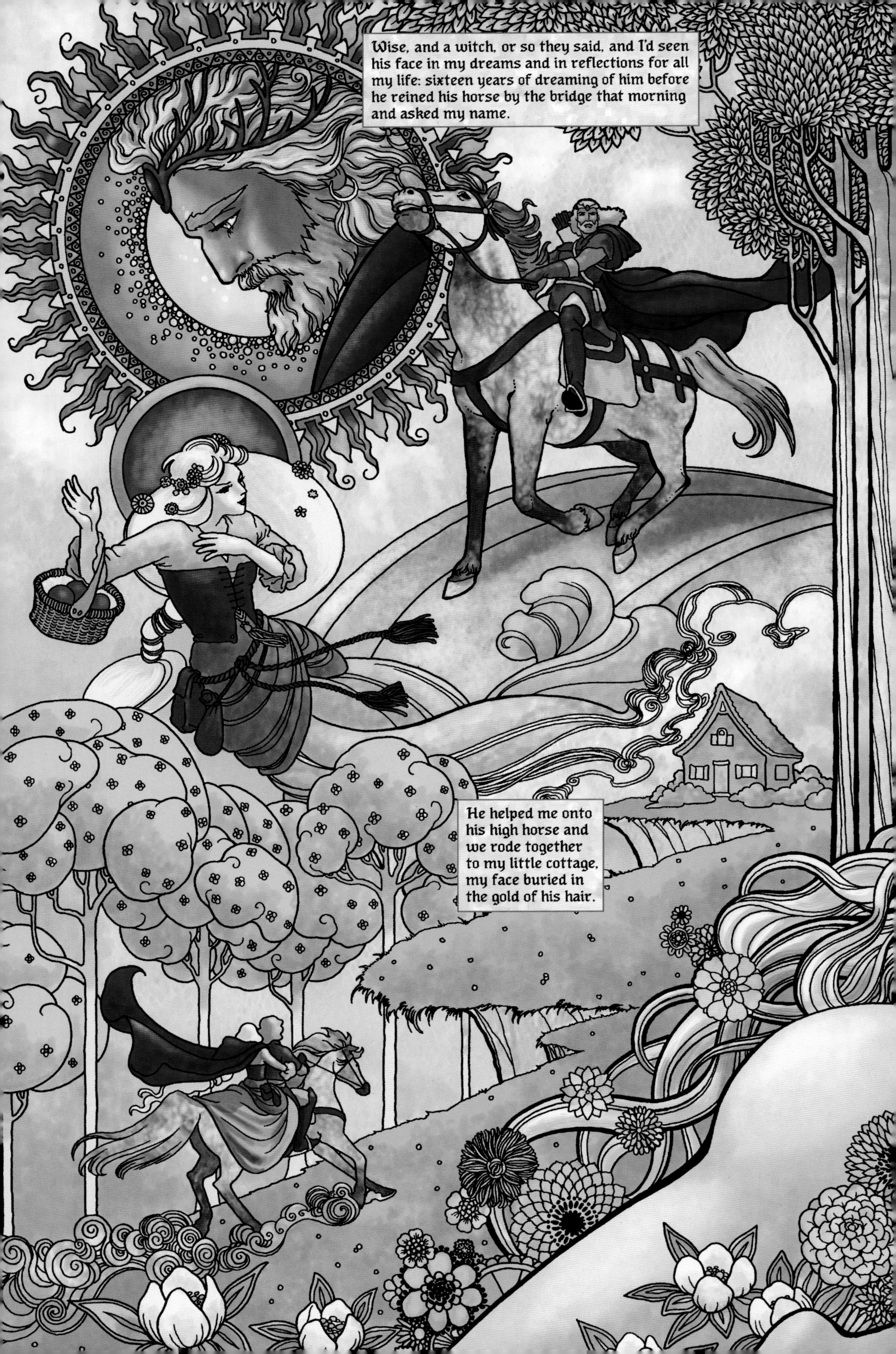
Wise, and a witch, or so they said, and I'd seen his face in my dreams and in reflections for all my life: sixteen years of dreaming of him before he reined his horse by the bridge that morning and asked my name.
He helped me onto his high horse and we rode together to my little cottage, my face buried in the gold of his hair.

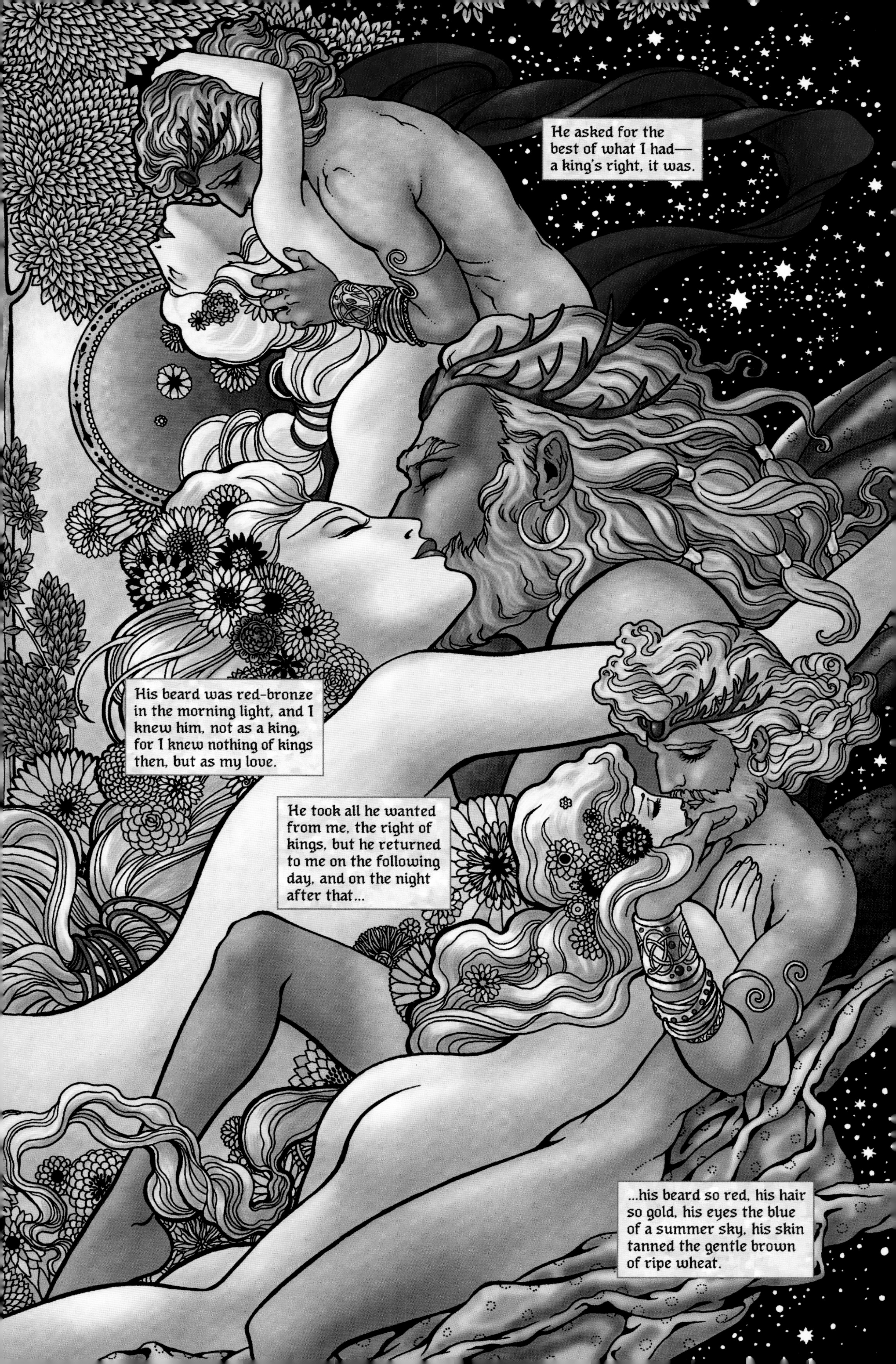
He asked for the best of what I had— a king's right, it was.
His beard was red-bronze in the morning light, and I knew him, not as a king, for I knew nothing of kings then, but as my love.
He took all he wanted from me, the right of kings, but he returned to me on the following day, and on the night after that...
...his beard so red, his hair so gold, his eyes the blue of a summer sky, his skin tanned the gentle brown of ripe wheat.

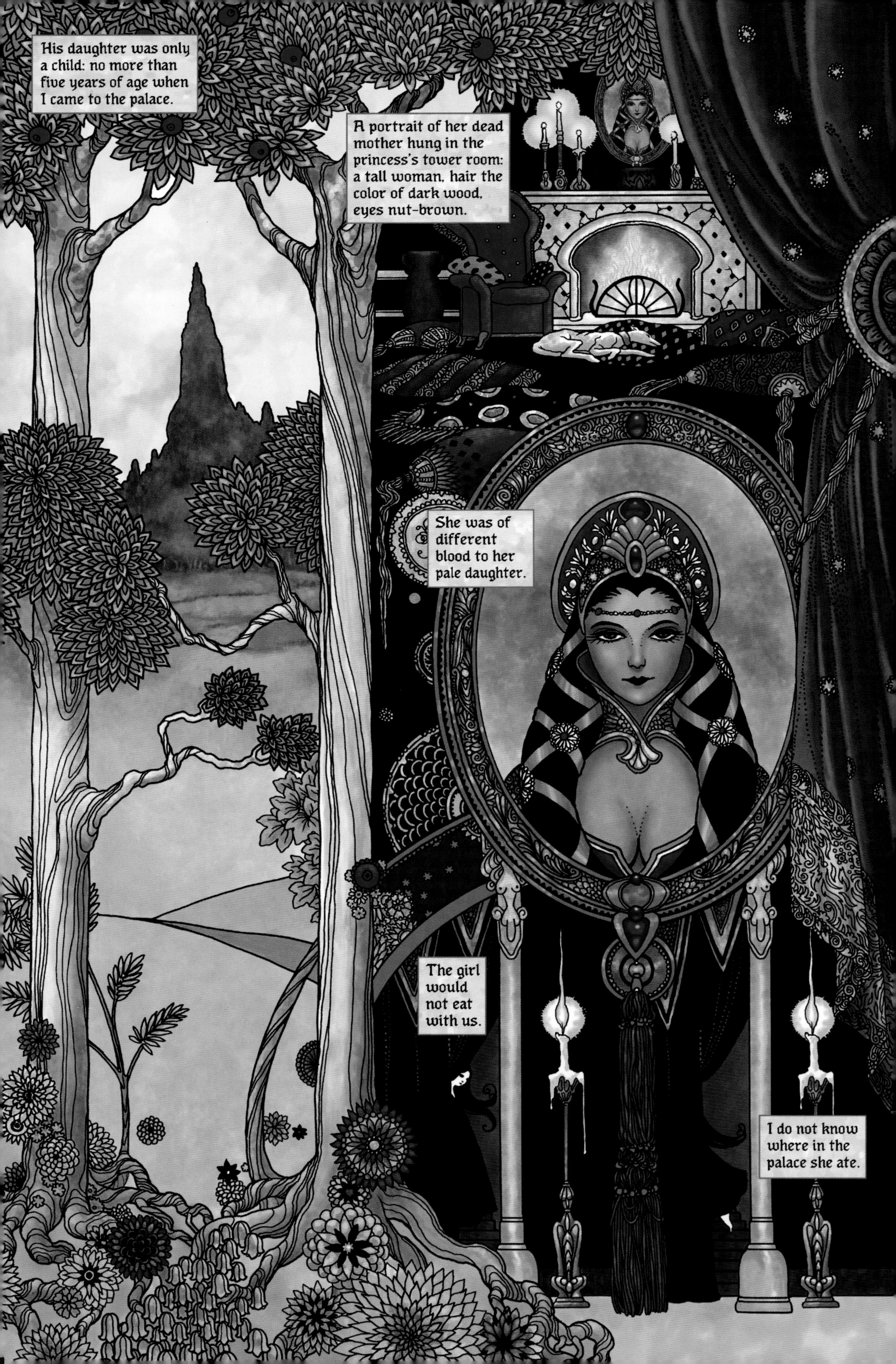
His daughter was only a child: no more than five years of age when I came to the palace.
A portrait of her dead mother hung in the princess's tower room: a tall woman, hair the color of dark wood, eyes nut-brown.
She was of different blood to her pale daughter.
The girl would not eat with us.
I do not know where in the palace she ate.

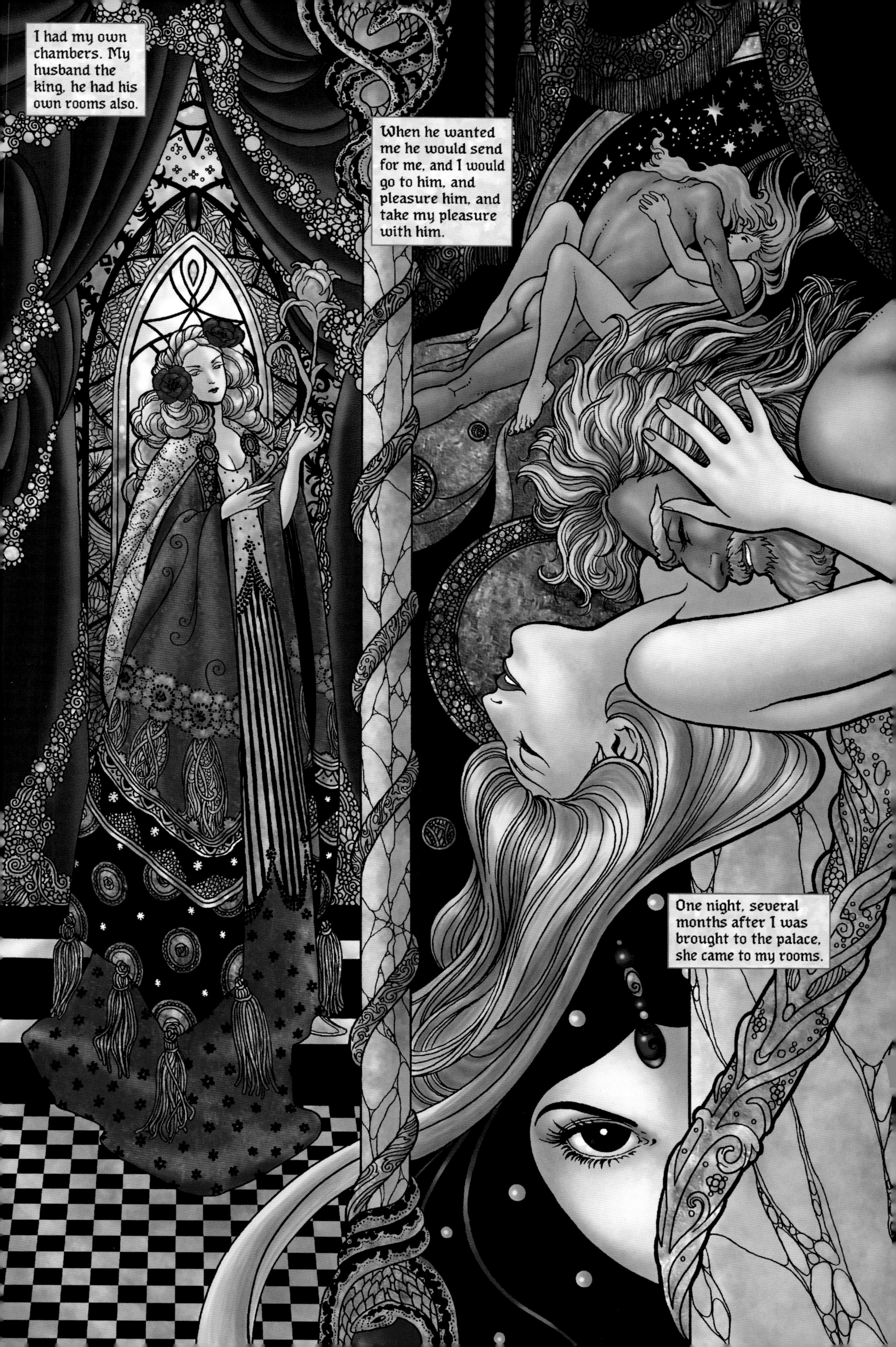
I had my own chambers. My husband the king, he had his own rooms also.
When he wanted me he would send for me, and I would go to him, and pleasure him, and take my pleasure with him.
One night, several months after I was brought to the palace, she came to my rooms.

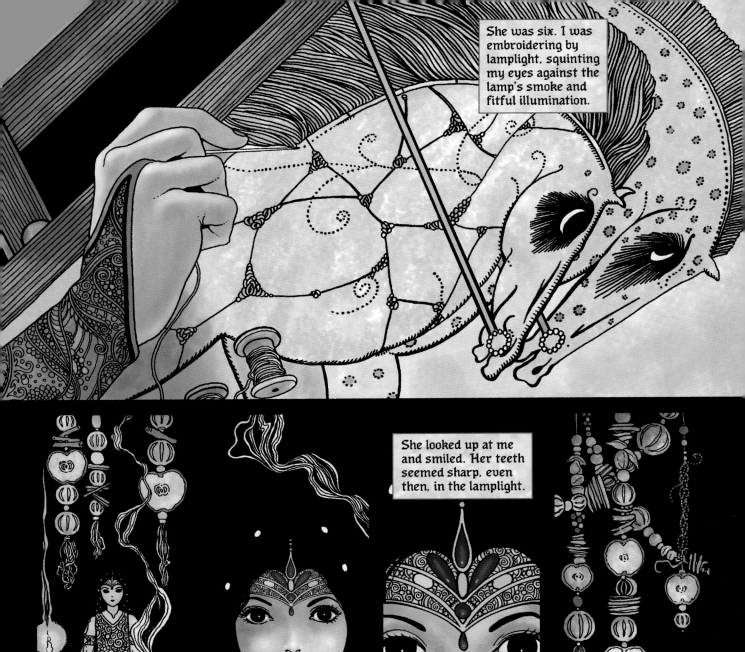

She was six. I was embroidering by lamplight, squinting my eyes against the lamp's smoke and fitful illumination.

She looked up at me and smiled. Her teeth seemed sharp, even then, in the lamplight.

PRINCESS?

She said nothing. Her eyes were black as coal, black as her hair—her lips were redder than blood.

WHAT ARE YOU DOING AWAY FROM YOUR ROOM?

I'M HUNGRY.

It was winter, when fresh food is a dream of warmth and sunlight—but I had strings of whole apples, cored and dried, hanging from the beams of my chamber.

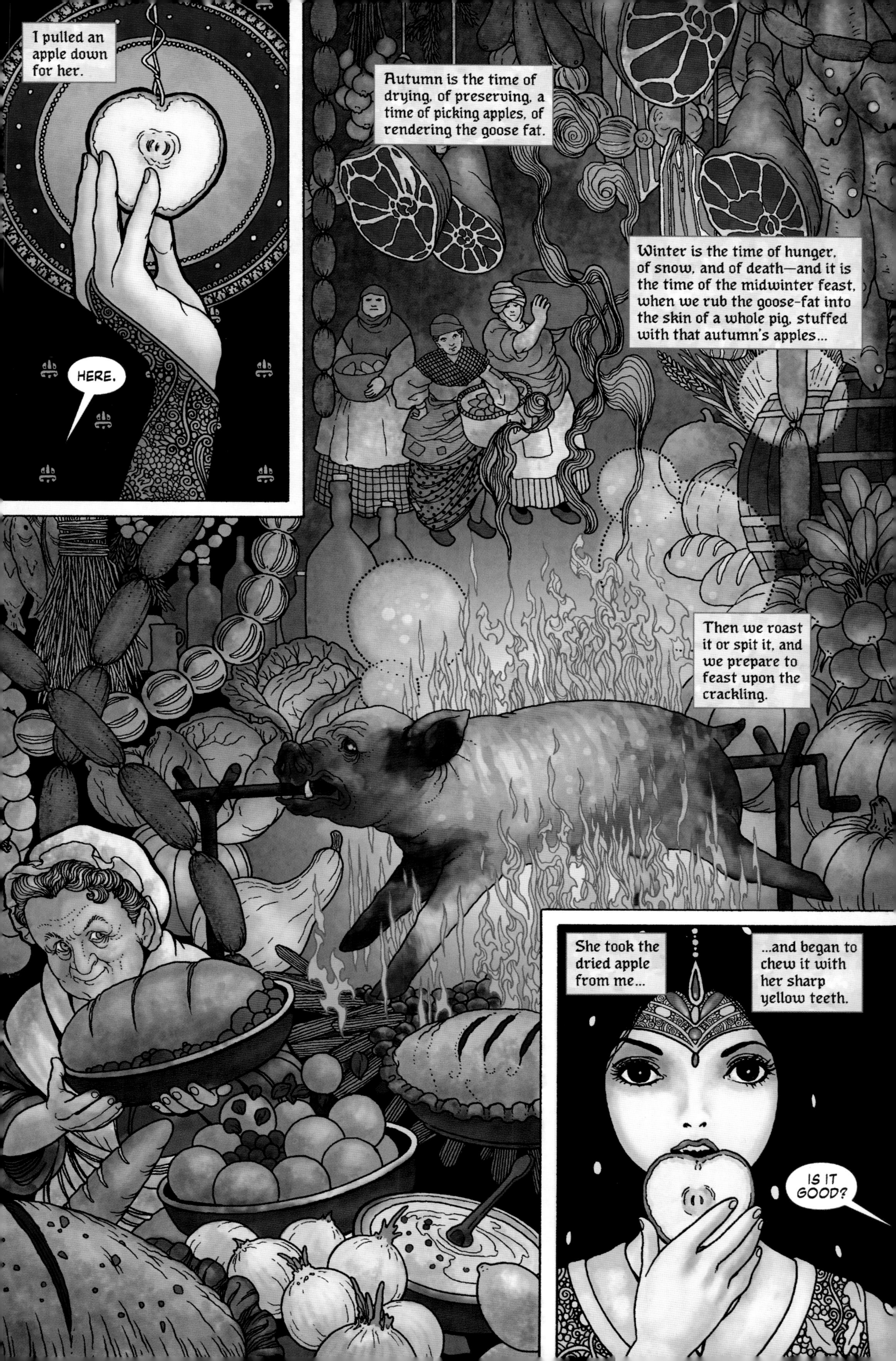
I pulled an apple down for her.
HERE.
Autumn is the time of drying, of preserving, a time of picking apples, of rendering the goose fat.
Winter is the time of hunger, of snow, and of death—and it is the time of the midwinter feast, when we rub the goose-fat into the skin of a whole pig, stuffed with that autumn's apples...
Then we roast it or spit it, and we prepare to feast upon the crackling.
She took the dried apple from me...
...and began to chew it with her sharp yellow teeth.
IS IT GOOD?

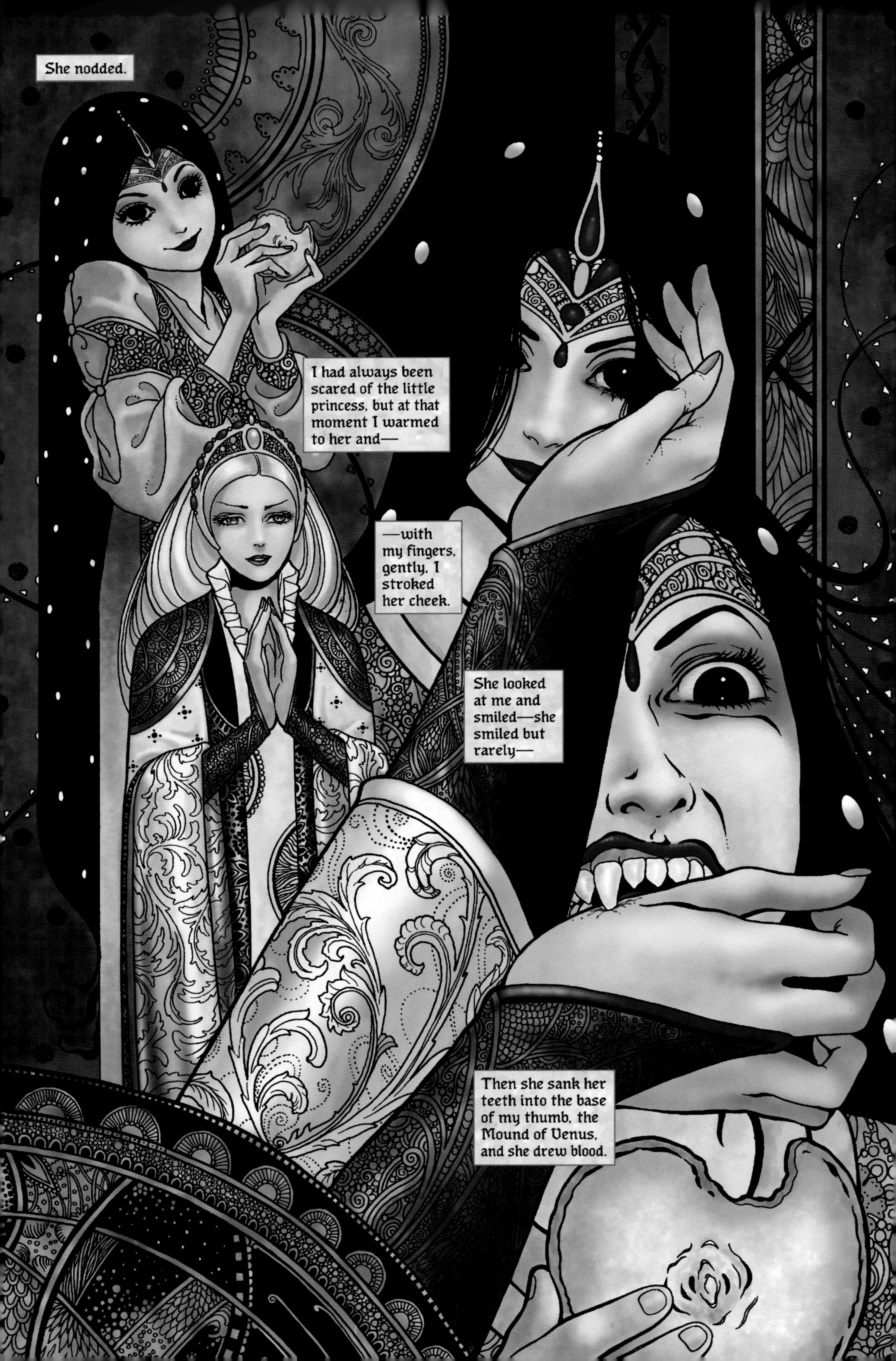
She nodded.
I had always been scared of the little princess, but at that moment I warmed to her and—
—with my fingers, gently, I stroked her cheek.
She looked at me and smiled—she smiled but rarely—
Then she sank her teeth into the base of my thumb, the Mound of Venus, and she drew blood.

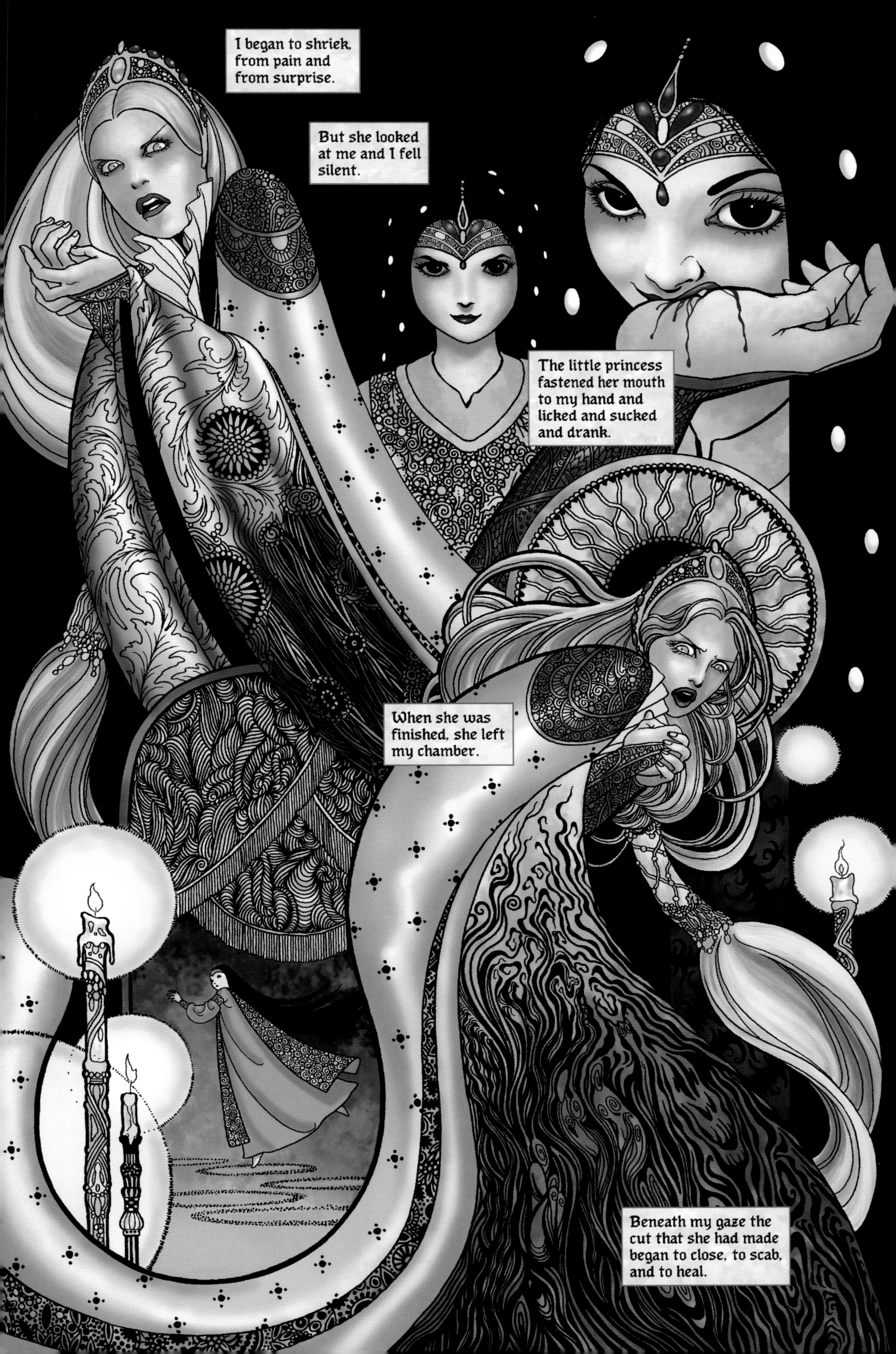
I began to shriek, from pain and from surprise.
But she looked at me and I fell silent.
The little princess fastened her mouth to my hand and licked and sucked and drank.
When she was finished, she left my chamber.
Beneath my gaze the cut that she had made began to close, to scab, and to heal.

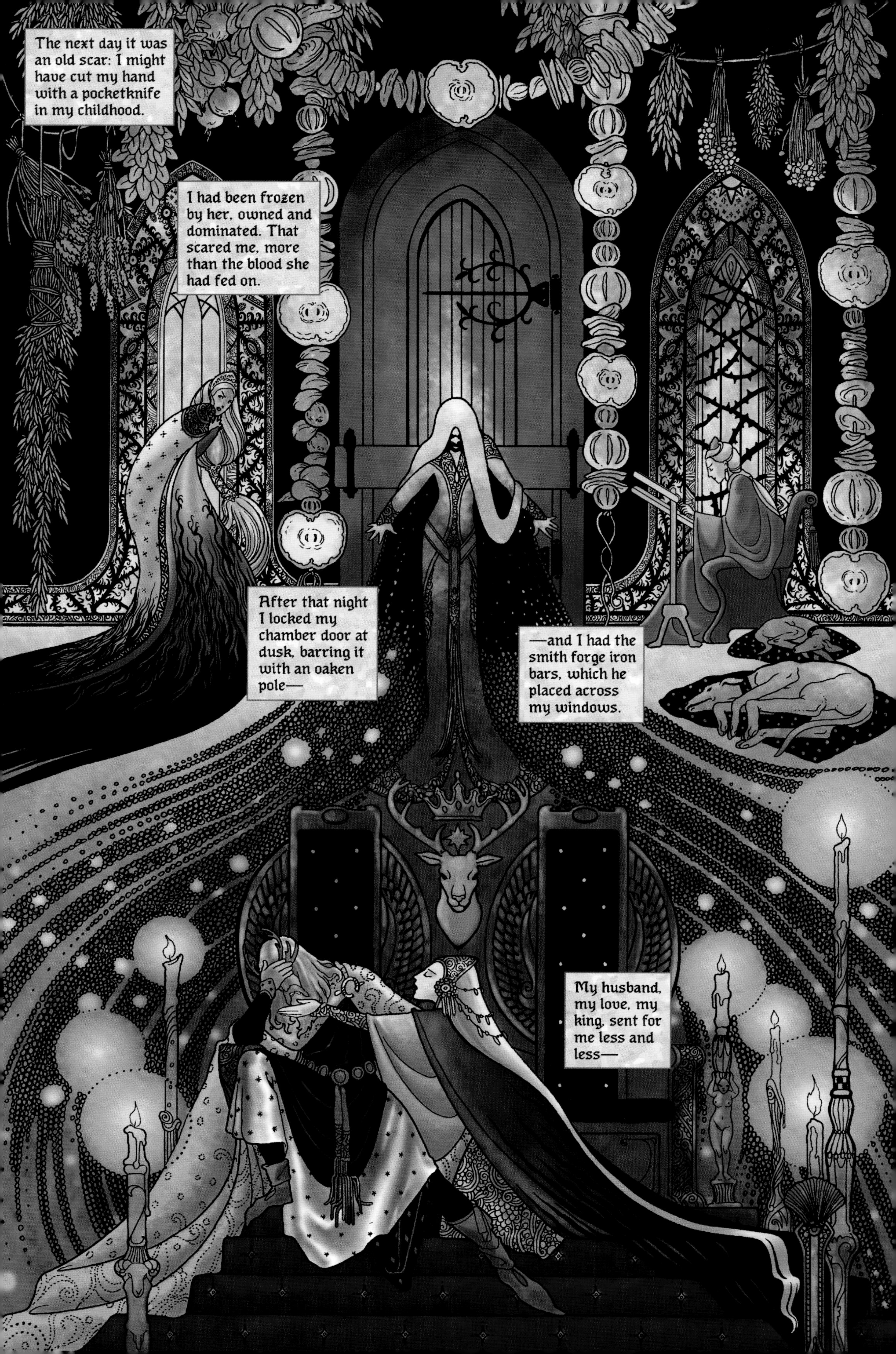
The next day it was an old scar: I might have cut my hand with a pocketknife in my childhood.
I had been frozen by her, owned and dominated. That scared me, more than the blood she had fed on.
After that night I locked my chamber door at dusk, barring it with an oaken pole—
—and I had the smith forge iron bars, which he placed across my windows.
My husband, my love, my king, sent for me less and less—

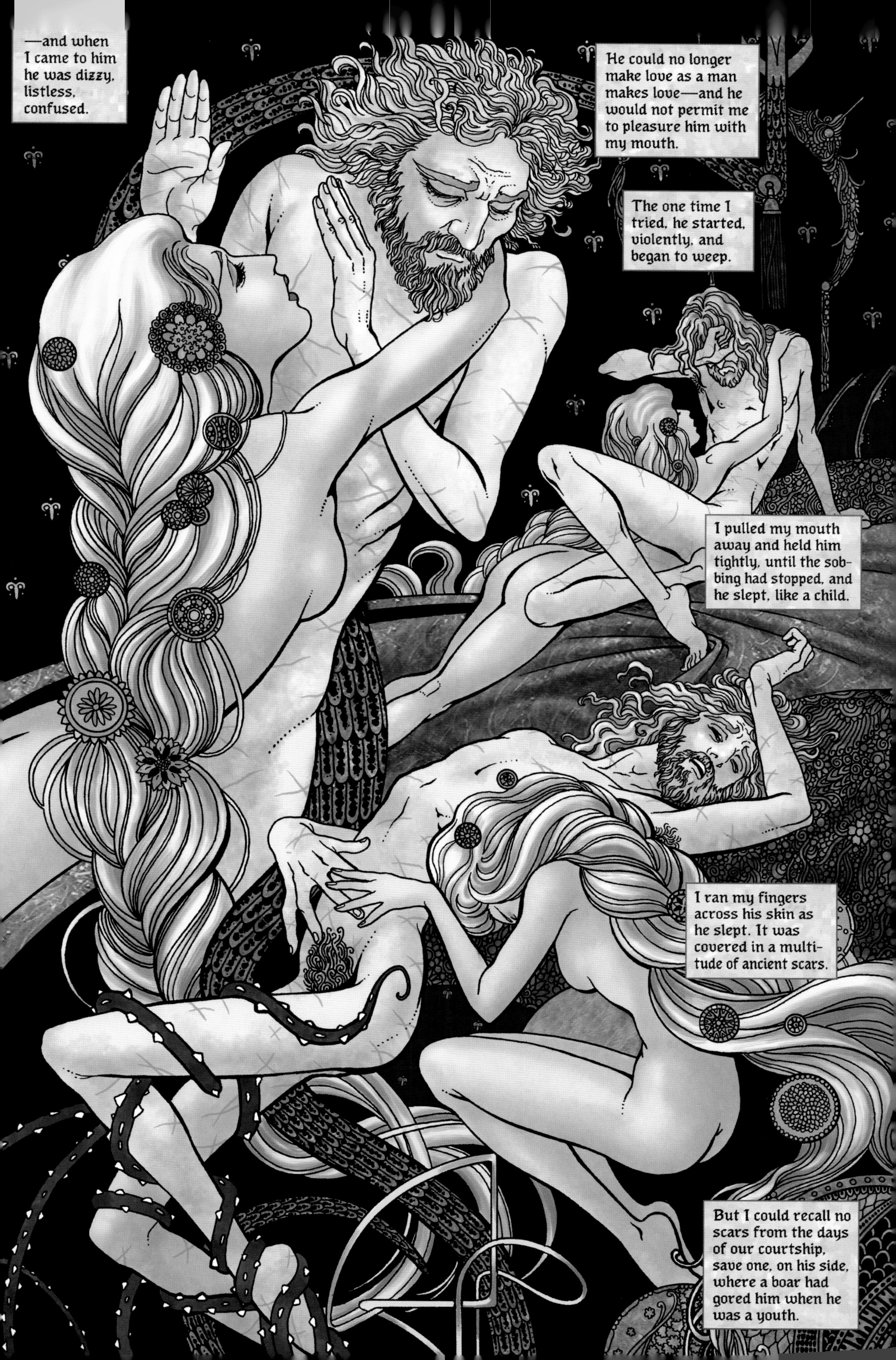
—and when I came to him he was dizzy, listless, confused.
He could no longer make love as a man makes love—and he would not permit me to pleasure him with my mouth.
The one time I tried, he started, violently, and began to weep.
I pulled my mouth away and held him tightly, until the sobbing had stopped, and he slept, like a child.
I ran my fingers across his skin as he slept. It was covered in a multitude of ancient scars.
But I could recall no scars from the days of our courtship, save one, on his side, where a boar had gored him when he was a youth.

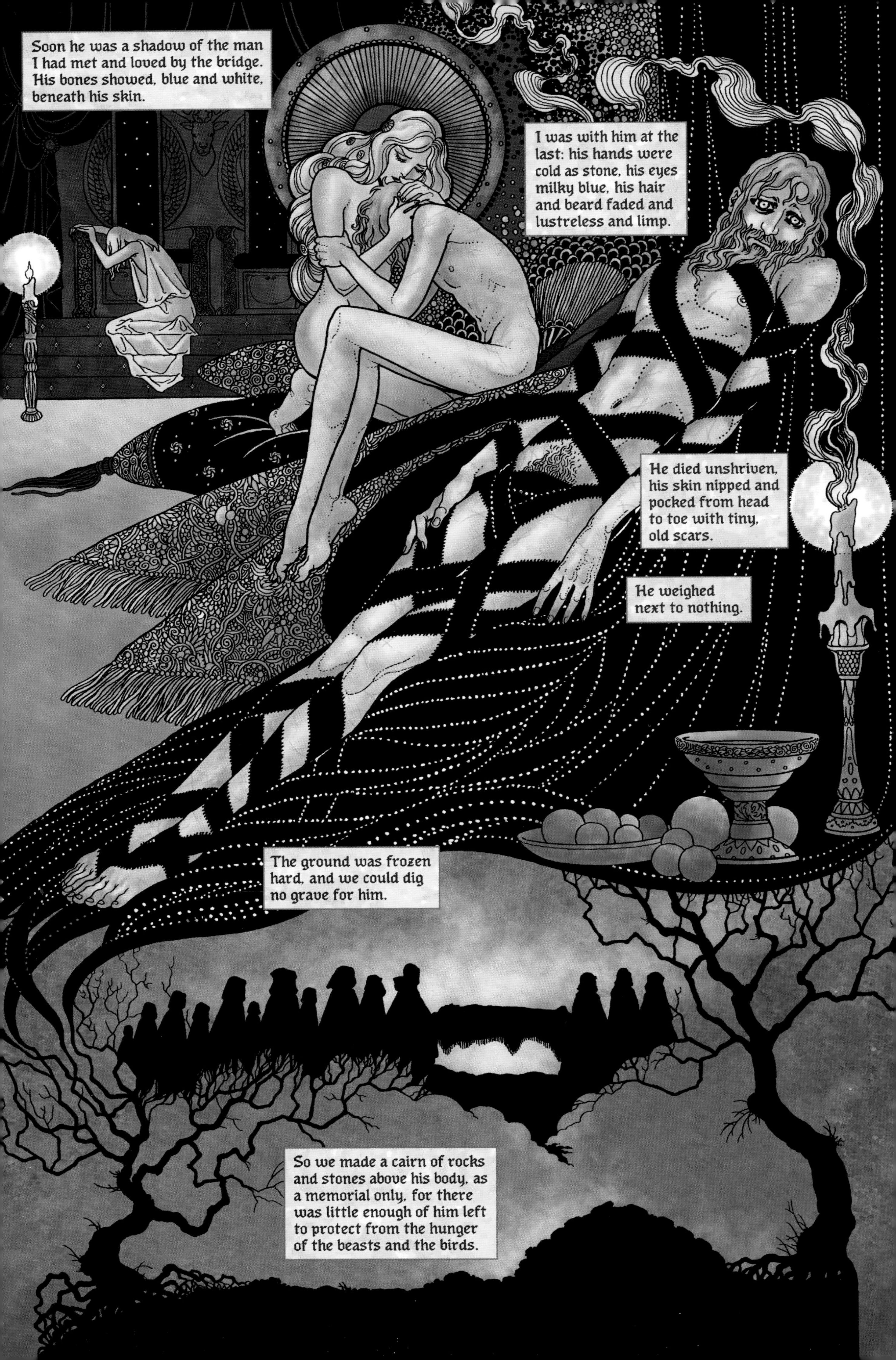
Soon he was a shadow of the man I had met and loved by the bridge. His bones showed, blue and white, beneath his skin.
I was with him at the last: his hands were cold as stone, his eyes milky blue, his hair and beard faded and lustreless and limp.
He died unshriven, his skin nipped and pocked from head to toe with tiny, old scars.
He weighed next to nothing.
The ground was frozen hard, and we could dig no grave for him.
So we made a cairn of rocks and stones above his body, as a memorial only, for there was little enough of him left to protect from the hunger of the beasts and the birds.

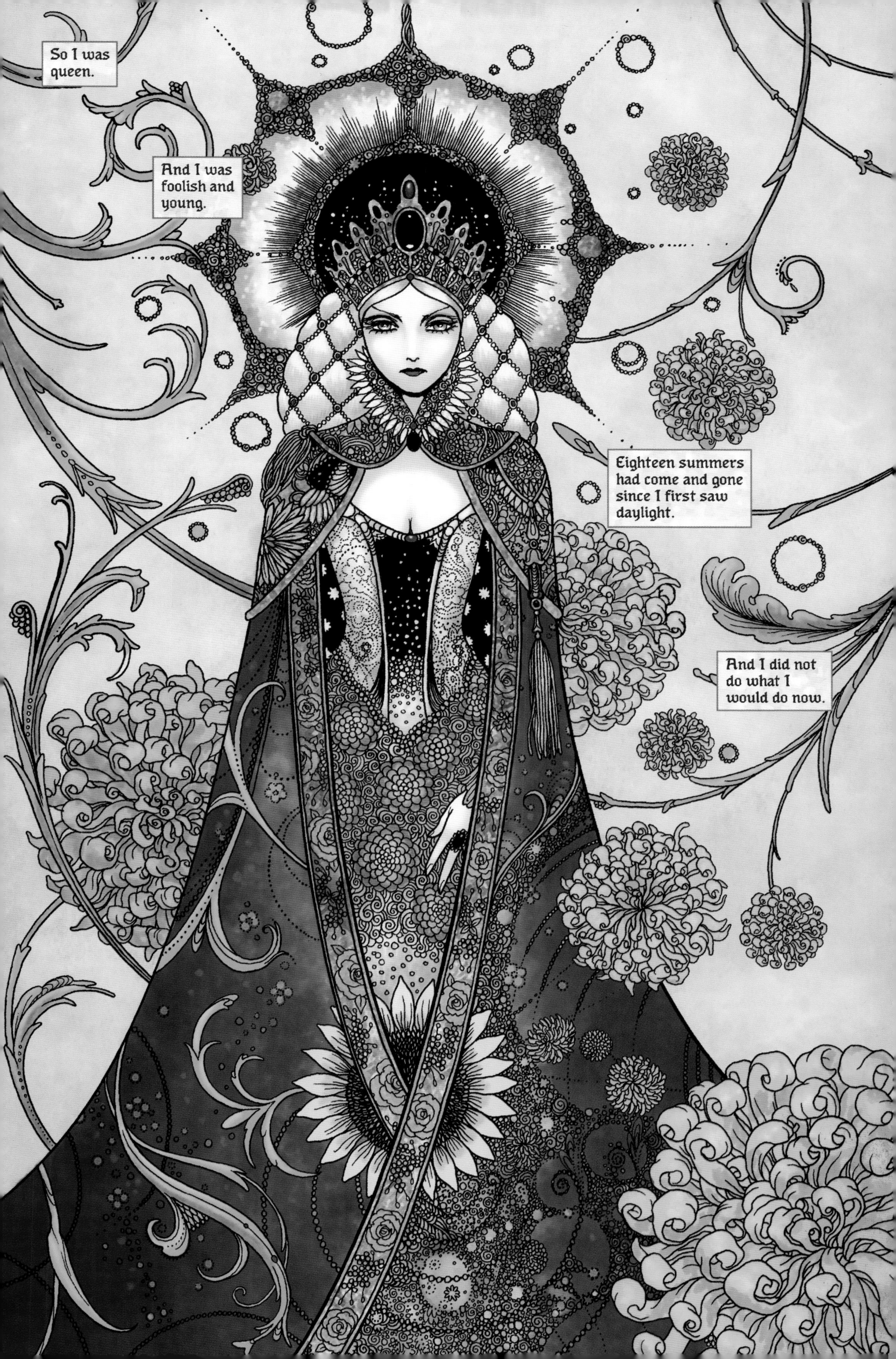
So I was queen.
And I was foolish and young.
Eighteen summers had come and gone since I first saw daylight.
And I did not do what I would do now.

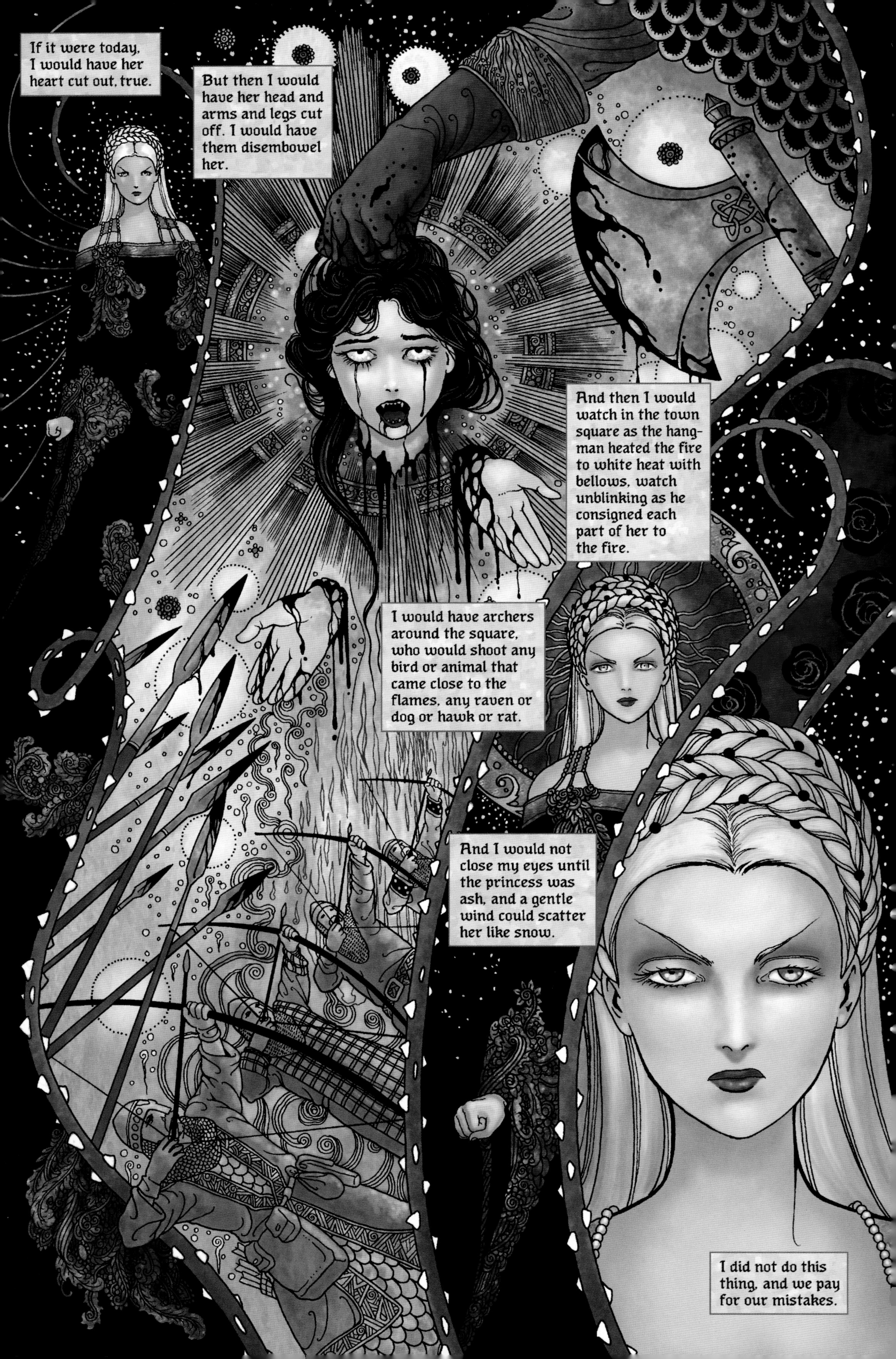
If it were today, I would have her heart cut out, true.
But then I would have her head and arms and legs cut off. I would have them disembowel her.
And then I would watch in the town square as the hang-man heated the fire to white heat with bellows, watch unblinking as he consigned each part of her to the fire.
I would have archers around the square, who would shoot any bird or animal that came close to the flames, any raven or dog or hawk or rat.
And I would not close my eyes until the princess was ash, and a gentle wind could scatter her like snow.
I did not do this thing, and we pay for our mistakes.

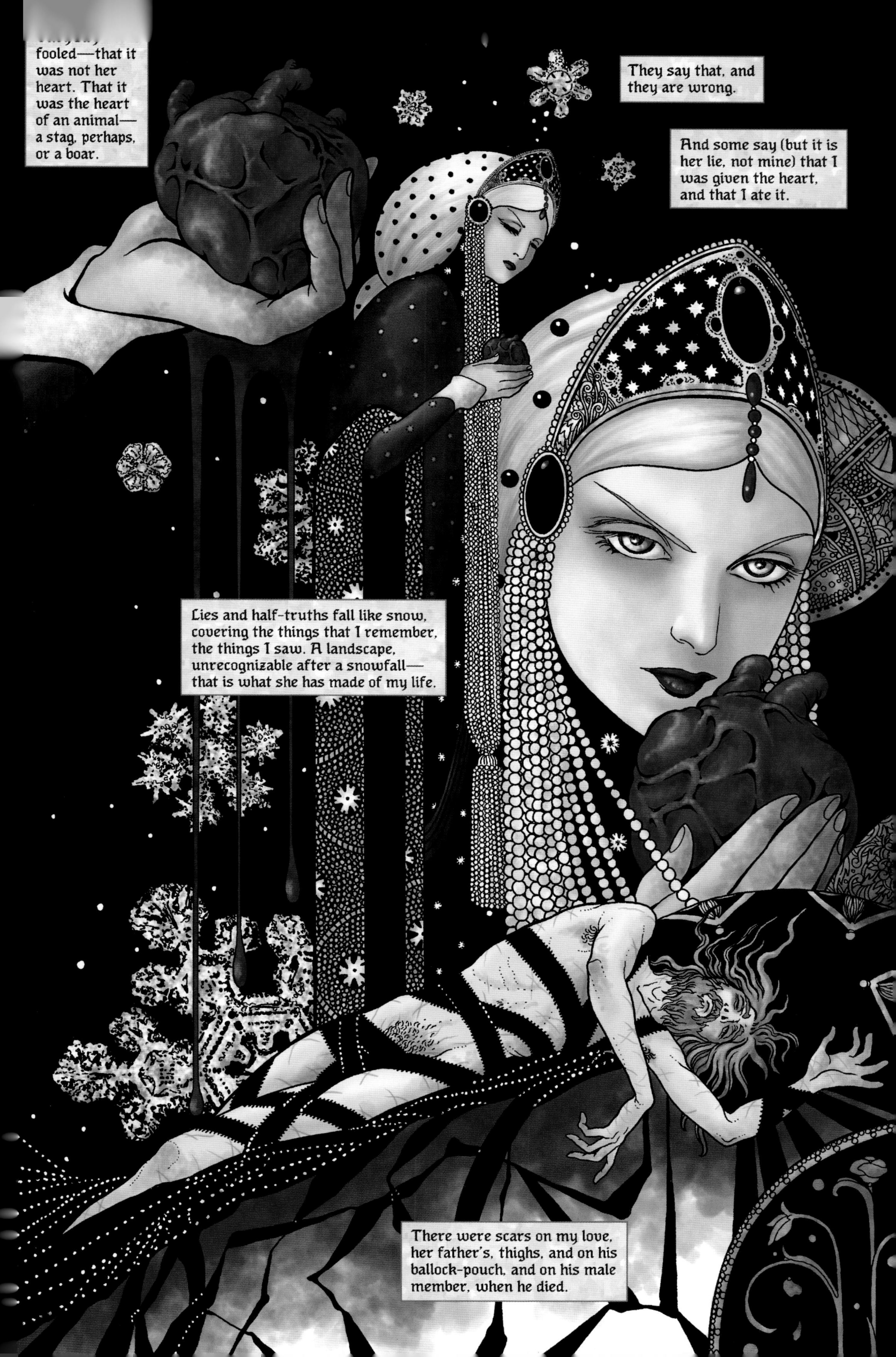
fooled—that it was not her heart. That it was the heart of an animal—a stag, perhaps, or a boar.
They say that, and they are wrong.
And some say (but it is her lie, not mine) that I was given the heart, and that I ate it.
Lies and half-truths fall like snow, covering the things that I remember, the things I saw. A landscape, unrecognizable after a snowfall—that is what she has made of my life.
There were scars on my love, her father's, thighs, and on his ballock-pouch, and on his male member, when he died.

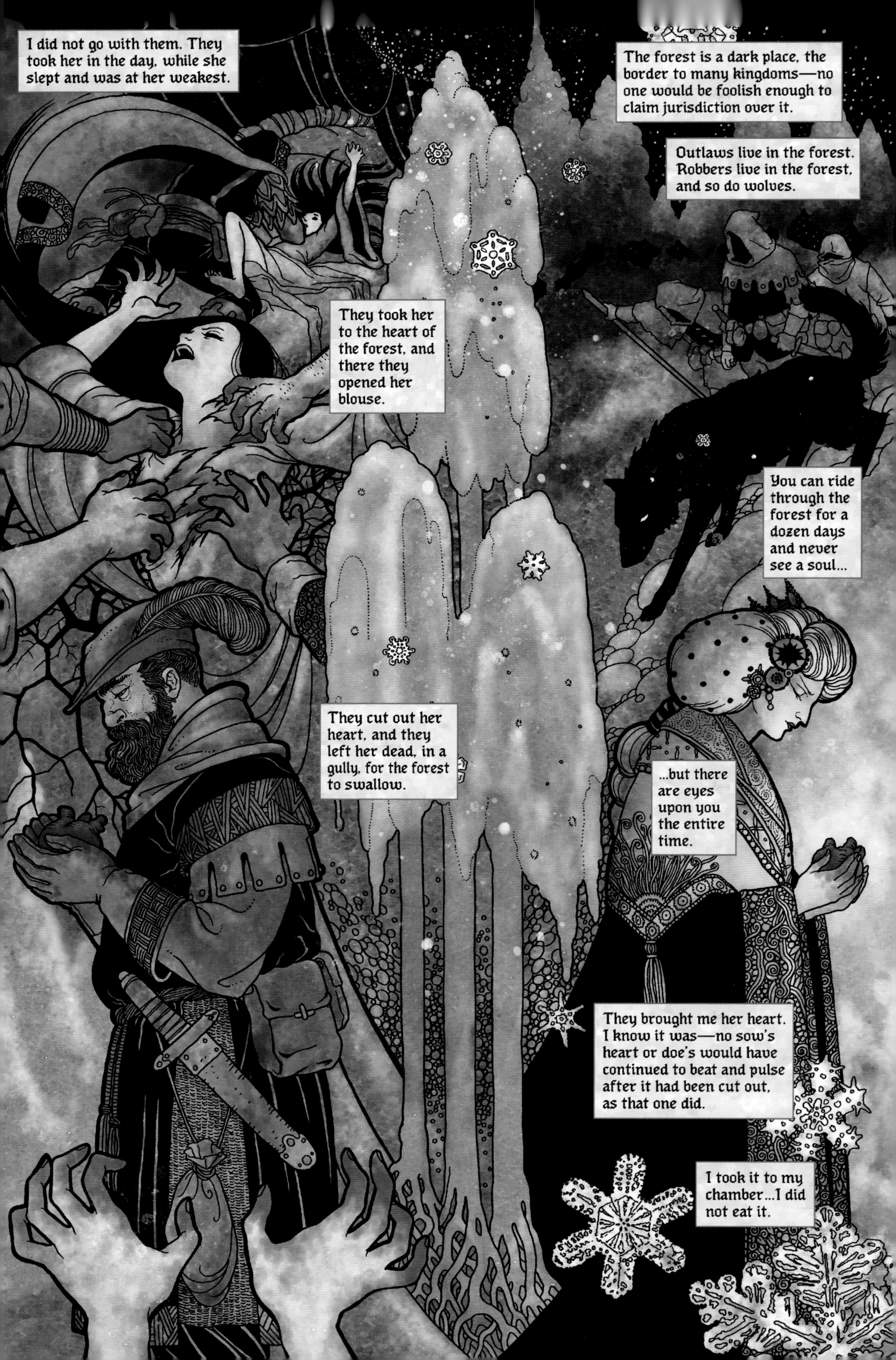
I did not go with them. They took her in the day, while she slept and was at her weakest.
They took her to the heart of the forest, and there they opened her blouse.
They cut out her heart, and they left her dead, in a gully, for the forest to swallow.
The forest is a dark place, the border to many kingdoms—no one would be foolish enough to claim jurisdiction over it.
Outlaws live in the forest. Robbers live in the forest, and so do wolves.
You can ride through the forest for a dozen days and never see a soul...
...but there are eyes upon you the entire time.
They brought me her heart. I know it was—no sow's heart or doe's would have continued to beat and pulse after it had been cut out, as that one did.
I took it to my chamber...I did not eat it.

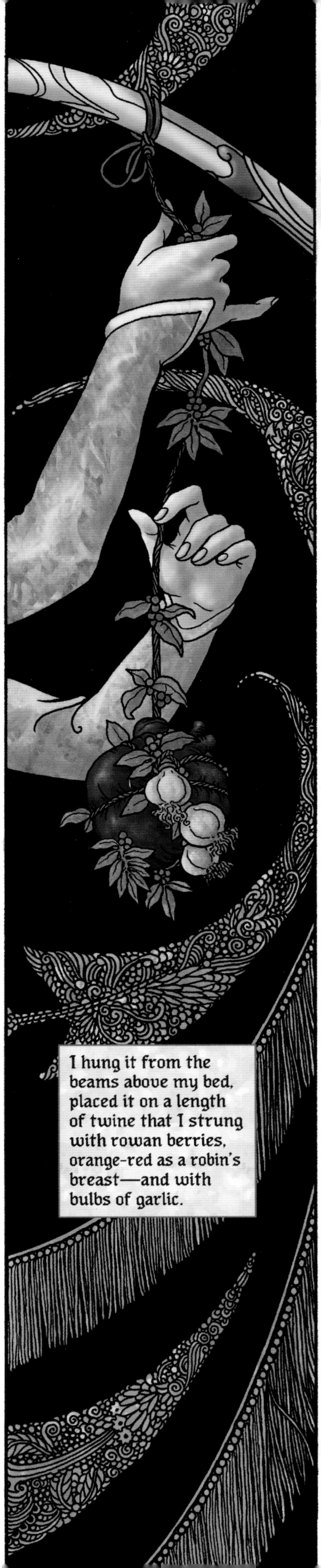
I hung it from the beams above my bed, placed it on a length of twine that I strung with rowan berries, orange-red as a robin's breast—and with bulbs of garlic.

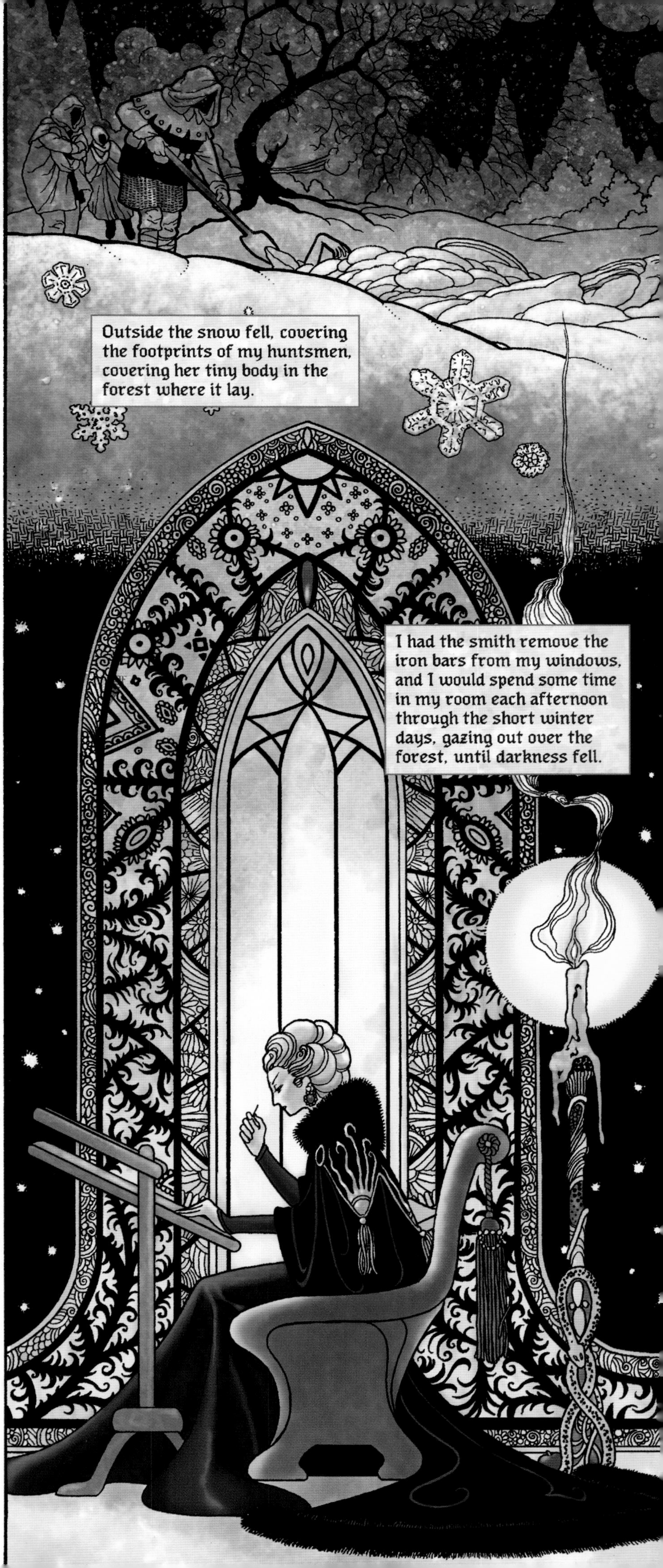
Outside the snow fell, covering the footprints of my huntsmen, covering her tiny body in the forest where it lay.
I had the smith remove the iron bars from my windows, and I would spend some time in my room each afternoon through the short winter days, gazing out over the forest, until darkness fell.

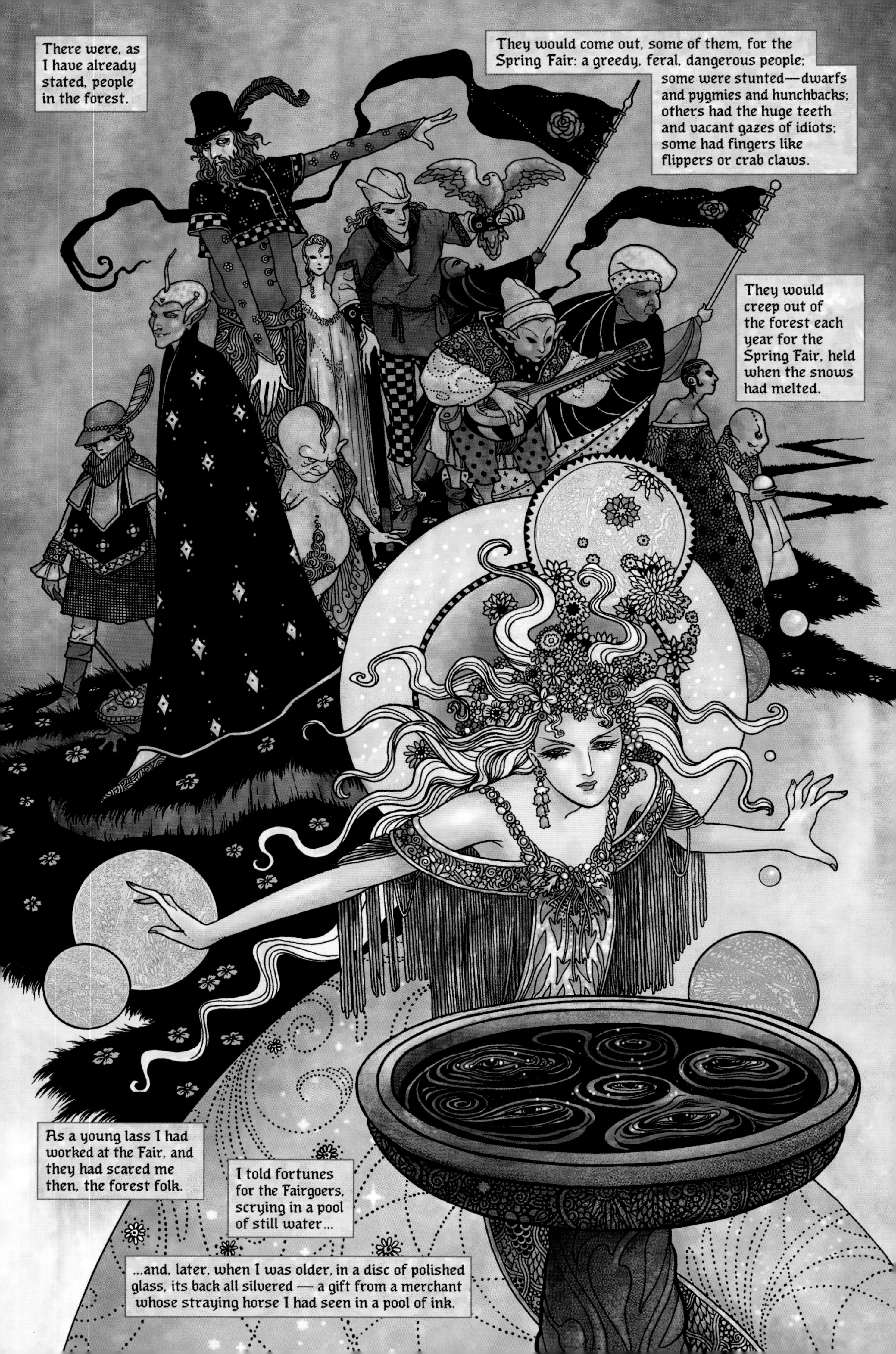
There were, as I have already stated, people in the forest.
They would come out, some of them, for the Spring Fair: a greedy, feral, dangerous people;
some were stunted—dwarfs and pygmies and hunchbacks; others had the huge teeth and vacant gazes of idiots; some had fingers like flippers or crab claws.
They would creep out of the forest each year for the Spring Fair, held when the snows had melted.
As a young lass I had worked at the Fair, and they had scared me then, the forest folk.
I told fortunes for the Fairgoers, scrying in a pool of still water...
...and, later, when I was older, in a disc of polished glass, its back all silvered — a gift from a merchant whose straying horse I had seen in a pool of ink.

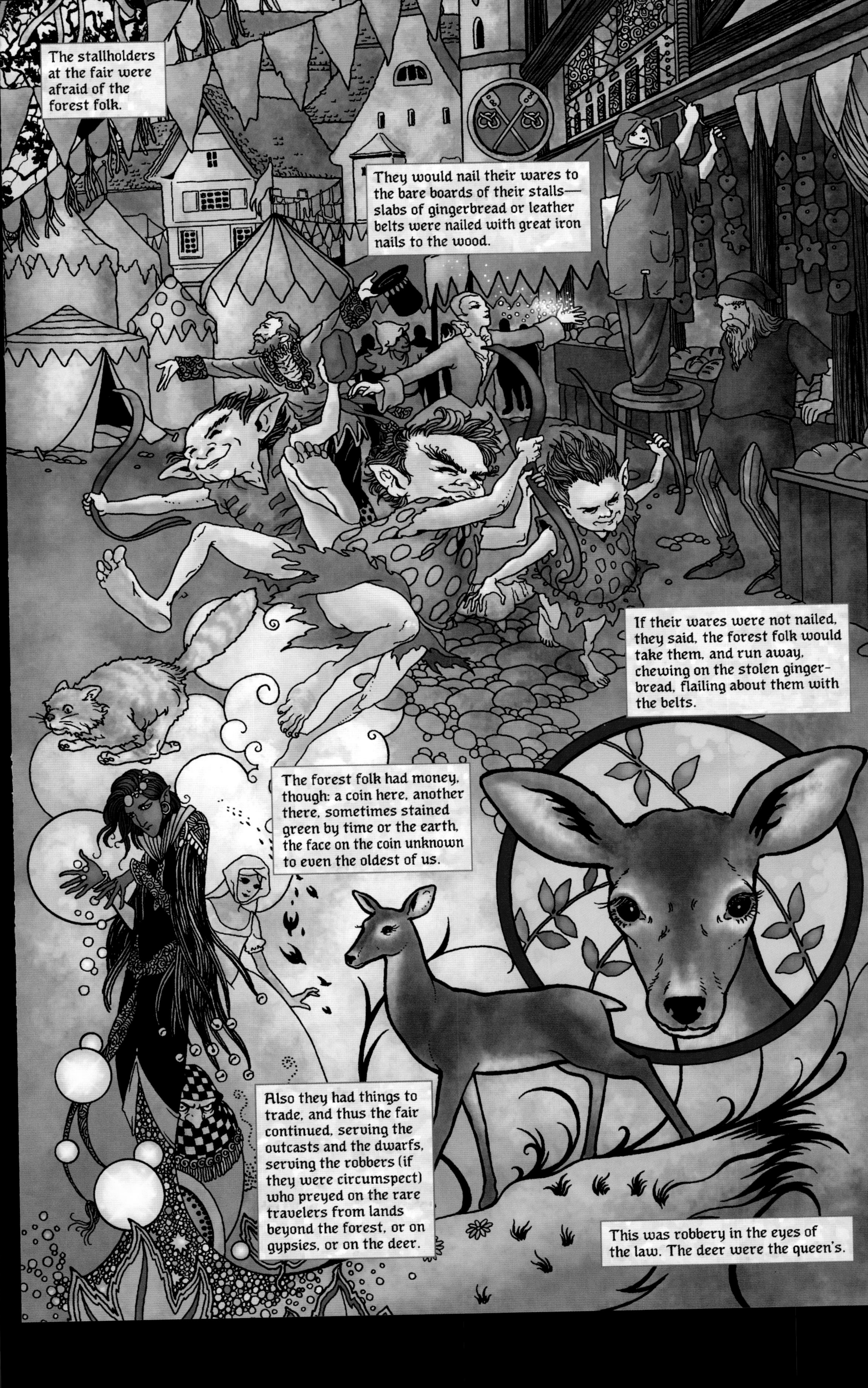
The stallholders at the fair were afraid of the forest folk.
They would nail their wares to the bare boards of their stalls—slabs of gingerbread or leather belts were nailed with great iron nails to the wood.
If their wares were not nailed, they said, the forest folk would take them, and run away, chewing on the stolen ginger-bread, flailing about them with the belts.
The forest folk had money, though: a coin here, another there, sometimes stained green by time or the earth, the face on the coin unknown to even the oldest of us.
Also they had things to trade, and thus the fair continued, serving the outcasts and the dwarfs, serving the robbers (if they were circumspect) who preyed on the rare travelers from lands beyond the forest, or on gypsies, or on the deer.
This was robbery in the eyes of the law. The deer were the queen's.

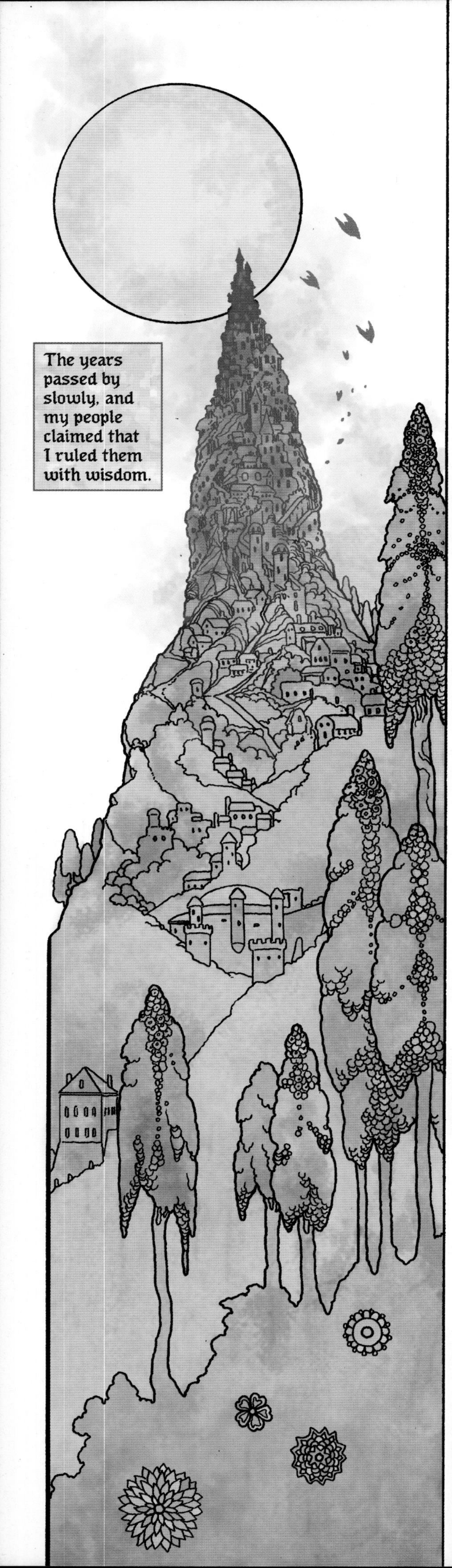
The years passed by slowly, and my people claimed that I ruled them with wisdom.

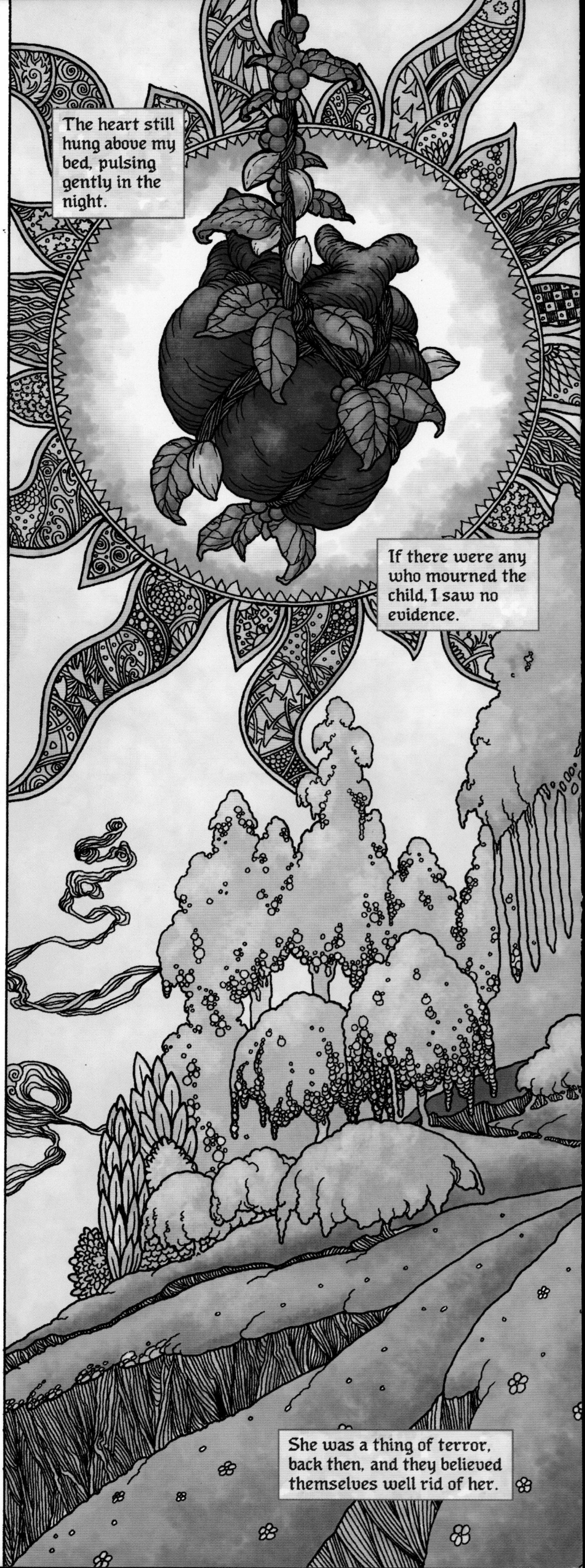
The heart still hung above my bed, pulsing gently in the night.
If there were any who mourned the child, I saw no evidence.
She was a thing of terror, back then, and they believed themselves well rid of her.

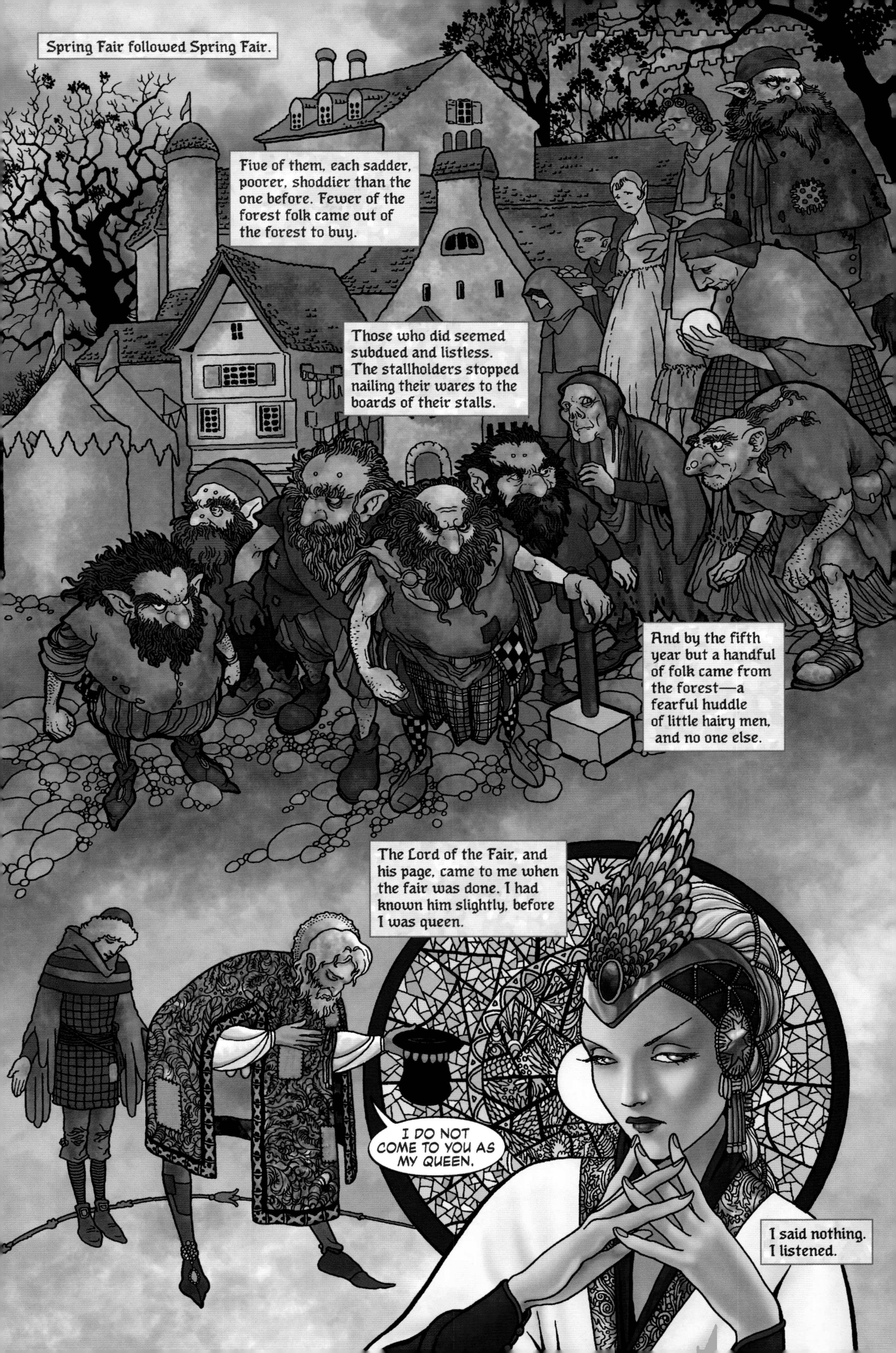
Spring Fair followed Spring Fair.
Five of them, each sadder, poorer, shoddier than the one before. Fewer of the forest folk came out of the forest to buy.
Those who did seemed subdued and listless. The stallholders stopped nailing their wares to the boards of their stalls.
And by the fifth year but a handful of folk came from the forest—a fearful huddle of little hairy men, and no one else.
The Lord of the Fair, and his page, came to me when the fair was done. I had known him slightly, before I was queen.
I DO NOT COME TO YOU AS MY QUEEN.
I said nothing. I listened.

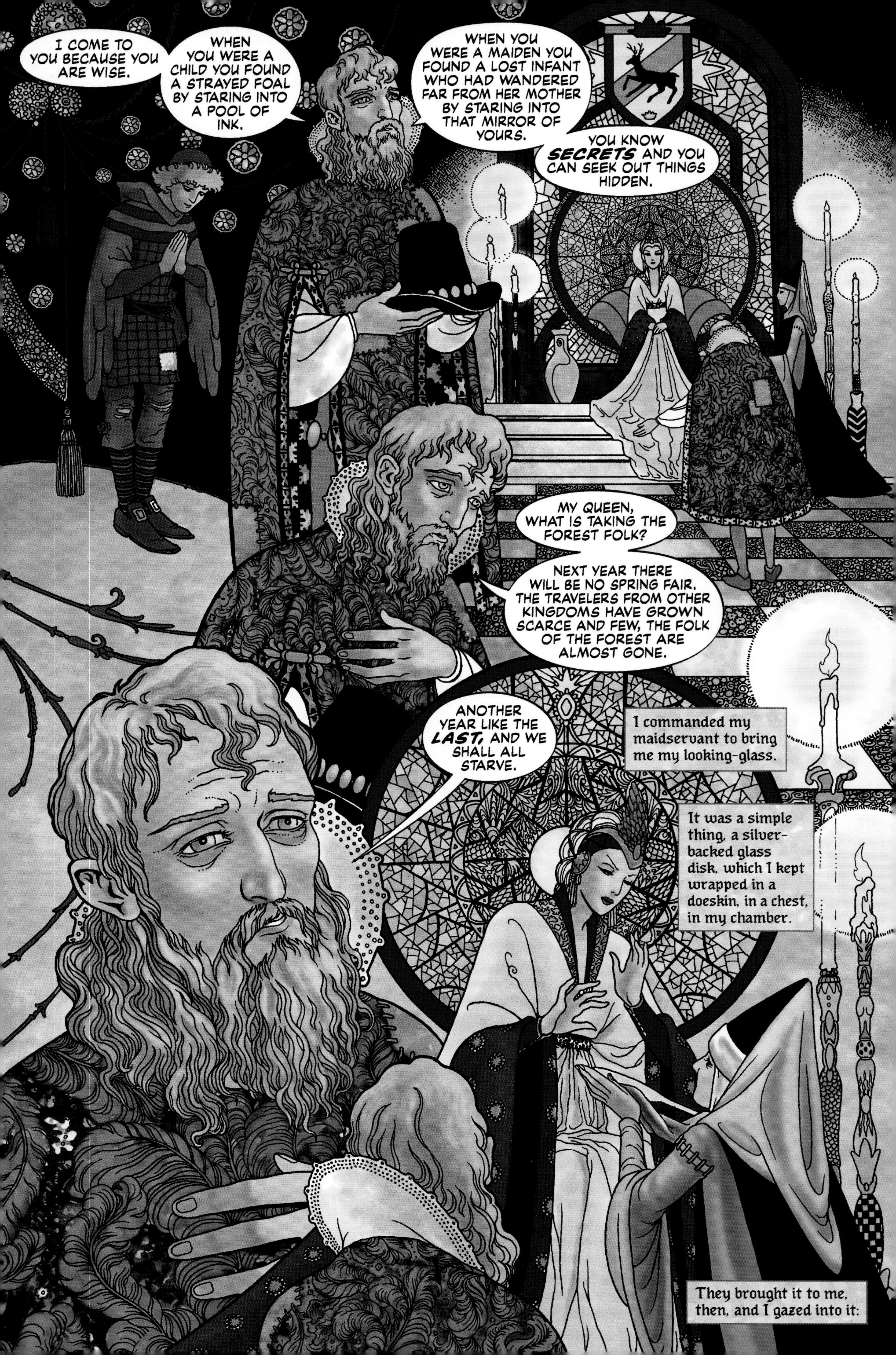
I COME TO YOU BECAUSE YOU ARE WISE.
WHEN YOU WERE A CHILD YOU FOUND A STRAYED FOAL BY STARING INTO A POOL OF INK.
WHEN YOU WERE A MAIDEN YOU FOUND A LOST INFANT WHO HAD WANDERED FAR FROM HER MOTHER BY STARING INTO THAT MIRROR OF YOURS.
YOU KNOW SECRETS AND YOU CAN SEEK OUT THINGS HIDDEN.
MY QUEEN, WHAT IS TAKING THE FOREST FOLK?
NEXT YEAR THERE WILL BE NO SPRING FAIR. THE TRAVELERS FROM OTHER KINGDOMS HAVE GROWN SCARCE AND FEW, THE FOLK OF THE FOREST ARE ALMOST GONE.
ANOTHER YEAR LIKE THE LAST, AND WE SHALL ALL STARVE.
I commanded my maidservant to bring me my looking-glass.
It was a simple thing, a silver-backed glass disk, which I kept wrapped in a doeskin, in a chest, in my chamber.
They brought it to me, then, and I gazed into it:

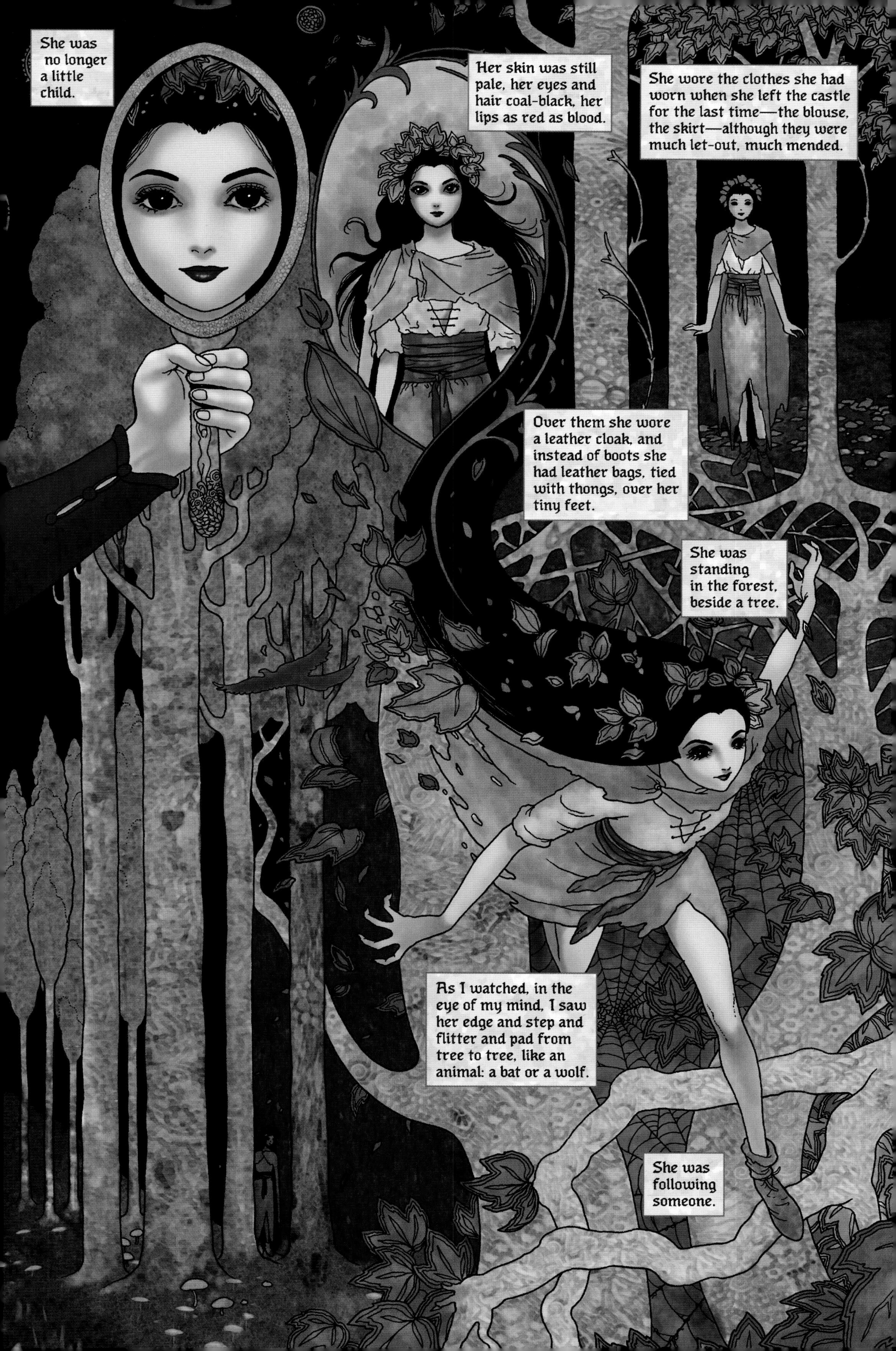
She was no longer a little child.
Her skin was still pale, her eyes and hair coal-black, her lips as red as blood.
She wore the clothes she had worn when she left the castle for the last time—the blouse, the skirt—although they were much let-out, much mended.
Over them she wore a leather cloak, and instead of boots she had leather bags, tied with thongs, over her tiny feet.
She was standing in the forest, beside a tree.
As I watched, in the eye of my mind, I saw her edge and step and flitter and pad from tree to tree, like an animal: a bat or a wolf.
She was following someone.

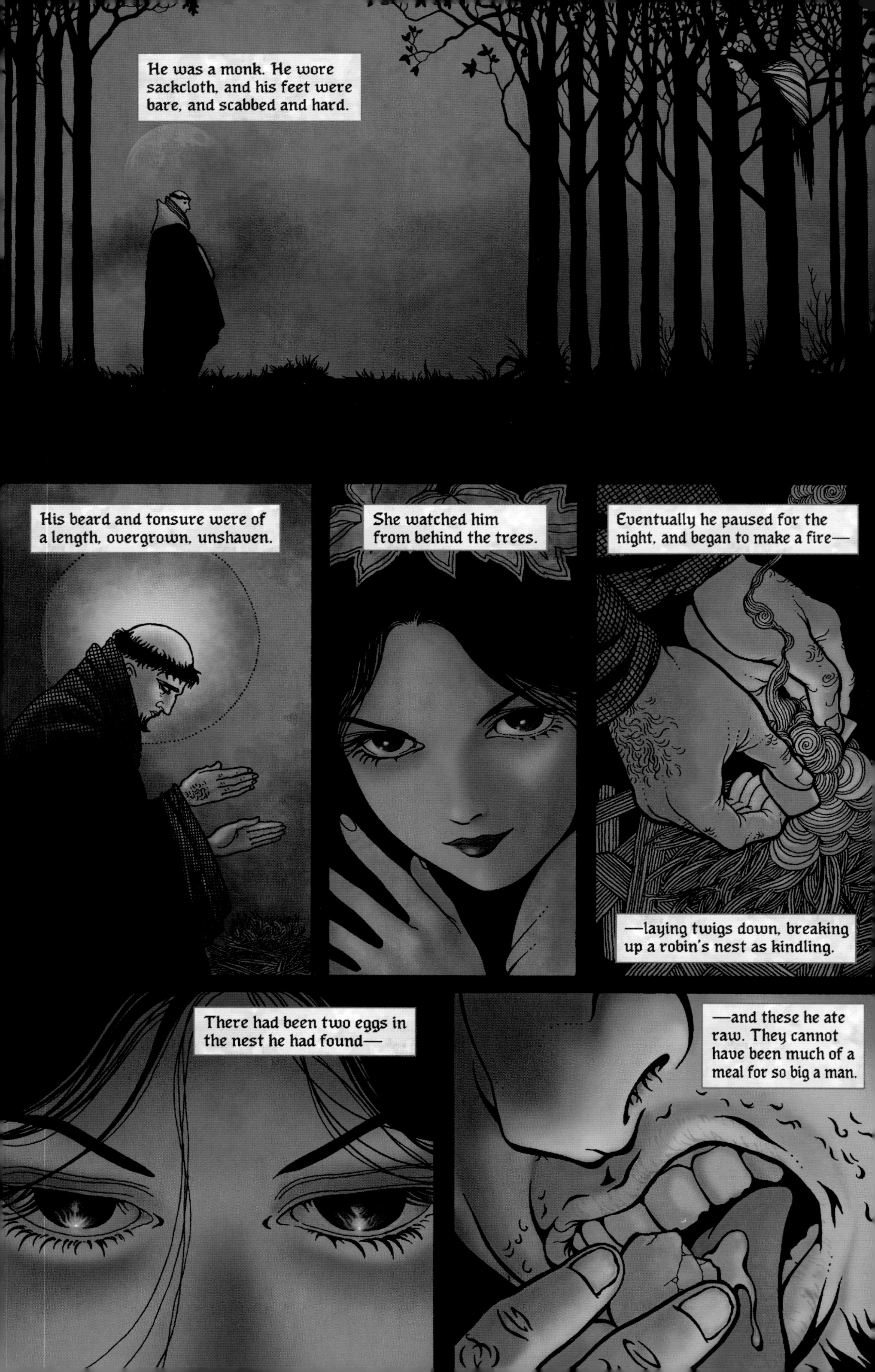
He was a monk. He wore sackcloth, and his feet were bare, and scabbed and hard.
His beard and tonsure were of a length, overgrown, unshaven.
She watched him from behind the trees.
Eventually he paused for the night, and began to make a fire—
—laying twigs down, breaking up a robin's nest as kindling.
There had been two eggs in the nest he had found—
—and these he ate raw. They cannot have been much of a meal for so big a man.

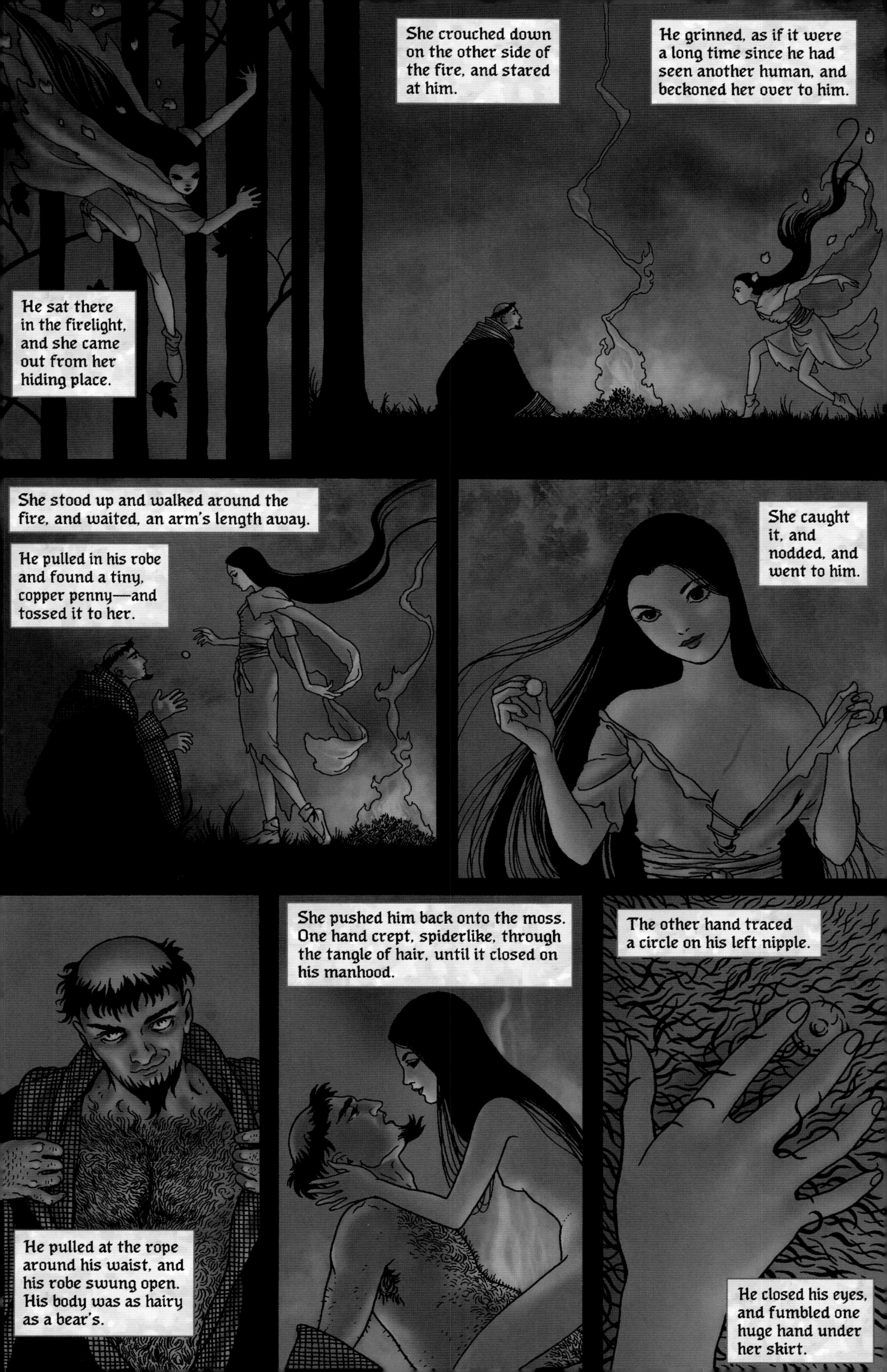
He sat there in the firelight, and she came out from her hiding place.
She crouched down on the other side of the fire, and stared at him.
He grinned, as if it were a long time since he had seen another human, and beckoned her over to him.
She stood up and walked around the fire, and waited, an arm's length away.
He pulled in his robe and found a tiny, copper penny—and tossed it to her.
She caught it, and nodded, and went to him.
He pulled at the rope around his waist, and his robe swung open. His body was as hairy as a bear's.
She pushed him back onto the moss. One hand crept, spiderlike, through the tangle of hair, until it closed on his manhood.
The other hand traced a circle on his left nipple.
He closed his eyes, and fumbled one huge hand under her skirt.

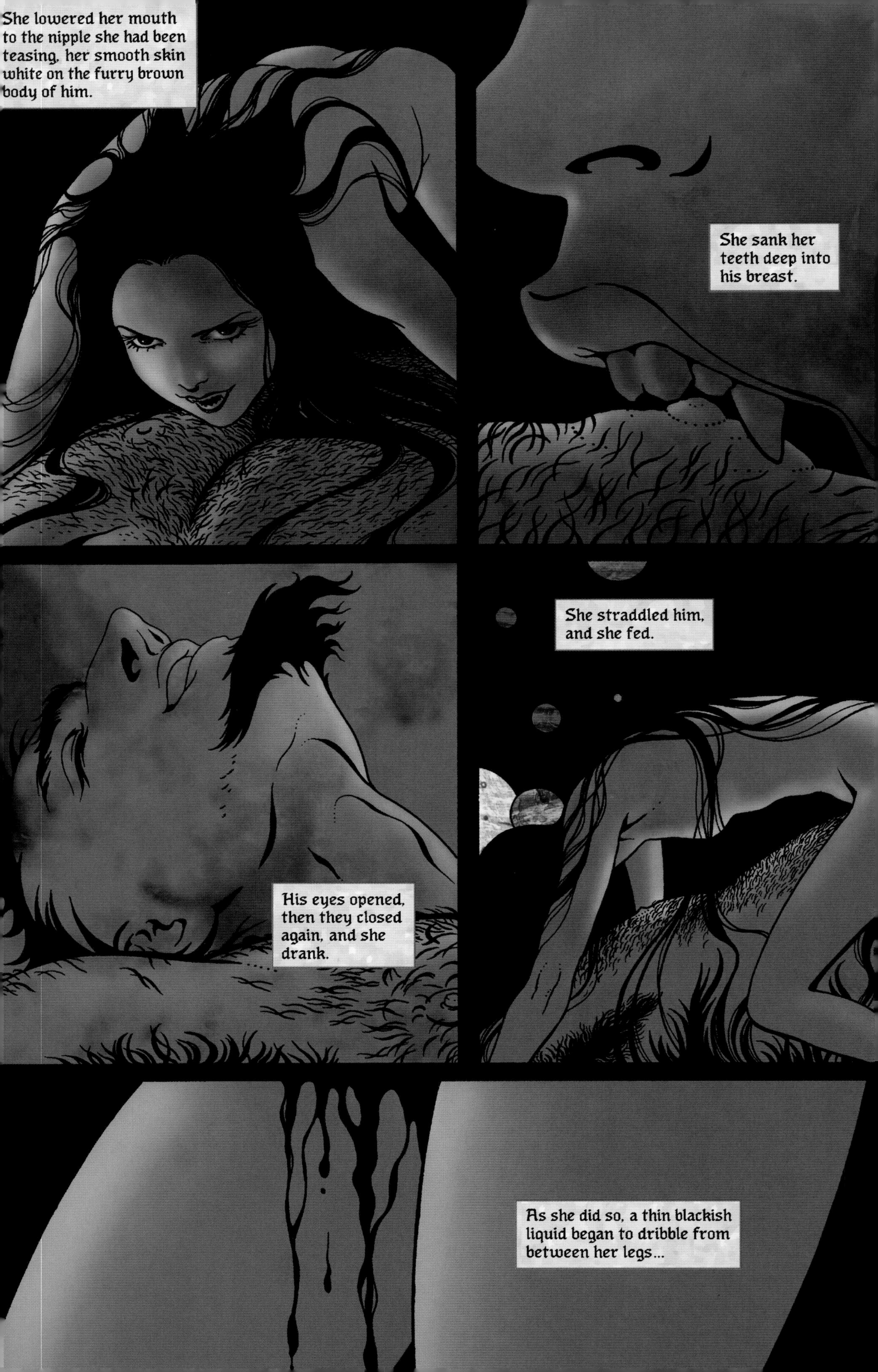
She lowered her mouth to the nipple she had been teasing, her smooth skin white on the furry brown body of him.
She sank her teeth deep into his breast.
His eyes opened, then they closed again, and she drank.
She straddled him, and she fed.
As she did so, a thin blackish liquid began to dribble from between her legs...

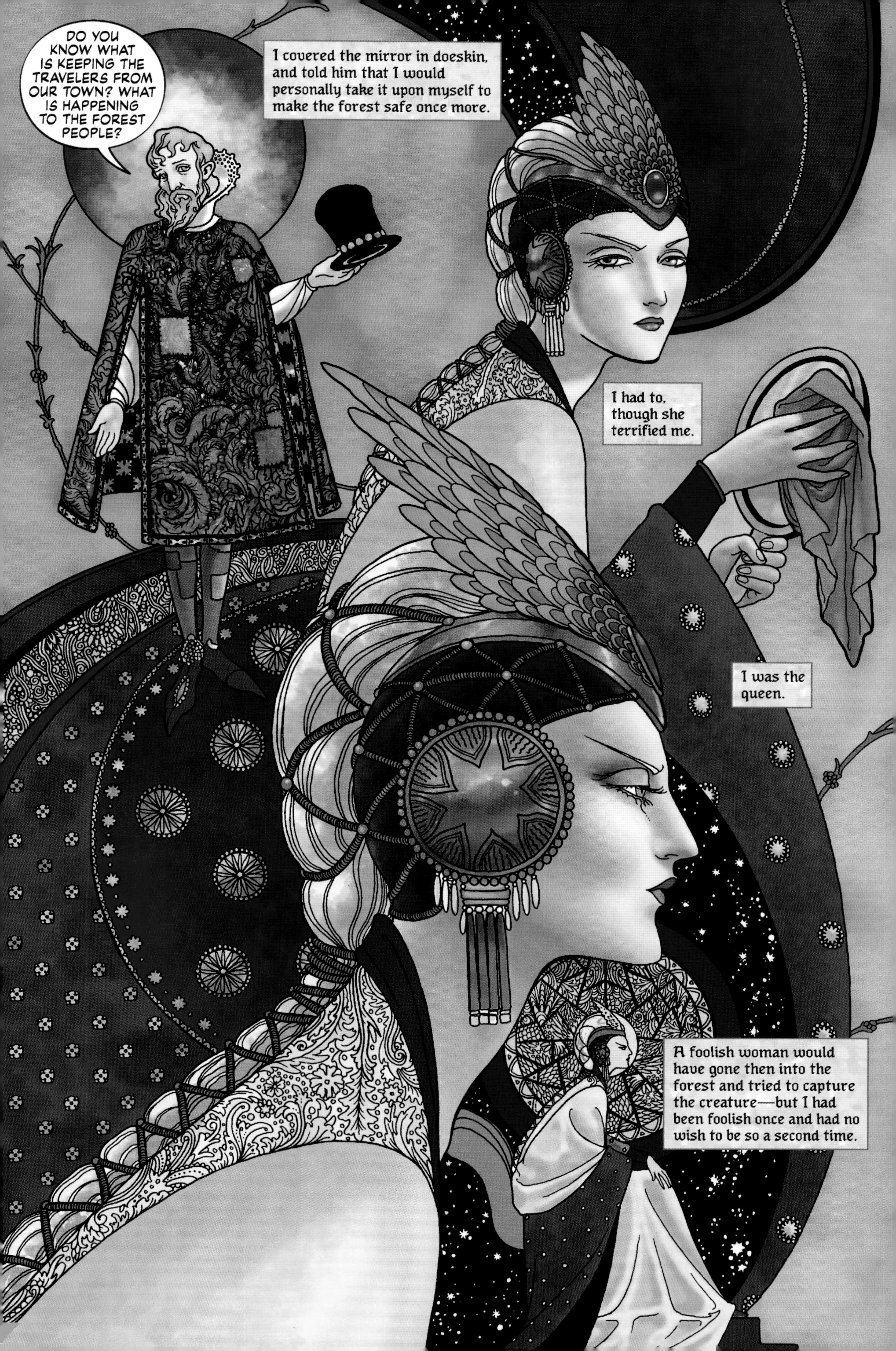
DO YOU KNOW WHAT IS KEEPING THE TRAVELERS FROM OUR TOWN? WHAT IS HAPPENING TO THE FOREST PEOPLE?
I covered the mirror in doeskin, and told him that I would personally take it upon myself to make the forest safe once more.
I had to, though she terrified me.
I was the queen.
A foolish woman would have gone then into the forest and tried to capture the creature—but I had been foolish once and had no wish to be so a second time.

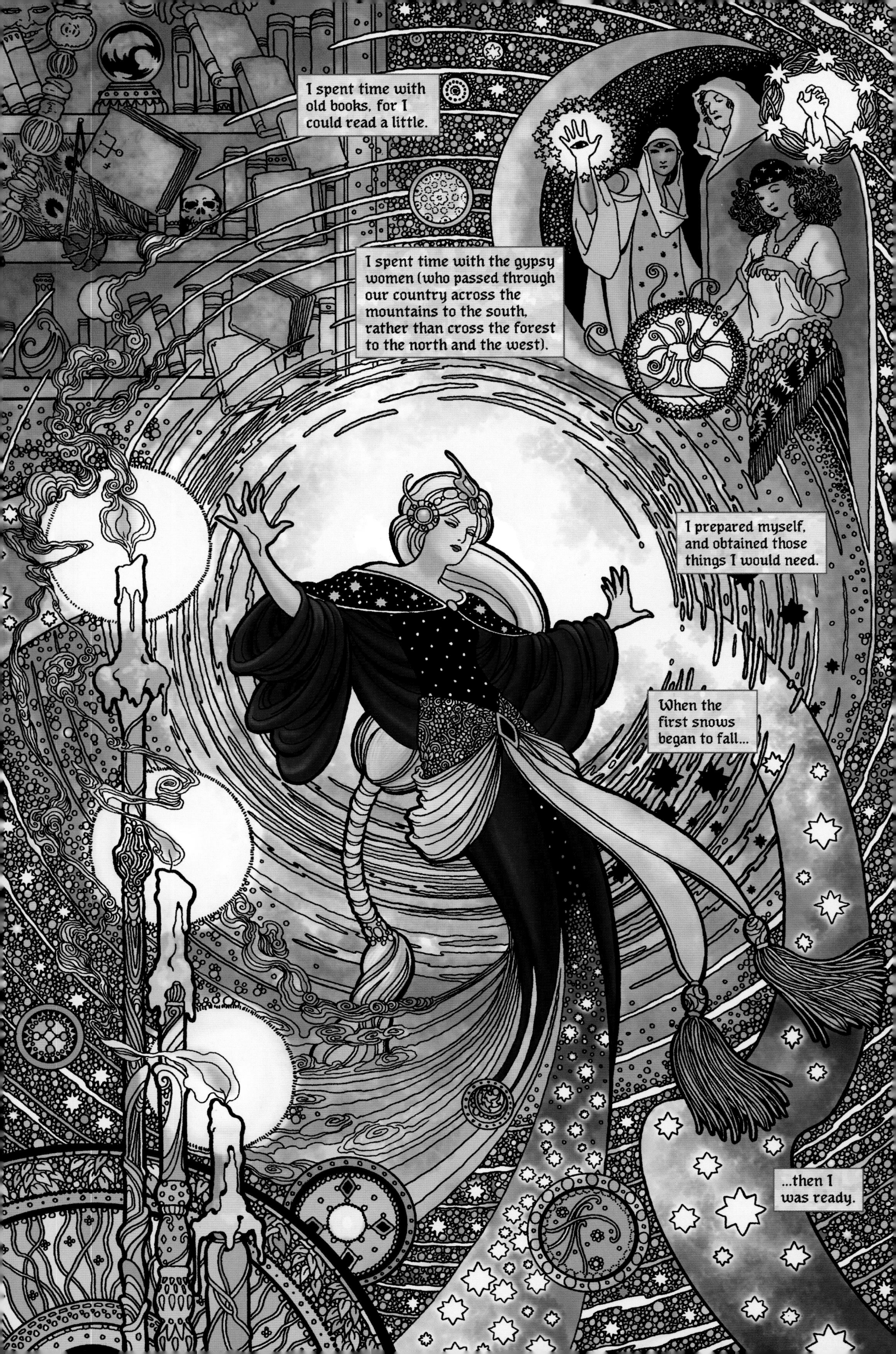
I spent time with old books, for I could read a little.
I spent time with the gypsy women (who passed through our country across the mountains to the south, rather than cross the forest to the north and the west).
I prepared myself, and obtained those things I would need.
When the first snows began to fall...
...then I was ready.

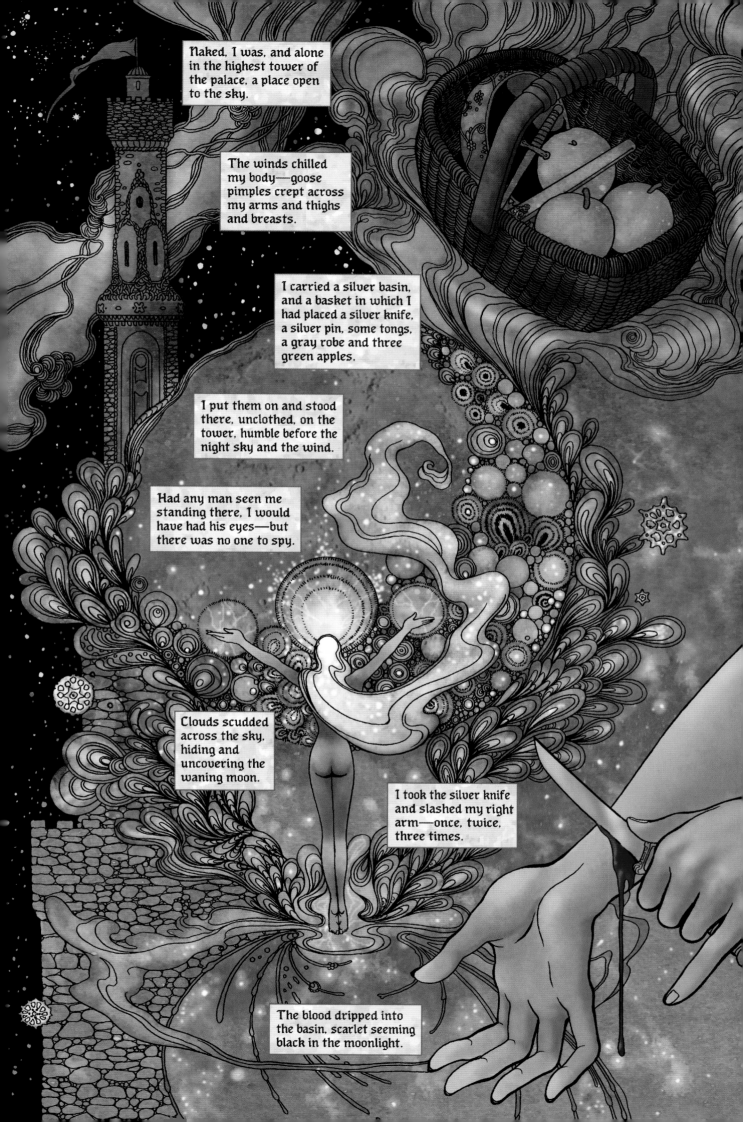

Naked, I was, and alone in the highest tower of the palace, a place open to the sky.

The winds chilled my body—goose pimples crept across my arms and thighs and breasts.

I carried a silver basin, and a basket in which I had placed a silver knife, a silver pin, some tongs, a gray robe and three green apples.

I put them on and stood there, unclothed, on the tower, humble before the night sky and the wind.

Had any man seen me standing there, I would have had his eyes—but there was no one to spy.

Clouds scudded across the sky, hiding and uncovering the waning moon.

I took the silver knife and slashed my right arm—once, twice, three times.

The blood dripped into the basin, scarlet seeming black in the moonlight.

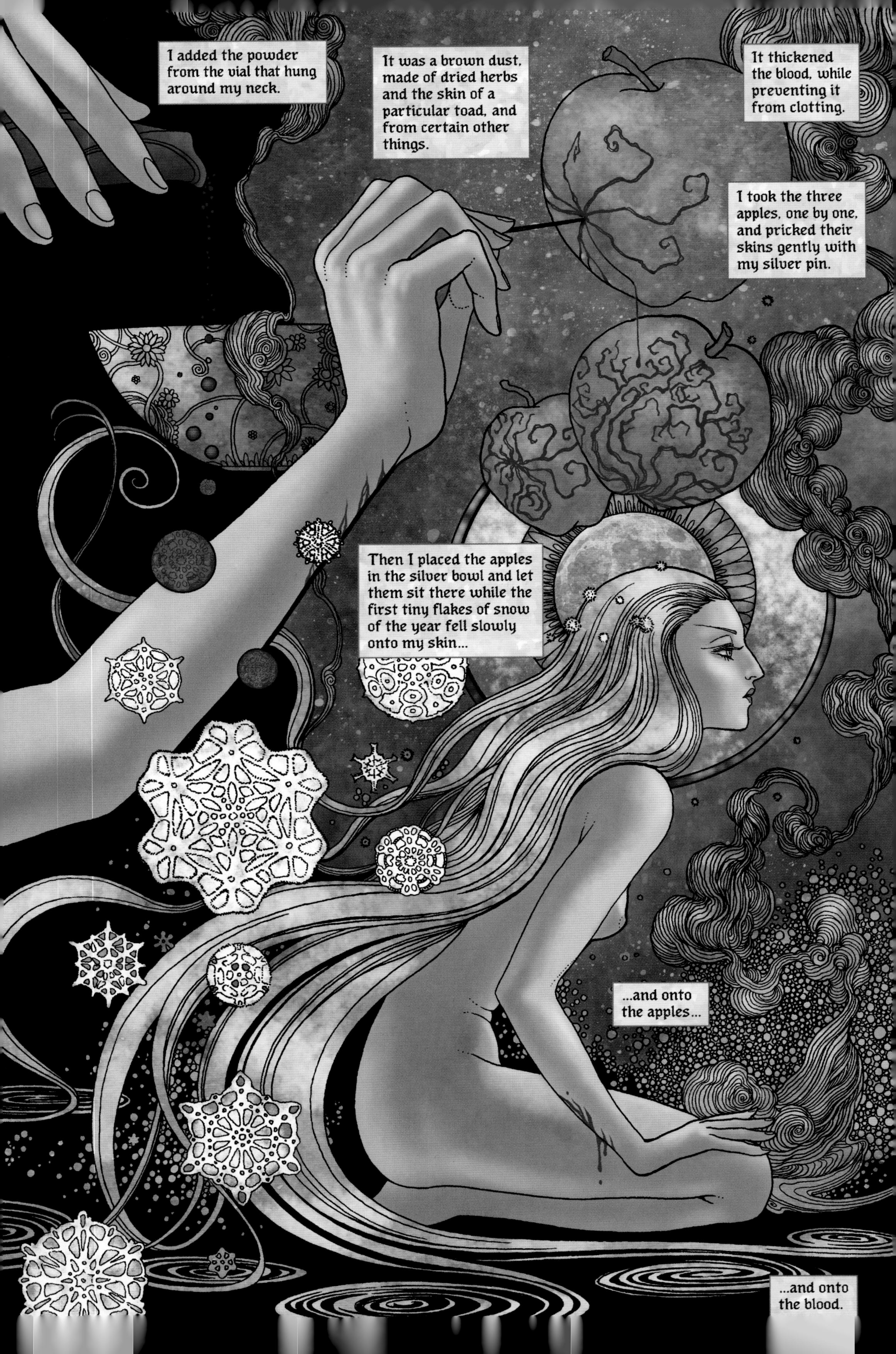
I added the powder from the vial that hung around my neck.
It was a brown dust, made of dried herbs and the skin of a particular toad, and from certain other things.
It thickened the blood, while preventing it from clotting.
I took the three apples, one by one, and pricked their skins gently with my silver pin.
Then I placed the apples in the silver bowl and let them sit there while the first tiny flakes of snow of the year fell slowly onto my skin...
...and onto the apples...
...and onto the blood.

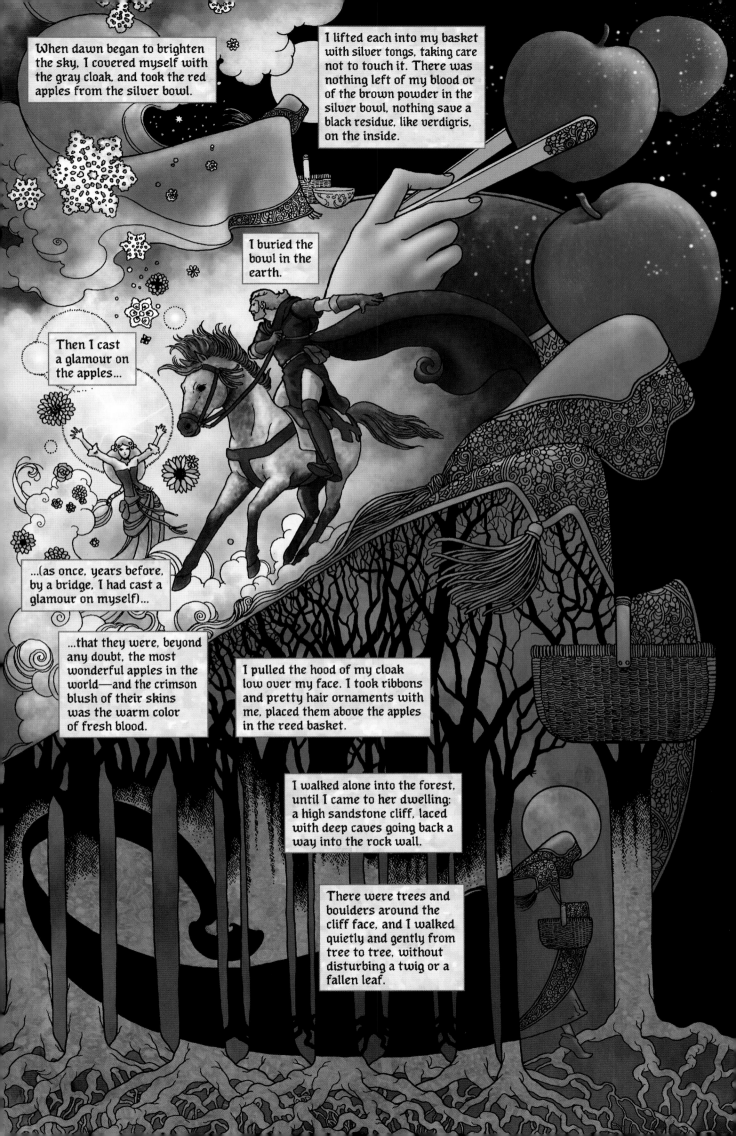

When dawn began to brighten the sky, I covered myself with the gray cloak, and took the red apples from the silver bowl.

I lifted each into my basket with silver tongs, taking care not to touch it. There was nothing left of my blood or of the brown powder in the silver bowl, nothing save a black residue, like verdigris, on the inside.

I buried the bowl in the earth.

Then I cast a glamour on the apples...

...(as once, years before, by a bridge, I had cast a glamour on myself)...

...that they were, beyond any doubt, the most wonderful apples in the world—and the crimson blush of their skins was the warm color of fresh blood.

I pulled the hood of my cloak low over my face. I took ribbons and pretty hair ornaments with me, placed them above the apples in the reed basket.

I walked alone into the forest, until I came to her dwelling: a high sandstone cliff, laced with deep caves going back a way into the rock wall.

There were trees and boulders around the cliff face, and I walked quietly and gently from tree to tree, without disturbing a twig or a fallen leaf.

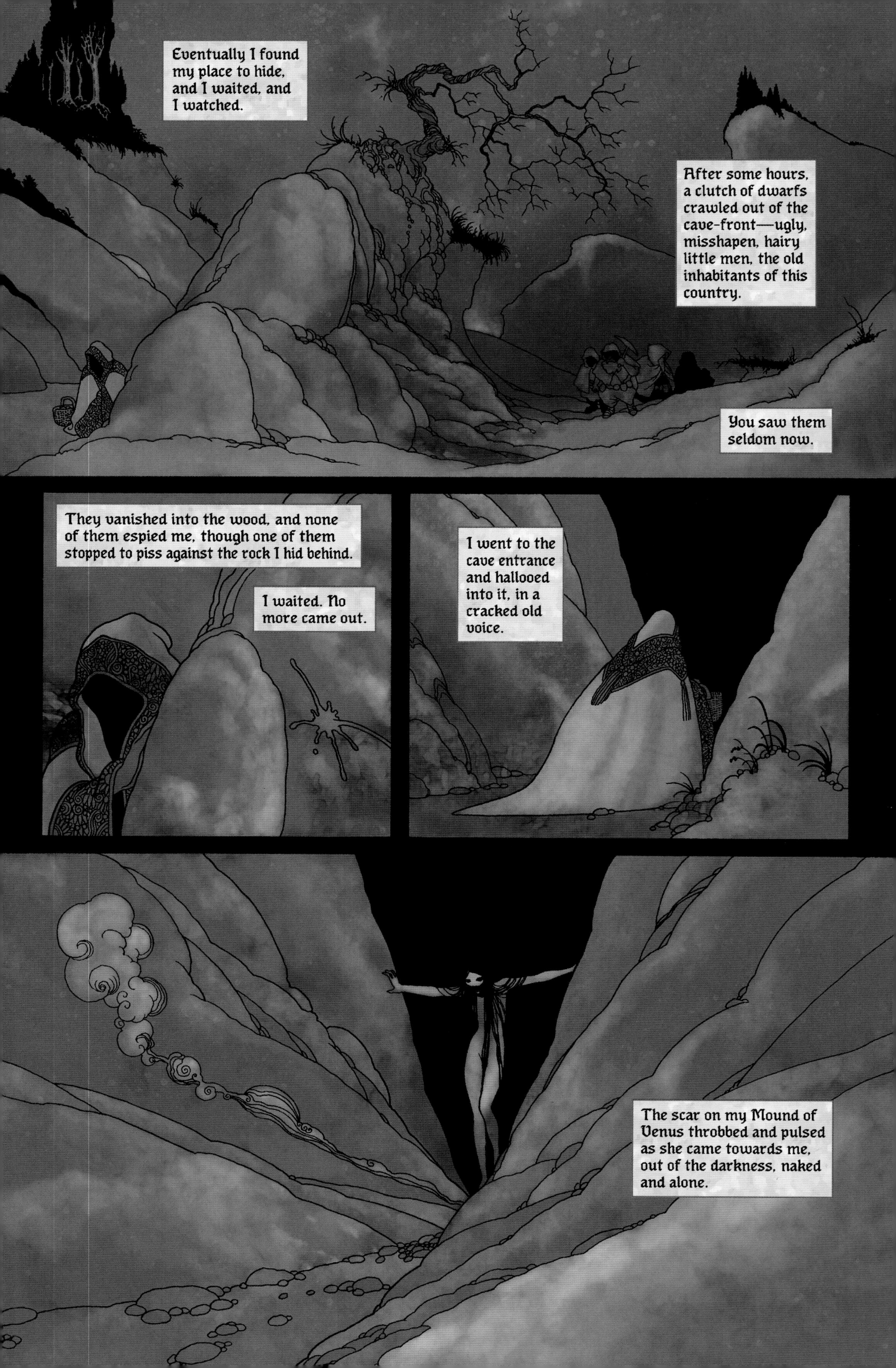
Eventually I found my place to hide, and I waited, and I watched.
After some hours, a clutch of dwarfs crawled out of the cave-front—ugly, misshapen, hairy little men, the old inhabitants of this country.
You saw them seldom now.
They vanished into the wood, and none of them espied me, though one of them stopped to piss against the rock I hid behind.
I waited. No more came out.
I went to the cave entrance and hallooed into it, in a cracked old voice.
The scar on my Mound of Venus throbbed and pulsed as she came towards me, out of the darkness, naked and alone.

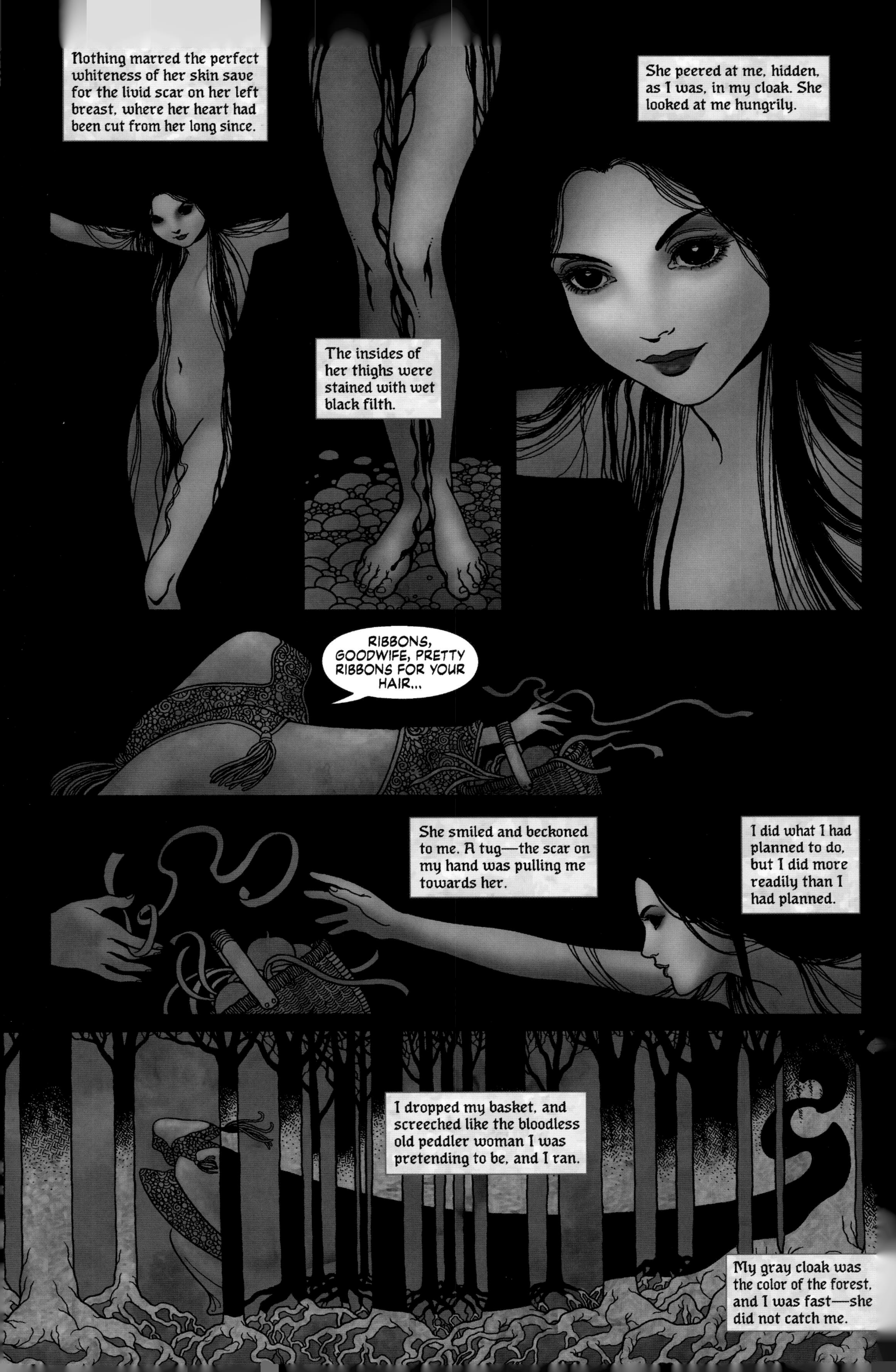
Nothing marred the perfect whiteness of her skin save for the livid scar on her left breast, where her heart had been cut from her long since.
The insides of her thighs were stained with wet black filth.
She peered at me, hidden, as I was, in my cloak. She looked at me hungrily.
RIBBONS, GOODWIFE, PRETTY RIBBONS FOR YOUR HAIR...
She smiled and beckoned to me. A tug—the scar on my hand was pulling me towards her.
I did what I had planned to do, but I did more readily than I had planned.
I dropped my basket, and screeched like the bloodless old peddler woman I was pretending to be, and I ran.
My gray cloak was the color of the forest, and I was fast—she did not catch me.

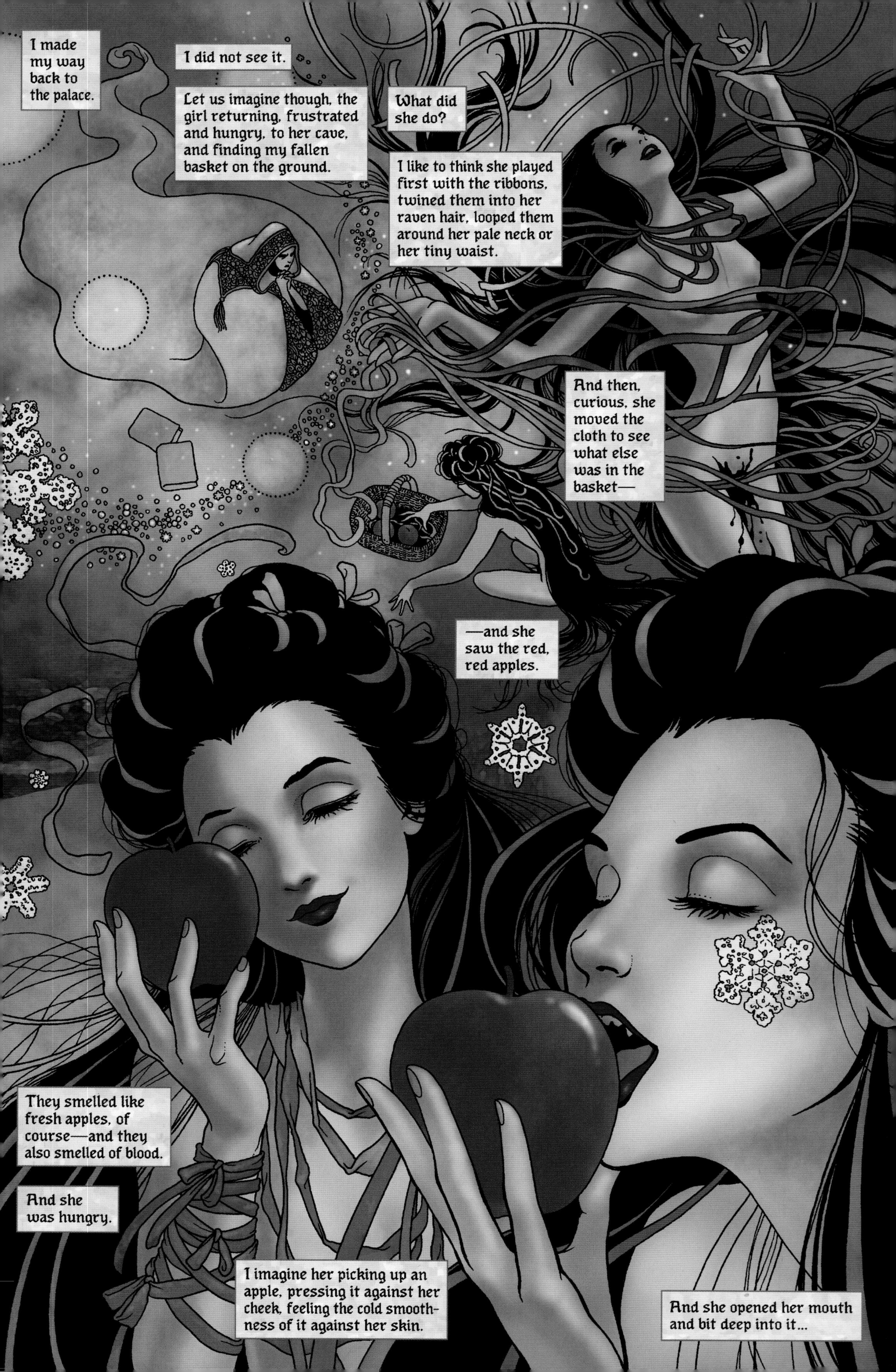

I made my way back to the palace.
I did not see it.
Let us imagine though, the girl returning, frustrated and hungry, to her cave, and finding my fallen basket on the ground.
What did she do?
I like to think she played first with the ribbons, twined them into her raven hair, looped them around her pale neck or her tiny waist.
And then, curious, she moved the cloth to see what else was in the basket—
—and she saw the red, red apples.
They smelled like fresh apples, of course—and they also smelled of blood.
And she was hungry.
I imagine her picking up an apple, pressing it against her cheek, feeling the cold smoothness of it against her skin.
And she opened her mouth and bit deep into it...

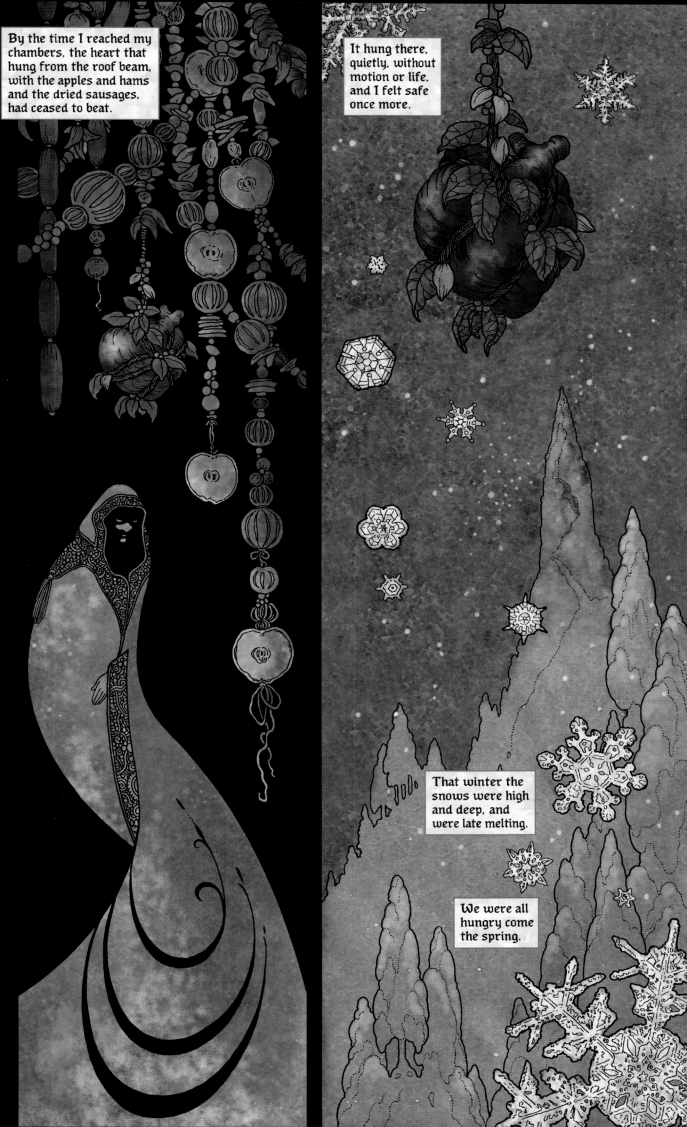

By the time I reached my chambers, the heart that hung from the roof beam, with the apples and hams and the dried sausages, had ceased to beat.

It hung there, quietly, without motion or life, and I felt safe once more.

That winter the snows were high and deep, and were late melting.

We were all hungry come the spring.

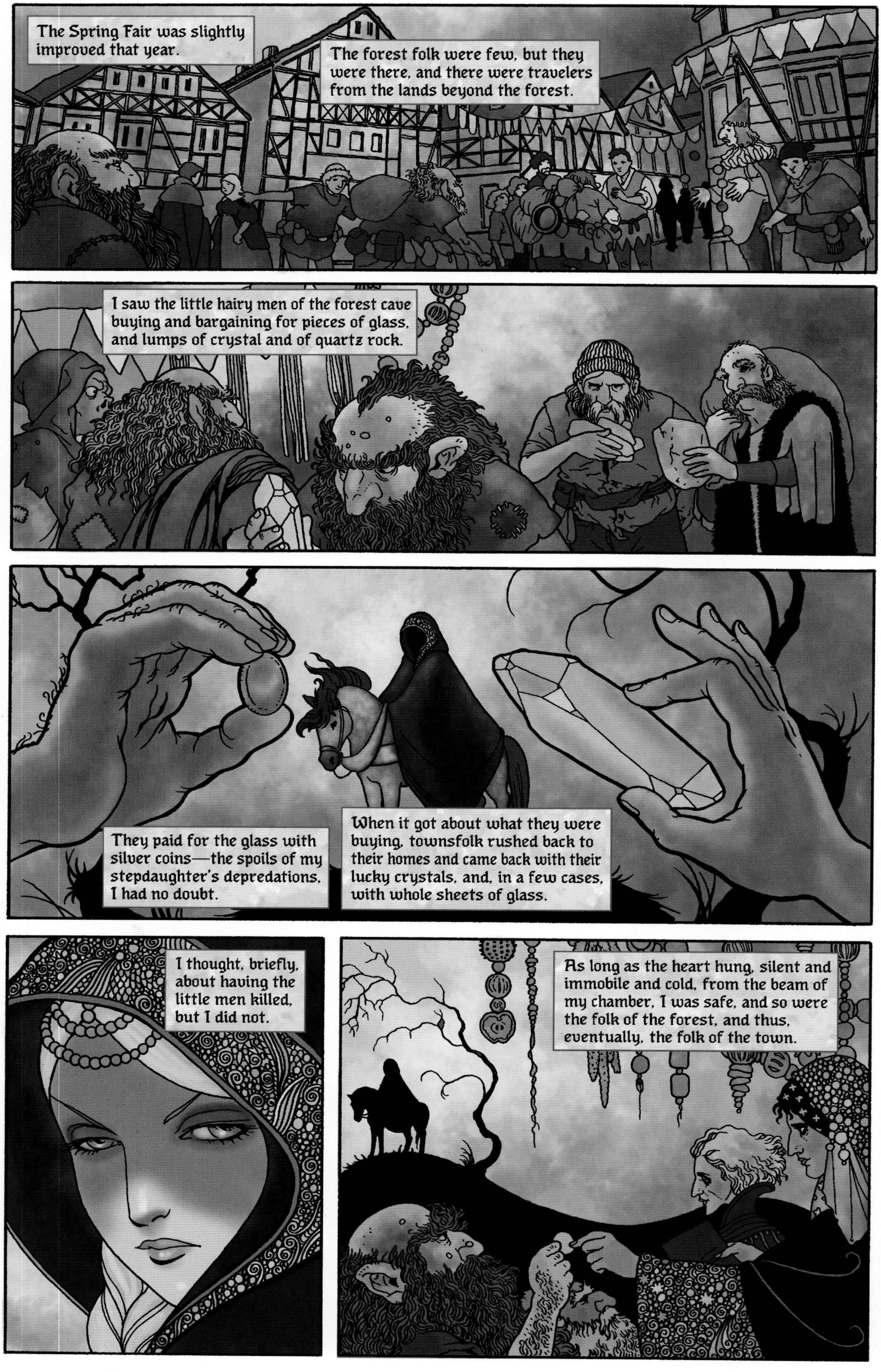
The Spring Fair was slightly improved that year.
The forest folk were few, but they were there, and there were travelers from the lands beyond the forest.
I saw the little hairy men of the forest cave buying and bargaining for pieces of glass, and lumps of crystal and of quartz rock.
They paid for the glass with silver coins—the spoils of my stepdaughter's depredations, I had no doubt.
When it got about what they were buying, townsfolk rushed back to their homes and came back with their lucky crystals, and, in a few cases, with whole sheets of glass.
I thought, briefly, about having the little men killed, but I did not.
As long as the heart hung, silent and immobile and cold, from the beam of my chamber, I was safe, and so were the folk of the forest, and thus, eventually, the folk of the town.

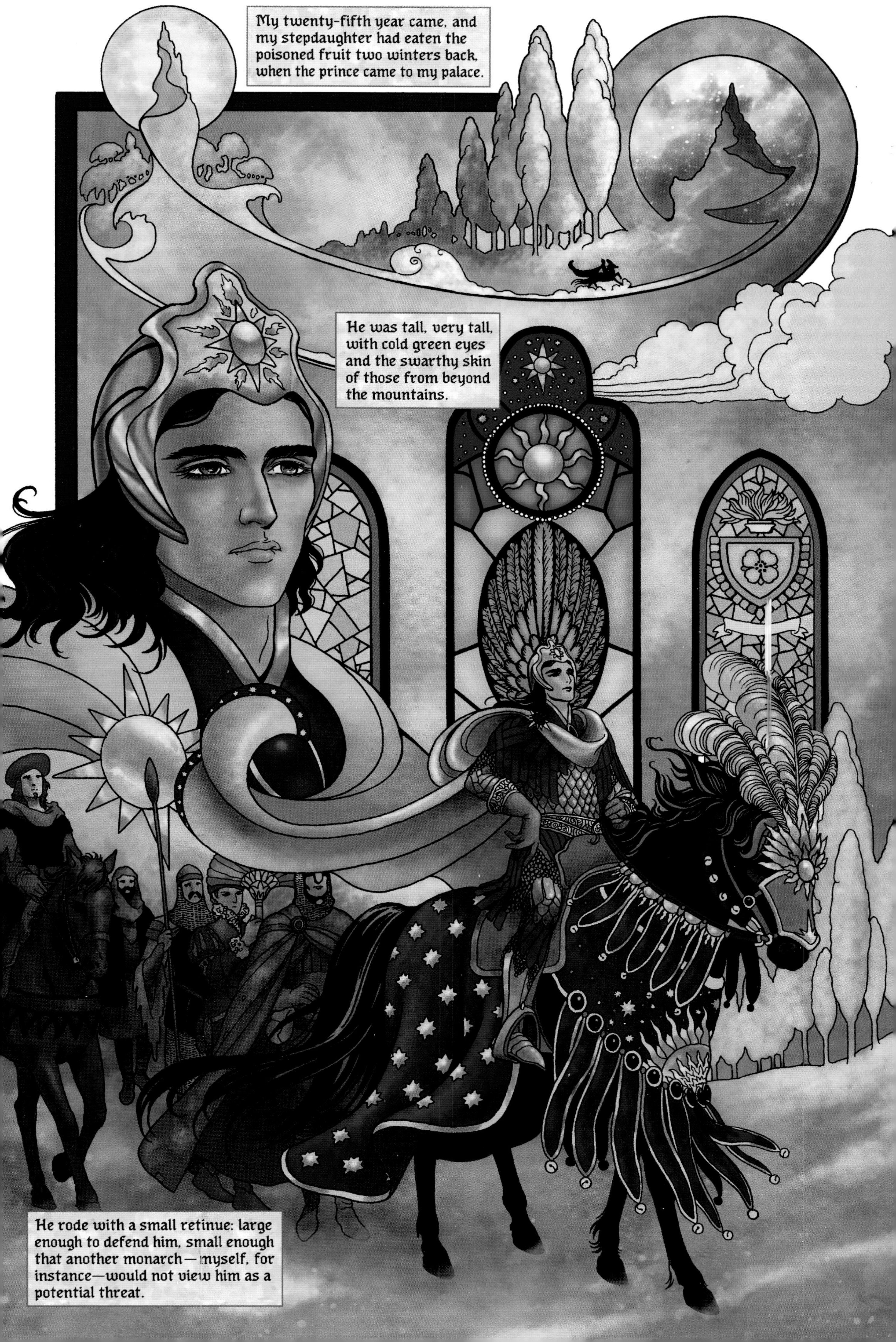
My twenty-fifth year came, and my stepdaughter had eaten the poisoned fruit two winters back, when the prince came to my palace.
He was tall, very tall, with cold green eyes and the swarthy skin of those from beyond the mountains.
He rode with a small retinue: large enough to defend him, small enough that another monarch—myself, for instance—would not view him as a potential threat.

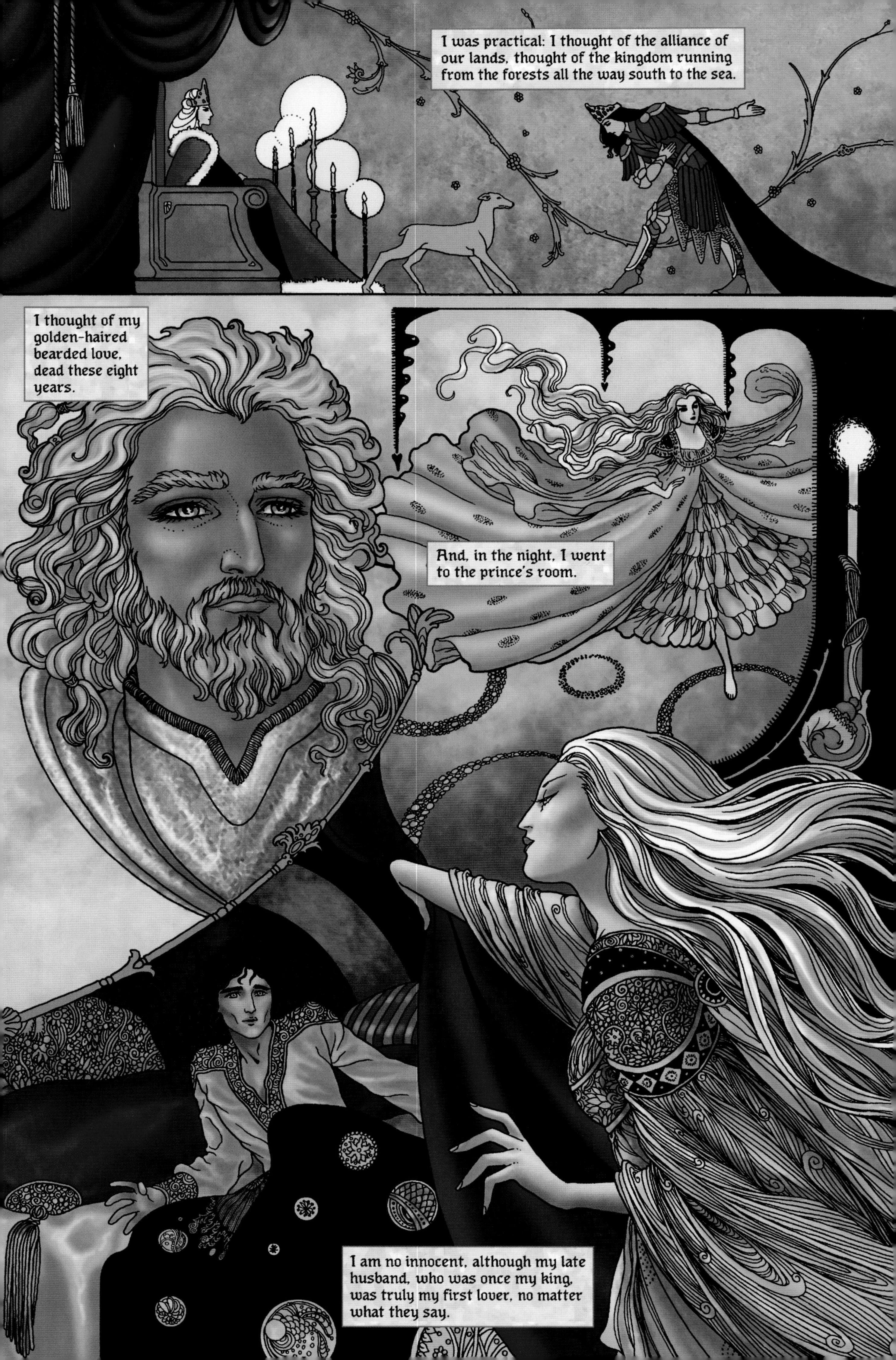
I was practical: I thought of the alliance of our lands, thought of the kingdom running from the forests all the way south to the sea.
I thought of my golden-haired bearded love, dead these eight years.
And, in the night, I went to the prince's room.
I am no innocent, although my late husband, who was once my king, was truly my first lover, no matter what they say.

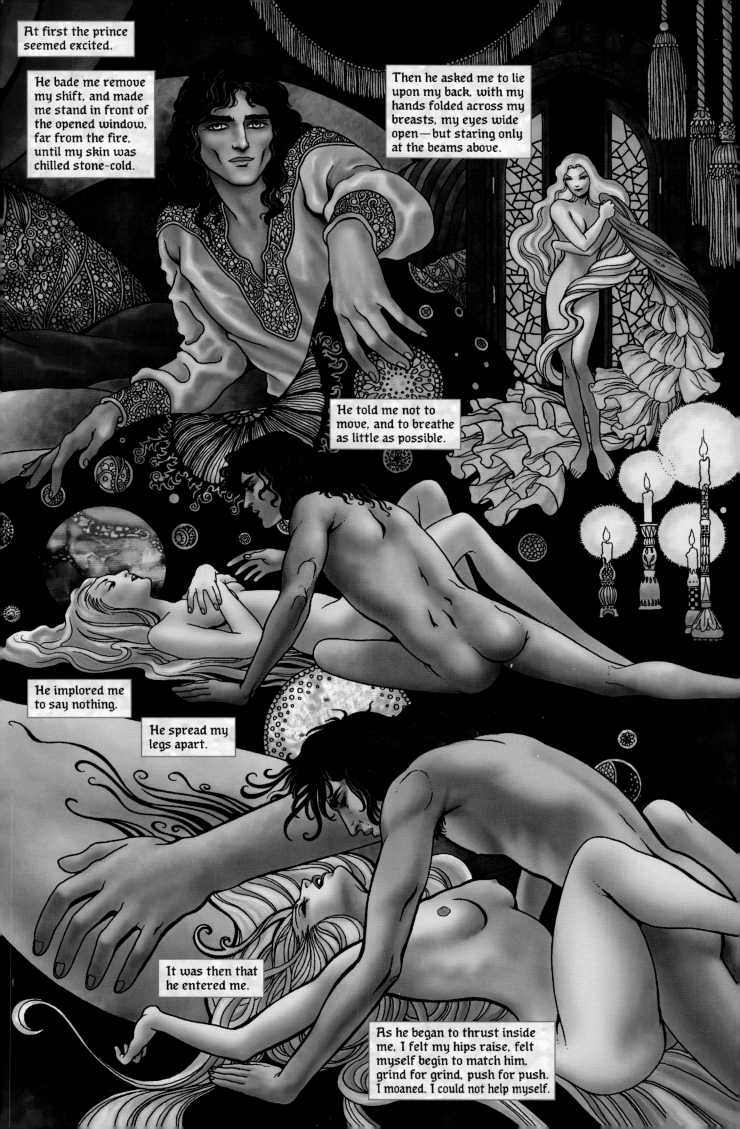

At first the prince seemed excited.

He bade me remove my shift, and made me stand in front of the opened window, far from the fire, until my skin was chilled stone-cold.

Then he asked me to lie upon my back, with my hands folded across my breasts, my eyes wide open—but staring only at the beams above.

He told me not to move, and to breathe as little as possible.

He implored me to say nothing.

He spread my legs apart.

It was then that he entered me.

As he began to thrust inside me, I felt my hips raise, felt myself begin to match him, grind for grind, push for push. I moaned. I could not help myself.

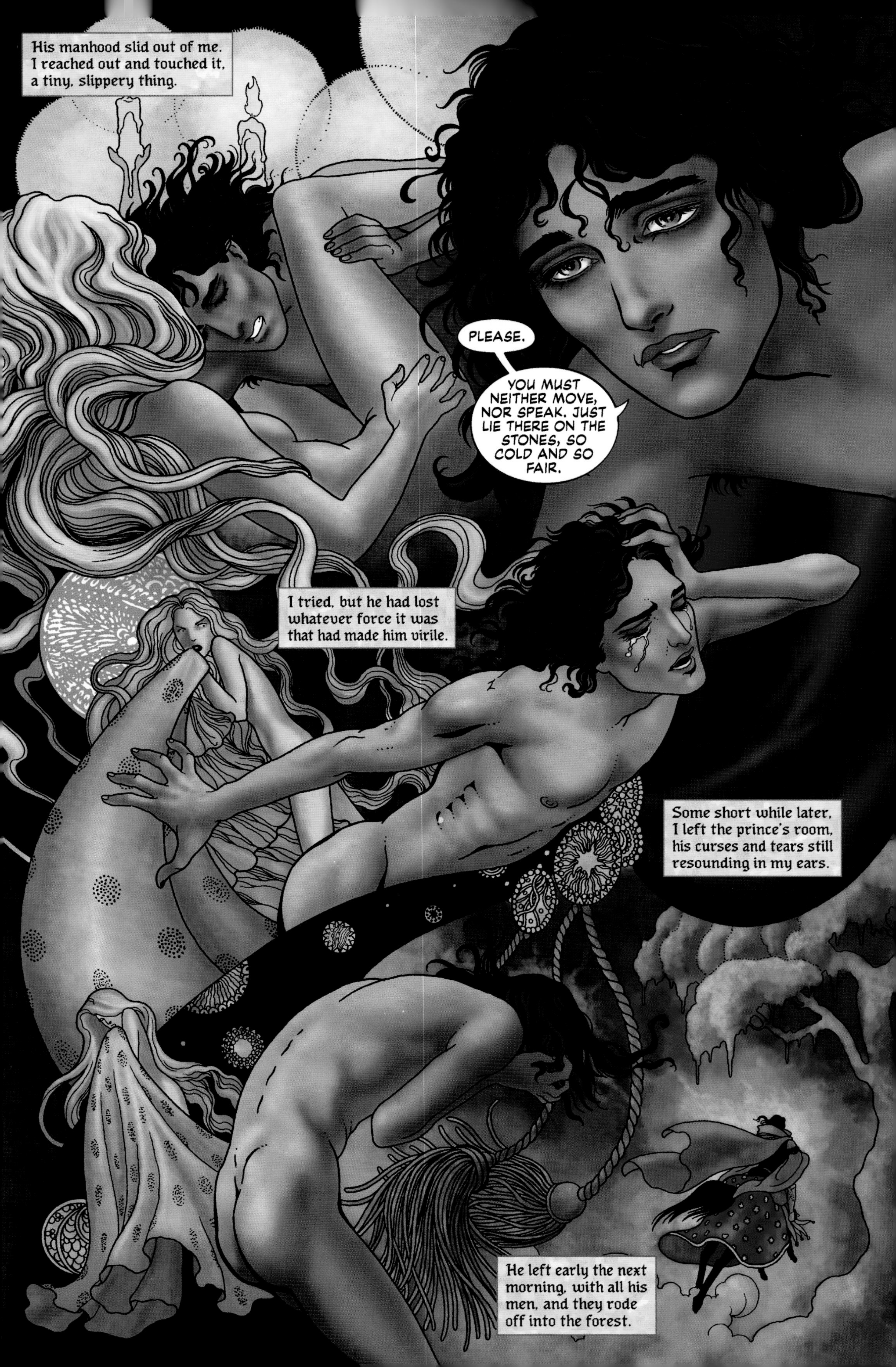
His manhood slid out of me. I reached out and touched it, a tiny, slippery thing.
PLEASE.
YOU MUST NEITHER MOVE, NOR SPEAK. JUST LIE THERE ON THE STONES, SO COLD AND SO FAIR.
I tried, but he had lost whatever force it was that had made him virile.
Some short while later, I left the prince's room, his curses and tears still resounding in my ears.
He left early the next morning, with all his men, and they rode off into the forest.

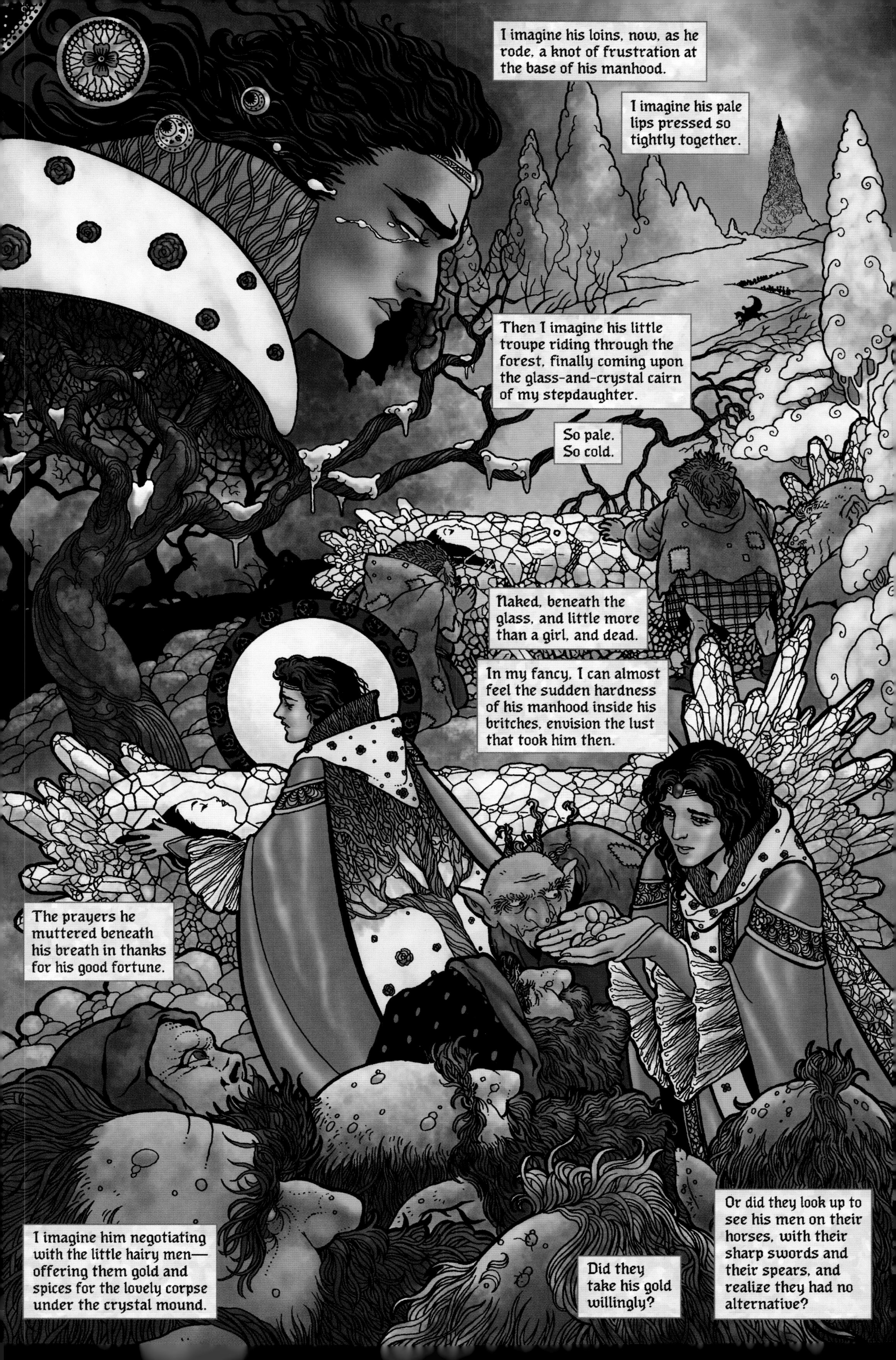
I imagine his loins, now, as he rode, a knot of frustration at the base of his manhood.
I imagine his pale lips pressed so tightly together.
Then I imagine his little troupe riding through the forest, finally coming upon the glass-and-crystal cairn of my stepdaughter.
So pale. So cold.
Naked, beneath the glass, and little more than a girl, and dead.
In my fancy, I can almost feel the sudden hardness of his manhood inside his britches, envision the lust that took him then.
The prayers he muttered beneath his breath in thanks for his good fortune.
I imagine him negotiating with the little hairy men—offering them gold and spices for the lovely corpse under the crystal mound.
Did they take his gold willingly?
Or did they look up to see his men on their horses, with their sharp swords and their spears, and realize they had no alternative?

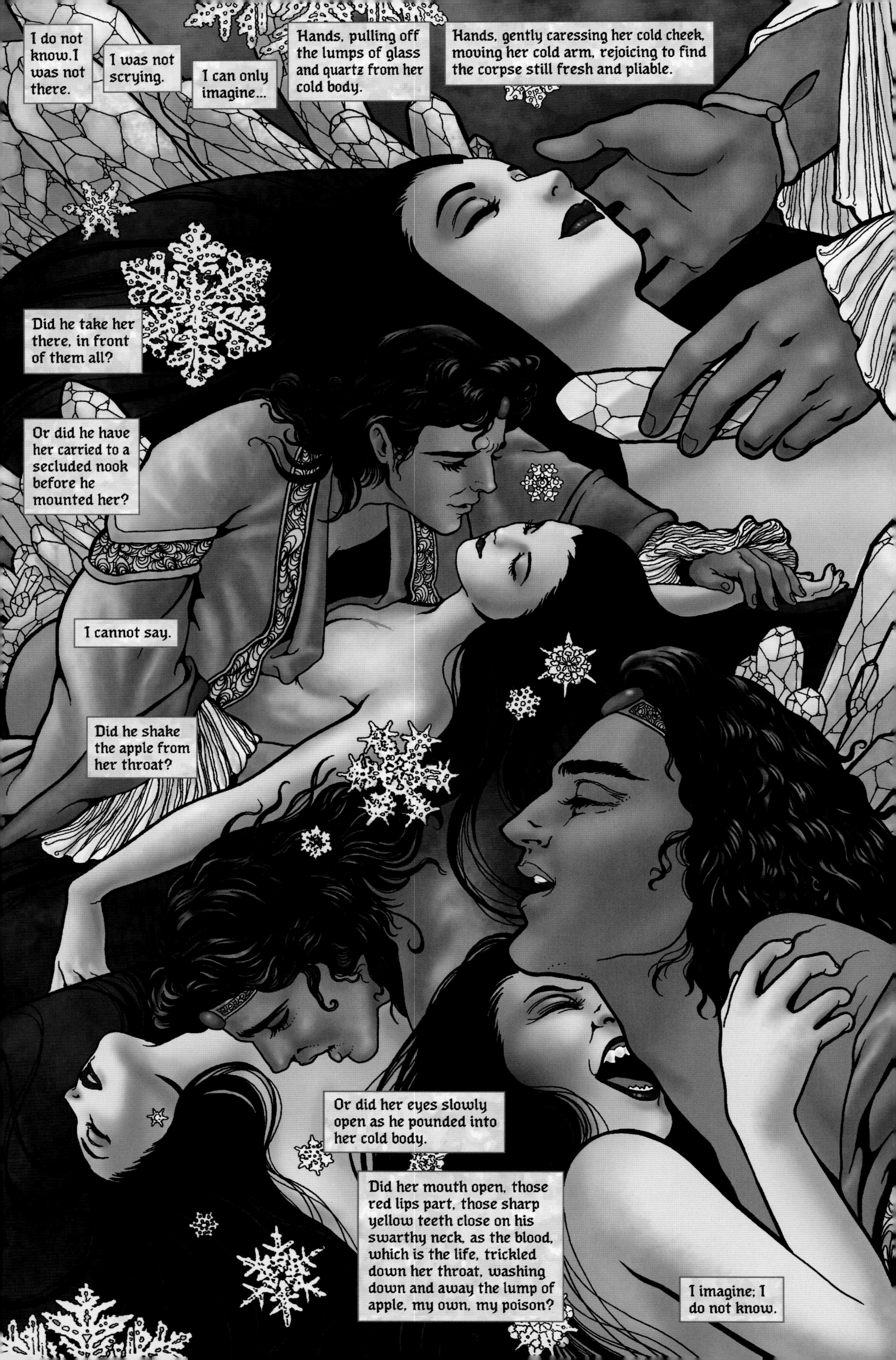

I do not know. I was not there.
I was not scrying.
I can only imagine...
Hands, pulling off the lumps of glass and quartz from her cold body.
Hands, gently caressing her cold cheek, moving her cold arm, rejoicing to find the corpse still fresh and pliable.
Did he take her there, in front of them all?
Or did he have her carried to a secluded nook before he mounted her?
I cannot say.
Did he shake the apple from her throat?
Or did her eyes slowly open as he pounded into her cold body.
Did her mouth open, those red lips part, those sharp yellow teeth close on his swarthy neck, as the blood, which is the life, trickled down her throat, washing down and away the lump of apple, my own, my poison?
I imagine; I do not know.

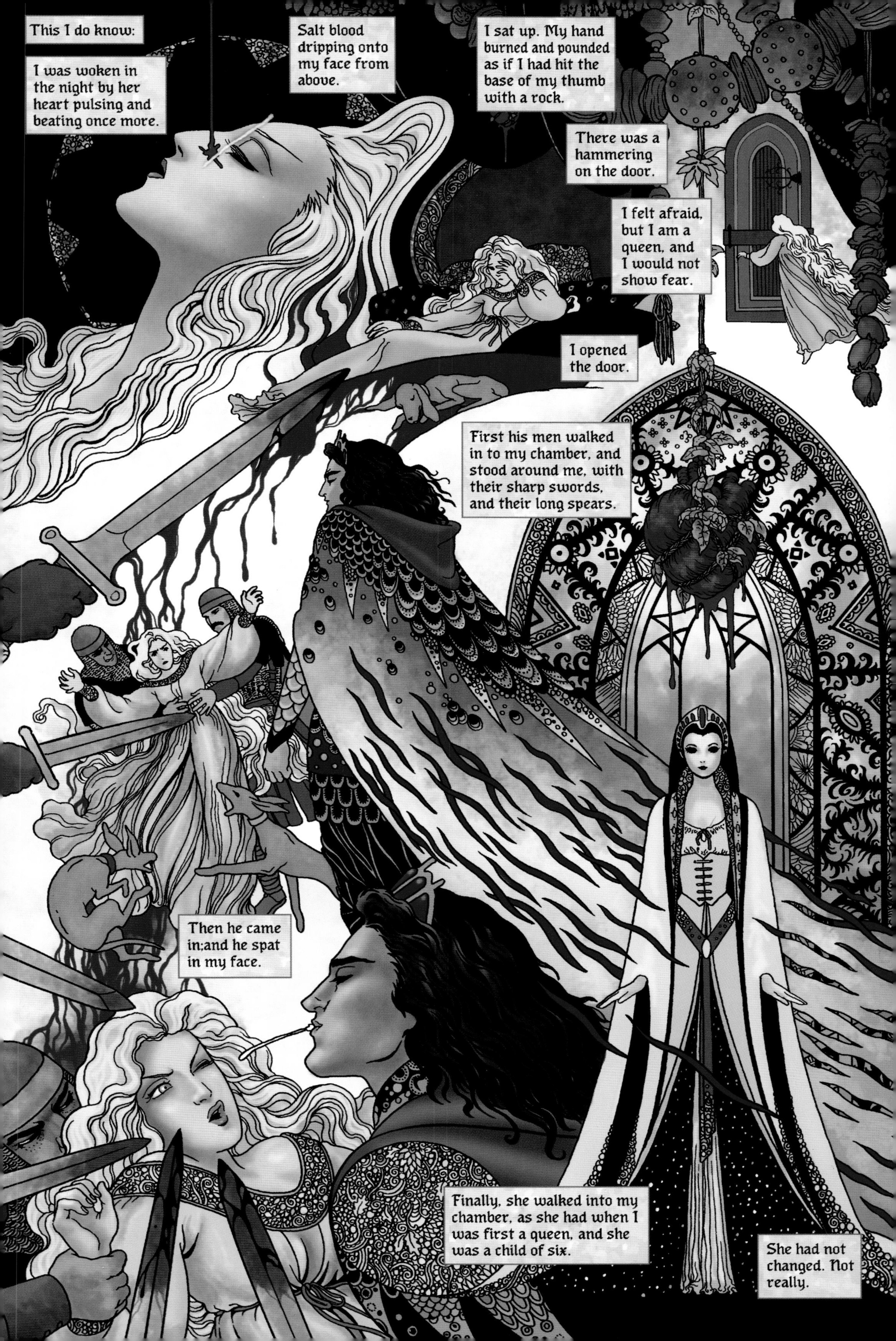
This I do know:
I was woken in the night by her heart pulsing and beating once more.
Salt blood dripping onto my face from above.
I sat up. My hand burned and pounded as if I had hit the base of my thumb with a rock.
There was a hammering on the door.
I felt afraid, but I am a queen, and I would not show fear.
I opened the door.
First his men walked in to my chamber, and stood around me, with their sharp swords, and their long spears.
Then he came in;and he spat in my face.
Finally, she walked into my chamber, as she had when I was first a queen, and she was a child of six.
She had not changed. Not really.

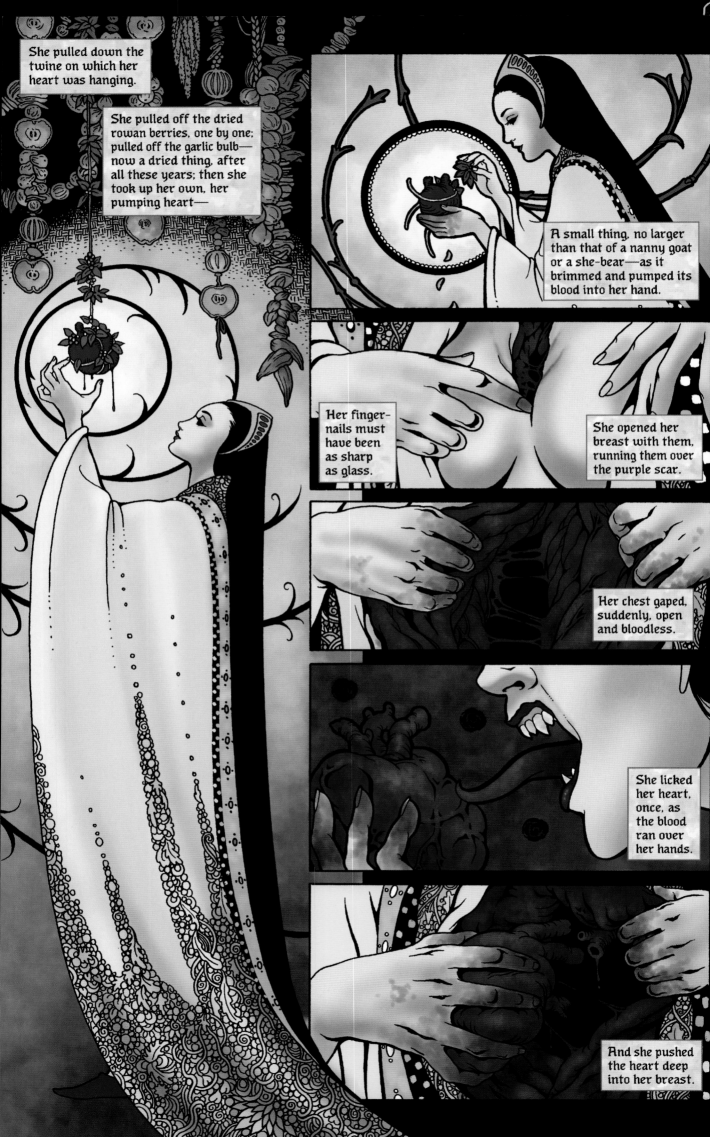

She pulled down the twine on which her heart was hanging.

She pulled off the dried rowan berries, one by one; pulled off the garlic bulb—now a dried thing, after all these years; then she took up her own, her pumping heart—

A small thing, no larger than that of a nanny goat or a she-bear—as it brimmed and pumped its blood into her hand.

Her finger-nails must have been as sharp as glass.

She opened her breast with them, running them over the purple scar.

Her chest gaped, suddenly, open and bloodless.

She licked her heart, once, as the blood ran over her hands.

And she pushed the heart deep into her breast.

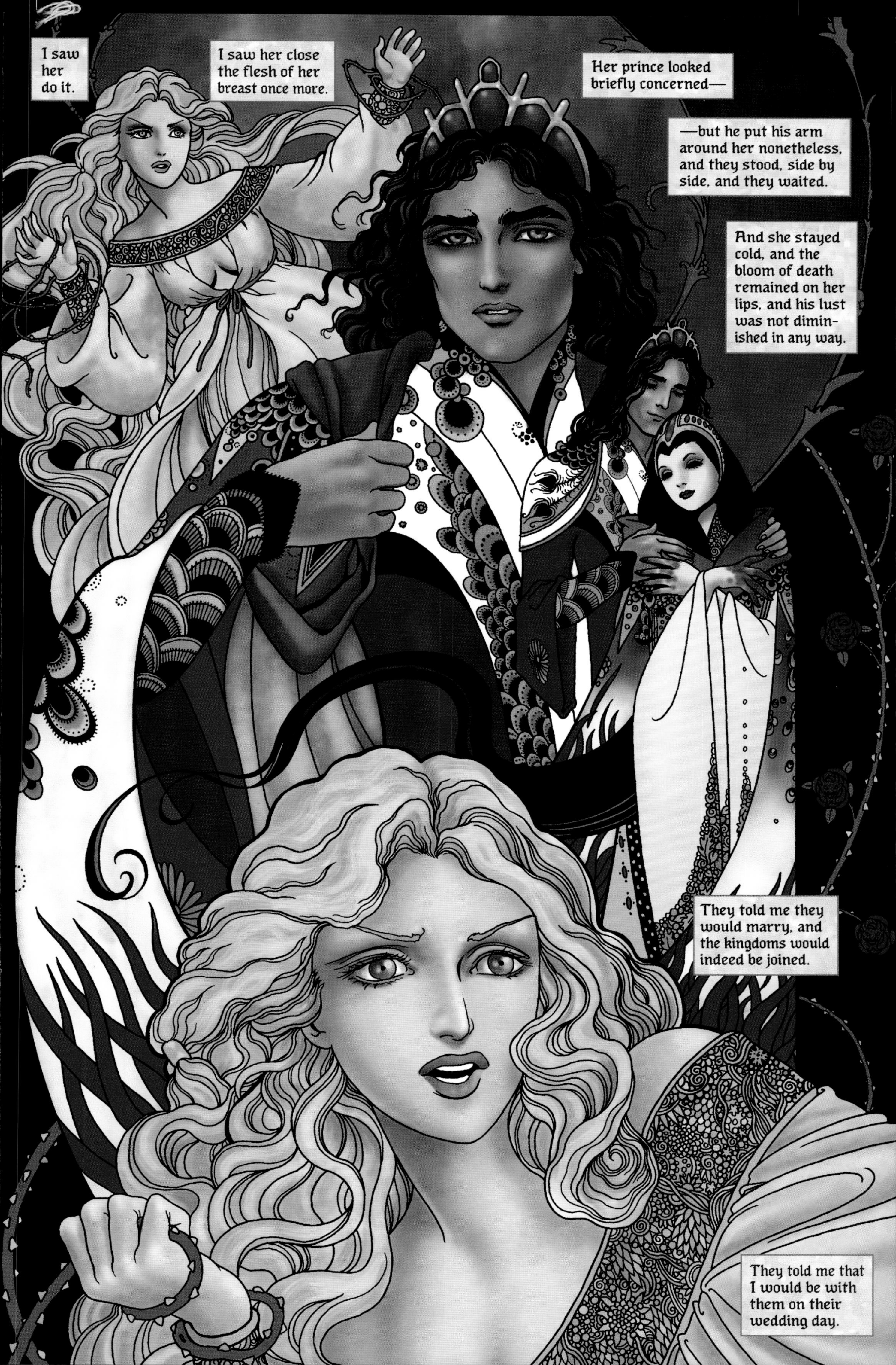
I saw her do it.
I saw her close the flesh of her breast once more.
Her prince looked briefly concerned—
—but he put his arm around her nonetheless, and they stood, side by side, and they waited.
And she stayed cold, and the bloom of death remained on her lips, and his lust was not diminished in any way.
They told me they would marry, and the kingdoms would indeed be joined.
They told me that I would be with them on their wedding day.

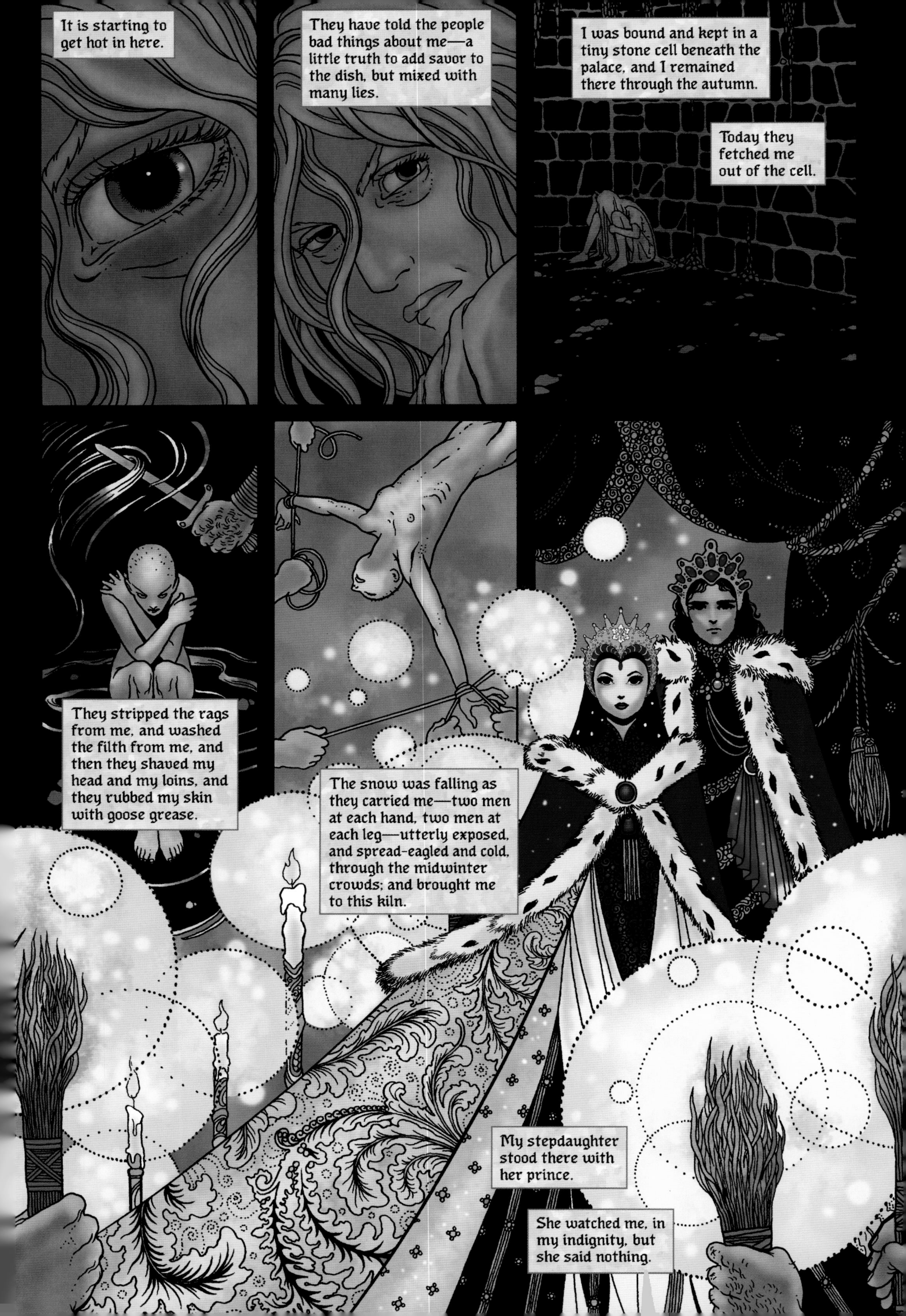

It is starting to get hot in here.
They have told the people bad things about me—a little truth to add savor to the dish, but mixed with many lies.
I was bound and kept in a tiny stone cell beneath the palace, and I remained there through the autumn.
Today they fetched me out of the cell.
They stripped the rags from me, and washed the filth from me, and then they shaved my head and my loins, and they rubbed my skin with goose grease.
The snow was falling as they carried me—two men at each hand, two men at each leg—utterly exposed, and spread-eagled and cold, through the midwinter crowds; and brought me to this kiln.
My stepdaughter stood there with her prince.
She watched me, in my indignity, but she said nothing.

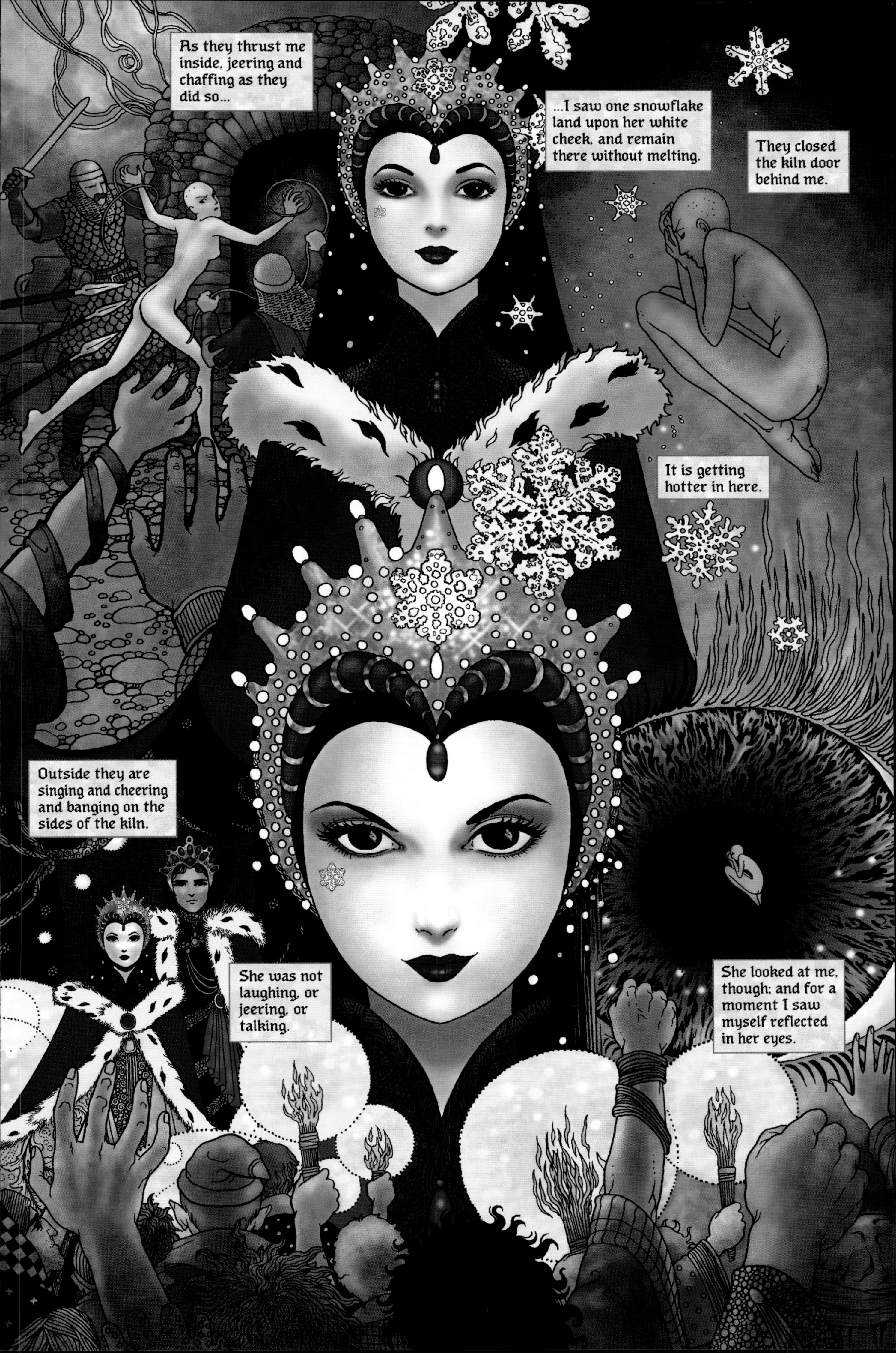

As they thrust me inside, jeering and chaffing as they did so...
...I saw one snowflake land upon her white cheek, and remain there without melting.
They closed the kiln door behind me.
It is getting hotter in here.
Outside they are singing and cheering and banging on the sides of the kiln.
She was not laughing, or jeering, or talking.
She looked at me, though; and for a moment I saw myself reflected in her eyes.

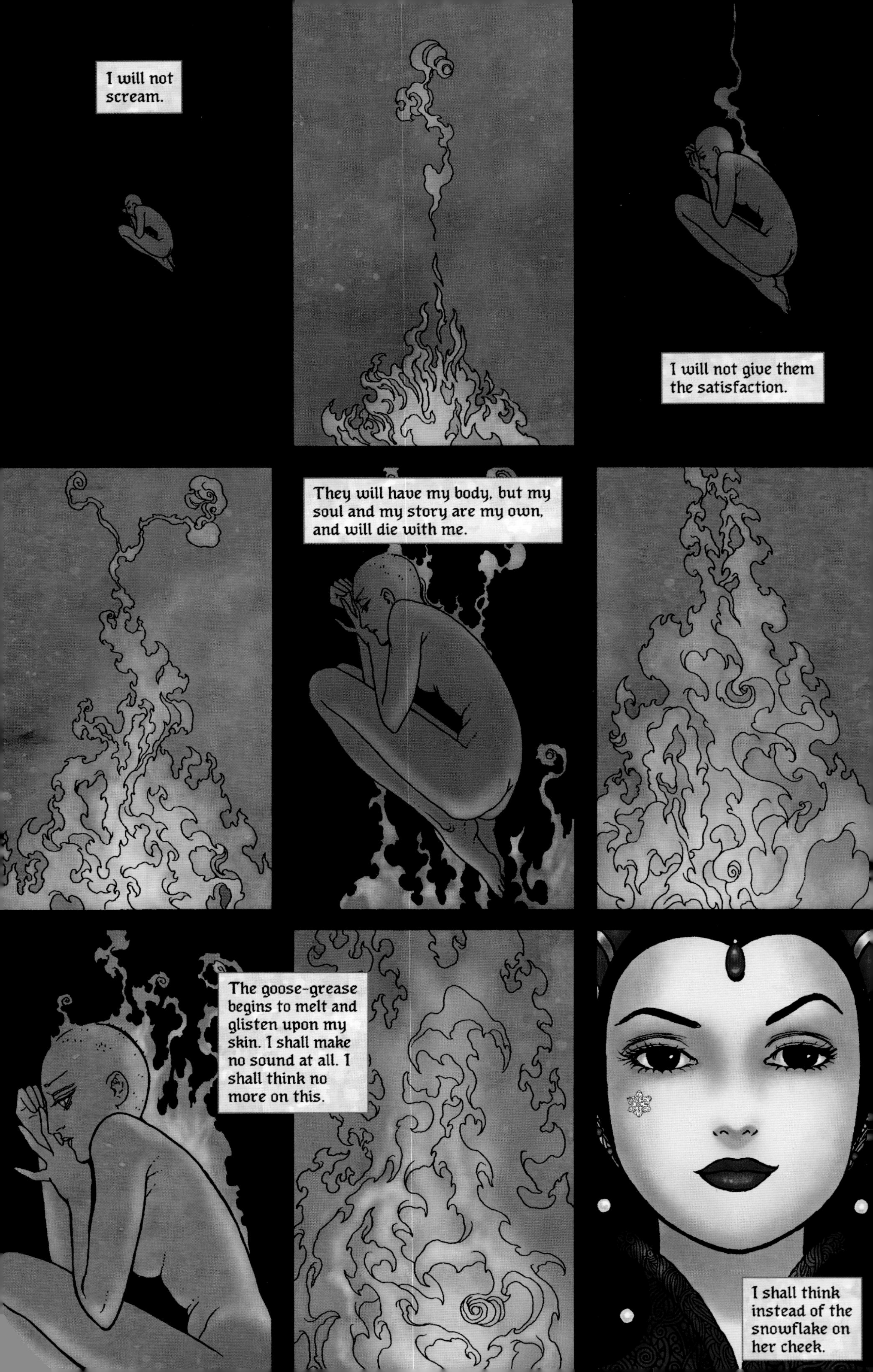
I will not scream.
I will not give them the satisfaction.
They will have my body, but my soul and my story are my own, and will die with me.
The goose-grease begins to melt and glisten upon my skin. I shall make no sound at all. I shall think no more on this.
I shall think instead of the snowflake on her cheek.

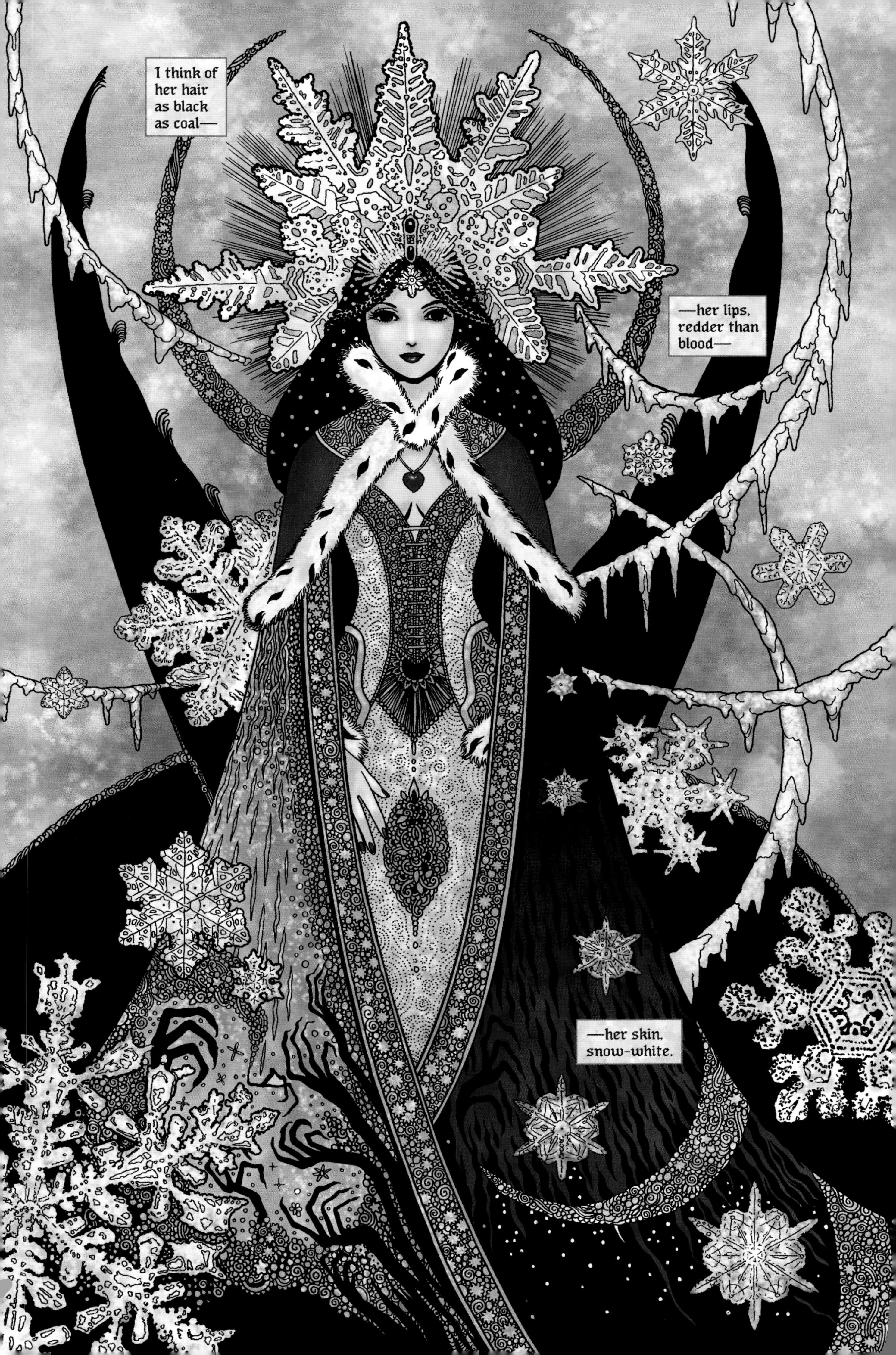
I think of her hair as black as coal—
—her lips, redder than blood—
—her skin, snow-white.

The Problem of Susan and Other Stories

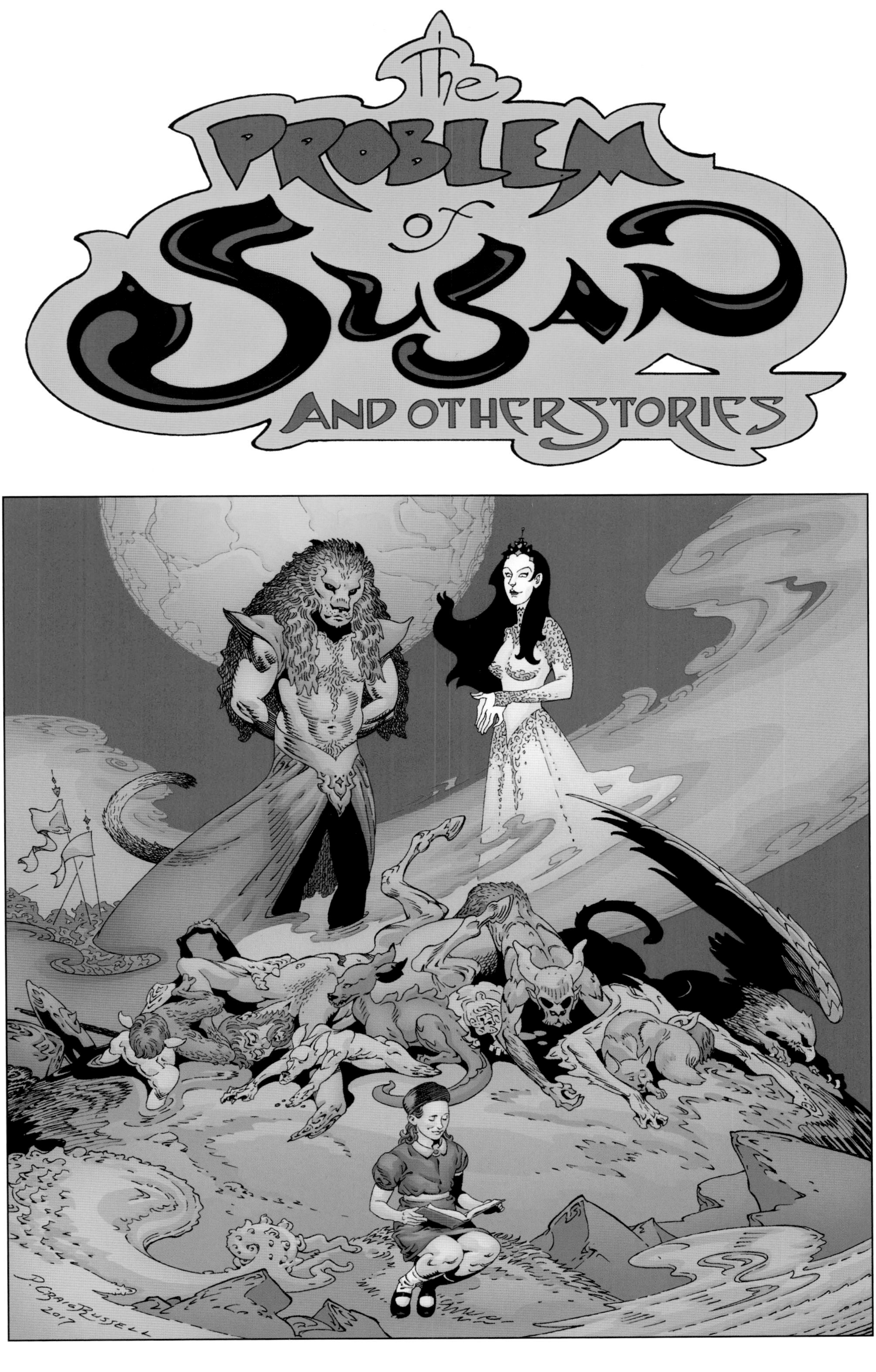
P. CRAIG RUSSELL
2017

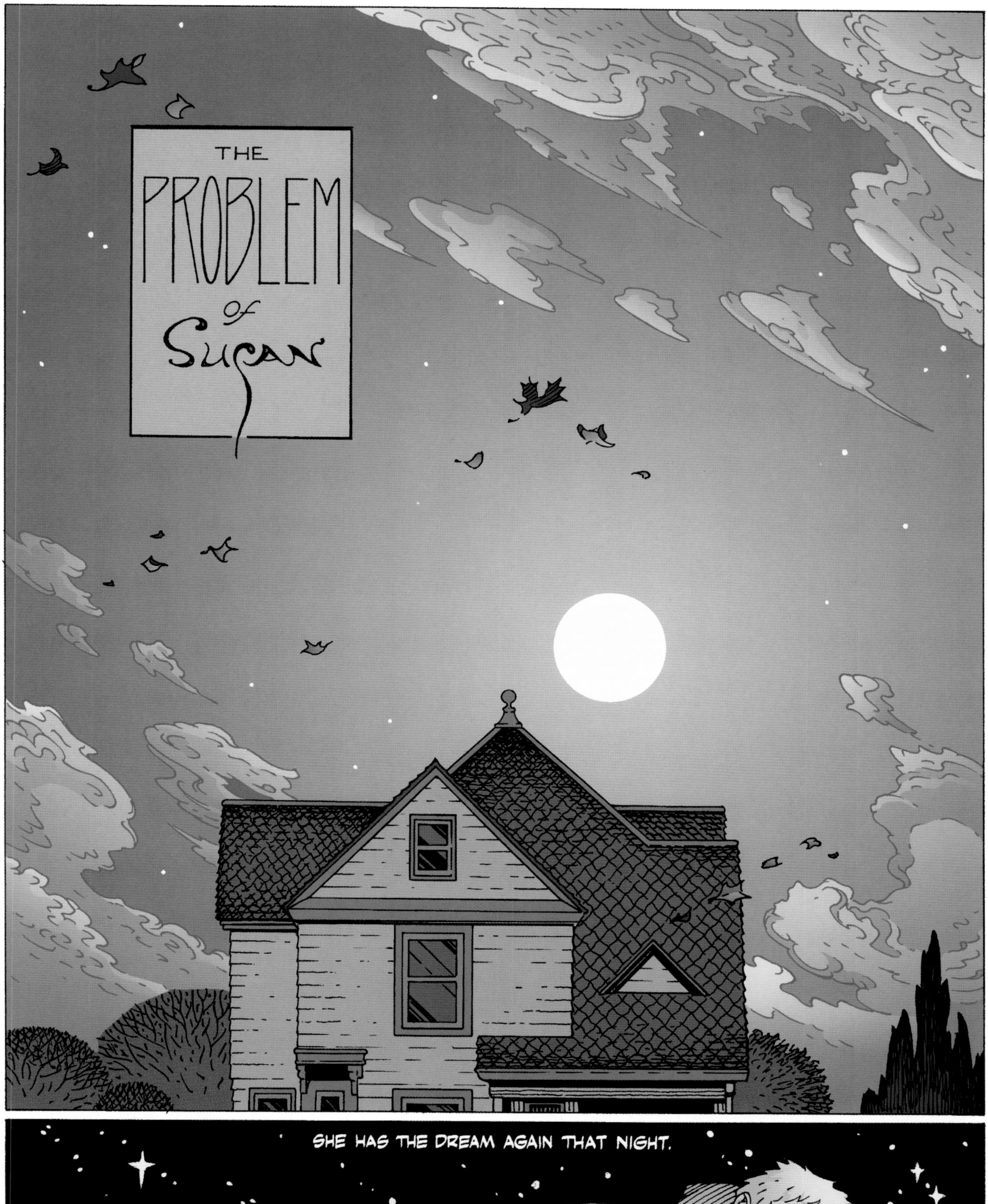
THE PROBLEM of SUSAN

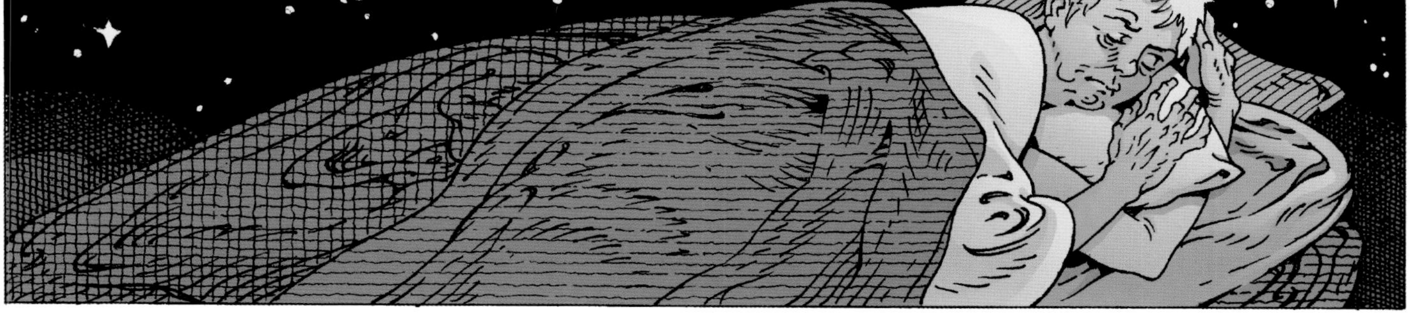
SHE HAS THE DREAM AGAIN THAT NIGHT.

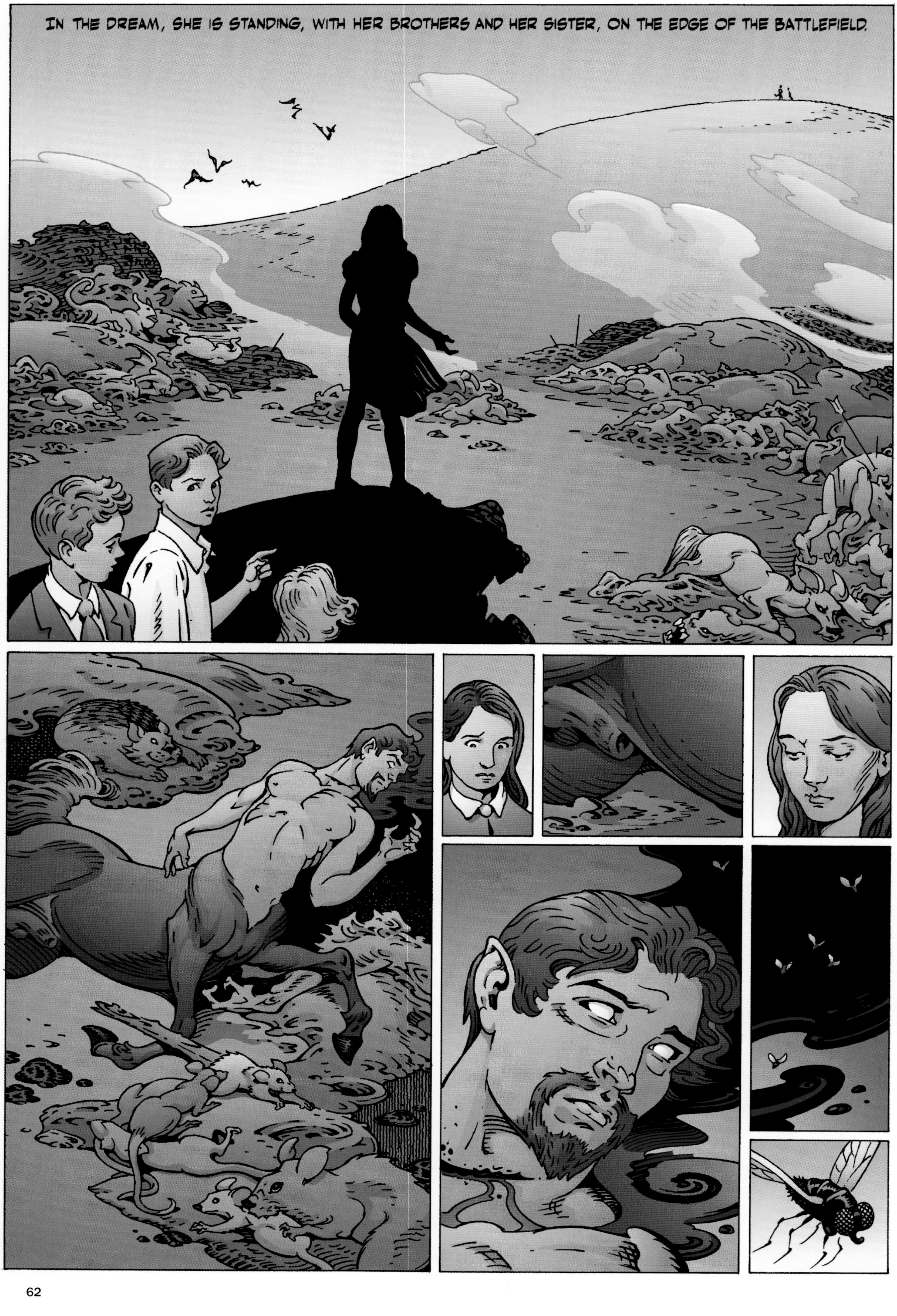
IN THE DREAM, SHE IS STANDING, WITH HER BROTHERS AND HER SISTER, ON THE EDGE OF THE BATTLEFIELD.

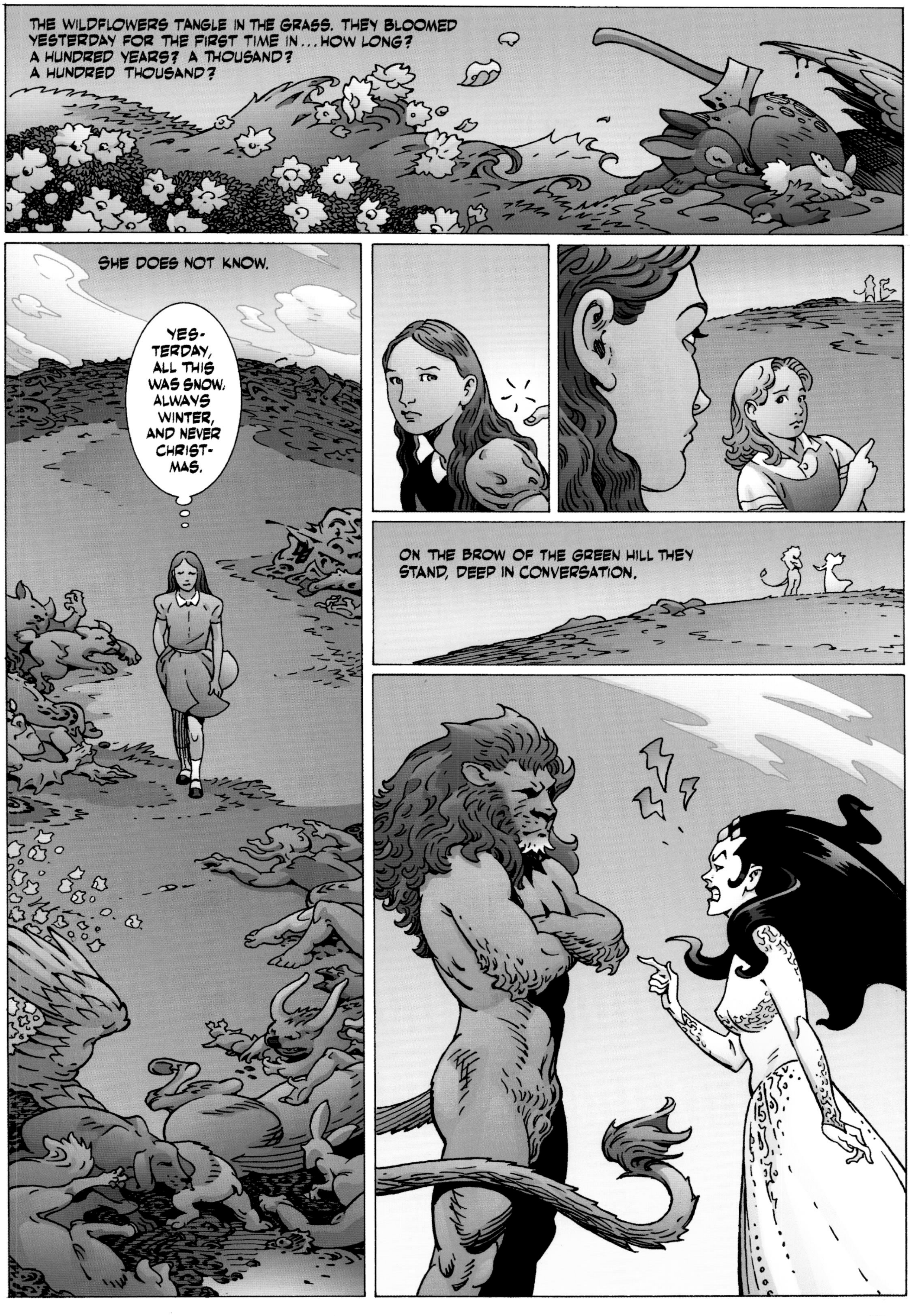
THE WILDFLOWERS TANGLE IN THE GRASS. THEY BLOOMED YESTERDAY FOR THE FIRST TIME IN... HOW LONG? A HUNDRED YEARS? A THOUSAND? A HUNDRED THOUSAND?
SHE DOES NOT KNOW.
YES-TERDAY, ALL THIS WAS SNOW: ALWAYS WINTER, AND NEVER CHRIST-MAS.
ON THE BROW OF THE GREEN HILL THEY STAND, DEEP IN CONVERSATION.

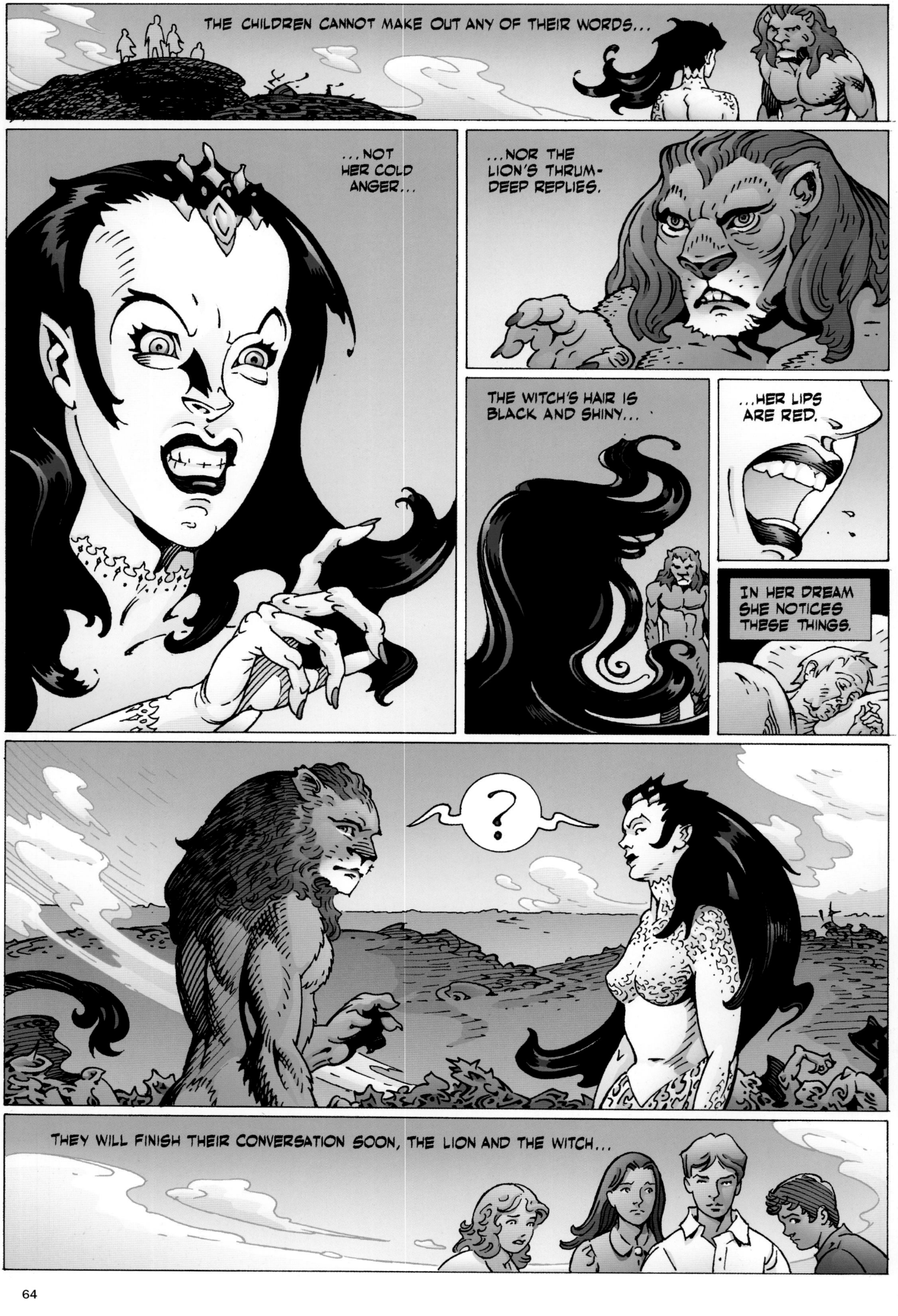
THE CHILDREN CANNOT MAKE OUT ANY OF THEIR WORDS...
...NOT HER COLD ANGER...
...NOR THE LION'S THRUM-DEEP REPLIES.
THE WITCH'S HAIR IS BLACK AND SHINY...
...HER LIPS ARE RED.
IN HER DREAM SHE NOTICES THESE THINGS.
?
THEY WILL FINISH THEIR CONVERSATION SOON, THE LION AND THE WITCH...

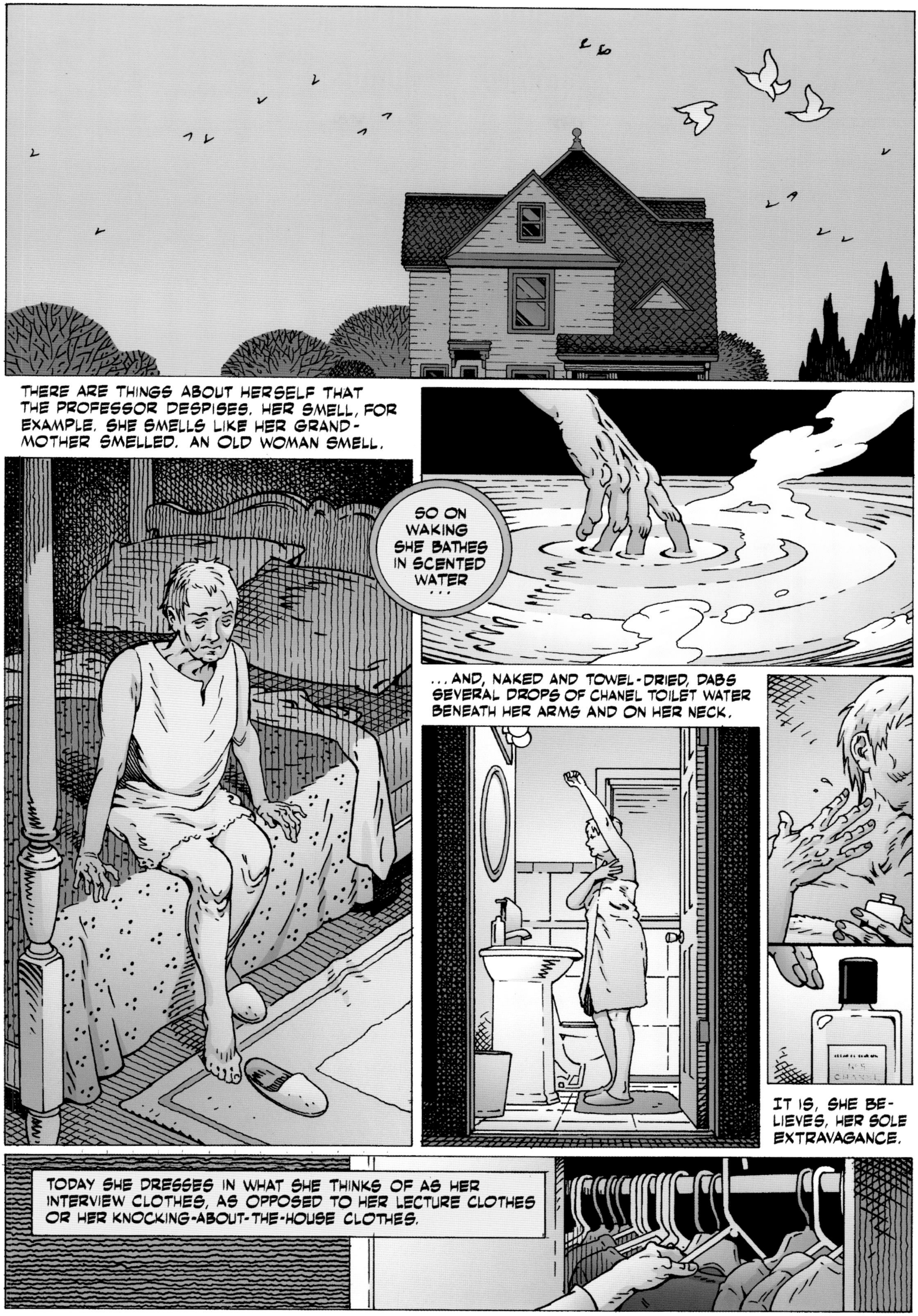

THERE ARE THINGS ABOUT HERSELF THAT THE PROFESSOR DESPISES. HER SMELL, FOR EXAMPLE. SHE SMELLS LIKE HER GRAND-MOTHER SMELLED. AN OLD WOMAN SMELL.
SO ON WAKING SHE BATHES IN SCENTED WATER ...
... AND, NAKED AND TOWEL-DRIED, DABS SEVERAL DROPS OF CHANEL TOILET WATER BENEATH HER ARMS AND ON HER NECK.
IT IS, SHE BE-LIEVES, HER SOLE EXTRAVAGANCE.
TODAY SHE DRESSES IN WHAT SHE THINKS OF AS HER INTERVIEW CLOTHES, AS OPPOSED TO HER LECTURE CLOTHES OR HER KNOCKING-ABOUT-THE-HOUSE CLOTHES.

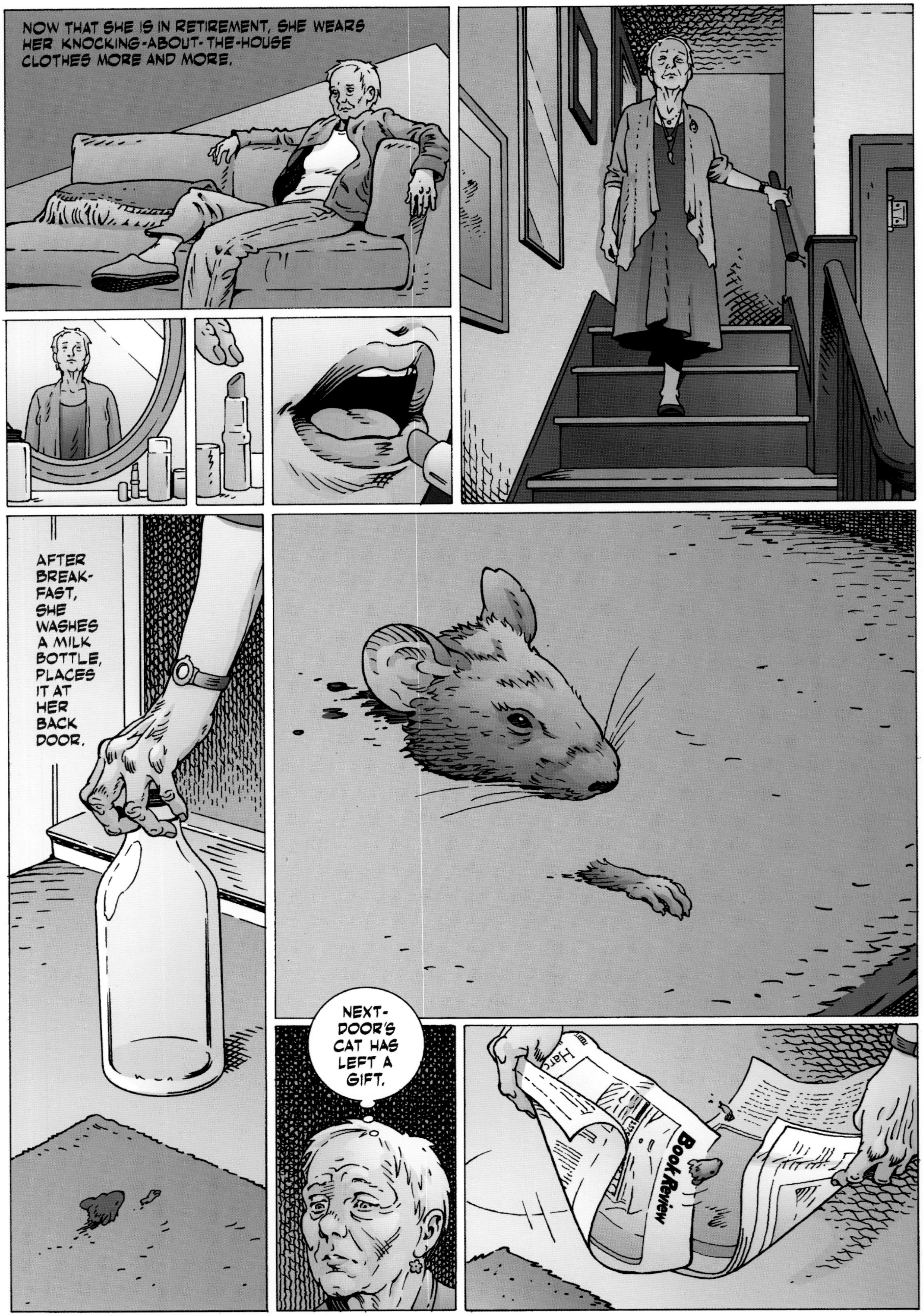
NOW THAT SHE IS IN RETIREMENT, SHE WEARS HER KNOCKING-ABOUT-THE-HOUSE CLOTHES MORE AND MORE.
AFTER BREAKFAST, SHE WASHES A MILK BOTTLE, PLACES IT AT HER BACK DOOR.
NEXT-DOOR'S CAT HAS LEFT A GIFT.
Book Review

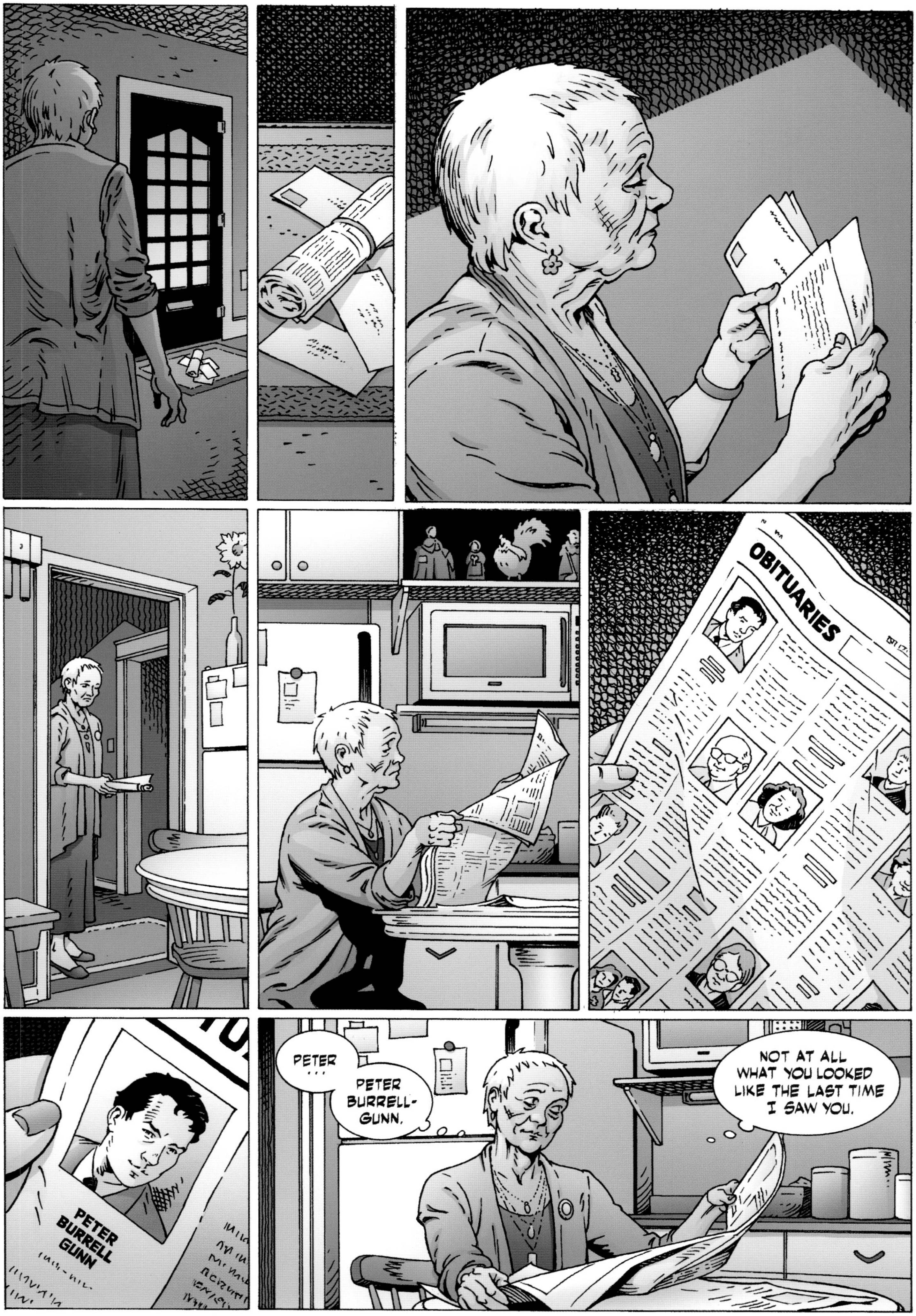
OBITUARIES
PETER BURRELL GUNN
PETER . . .
PETER BURRELL-GUNN.
NOT AT ALL WHAT YOU LOOKED LIKE THE LAST TIME I SAW YOU.

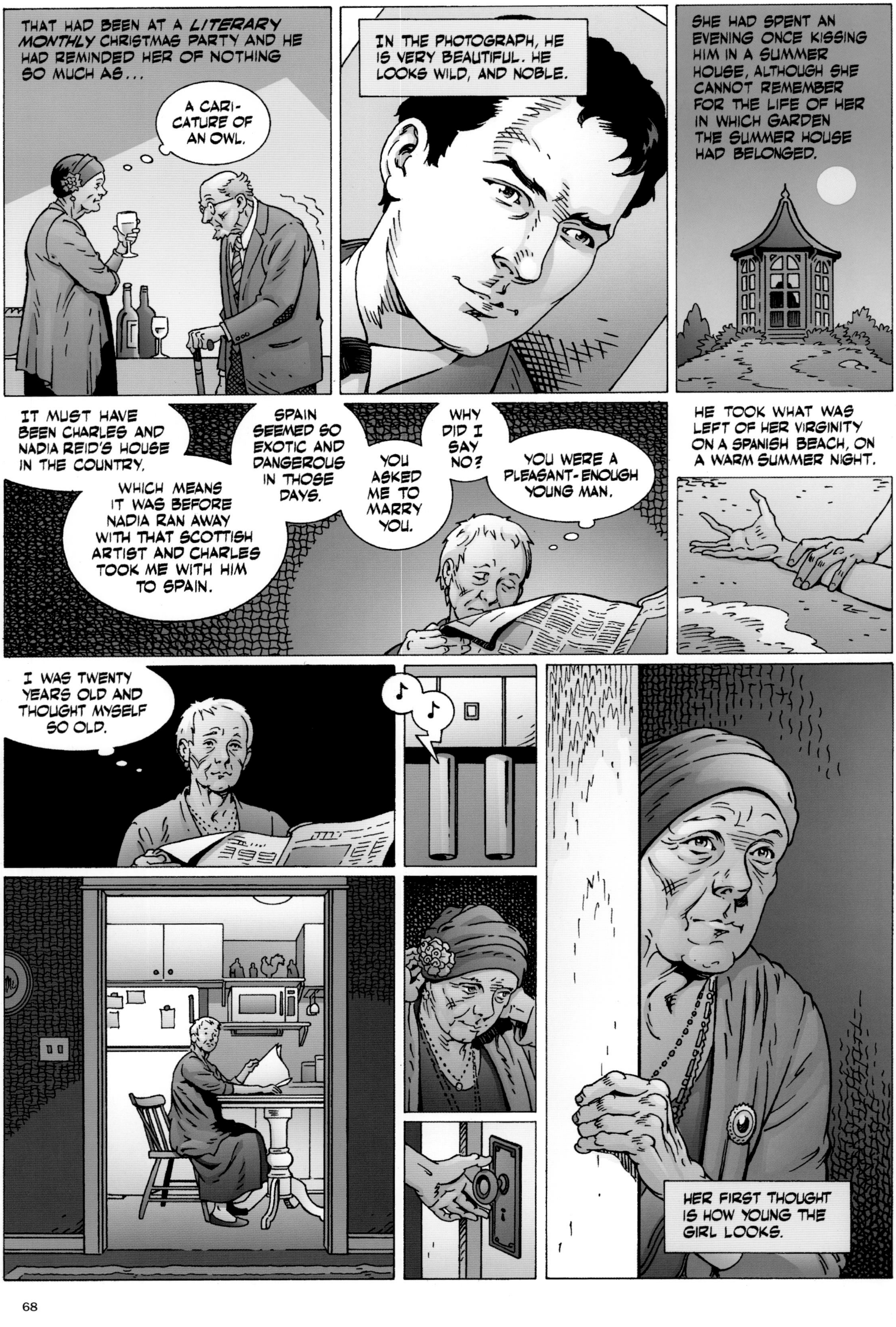
THAT HAD BEEN AT A *LITERARY MONTHLY* CHRISTMAS PARTY AND HE HAD REMINDED HER OF NOTHING SO MUCH AS...
A CARI-CATURE OF AN OWL.
IN THE PHOTOGRAPH, HE IS VERY BEAUTIFUL. HE LOOKS WILD, AND NOBLE.
SHE HAD SPENT AN EVENING ONCE KISSING HIM IN A SUMMER HOUSE, ALTHOUGH SHE CANNOT REMEMBER FOR THE LIFE OF HER IN WHICH GARDEN THE SUMMER HOUSE HAD BELONGED.
IT MUST HAVE BEEN CHARLES AND NADIA REID'S HOUSE IN THE COUNTRY.
WHICH MEANS IT WAS BEFORE NADIA RAN AWAY WITH THAT SCOTTISH ARTIST AND CHARLES TOOK ME WITH HIM TO SPAIN.
SPAIN SEEMED SO EXOTIC AND DANGEROUS IN THOSE DAYS.
YOU ASKED ME TO MARRY YOU.
WHY DID I SAY NO?
YOU WERE A PLEASANT-ENOUGH YOUNG MAN.
HE TOOK WHAT WAS LEFT OF HER VIRGINITY ON A SPANISH BEACH, ON A WARM SUMMER NIGHT.
I WAS TWENTY YEARS OLD AND THOUGHT MYSELF SO OLD.
♪
♪
HER FIRST THOUGHT IS HOW YOUNG THE GIRL LOOKS.

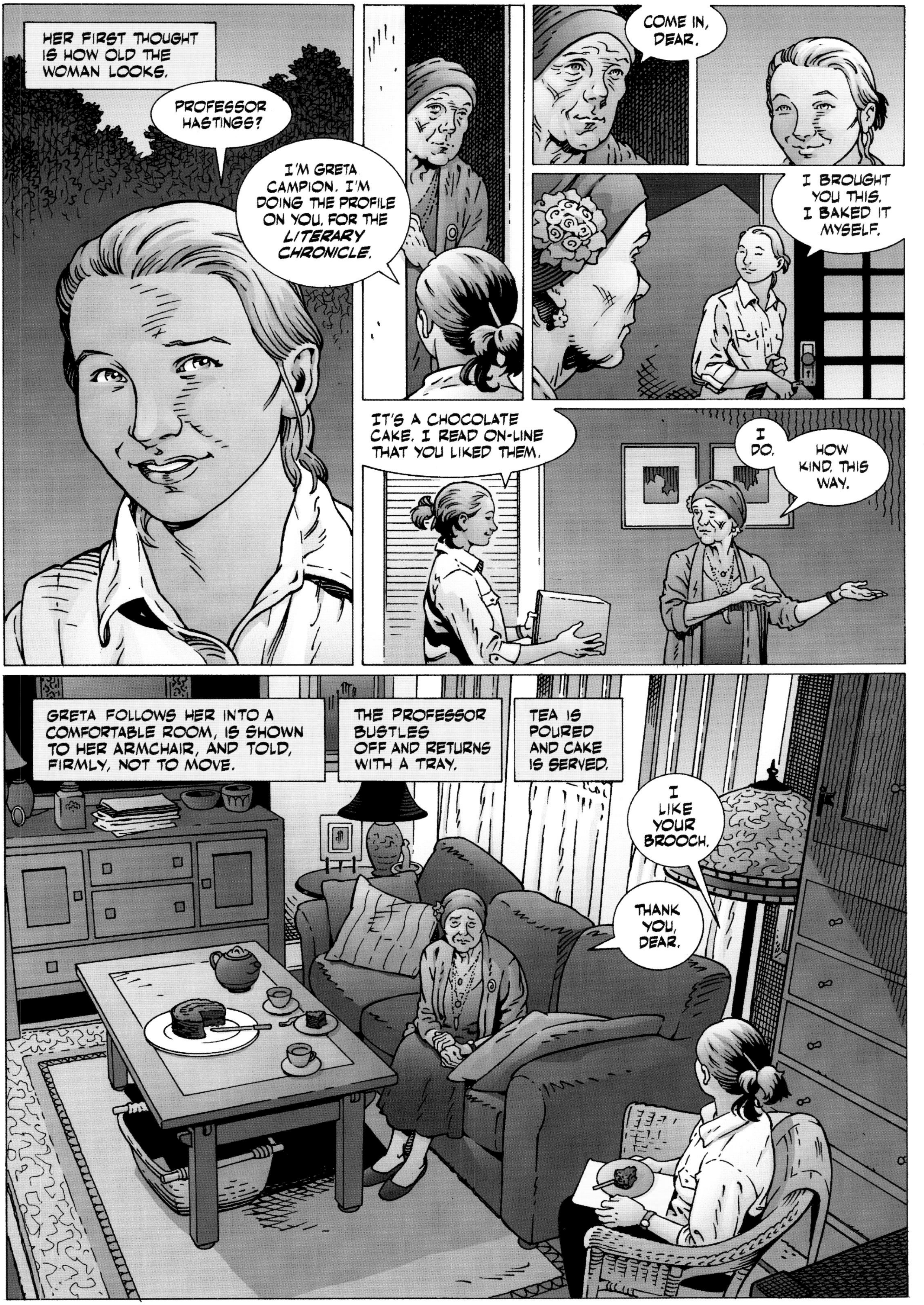
HER FIRST THOUGHT IS HOW OLD THE WOMAN LOOKS.
PROFESSOR HASTINGS?
I'M GRETA CAMPION. I'M DOING THE PROFILE ON YOU, FOR THE *LITERARY CHRONICLE*.
COME IN, DEAR.
I BROUGHT YOU THIS. I BAKED IT MYSELF.
IT'S A CHOCOLATE CAKE. I READ ON-LINE THAT YOU LIKED THEM.
I DO.
HOW KIND. THIS WAY.
GRETA FOLLOWS HER INTO A COMFORTABLE ROOM, IS SHOWN TO HER ARMCHAIR, AND TOLD, FIRMLY, NOT TO MOVE.
THE PROFESSOR BUSTLES OFF AND RETURNS WITH A TRAY.
TEA IS POURED AND CAKE IS SERVED.
I LIKE YOUR BROOCH.
THANK YOU, DEAR.

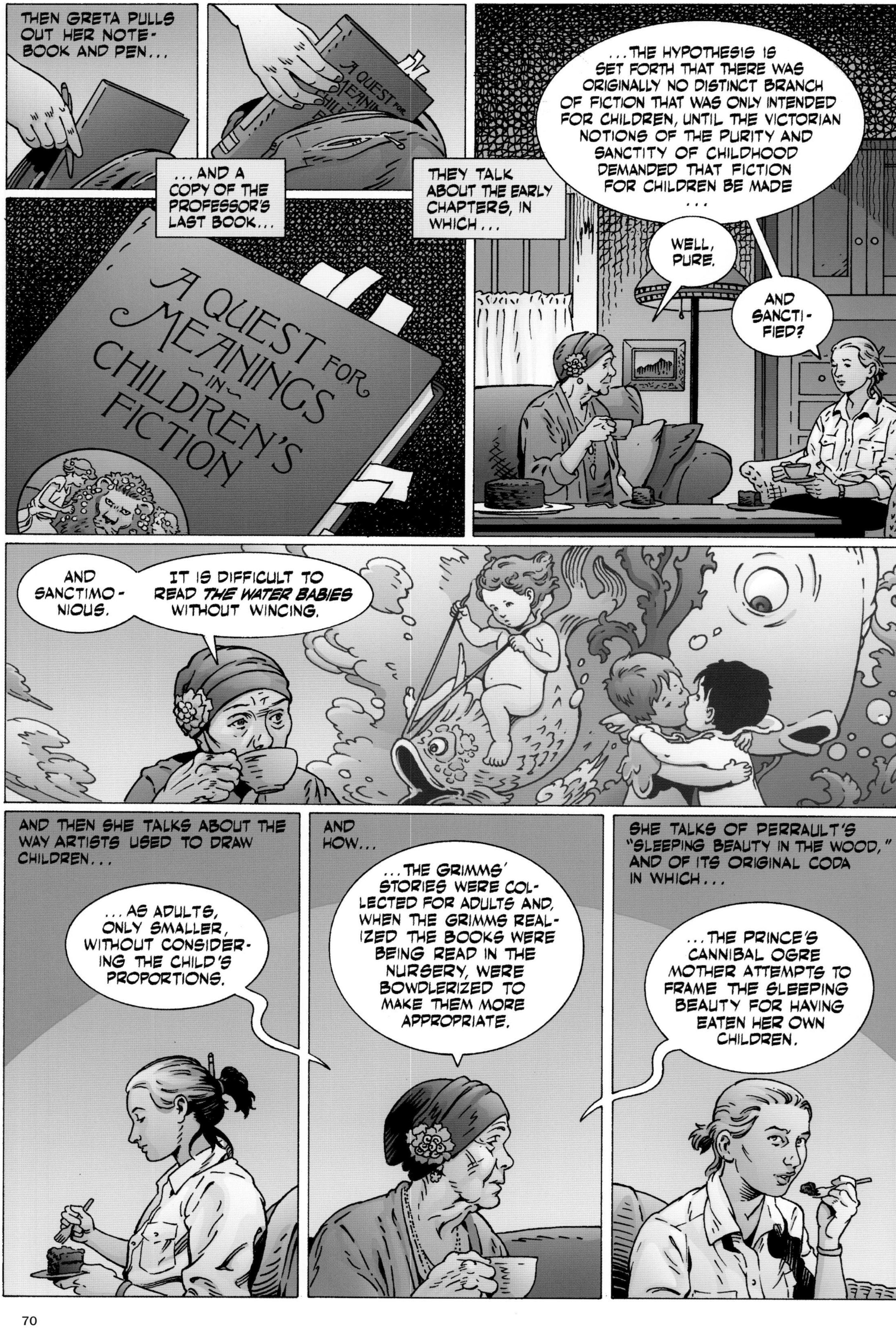
THEN GRETA PULLS OUT HER NOTE-BOOK AND PEN...
...AND A COPY OF THE PROFESSOR'S LAST BOOK...
A QUEST FOR MEANINGS IN CHILDREN'S FICTION
THEY TALK ABOUT THE EARLY CHAPTERS, IN WHICH...
...THE HYPOTHESIS IS SET FORTH THAT THERE WAS ORIGINALLY NO DISTINCT BRANCH OF FICTION THAT WAS ONLY INTENDED FOR CHILDREN, UNTIL THE VICTORIAN NOTIONS OF THE PURITY AND SANCTITY OF CHILDHOOD DEMANDED THAT FICTION FOR CHILDREN BE MADE ...
WELL, PURE.
AND SANCTI-FIED?
AND SANCTIMO-NIOUS.
IT IS DIFFICULT TO READ *THE WATER BABIES* WITHOUT WINCING.
AND THEN SHE TALKS ABOUT THE WAY ARTISTS USED TO DRAW CHILDREN...
...AS ADULTS, ONLY SMALLER, WITHOUT CONSIDER-ING THE CHILD'S PROPORTIONS.
AND HOW...
...THE GRIMMS' STORIES WERE COL-LECTED FOR ADULTS AND, WHEN THE GRIMMS REAL-IZED THE BOOKS WERE BEING READ IN THE NURSERY, WERE BOWDLERIZED TO MAKE THEM MORE APPROPRIATE.
SHE TALKS OF PERRAULT'S "SLEEPING BEAUTY IN THE WOOD," AND OF ITS ORIGINAL CODA IN WHICH...
...THE PRINCE'S CANNIBAL OGRE MOTHER ATTEMPTS TO FRAME THE SLEEPING BEAUTY FOR HAVING EATEN HER OWN CHILDREN.

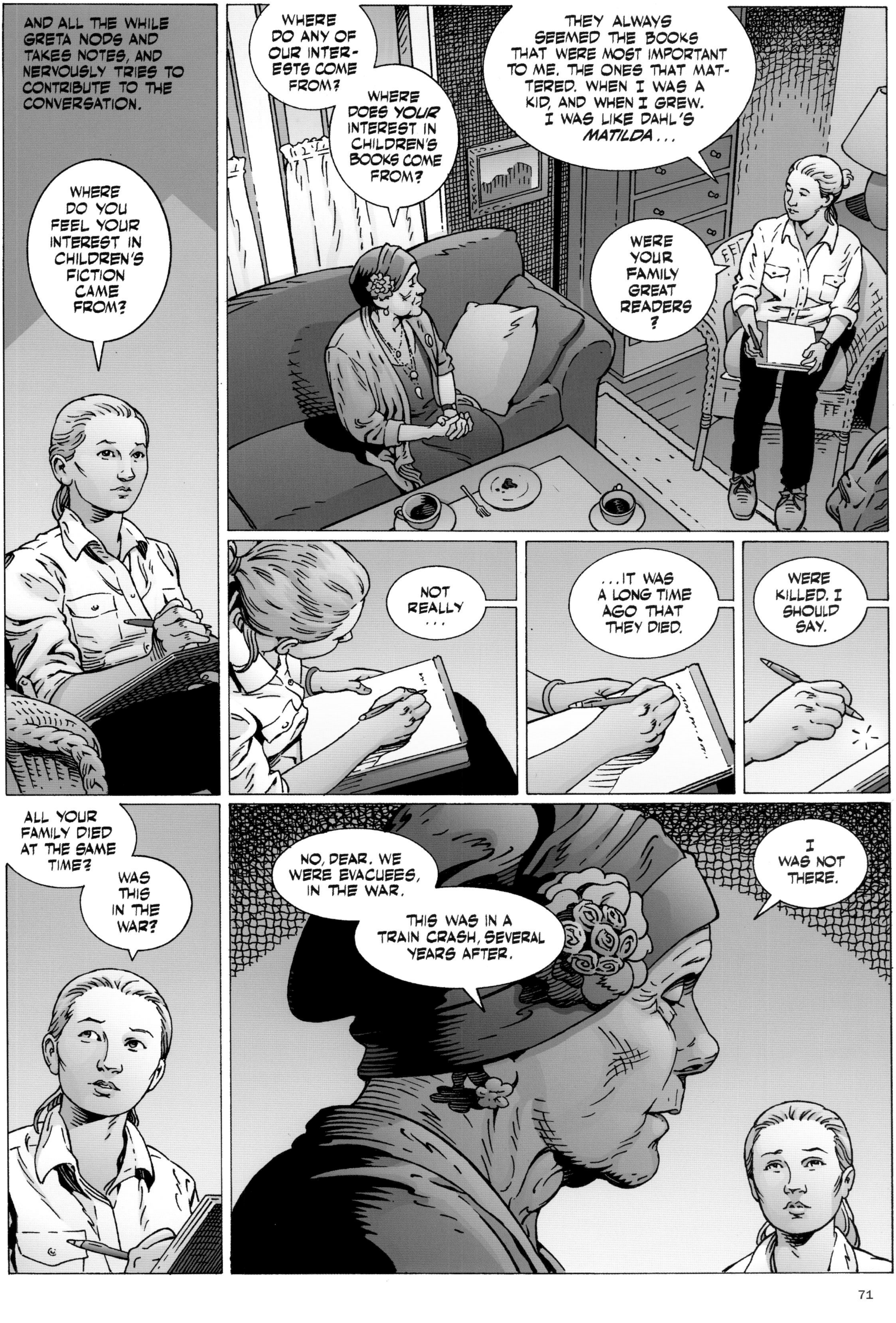
AND ALL THE WHILE GRETA NODS AND TAKES NOTES, AND NERVOUSLY TRIES TO CONTRIBUTE TO THE CONVERSATION.
WHERE DO YOU FEEL YOUR INTEREST IN CHILDREN'S FICTION CAME FROM?
WHERE DO ANY OF OUR INTERESTS COME FROM?
WHERE DOES *YOUR* INTEREST IN CHILDREN'S BOOKS COME FROM?
THEY ALWAYS SEEMED THE BOOKS THAT WERE MOST IMPORTANT TO ME. THE ONES THAT MATTERED. WHEN I WAS A KID, AND WHEN I GREW. I WAS LIKE DAHL'S *MATILDA*...
WERE YOUR FAMILY GREAT READERS?
NOT REALLY...
...IT WAS A LONG TIME AGO THAT THEY DIED.
WERE KILLED, I SHOULD SAY.
ALL YOUR FAMILY DIED AT THE SAME TIME?
WAS THIS IN THE WAR?
NO, DEAR. WE WERE EVACUEES, IN THE WAR.
THIS WAS IN A TRAIN CRASH, SEVERAL YEARS AFTER.
I WAS NOT THERE.

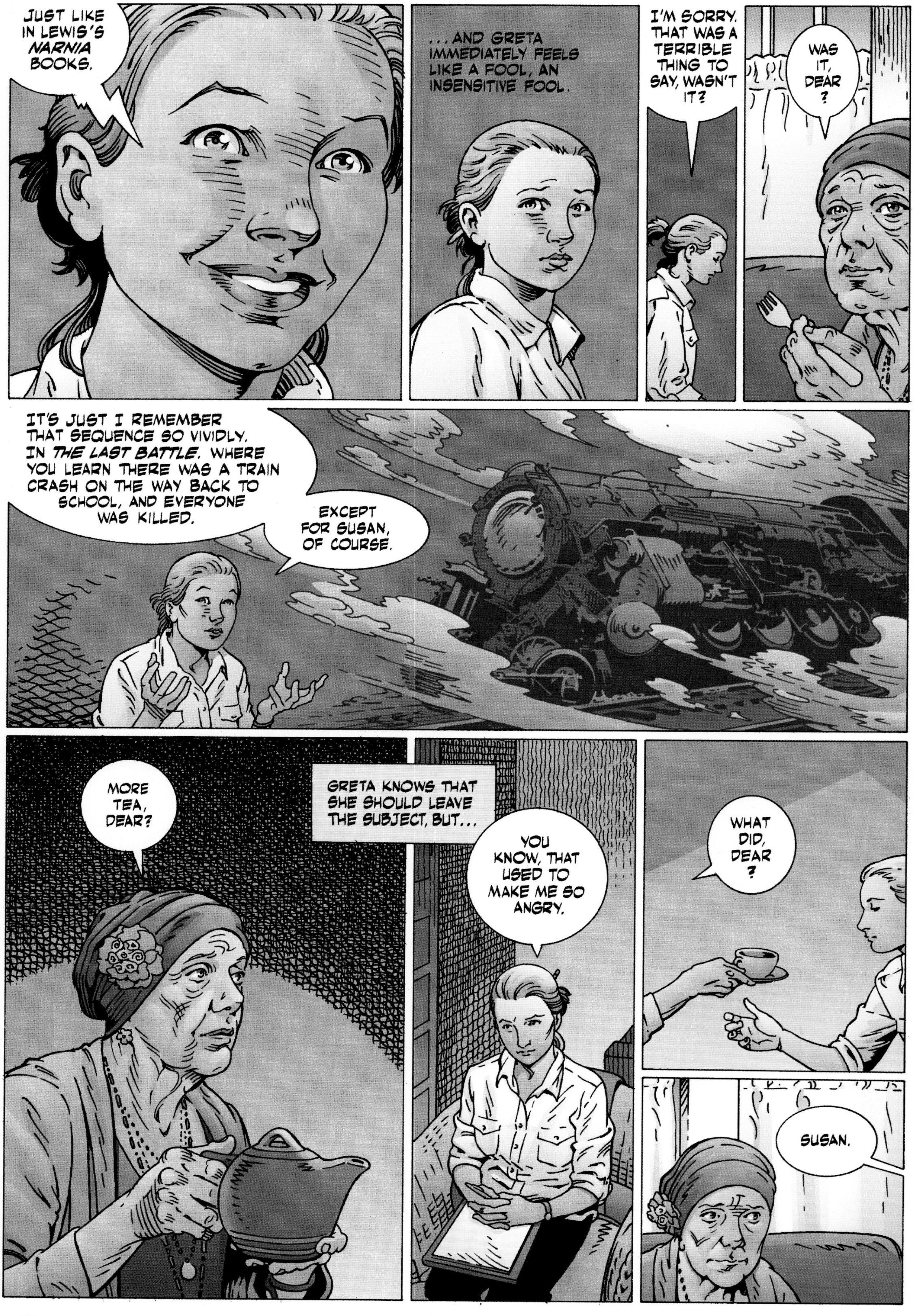

JUST LIKE IN LEWIS'S *NARNIA* BOOKS.
...AND GRETA IMMEDIATELY FEELS LIKE A FOOL, AN INSENSITIVE FOOL.
I'M SORRY. THAT WAS A TERRIBLE THING TO SAY, WASN'T IT?
WAS IT, DEAR?
IT'S JUST I REMEMBER THAT SEQUENCE SO VIVIDLY. IN *THE LAST BATTLE*. WHERE YOU LEARN THERE WAS A TRAIN CRASH ON THE WAY BACK TO SCHOOL, AND EVERYONE WAS KILLED.
EXCEPT FOR SUSAN, OF COURSE.
MORE TEA, DEAR?
GRETA KNOWS THAT SHE SHOULD LEAVE THE SUBJECT, BUT...
YOU KNOW, THAT USED TO MAKE ME SO ANGRY.
WHAT DID, DEAR?
SUSAN.

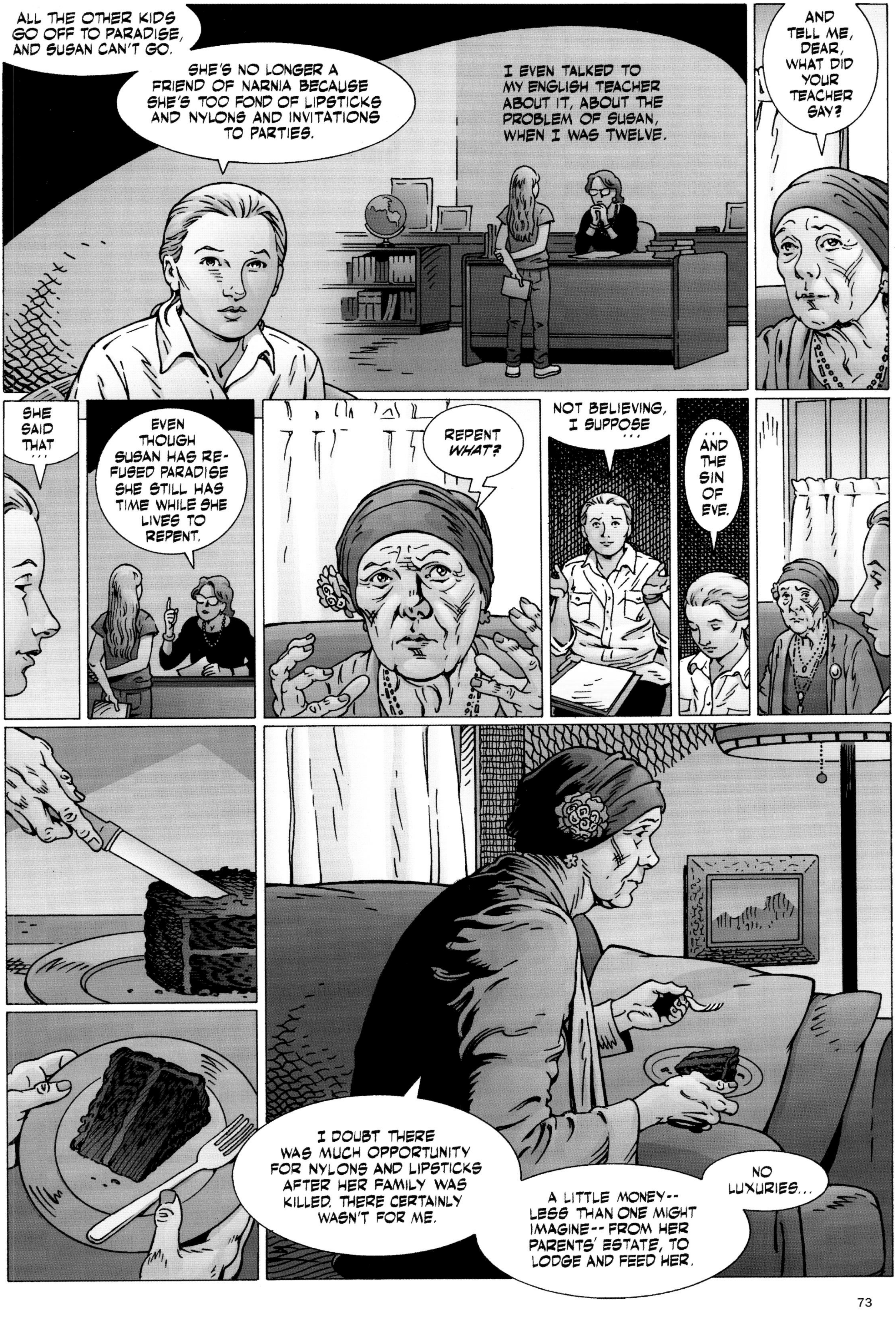
ALL THE OTHER KIDS GO OFF TO PARADISE, AND SUSAN CAN'T GO.
SHE'S NO LONGER A FRIEND OF NARNIA BECAUSE SHE'S TOO FOND OF LIPSTICKS AND NYLONS AND INVITATIONS TO PARTIES.
I EVEN TALKED TO MY ENGLISH TEACHER ABOUT IT, ABOUT THE PROBLEM OF SUSAN, WHEN I WAS TWELVE.
AND TELL ME, DEAR, WHAT DID YOUR TEACHER SAY?
SHE SAID THAT . . .
EVEN THOUGH SUSAN HAS REFUSED PARADISE SHE STILL HAS TIME WHILE SHE LIVES TO REPENT.
REPENT *WHAT?*
NOT BELIEVING, I SUPPOSE . . .
. . . AND THE SIN OF EVE.
I DOUBT THERE WAS MUCH OPPORTUNITY FOR NYLONS AND LIPSTICKS AFTER HER FAMILY WAS KILLED. THERE CERTAINLY WASN'T FOR ME.
A LITTLE MONEY-- LESS THAN ONE MIGHT IMAGINE-- FROM HER PARENTS' ESTATE, TO LODGE AND FEED HER.
NO LUXURIES...

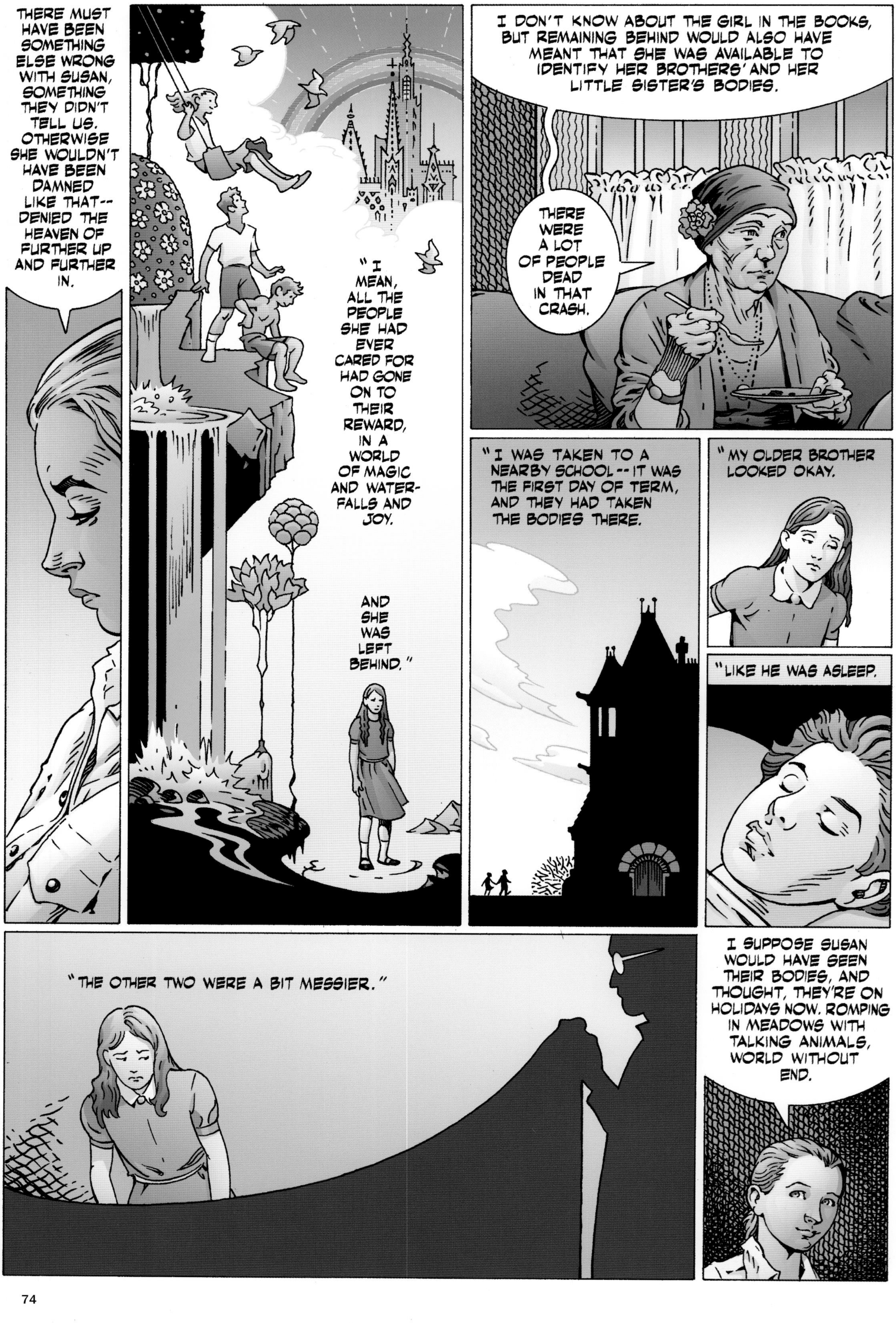
THERE MUST HAVE BEEN SOMETHING ELSE WRONG WITH SUSAN, SOMETHING THEY DIDN'T TELL US. OTHERWISE SHE WOULDN'T HAVE BEEN DAMNED LIKE THAT-- DENIED THE HEAVEN OF FURTHER UP AND FURTHER IN.
"I MEAN, ALL THE PEOPLE SHE HAD EVER CARED FOR HAD GONE ON TO THEIR REWARD, IN A WORLD OF MAGIC AND WATER-FALLS AND JOY.
AND SHE WAS LEFT BEHIND."
I DON'T KNOW ABOUT THE GIRL IN THE BOOKS, BUT REMAINING BEHIND WOULD ALSO HAVE MEANT THAT SHE WAS AVAILABLE TO IDENTIFY HER BROTHERS' AND HER LITTLE SISTER'S BODIES.
THERE WERE A LOT OF PEOPLE DEAD IN THAT CRASH.
"I WAS TAKEN TO A NEARBY SCHOOL -- IT WAS THE FIRST DAY OF TERM, AND THEY HAD TAKEN THE BODIES THERE.
"MY OLDER BROTHER LOOKED OKAY.
"LIKE HE WAS ASLEEP.
"THE OTHER TWO WERE A BIT MESSIER."
I SUPPOSE SUSAN WOULD HAVE SEEN THEIR BODIES, AND THOUGHT, THEY'RE ON HOLIDAYS NOW. ROMPING IN MEADOWS WITH TALKING ANIMALS, WORLD WITHOUT END.

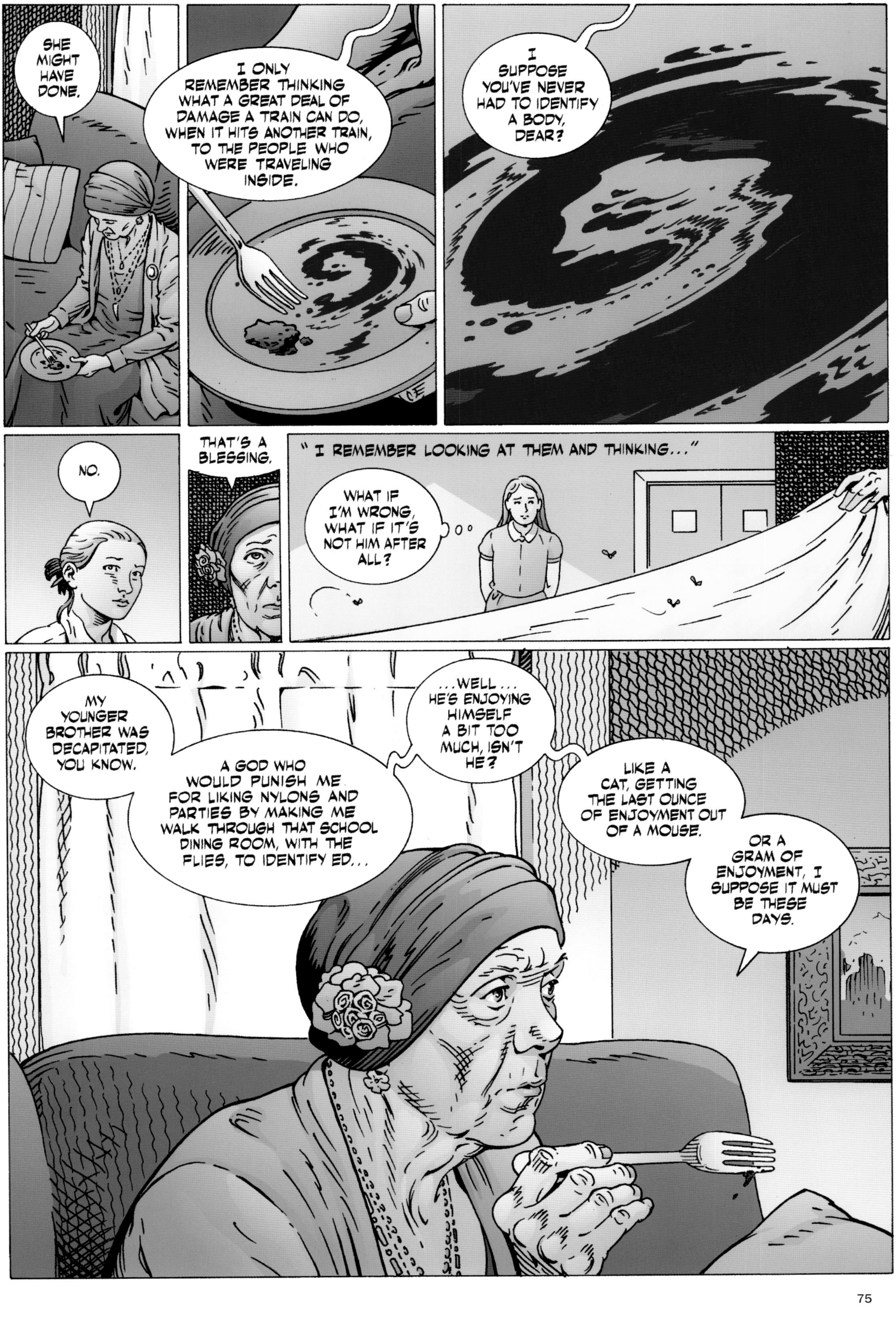
SHE MIGHT HAVE DONE.
I ONLY REMEMBER THINKING WHAT A GREAT DEAL OF DAMAGE A TRAIN CAN DO, WHEN IT HITS ANOTHER TRAIN, TO THE PEOPLE WHO WERE TRAVELING INSIDE.
I SUPPOSE YOU'VE NEVER HAD TO IDENTIFY A BODY, DEAR?
NO.
THAT'S A BLESSING.
" I REMEMBER LOOKING AT THEM AND THINKING..."
WHAT IF I'M WRONG, WHAT IF IT'S NOT HIM AFTER ALL?
MY YOUNGER BROTHER WAS DECAPITATED, YOU KNOW.
A GOD WHO WOULD PUNISH ME FOR LIKING NYLONS AND PARTIES BY MAKING ME WALK THROUGH THAT SCHOOL DINING ROOM, WITH THE FLIES, TO IDENTIFY ED...
...WELL... HE'S ENJOYING HIMSELF A BIT TOO MUCH, ISN'T HE?
LIKE A CAT, GETTING THE LAST OUNCE OF ENJOYMENT OUT OF A MOUSE.
OR A GRAM OF ENJOYMENT, I SUPPOSE IT MUST BE THESE DAYS.

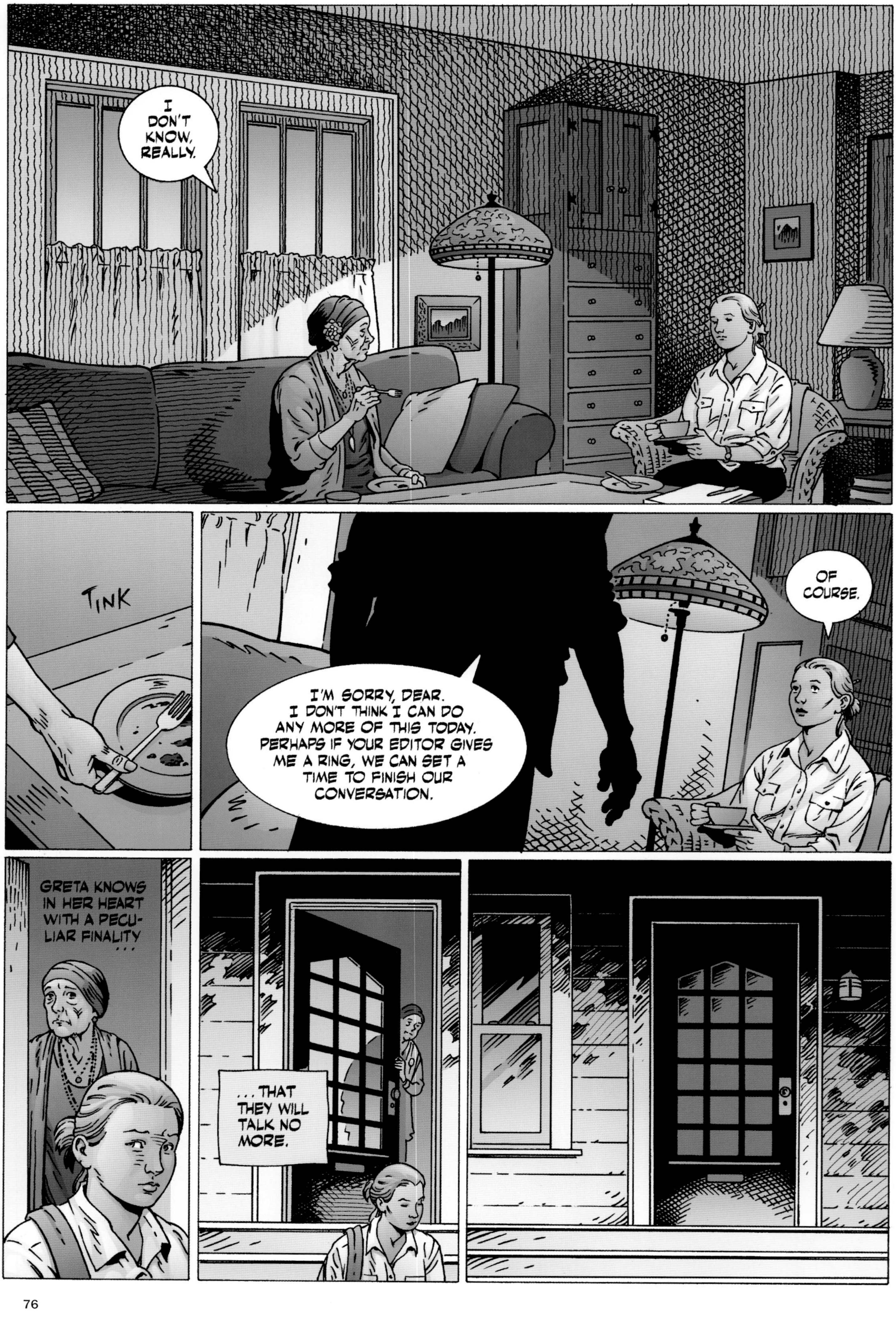

I DON'T KNOW, REALLY.
TINK
I'M SORRY, DEAR. I DON'T THINK I CAN DO ANY MORE OF THIS TODAY. PERHAPS IF YOUR EDITOR GIVES ME A RING, WE CAN SET A TIME TO FINISH OUR CONVERSATION.
OF COURSE.
GRETA KNOWS IN HER HEART WITH A PECULIAR FINALITY . . .
. . . THAT THEY WILL TALK NO MORE.

THAT NIGHT, THE PROFESSOR CLIMBS THE STAIRS OF HER HOUSE, SLOWLY, PAINSTAKINGLY, FLOOR BY FLOOR.

SHE MAKES UP A BED IN THE SPARE BEDROOM, AT THE BACK...

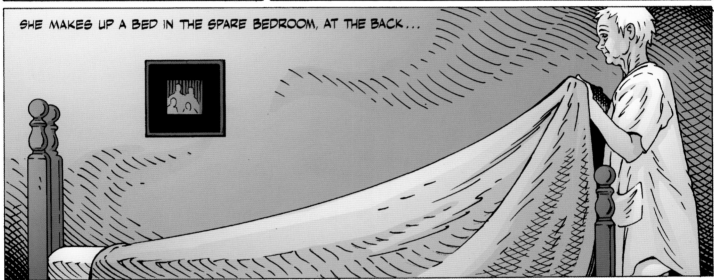

SHE PLACES A VASE ON THE DRESSING TABLE, CONTAINING PURPLE RHODODENDRON FLOWERS, STICKY AND VULGAR...

...TAKES FROM A BOX IN THE WARDROBE A PLASTIC SHOPPING BAG CONTAINING FOUR OLD PHOTOGRAPHIC ALBUMS...

...AND CLIMBS INTO THE BED THAT WAS HERS AS A CHILD.

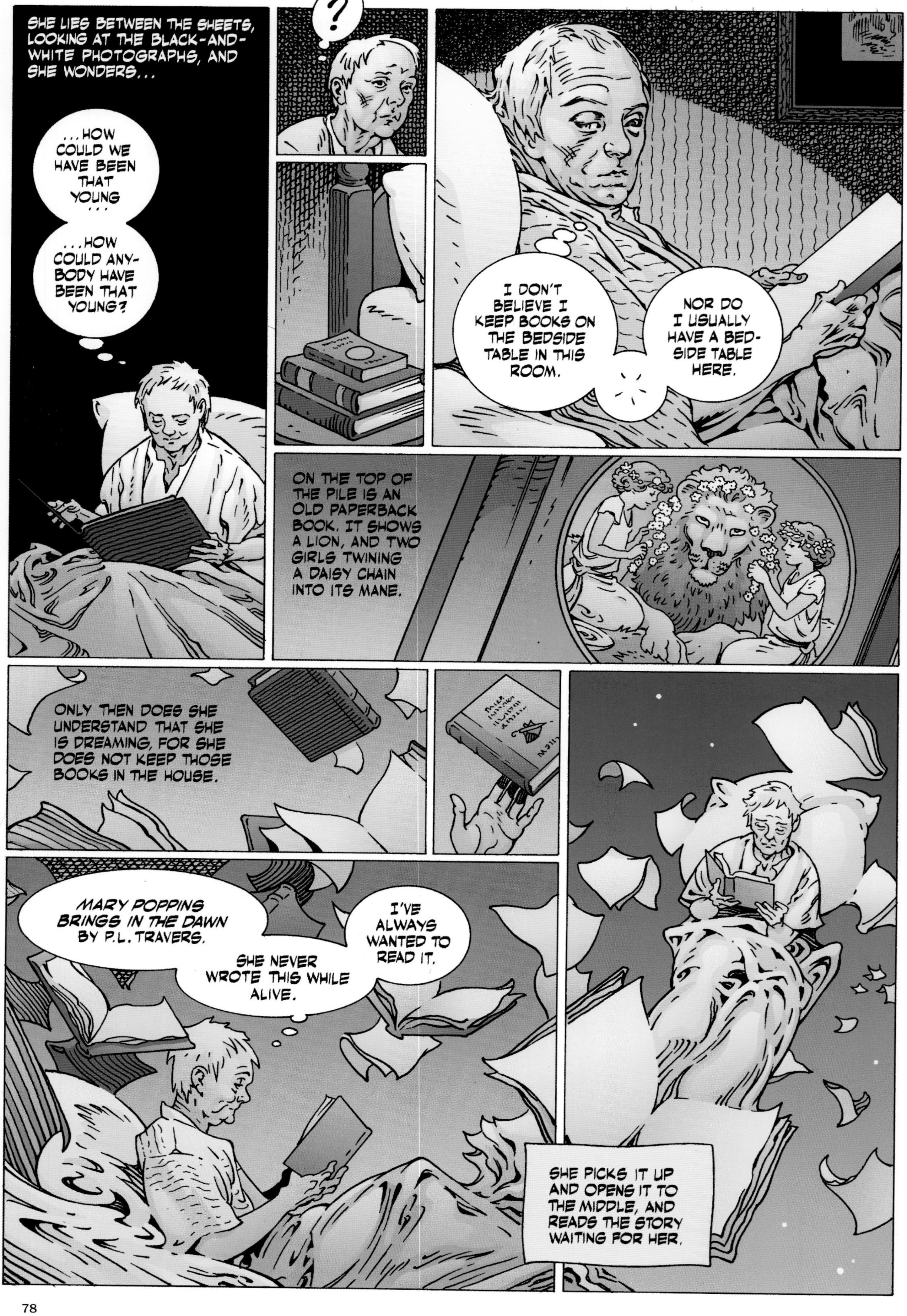
SHE LIES BETWEEN THE SHEETS, LOOKING AT THE BLACK-AND-WHITE PHOTOGRAPHS, AND SHE WONDERS...
...HOW COULD WE HAVE BEEN THAT YOUNG ...
...HOW COULD ANY-BODY HAVE BEEN THAT YOUNG?
?
I DON'T BELIEVE I KEEP BOOKS ON THE BEDSIDE TABLE IN THIS ROOM.
NOR DO I USUALLY HAVE A BED-SIDE TABLE HERE.
ON THE TOP OF THE PILE IS AN OLD PAPERBACK BOOK. IT SHOWS A LION, AND TWO GIRLS TWINING A DAISY CHAIN INTO ITS MANE.
ONLY THEN DOES SHE UNDERSTAND THAT SHE IS DREAMING, FOR SHE DOES NOT KEEP THOSE BOOKS IN THE HOUSE.
MARY POPPINS BRINGS IN THE DAWN BY P.L. TRAVERS.
SHE NEVER WROTE THIS WHILE ALIVE.
I'VE ALWAYS WANTED TO READ IT.
SHE PICKS IT UP AND OPENS IT TO THE MIDDLE, AND READS THE STORY WAITING FOR HER.

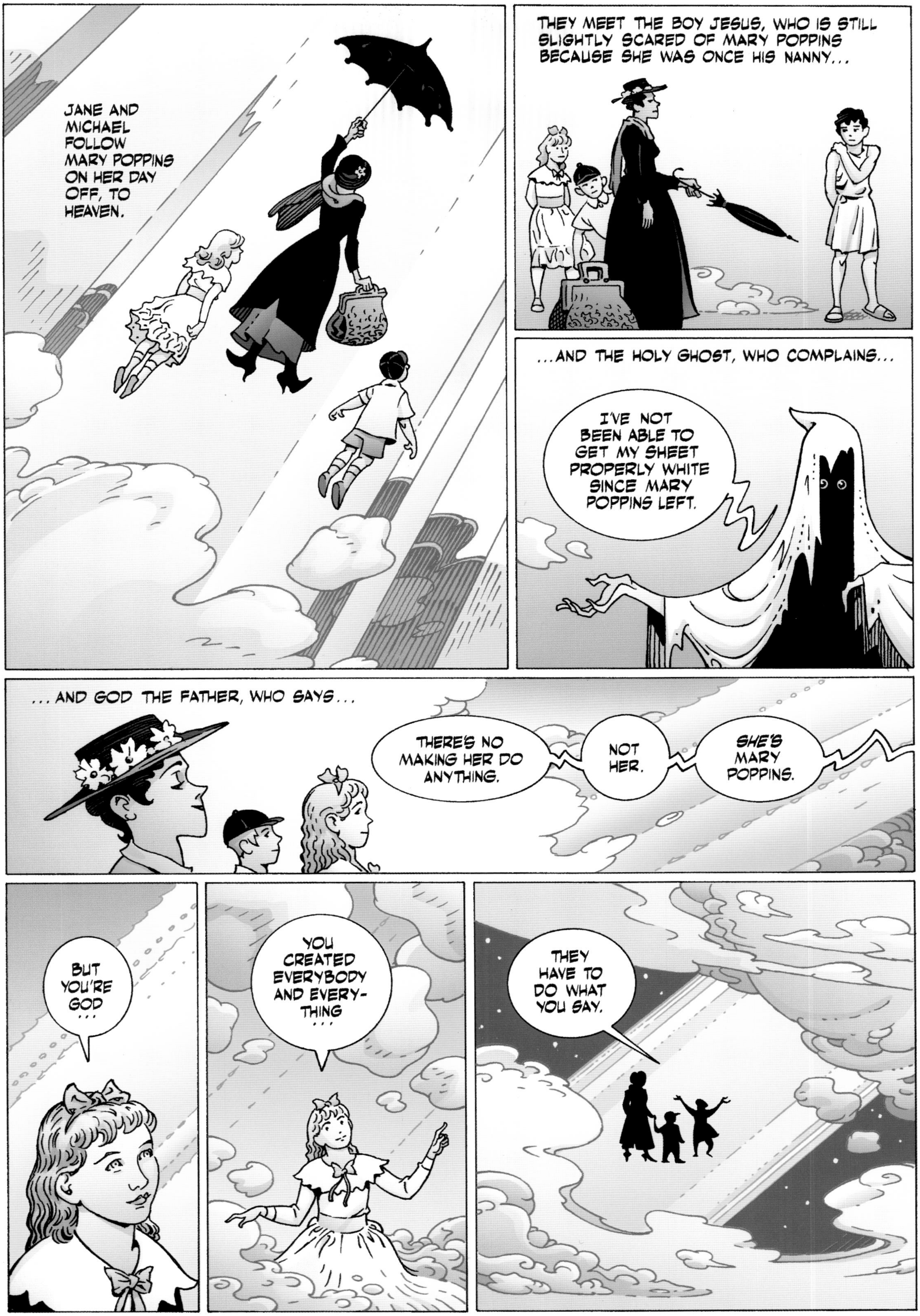
JANE AND MICHAEL FOLLOW MARY POPPINS ON HER DAY OFF, TO HEAVEN.
THEY MEET THE BOY JESUS, WHO IS STILL SLIGHTLY SCARED OF MARY POPPINS BECAUSE SHE WAS ONCE HIS NANNY...
...AND THE HOLY GHOST, WHO COMPLAINS...
I'VE NOT BEEN ABLE TO GET MY SHEET PROPERLY WHITE SINCE MARY POPPINS LEFT.
...AND GOD THE FATHER, WHO SAYS...
THERE'S NO MAKING HER DO ANYTHING.
NOT HER.
SHE'S MARY POPPINS.
BUT YOU'RE GOD...
YOU CREATED EVERYBODY AND EVERY-THING...
THEY HAVE TO DO WHAT YOU SAY.

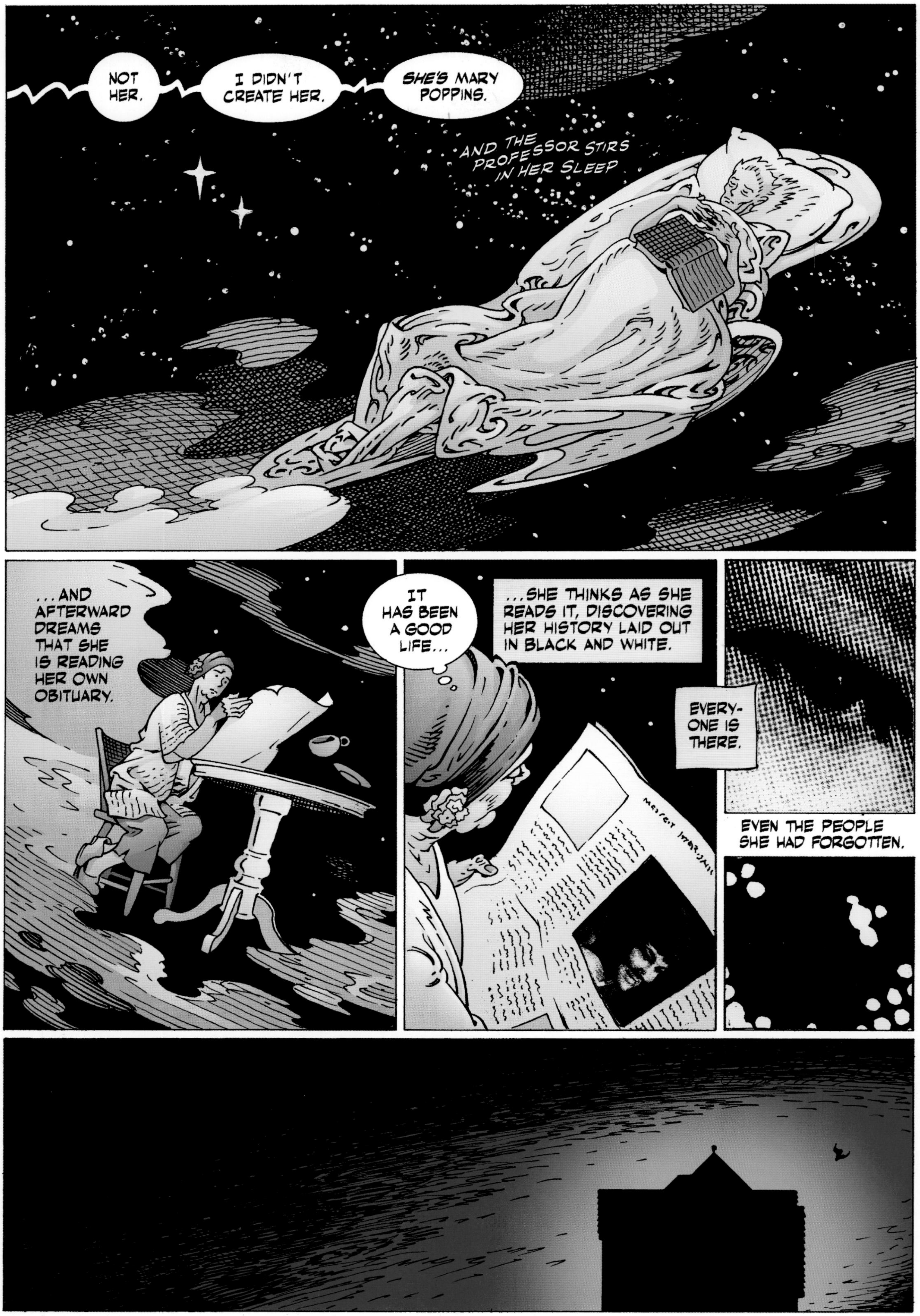
NOT HER.
I DIDN'T CREATE HER.
SHE'S MARY POPPINS.
AND THE PROFESSOR STIRS IN HER SLEEP
...AND AFTERWARD DREAMS THAT SHE IS READING HER OWN OBITUARY.
IT HAS BEEN A GOOD LIFE...
...SHE THINKS AS SHE READS IT, DISCOVERING HER HISTORY LAID OUT IN BLACK AND WHITE.
EVERY-ONE IS THERE.
EVEN THE PEOPLE SHE HAD FORGOTTEN.

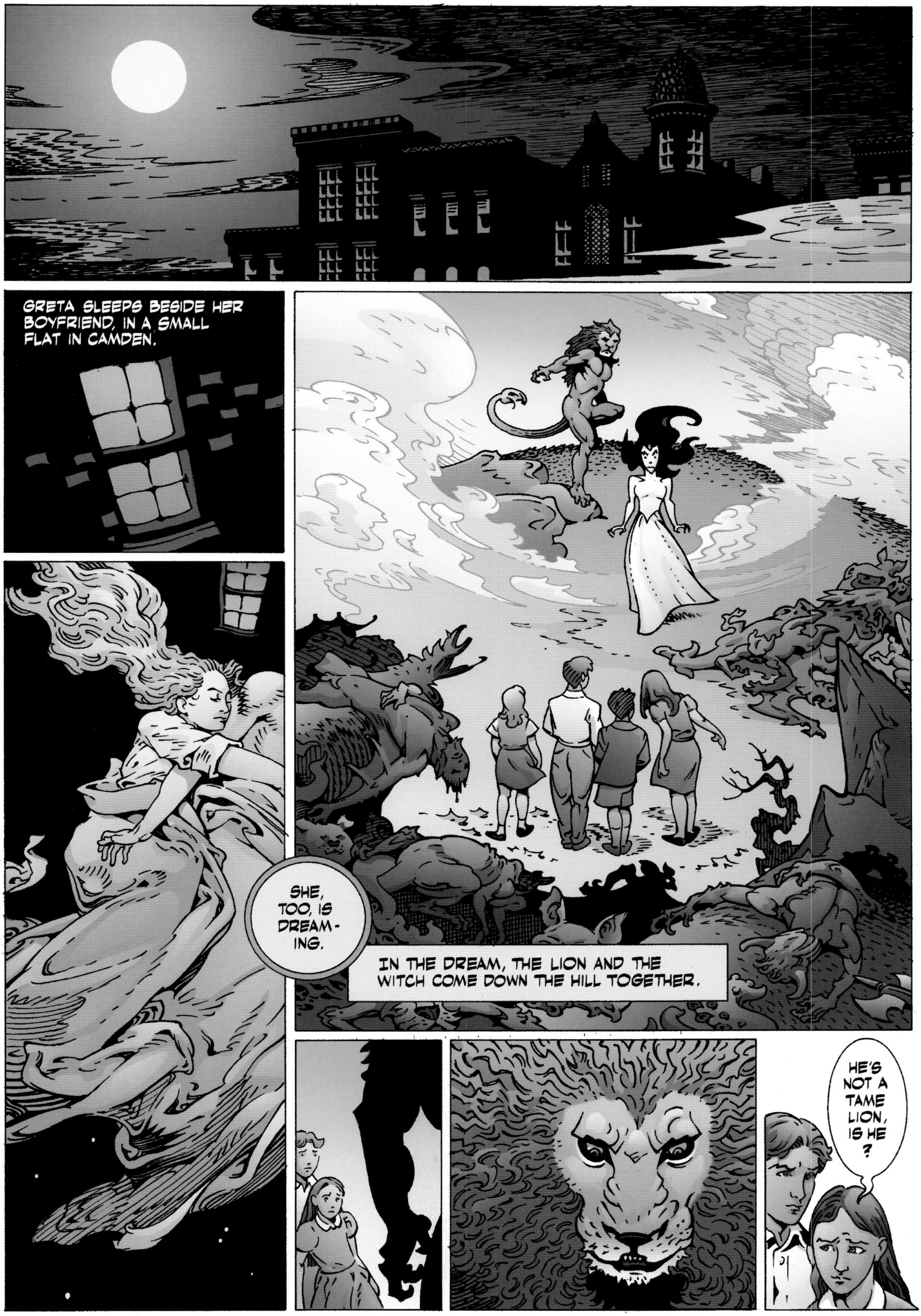
GRETA SLEEPS BESIDE HER BOYFRIEND, IN A SMALL FLAT IN CAMDEN.
SHE, TOO, IS DREAM-ING.
IN THE DREAM, THE LION AND THE WITCH COME DOWN THE HILL TOGETHER.
HE'S NOT A TAME LION, IS HE ?

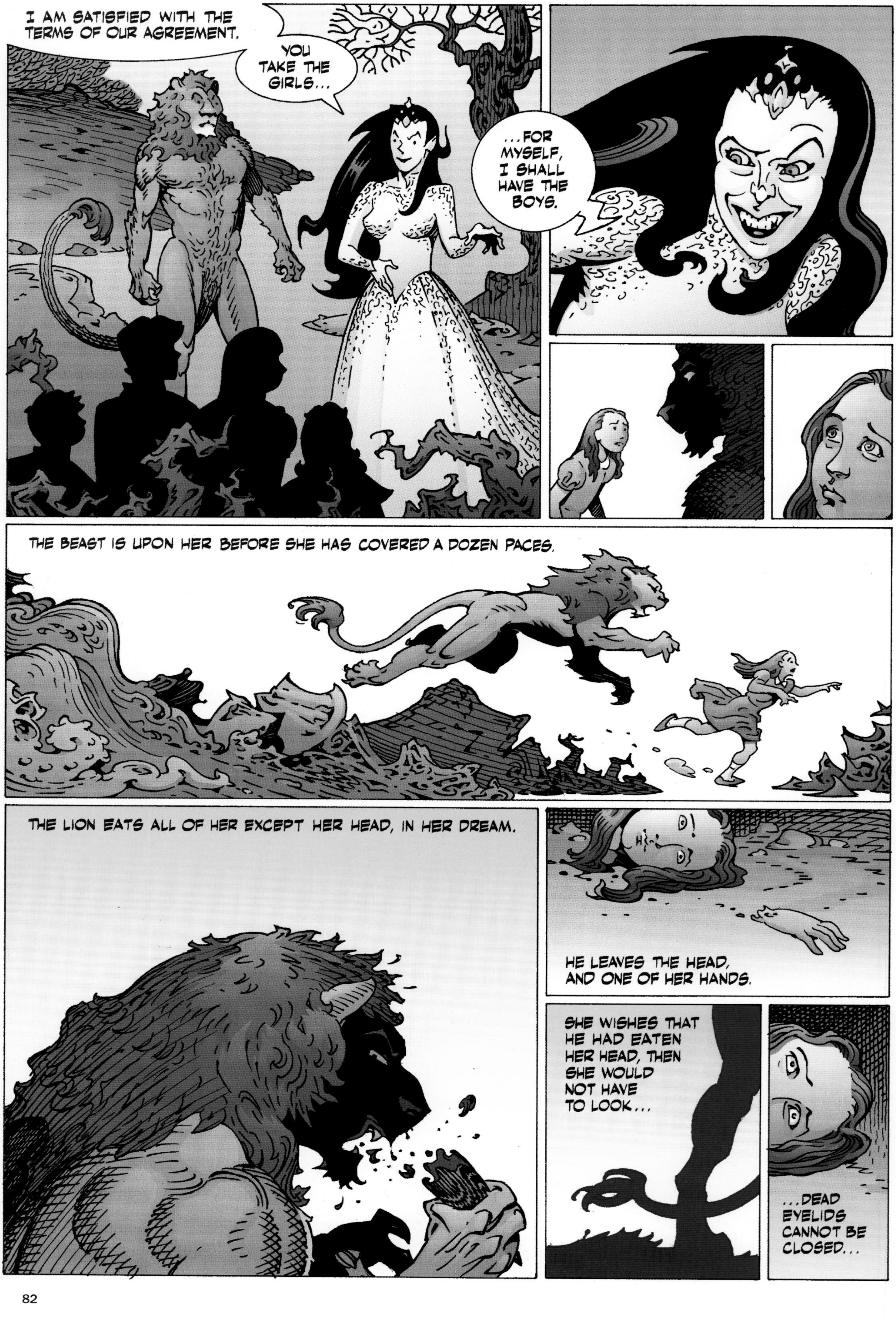
I AM SATISFIED WITH THE TERMS OF OUR AGREEMENT.
YOU TAKE THE GIRLS...
...FOR MYSELF, I SHALL HAVE THE BOYS.
THE BEAST IS UPON HER BEFORE SHE HAS COVERED A DOZEN PACES.
THE LION EATS ALL OF HER EXCEPT HER HEAD, IN HER DREAM.
HE LEAVES THE HEAD, AND ONE OF HER HANDS.
SHE WISHES THAT HE HAD EATEN HER HEAD, THEN SHE WOULD NOT HAVE TO LOOK...
...DEAD EYELIDS CANNOT BE CLOSED...

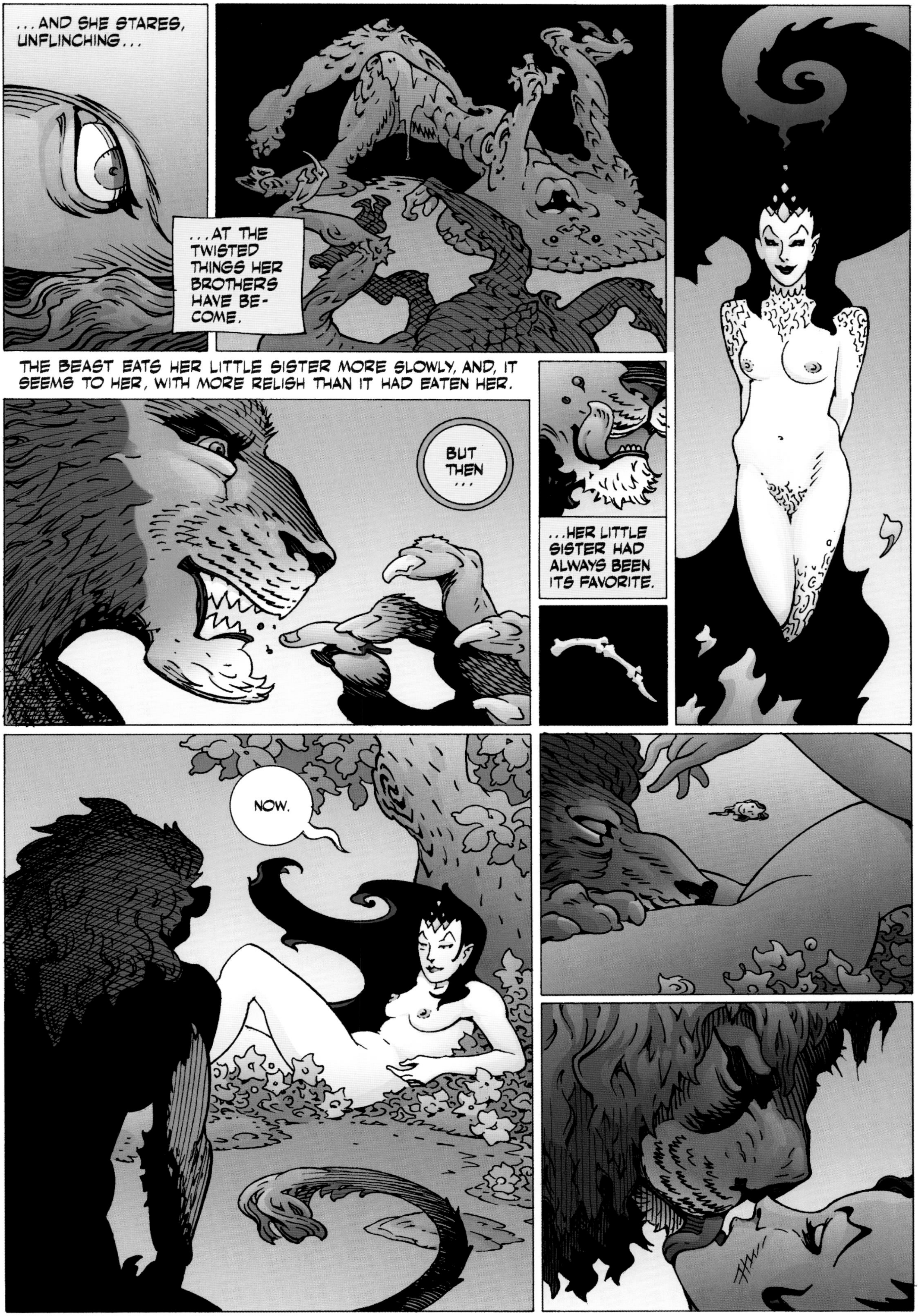
...AND SHE STARES, UNFLINCHING...
...AT THE TWISTED THINGS HER BROTHERS HAVE BE-COME.
THE BEAST EATS HER LITTLE SISTER MORE SLOWLY, AND, IT SEEMS TO HER, WITH MORE RELISH THAN IT HAD EATEN HER.
BUT THEN ...
...HER LITTLE SISTER HAD ALWAYS BEEN ITS FAVORITE.
NOW.

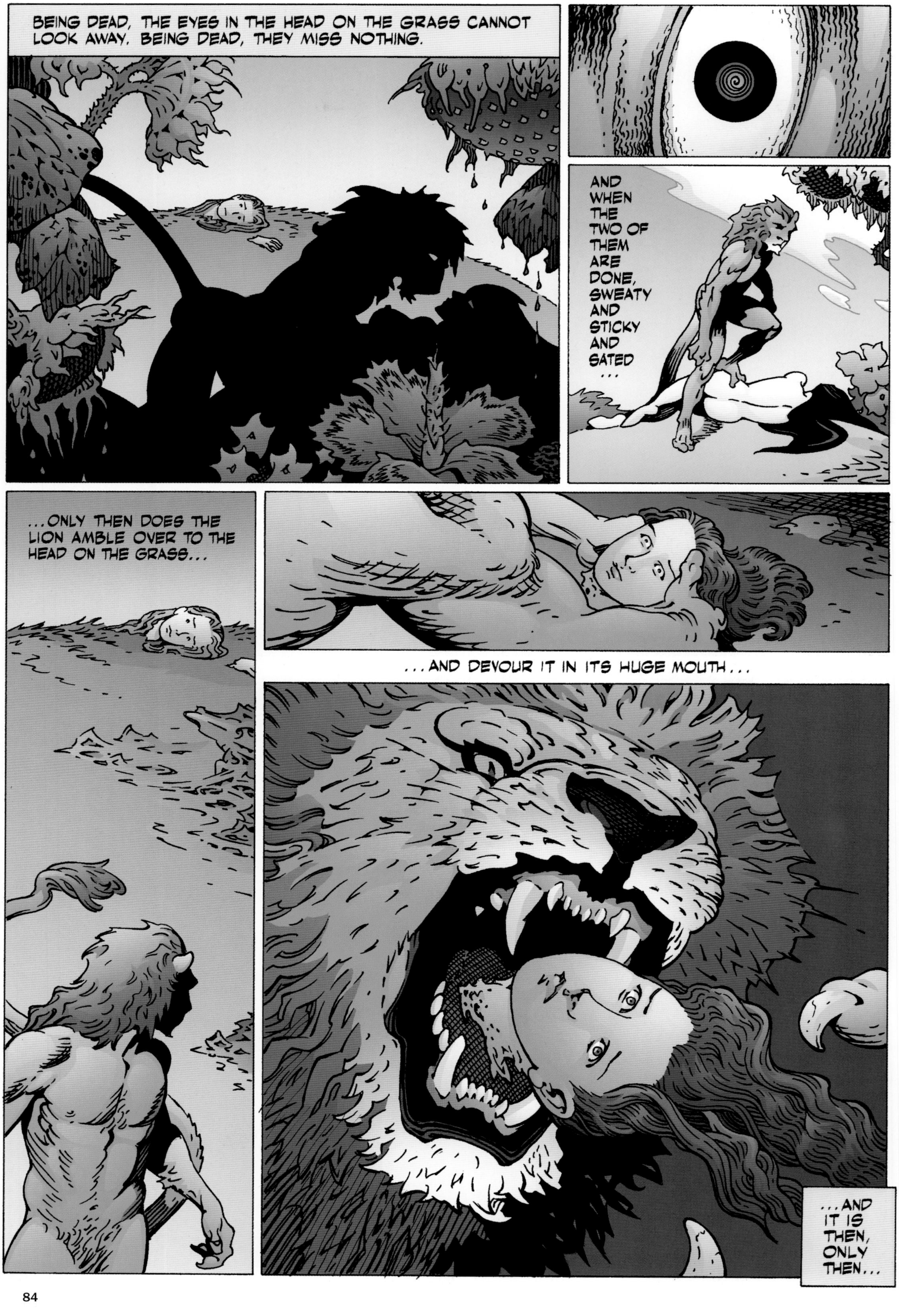

BEING DEAD, THE EYES IN THE HEAD ON THE GRASS CANNOT LOOK AWAY. BEING DEAD, THEY MISS NOTHING.
AND WHEN THE TWO OF THEM ARE DONE, SWEATY AND STICKY AND SATED ...
...ONLY THEN DOES THE LION AMBLE OVER TO THE HEAD ON THE GRASS...
...AND DEVOUR IT IN ITS HUGE MOUTH...
...AND IT IS THEN, ONLY THEN...

AHH H!

SHE TRIES TO WAKE HER BOY-FRIEND, BUT HE SNORES AND GRUNTS AND WILL NOT BE ROUSED.

IT'S TRUE.

SHE GREW UP.

SHE CARRIED ON.

SHE DIDN'T DIE.

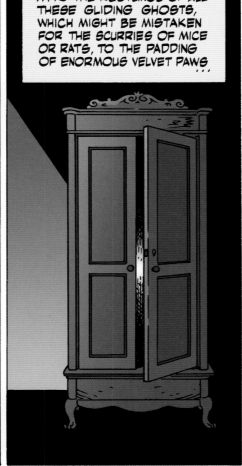

SHE IMAGINES THE PRO-FESSOR, WAKING IN THE NIGHT AND LISTENING TO THE NOISES COMING FROM THE OLD WARDROBE IN THE CORNER...

...TO THE RUSTLINGS OF ALL THESE GLIDING GHOSTS, WHICH MIGHT BE MISTAKEN FOR THE SCURRIES OF MICE OR RATS, TO THE PADDING OF ENORMOUS VELVET PAWS...

...AND THE DISTANT, DANGEROUS MUSIC OF A HUNTING HORN.

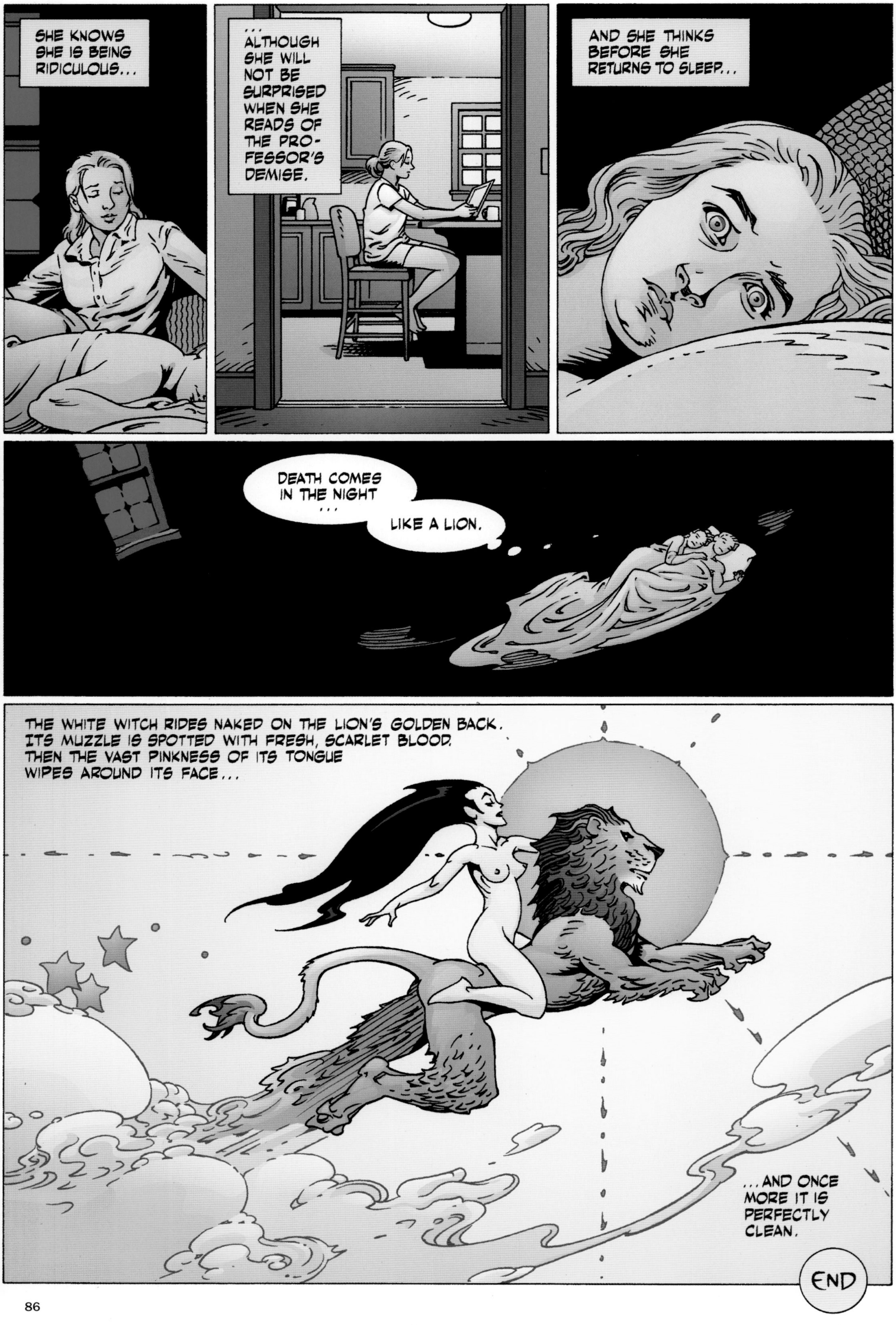
SHE KNOWS SHE IS BEING RIDICULOUS...
...ALTHOUGH SHE WILL NOT BE SURPRISED WHEN SHE READS OF THE PRO-FESSOR'S DEMISE.
AND SHE THINKS BEFORE SHE RETURNS TO SLEEP...
DEATH COMES IN THE NIGHT ...
LIKE A LION.
THE WHITE WITCH RIDES NAKED ON THE LION'S GOLDEN BACK. ITS MUZZLE IS SPOTTED WITH FRESH, SCARLET BLOOD. THEN THE VAST PINKNESS OF ITS TONGUE WIPES AROUND ITS FACE...
...AND ONCE MORE IT IS PERFECTLY CLEAN.
END

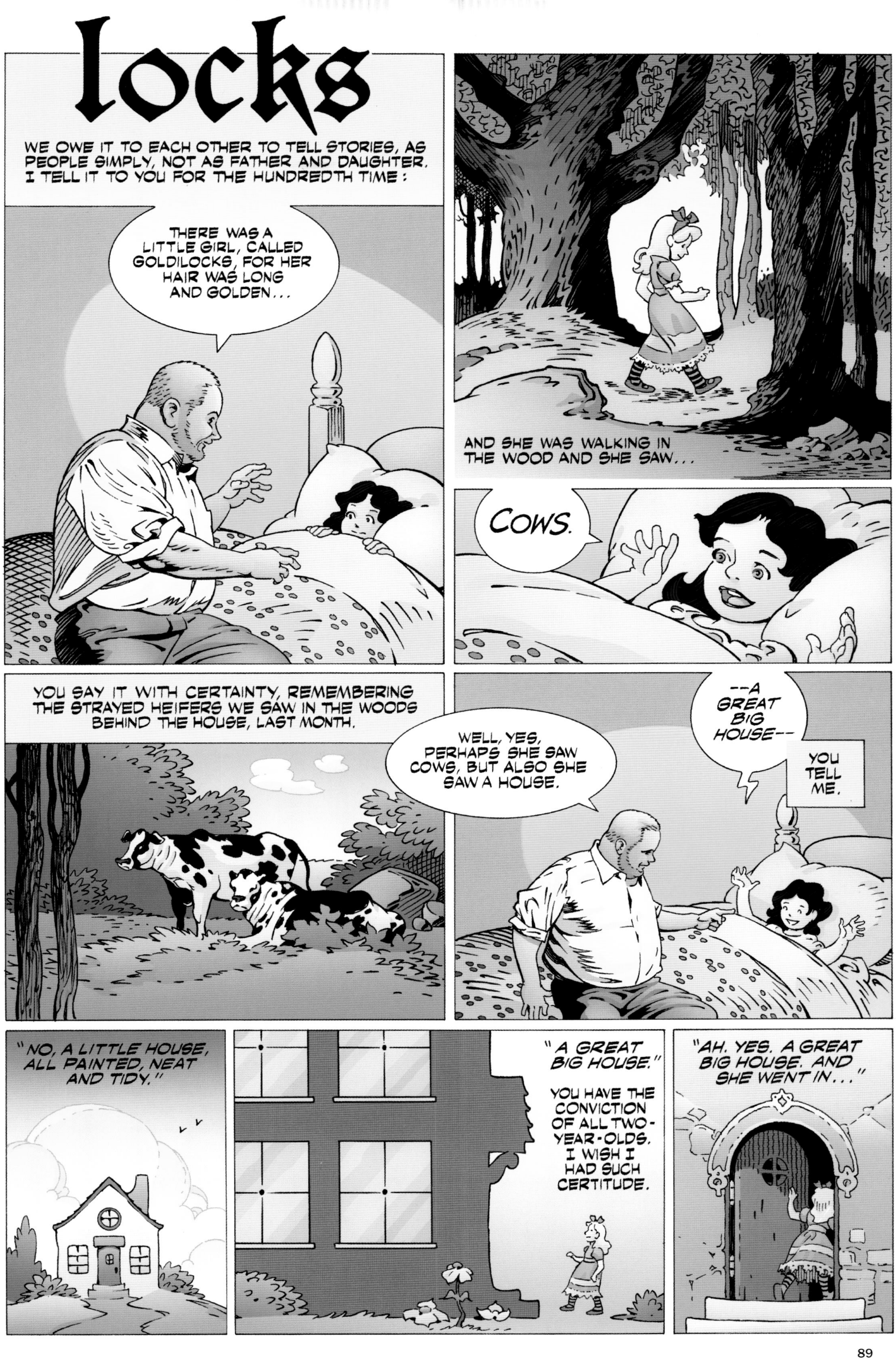
locks
WE OWE IT TO EACH OTHER TO TELL STORIES, AS PEOPLE SIMPLY, NOT AS FATHER AND DAUGHTER. I TELL IT TO YOU FOR THE HUNDREDTH TIME:
THERE WAS A LITTLE GIRL, CALLED GOLDILOCKS, FOR HER HAIR WAS LONG AND GOLDEN...
AND SHE WAS WALKING IN THE WOOD AND SHE SAW...
COWS.
YOU SAY IT WITH CERTAINTY, REMEMBERING THE STRAYED HEIFERS WE SAW IN THE WOODS BEHIND THE HOUSE, LAST MONTH.
WELL, YES, PERHAPS SHE SAW COWS, BUT ALSO SHE SAW A HOUSE.
--A GREAT BIG HOUSE--
YOU TELL ME.
"NO, A LITTLE HOUSE, ALL PAINTED, NEAT AND TIDY."
"A GREAT BIG HOUSE."
YOU HAVE THE CONVICTION OF ALL TWO-YEAR-OLDS. I WISH I HAD SUCH CERTITUDE.
"AH. YES. A GREAT BIG HOUSE. AND SHE WENT IN..."

I REMEMBER, AS I TELL IT, THAT THE LOCKS OF SOUTHEY'S HEROINE HAD SILVERED WITH AGE. THE OLD WOMAN AND THE THREE BEARS...

PERHAPS THEY HAD BEEN GOLDEN ONCE, WHEN SHE WAS A CHILD.

AND NOW, WE ARE ALREADY UP TO THE PORRIDGE...

AND IT WAS TOO--

HOT!

AND IT WAS TOO--

COLD!

AND THEN IT WAS, WE CHORUS...

JUST RIGHT.

THE PORRIDGE IS EATEN, THE BABY'S CHAIR IS SHATTERED.

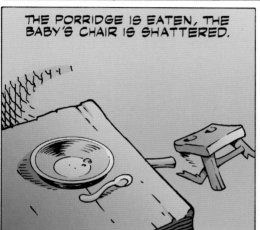

GOLDILOCKS GOES UPSTAIRS, EXAMINES BEDS, AND SLEEPS, UNWISELY.

BUT THEN THE BEARS RETURN.

REMEMBERING SOUTHEY STILL, I DO THE VOICES: FATHER BEAR'S GRUFF BOOM SCARES YOU, AND YOU DELIGHT IN IT.

WHEN I WAS A SMALL CHILD AND HEARD THE TALE, IF I WAS ANYONE I WAS BABY BEAR, MY PORRIDGE EATEN, AND MY CHAIR DESTROYED, MY BED INHABITED BY SOME STRANGE GIRL.

YOU GIGGLE WHEN I DO THE BABY'S WAIL...

SOMEONE'S BEEN EATING MY PORRIDGE, AND THEY'VE EATEN IT...

ALL UP...

YOU SAY. A RESPONSE IT IS, OR AN AMEN.

THE BEARS GO UPSTAIRS HESITANTLY, THEIR HOUSE NOW FEELS DESECRATED. THEY REALIZE WHAT LOCKS ARE FOR.

THEY REACH THE BEDROOM. "SOMEONE'S BEEN SLEEPING IN MY BED."

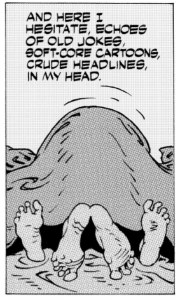

AND HERE I HESITATE, ECHOES OF OLD JOKES, SOFT-CORE CARTOONS, CRUDE HEADLINES, IN MY HEAD.

ONE DAY YOUR MOUTH WILL CURL AT THAT LINE. A LOSS OF INTEREST, LATER, INNOCENCE. INNOCENCE, AS IF IT WERE A COMMODITY.

And if I could,
-- MY FATHER WROTE TO ME, HUGE AS A BEAR HIMSELF, WHEN I WAS YOUNGER . . .

I WOULD DOWER YOU WITH EXPERIENCE, WITHOUT EXPERIENCE.

AND I, IN MY TURN, WOULD PASS THAT ON TO YOU. BUT WE MAKE OUR OWN MISTAKES.

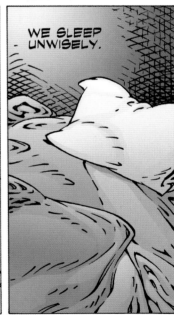

WE SLEEP - UNWISELY.

THE REPETITION ECHOES DOWN THE YEARS. WHEN YOUR CHILDREN GROW, WHEN YOUR DARK LOCKS BEGIN TO SILVER, WHEN YOU ARE AN OLD WOMAN, ALONE WITH YOUR THREE BEARS, WHAT WILL YOU SEE? WHAT STORIES WILL YOU TELL?

"AND THEN GOLDILOCKS JUMPED OUT OF THE WINDOW AND SHE RAN--"

TOGETHER, NOW:

ALL THE WAY HOME.

AND THEN YOU SAY...

AGAIN. AGAIN. AGAIN.

WE OWE IT TO EACH OTHER TO TELL STORIES.

THESE DAYS, MY SYMPATHY'S WITH FATHER BEAR.

BEFORE I LEAVE MY HOUSE I LOCK THE DOOR...

...AND CHECK EACH BED AND CHAIR ON MY RETURN.

AGAIN.

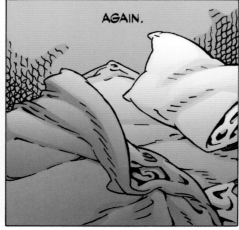

AGAIN.

AGAIN.

END

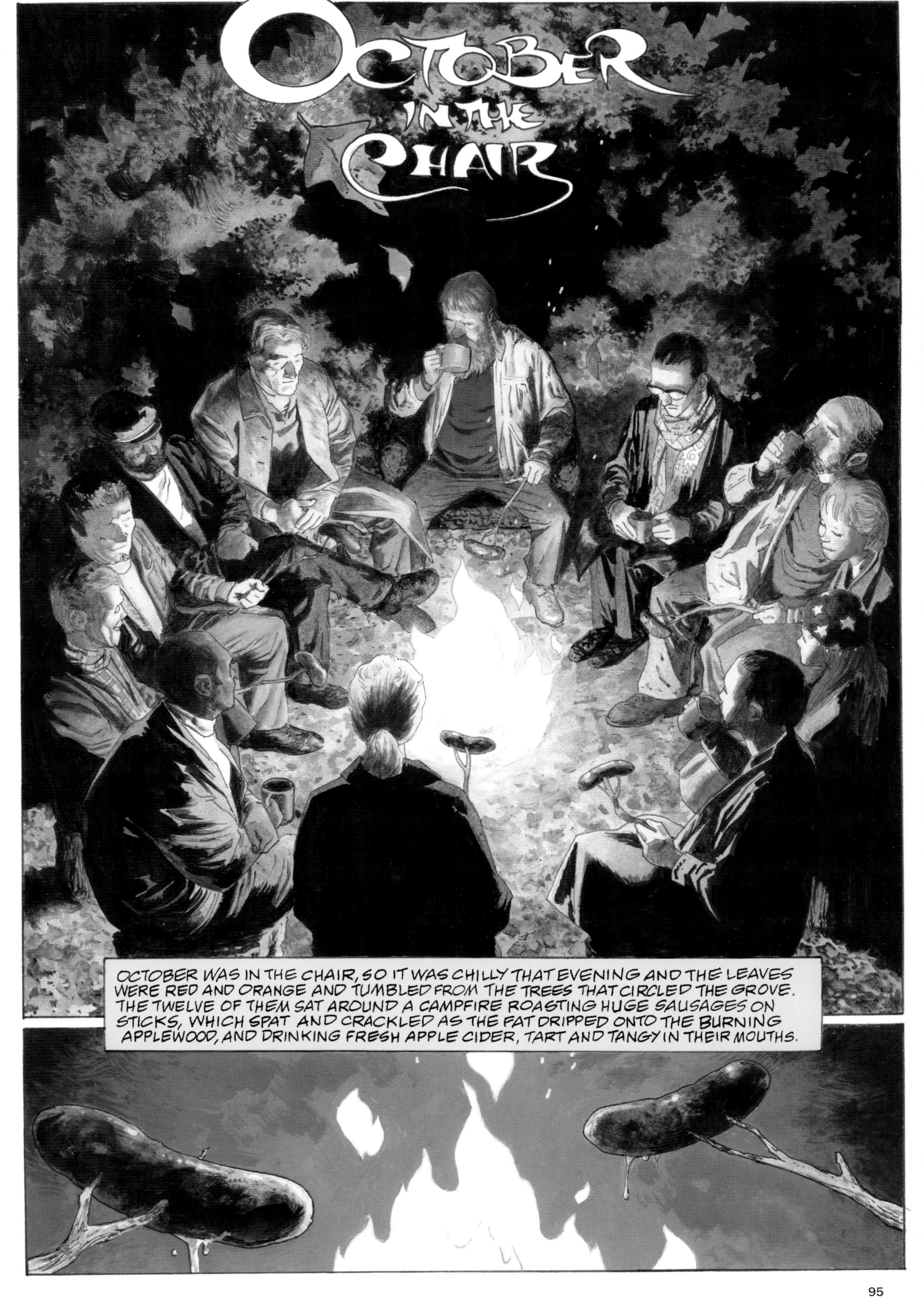
OCTOBER IN THE CHAIR
OCTOBER WAS IN THE CHAIR, SO IT WAS CHILLY THAT EVENING AND THE LEAVES WERE RED AND ORANGE AND TUMBLED FROM THE TREES THAT CIRCLED THE GROVE. THE TWELVE OF THEM SAT AROUND A CAMPFIRE ROASTING HUGE SAUSAGES ON STICKS, WHICH SPAT AND CRACKLED AS THE FAT DRIPPED ONTO THE BURNING APPLEWOOD, AND DRINKING FRESH APPLE CIDER, TART AND TANGY IN THEIR MOUTHS.

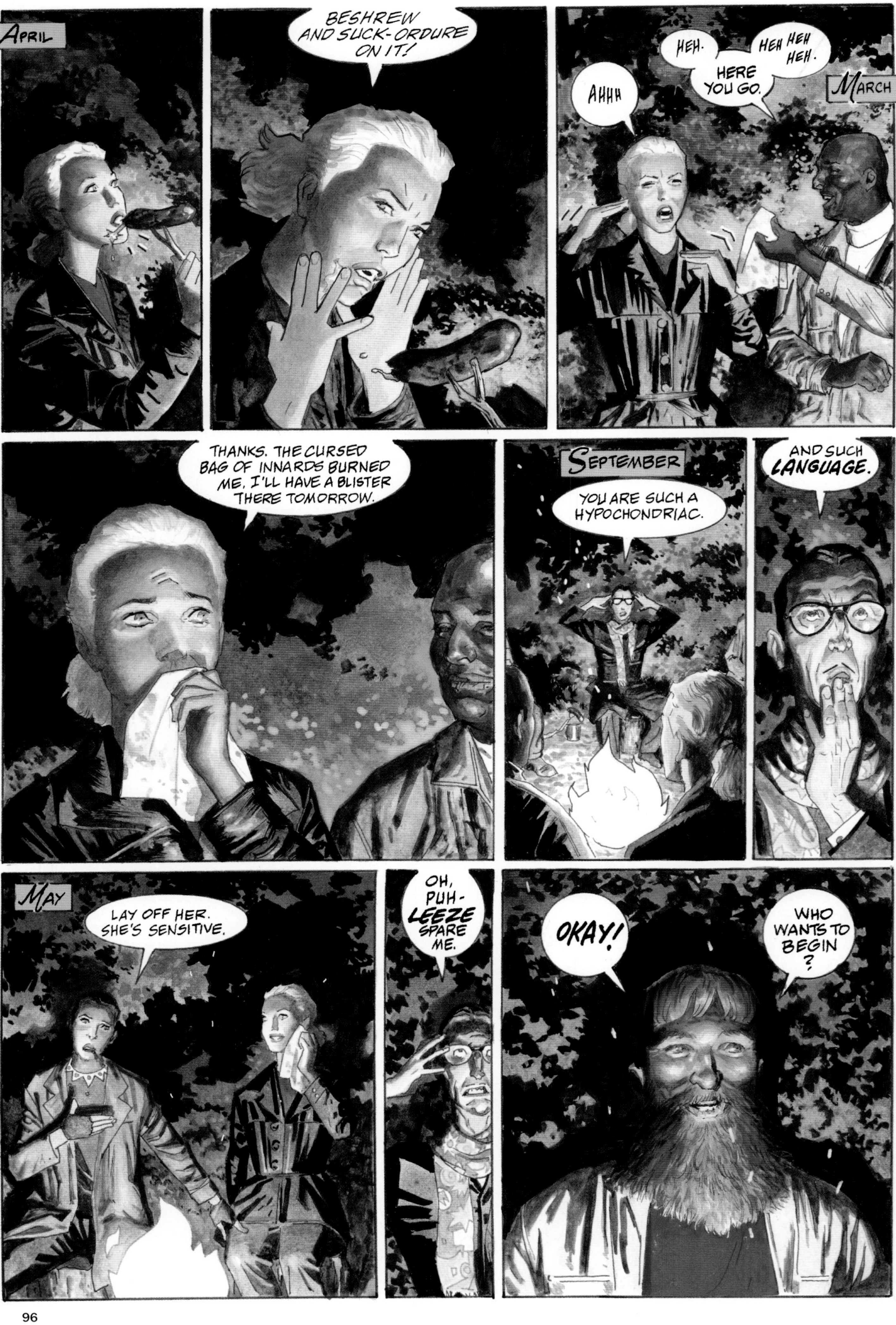
April
BESHREW AND SUCK-ORDURE ON IT!
AHHH
HEH.
HERE YOU GO.
HEH HEH HEH.
March
THANKS. THE CURSED BAG OF INNARDS BURNED ME. I'LL HAVE A BLISTER THERE TOMORROW.
September
YOU ARE SUCH A HYPOCHONDRIAC.
AND SUCH LANGUAGE.
May
LAY OFF HER. SHE'S SENSITIVE.
OH, PUH-LEEZE SPARE ME.
OKAY!
WHO WANTS TO BEGIN?

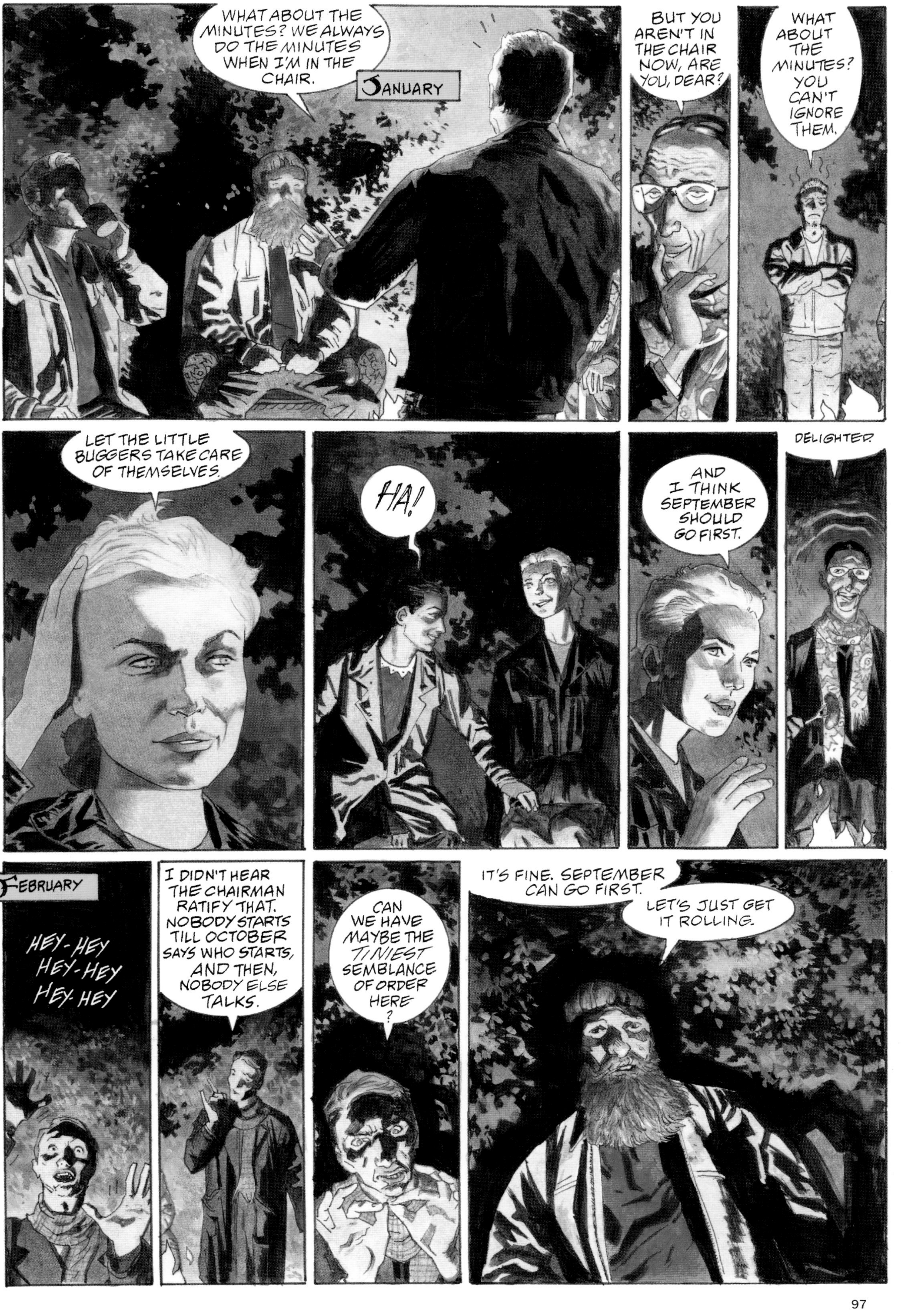
WHAT ABOUT THE MINUTES? WE ALWAYS DO THE MINUTES WHEN I'M IN THE CHAIR.
JANUARY
BUT YOU AREN'T IN THE CHAIR NOW, ARE YOU, DEAR?
WHAT ABOUT THE MINUTES? YOU CAN'T IGNORE THEM.
LET THE LITTLE BUGGERS TAKE CARE OF THEMSELVES.
HA!
AND I THINK SEPTEMBER SHOULD GO FIRST.
DELIGHTED.
FEBRUARY
HEY-HEY HEY-HEY HEY-HEY
I DIDN'T HEAR THE CHAIRMAN RATIFY THAT. NOBODY STARTS TILL OCTOBER SAYS WHO STARTS, AND THEN, NOBODY ELSE TALKS.
CAN WE HAVE MAYBE THE TINIEST SEMBLANCE OF ORDER HERE?
IT'S FINE. SEPTEMBER CAN GO FIRST.
LET'S JUST GET IT ROLLING.

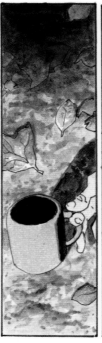

=AHEM=

LAURENT DELISLE WAS THE FINEST CHEF IN ALL OF SEATTLE...

"...AT LEAST, LAURENT DELISLE THOUGHT SO, AND THE THREE MICHELIN STARS ON HIS DOOR CONFIRMED HIM IN HIS OPINION.

"HE WAS A REMARKABLE CHEF, IT IS TRUE-- HIS MINCED LAMB BRIOCHE HAD WON SEVERAL AWARDS.

"HIS SMOKED QUAIL AND WHITE TRUFFLE RAVIOLI HAD BEEN DESCRIBED IN THE GASTRONOME AS..."

THE TENTH WONDER OF THE WORLD!

"BUT IT WAS HIS WINE CELLAR... AH, HIS WINE CELLAR. THAT WAS THE SOURCE OF HIS PRIDE AND HIS PASSION."

I UNDERSTAND THAT. THE LAST OF THE WHITE GRAPES ARE HARVESTED IN ME. I APPRECIATE FINE WINES, THE AROMA, THE TASTE.

"THE TREASURE -- THE JEWEL -- THE RAREST OF THE RARE -- AND THE NE PLUS ULTRA OF HIS TEMPERATURE-CONTROLLED WINE CELLAR WAS A BOTTLE OF 1902 CHATEAU LAFITTE."

EXCUSE ME.

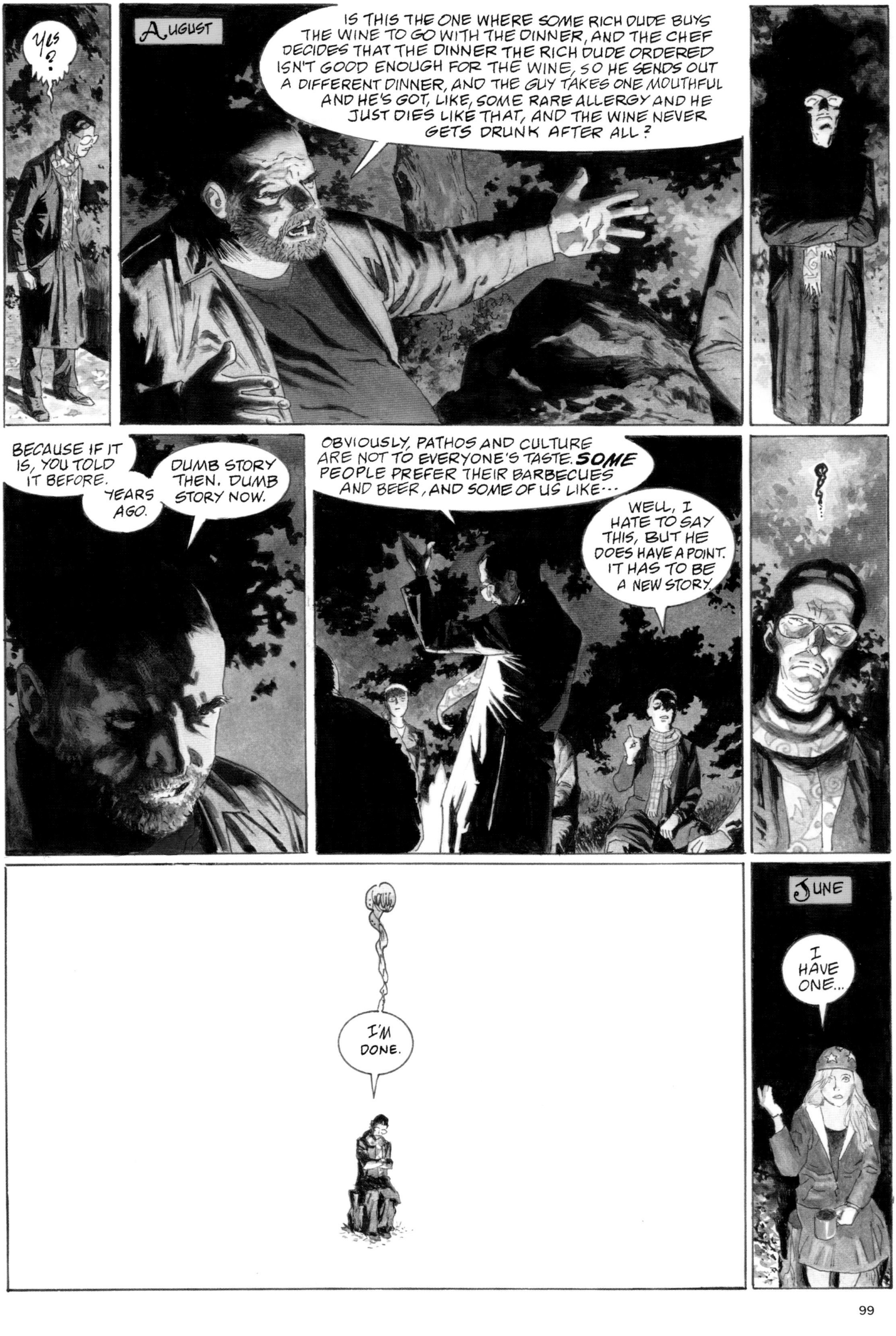
Yes?
August
IS THIS THE ONE WHERE SOME RICH DUDE BUYS THE WINE TO GO WITH THE DINNER, AND THE CHEF DECIDES THAT THE DINNER THE RICH DUDE ORDERED ISN'T GOOD ENOUGH FOR THE WINE, SO HE SENDS OUT A DIFFERENT DINNER, AND THE GUY TAKES ONE MOUTHFUL AND HE'S GOT, LIKE, SOME RARE ALLERGY AND HE JUST DIES LIKE THAT, AND THE WINE NEVER GETS DRUNK AFTER ALL?
BECAUSE IF IT IS, YOU TOLD IT BEFORE.
YEARS AGO.
DUMB STORY THEN. DUMB STORY NOW.
OBVIOUSLY, PATHOS AND CULTURE ARE NOT TO EVERYONE'S TASTE. SOME PEOPLE PREFER THEIR BARBECUES AND BEER, AND SOME OF US LIKE...
WELL, I HATE TO SAY THIS, BUT HE DOES HAVE A POINT. IT HAS TO BE A NEW STORY.
I'M DONE.
June
I HAVE ONE...

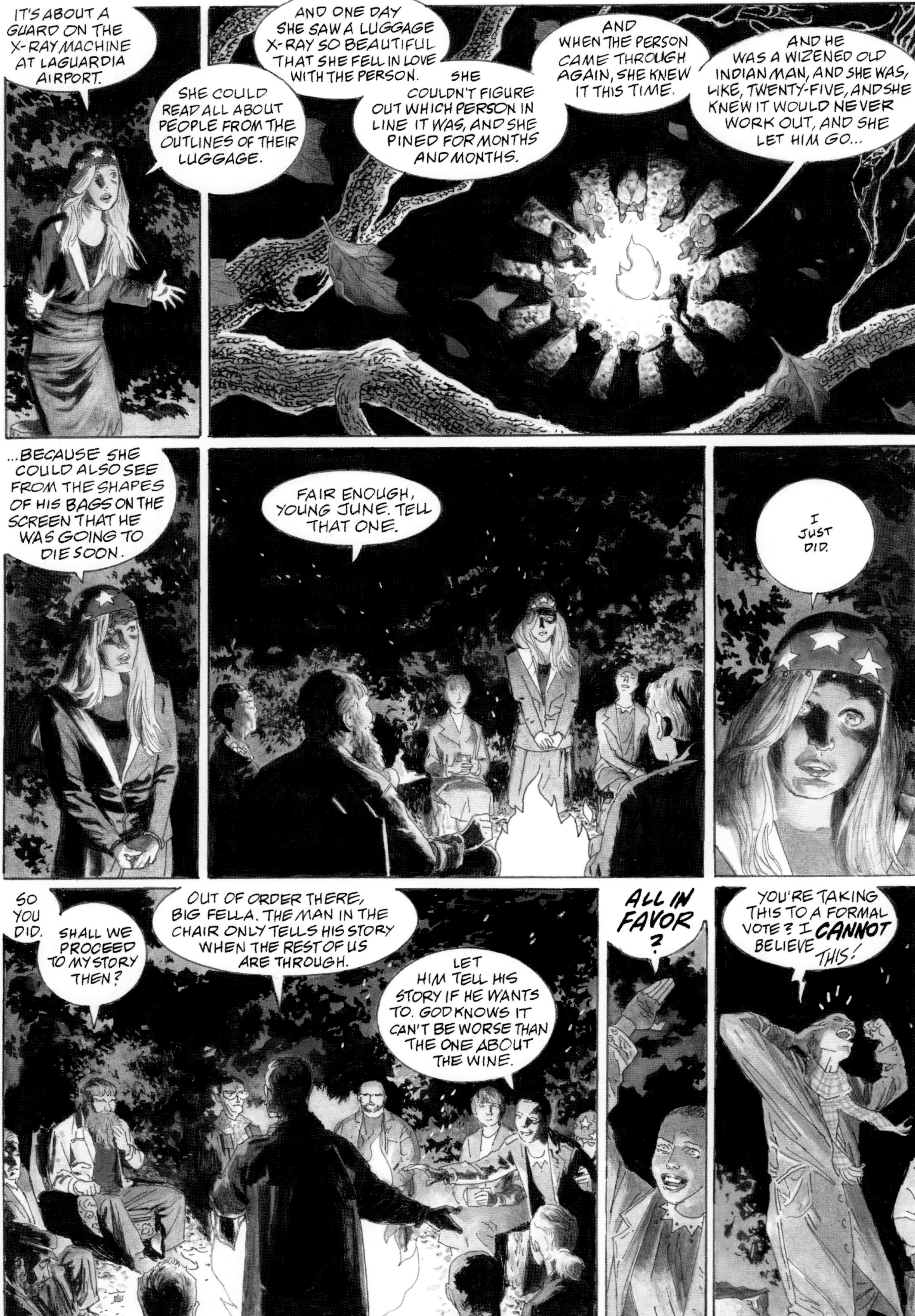
IT'S ABOUT A GUARD ON THE X-RAY MACHINE AT LAGUARDIA AIRPORT.
SHE COULD READ ALL ABOUT PEOPLE FROM THE OUTLINES OF THEIR LUGGAGE.
AND ONE DAY SHE SAW A LUGGAGE X-RAY SO BEAUTIFUL THAT SHE FELL IN LOVE WITH THE PERSON.
SHE COULDN'T FIGURE OUT WHICH PERSON IN LINE IT WAS, AND SHE PINED FOR MONTHS AND MONTHS.
AND WHEN THE PERSON CAME THROUGH AGAIN, SHE KNEW IT THIS TIME.
AND HE WAS A WIZENED OLD INDIAN MAN, AND SHE WAS, LIKE, TWENTY-FIVE, AND SHE KNEW IT WOULD NEVER WORK OUT, AND SHE LET HIM GO...
...BECAUSE SHE COULD ALSO SEE FROM THE SHAPES OF HIS BAGS ON THE SCREEN THAT HE WAS GOING TO DIE SOON.
FAIR ENOUGH, YOUNG JUNE. TELL THAT ONE.
I JUST DID.
SO YOU DID.
SHALL WE PROCEED TO MY STORY THEN?
OUT OF ORDER THERE, BIG FELLA. THE MAN IN THE CHAIR ONLY TELLS HIS STORY WHEN THE REST OF US ARE THROUGH.
LET HIM TELL HIS STORY IF HE WANTS TO. GOD KNOWS IT CAN'T BE WORSE THAN THE ONE ABOUT THE WINE.
ALL IN FAVOR?
YOU'RE TAKING THIS TO A FORMAL VOTE? I CANNOT BELIEVE THIS!

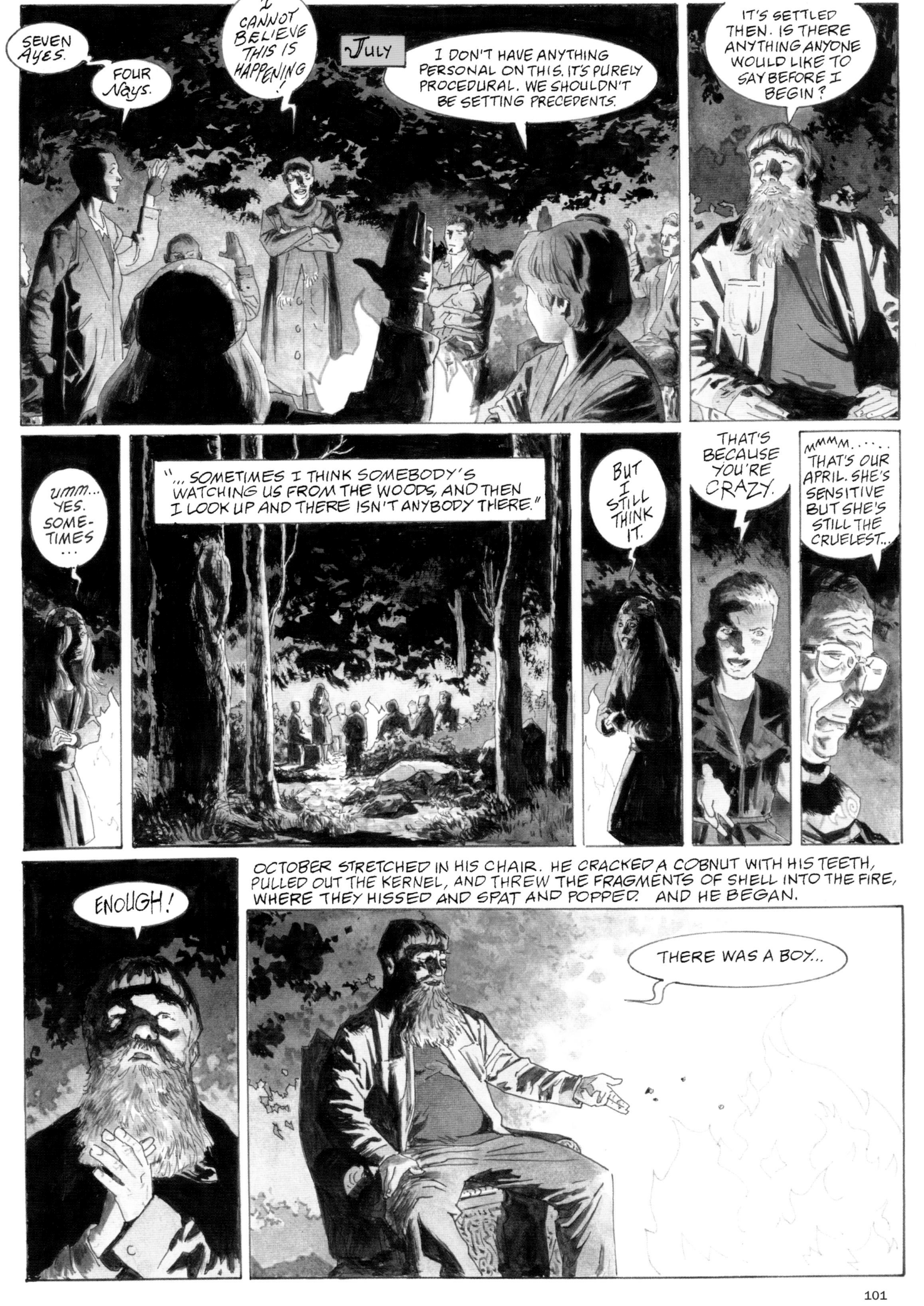
SEVEN AYES.
FOUR NAYS.
I CANNOT BELIEVE THIS IS HAPPENING!
JULY
I DON'T HAVE ANYTHING PERSONAL ON THIS. IT'S PURELY PROCEDURAL. WE SHOULDN'T BE SETTING PRECEDENTS.
IT'S SETTLED THEN. IS THERE ANYTHING ANYONE WOULD LIKE TO SAY BEFORE I BEGIN?
UMM... YES. SOMETIMES...
"...SOMETIMES I THINK SOMEBODY'S WATCHING US FROM THE WOODS, AND THEN I LOOK UP AND THERE ISN'T ANYBODY THERE."
BUT I STILL THINK IT.
THAT'S BECAUSE YOU'RE CRAZY.
MMMM..... THAT'S OUR APRIL. SHE'S SENSITIVE BUT SHE'S STILL THE CRUELEST...
ENOUGH!
OCTOBER STRETCHED IN HIS CHAIR. HE CRACKED A COBNUT WITH HIS TEETH, PULLED OUT THE KERNEL, AND THREW THE FRAGMENTS OF SHELL INTO THE FIRE, WHERE THEY HISSED AND SPAT AND POPPED. AND HE BEGAN.
THERE WAS A BOY...

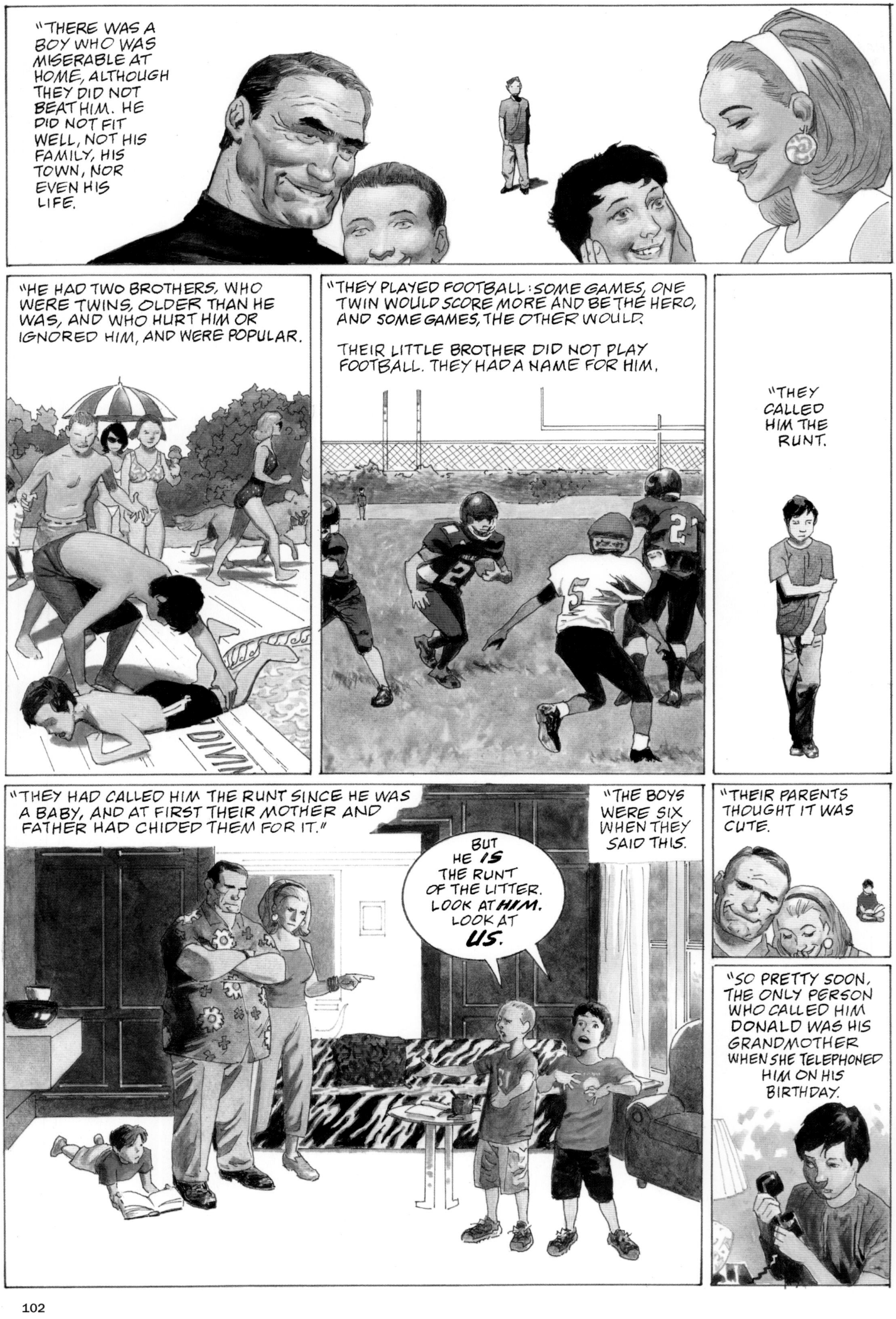

"THERE WAS A BOY WHO WAS MISERABLE AT HOME, ALTHOUGH THEY DID NOT BEAT HIM. HE DID NOT FIT WELL, NOT HIS FAMILY, HIS TOWN, NOR EVEN HIS LIFE.
"HE HAD TWO BROTHERS, WHO WERE TWINS, OLDER THAN HE WAS, AND WHO HURT HIM OR IGNORED HIM, AND WERE POPULAR.
"THEY PLAYED FOOTBALL: SOME GAMES, ONE TWIN WOULD SCORE MORE AND BE THE HERO, AND SOME GAMES, THE OTHER WOULD.
THEIR LITTLE BROTHER DID NOT PLAY FOOTBALL. THEY HAD A NAME FOR HIM.
"THEY CALLED HIM THE RUNT.
"THEY HAD CALLED HIM THE RUNT SINCE HE WAS A BABY, AND AT FIRST THEIR MOTHER AND FATHER HAD CHIDED THEM FOR IT."
"THE BOYS WERE SIX WHEN THEY SAID THIS.
BUT HE IS THE RUNT OF THE LITTER. LOOK AT HIM. LOOK AT US.
"THEIR PARENTS THOUGHT IT WAS CUTE.
"SO PRETTY SOON, THE ONLY PERSON WHO CALLED HIM DONALD WAS HIS GRANDMOTHER WHEN SHE TELEPHONED HIM ON HIS BIRTHDAY.

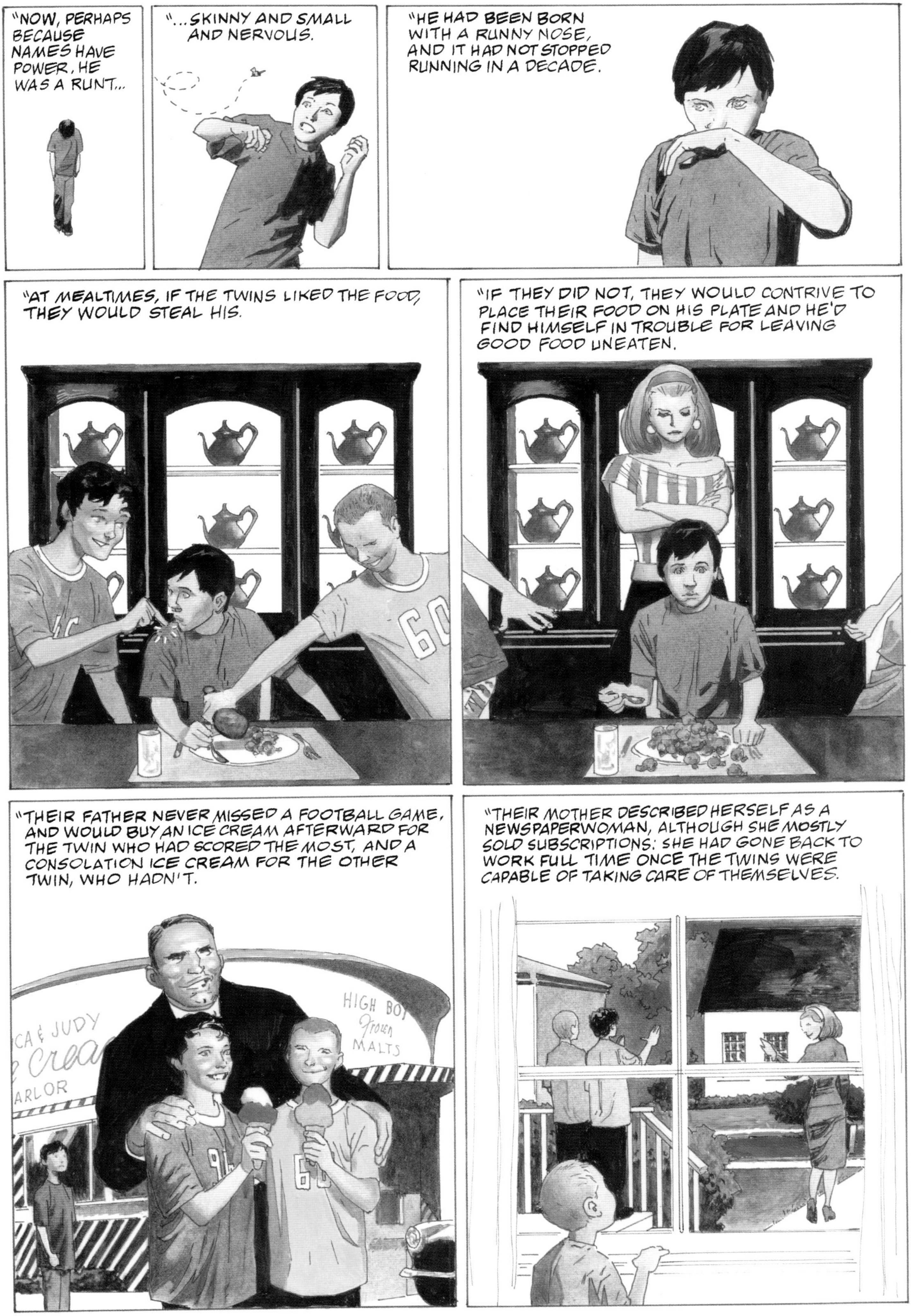
"NOW, PERHAPS BECAUSE NAMES HAVE POWER, HE WAS A RUNT...
"...SKINNY AND SMALL AND NERVOUS.
"HE HAD BEEN BORN WITH A RUNNY NOSE, AND IT HAD NOT STOPPED RUNNING IN A DECADE.
"AT MEALTIMES, IF THE TWINS LIKED THE FOOD, THEY WOULD STEAL HIS.
"IF THEY DID NOT, THEY WOULD CONTRIVE TO PLACE THEIR FOOD ON HIS PLATE AND HE'D FIND HIMSELF IN TROUBLE FOR LEAVING GOOD FOOD UNEATEN.
"THEIR FATHER NEVER MISSED A FOOTBALL GAME, AND WOULD BUY AN ICE CREAM AFTERWARD FOR THE TWIN WHO HAD SCORED THE MOST, AND A CONSOLATION ICE CREAM FOR THE OTHER TWIN, WHO HADN'T.
HIGH BOY
Frozen
MALTS
"THEIR MOTHER DESCRIBED HERSELF AS A NEWSPAPERWOMAN, ALTHOUGH SHE MOSTLY SOLD SUBSCRIPTIONS: SHE HAD GONE BACK TO WORK FULL TIME ONCE THE TWINS WERE CAPABLE OF TAKING CARE OF THEMSELVES.

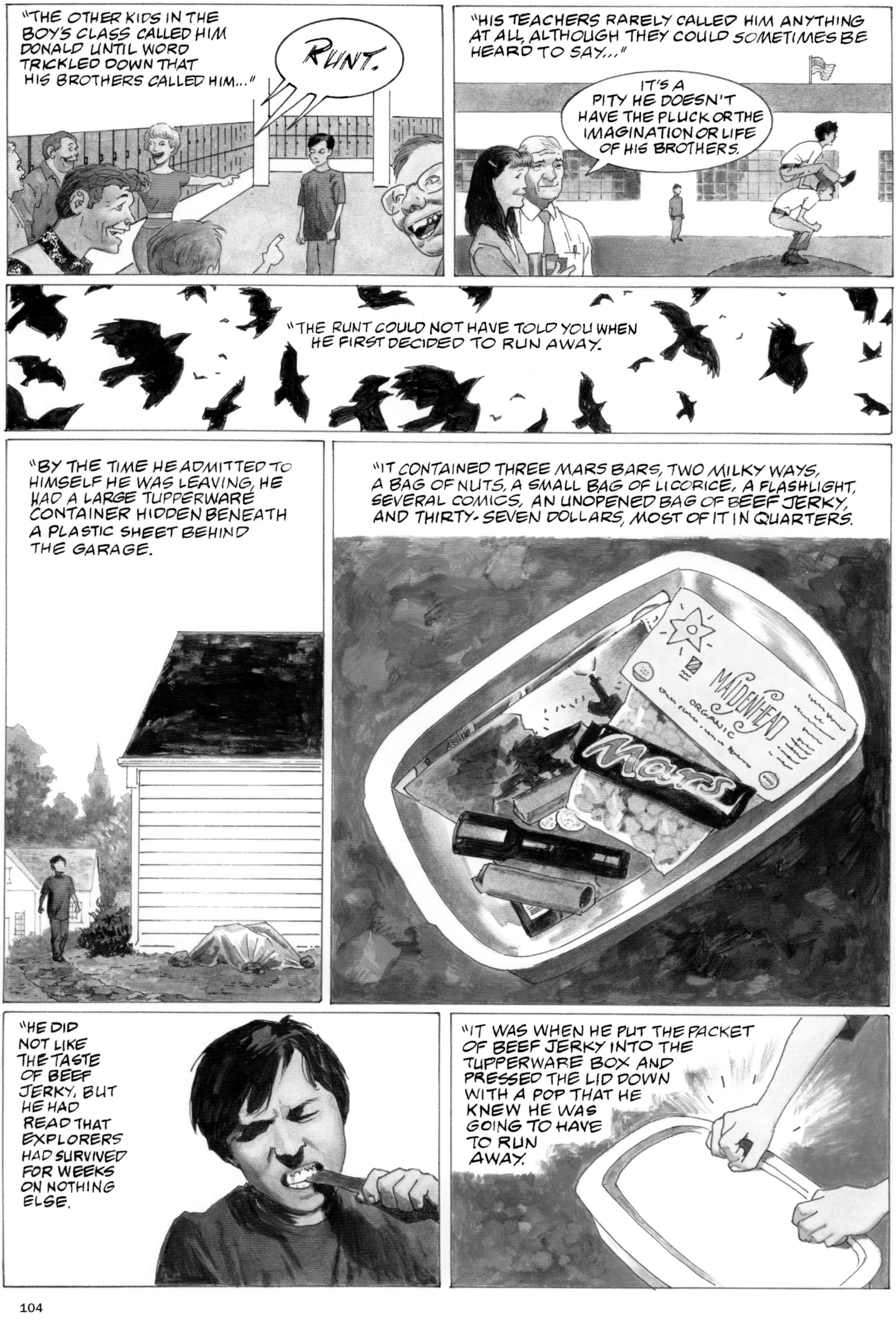
"THE OTHER KIDS IN THE BOY'S CLASS CALLED HIM DONALD UNTIL WORD TRICKLED DOWN THAT HIS BROTHERS CALLED HIM..."
RUNT.
"HIS TEACHERS RARELY CALLED HIM ANYTHING AT ALL, ALTHOUGH THEY COULD SOMETIMES BE HEARD TO SAY..."
IT'S A PITY HE DOESN'T HAVE THE PLUCK OR THE IMAGINATION OR LIFE OF HIS BROTHERS.
"THE RUNT COULD NOT HAVE TOLD YOU WHEN HE FIRST DECIDED TO RUN AWAY.
"BY THE TIME HE ADMITTED TO HIMSELF HE WAS LEAVING, HE HAD A LARGE TUPPERWARE CONTAINER HIDDEN BENEATH A PLASTIC SHEET BEHIND THE GARAGE.
"IT CONTAINED THREE MARS BARS, TWO MILKY WAYS, A BAG OF NUTS, A SMALL BAG OF LICORICE, A FLASHLIGHT, SEVERAL COMICS, AN UNOPENED BAG OF BEEF JERKY, AND THIRTY-SEVEN DOLLARS, MOST OF IT IN QUARTERS.
MAIDENHEAD
ORGANIC
Mars
"HE DID NOT LIKE THE TASTE OF BEEF JERKY, BUT HE HAD READ THAT EXPLORERS HAD SURVIVED FOR WEEKS ON NOTHING ELSE.
"IT WAS WHEN HE PUT THE PACKET OF BEEF JERKY INTO THE TUPPERWARE BOX AND PRESSED THE LID DOWN WITH A POP THAT HE KNEW HE WAS GOING TO HAVE TO RUN AWAY.

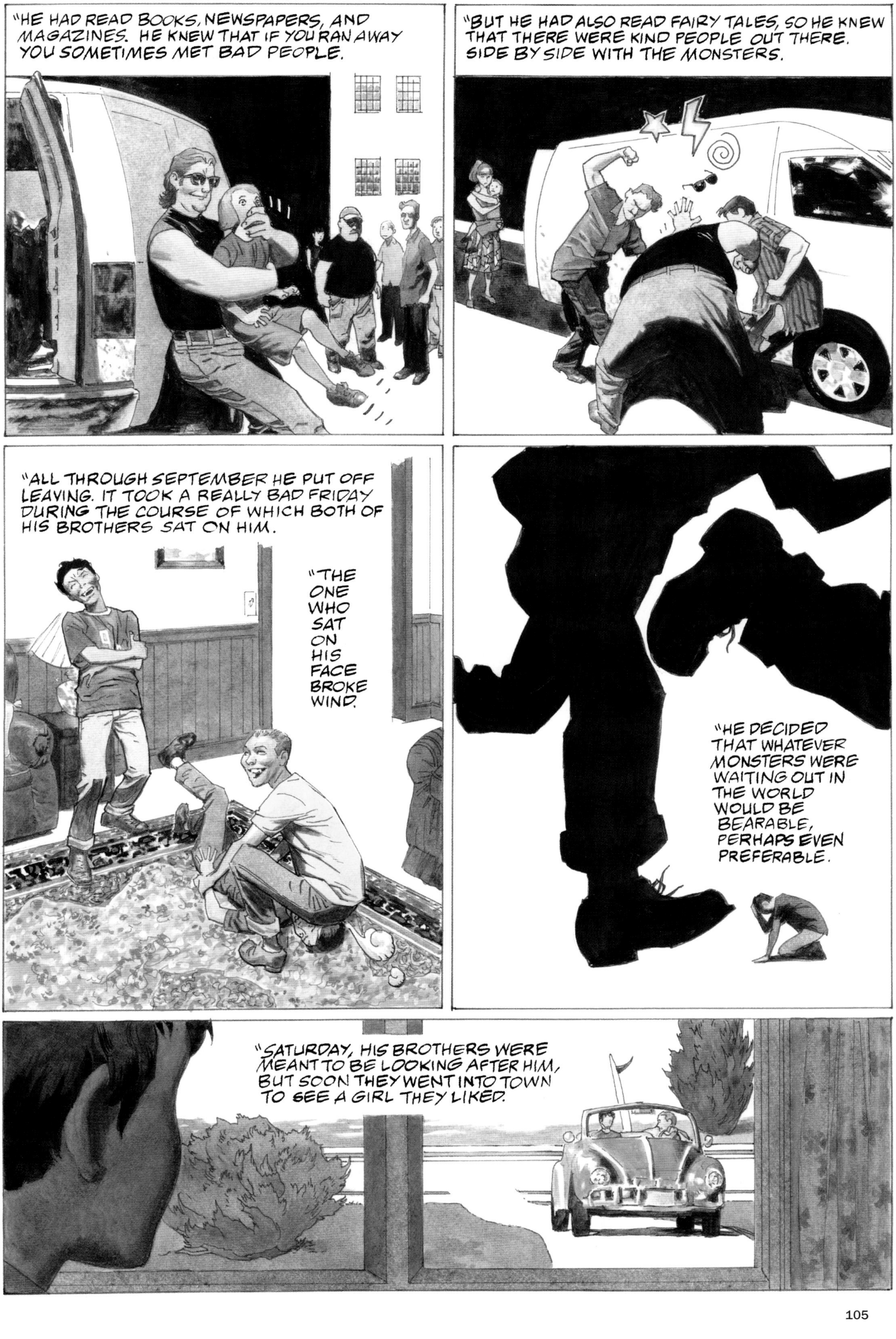
"HE HAD READ BOOKS, NEWSPAPERS, AND MAGAZINES. HE KNEW THAT IF YOU RAN AWAY YOU SOMETIMES MET BAD PEOPLE.
"BUT HE HAD ALSO READ FAIRY TALES, SO HE KNEW THAT THERE WERE KIND PEOPLE OUT THERE. SIDE BY SIDE WITH THE MONSTERS.
"ALL THROUGH SEPTEMBER HE PUT OFF LEAVING. IT TOOK A REALLY BAD FRIDAY DURING THE COURSE OF WHICH BOTH OF HIS BROTHERS SAT ON HIM.
"THE ONE WHO SAT ON HIS FACE BROKE WIND.
"HE DECIDED THAT WHATEVER MONSTERS WERE WAITING OUT IN THE WORLD WOULD BE BEARABLE, PERHAPS EVEN PREFERABLE.
"SATURDAY, HIS BROTHERS WERE MEANT TO BE LOOKING AFTER HIM, BUT SOON THEY WENT INTO TOWN TO SEE A GIRL THEY LIKED.

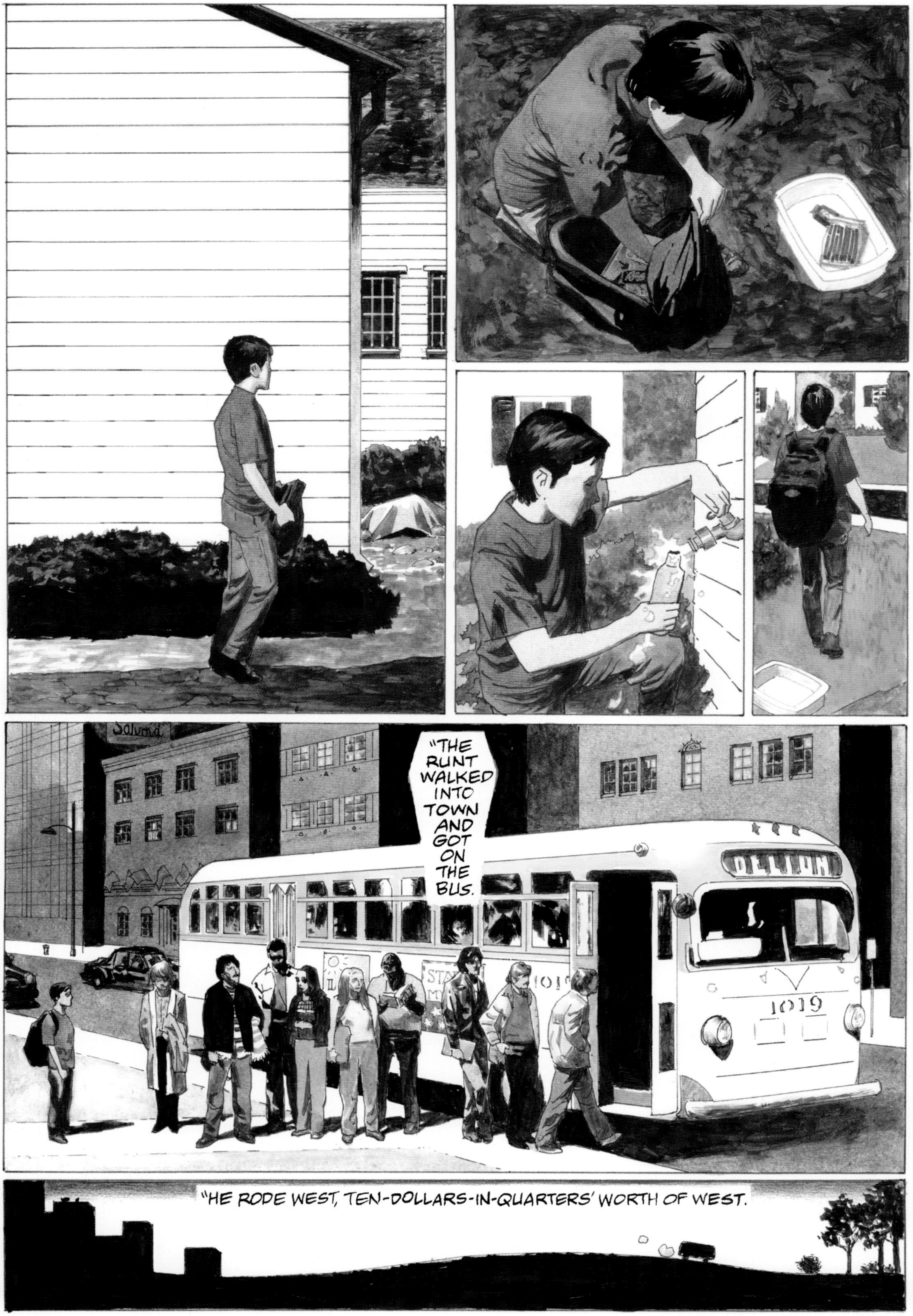
"THE RUNT WALKED INTO TOWN AND GOT ON THE BUS.
1019
"HE RODE WEST, TEN-DOLLARS-IN-QUARTERS' WORTH OF WEST.

"THEN HE GOT OFF THE BUS.

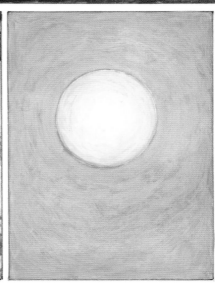

"HE HAD THOUGHT THAT ONCE HE GOT OUT OF TOWN HE WOULD SEE SPRINGS OF FRESH WATER EVERYWHERE BUT THERE WERE NONE TO BE FOUND. HE REMEMBERED SOMETHING HE HAD BEEN TOLD IN SCHOOL..."

IN THE END, ALL RIVERS FLOW INTO THE SEA.

I'VE NEVER BEEN TO THE SEASHORE.

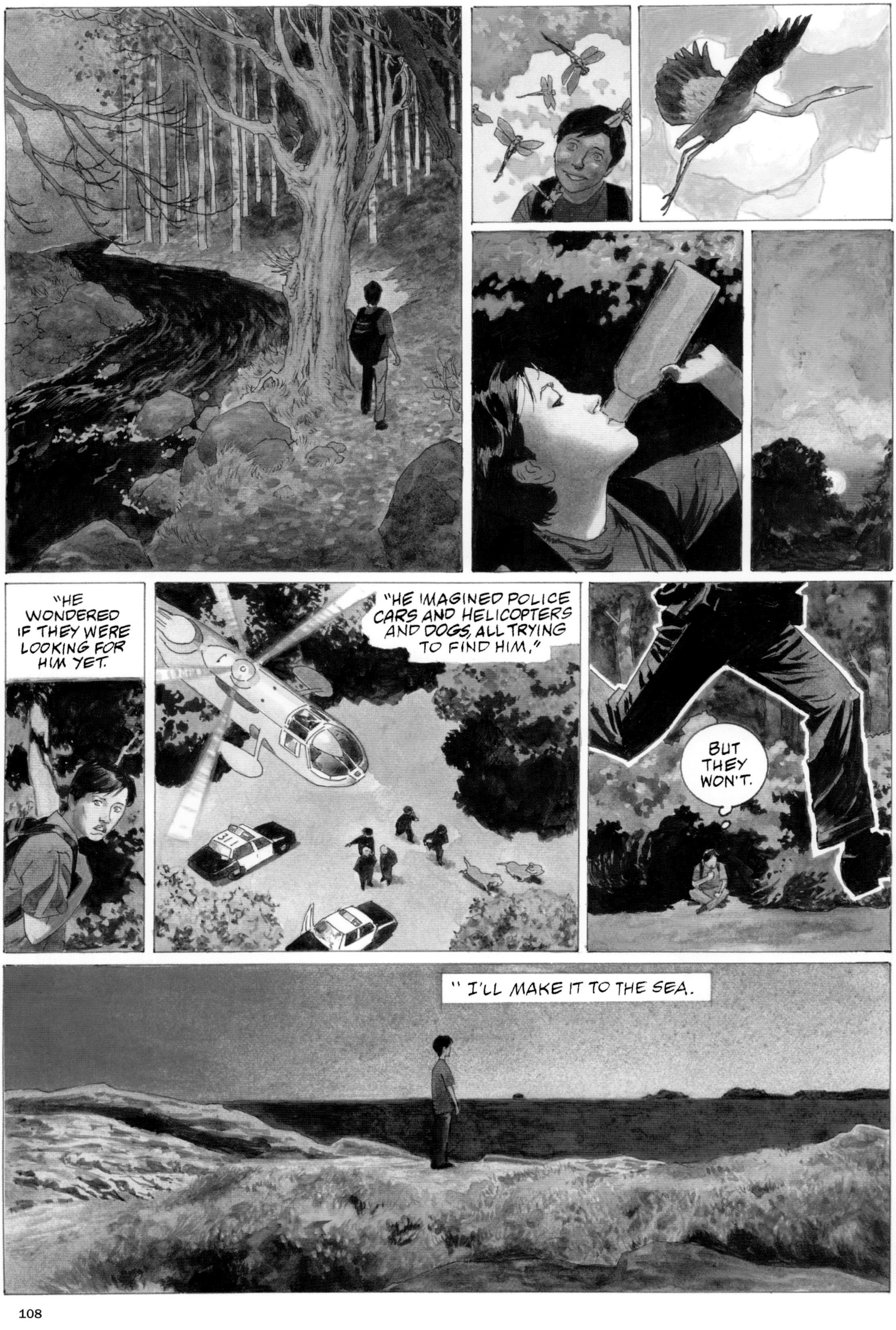
"HE WONDERED IF THEY WERE LOOKING FOR HIM YET.
"HE IMAGINED POLICE CARS AND HELICOPTERS AND DOGS, ALL TRYING TO FIND HIM."
311
BUT THEY WON'T.
" I'LL MAKE IT TO THE SEA.

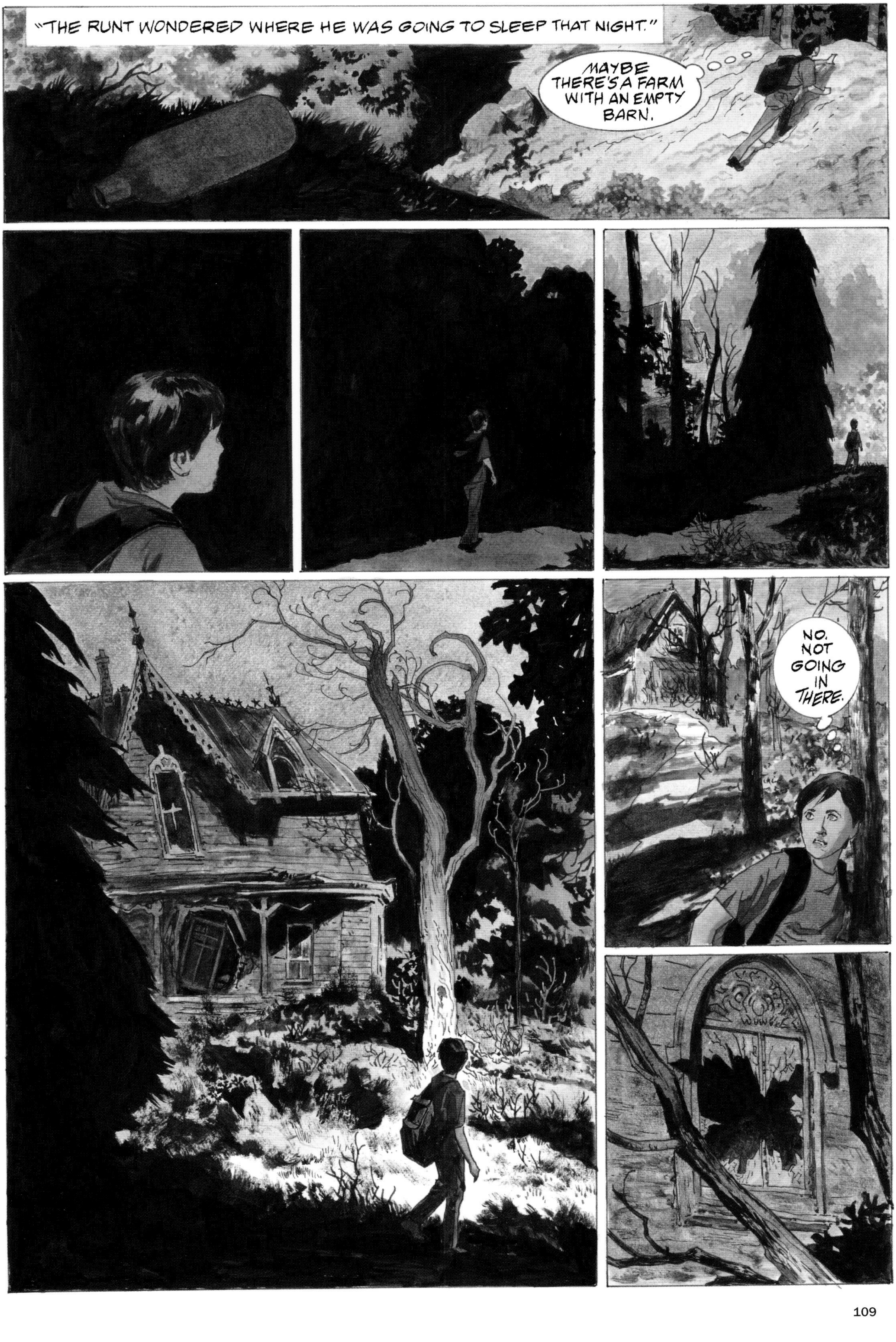
"THE RUNT WONDERED WHERE HE WAS GOING TO SLEEP THAT NIGHT."
MAYBE THERE'S A FARM WITH AN EMPTY BARN.
NO. NOT GOING IN THERE.

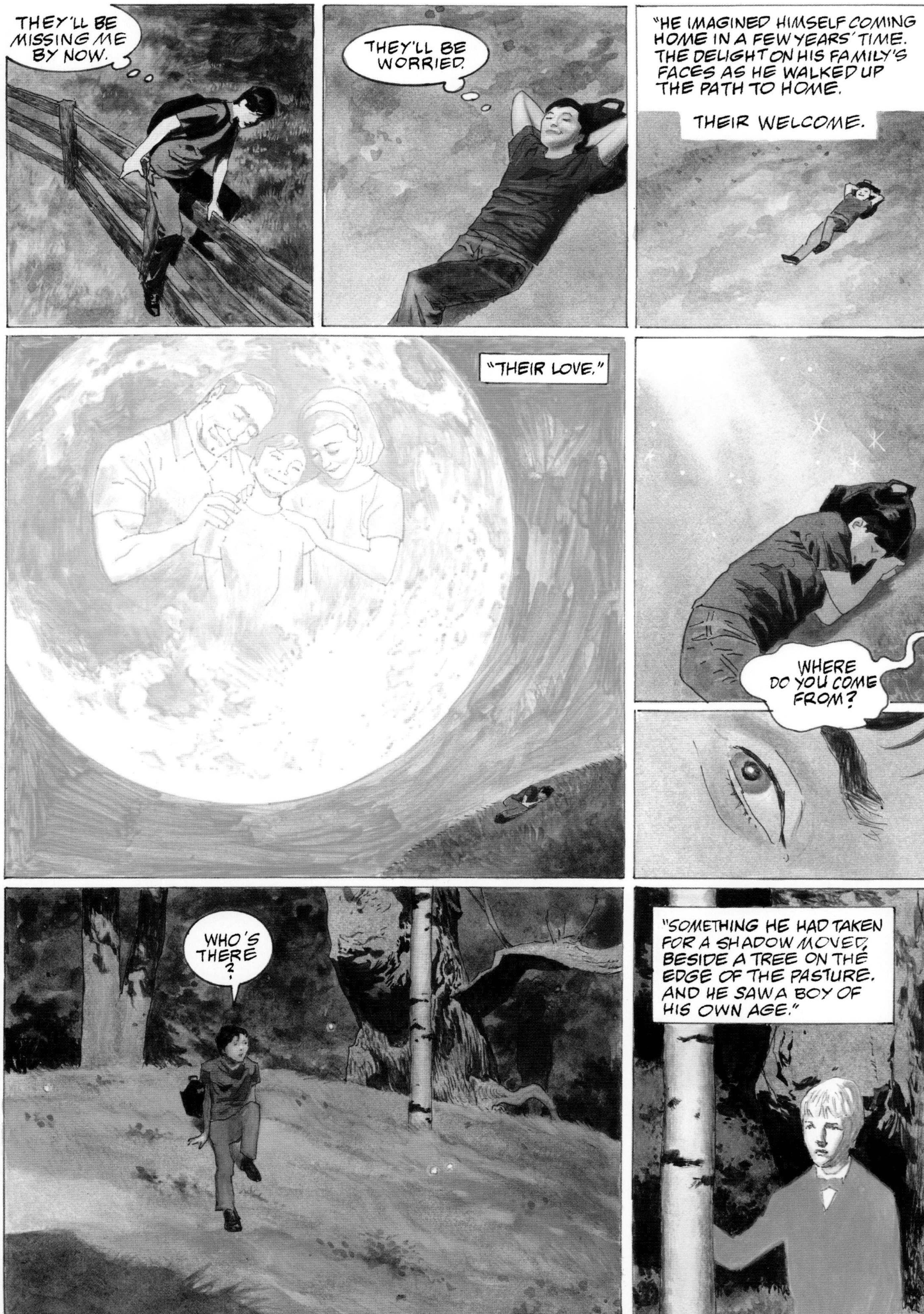
THEY'LL BE MISSING ME BY NOW.
THEY'LL BE WORRIED.
"HE IMAGINED HIMSELF COMING HOME IN A FEW YEARS' TIME. THE DELIGHT ON HIS FAMILY'S FACES AS HE WALKED UP THE PATH TO HOME.
THEIR WELCOME.
"THEIR LOVE."
WHERE DO YOU COME FROM?
WHO'S THERE?
"SOMETHING HE HAD TAKEN FOR A SHADOW MOVED, BESIDE A TREE ON THE EDGE OF THE PASTURE. AND HE SAW A BOY OF HIS OWN AGE."

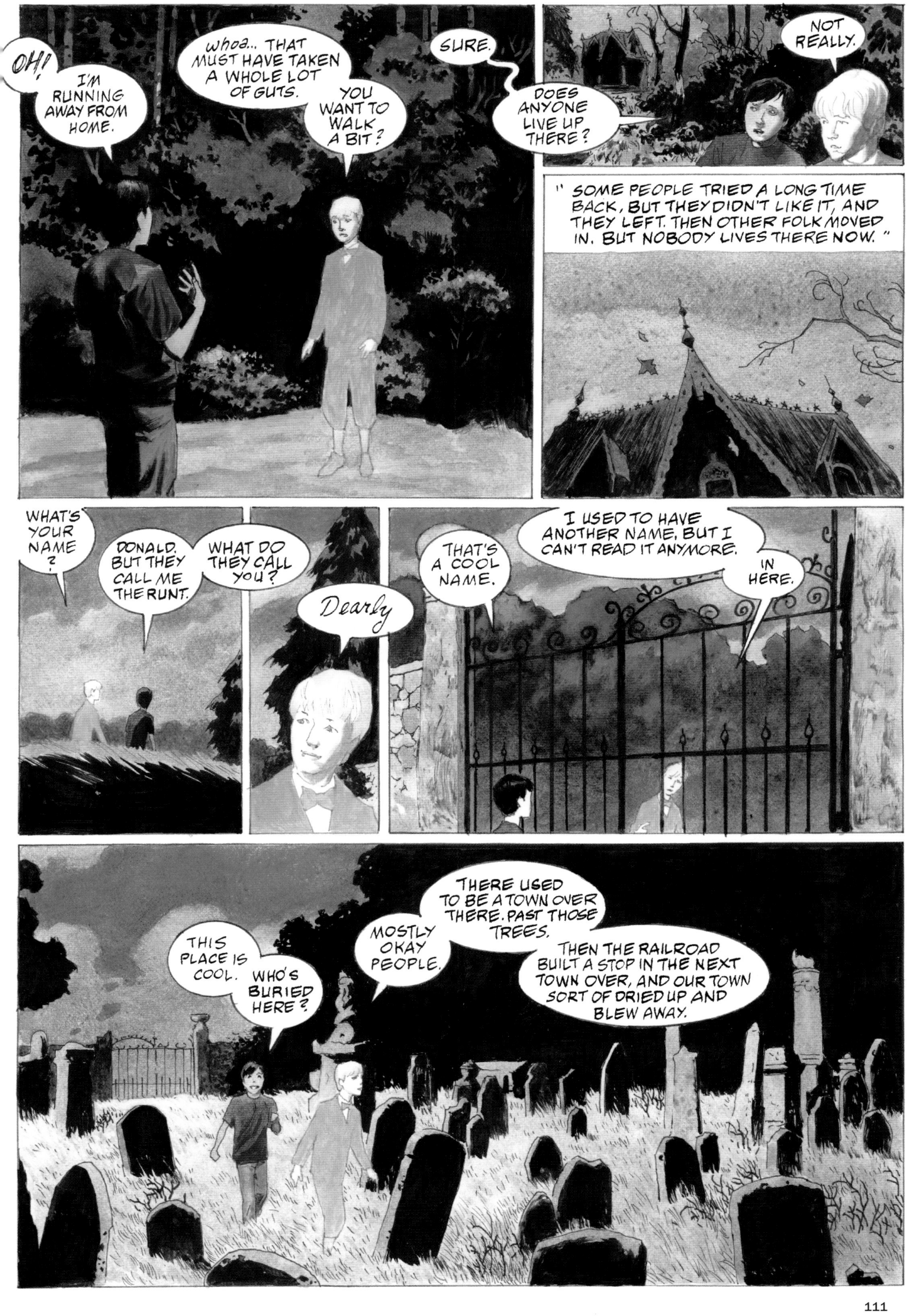
OH!
I'M RUNNING AWAY FROM HOME.
whoa... THAT MUST HAVE TAKEN A WHOLE LOT OF GUTS.
YOU WANT TO WALK A BIT?
SURE.
DOES ANYONE LIVE UP THERE?
NOT REALLY.
" SOME PEOPLE TRIED A LONG TIME BACK, BUT THEY DIDN'T LIKE IT, AND THEY LEFT. THEN OTHER FOLK MOVED IN. BUT NOBODY LIVES THERE NOW. "
WHAT'S YOUR NAME?
DONALD. BUT THEY CALL ME THE RUNT.
WHAT DO THEY CALL YOU?
Dearly
THAT'S A COOL NAME.
I USED TO HAVE ANOTHER NAME, BUT I CAN'T READ IT ANYMORE.
IN HERE.
THIS PLACE IS COOL.
WHO'S BURIED HERE?
MOSTLY OKAY PEOPLE.
THERE USED TO BE A TOWN OVER THERE. PAST THOSE TREES.
THEN THE RAILROAD BUILT A STOP IN THE NEXT TOWN OVER, AND OUR TOWN SORT OF DRIED UP AND BLEW AWAY.

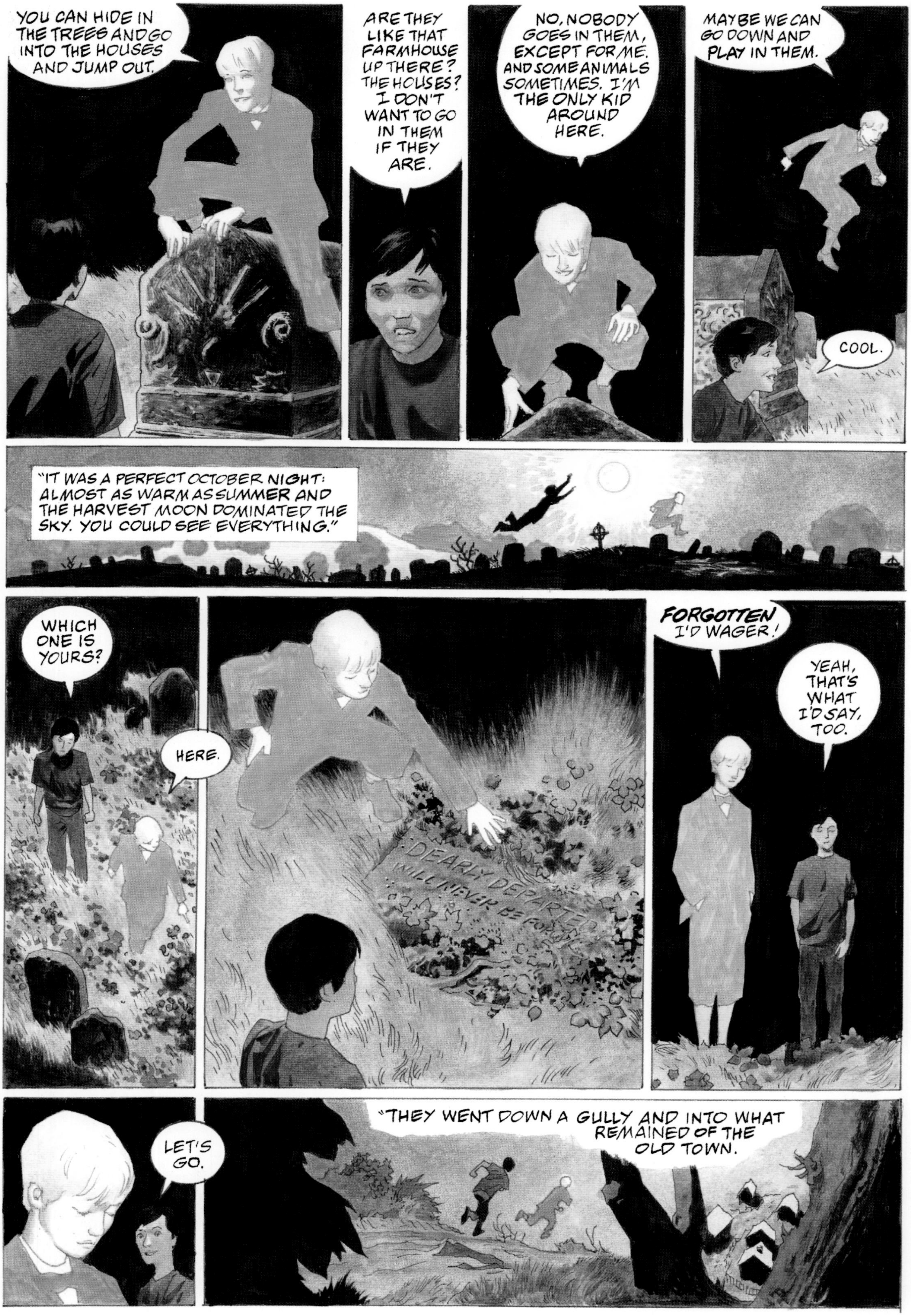

YOU CAN HIDE IN THE TREES AND GO INTO THE HOUSES AND JUMP OUT.
ARE THEY LIKE THAT FARMHOUSE UP THERE? THE HOUSES? I DON'T WANT TO GO IN THEM IF THEY ARE.
NO, NOBODY GOES IN THEM, EXCEPT FOR ME. AND SOME ANIMALS SOMETIMES. I'M THE ONLY KID AROUND HERE.
MAYBE WE CAN GO DOWN AND PLAY IN THEM.
COOL.
"IT WAS A PERFECT OCTOBER NIGHT: ALMOST AS WARM AS SUMMER AND THE HARVEST MOON DOMINATED THE SKY. YOU COULD SEE EVERYTHING."
WHICH ONE IS YOURS?
HERE.
DEARLY DEPARTED
FORGOTTEN I'D WAGER!
YEAH, THAT'S WHAT I'D SAY, TOO.
LET'S GO.
"THEY WENT DOWN A GULLY AND INTO WHAT REMAINED OF THE OLD TOWN.

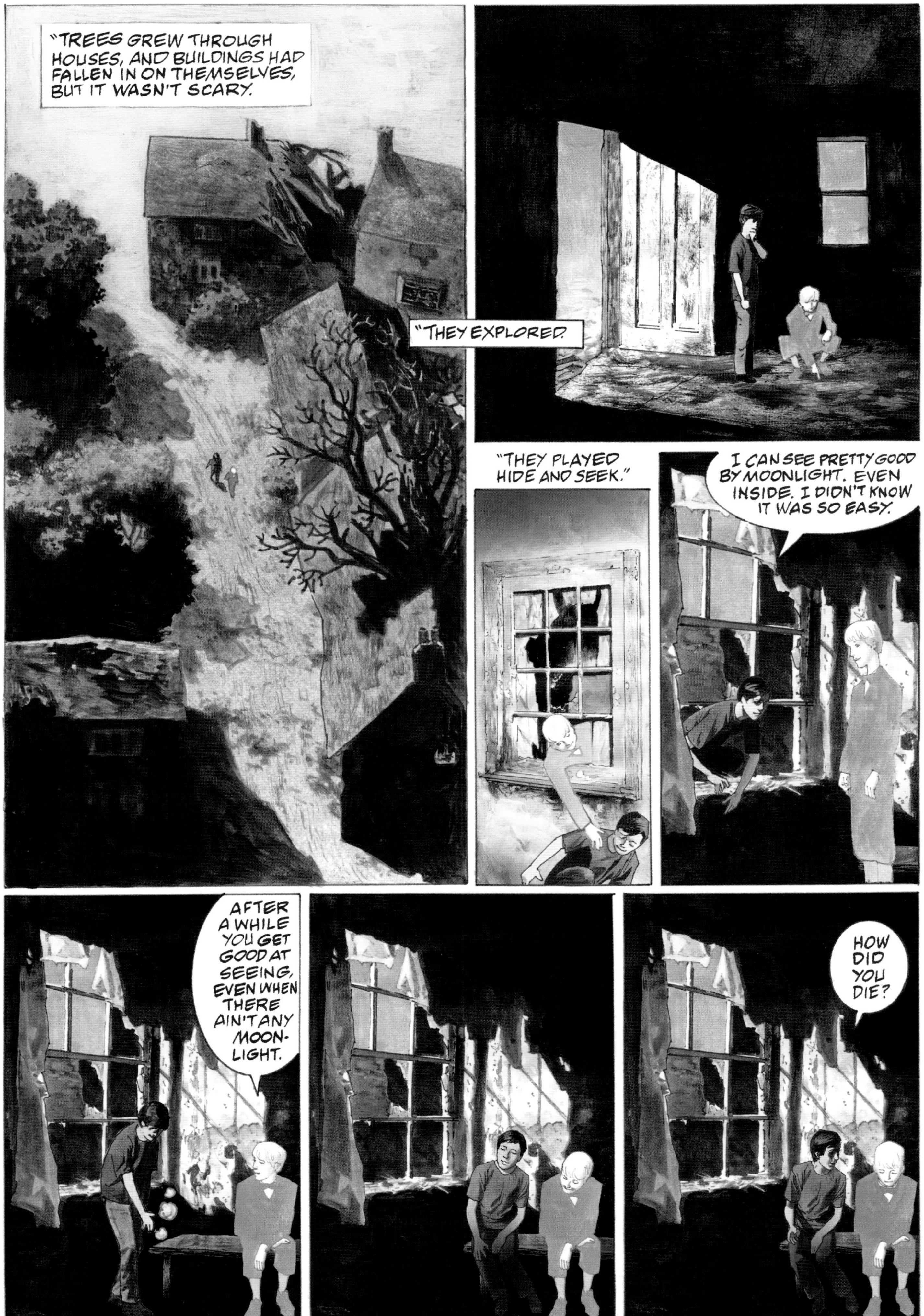
"TREES GREW THROUGH HOUSES, AND BUILDINGS HAD FALLEN IN ON THEMSELVES, BUT IT WASN'T SCARY.
"THEY EXPLORED.
"THEY PLAYED HIDE AND SEEK."
I CAN SEE PRETTY GOOD BY MOONLIGHT. EVEN INSIDE. I DIDN'T KNOW IT WAS SO EASY.
AFTER A WHILE YOU GET GOOD AT SEEING, EVEN WHEN THERE AIN'T ANY MOON-LIGHT.
HOW DID YOU DIE?

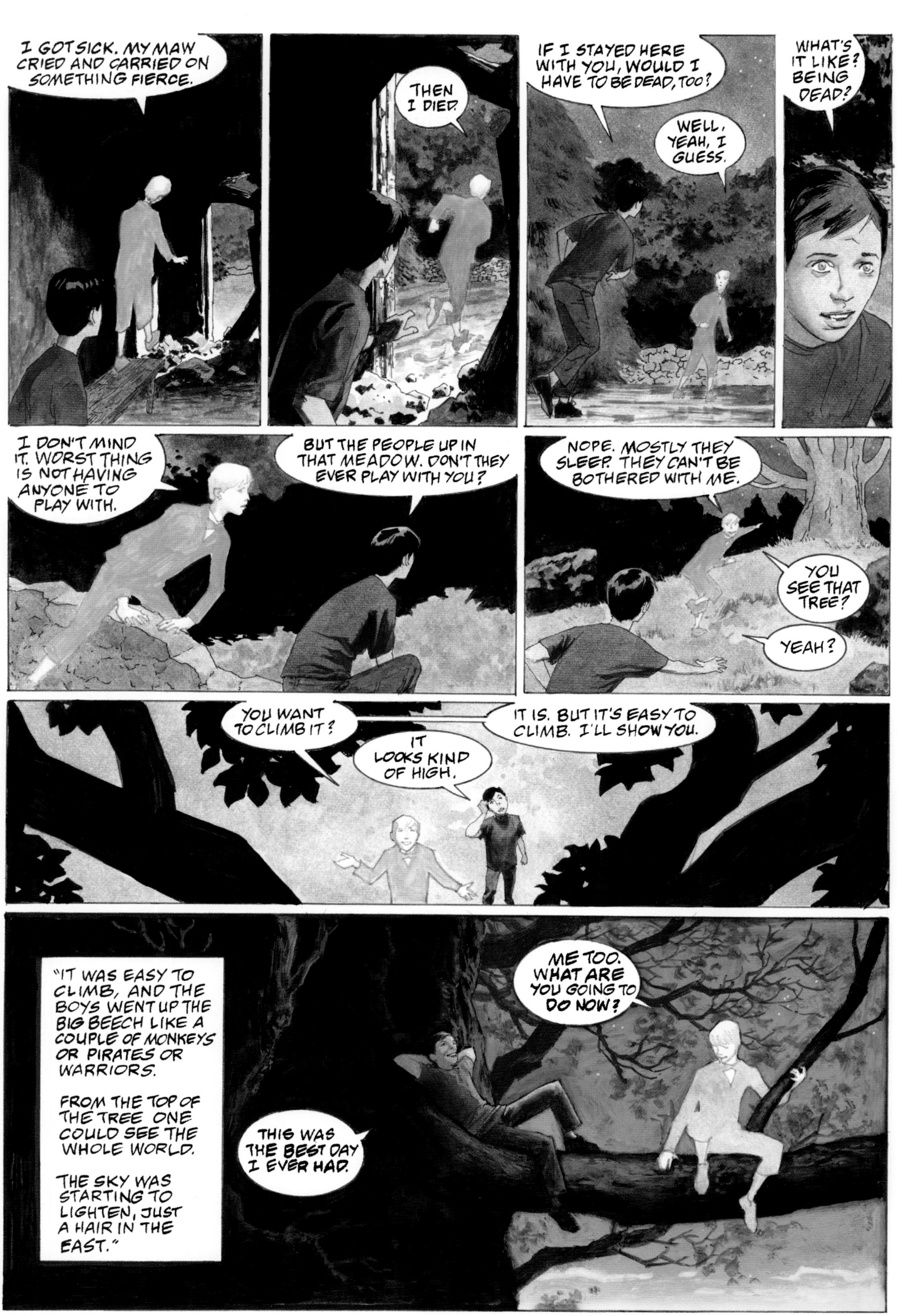
I GOT SICK. MY MAW CRIED AND CARRIED ON SOMETHING FIERCE.
THEN I DIED.
IF I STAYED HERE WITH YOU, WOULD I HAVE TO BE DEAD, TOO?
WELL, YEAH, I GUESS.
WHAT'S IT LIKE? BEING DEAD?
I DON'T MIND IT. WORST THING IS NOT HAVING ANYONE TO PLAY WITH.
BUT THE PEOPLE UP IN THAT MEADOW. DON'T THEY EVER PLAY WITH YOU?
NOPE. MOSTLY THEY SLEEP. THEY CAN'T BE BOTHERED WITH ME.
YOU SEE THAT TREE?
YEAH?
YOU WANT TO CLIMB IT?
IT LOOKS KIND OF HIGH.
IT IS. BUT IT'S EASY TO CLIMB. I'LL SHOW YOU.
"IT WAS EASY TO CLIMB, AND THE BOYS WENT UP THE BIG BEECH LIKE A COUPLE OF MONKEYS OR PIRATES OR WARRIORS.
FROM THE TOP OF THE TREE ONE COULD SEE THE WHOLE WORLD.
THE SKY WAS STARTING TO LIGHTEN, JUST A HAIR IN THE EAST."
THIS WAS THE BEST DAY I EVER HAD.
ME TOO. WHAT ARE YOU GOING TO DO NOW?

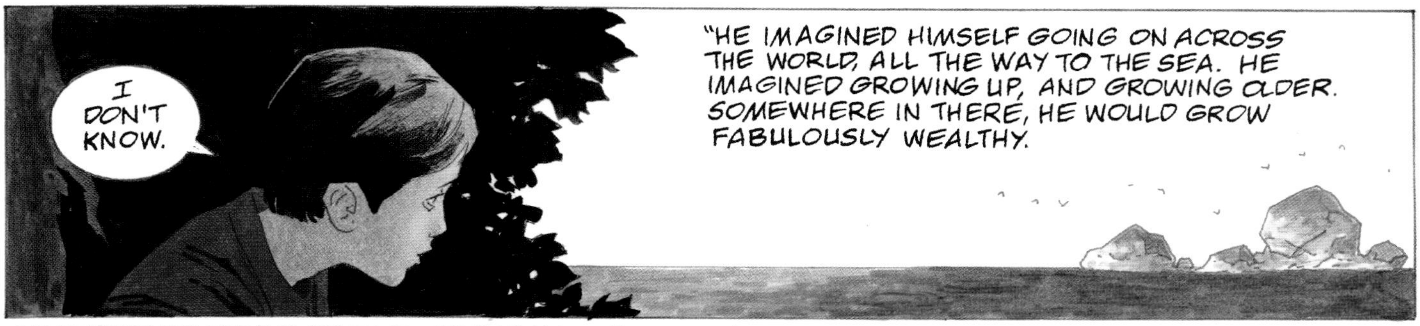
I DON'T KNOW.
"HE IMAGINED HIMSELF GOING ON ACROSS THE WORLD, ALL THE WAY TO THE SEA. HE IMAGINED GROWING UP, AND GROWING OLDER. SOMEWHERE IN THERE, HE WOULD GROW FABULOUSLY WEALTHY.

"AND THEN HE WOULD GO BACK TO THE HOUSE WITH THE TWINS IN IT, AND HE WOULD DRIVE UP TO THE DOOR IN HIS WONDERFUL CAR.

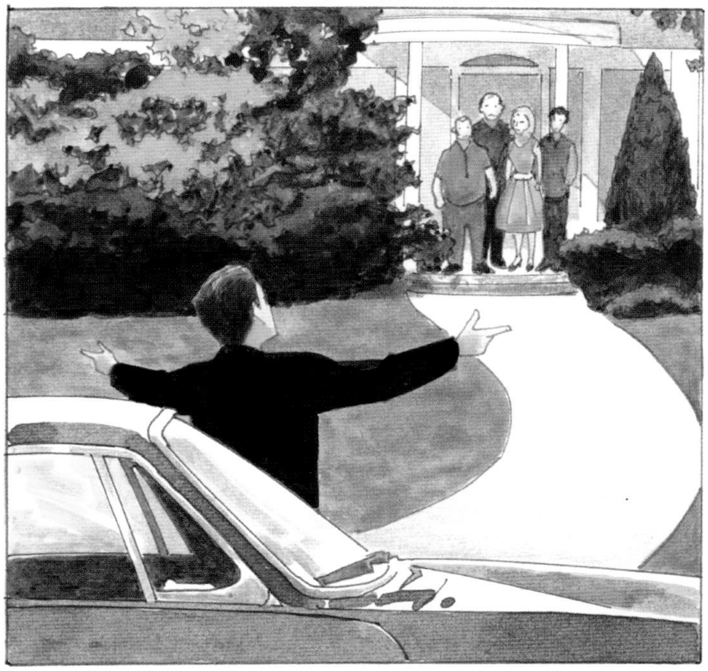

"HE WOULD BUY THEM ALL, THE TWINS, HIS PARENTS, A MEAL AT THE FINEST RESTAURANT IN THE CITY.

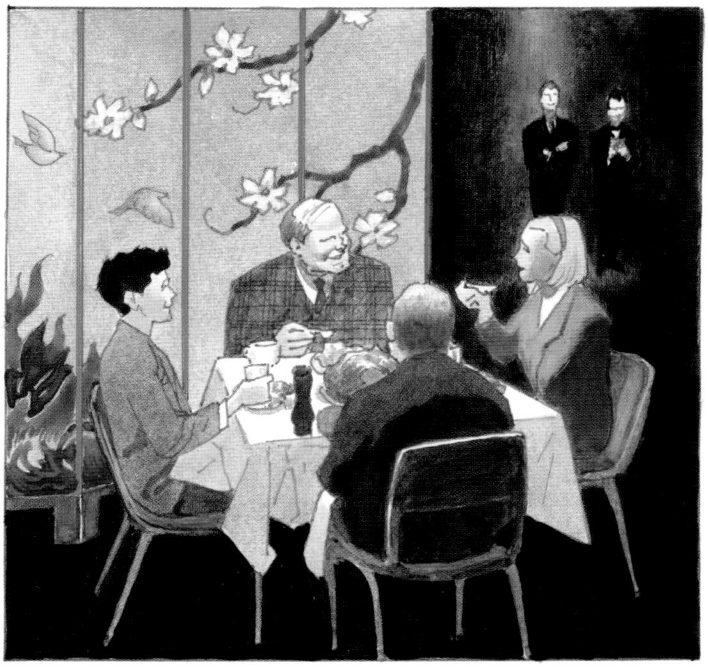

"AND THEY WOULD TELL HIM HOW BADLY THEY HAD MISTREATED HIM. THEY APOLOGIZED AND WEPT AND THROUGH IT ALL HE SAID NOTHING.

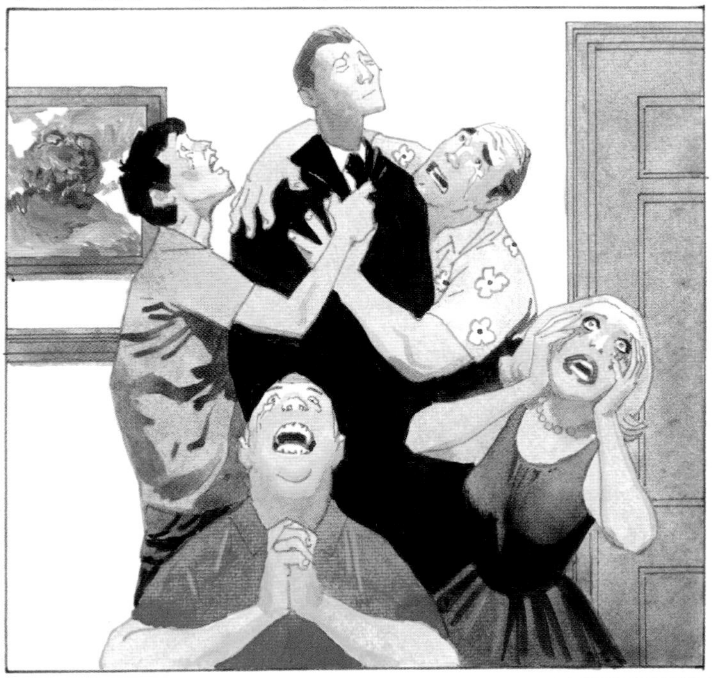

"AND THEN HE WOULD GIVE EACH OF THEM A GIFT. AND AFTERWARD HE WOULD LEAVE THEIR LIVES ONCE MORE, THIS TIME FOR GOOD.

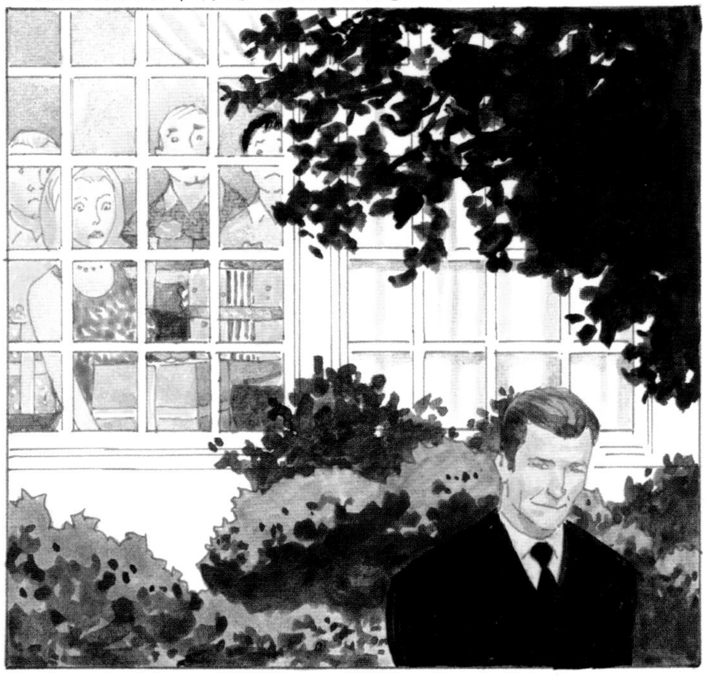

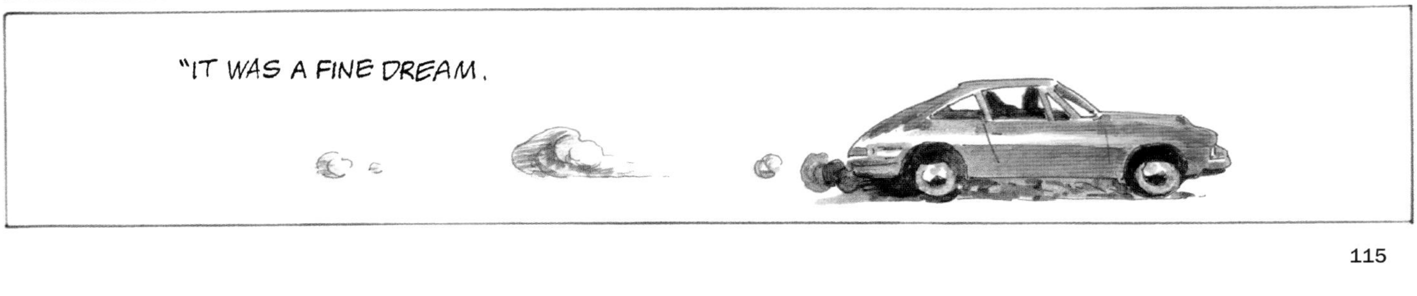
"IT WAS A FINE DREAM.

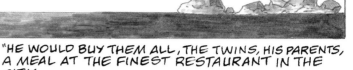

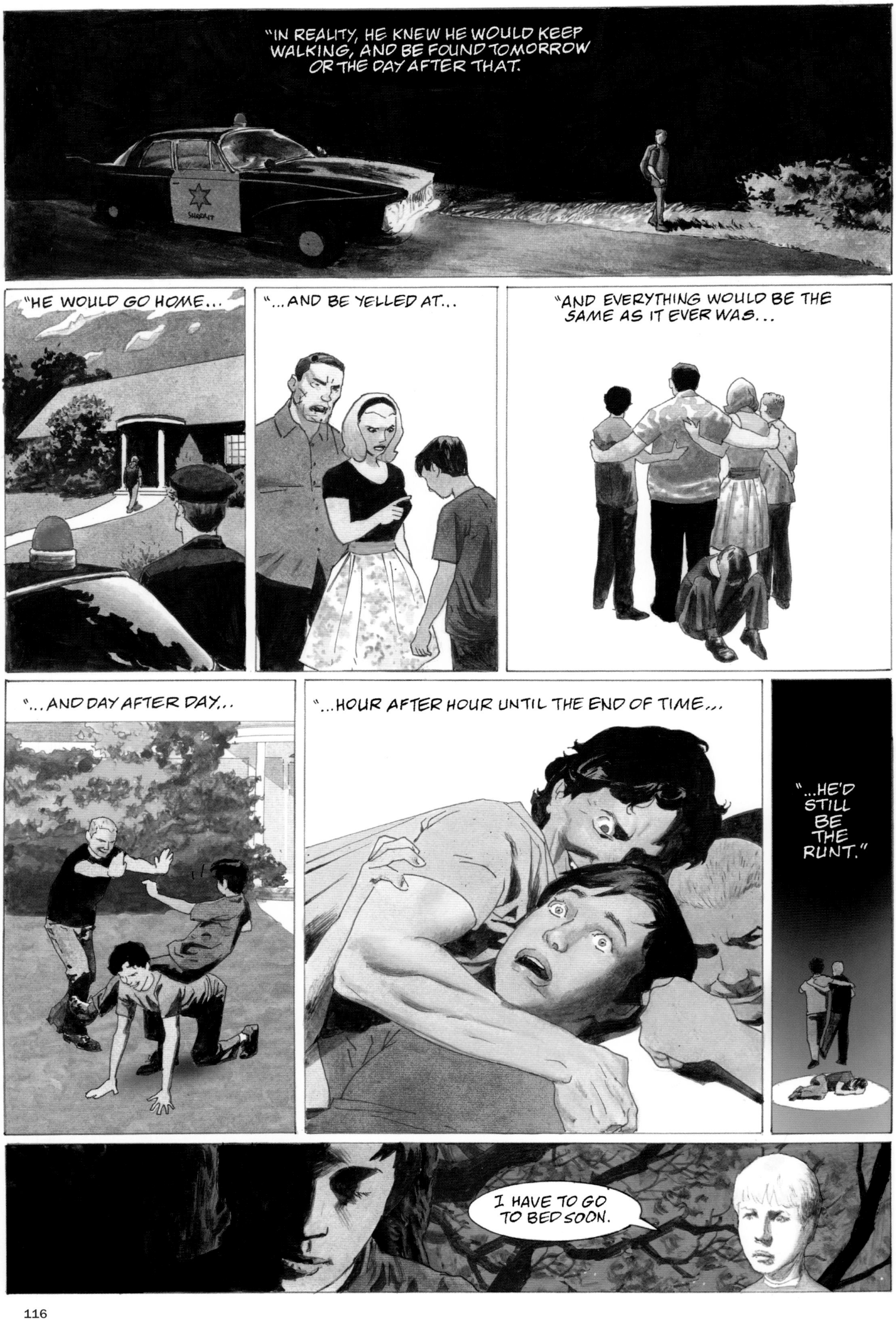
"IN REALITY, HE KNEW HE WOULD KEEP WALKING, AND BE FOUND TOMORROW OR THE DAY AFTER THAT.
"HE WOULD GO HOME...
"...AND BE YELLED AT...
"AND EVERYTHING WOULD BE THE SAME AS IT EVER WAS...
"...AND DAY AFTER DAY...
"...HOUR AFTER HOUR UNTIL THE END OF TIME...
"...HE'D STILL BE THE RUNT."
I HAVE TO GO TO BED SOON.

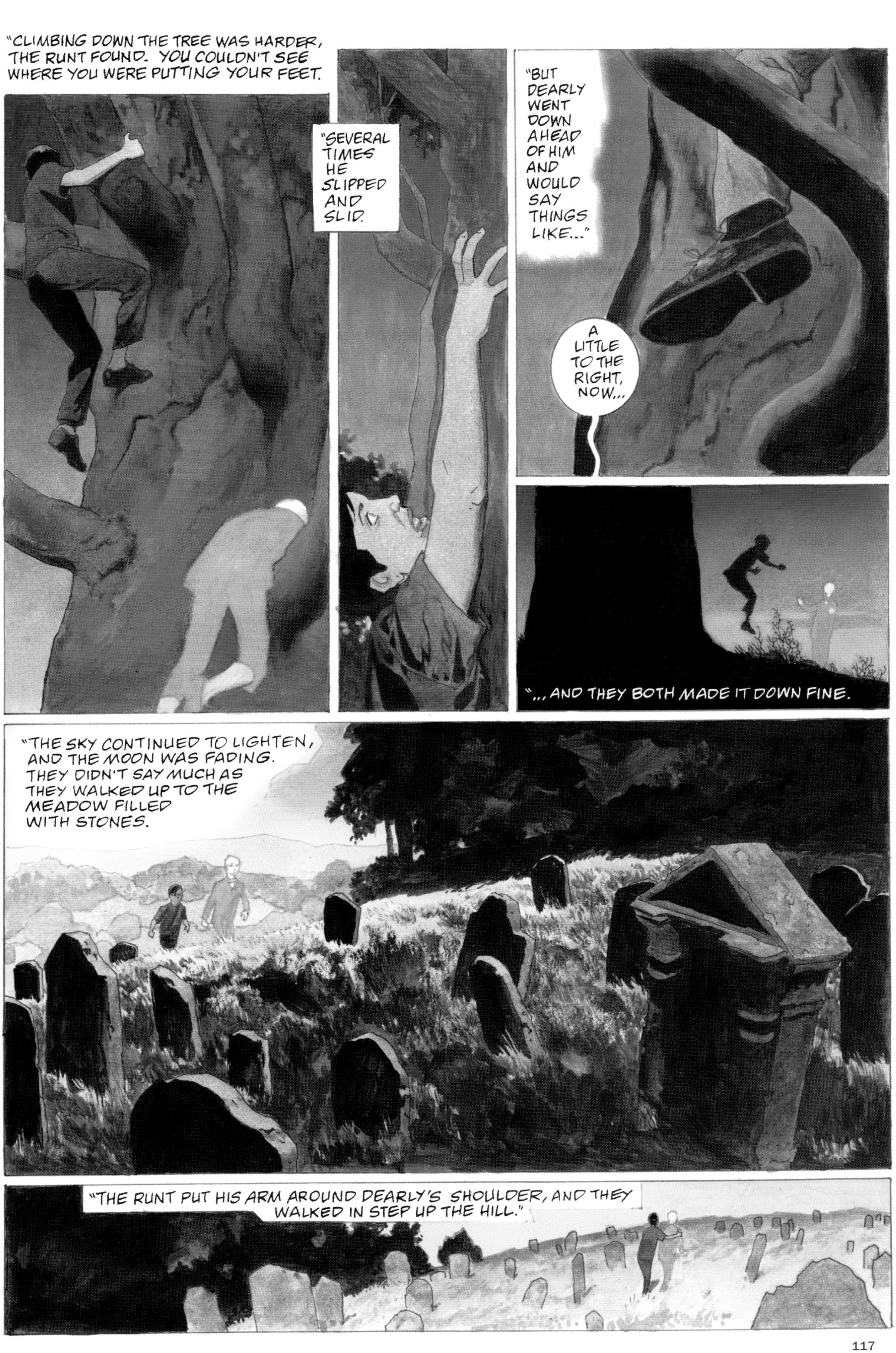
"CLIMBING DOWN THE TREE WAS HARDER, THE RUNT FOUND. YOU COULDN'T SEE WHERE YOU WERE PUTTING YOUR FEET.
"SEVERAL TIMES HE SLIPPED AND SLID.
"BUT DEARLY WENT DOWN AHEAD OF HIM AND WOULD SAY THINGS LIKE..."
A LITTLE TO THE RIGHT, NOW...
"...AND THEY BOTH MADE IT DOWN FINE.
"THE SKY CONTINUED TO LIGHTEN, AND THE MOON WAS FADING. THEY DIDN'T SAY MUCH AS THEY WALKED UP TO THE MEADOW FILLED WITH STONES.
"THE RUNT PUT HIS ARM AROUND DEARLY'S SHOULDER, AND THEY WALKED IN STEP UP THE HILL."

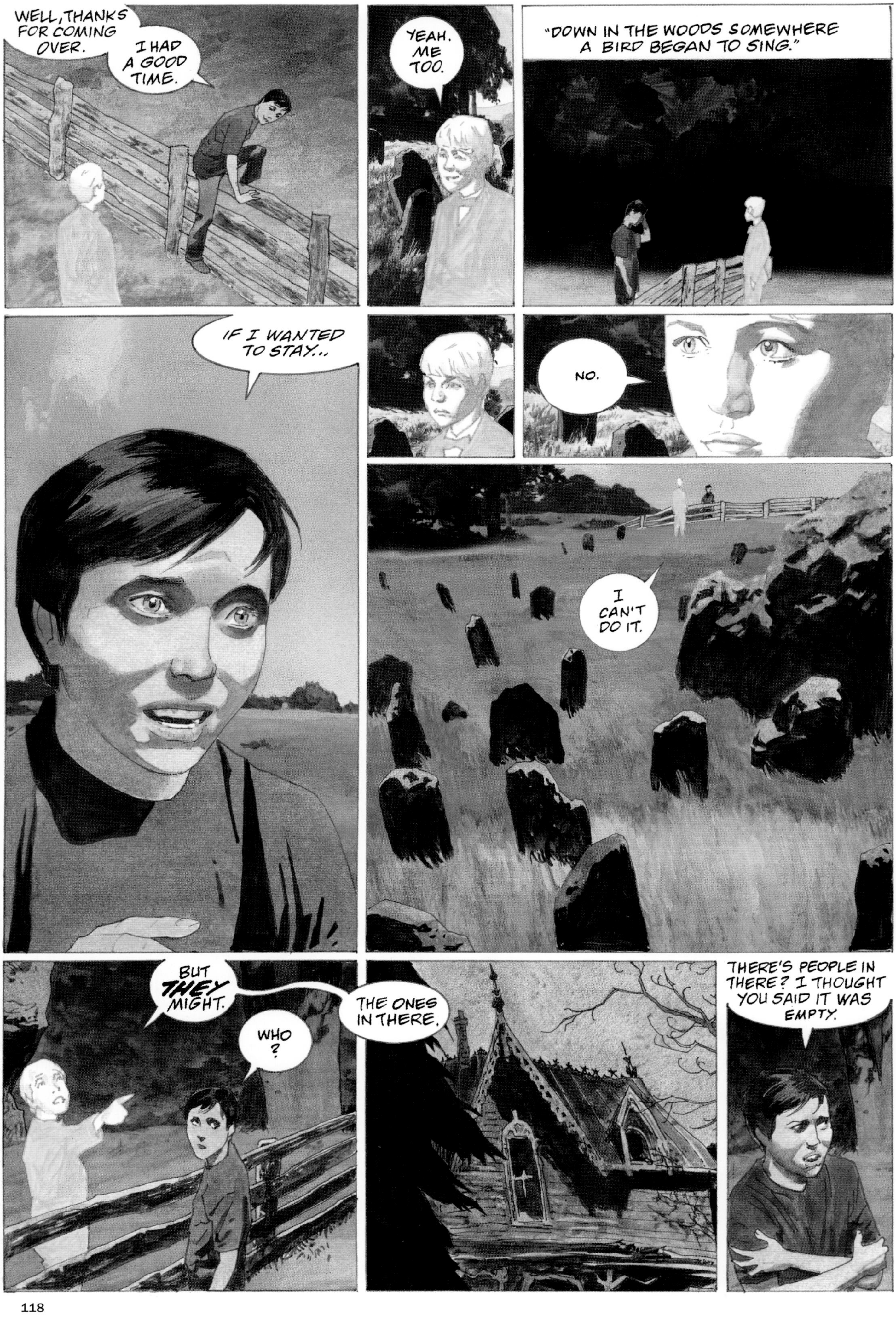
WELL, THANKS FOR COMING OVER.
I HAD A GOOD TIME.
YEAH. ME TOO.
"DOWN IN THE WOODS SOMEWHERE A BIRD BEGAN TO SING."
IF I WANTED TO STAY...
NO.
I CAN'T DO IT.
BUT THEY MIGHT.
WHO?
THE ONES IN THERE.
THERE'S PEOPLE IN THERE? I THOUGHT YOU SAID IT WAS EMPTY.

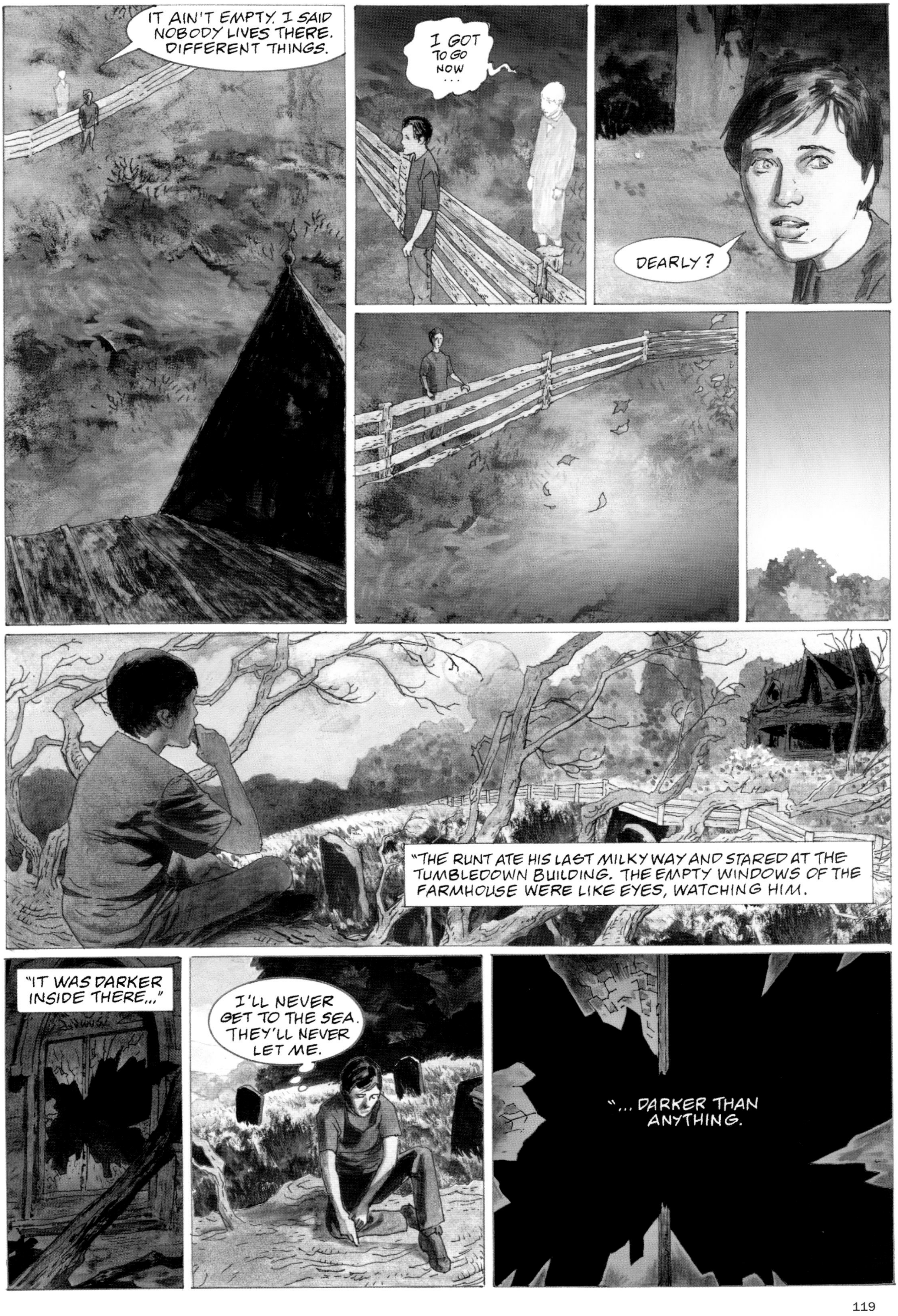

IT AIN'T EMPTY. I SAID NOBODY LIVES THERE. DIFFERENT THINGS.
I GOT TO GO NOW . . .
DEARLY?
"THE RUNT ATE HIS LAST MILKY WAY AND STARED AT THE TUMBLEDOWN BUILDING. THE EMPTY WINDOWS OF THE FARMHOUSE WERE LIKE EYES, WATCHING HIM.
"IT WAS DARKER INSIDE THERE..."
I'LL NEVER GET TO THE SEA. THEY'LL NEVER LET ME.
"... DARKER THAN ANYTHING.

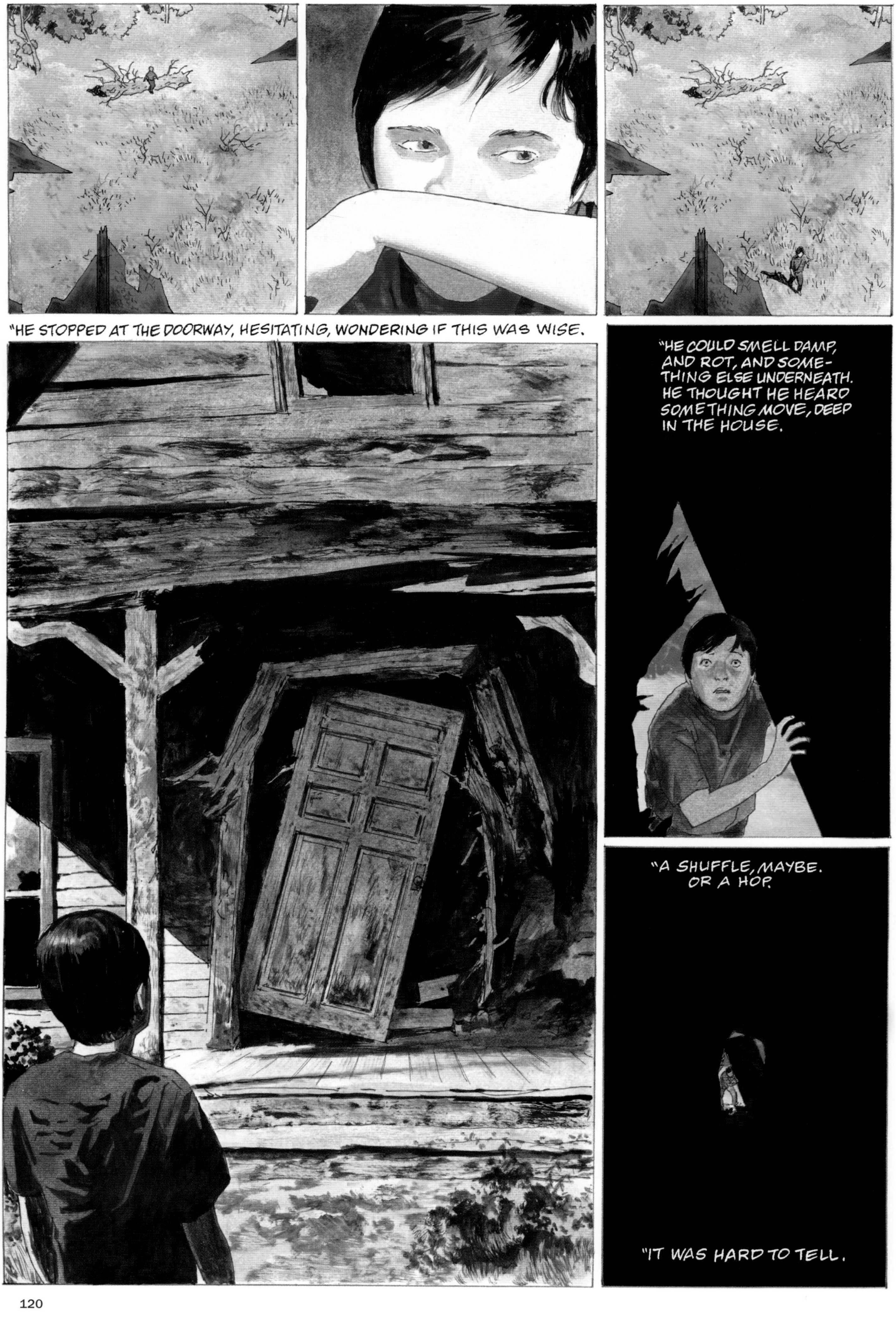
"HE STOPPED AT THE DOORWAY, HESITATING, WONDERING IF THIS WAS WISE.
"HE COULD SMELL DAMP, AND ROT, AND SOMETHING ELSE UNDERNEATH. HE THOUGHT HE HEARD SOMETHING MOVE, DEEP IN THE HOUSE.
"A SHUFFLE, MAYBE. OR A HOP.
"IT WAS HARD TO TELL.

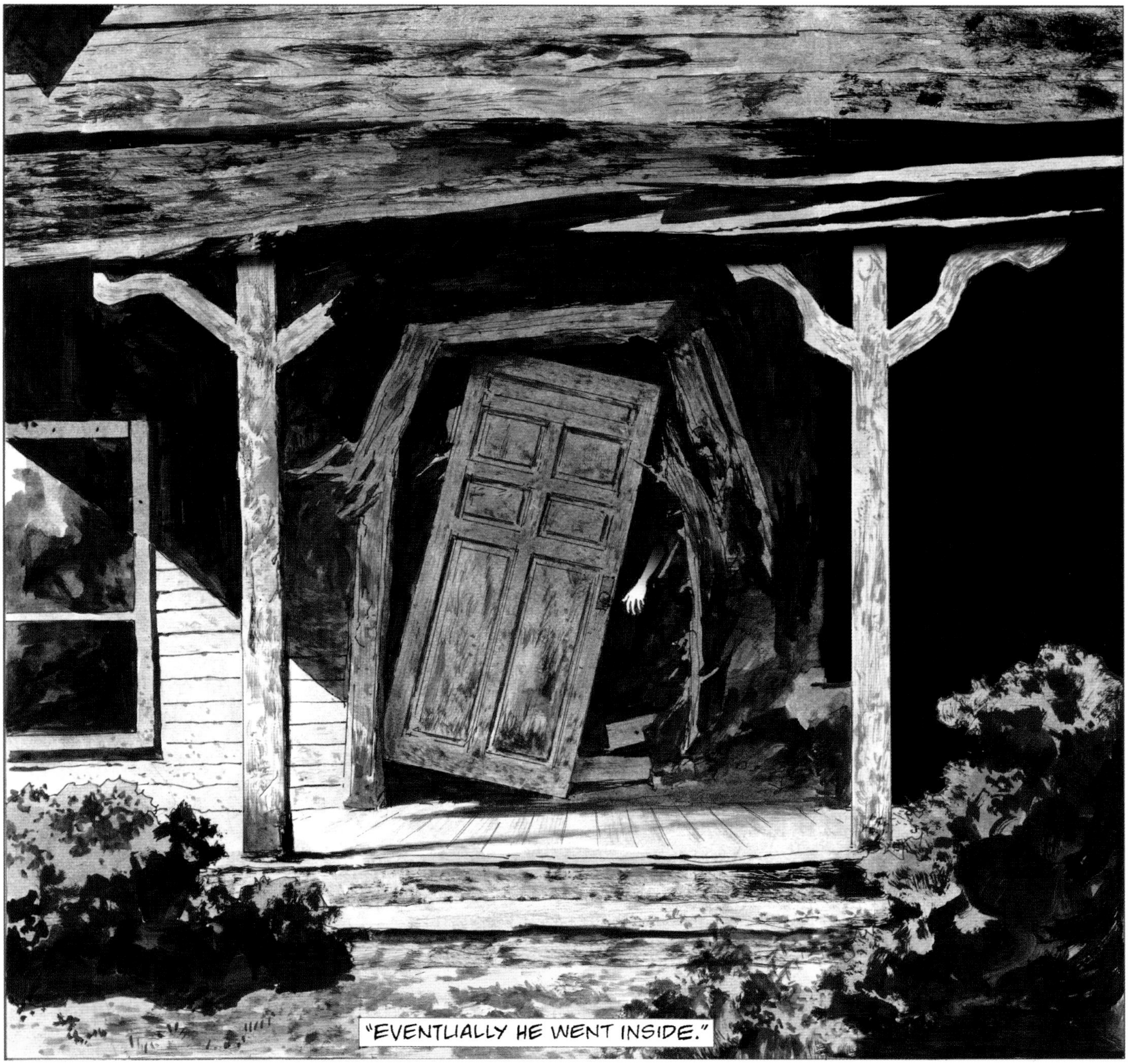
"EVENTUALLY HE WENT INSIDE."

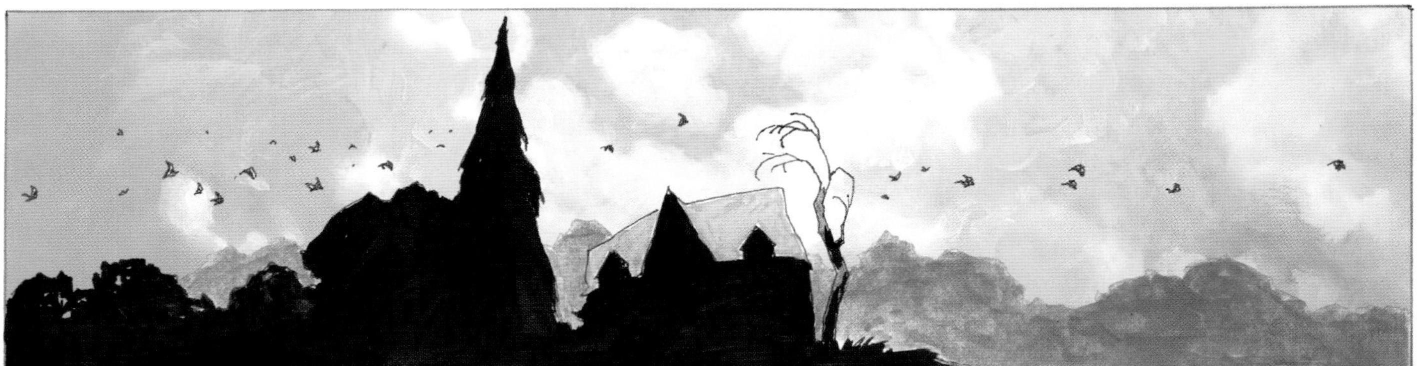

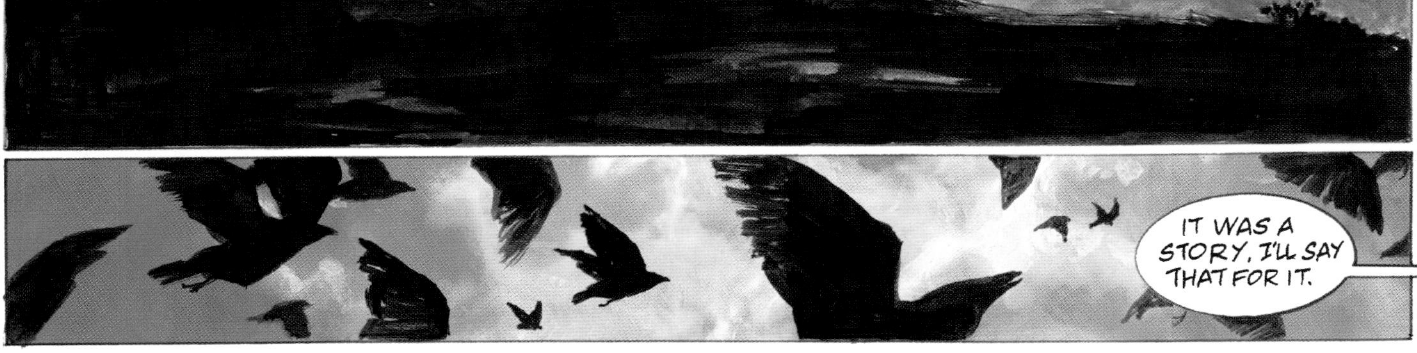
IT WAS A STORY, I'LL SAY THAT FOR IT.

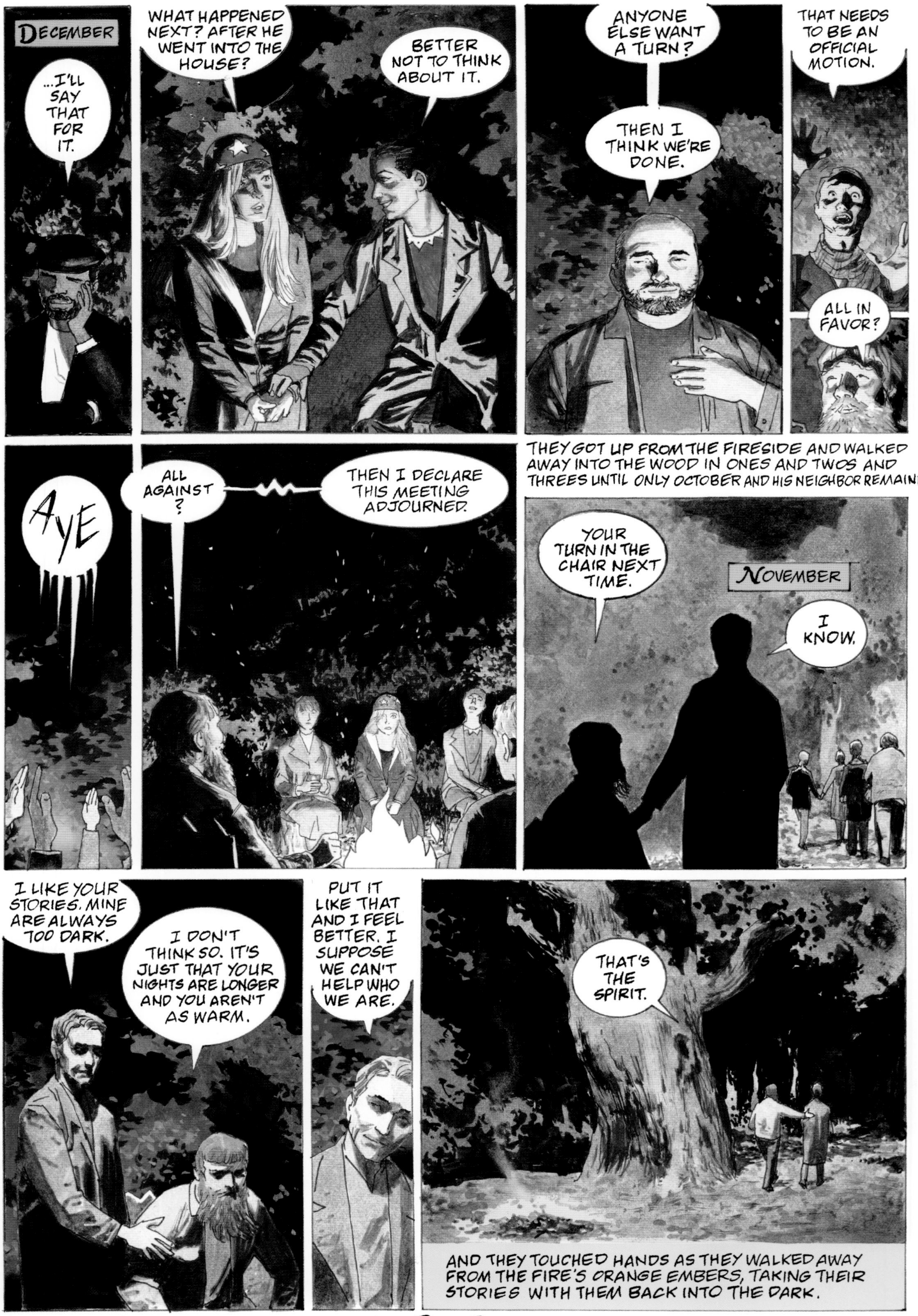
DECEMBER
...I'LL SAY THAT FOR IT.
WHAT HAPPENED NEXT? AFTER HE WENT INTO THE HOUSE?
BETTER NOT TO THINK ABOUT IT.
ANYONE ELSE WANT A TURN?
THEN I THINK WE'RE DONE.
THAT NEEDS TO BE AN OFFICIAL MOTION.
ALL IN FAVOR?
AYE
ALL AGAINST?
THEN I DECLARE THIS MEETING ADJOURNED.
THEY GOT UP FROM THE FIRESIDE AND WALKED AWAY INTO THE WOOD IN ONES AND TWOS AND THREES UNTIL ONLY OCTOBER AND HIS NEIGHBOR REMAINED.
YOUR TURN IN THE CHAIR NEXT TIME.
NOVEMBER
I KNOW.
I LIKE YOUR STORIES. MINE ARE ALWAYS TOO DARK.
I DON'T THINK SO. IT'S JUST THAT YOUR NIGHTS ARE LONGER AND YOU AREN'T AS WARM.
PUT IT LIKE THAT AND I FEEL BETTER. I SUPPOSE WE CAN'T HELP WHO WE ARE.
THAT'S THE SPIRIT.
AND THEY TOUCHED HANDS AS THEY WALKED AWAY FROM THE FIRE'S ORANGE EMBERS, TAKING THEIR STORIES WITH THEM BACK INTO THE DARK.

FOR RAY BRADBURY

THE DAY THE SAUCERS CAME

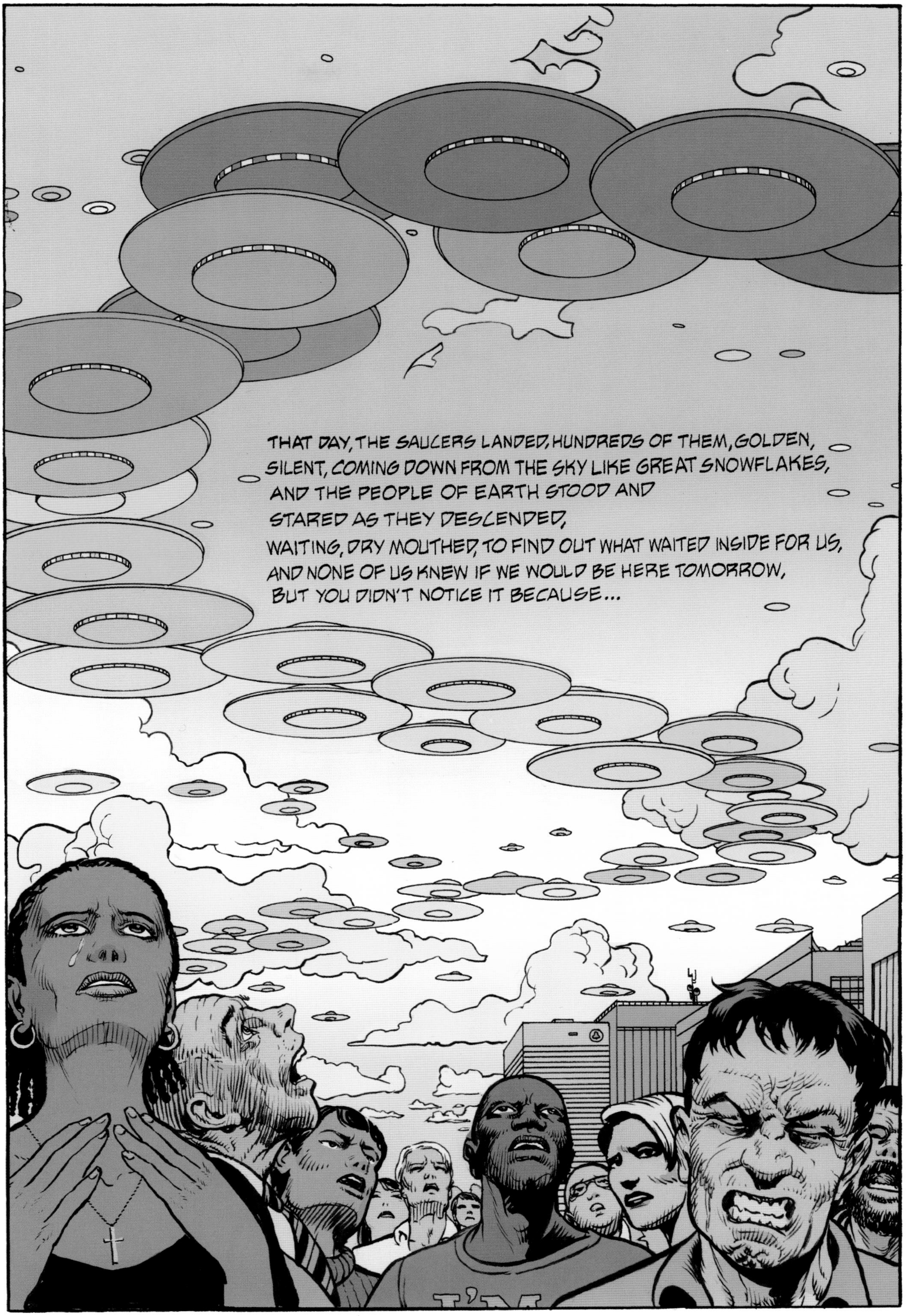
THAT DAY, THE SAUCERS LANDED, HUNDREDS OF THEM, GOLDEN, SILENT, COMING DOWN FROM THE SKY LIKE GREAT SNOWFLAKES, AND THE PEOPLE OF EARTH STOOD AND STARED AS THEY DESCENDED, WAITING, DRY MOUTHED, TO FIND OUT WHAT WAITED INSIDE FOR US, AND NONE OF US KNEW IF WE WOULD BE HERE TOMORROW, BUT YOU DIDN'T NOTICE IT BECAUSE...

Story by **Neil Gaiman** Art by **Paul Chadwick** Lettering by **Gaspar Saladino**

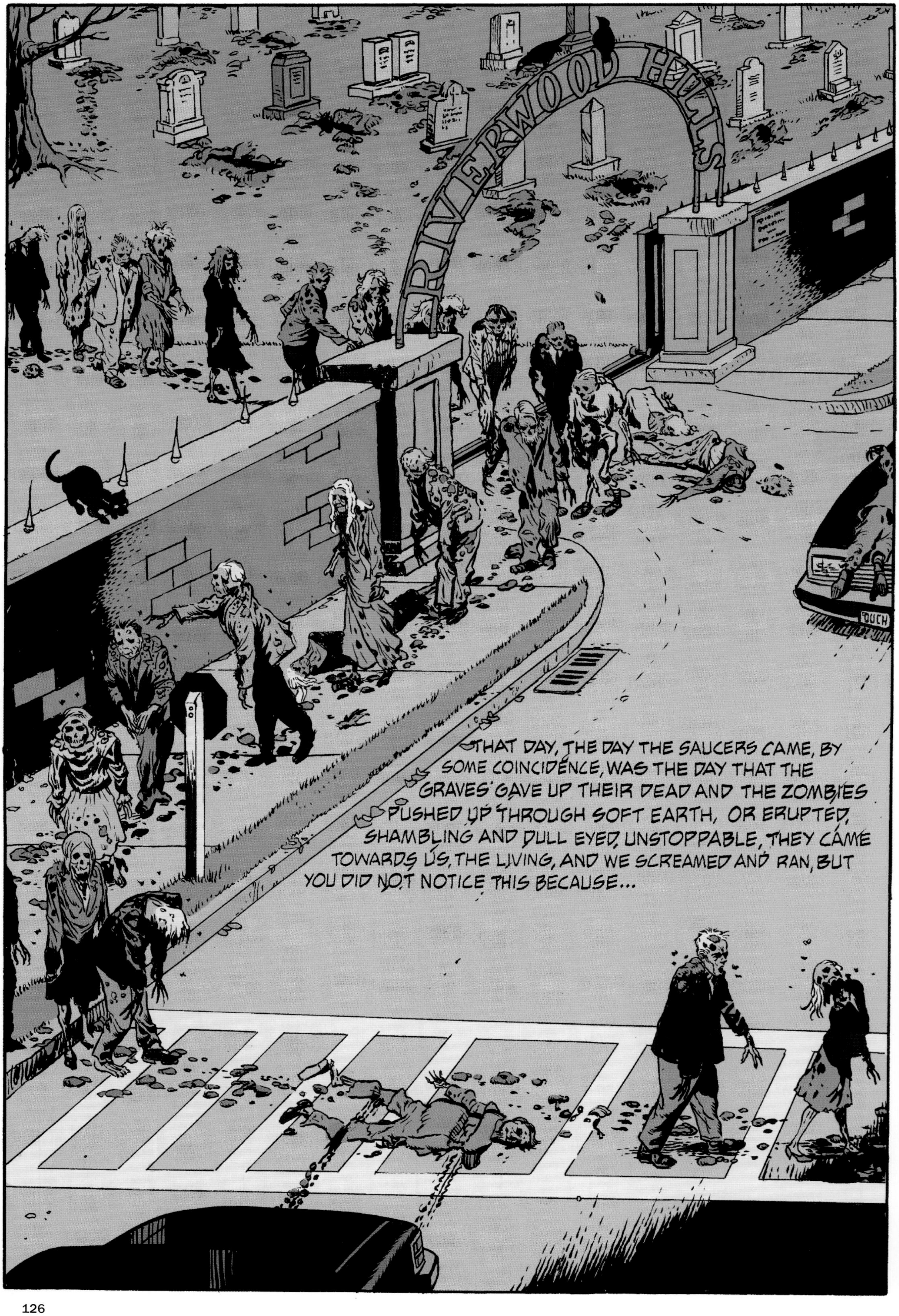
RIVERWOOD HILLS
THAT DAY, THE DAY THE SAUCERS CAME, BY SOME COINCIDENCE, WAS THE DAY THAT THE GRAVES GAVE UP THEIR DEAD AND THE ZOMBIES PUSHED UP THROUGH SOFT EARTH, OR ERUPTED, SHAMBLING AND DULL EYED, UNSTOPPABLE, THEY CAME TOWARDS US, THE LIVING, AND WE SCREAMED AND RAN, BUT YOU DID NOT NOTICE THIS BECAUSE...

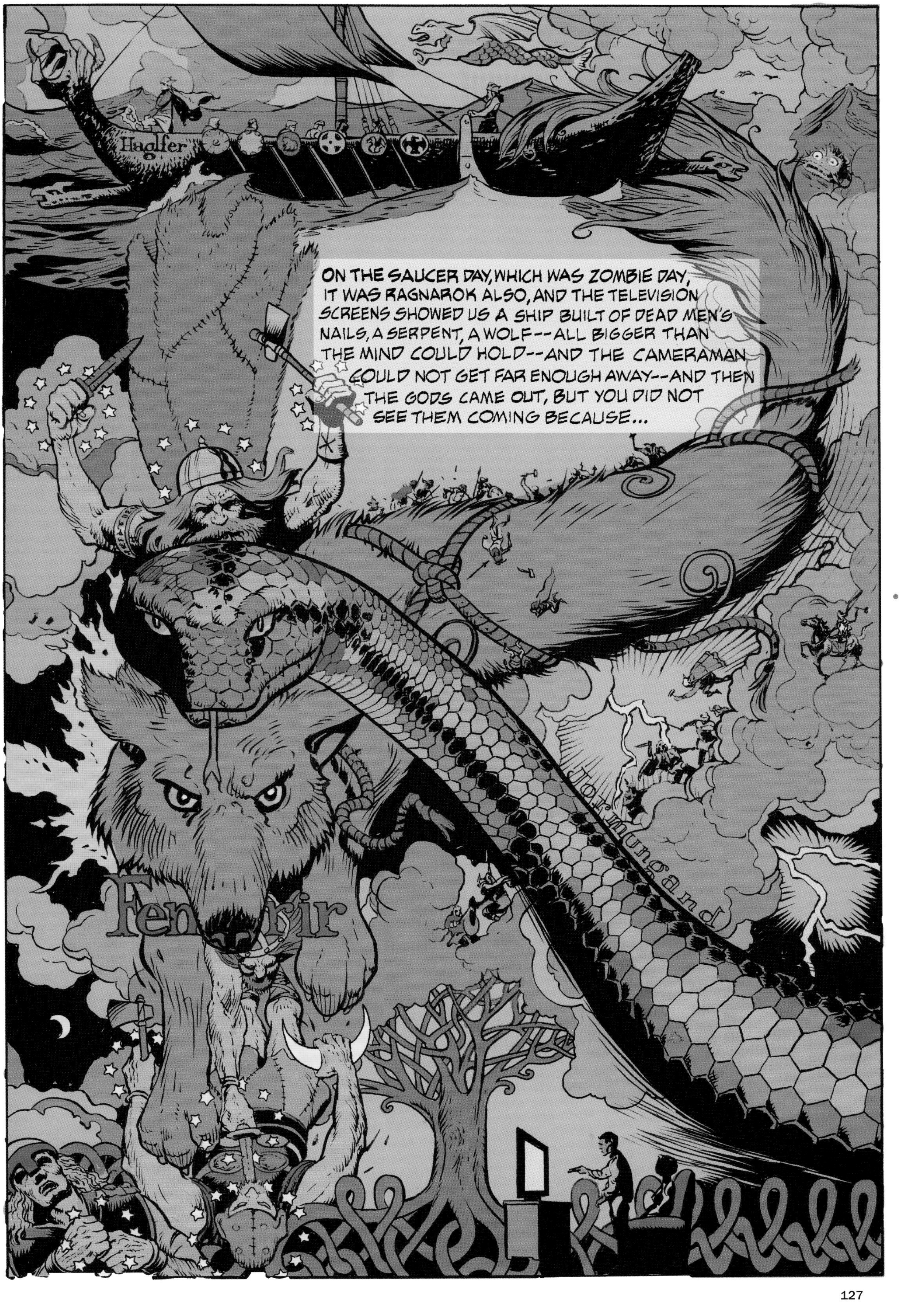
Haglfer
ON THE SAUCER DAY, WHICH WAS ZOMBIE DAY, IT WAS RAGNAROK ALSO, AND THE TELEVISION SCREENS SHOWED US A SHIP BUILT OF DEAD MEN'S NAILS, A SERPENT, A WOLF--ALL BIGGER THAN THE MIND COULD HOLD--AND THE CAMERAMAN COULD NOT GET FAR ENOUGH AWAY--AND THEN THE GODS CAME OUT, BUT YOU DID NOT SEE THEM COMING BECAUSE...

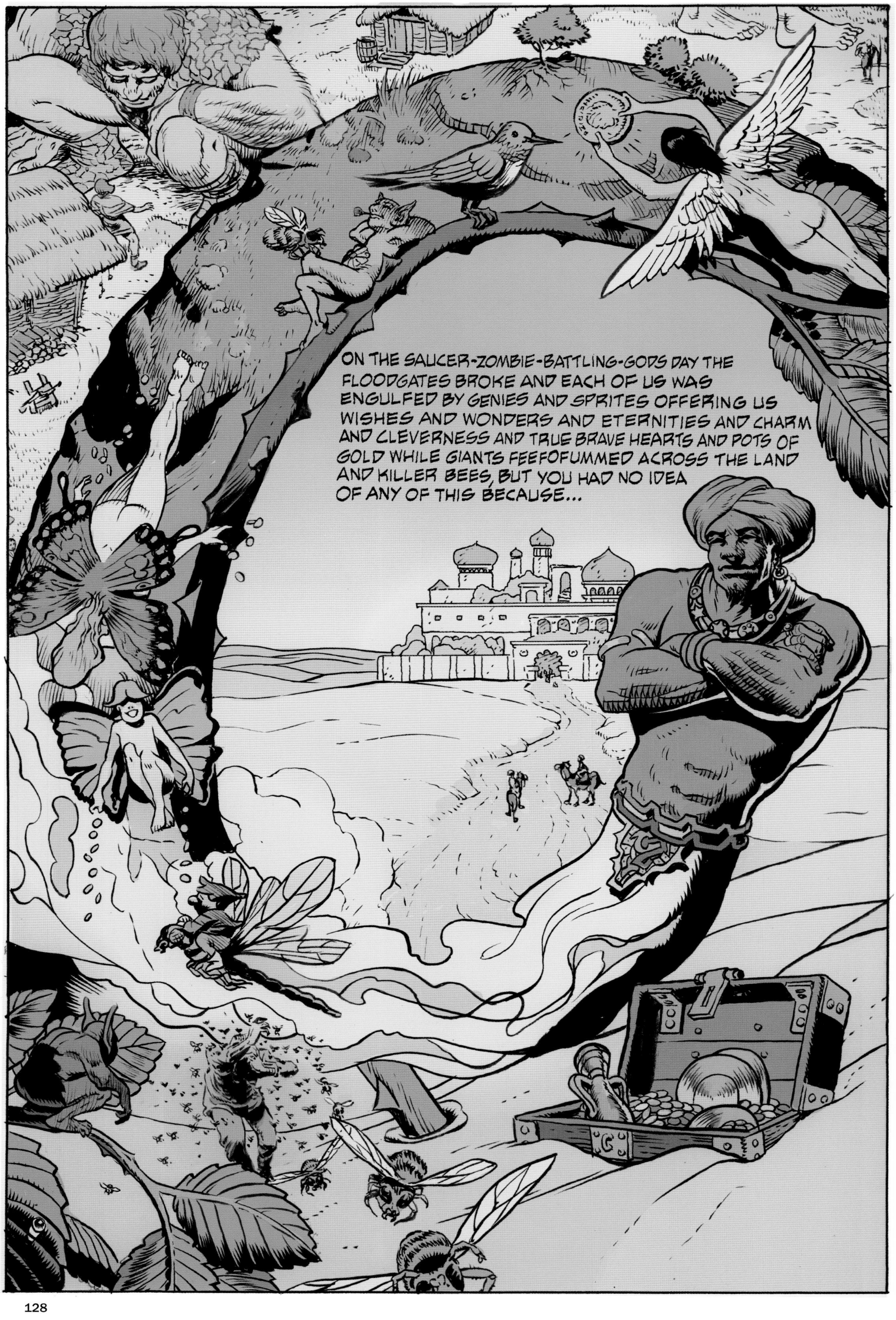
ON THE SAUCER-ZOMBIE-BATTLING-GODS DAY THE FLOODGATES BROKE AND EACH OF US WAS ENGULFED BY GENIES AND SPRITES OFFERING US WISHES AND WONDERS AND ETERNITIES AND CHARM AND CLEVERNESS AND TRUE BRAVE HEARTS AND POTS OF GOLD WHILE GIANTS FEEFOFUMMED ACROSS THE LAND AND KILLER BEES, BUT YOU HAD NO IDEA OF ANY OF THIS BECAUSE...

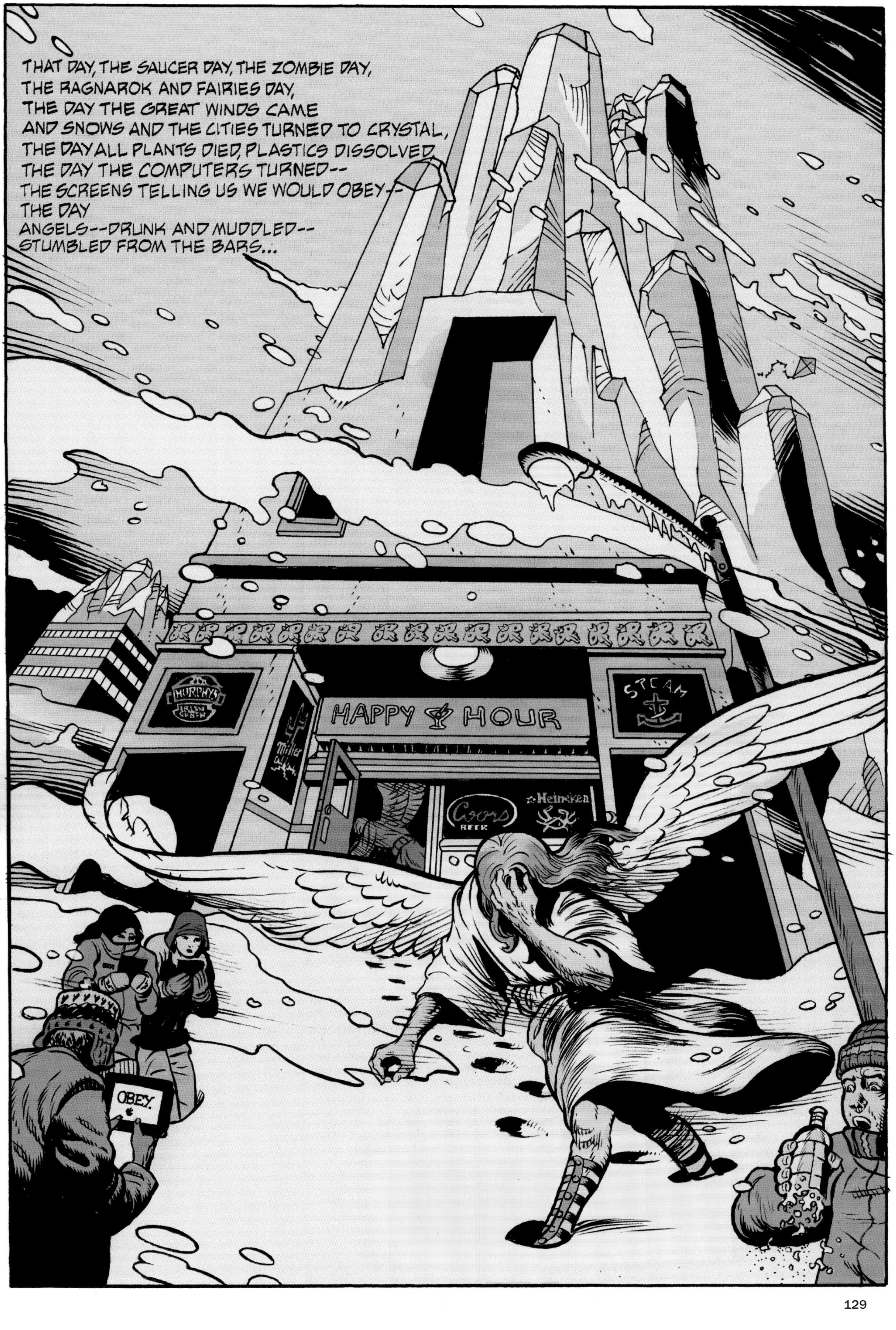
THAT DAY, THE SAUCER DAY, THE ZOMBIE DAY,
THE RAGNAROK AND FAIRIES DAY,
THE DAY THE GREAT WINDS CAME
AND SNOWS AND THE CITIES TURNED TO CRYSTAL,
THE DAY ALL PLANTS DIED, PLASTICS DISSOLVED,
THE DAY THE COMPUTERS TURNED--
THE SCREENS TELLING US WE WOULD OBEY--
THE DAY
ANGELS--DRUNK AND MUDDLED--
STUMBLED FROM THE BARS...
HAPPY HOUR
Miller
Coors BEER
Heineken
OBEY.

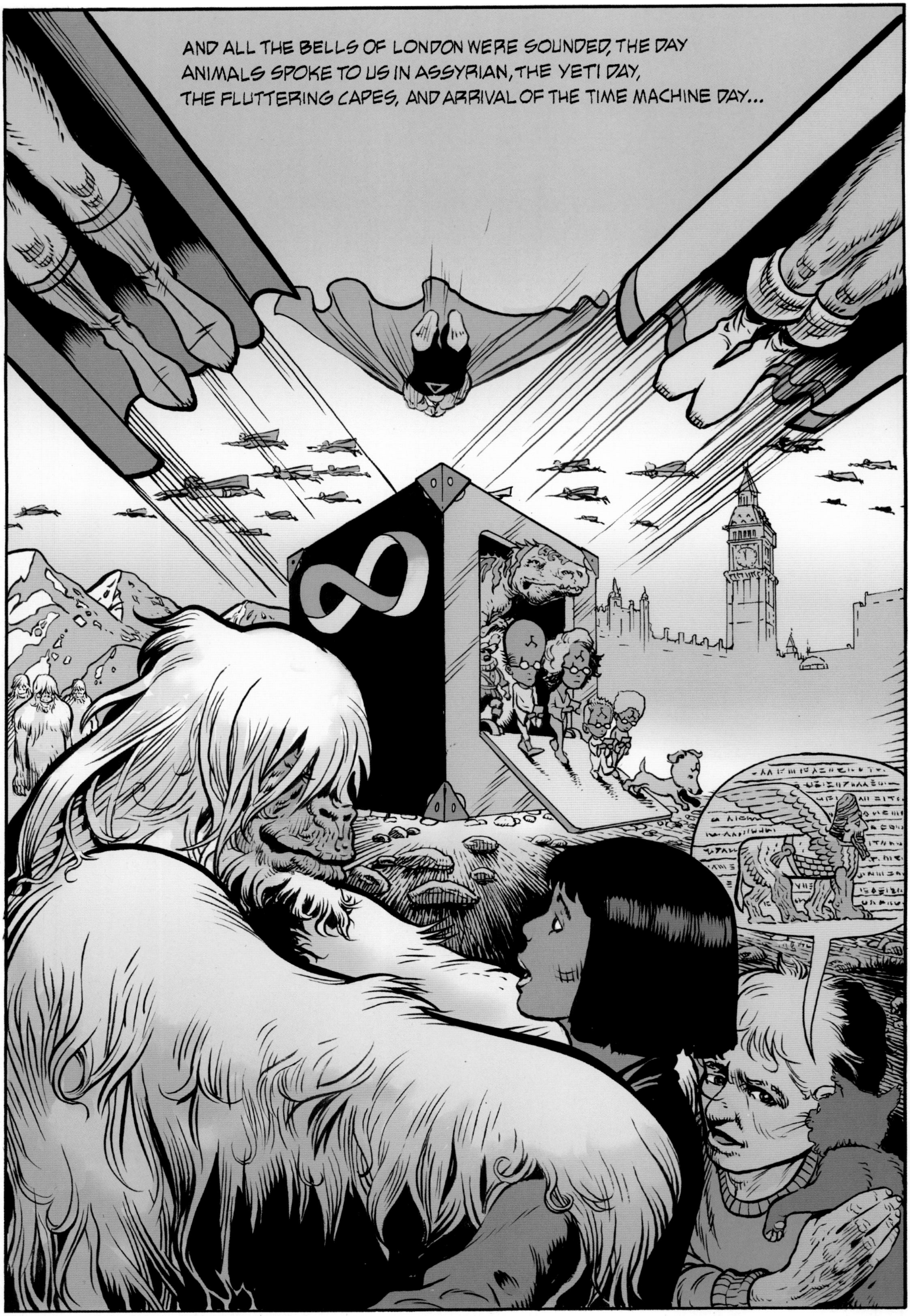
AND ALL THE BELLS OF LONDON WERE SOUNDED, THE DAY ANIMALS SPOKE TO US IN ASSYRIAN, THE YETI DAY, THE FLUTTERING CAPES, AND ARRIVAL OF THE TIME MACHINE DAY...

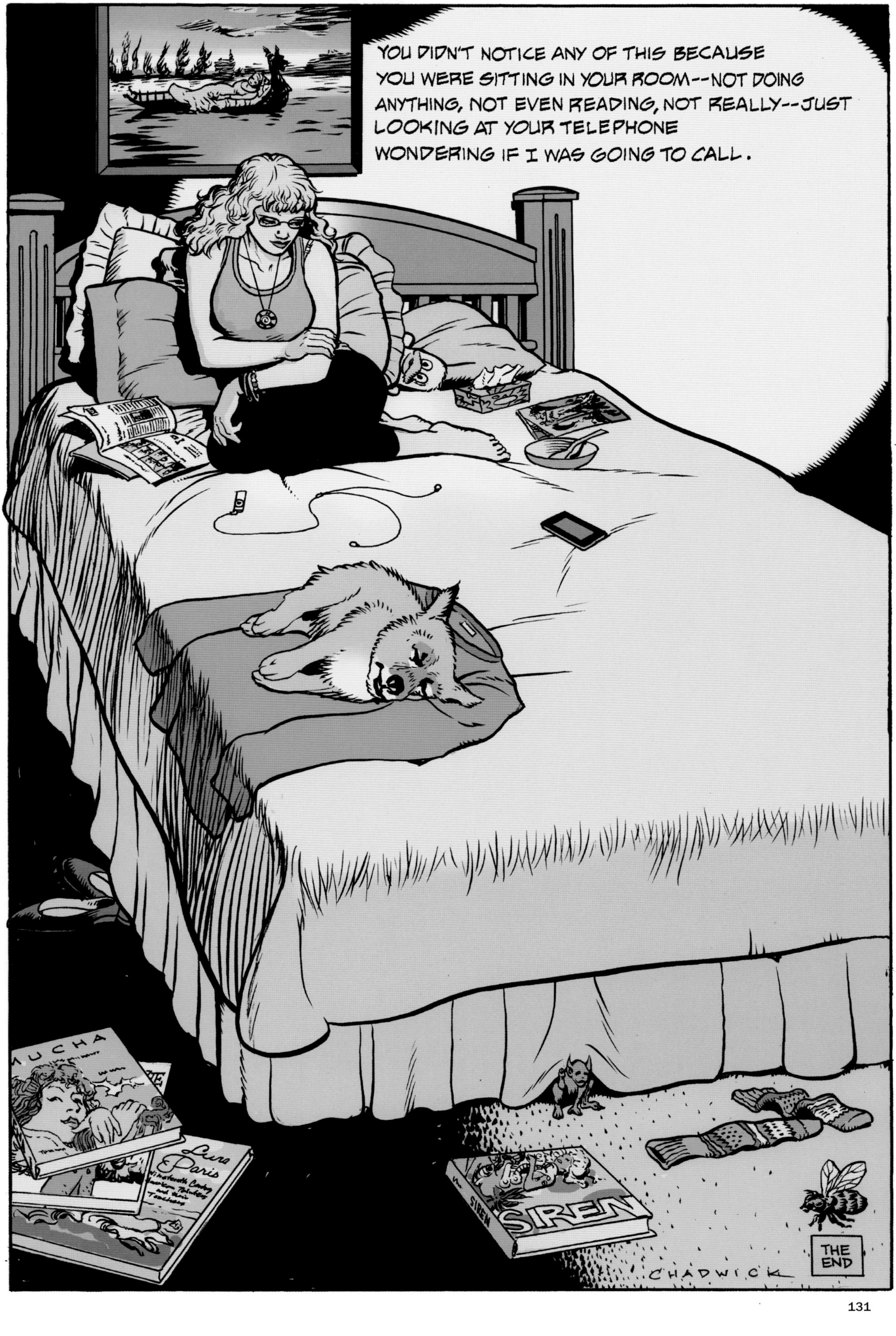
YOU DIDN'T NOTICE ANY OF THIS BECAUSE YOU WERE SITTING IN YOUR ROOM--NOT DOING ANYTHING, NOT EVEN READING, NOT REALLY--JUST LOOKING AT YOUR TELEPHONE WONDERING IF I WAS GOING TO CALL.
MUCHA
SIREN
CHADWICK
THE END

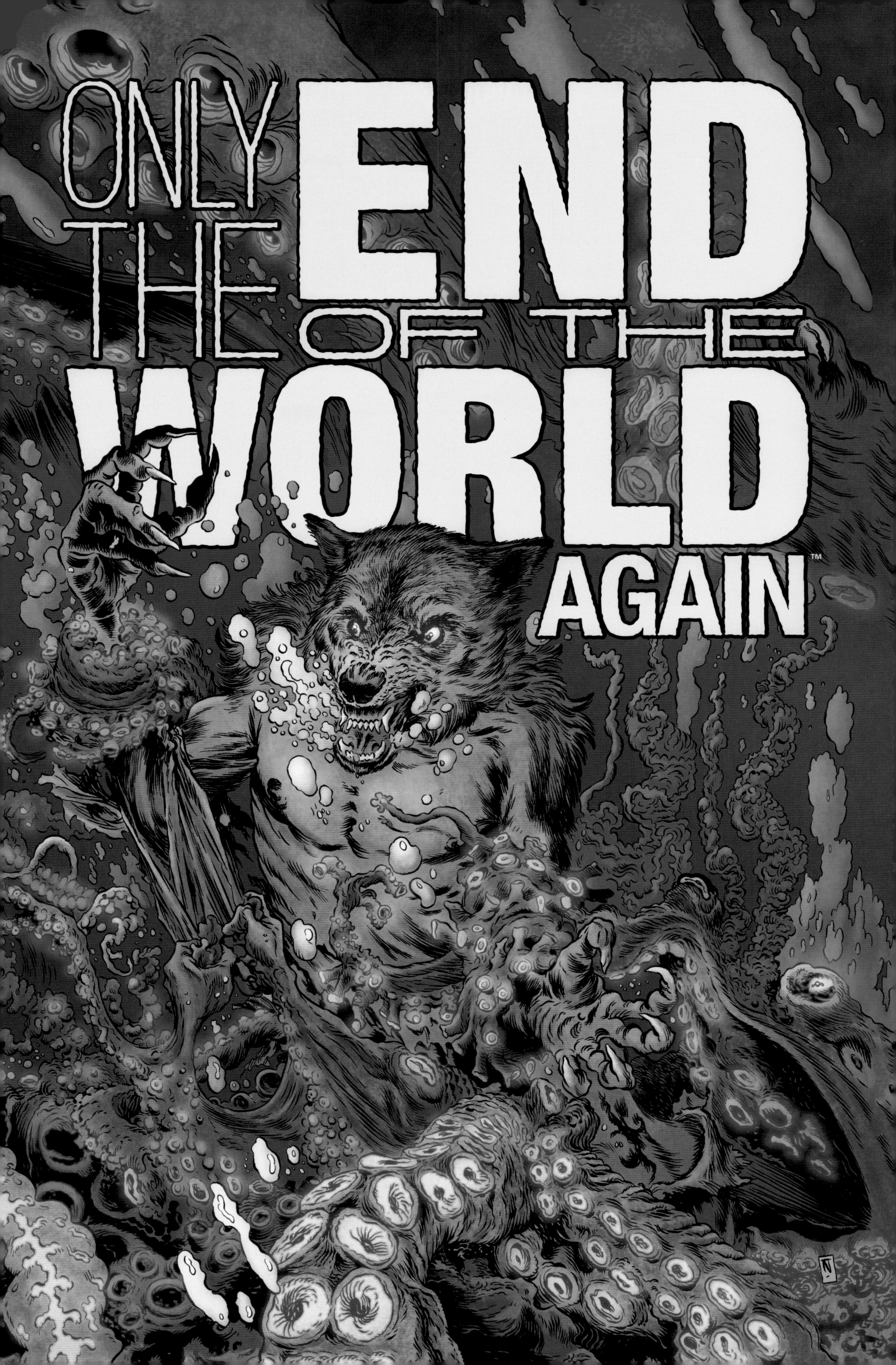
ONLY THE END OF THE WORLD AGAIN™

It was a bad day.

I woke up naked in the bed, with a cramp in my stomach, feeling more or less like hell. Something about the quality of the light, stretched and metallic, like the colon of a migraine, told me it was afternoon.

The room was freezing,... literally: there was a thin crust of ice on the inside of the windows. The sheets on the bed around me were ripped and clawed, and there was animal hair in the bed.

It itched.

ONLY THE END of the WORLD AGAIN™

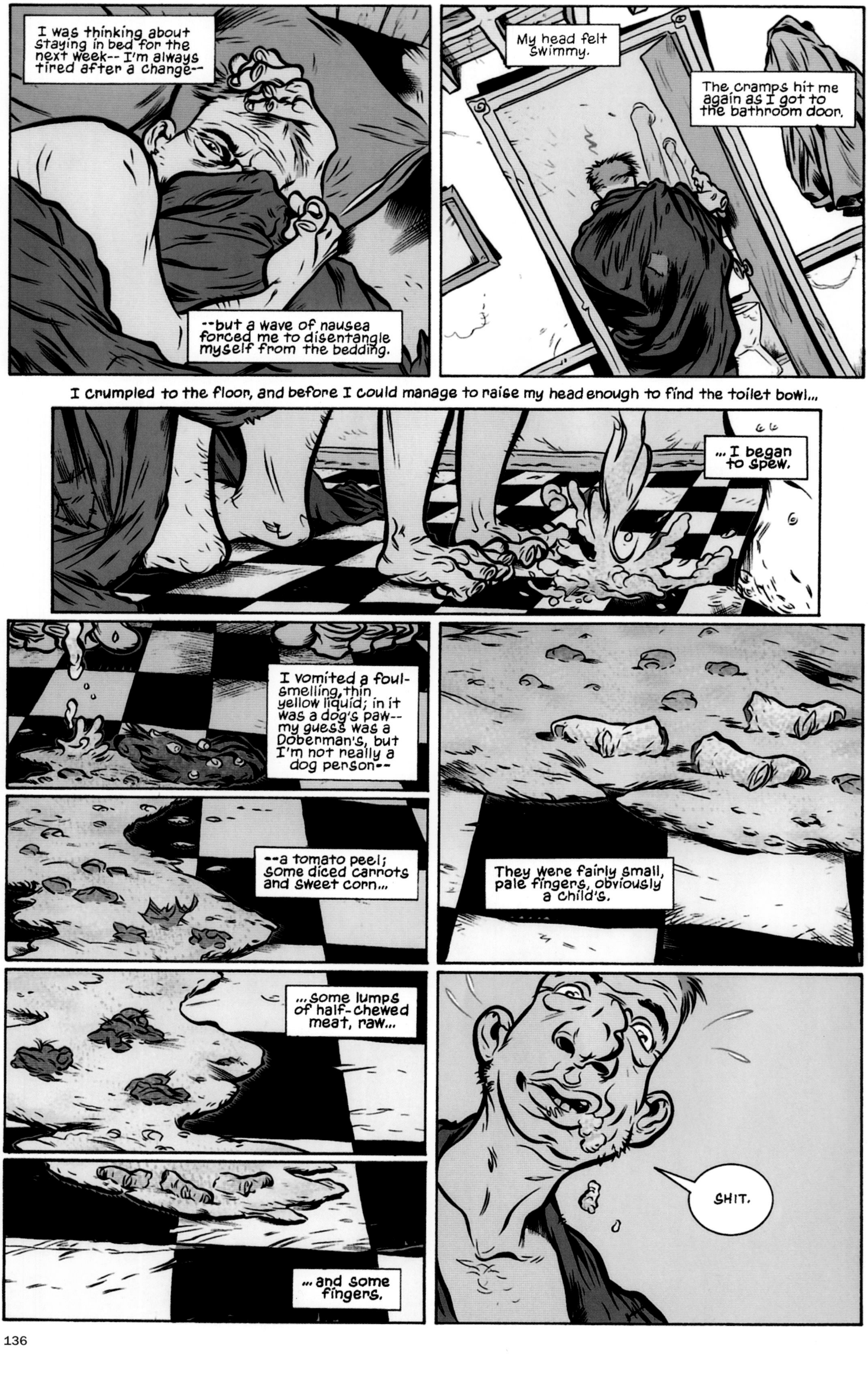
I was thinking about staying in bed for the next week-- I'm always tired after a change--
--but a wave of nausea forced me to disentangle myself from the bedding.
My head felt swimmy.
The cramps hit me again as I got to the bathroom door.
I crumpled to the floor, and before I could manage to raise my head enough to find the toilet bowl...
... I began to spew.
I vomited a foul-smelling, thin yellow liquid; in it was a dog's paw-- my guess was a Doberman's, but I'm not really a dog person--
--a tomato peel; some diced carrots and sweet corn...
...some lumps of half-chewed meat, raw...
... and some fingers.
They were fairly small, pale fingers, obviously a child's.
SHIT.

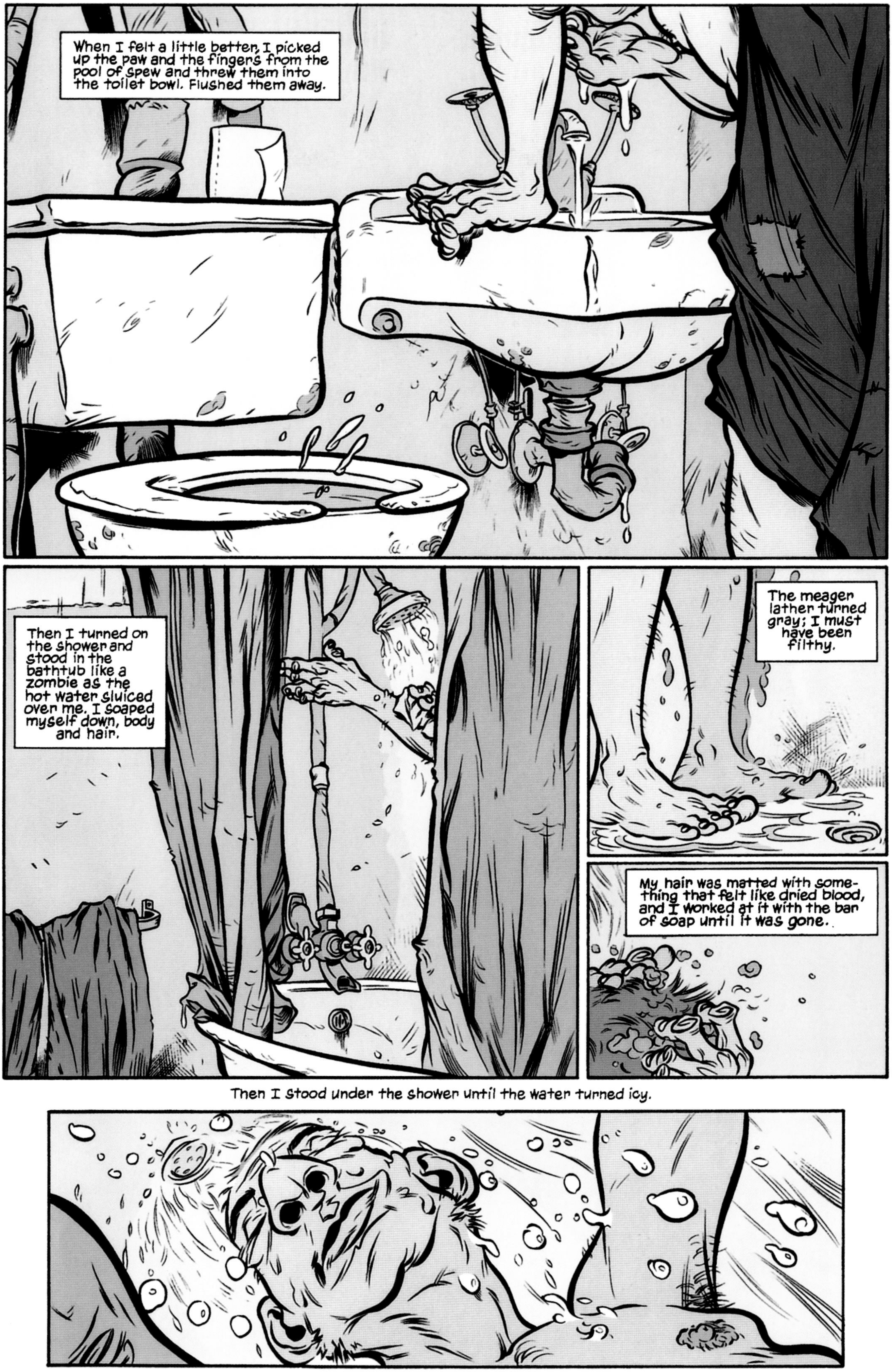
When I felt a little better, I picked up the paw and the fingers from the pool of spew and threw them into the toilet bowl. Flushed them away.
Then I turned on the shower and stood in the bathtub like a zombie as the hot water sluiced over me. I soaped myself down, body and hair.
The meager lather turned gray; I must have been filthy.
My hair was matted with something that felt like dried blood, and I worked at it with the bar of soap until it was gone.
Then I stood under the shower until the water turned icy.

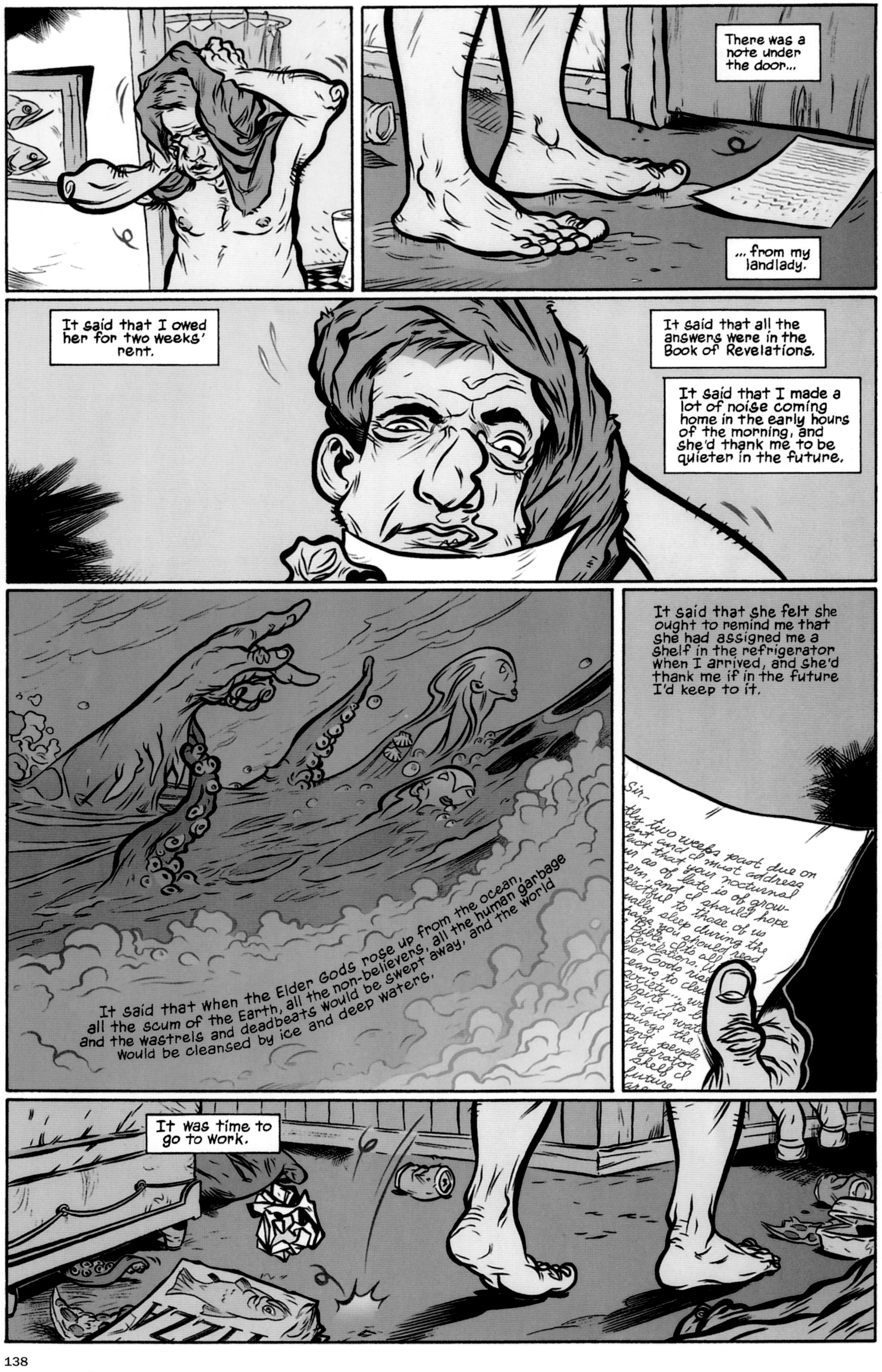
There was a note under the door...
...from my landlady.
It said that I owed her for two weeks' rent.
It said that all the answers were in the Book of Revelations.
It said that I made a lot of noise coming home in the early hours of the morning, and she'd thank me to be quieter in the future.
It said that she felt she ought to remind me that she had assigned me a shelf in the refrigerator when I arrived, and she'd thank me if in the future I'd keep to it.
Sir-
It said that when the Elder Gods rose up from the ocean, all the scum of the Earth, all the non-believers, all the human garbage and the wastrels and deadbeats would be swept away, and the world would be cleansed by ice and deep waters.
It was time to go to work.

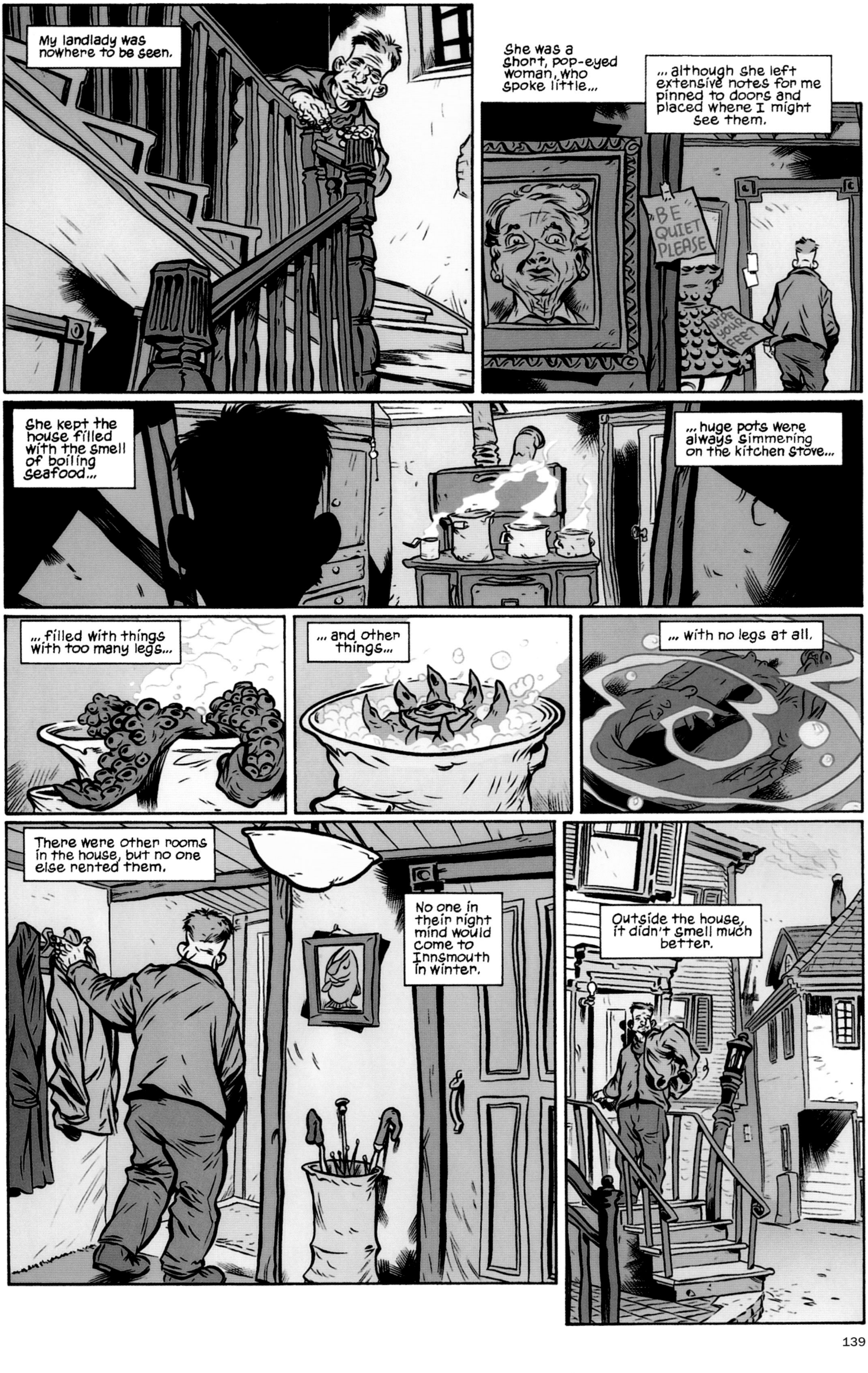

My landlady was nowhere to be seen.
She was a short, pop-eyed woman, who spoke little...
...although she left extensive notes for me pinned to doors and placed where I might see them.
BE QUIET PLEASE
WIPE YOUR FEET
She kept the house filled with the smell of boiling seafood...
...huge pots were always simmering on the kitchen stove...
...filled with things with too many legs...
...and other things...
...with no legs at all.
There were other rooms in the house, but no one else rented them.
No one in their right mind would come to Innsmouth in winter.
Outside the house, it didn't smell much better.

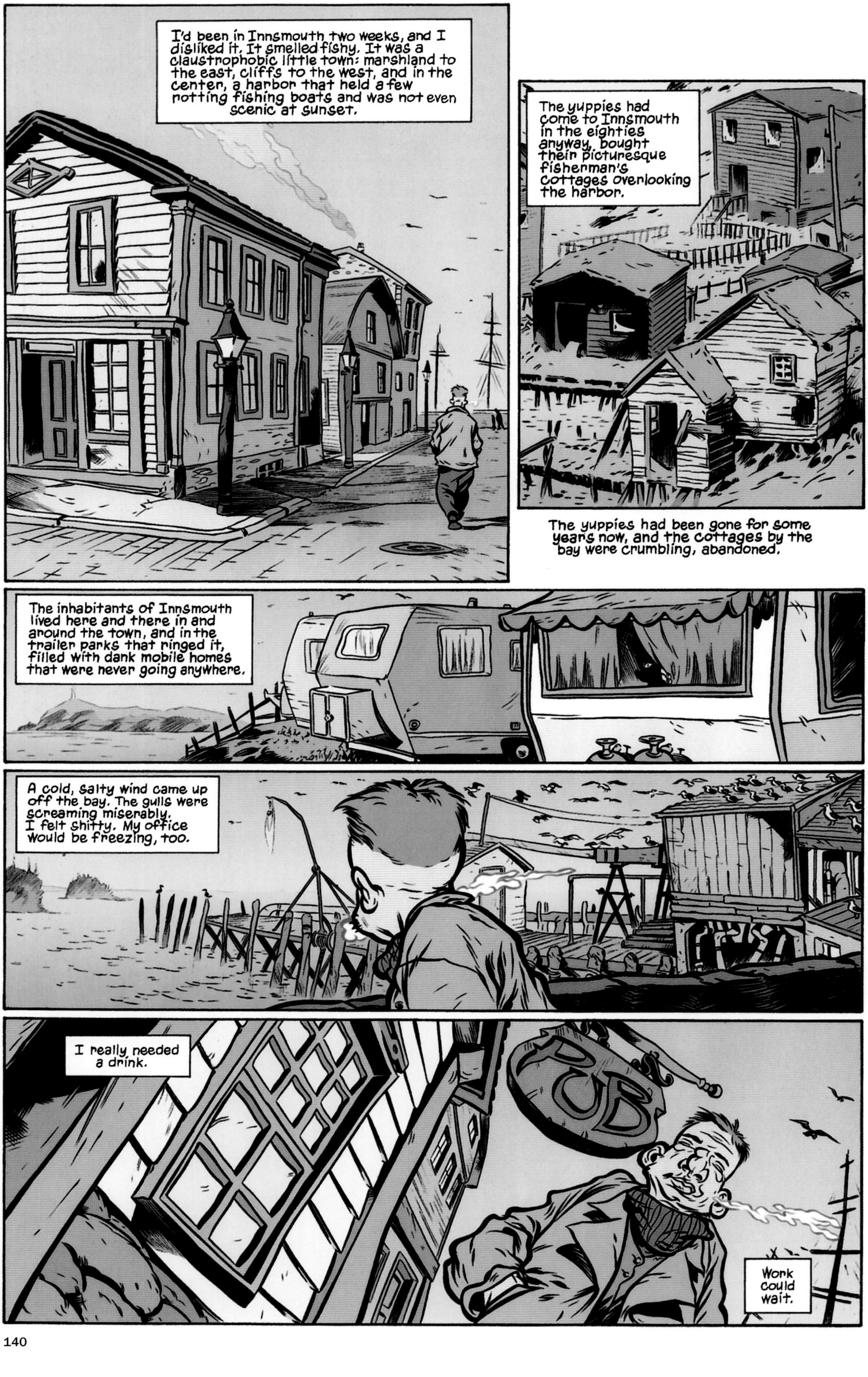

I'd been in Innsmouth two weeks, and I disliked it. It smelled fishy. It was a claustrophobic little town: marshland to the east, cliffs to the west, and in the center, a harbor that held a few rotting fishing boats and was not even scenic at sunset.
The yuppies had come to Innsmouth in the eighties anyway, bought their picturesque fisherman's cottages overlooking the harbor.
The yuppies had been gone for some years now, and the cottages by the bay were crumbling, abandoned.
The inhabitants of Innsmouth lived here and there in and around the town, and in the trailer parks that ringed it, filled with dank mobile homes that were never going anywhere.
A cold, salty wind came up off the bay. The gulls were screaming miserably. I felt shitty. My office would be freezing, too.
I really needed a drink.
PUB
Work could wait.

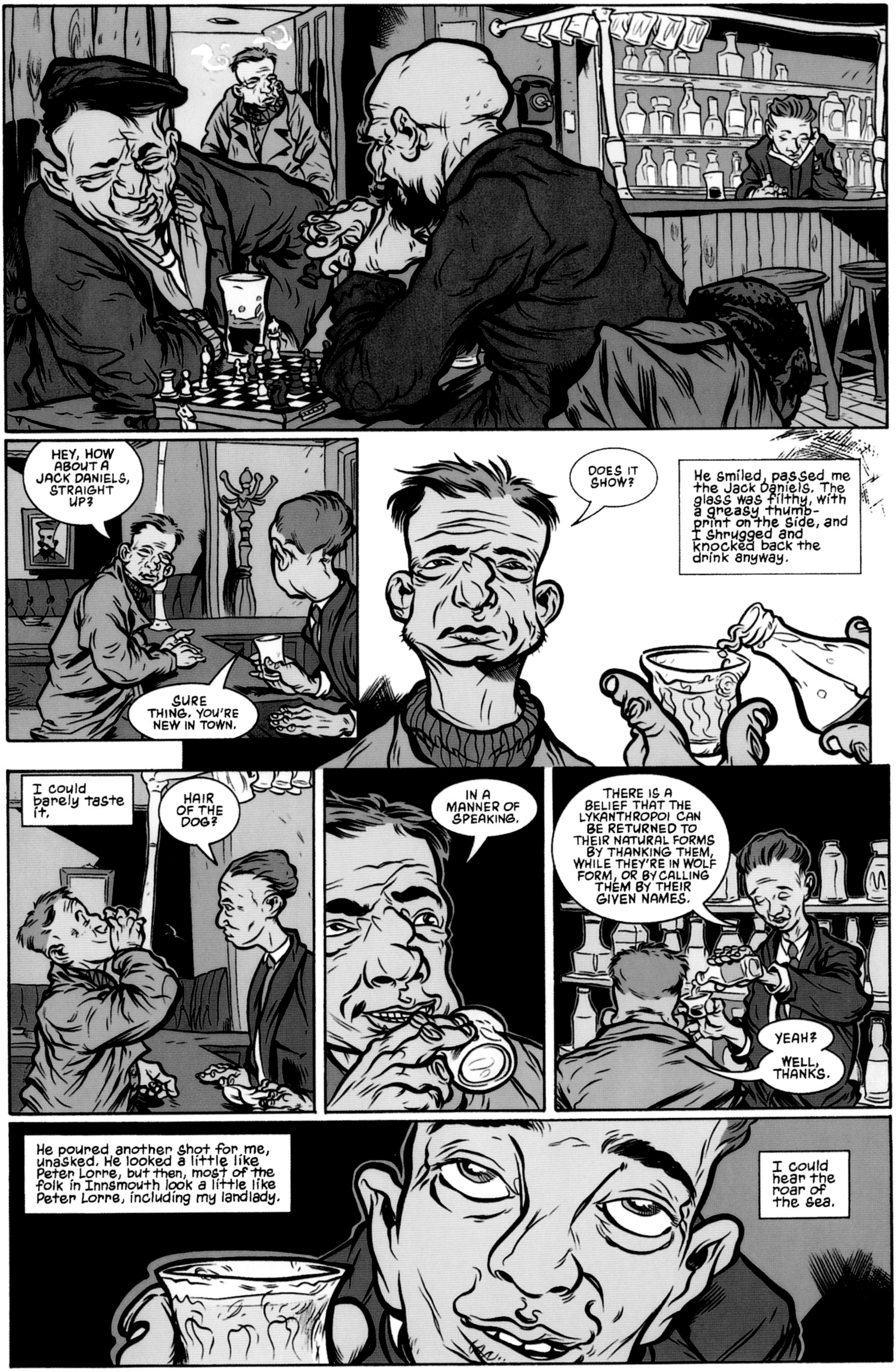
HEY, HOW ABOUT A JACK DANIELS, STRAIGHT UP?
SURE THING. YOU'RE NEW IN TOWN.
DOES IT SHOW?
He smiled, passed me the Jack Daniels. The glass was filthy, with a greasy thumb-print on the side, and I shrugged and knocked back the drink anyway.
I could barely taste it.
HAIR OF THE DOG?
IN A MANNER OF SPEAKING.
THERE IS A BELIEF THAT THE LYKANTHROPOI CAN BE RETURNED TO THEIR NATURAL FORMS BY THANKING THEM, WHILE THEY'RE IN WOLF FORM, OR BY CALLING THEM BY THEIR GIVEN NAMES.
YEAH?
WELL, THANKS.
He poured another shot for me, unasked. He looked a little like Peter Lorre, but then, most of the folk in Innsmouth look a little like Peter Lorre, including my landlady.
I could hear the roar of the sea.

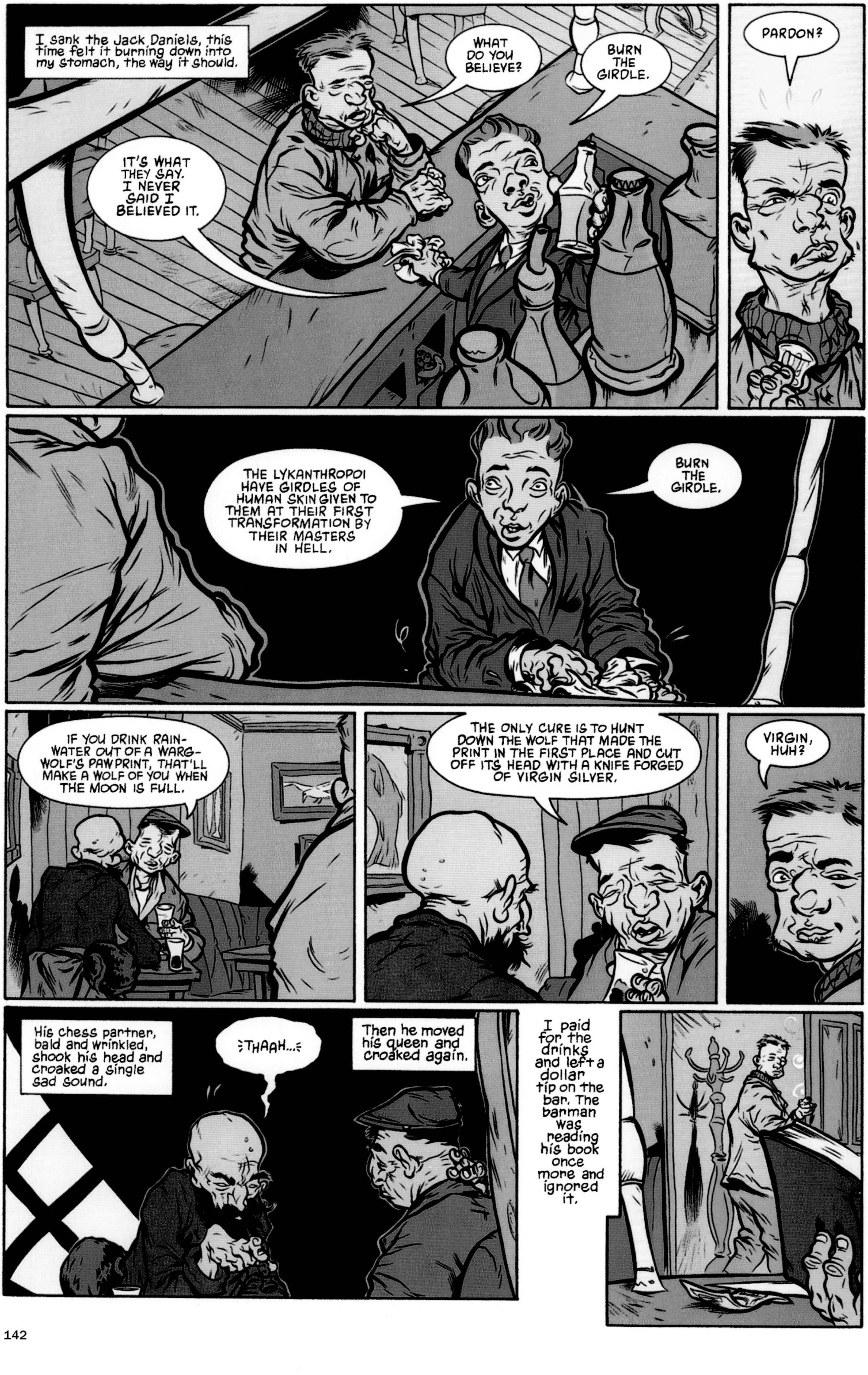

I sank the Jack Daniels, this time felt it burning down into my stomach, the way it should.
WHAT DO YOU BELIEVE?
BURN THE GIRDLE.
IT'S WHAT THEY SAY. I NEVER SAID I BELIEVED IT.
PARDON?
THE LYKANTHROPOI HAVE GIRDLES OF HUMAN SKIN GIVEN TO THEM AT THEIR FIRST TRANSFORMATION BY THEIR MASTERS IN HELL.
BURN THE GIRDLE.
IF YOU DRINK RAIN-WATER OUT OF A WARG-WOLF'S PAWPRINT, THAT'LL MAKE A WOLF OF YOU WHEN THE MOON IS FULL.
THE ONLY CURE IS TO HUNT DOWN THE WOLF THAT MADE THE PRINT IN THE FIRST PLACE AND CUT OFF ITS HEAD WITH A KNIFE FORGED OF VIRGIN SILVER.
VIRGIN, HUH?
His chess partner, bald and wrinkled, shook his head and croaked a single sad sound.
THAAH...
Then he moved his queen and croaked again.
I paid for the drinks and left a dollar tip on the bar. The barman was reading his book once more and ignored it.

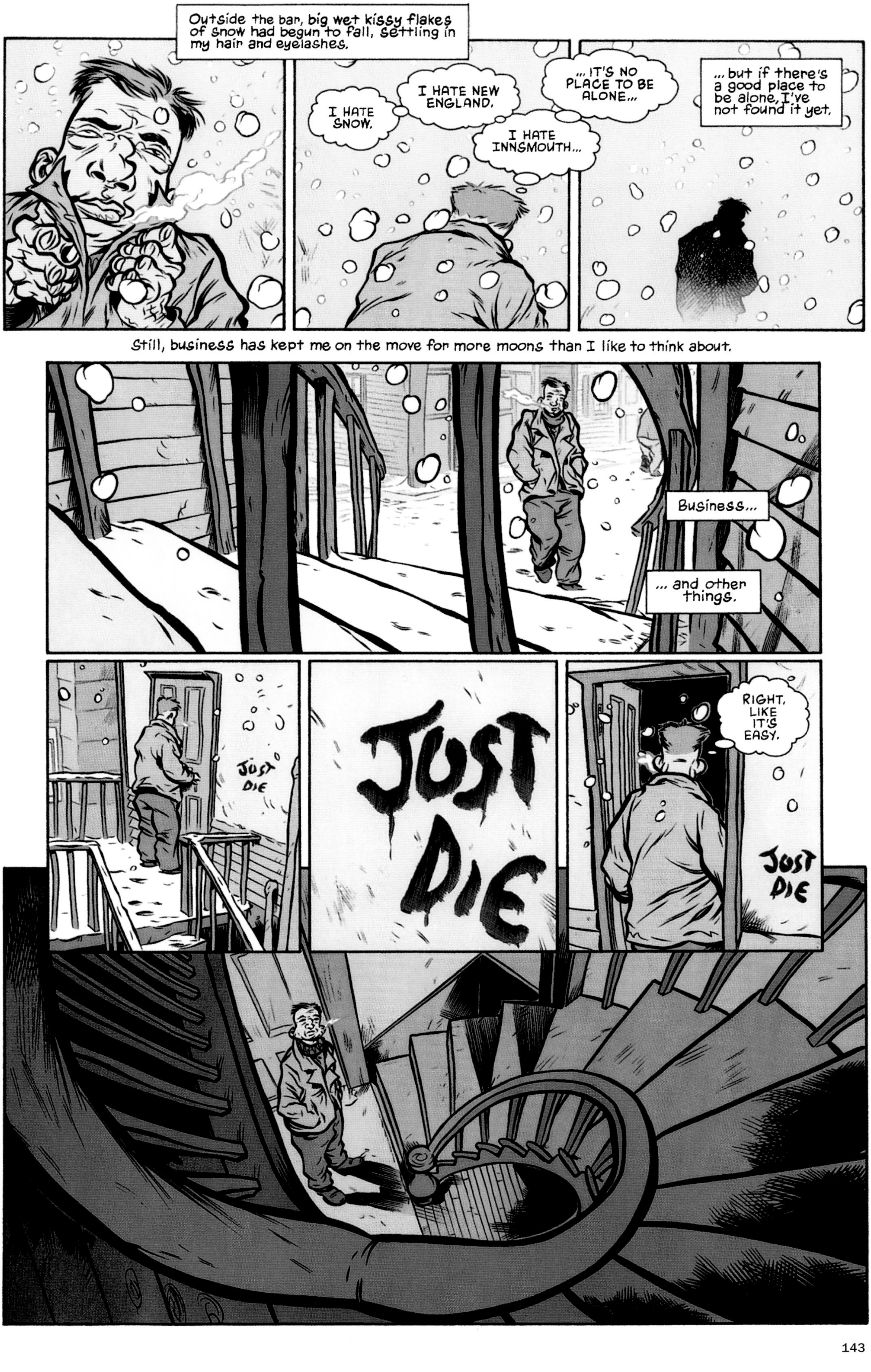

Outside the bar, big wet kissy flakes of snow had begun to fall, settling in my hair and eyelashes.
I HATE SNOW.
I HATE NEW ENGLAND.
I HATE INNSMOUTH...
...IT'S NO PLACE TO BE ALONE...
...but if there's a good place to be alone, I've not found it yet.
Still, business has kept me on the move for more moons than I like to think about.
Business...
...and other things.
JUST DIE
JUST DIE
RIGHT, LIKE IT'S EASY.
JUST DIE

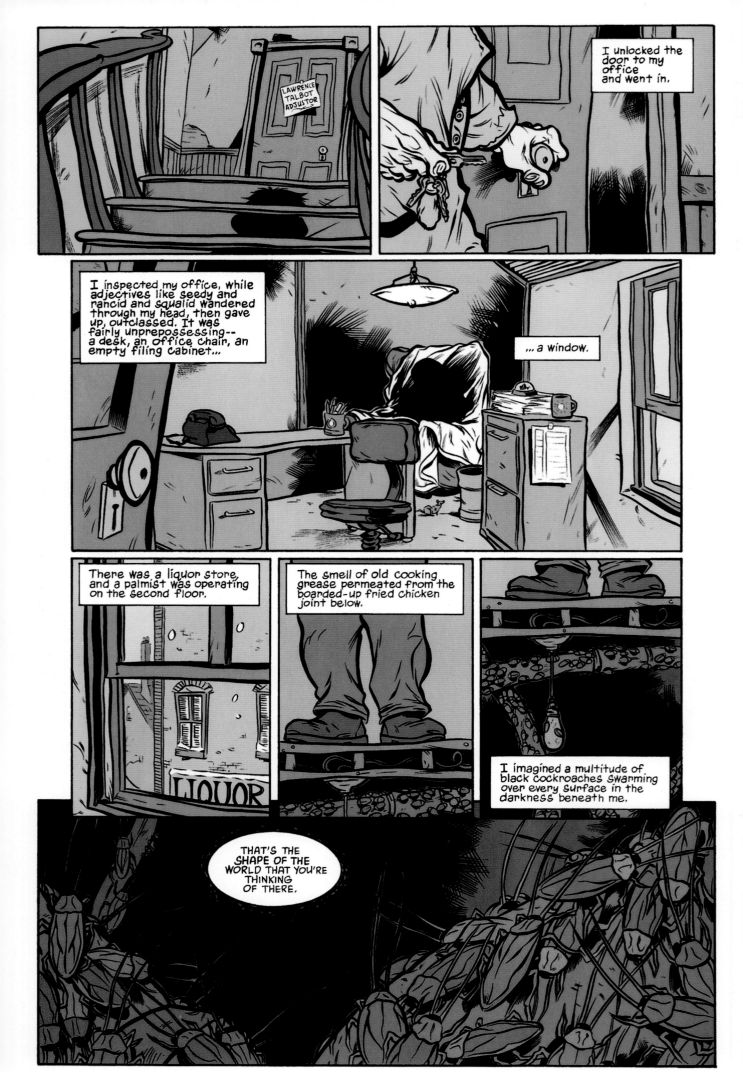

LAWRENCE TALBOT ADJUSTOR

I unlocked the door to my office and went in.

I inspected my office, while adjectives like seedy and rancid and squalid wandered through my head, then gave up, outclassed. It was fairly unprepossessing-- a desk, an office chair, an empty filing cabinet...

...a window.

There was a liquor store, and a palmist was operating on the second floor.

The smell of old cooking grease permeated from the boarded-up fried chicken joint below.

I imagined a multitude of black cockroaches swarming over every surface in the darkness beneath me.

THAT'S THE SHAPE OF THE WORLD THAT YOU'RE THINKING OF THERE.

LIQUOR

It was said with a deep, dark voice, deep enough that I felt it in the pit of my stomach.

WE LOOK ABOUT IN PUZZLEMENT AT OUR WORLD, WITH A SENSE OF UNEASE AND DISQUIET.

WE THINK OF OUR-SELVES AS SCHOLARS IN ARCANE LITURGIES, SINGLE MEN TRAPPED IN WORLDS BEYOND OUR DEVISING.

THE TRUTH IS FAR SIMPLER: THERE ARE THINGS IN THE DARKNESS BENEATH US THAT WISH US HARM.

The man in the armchair took a slow deep breath that rattled in the back of his throat.

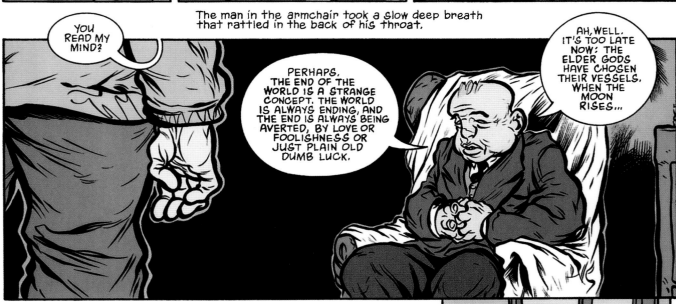

YOU READ MY MIND?

PERHAPS, THE END OF THE WORLD IS A STRANGE CONCEPT. THE WORLD IS ALWAYS ENDING, AND THE END IS ALWAYS BEING AVERTED, BY LOVE OR FOOLISHNESS OR JUST PLAIN OLD DUMB LUCK.

AH, WELL. IT'S TOO LATE NOW: THE ELDER GODS HAVE CHOSEN THEIR VESSELS, WHEN THE MOON RISES...

A thin trickle of drool came from one corner of his mouth...

...trickled down in a thread of silver to his collar.

Something scuttled down into the shadows of his coat.

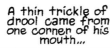

YEAH? WHAT HAPPENS WHEN THE MOON RISES?

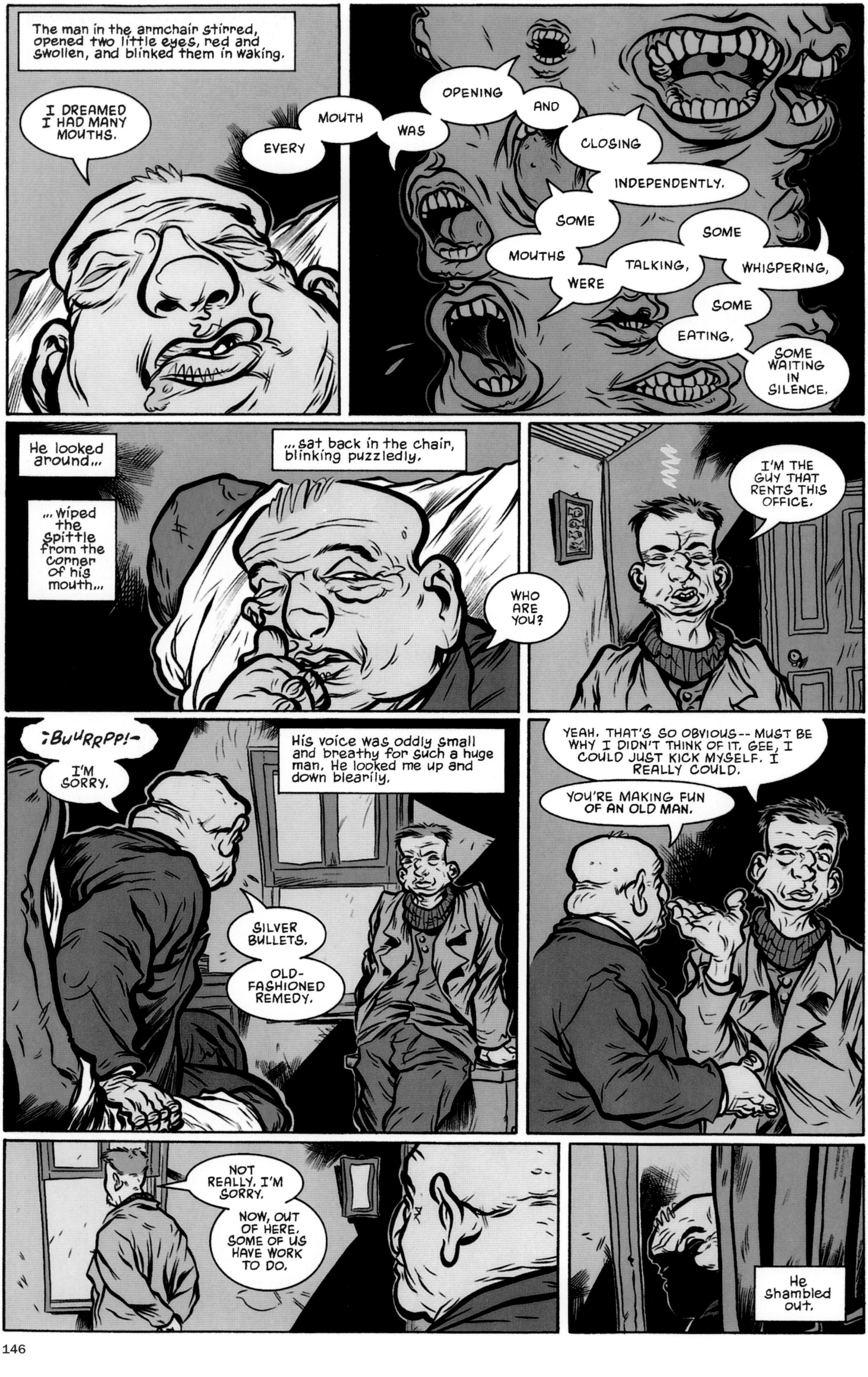

The man in the armchair stirred, opened two little eyes, red and swollen, and blinked them in waking.
I DREAMED I HAD MANY MOUTHS.
EVERY
MOUTH
WAS
OPENING
AND
CLOSING
INDEPENDENTLY.
SOME
MOUTHS
WERE
TALKING,
SOME
WHISPERING,
SOME
EATING,
SOME WAITING IN SILENCE.
He looked around...
...wiped the spittle from the corner of his mouth...
...sat back in the chair, blinking puzzledly.
WHO ARE YOU?
I'M THE GUY THAT RENTS THIS OFFICE.
-BUURRPP!-
I'M SORRY.
His voice was oddly small and breathy for such a huge man. He looked me up and down blearily.
SILVER BULLETS.
OLD-FASHIONED REMEDY.
YEAH. THAT'S SO OBVIOUS-- MUST BE WHY I DIDN'T THINK OF IT. GEE, I COULD JUST KICK MYSELF. I REALLY COULD.
YOU'RE MAKING FUN OF AN OLD MAN.
NOT REALLY. I'M SORRY.
NOW, OUT OF HERE. SOME OF US HAVE WORK TO DO.
He shambled out.

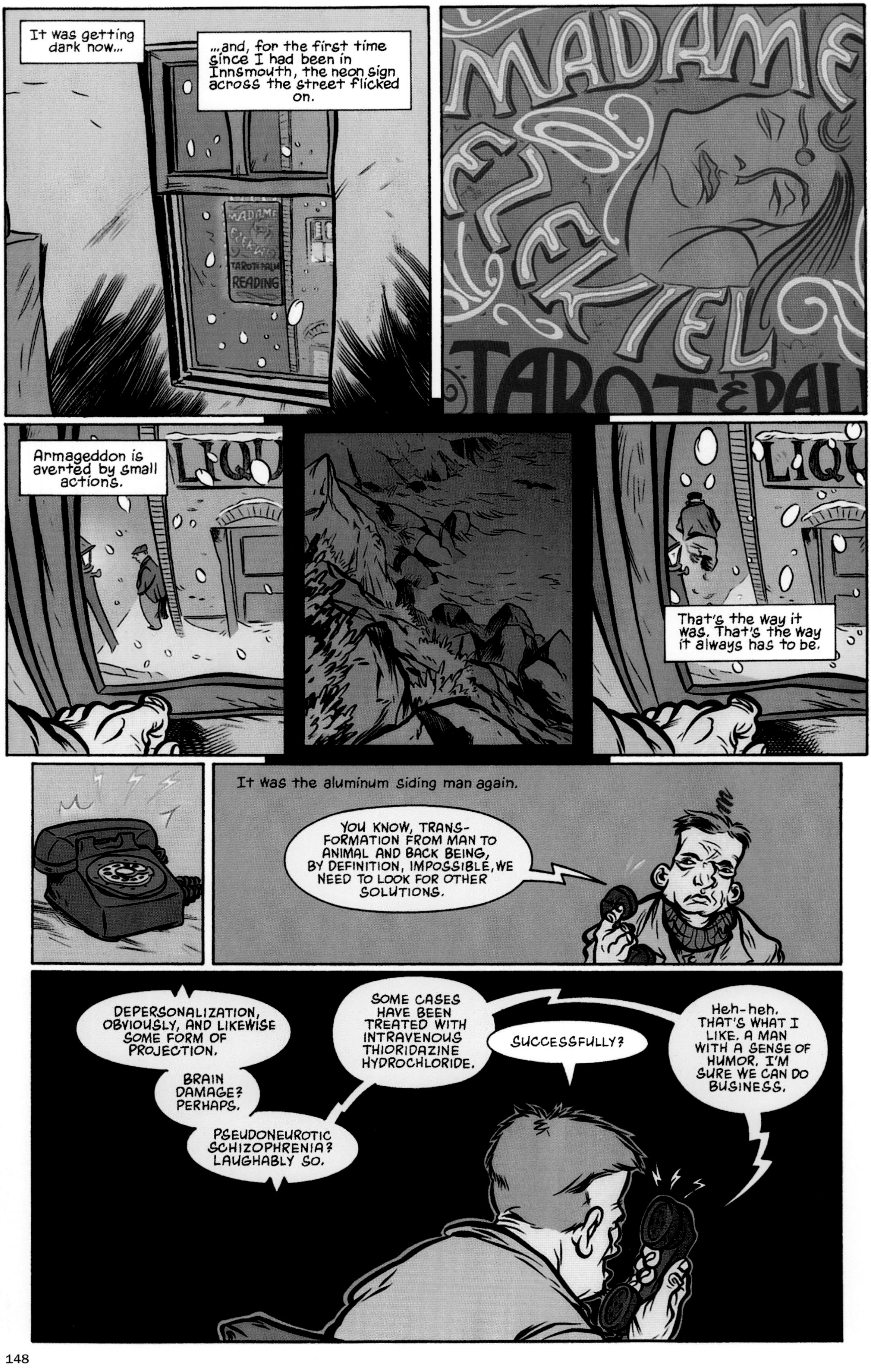
It was getting dark now...
...and, for the first time since I had been in Innsmouth, the neon sign across the street flicked on.
MADAME EZEKIEL TAROT & PALM
Armageddon is averted by small actions.
That's the way it was. That's the way it always has to be.
It was the aluminum siding man again.
YOU KNOW, TRANSFORMATION FROM MAN TO ANIMAL AND BACK BEING, BY DEFINITION, IMPOSSIBLE, WE NEED TO LOOK FOR OTHER SOLUTIONS.
DEPERSONALIZATION, OBVIOUSLY, AND LIKEWISE SOME FORM OF PROJECTION.
BRAIN DAMAGE? PERHAPS.
PSEUDONEUROTIC SCHIZOPHRENIA? LAUGHABLY SO.
SOME CASES HAVE BEEN TREATED WITH INTRAVENOUS THIORIDAZINE HYDROCHLORIDE.
SUCCESSFULLY?
Heh-heh. THAT'S WHAT I LIKE. A MAN WITH A SENSE OF HUMOR. I'M SURE WE CAN DO BUSINESS.

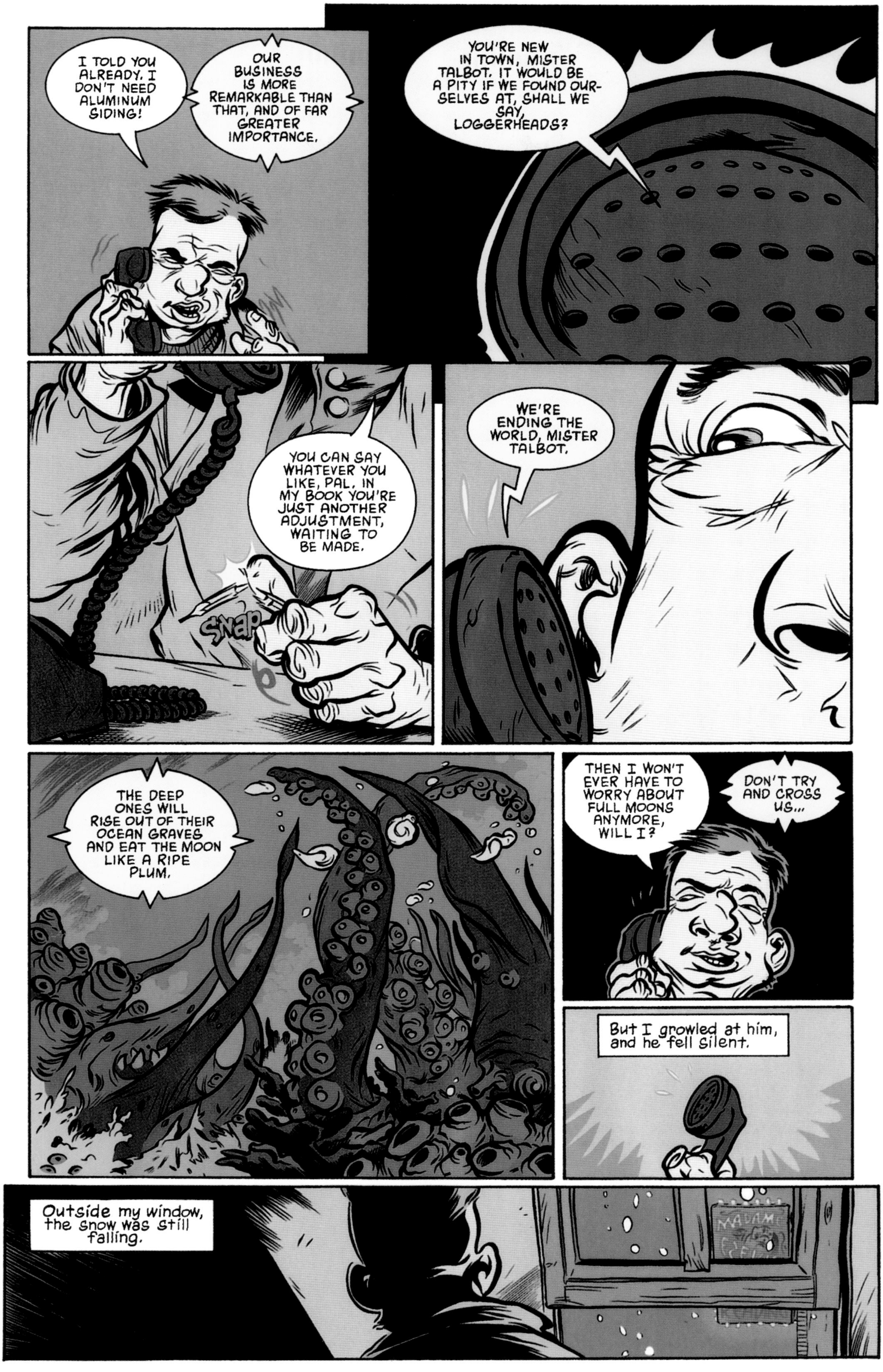
I TOLD YOU ALREADY. I DON'T NEED ALUMINUM SIDING!
OUR BUSINESS IS MORE REMARKABLE THAN THAT, AND OF FAR GREATER IMPORTANCE.
YOU'RE NEW IN TOWN, MISTER TALBOT. IT WOULD BE A PITY IF WE FOUND OURSELVES AT, SHALL WE SAY, LOGGERHEADS?
YOU CAN SAY WHATEVER YOU LIKE, PAL. IN MY BOOK YOU'RE JUST ANOTHER ADJUSTMENT, WAITING TO BE MADE.
SNAP
WE'RE ENDING THE WORLD, MISTER TALBOT.
THE DEEP ONES WILL RISE OUT OF THEIR OCEAN GRAVES AND EAT THE MOON LIKE A RIPE PLUM.
THEN I WON'T EVER HAVE TO WORRY ABOUT FULL MOONS ANYMORE, WILL I?
DON'T TRY AND CROSS US...
But I growled at him, and he fell silent.
Outside my window, the snow was still falling.

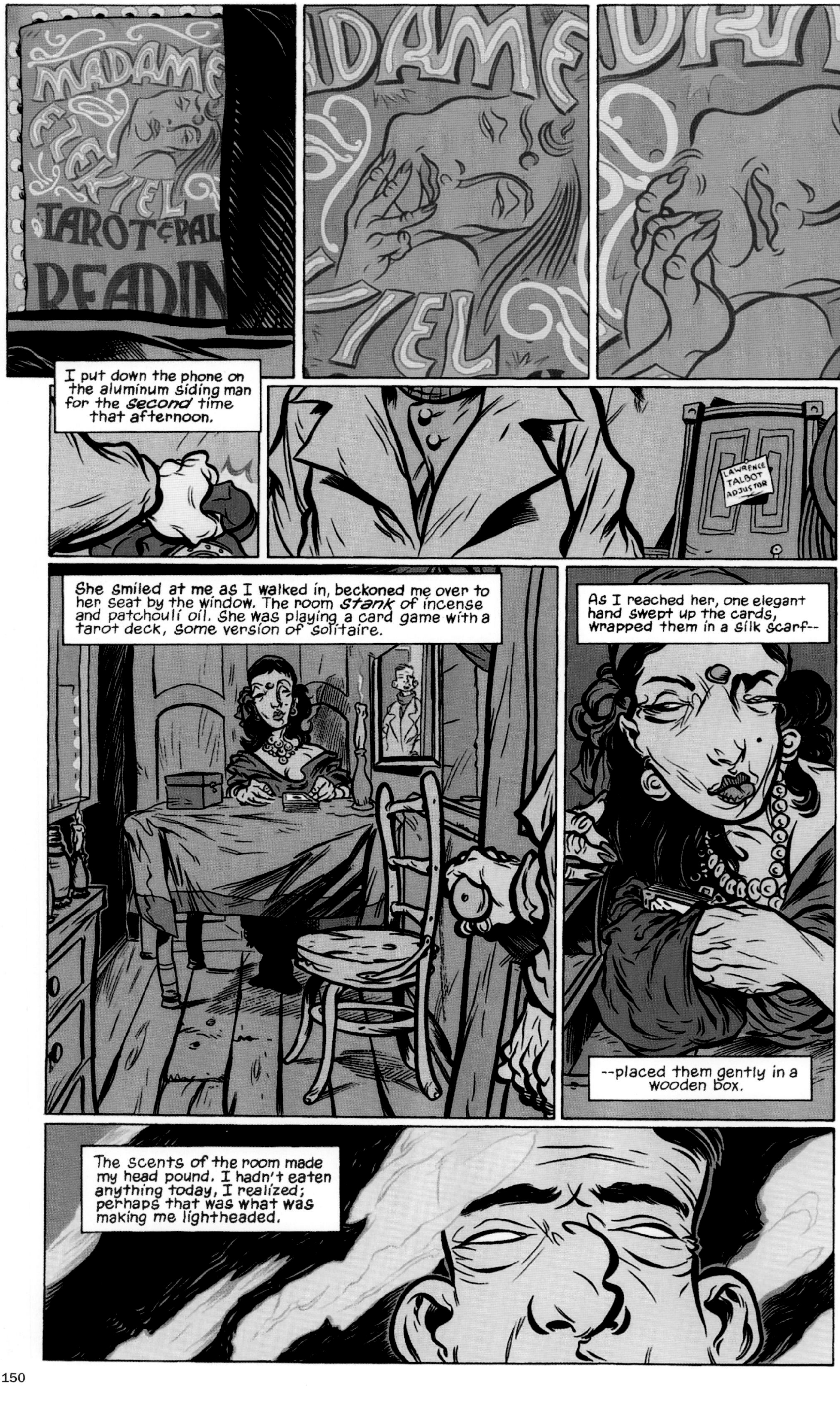
MADAME
TAROT & PAL
READIN
I put down the phone on the aluminum siding man for the *second* time that afternoon.
LAWRENCE TALBOT ADJUSTOR
She smiled at me as I walked in, beckoned me over to her seat by the window. The room *stank* of incense and patchouli oil. She was playing a card game with a tarot deck, some version of solitaire.
As I reached her, one elegant hand swept up the cards, wrapped them in a silk scarf--
--placed them gently in a wooden box.
The scents of the room made my head pound. I hadn't eaten anything today, I realized; perhaps that was what was making me lightheaded.

I sat down, across the table from her, in the candlelight. She extended her hand, and took my hand in hers.

HAIR?

YEAH, WELL, I'M ON MY OWN A LOT.

I grinned.

I hoped it was a friendly grin.

WHEN I LOOK AT YOU, THIS IS WHAT I SEE.

I SEE THE EYE OF A MAN.

ALSO, I SEE THE EYE OF A WOLF.

IN THE EYE OF A MAN, I SEE HONESTY, DECENCY, INNOCENCE.

I SEE AN UPRIGHT MAN WHO WALKS ON A SQUARE.

"AND IN THE EYE OF A WOLF, I SEE A GROANING AND A GROWLING, NIGHT HOWLS AND CRIES. I SEE A MONSTER RUNNING WITH BLOOD-FLECKED SPITTLE IN THE DARKNESS OF THE BORDERS OF THE TOWN."

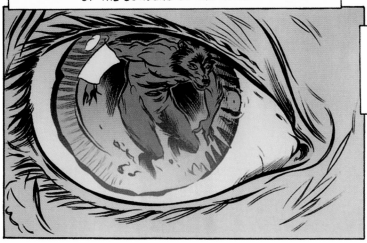

HOW CAN YOU SEE A GROWL OR A CRY?

Her accent was not American. It was Russian, or Maltese, or Egyptian, perhaps.

IT IS NOT HARD. IN THE EYE OF THE MIND, WE SEE MANY THINGS.

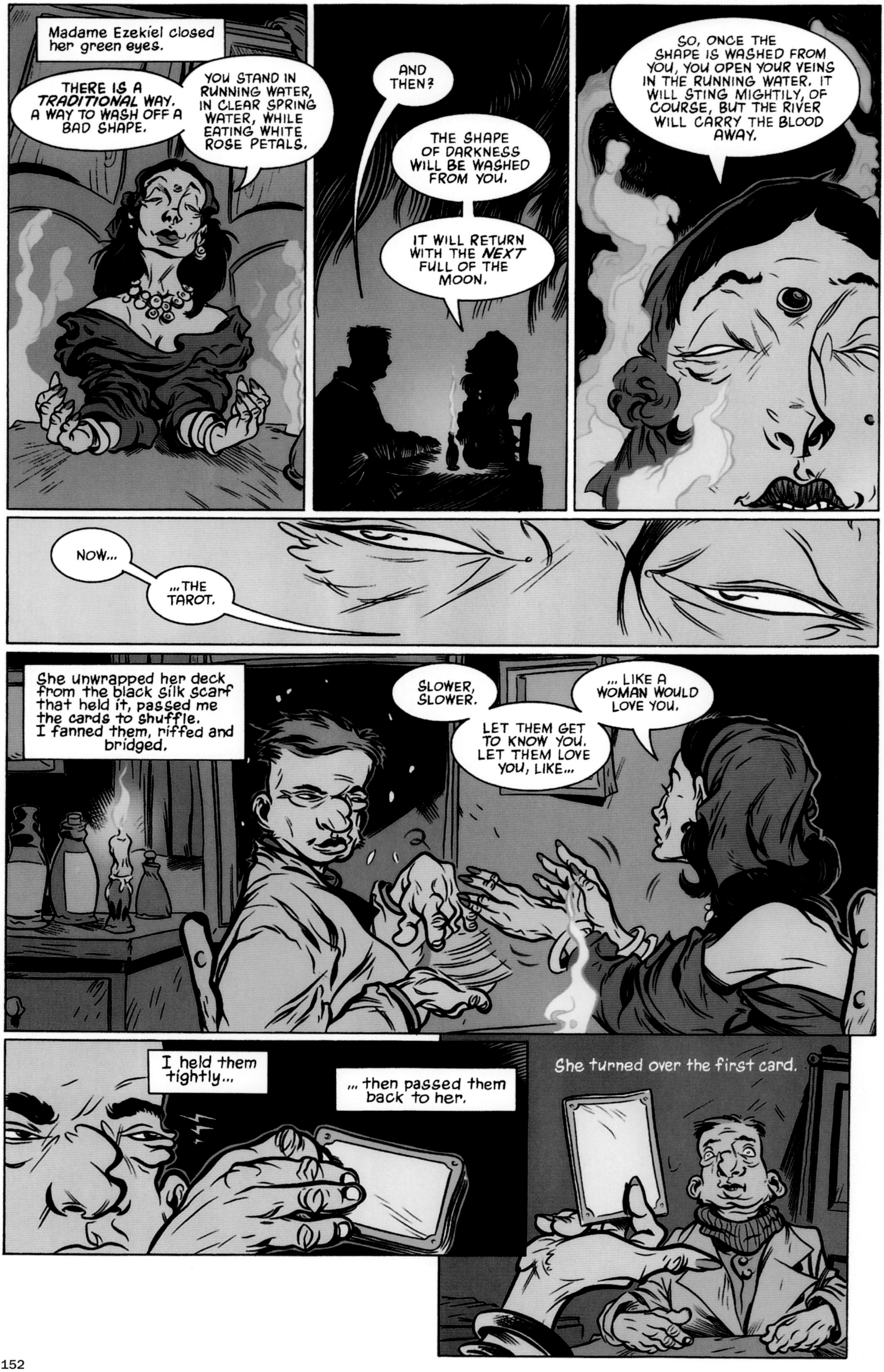

Madame Ezekiel closed her green eyes.
THERE IS A TRADITIONAL WAY. A WAY TO WASH OFF A BAD SHAPE.
YOU STAND IN RUNNING WATER, IN CLEAR SPRING WATER, WHILE EATING WHITE ROSE PETALS.
AND THEN?
THE SHAPE OF DARKNESS WILL BE WASHED FROM YOU.
IT WILL RETURN WITH THE NEXT FULL OF THE MOON.
SO, ONCE THE SHAPE IS WASHED FROM YOU, YOU OPEN YOUR VEINS IN THE RUNNING WATER. IT WILL STING MIGHTILY, OF COURSE, BUT THE RIVER WILL CARRY THE BLOOD AWAY.
NOW...
...THE TAROT.
She unwrapped her deck from the black silk scarf that held it, passed me the cards to shuffle. I fanned them, riffed and bridged.
SLOWER, SLOWER.
LET THEM GET TO KNOW YOU. LET THEM LOVE YOU, LIKE...
... LIKE A WOMAN WOULD LOVE YOU.
I held them tightly...
... then passed them back to her.
She turned over the first card.

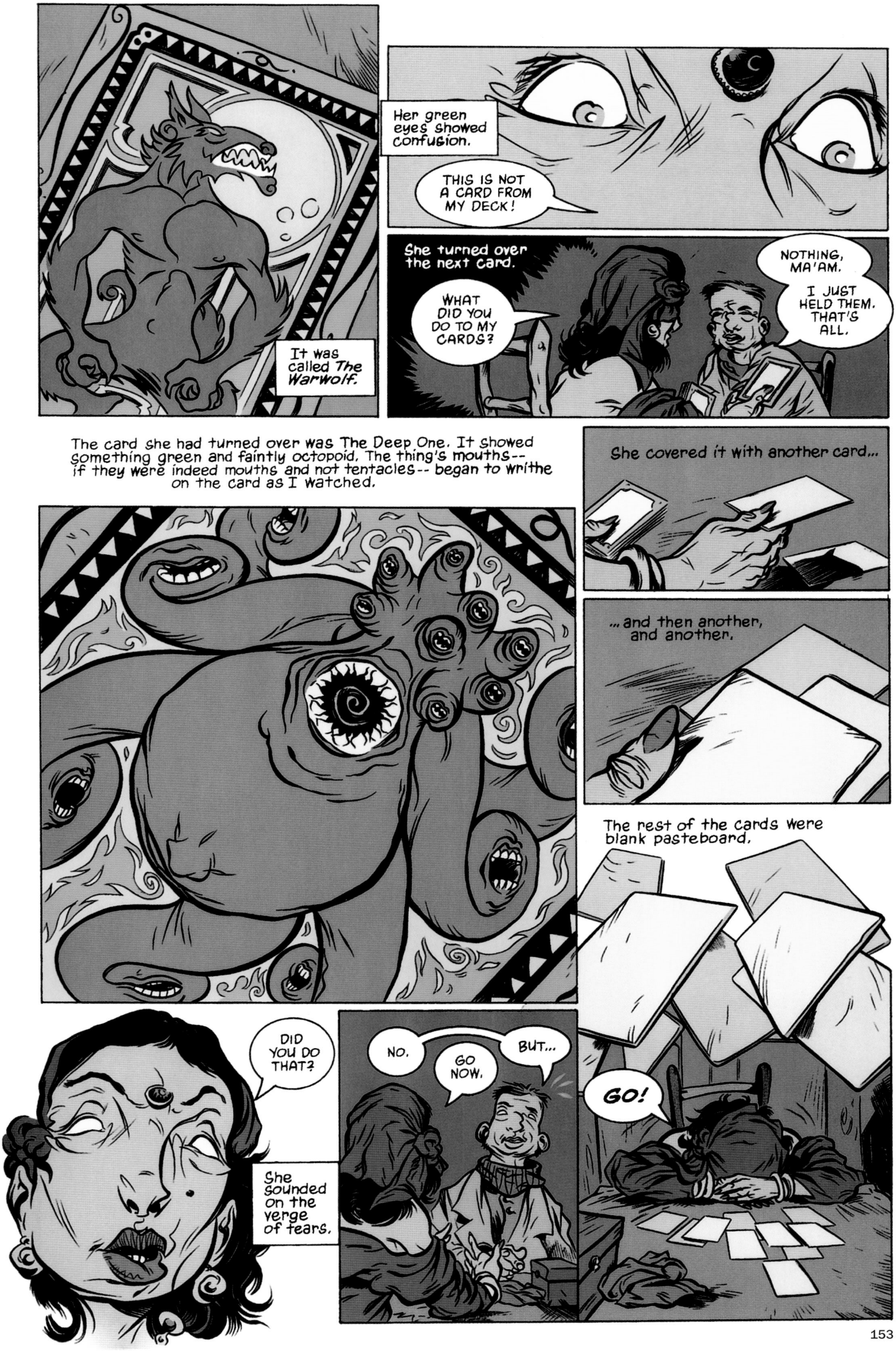
It was called *The Warwolf.*
Her green eyes showed confusion.
THIS IS NOT A CARD FROM MY DECK!
She turned over the next card.
WHAT DID YOU DO TO MY CARDS?
NOTHING, MA'AM.
I JUST HELD THEM. THAT'S ALL.
The card she had turned over was The Deep One. It showed something green and faintly octopoid. The thing's mouths-- if they were indeed mouths and not tentacles-- began to writhe on the card as I watched.
She covered it with another card...
...and then another, and another.
The rest of the cards were blank pasteboard.
DID YOU DO THAT?
She sounded on the verge of tears.
NO.
BUT...
GO NOW.
GO!

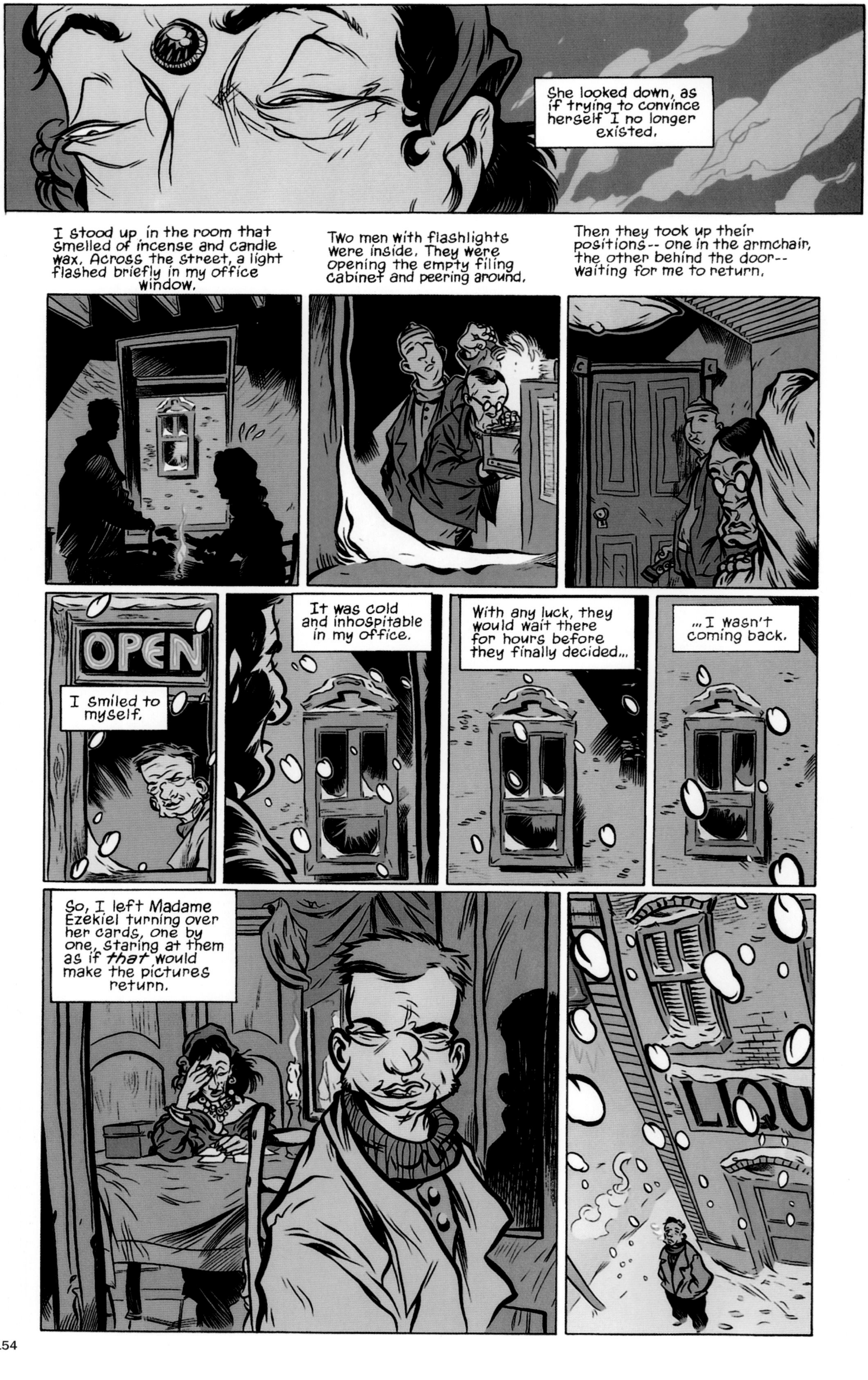
She looked down, as if trying to convince herself I no longer existed.
I stood up in the room that smelled of incense and candle wax. Across the street, a light flashed briefly in my office window.
Two men with flashlights were inside. They were opening the empty filing cabinet and peering around.
Then they took up their positions-- one in the armchair, the other behind the door-- waiting for me to return.
OPEN
I smiled to myself.
It was cold and inhospitable in my office.
With any luck, they would wait there for hours before they finally decided...
...I wasn't coming back.
So, I left Madame Ezekiel turning over her cards, one by one, staring at them as if *that* would make the pictures return.
LIQU

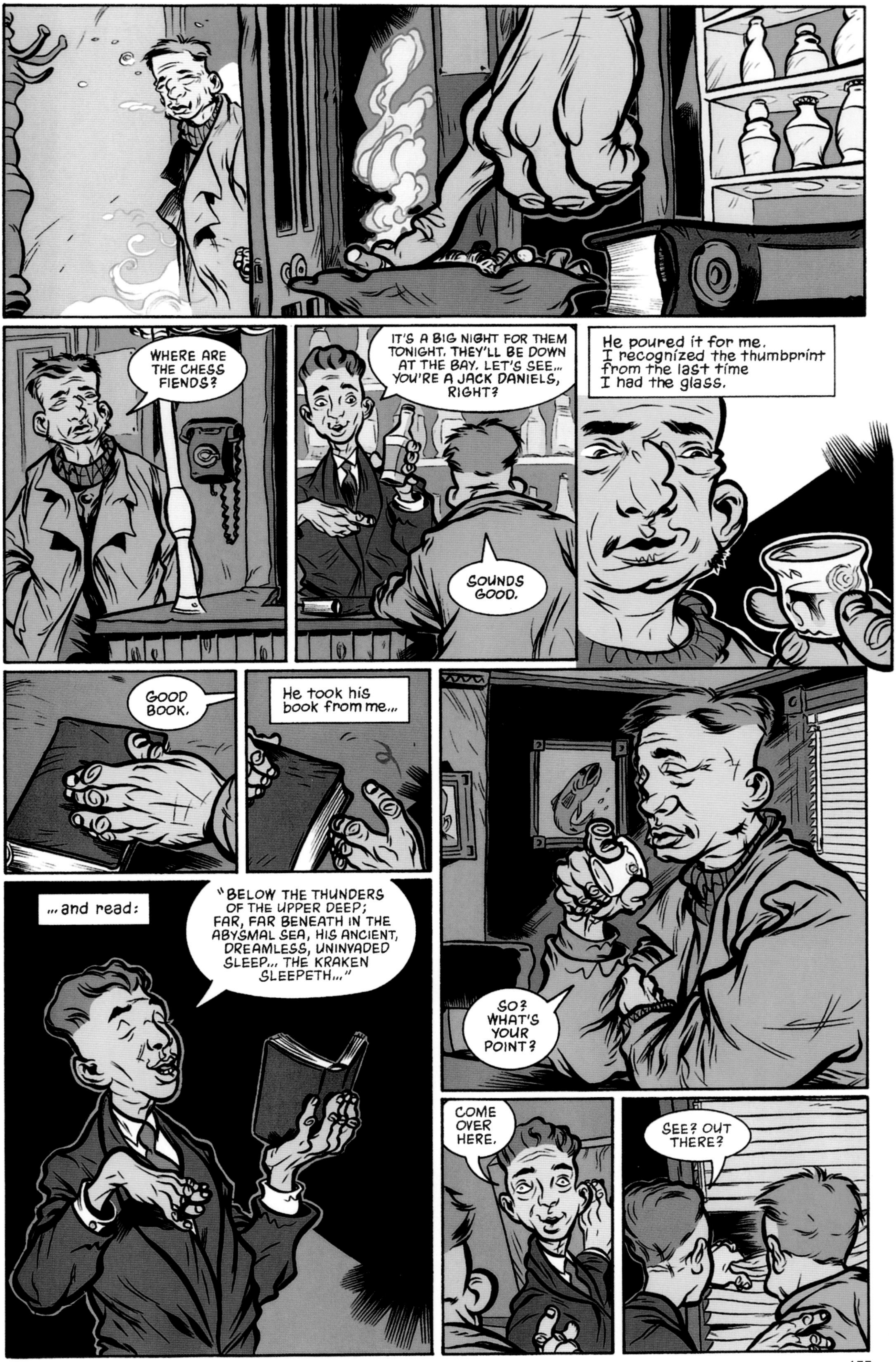
WHERE ARE THE CHESS FIENDS?
IT'S A BIG NIGHT FOR THEM TONIGHT. THEY'LL BE DOWN AT THE BAY. LET'S SEE... YOU'RE A JACK DANIELS, RIGHT?
SOUNDS GOOD.
He poured it for me. I recognized the thumbprint from the last time I had the glass.
GOOD BOOK.
He took his book from me...
...and read:
"BELOW THE THUNDERS OF THE UPPER DEEP; FAR, FAR BENEATH IN THE ABYSMAL SEA, HIS ANCIENT, DREAMLESS, UNINVADED SLEEP... THE KRAKEN SLEEPETH..."
SO? WHAT'S YOUR POINT?
COME OVER HERE.
SEE? OUT THERE?

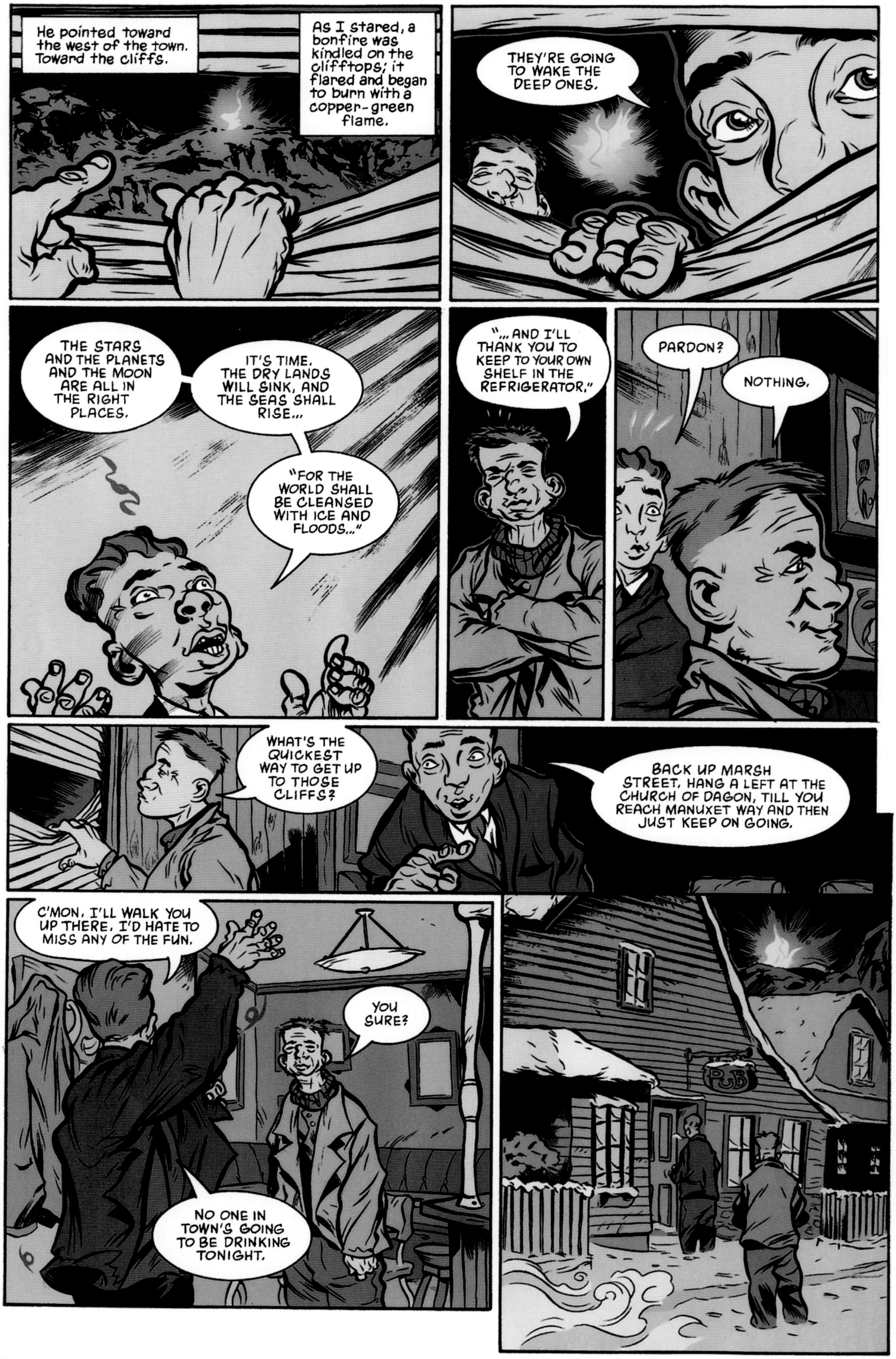
He pointed toward the west of the town. Toward the cliffs.
As I stared, a bonfire was kindled on the clifftops; it flared and began to burn with a copper-green flame.
THEY'RE GOING TO WAKE THE DEEP ONES.
THE STARS AND THE PLANETS AND THE MOON ARE ALL IN THE RIGHT PLACES.
IT'S TIME. THE DRY LANDS WILL SINK, AND THE SEAS SHALL RISE...
"FOR THE WORLD SHALL BE CLEANSED WITH ICE AND FLOODS..."
"...AND I'LL THANK YOU TO KEEP TO YOUR OWN SHELF IN THE REFRIGERATOR."
PARDON?
NOTHING.
WHAT'S THE QUICKEST WAY TO GET UP TO THOSE CLIFFS?
BACK UP MARSH STREET. HANG A LEFT AT THE CHURCH OF DAGON, TILL YOU REACH MANUXET WAY AND THEN JUST KEEP ON GOING.
C'MON. I'LL WALK YOU UP THERE. I'D HATE TO MISS ANY OF THE FUN.
YOU SURE?
NO ONE IN TOWN'S GOING TO BE DRINKING TONIGHT.
PUB

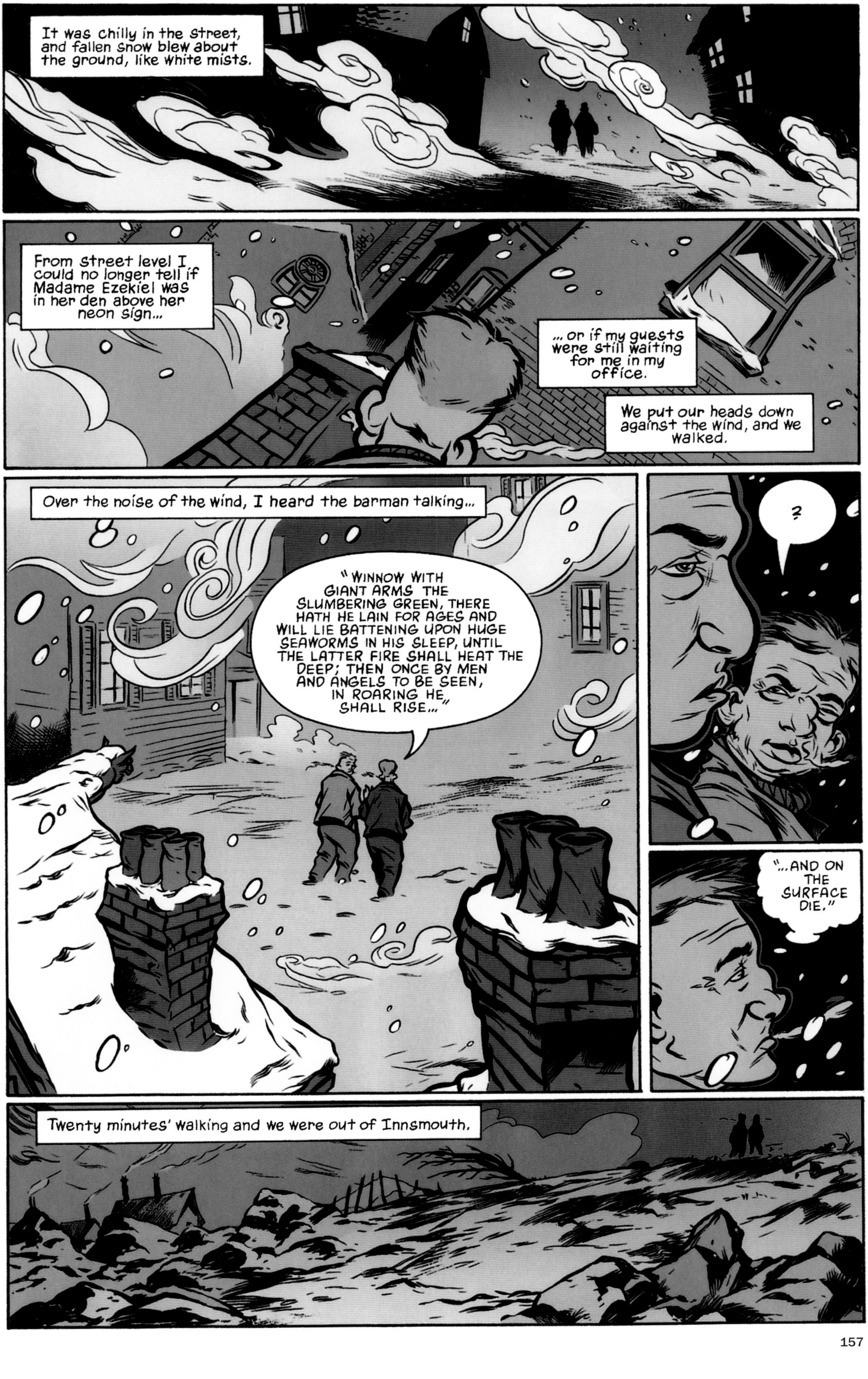

It was chilly in the street, and fallen snow blew about the ground, like white mists.
From street level I could no longer tell if Madame Ezekiel was in her den above her neon sign...
...or if my guests were still waiting for me in my office.
We put our heads down against the wind, and we walked.
Over the noise of the wind, I heard the barman talking...
"WINNOW WITH GIANT ARMS THE SLUMBERING GREEN, THERE HATH HE LAIN FOR AGES AND WILL LIE BATTENING UPON HUGE SEAWORMS IN HIS SLEEP, UNTIL THE LATTER FIRE SHALL HEAT THE DEEP; THEN ONCE BY MEN AND ANGELS TO BE SEEN, IN ROARING HE SHALL RISE..."
?
"...AND ON THE SURFACE DIE."
Twenty minutes' walking and we were out of Innsmouth.

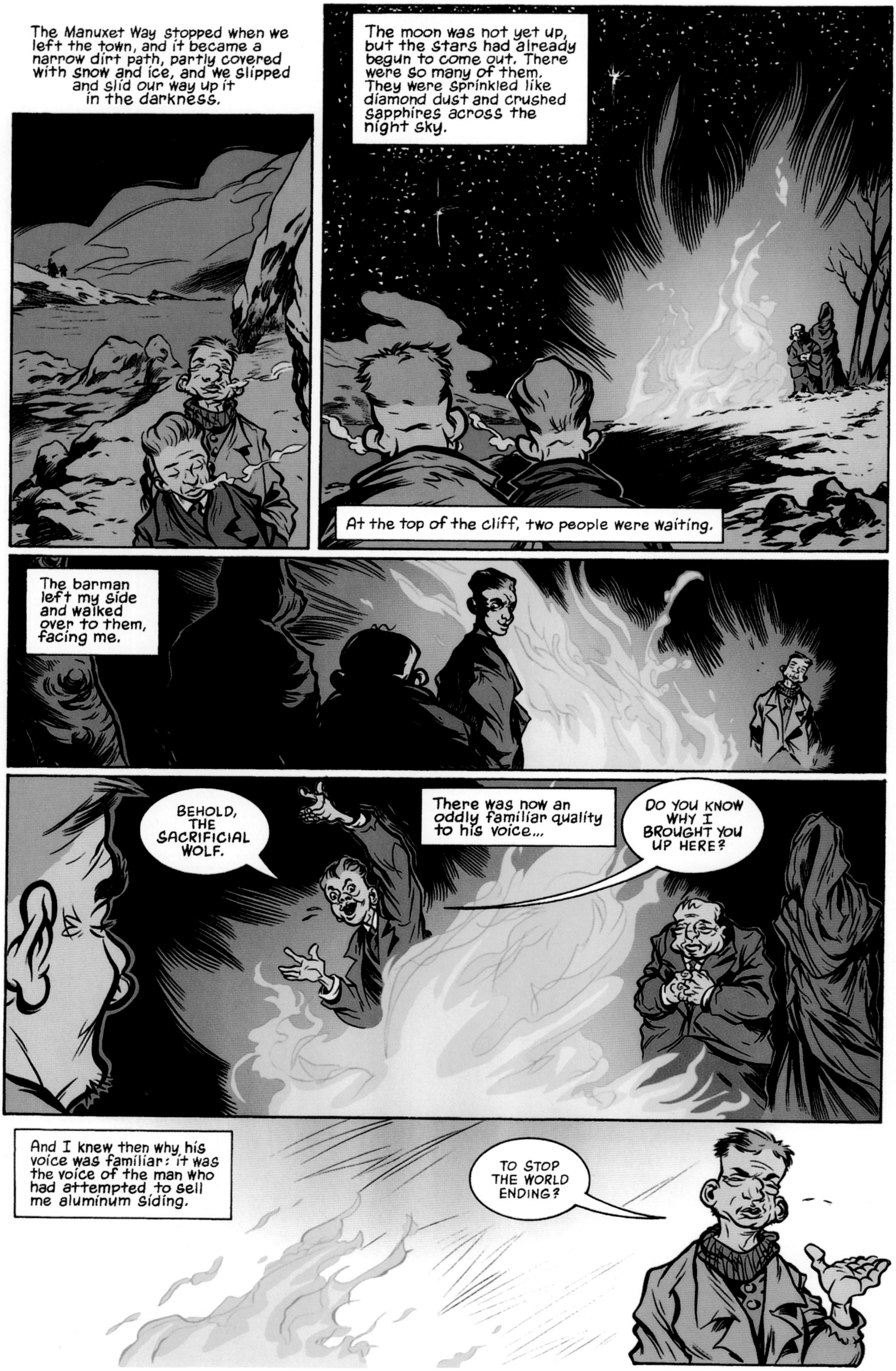
The Manuxet Way stopped when we left the town, and it became a narrow dirt path, partly covered with snow and ice, and we slipped and slid our way up it in the darkness.
The moon was not yet up, but the stars had already begun to come out. There were so many of them. They were sprinkled like diamond dust and crushed sapphires across the night sky.
At the top of the cliff, two people were waiting.
The barman left my side and walked over to them, facing me.
BEHOLD, THE SACRIFICIAL WOLF.
There was now an oddly familiar quality to his voice...
DO YOU KNOW WHY I BROUGHT YOU UP HERE?
And I knew then why his voice was familiar: it was the voice of the man who had attempted to sell me aluminum siding.
TO STOP THE WORLD ENDING?

He laughed at me, then.

The second figure was the fat man I had found asleep in my office.

He murmured in a voice deep enough to rattle walls...

WELL, IF YOU'RE GOING TO GET ESCHATOLOGICAL ABOUT IT...

His eyes were closed. He was fast asleep.

The third figure was shrouded in dark silks and smelled of patchouli oil.

It held a knife.

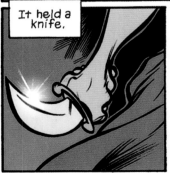

It said nothing.

THIS NIGHT, THE MOON IS THE MOON OF THE DEEP ONES...

THIS NIGHT ARE THE STARS CONFIGURED IN THE SHAPES AND PATTERNS OF THE DARK, OLD TIMES.

THIS NIGHT, IF WE CALL THEM, THEY WILL COME. IF OUR SACRIFICE IS WORTHY. IF OUR CRIES ARE HEARD.

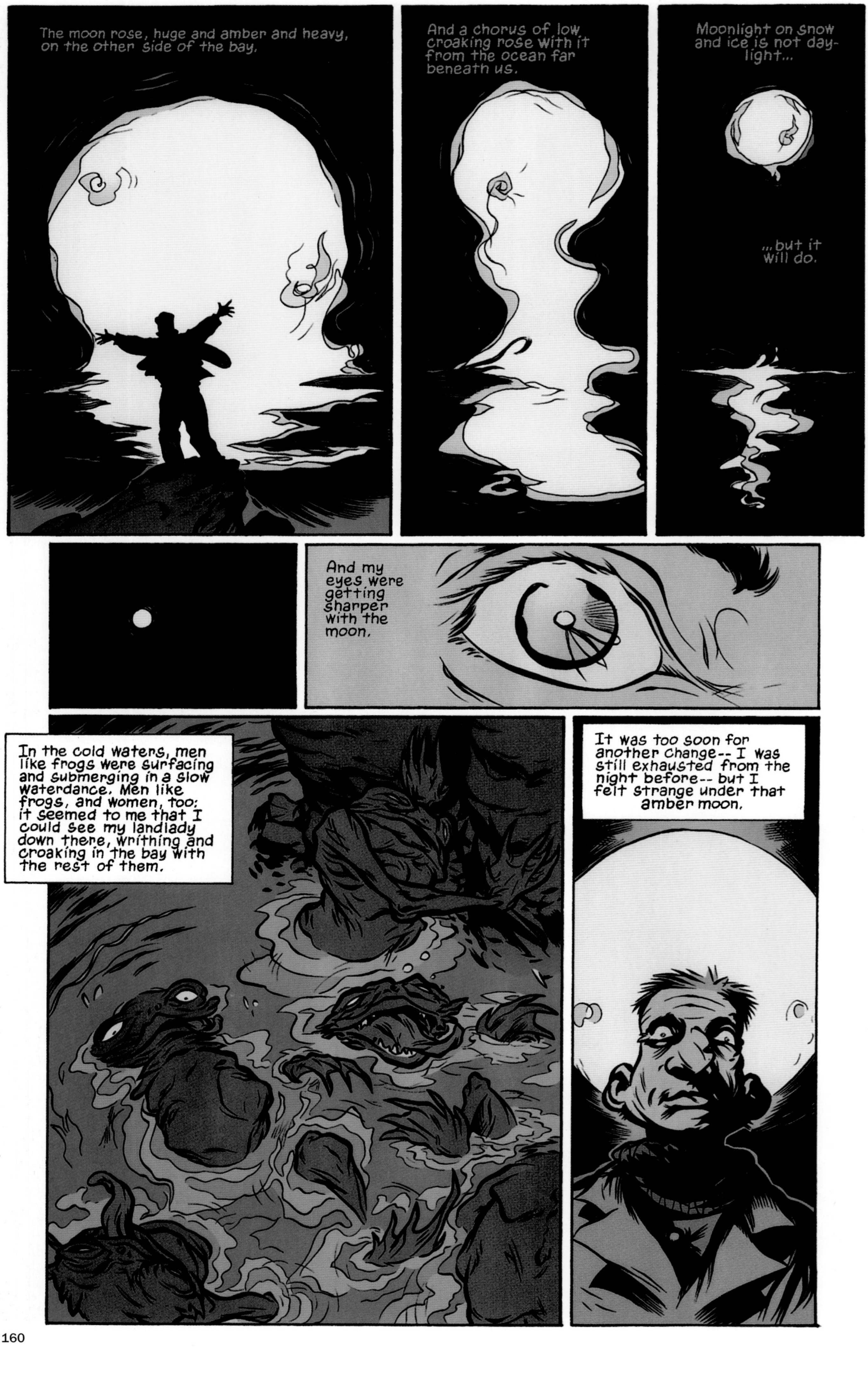

The moon rose, huge and amber and heavy, on the other side of the bay.
And a chorus of low croaking rose with it from the ocean far beneath us.
Moonlight on snow and ice is not daylight...
...but it will do.
And my eyes were getting sharper with the moon.
In the cold waters, men like frogs were surfacing and submerging in a slow waterdance. Men like frogs, and women, too: it seemed to me that I could see my landlady down there, writhing and croaking in the bay with the rest of them.
It was too soon for another change-- I was still exhausted from the night before-- but I felt strange under that amber moon.

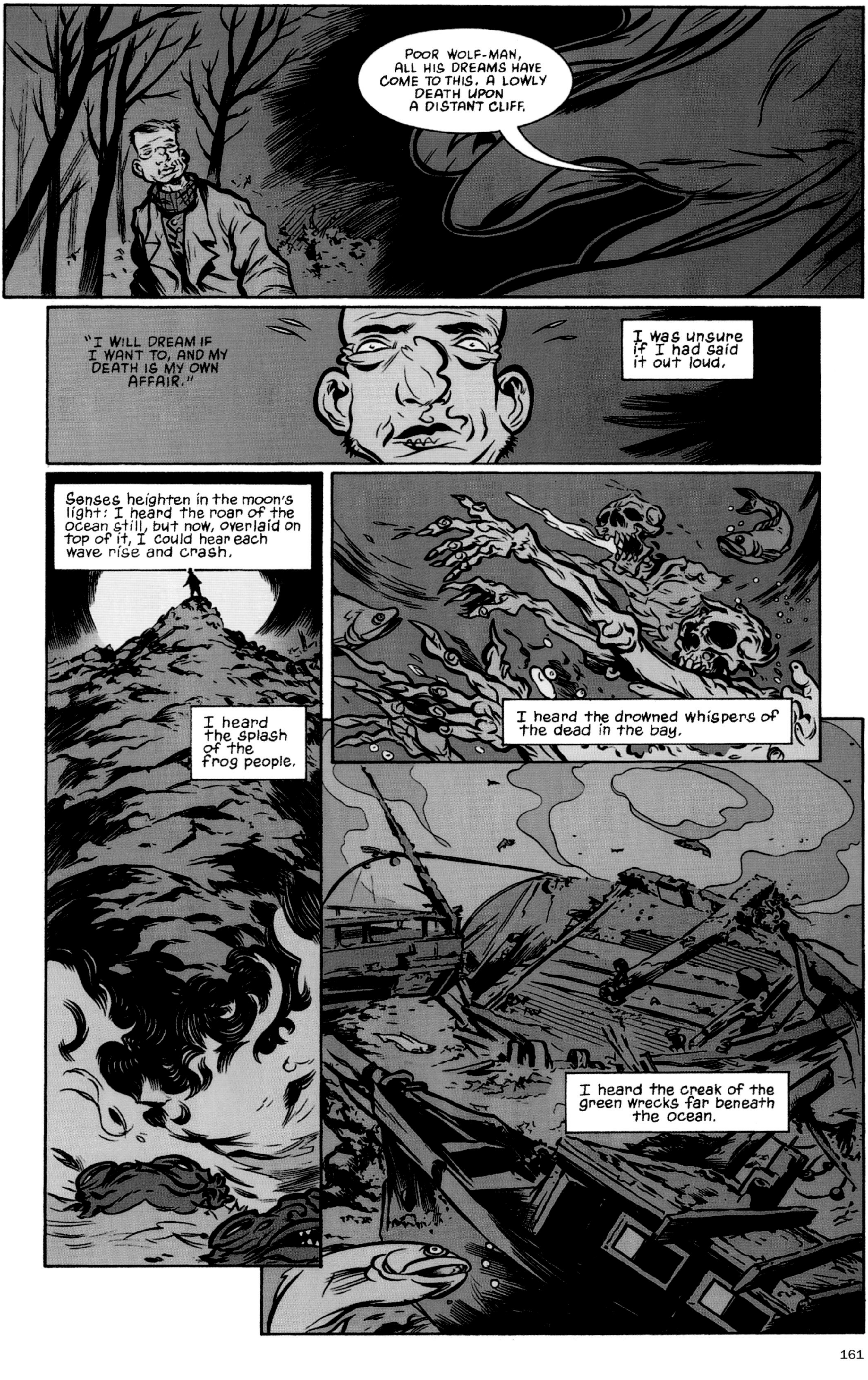
POOR WOLF-MAN, ALL HIS DREAMS HAVE COME TO THIS. A LOWLY DEATH UPON A DISTANT CLIFF.
"I WILL DREAM IF I WANT TO, AND MY DEATH IS MY OWN AFFAIR."
I was unsure if I had said it out loud.
Senses heighten in the moon's light: I heard the roar of the ocean still, but now, overlaid on top of it, I could hear each wave rise and crash.
I heard the drowned whispers of the dead in the bay.
I heard the splash of the frog people.
I heard the creak of the green wrecks far beneath the ocean.

Smell improves, too.

The aluminum siding man was human...

...while the fat man had other blood in him.

And the figure in the silks...

...I had smelled her perfume when I wore a man's shape. Now I could smell something else, less heady, beneath it. A smell of *decay*, of putrefying meat and rotten flesh.

The silk fluttered. She was moving toward me.

She held the knife.

MADAME EZEKIEL?

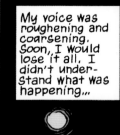

My voice was roughening and coarsening. Soon, I would lose it all. I didn't understand what was happening...

But the moon was rising higher and higher, losing its amber color and filling my mind with its pale light.

"MADAME EZEKIEL?"

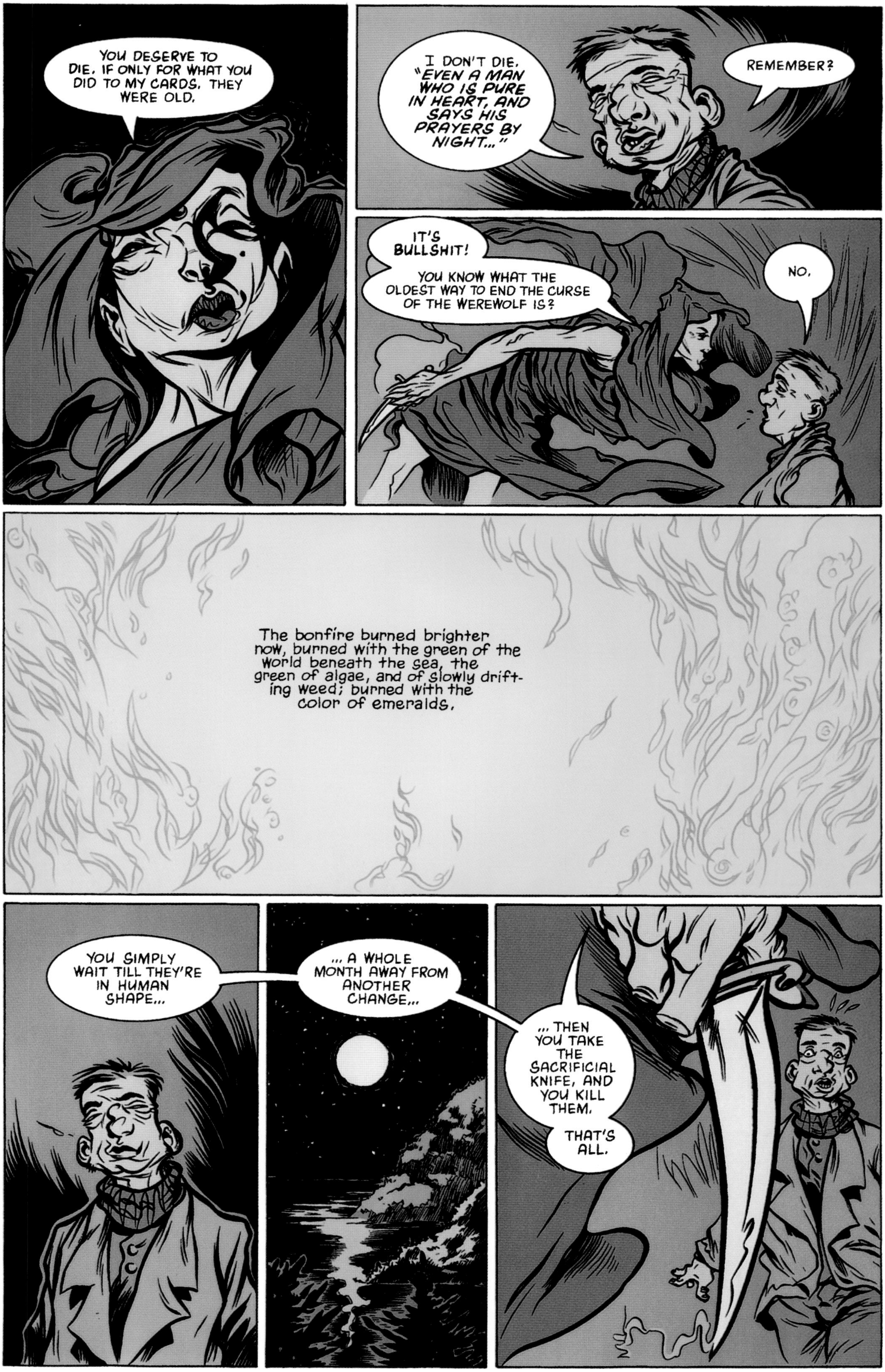

YOU DESERVE TO DIE. IF ONLY FOR WHAT YOU DID TO MY CARDS. THEY WERE OLD.
I DON'T DIE. "EVEN A MAN WHO IS PURE IN HEART, AND SAYS HIS PRAYERS BY NIGHT..."
REMEMBER?
IT'S BULLSHIT!
YOU KNOW WHAT THE OLDEST WAY TO END THE CURSE OF THE WEREWOLF IS?
NO.
The bonfire burned brighter now, burned with the green of the world beneath the sea, the green of algae, and of slowly drifting weed; burned with the color of emeralds.
YOU SIMPLY WAIT TILL THEY'RE IN HUMAN SHAPE...
...A WHOLE MONTH AWAY FROM ANOTHER CHANGE...
...THEN YOU TAKE THE SACRIFICIAL KNIFE, AND YOU KILL THEM.
THAT'S ALL.

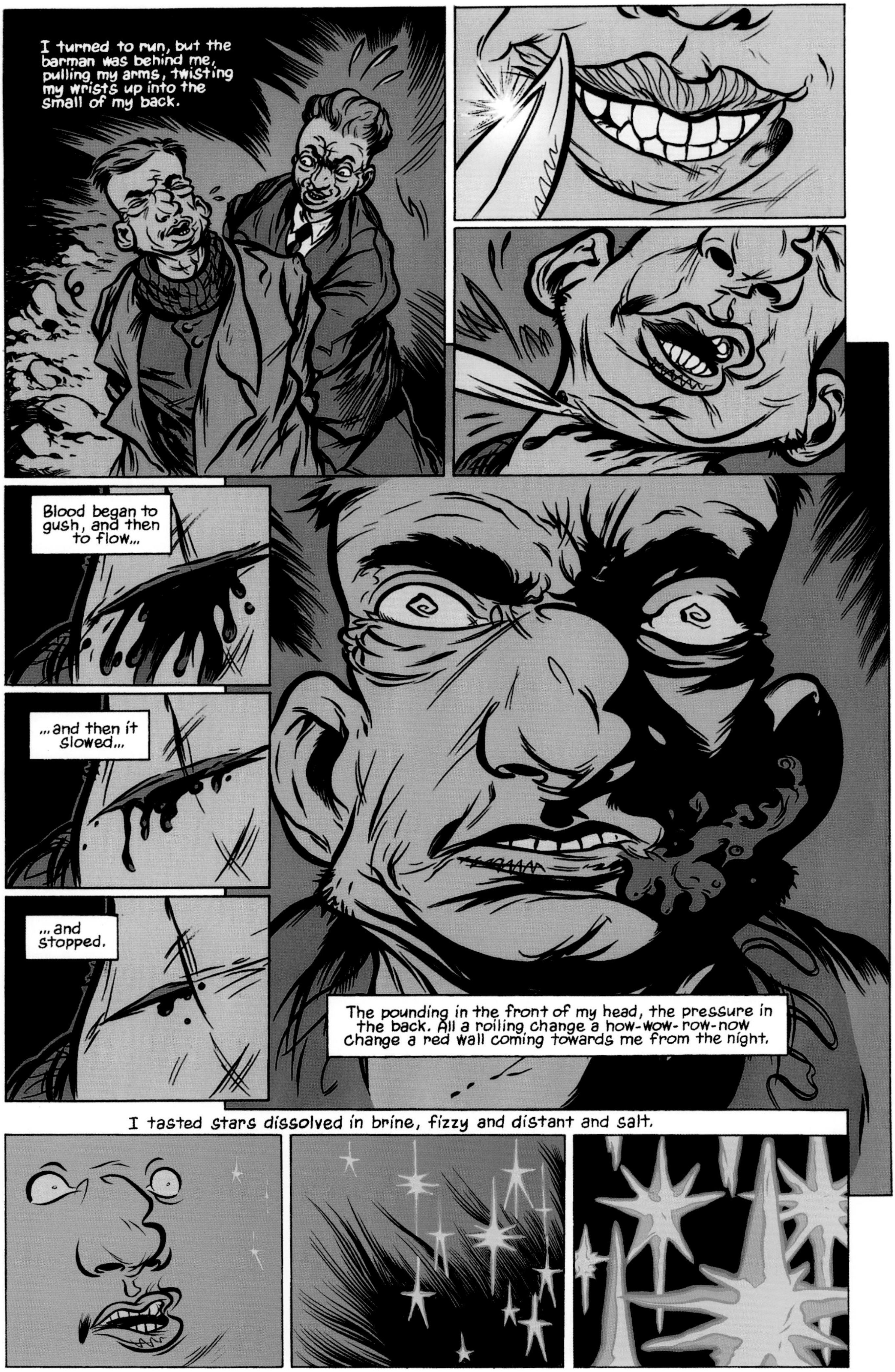

I turned to run, but the barman was behind me, pulling my arms, twisting my wrists up into the small of my back.
Blood began to gush, and then to flow...
...and then it slowed...
...and stopped.
The pounding in the front of my head, the pressure in the back. All a roiling change a how-wow-row-now change a red wall coming towards me from the night.
I tasted stars dissolved in brine, fizzy and distant and salt.

My fingers
prickled
with pins...

...and my skin was lashed with tongues of flame.

My eyes were topaz...

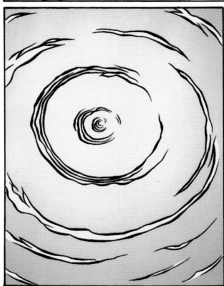

I could
taste the
night.

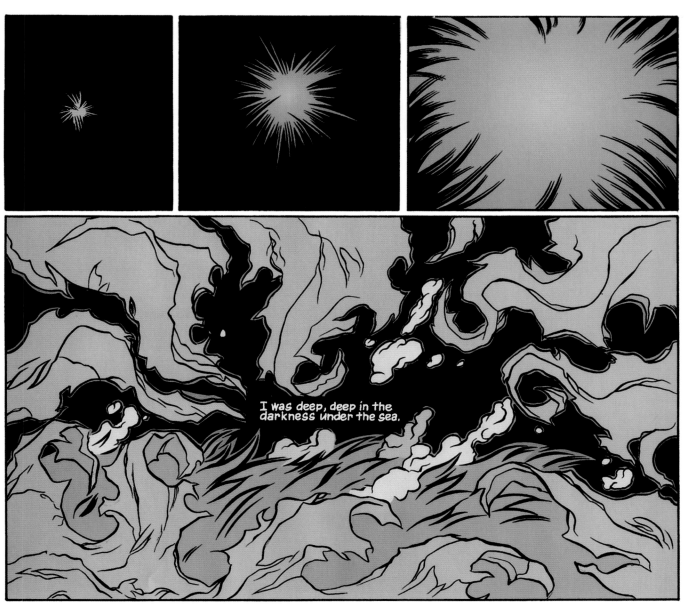

I was deep, deep in the darkness under the sea.

I was standing on all fours on a slimy rock floor, at the entrance of some kind of citadel, built of enormous, rough-hewn stones.

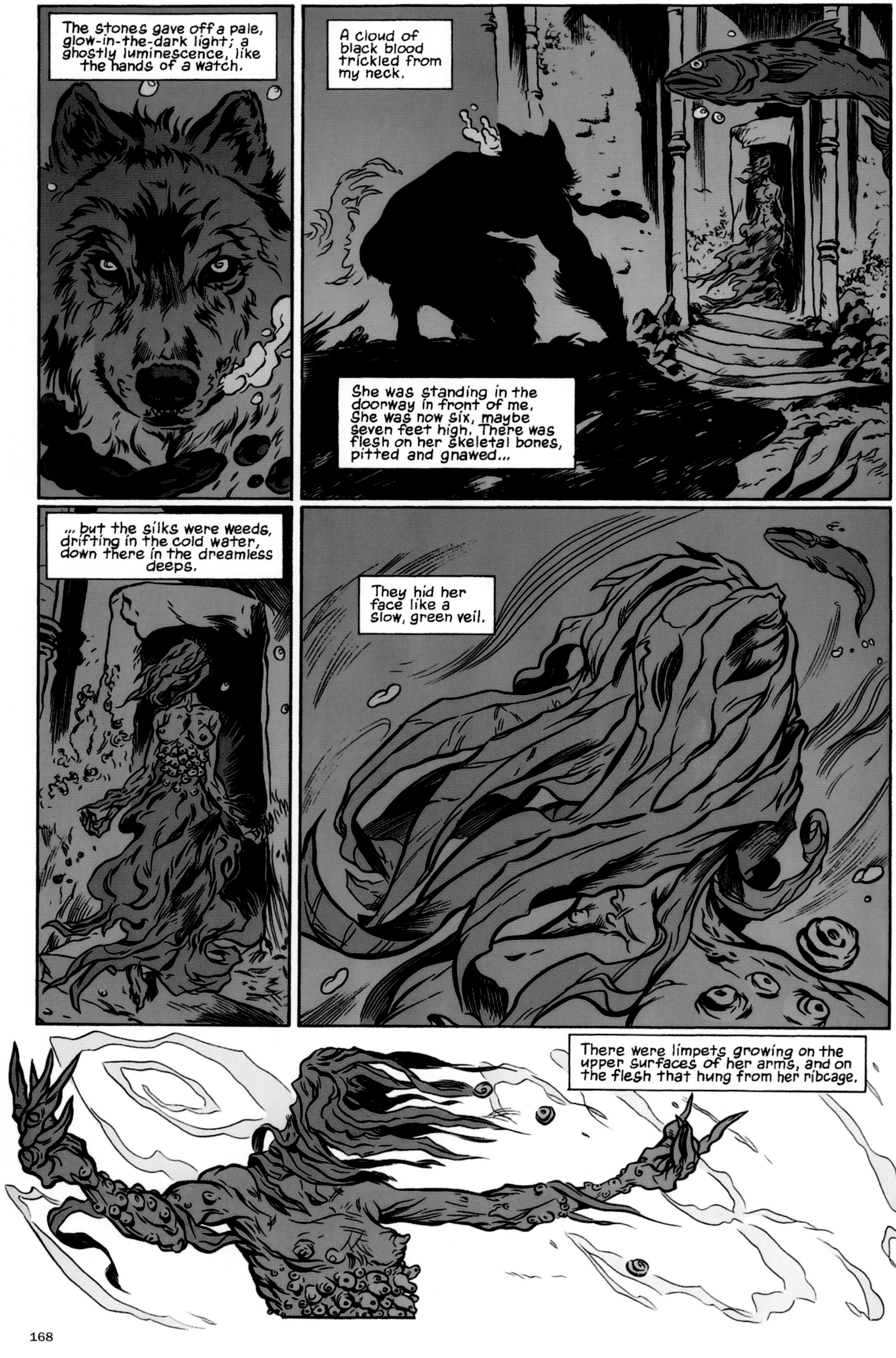
The stones gave off a pale, glow-in-the-dark light; a ghostly luminescence, like the hands of a watch.
A cloud of black blood trickled from my neck.
She was standing in the doorway in front of me. She was now six, maybe seven feet high. There was flesh on her skeletal bones, pitted and gnawed...
... but the silks were weeds, drifting in the cold water, down there in the dreamless deeps.
They hid her face like a slow, green veil.
There were limpets growing on the upper surfaces of her arms, and on the flesh that hung from her ribcage.

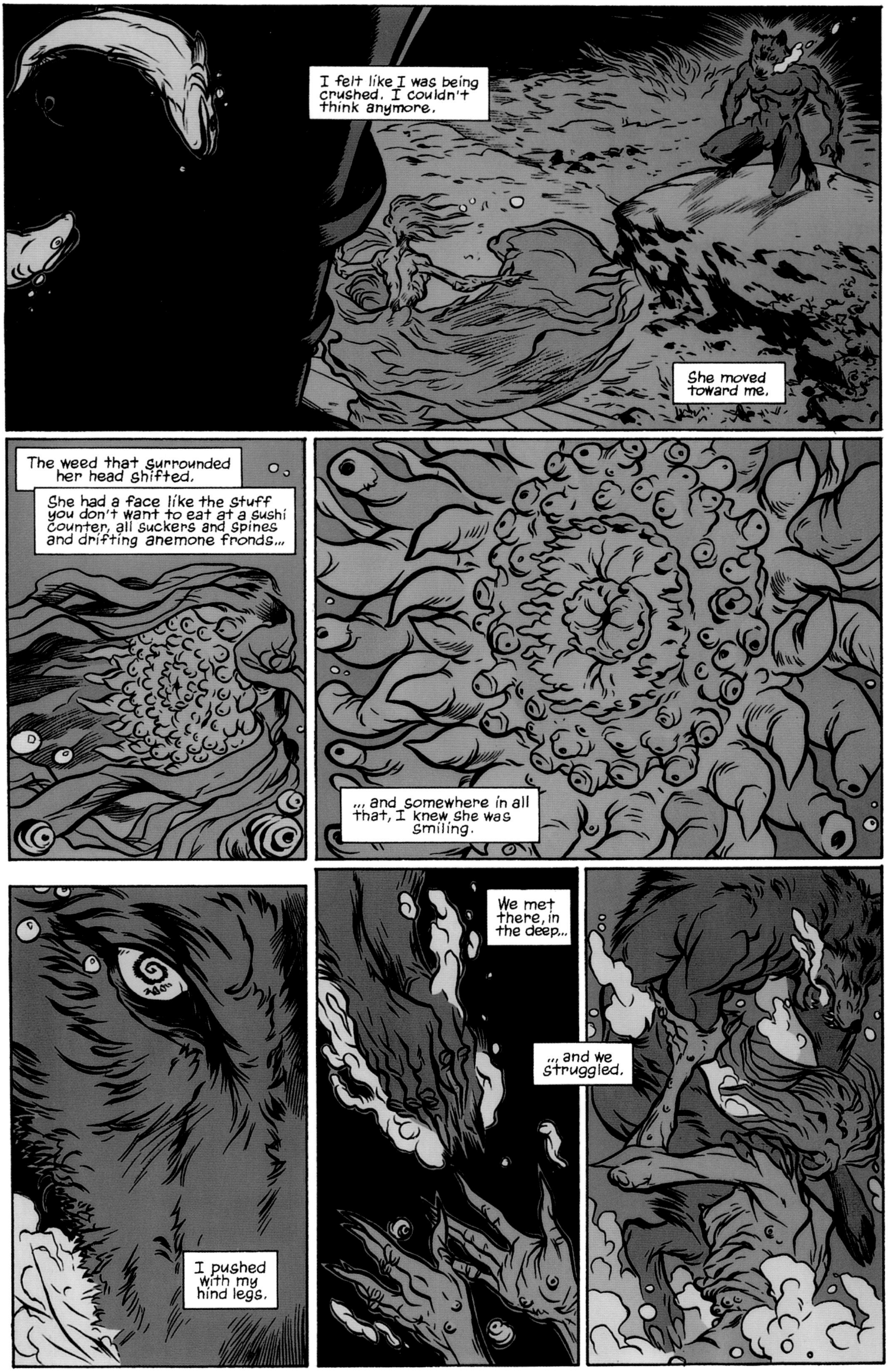
I felt like I was being crushed. I couldn't think anymore.
She moved toward me.
The weed that surrounded her head shifted.
She had a face like the stuff you don't want to eat at a sushi counter, all suckers and spines and drifting anemone fronds...
... and somewhere in all that, I knew she was smiling.
I pushed with my hind legs.
We met there, in the deep...
... and we struggled.

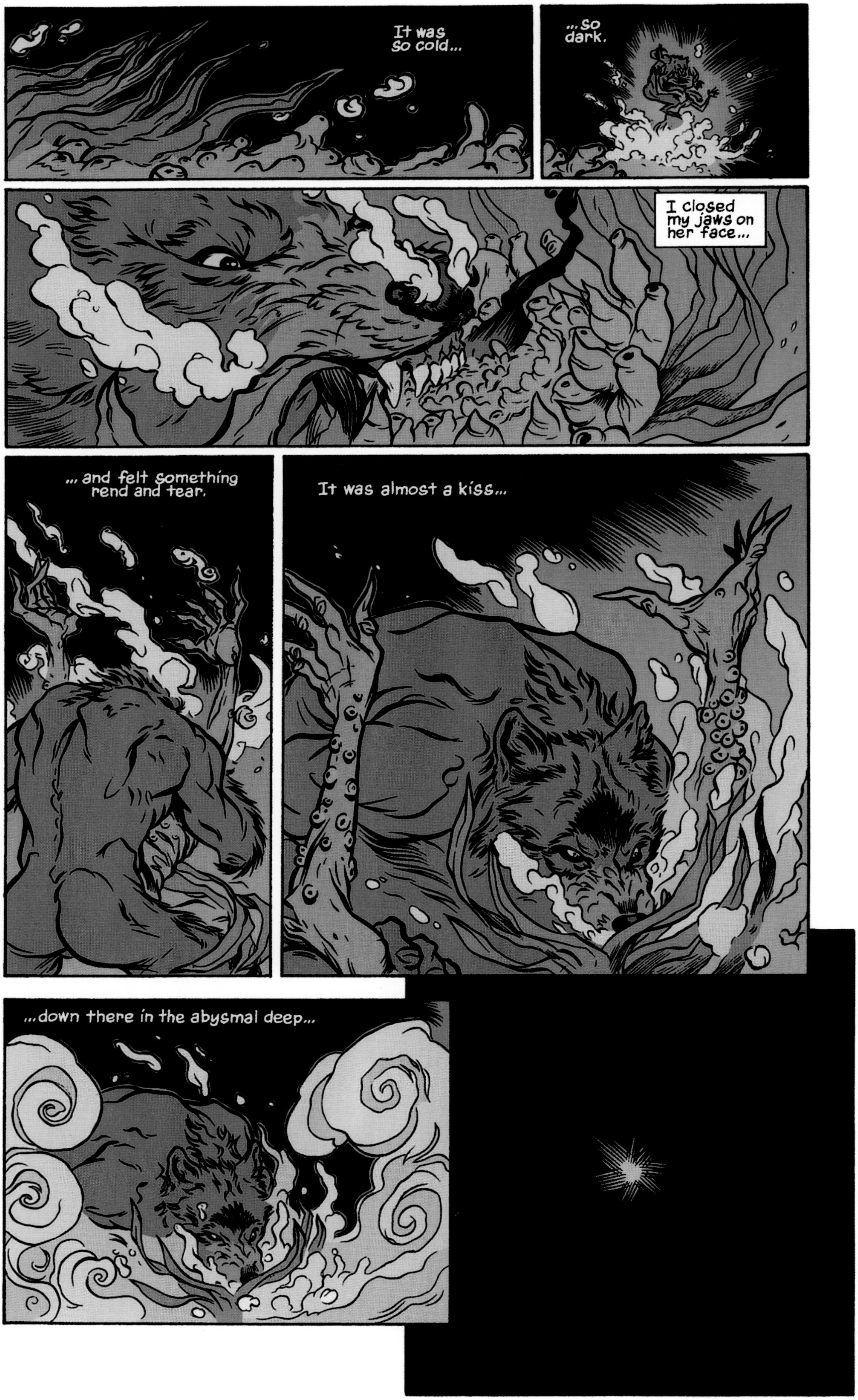
It was so cold...
...so dark.
I closed my jaws on her face...
...and felt something rend and tear.
It was almost a kiss...
...down there in the abysmal deep...

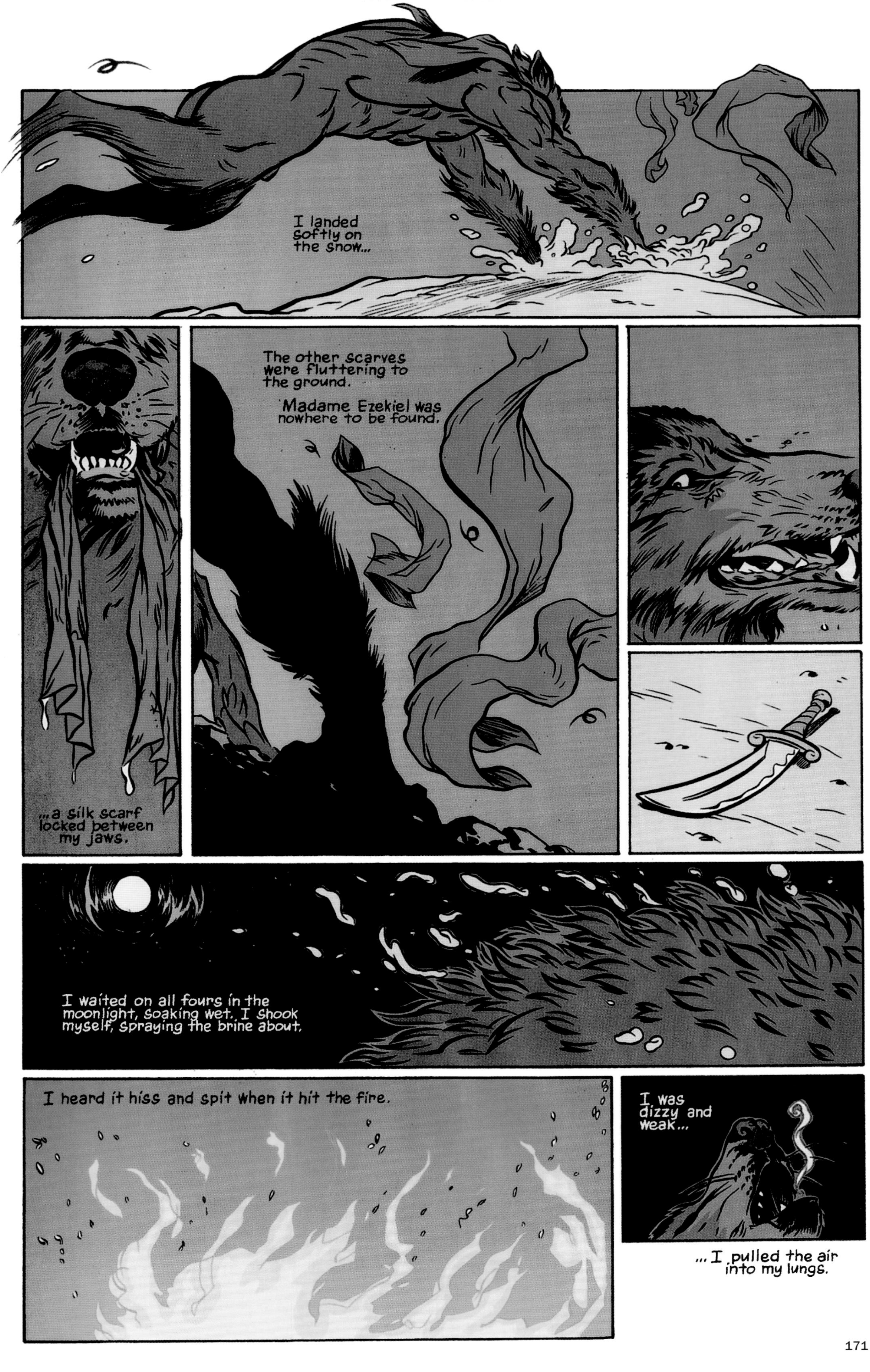
I landed softly on the snow...
...a silk scarf locked between my jaws.
The other scarves were fluttering to the ground.
Madame Ezekiel was nowhere to be found.
I waited on all fours in the moonlight, soaking wet. I shook myself, spraying the brine about.
I heard it hiss and spit when it hit the fire.
I was dizzy and weak...
...I pulled the air into my lungs.

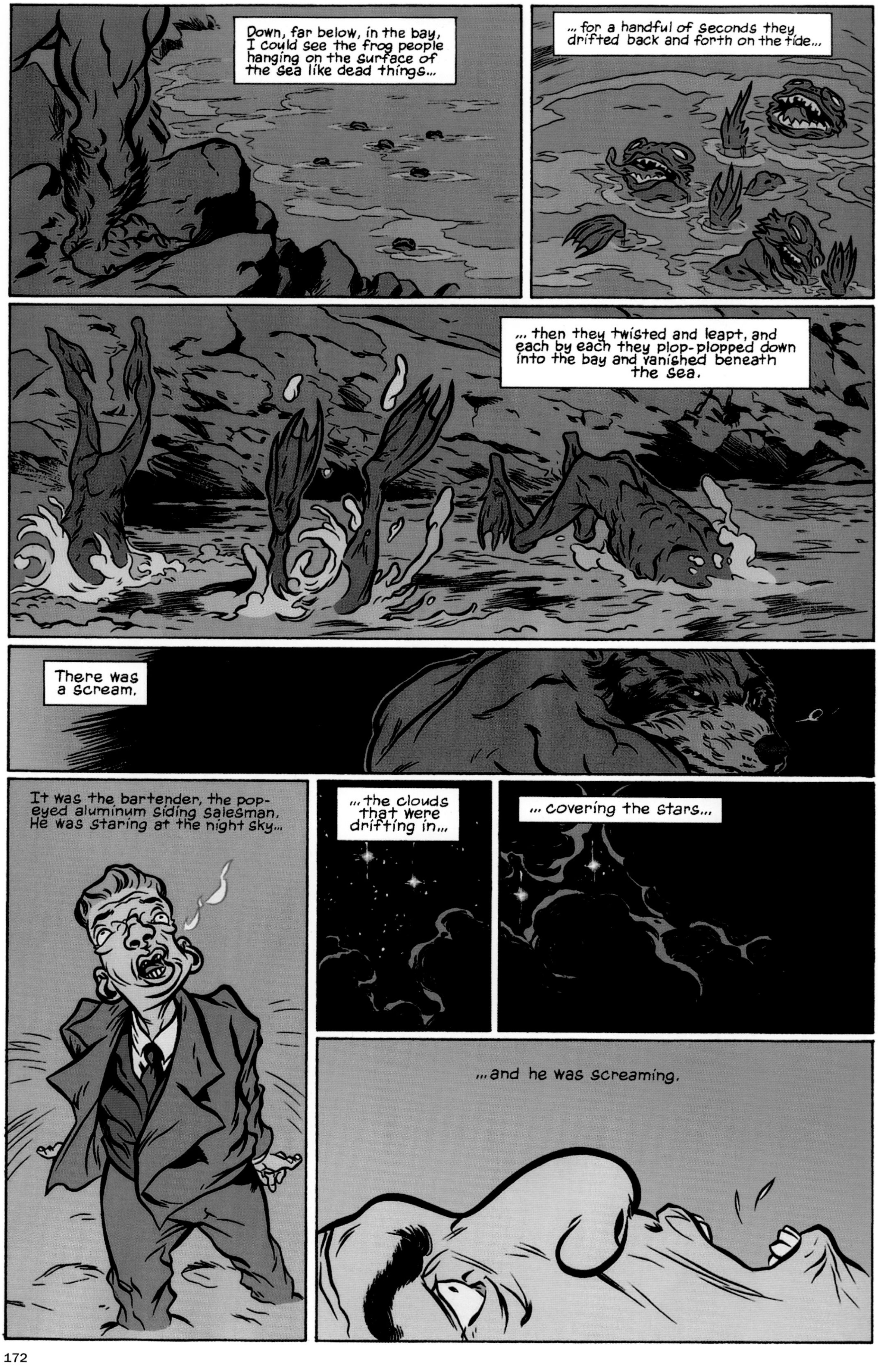
Down, far below, in the bay, I could see the frog people hanging on the surface of the sea like dead things...
... for a handful of seconds they drifted back and forth on the tide...
... then they twisted and leapt, and each by each they plop-plopped down into the bay and vanished beneath the sea.
There was a scream.
It was the bartender, the pop-eyed aluminum siding salesman. He was staring at the night sky...
... the clouds that were drifting in...
... covering the stars...
... and he was screaming.

YOU BASTARD,

WHAT DID YOU DO TO HER?

I would have told him I didn't do anything to her, that she was still on guard far beneath the ocean...

... but I couldn't talk anymore, only growl and whine and howl,

He was crying. He stank of insanity and disappointment.

He raised the knife...

... and ran at me,

I moved to one side,

Some people just can't adjust even to tiny changes, The barman stumbled past me...

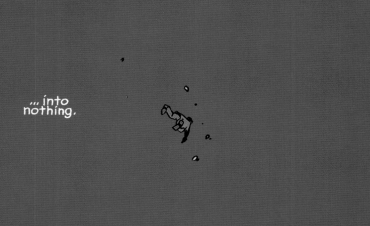

... into nothing.

Armageddon is averted by small actions...

In the moonlight, blood is black, not red, and the marks he left on the cliffside as he fell and bounced and fell were smudges of black and gray.

Then, finally, he lay still on the icy rocks at the base of the cliff...

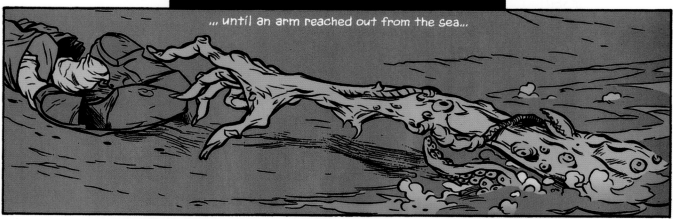

... until an arm reached out from the sea...

... and dragged him, with a slowness that was almost painful to watch...

... under the dark water.

174

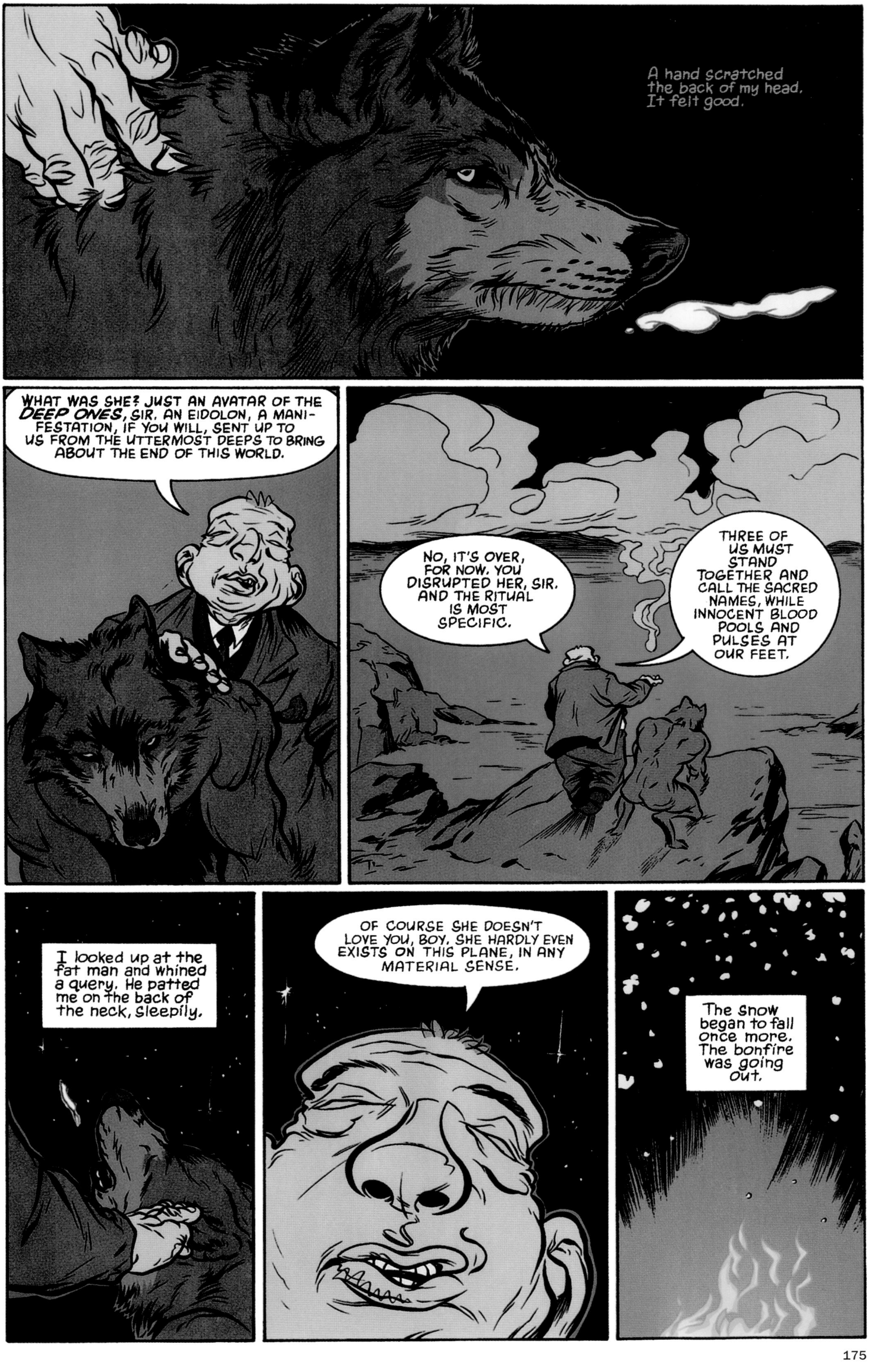
A hand scratched the back of my head. It felt good.
WHAT WAS SHE? JUST AN AVATAR OF THE DEEP ONES, SIR. AN EIDOLON, A MANIFESTATION, IF YOU WILL, SENT UP TO US FROM THE UTTERMOST DEEPS TO BRING ABOUT THE END OF THIS WORLD.
NO, IT'S OVER, FOR NOW. YOU DISRUPTED HER, SIR. AND THE RITUAL IS MOST SPECIFIC.
THREE OF US MUST STAND TOGETHER AND CALL THE SACRED NAMES, WHILE INNOCENT BLOOD POOLS AND PULSES AT OUR FEET.
I looked up at the fat man and whined a query. He patted me on the back of the neck, sleepily.
OF COURSE SHE DOESN'T LOVE YOU, BOY. SHE HARDLY EVEN EXISTS ON THIS PLANE, IN ANY MATERIAL SENSE.
The snow began to fall once more. The bonfire was going out.

I had no further interest in the sea or the clifftop or the fat man. There were deer running in the woods beyond the meadow: I could smell them on the winter night's air.

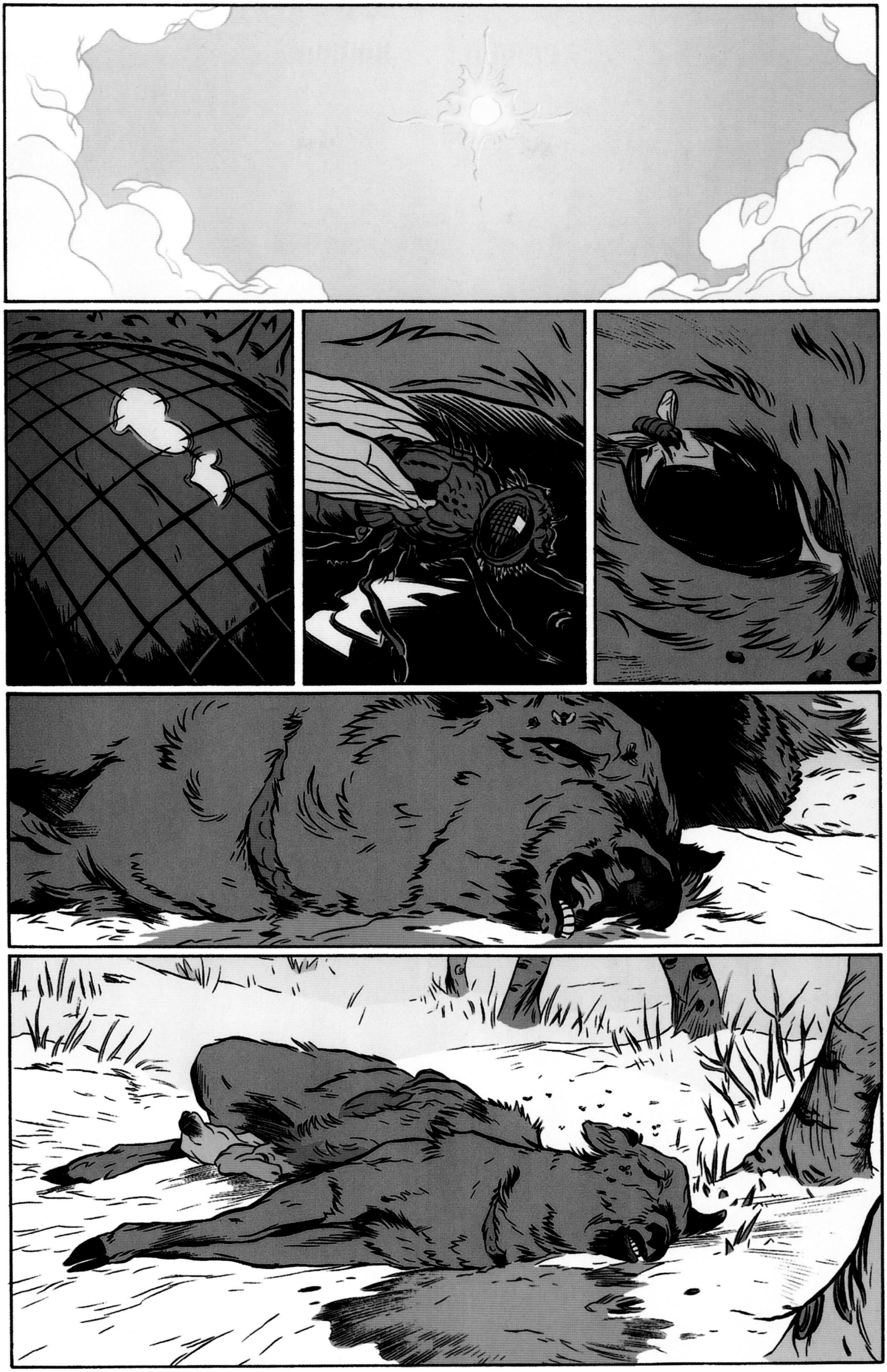

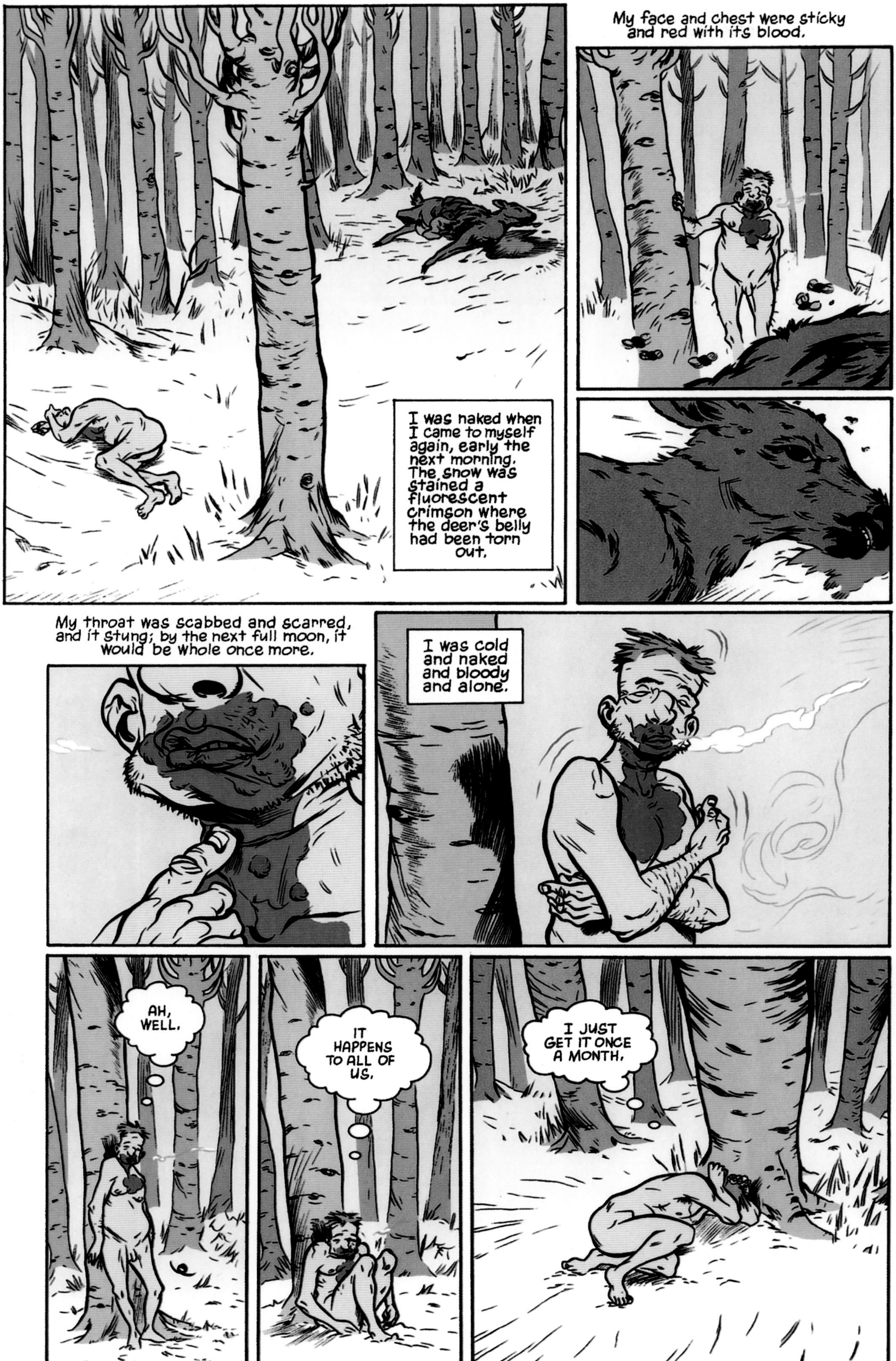

I was naked when I came to myself again, early the next morning. The snow was stained a fluorescent crimson where the deer's belly had been torn out.
My face and chest were sticky and red with its blood.
My throat was scabbed and scarred, and it stung; by the next full moon, it would be whole once more.
I was cold and naked and bloody and alone.
AH, WELL.
IT HAPPENS TO ALL OF US.
I JUST GET IT ONCE A MONTH.

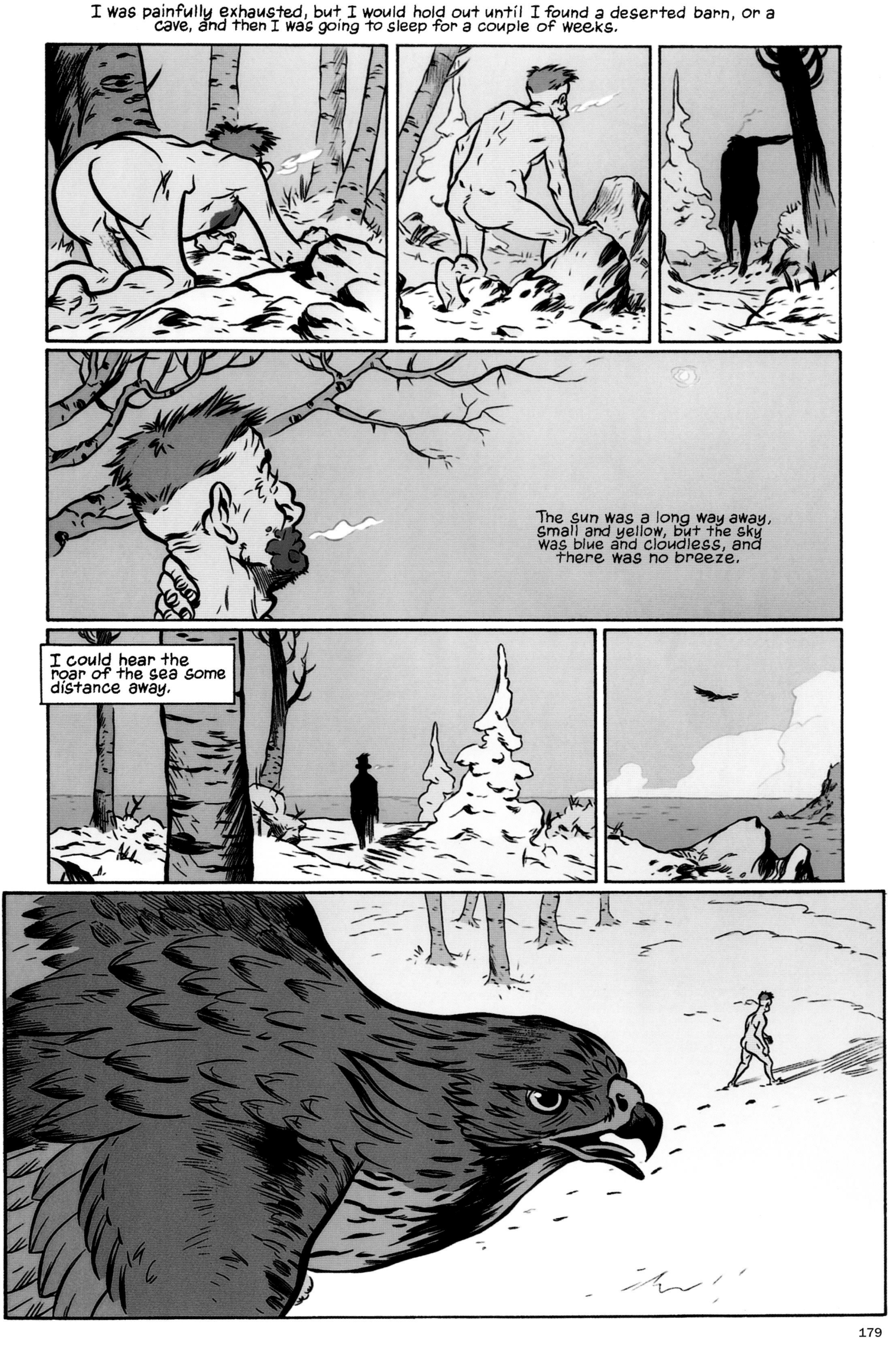
I was painfully exhausted, but I would hold out until I found a deserted barn, or a cave, and then I was going to sleep for a couple of weeks.
The sun was a long way away, small and yellow, but the sky was blue and cloudless, and there was no breeze.
I could hear the roar of the sea some distance away.

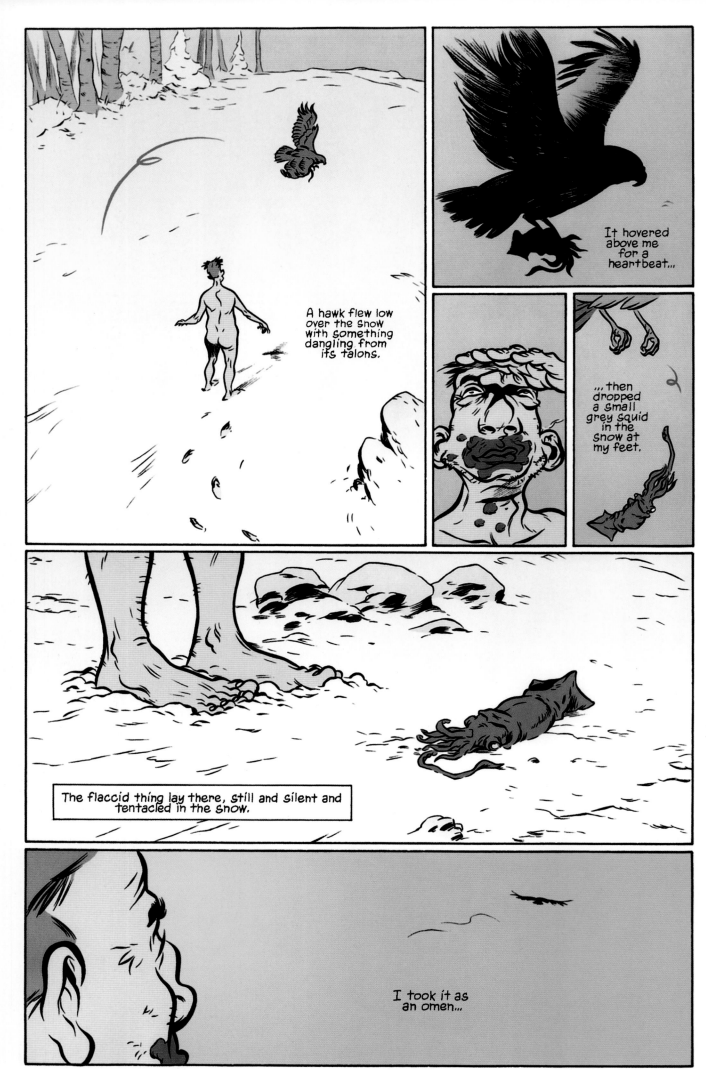

A hawk flew low over the snow with something dangling from its talons.

It hovered above me for a heartbeat...

...then dropped a small grey squid in the snow at my feet.

The flaccid thing lay there, still and silent and tentacled in the snow.

I took it as an omen...

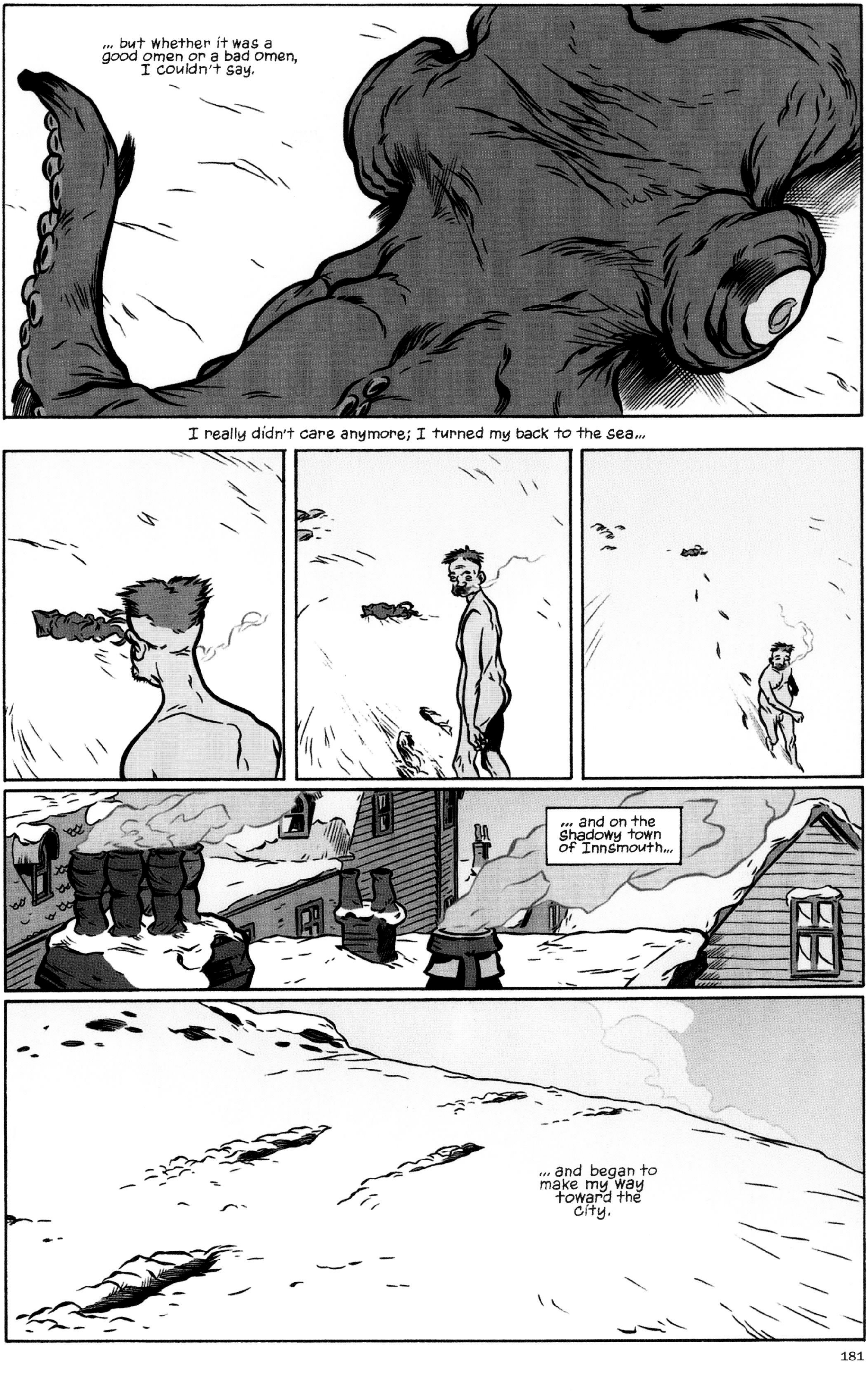
... but whether it was a good omen or a bad omen, I couldn't say.
I really didn't care anymore; I turned my back to the sea...
... and on the shadowy town of Innsmouth...
... and began to make my way toward the city.

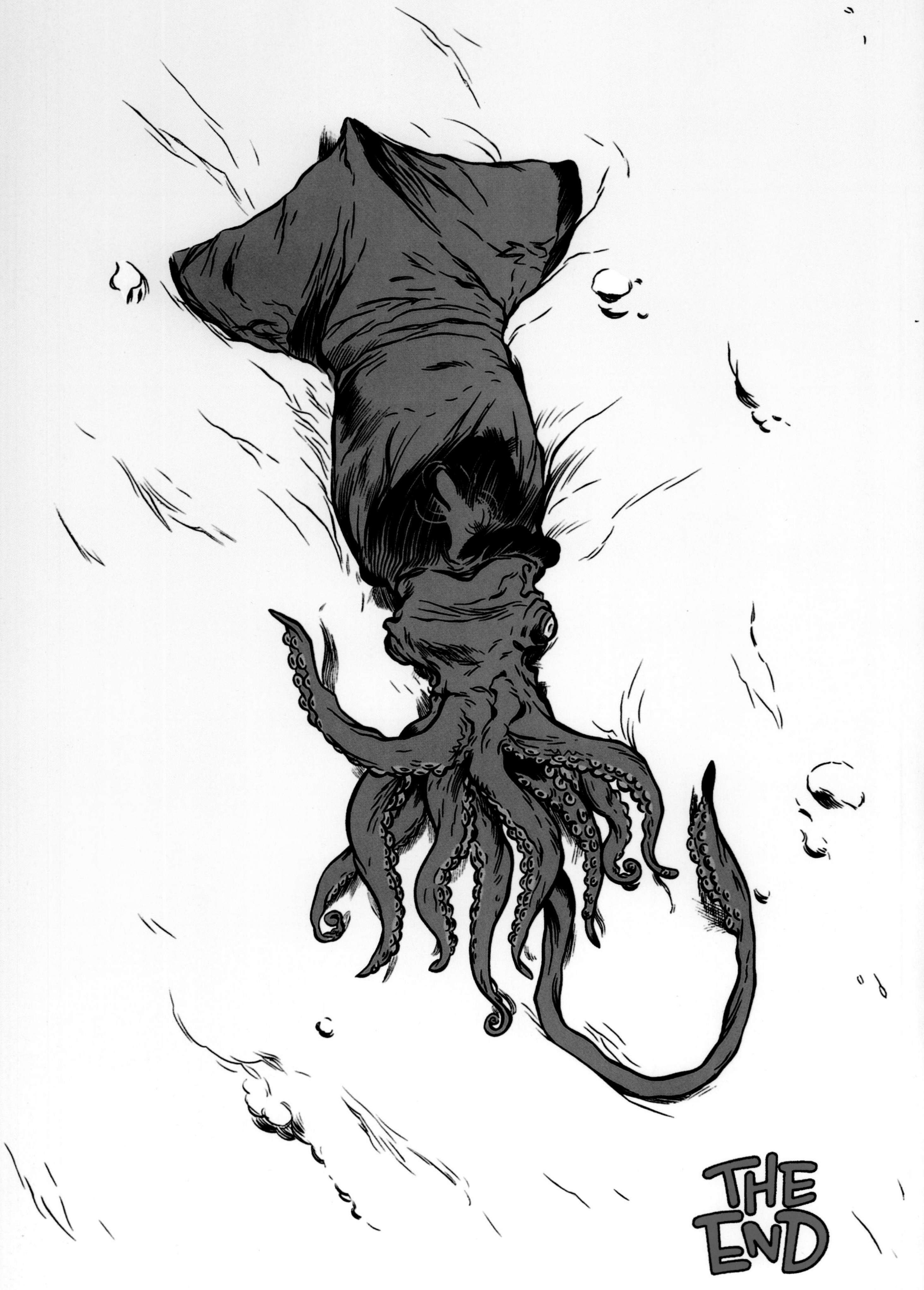
THE END

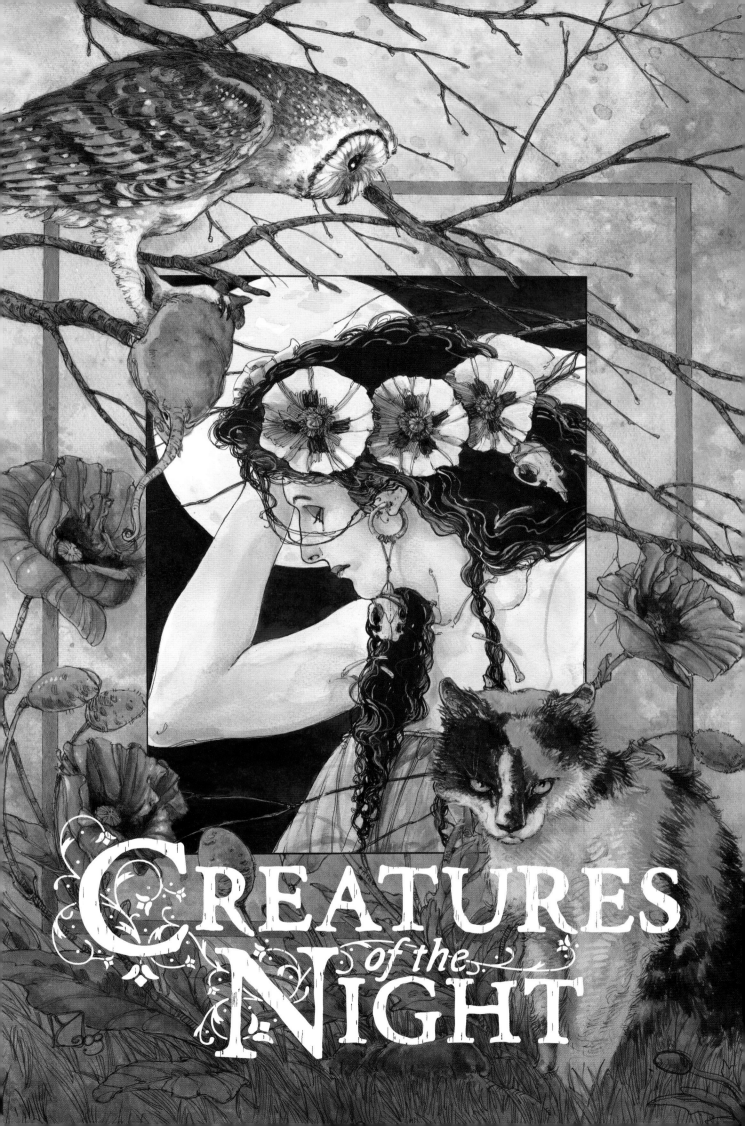

CREATURES of the NIGHT

DEDICATION

FIRST AND FOREMOST, THANKS MUST GO TO NEIL,
AS ALWAYS, FRIEND AND A HALF, AND NOT A
BAD-LOOKING GENT, WRITES A BIT, I'M TOLD.

TO THE THREE GRACES, DIANA, SHELLY, AND RE-
NAE. THEY HAVE ALL, IN ONE WAY OR ANOTHER,
MADE A GREAT JOB AN ABSOLUTE DELIGHT.

TO BWS, WHO'S SAVED ME FROM MYSELF, TWICE.

THIS BOOK IS FOR YOU.

—MICHAEL ZULLI
IN NEW ENGLAND.
IN A TOWER. ON A CLIFF. BY A RIVER.

the PRICE

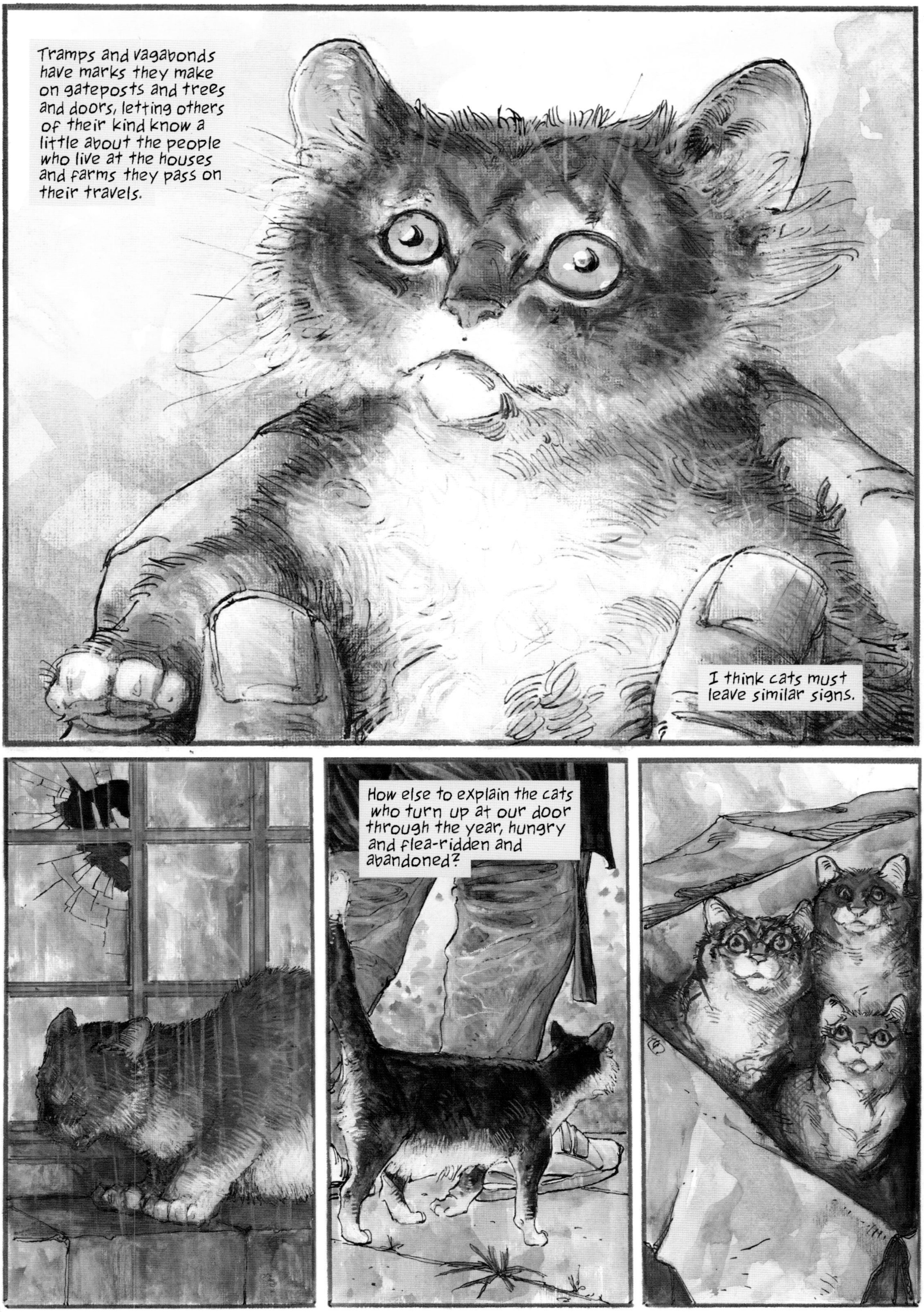
Tramps and vagabonds have marks they make on gateposts and trees and doors, letting others of their kind know a little about the people who live at the houses and farms they pass on their travels.
I think cats must leave similar signs.
How else to explain the cats who turn up at our door through the year, hungry and flea-ridden and abandoned?

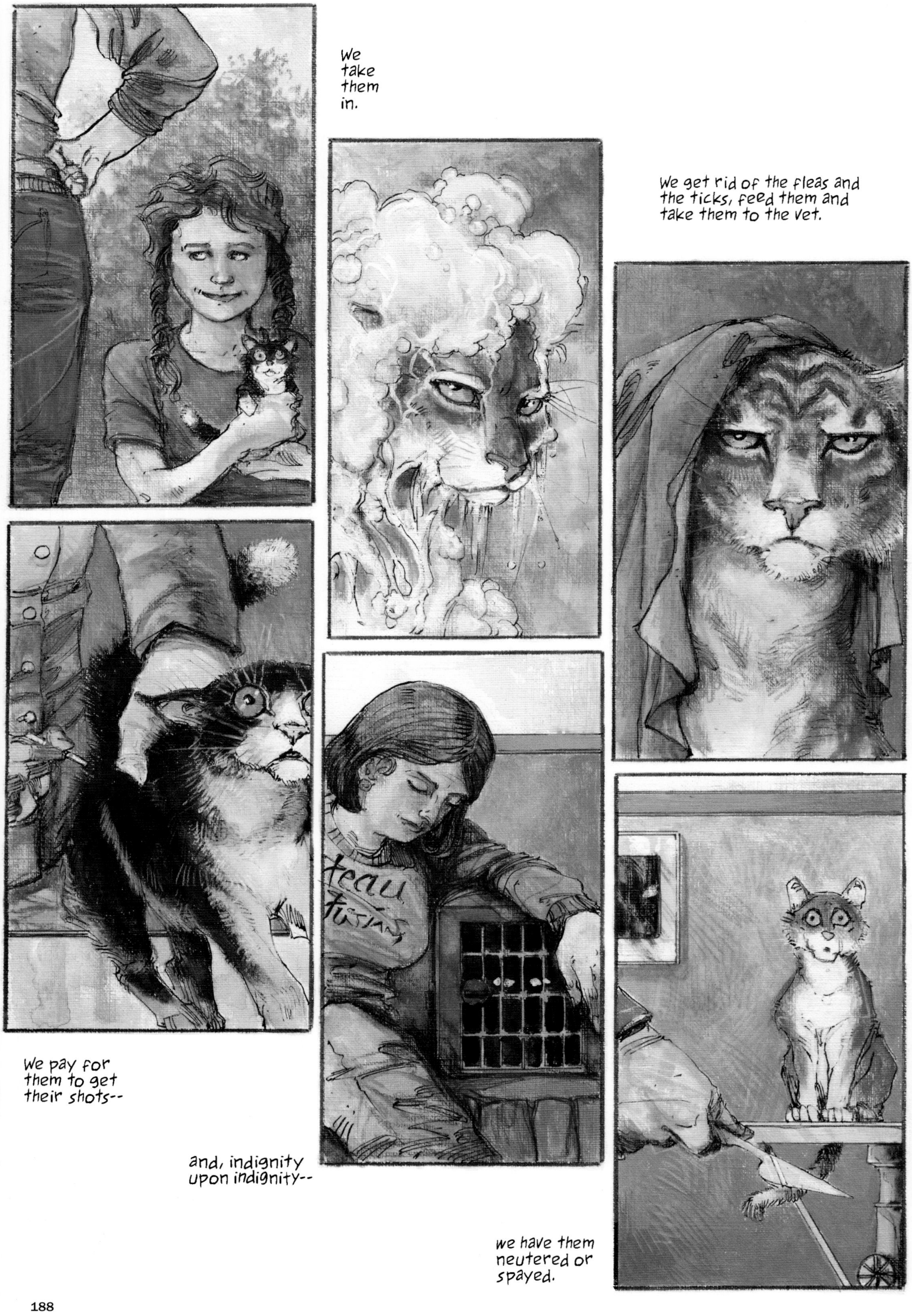
We take them in.
We get rid of the fleas and the ticks, feed them and take them to the vet.
We pay for them to get their shots--
and, indignity upon indignity--
we have them neutered or spayed.

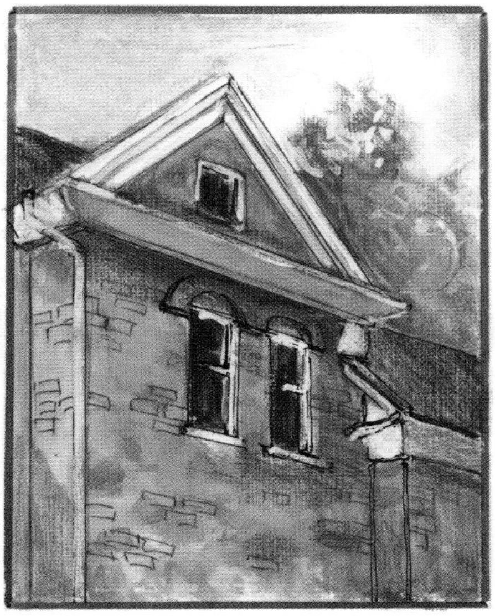

And they stay with us, for a few months, or for a year, or forever.

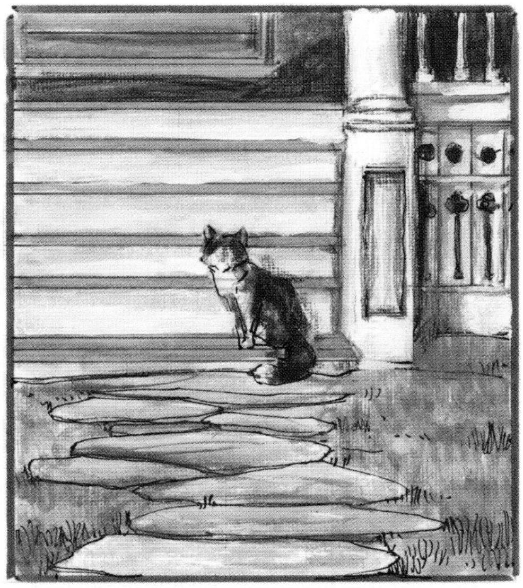

Most of them arrive in summer. We live in the country, just the right distance out of town for the city-dwellers to abandon their cats near us.

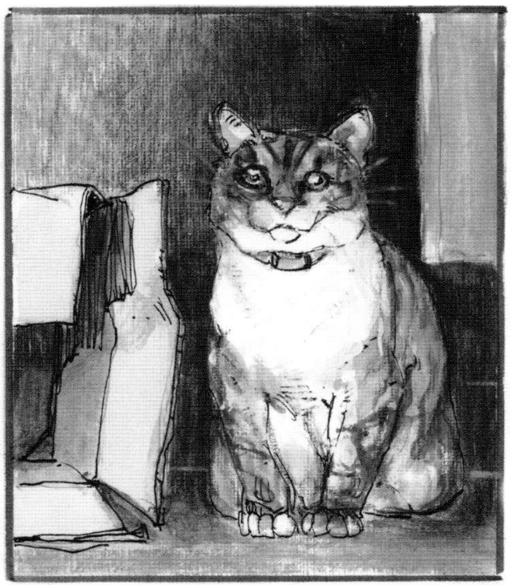

The cat population of my house is currently as follows:
Zoe, a half-Siamese, former barn-kitten, very gentle, very quiet.

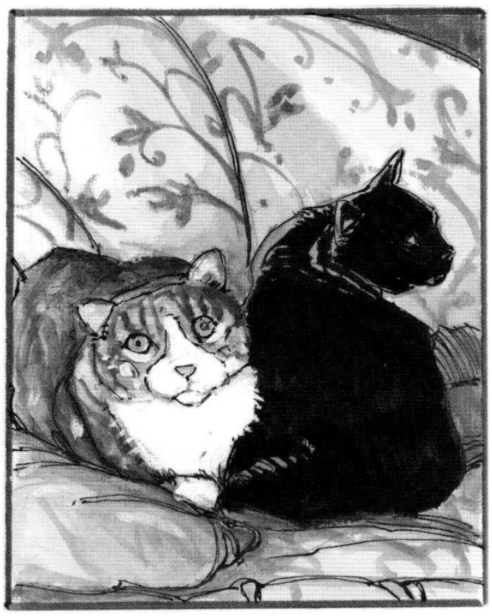

Hermione and Pod, tabby and black, respectively, the mad sisters who live in my attic office, and do not mingle.

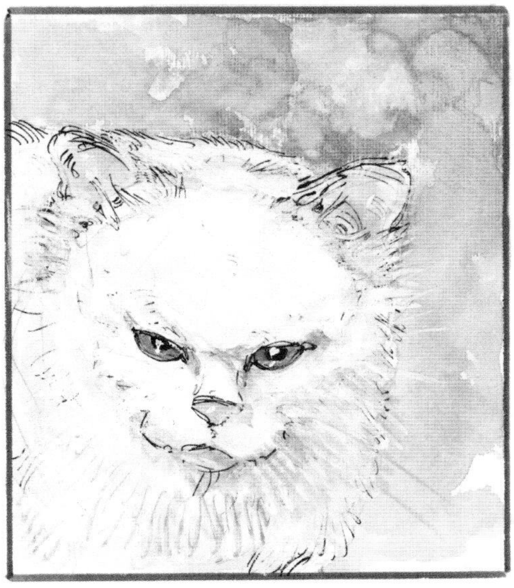

Princess, the blue-eyed long-haired white cat, who lived wild in the woods for years before she gave up her wild ways for soft sofas and beds.

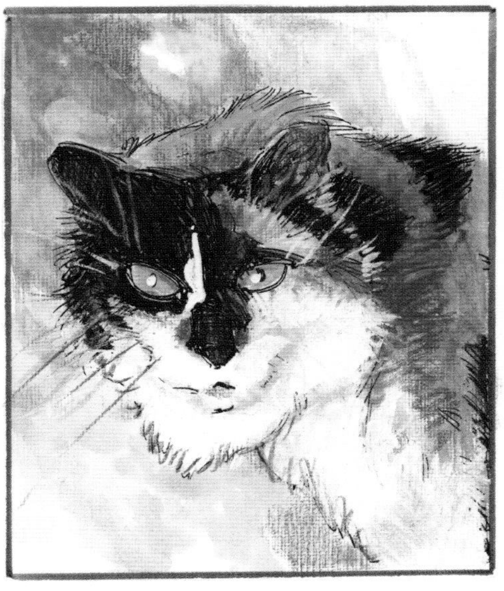

And, last but largest, Furball, Princess's cushion-like calico long-haired daughter, orange and black and white...

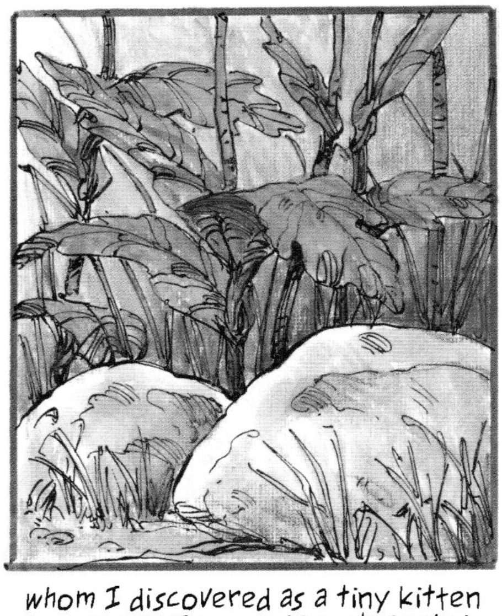

whom I discovered as a tiny kitten in our garage one day, strangled and almost dead, her head poked through an old badminton net...

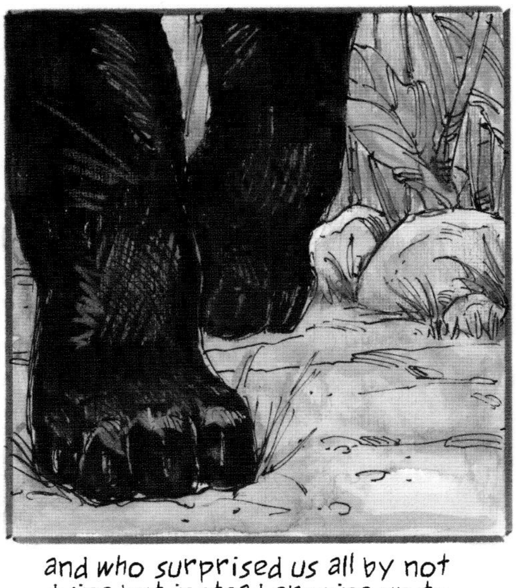

and who surprised us all by not dying but instead growing up to be the best-natured cat I have ever encountered.

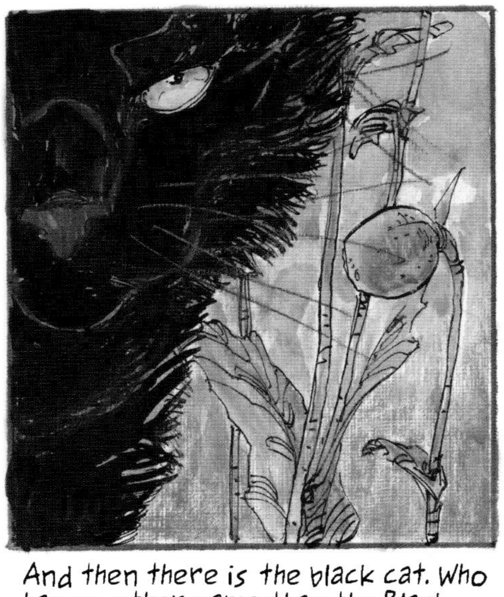

And then there is the black cat. Who has no other name than the Black Cat, and who turned up almost a month ago.

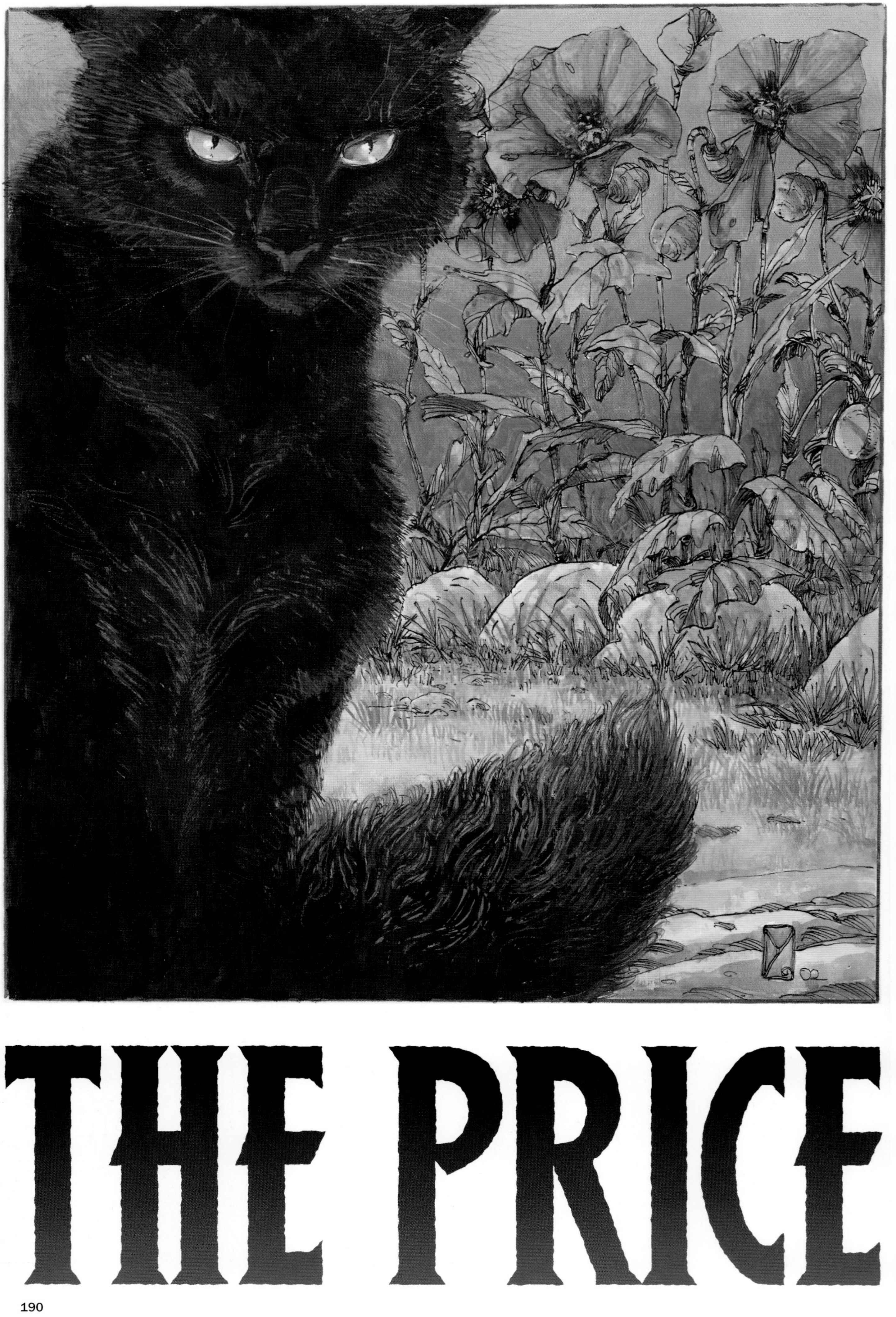

THE PRICE

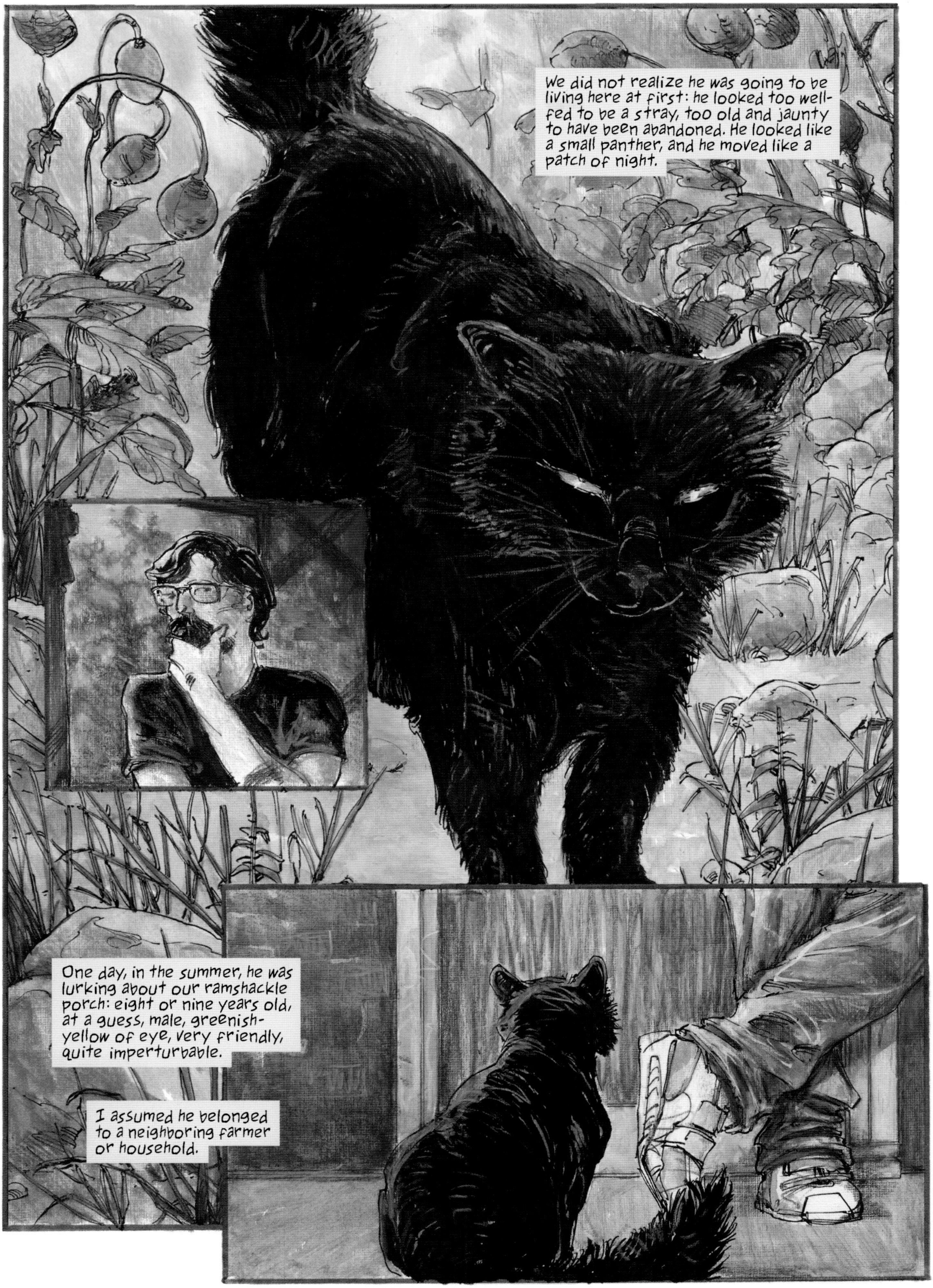
We did not realize he was going to be living here at first: he looked too well-fed to be a stray, too old and jaunty to have been abandoned. He looked like a small panther, and he moved like a patch of night.
One day, in the summer, he was lurking about our ramshackle porch: eight or nine years old, at a guess, male, greenish-yellow of eye, very friendly, quite imperturbable.
I assumed he belonged to a neighboring farmer or household.

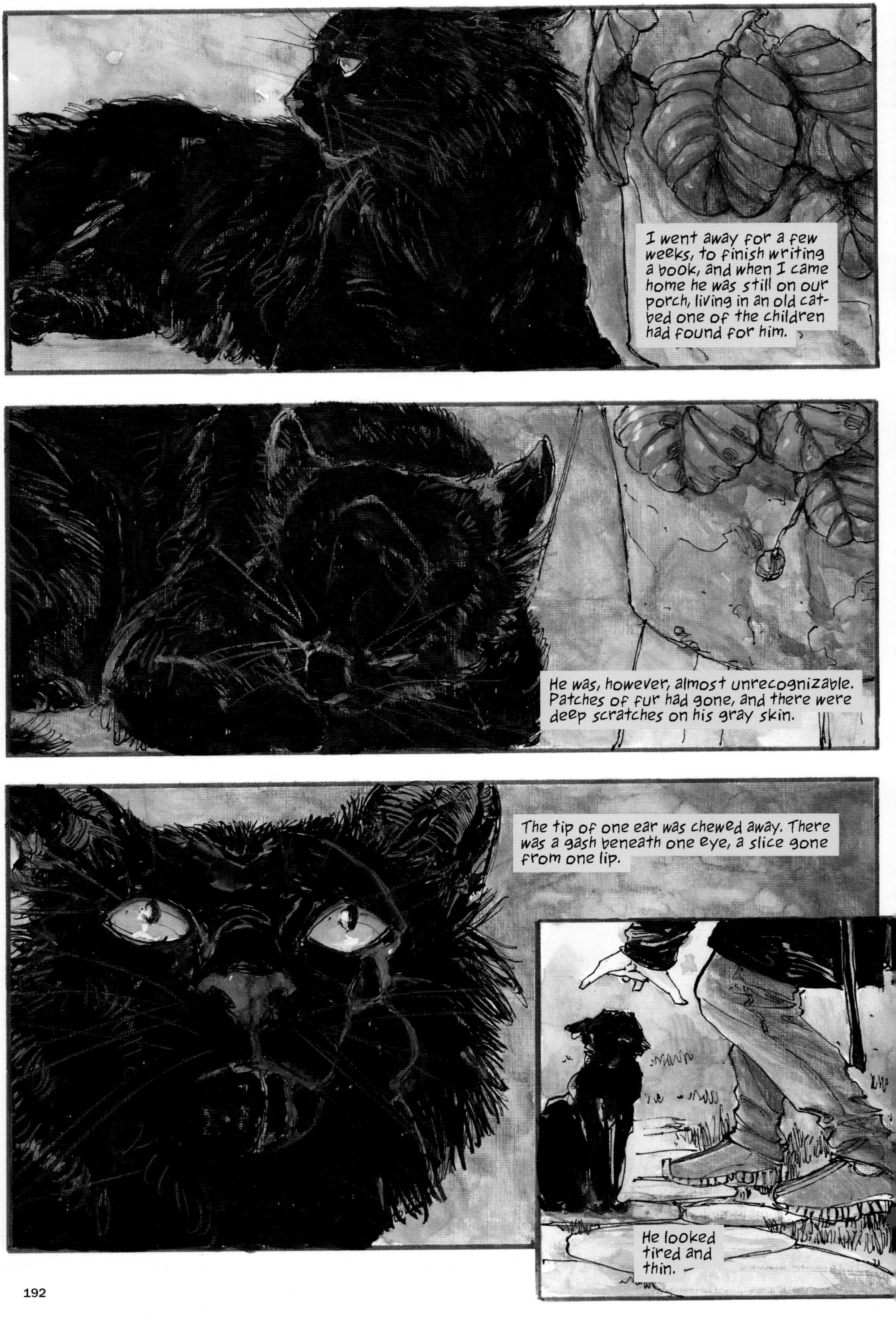
I went away for a few weeks, to finish writing a book, and when I came home he was still on our porch, living in an old cat-bed one of the children had found for him.
He was, however, almost unrecognizable. Patches of fur had gone, and there were deep scratches on his gray skin.
The tip of one ear was chewed away. There was a gash beneath one eye, a slice gone from one lip.
He looked tired and thin.

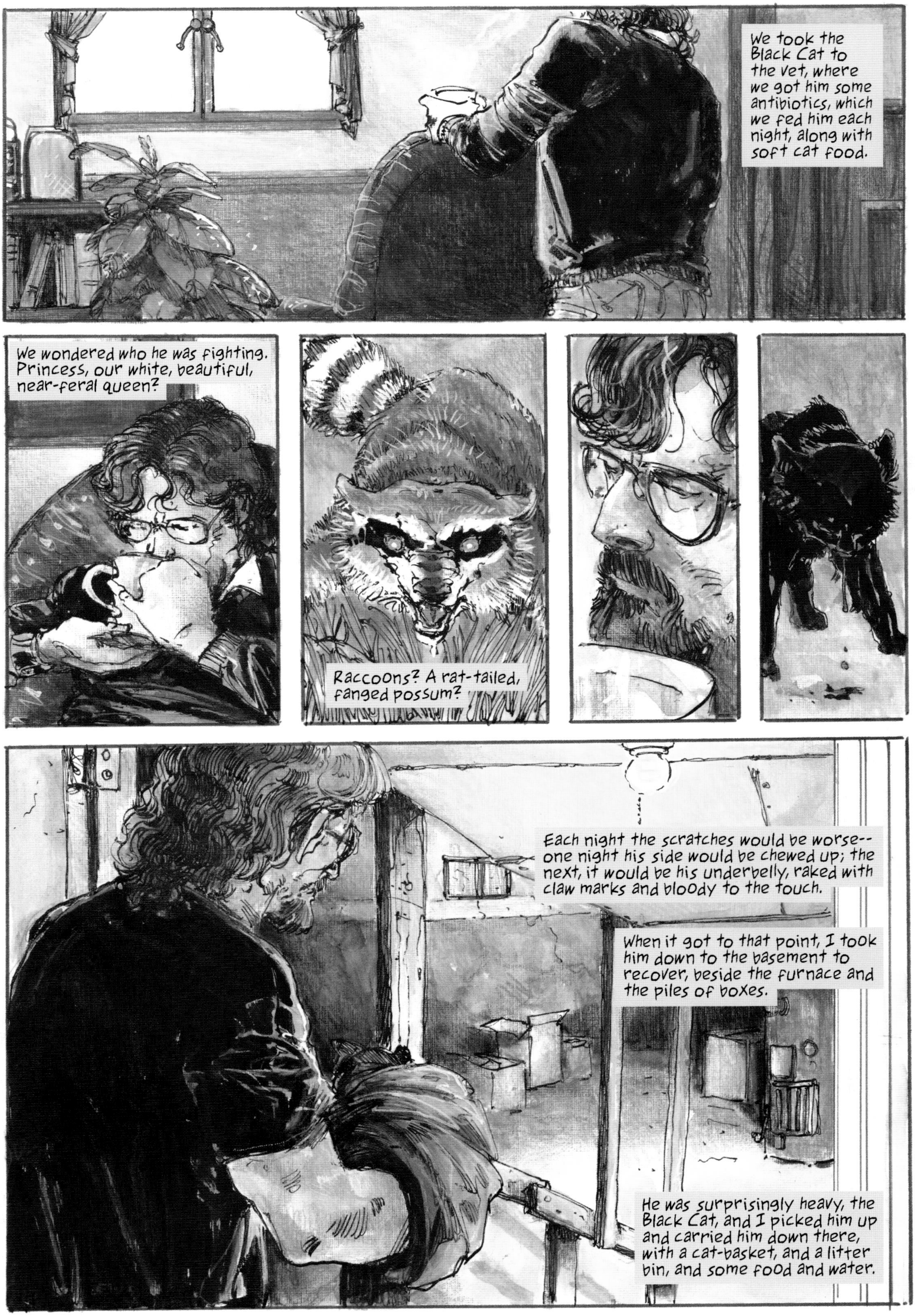

We took the Black Cat to the vet, where we got him some antibiotics, which we fed him each night, along with soft cat food.
We wondered who he was fighting. Princess, our white, beautiful, near-feral queen?
Raccoons? A rat-tailed, fanged possum?
Each night the scratches would be worse--one night his side would be chewed up; the next, it would be his underbelly, raked with claw marks and bloody to the touch.
When it got to that point, I took him down to the basement to recover, beside the furnace and the piles of boxes.
He was surprisingly heavy, the Black Cat, and I picked him up and carried him down there, with a cat-basket, and a litter bin, and some food and water.

I closed the door behind me.

I had to wash the blood from my hands, when I left the basement.

He stayed down there for four days.

At first he seemed too weak to feed himself: a cut beneath one eye had rendered him almost one-eyed, and he limped and lolled weakly, thick yellow pus oozing from the cut in his lip.

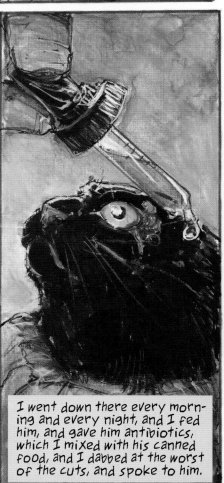

I went down there every morning and every night, and I fed him, and gave him antibiotics, which I mixed with his canned food, and I dabbed at the worst of the cuts, and spoke to him.

He had diarrhea, and, although I changed his litter daily, the basement stank evilly.

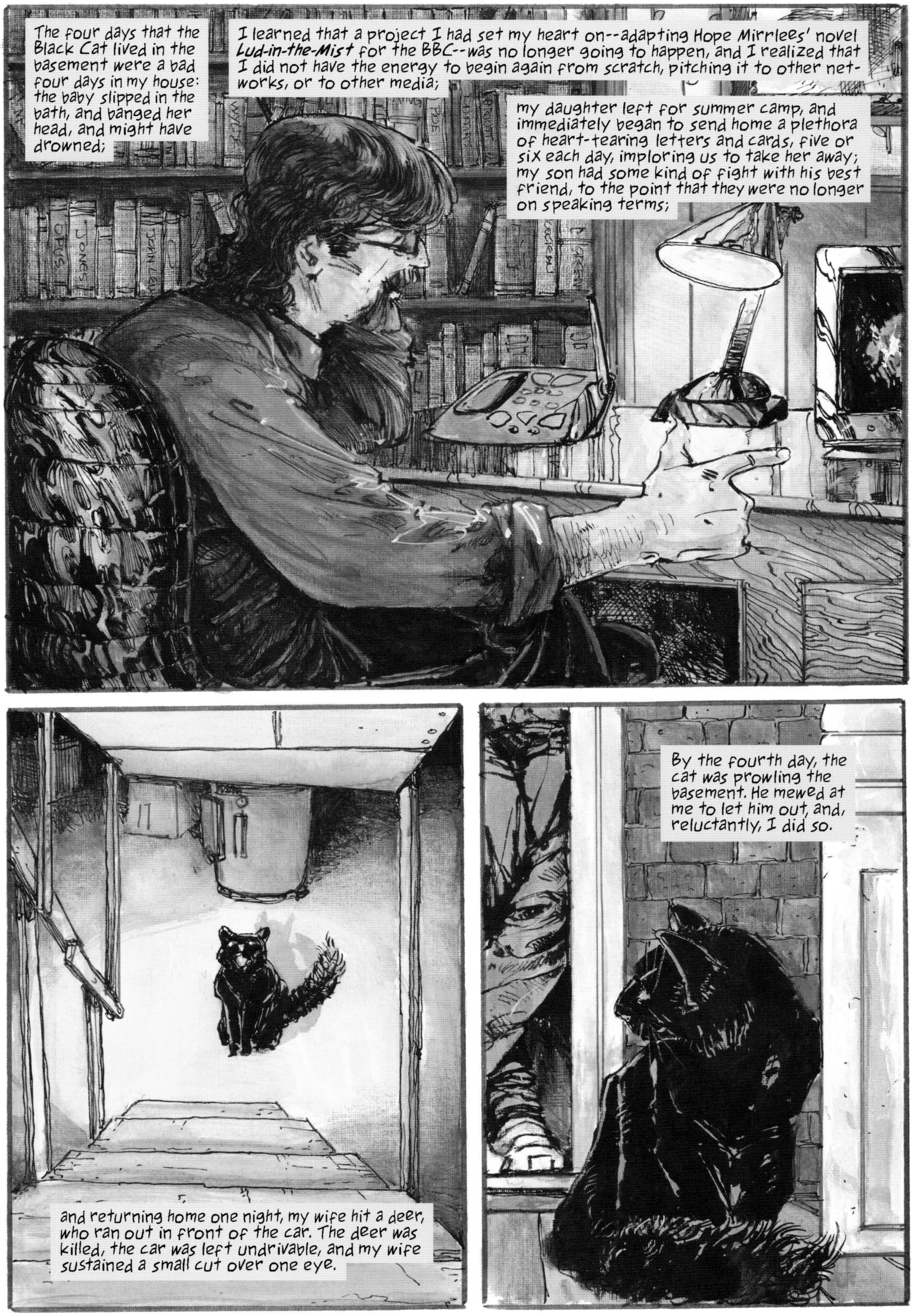
The four days that the Black Cat lived in the basement were a bad four days in my house: the baby slipped in the bath, and banged her head, and might have drowned;
I learned that a project I had set my heart on--adapting Hope Mirrlees' novel *Lud-in-the-Mist* for the BBC--was no longer going to happen, and I realized that I did not have the energy to begin again from scratch, pitching it to other net-works, or to other media;
my daughter left for summer camp, and immediately began to send home a plethora of heart-tearing letters and cards, five or six each day, imploring us to take her away; my son had some kind of fight with his best friend, to the point that they were no longer on speaking terms;
and returning home one night, my wife hit a deer, who ran out in front of the car. The deer was killed, the car was left undrivable, and my wife sustained a small cut over one eye.
By the fourth day, the cat was prowling the basement. He mewed at me to let him out, and, reluctantly, I did so.

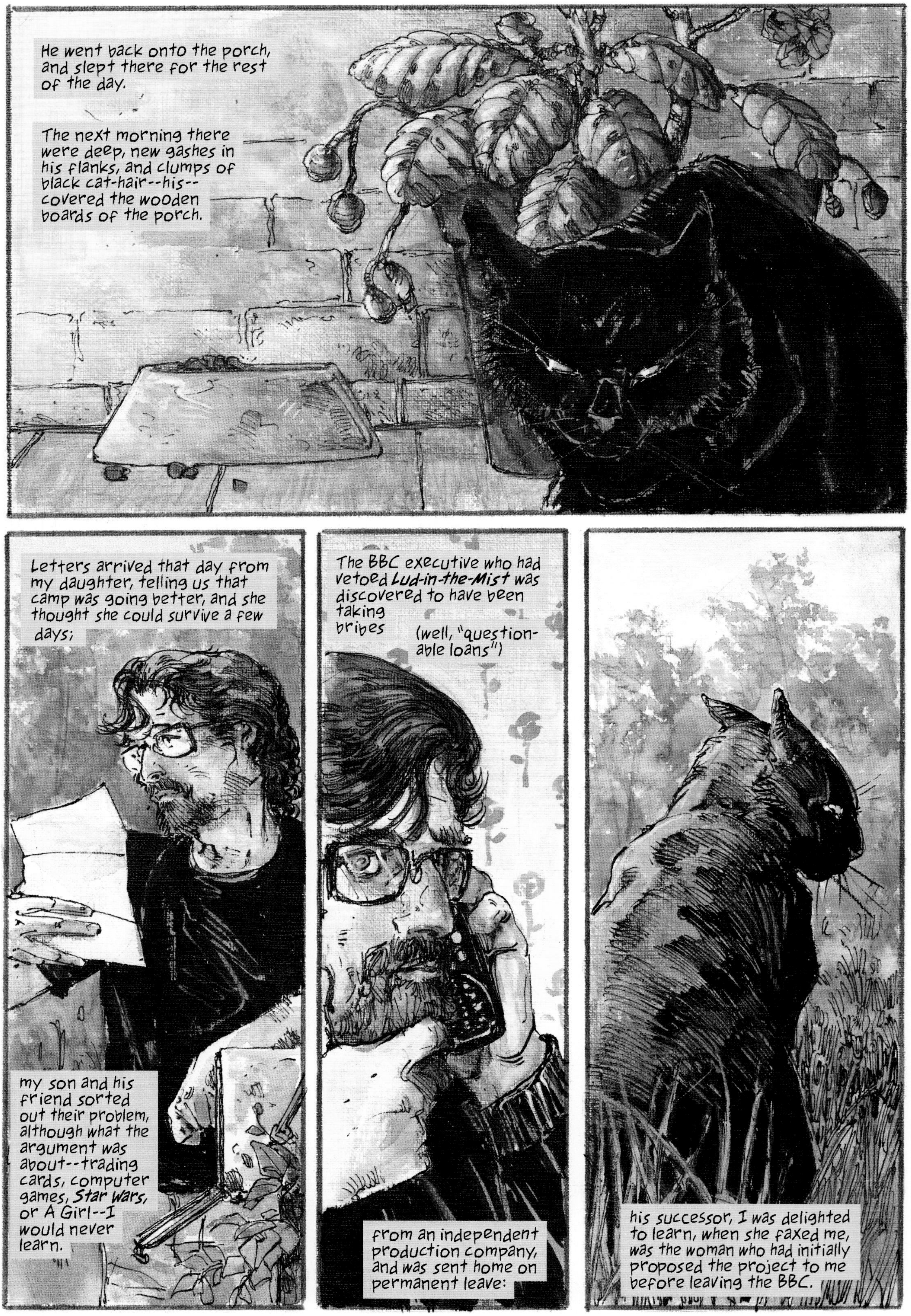
He went back onto the porch, and slept there for the rest of the day.
The next morning there were deep, new gashes in his flanks, and clumps of black cat-hair--his--covered the wooden boards of the porch.
Letters arrived that day from my daughter, telling us that camp was going better, and she thought she could survive a few days;
my son and his friend sorted out their problem, although what the argument was about--trading cards, computer games, ***Star Wars***, or A Girl--I would never learn.
The BBC executive who had vetoed ***Lud-in-the-Mist*** was discovered to have been taking bribes
(well, "question-able loans")
from an independent production company, and was sent home on permanent leave:
his successor, I was delighted to learn, when she faxed me, was the woman who had initially proposed the project to me before leaving the BBC.

I thought about returning the Black Cat to the basement, but decided against it. Instead, I resolved to try and discover what kind of animal was coming to our house each night, and from there to formulate a plan of action -- to trap it, perhaps.

for birthdays and at Christmas my family gives me gadgets and gizmos, pricey toys which excite my fancy but, ultimately, rarely leave their boxes.

There's a food dehydrator and an electric carving knife, a bread-making machine, and, last year's present...

a pair of see-in-the-dark binoculars.

Perhaps, I thought, if the creature, dog or cat or raccoon or what-have-you, were to see me sitting on the porch, it would not come...

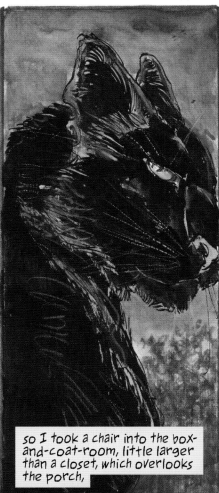

so I took a chair into the box-and-coat-room, little larger than a closet, which overlooks the porch,

and, when everyone in the house was asleep, I went out onto the porch, and bade the Black Cat good night.

197

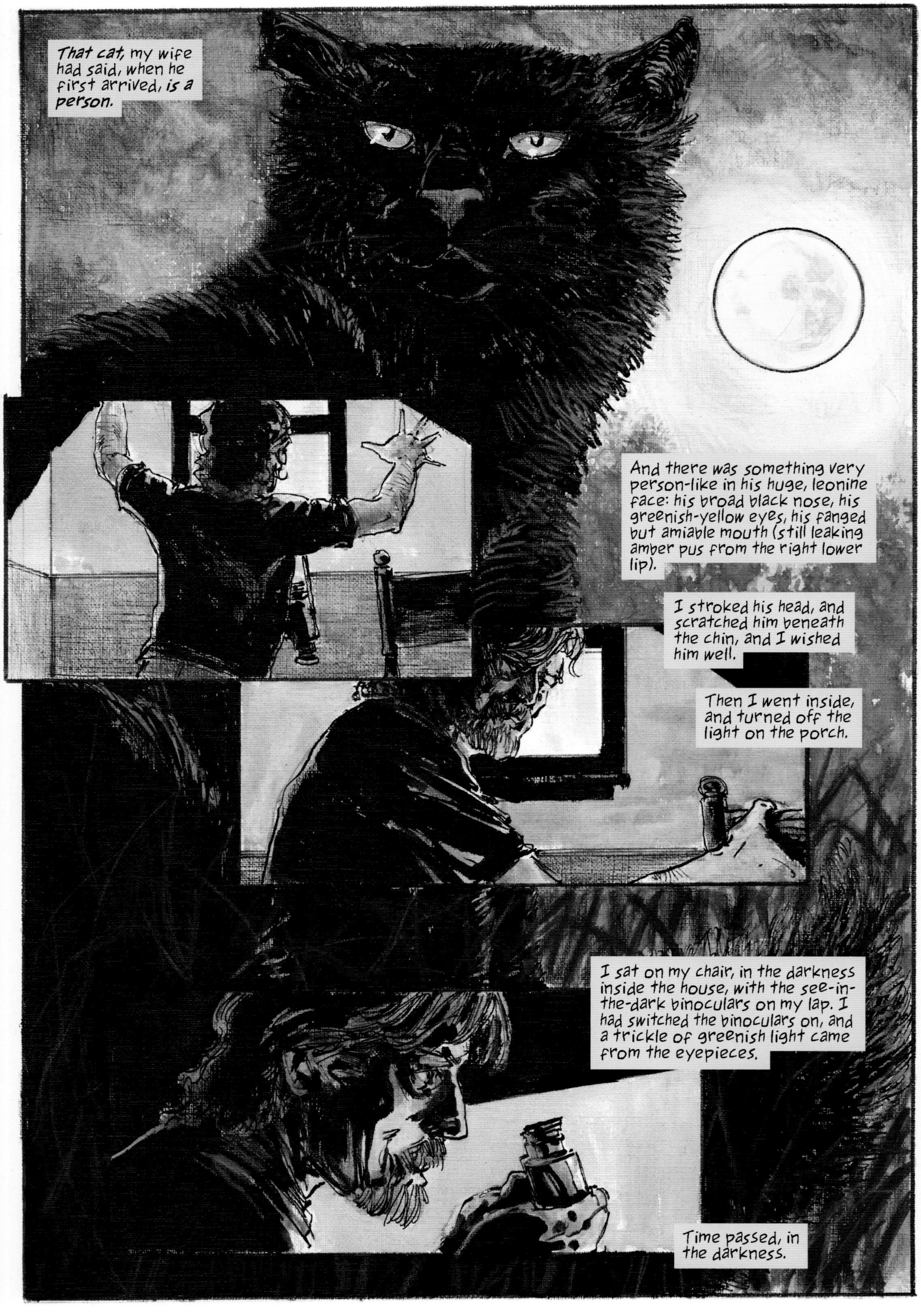
That cat, my wife had said, when he first arrived, ***is a person.***
And there was something very person-like in his huge, leonine face: his broad black nose, his greenish-yellow eyes, his fanged but amiable mouth (still leaking amber pus from the right lower lip).
I stroked his head, and scratched him beneath the chin, and I wished him well.
Then I went inside, and turned off the light on the porch.
I sat on my chair, in the darkness inside the house, with the see-in-the-dark binoculars on my lap. I had switched the binoculars on, and a trickle of greenish light came from the eyepieces.
Time passed, in the darkness.

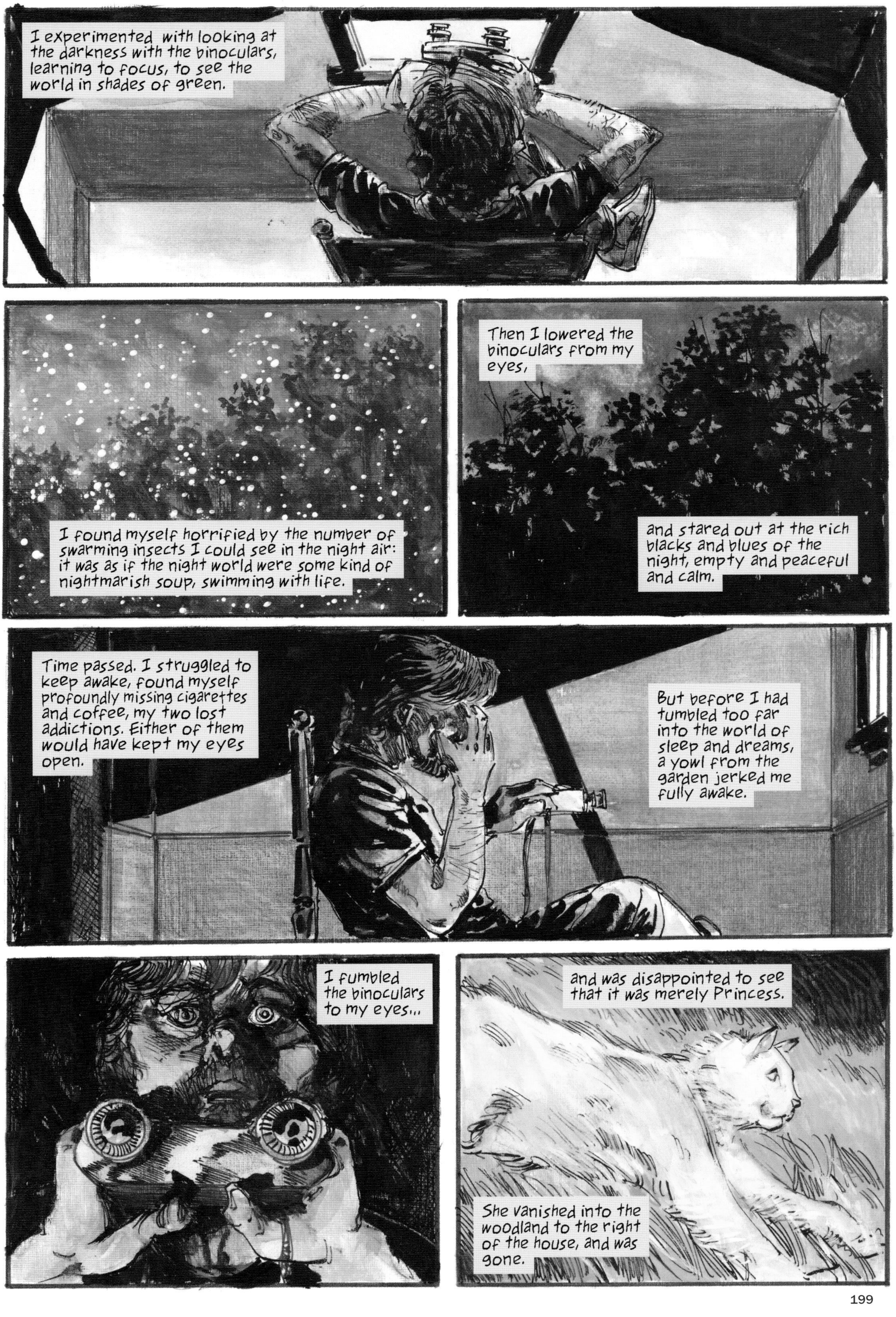
I experimented with looking at the darkness with the binoculars, learning to focus, to see the world in shades of green.
I found myself horrified by the number of swarming insects I could see in the night air: it was as if the night world were some kind of nightmarish soup, swimming with life.
Then I lowered the binoculars from my eyes,
and stared out at the rich blacks and blues of the night, empty and peaceful and calm.
Time passed. I struggled to keep awake, found myself profoundly missing cigarettes and coffee, my two lost addictions. Either of them would have kept my eyes open.
But before I had tumbled too far into the world of sleep and dreams, a yowl from the garden jerked me fully awake.
I fumbled the binoculars to my eyes...
and was disappointed to see that it was merely Princess.
She vanished into the woodland to the right of the house, and was gone.

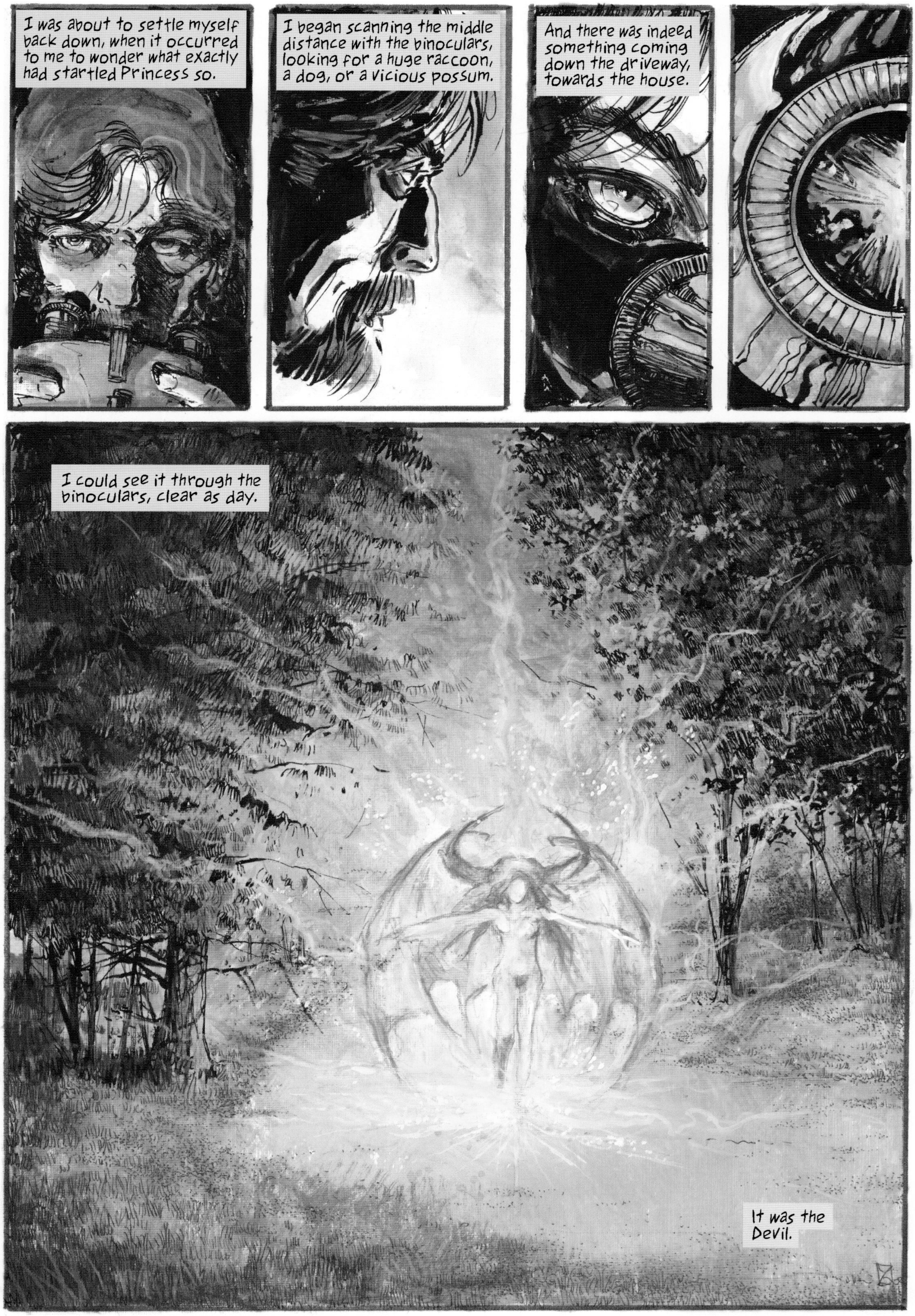
I was about to settle myself back down, when it occurred to me to wonder what exactly had startled Princess so.
I began scanning the middle distance with the binoculars, looking for a huge raccoon, a dog, or a vicious possum.
And there was indeed something coming down the driveway, towards the house.
I could see it through the binoculars, clear as day.
It was the Devil.

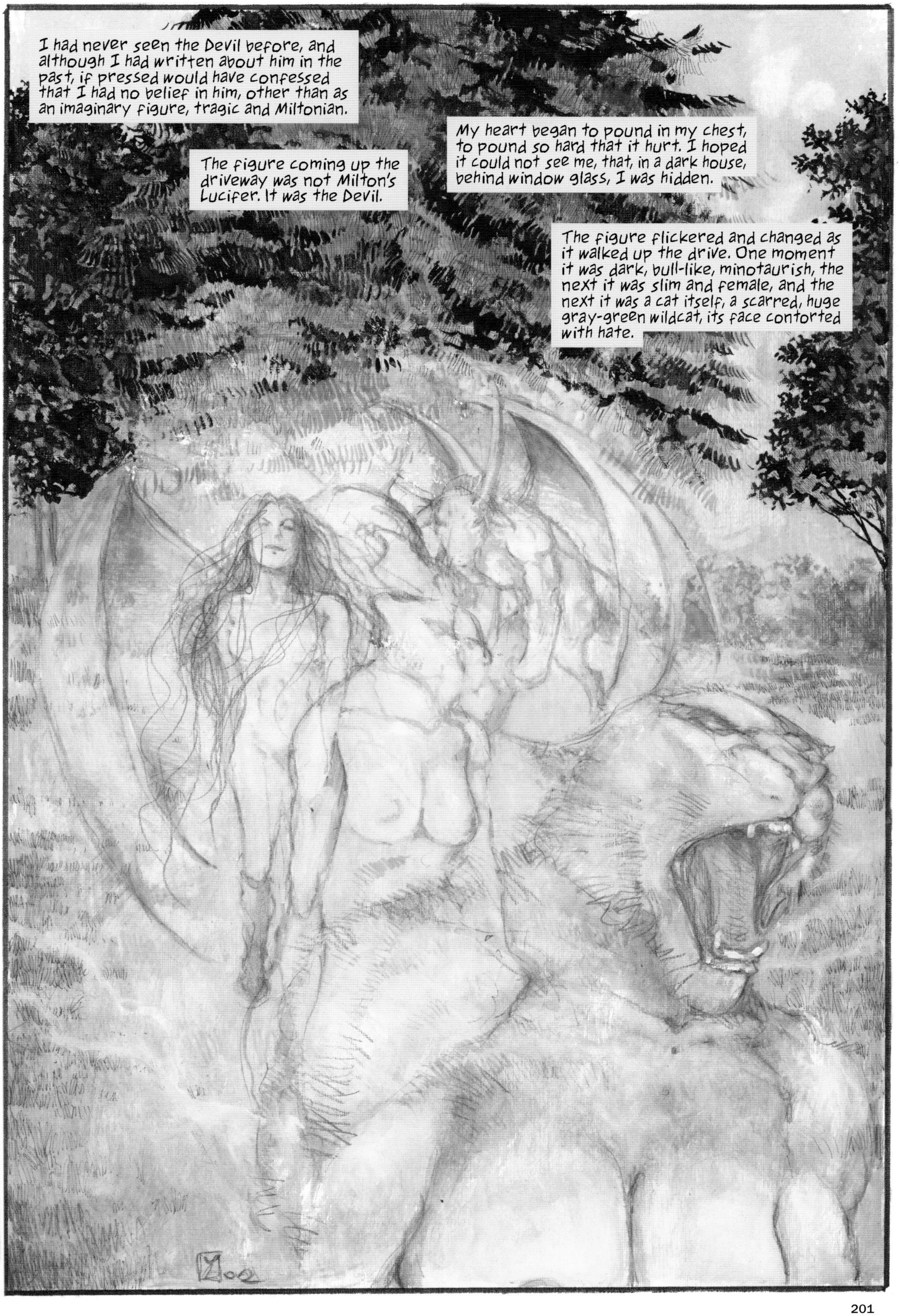
I had never seen the Devil before, and although I had written about him in the past, if pressed would have confessed that I had no belief in him, other than as an imaginary figure, tragic and Miltonian.
The figure coming up the driveway was not Milton's Lucifer. It was the Devil.
My heart began to pound in my chest, to pound so hard that it hurt. I hoped it could not see me, that, in a dark house, behind window glass, I was hidden.
The figure flickered and changed as it walked up the drive. One moment it was dark, bull-like, minotaurish, the next it was slim and female, and the next it was a cat itself, a scarred, huge gray-green wildcat, its face contorted with hate.

At the bottom of the steps, the Devil stopped, and called out something that I could not understand, three, perhaps four words in a whining, howling language that must have been old and forgotten when Babylon was young.

Although I did not understand the words, I felt the hairs rise on the back of my head as it called.

And then I heard, muffled through the glass, but still audible, a low growl, a challenge, and, slowly, unsteadily, a black figure walked down the steps of the house, away from me, towards the Devil.

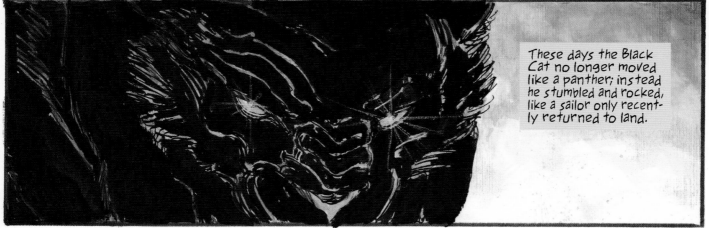

These days the Black Cat no longer moved like a panther; instead he stumbled and rocked, like a sailor only recently returned to land.

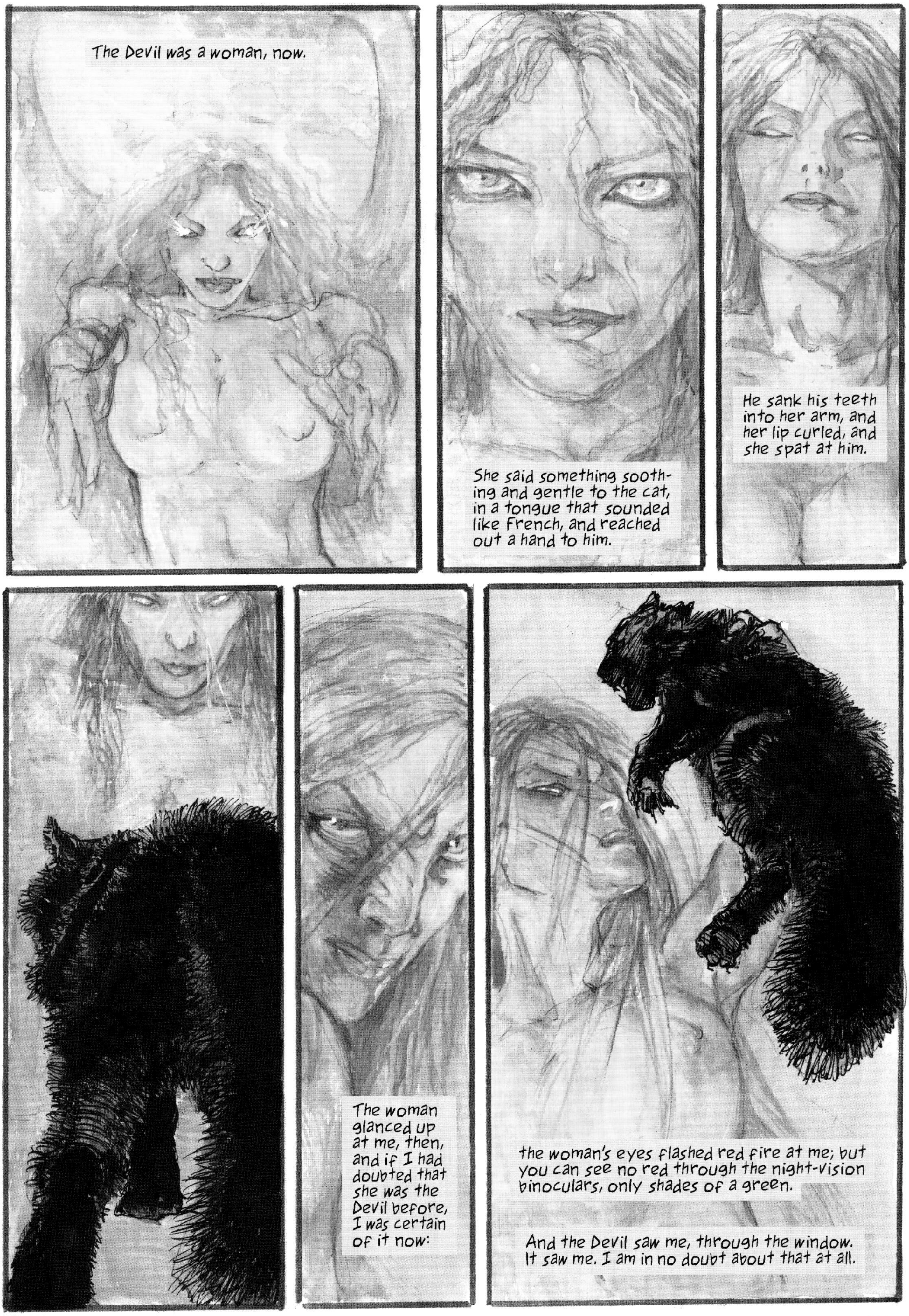
The Devil was a woman, now.
She said something soothing and gentle to the cat, in a tongue that sounded like French, and reached out a hand to him.
He sank his teeth into her arm, and her lip curled, and she spat at him.
The woman glanced up at me, then, and if I had doubted that she was the Devil before, I was certain of it now:
the woman's eyes flashed red fire at me; but you can see no red through the night-vision binoculars, only shades of a green.
And the Devil saw me, through the window. It saw me. I am in no doubt about that at all.

The Devil twisted and writhed,

and now it was some kind of jackal, a flat-faced, huge-headed, bull-necked creature,

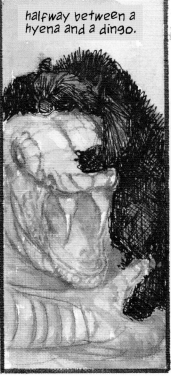

halfway between a hyena and a dingo.

There were maggots squirming in its mangy fur,

and it walked closer, approaching the steps.

Approaching my house.

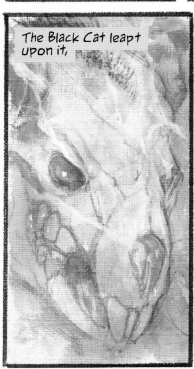

The Black Cat leapt upon it,

and in seconds they became a rolling, writhing thing,

moving faster than my eyes could follow.

All this in silence.

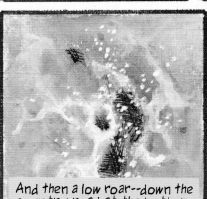

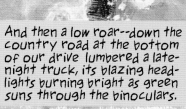

And then a low roar--down the country road at the bottom of our drive lumbered a late-night truck, its blazing headlights burning bright as green suns through the binoculars.

I lowered them from my eyes, and saw only darkness, and the gentle yellow of headlights, and then the red of rear lights as it vanished off again into the nowhere at all.

204

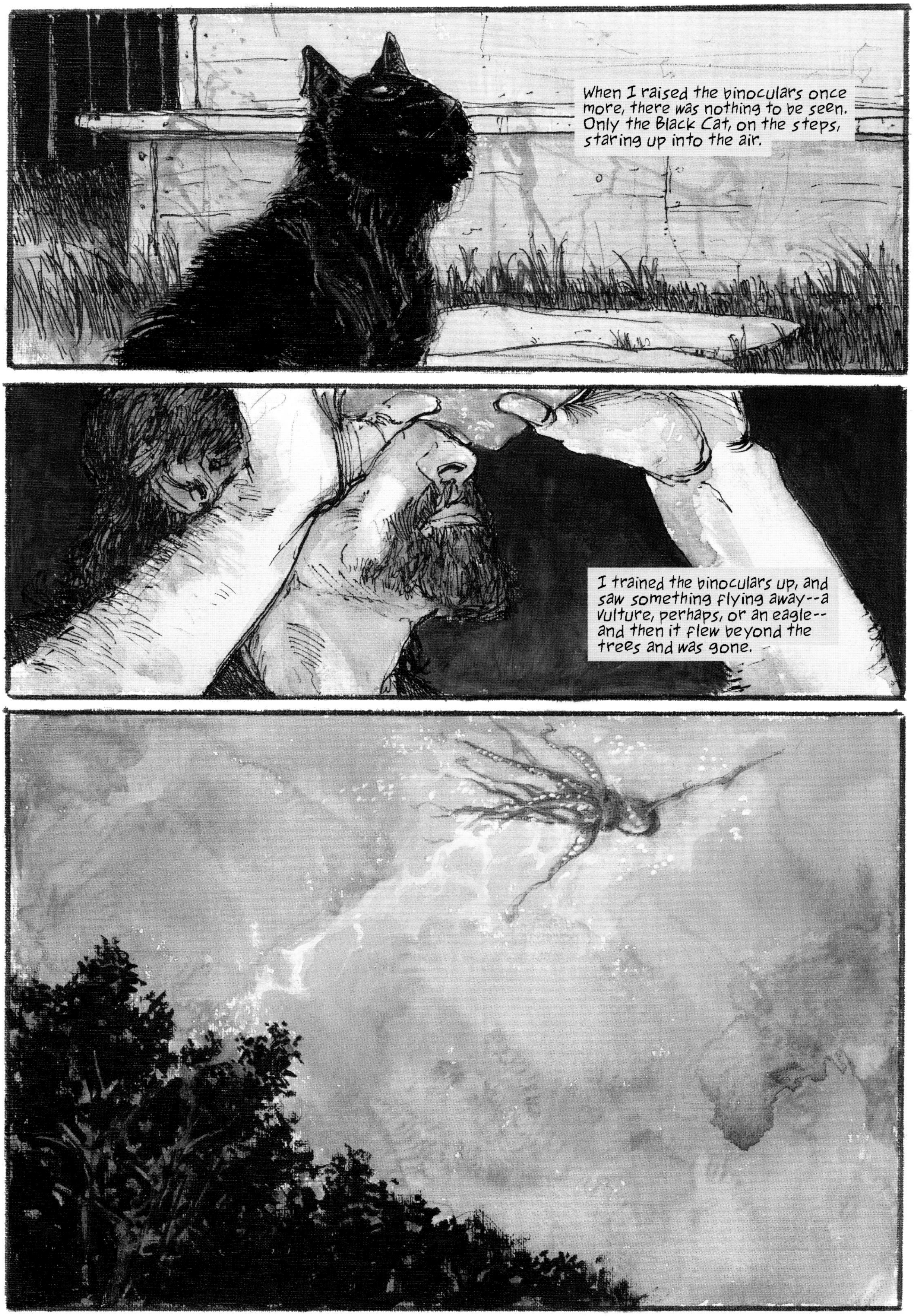
When I raised the binoculars once more, there was nothing to be seen. Only the Black Cat, on the steps, staring up into the air.
I trained the binoculars up, and saw something flying away--a vulture, perhaps, or an eagle--and then it flew beyond the trees and was gone.

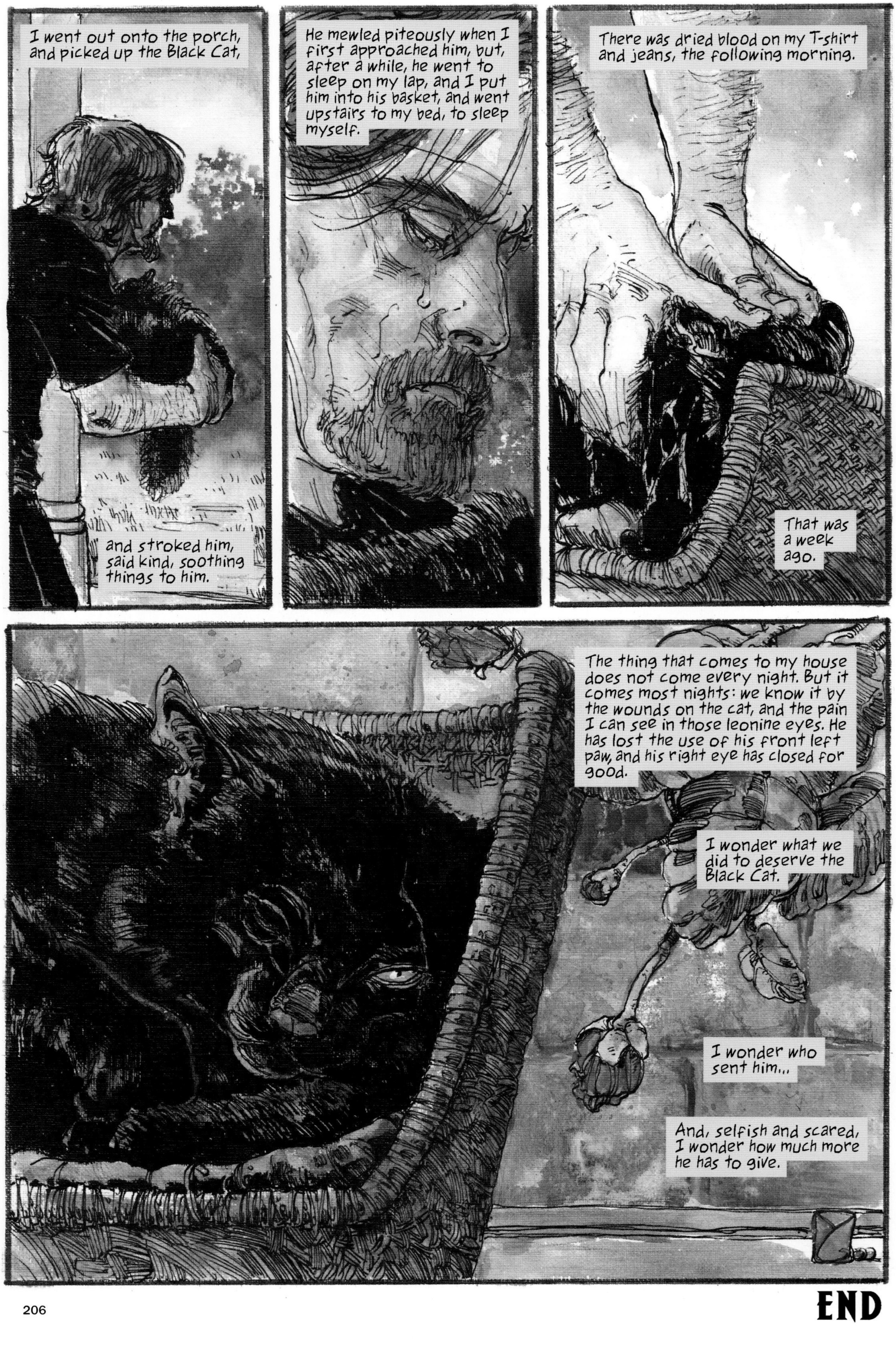
I went out onto the porch, and picked up the Black Cat,
and stroked him, said kind, soothing things to him.
He mewled piteously when I first approached him, but, after a while, he went to sleep on my lap, and I put him into his basket, and went upstairs to my bed, to sleep myself.
There was dried blood on my T-shirt and jeans, the following morning.
That was a week ago.
The thing that comes to my house does not come every night. But it comes most nights: we know it by the wounds on the cat, and the pain I can see in those leonine eyes. He has lost the use of his front left paw, and his right eye has closed for good.
I wonder what we did to deserve the Black Cat.
I wonder who sent him...
And, selfish and scared, I wonder how much more he has to give.

END

the DAUGHTER of OWLS

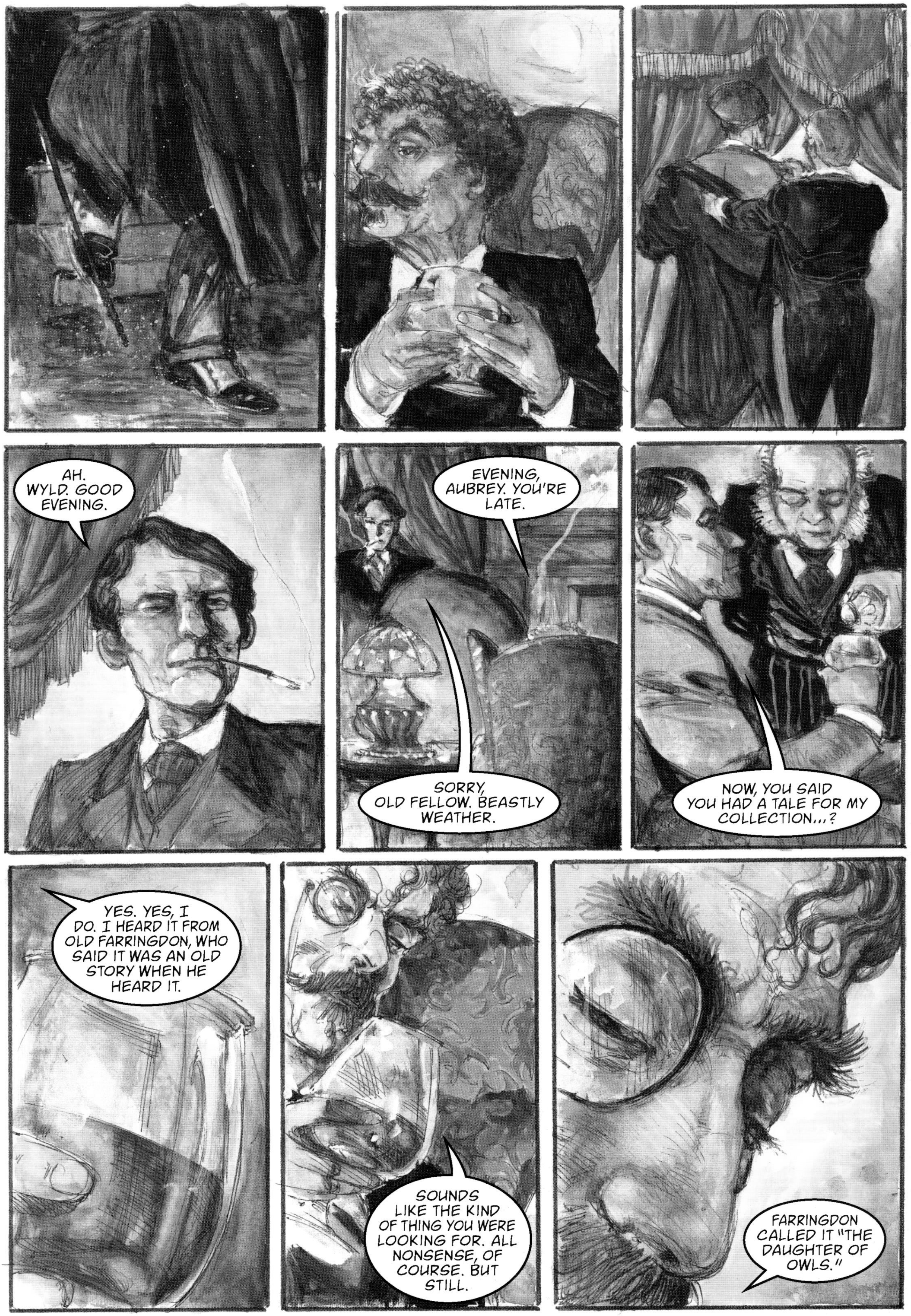
AH. WYLD. GOOD EVENING.
EVENING, AUBREY. YOU'RE LATE.
SORRY, OLD FELLOW. BEASTLY WEATHER.
NOW, YOU SAID YOU HAD A TALE FOR MY COLLECTION...?
YES. YES, I DO. I HEARD IT FROM OLD FARRINGDON, WHO SAID IT WAS AN OLD STORY WHEN HE HEARD IT.
SOUNDS LIKE THE KIND OF THING YOU WERE LOOKING FOR. ALL NONSENSE, OF COURSE. BUT STILL.
FARRINGDON CALLED IT "THE DAUGHTER OF OWLS."

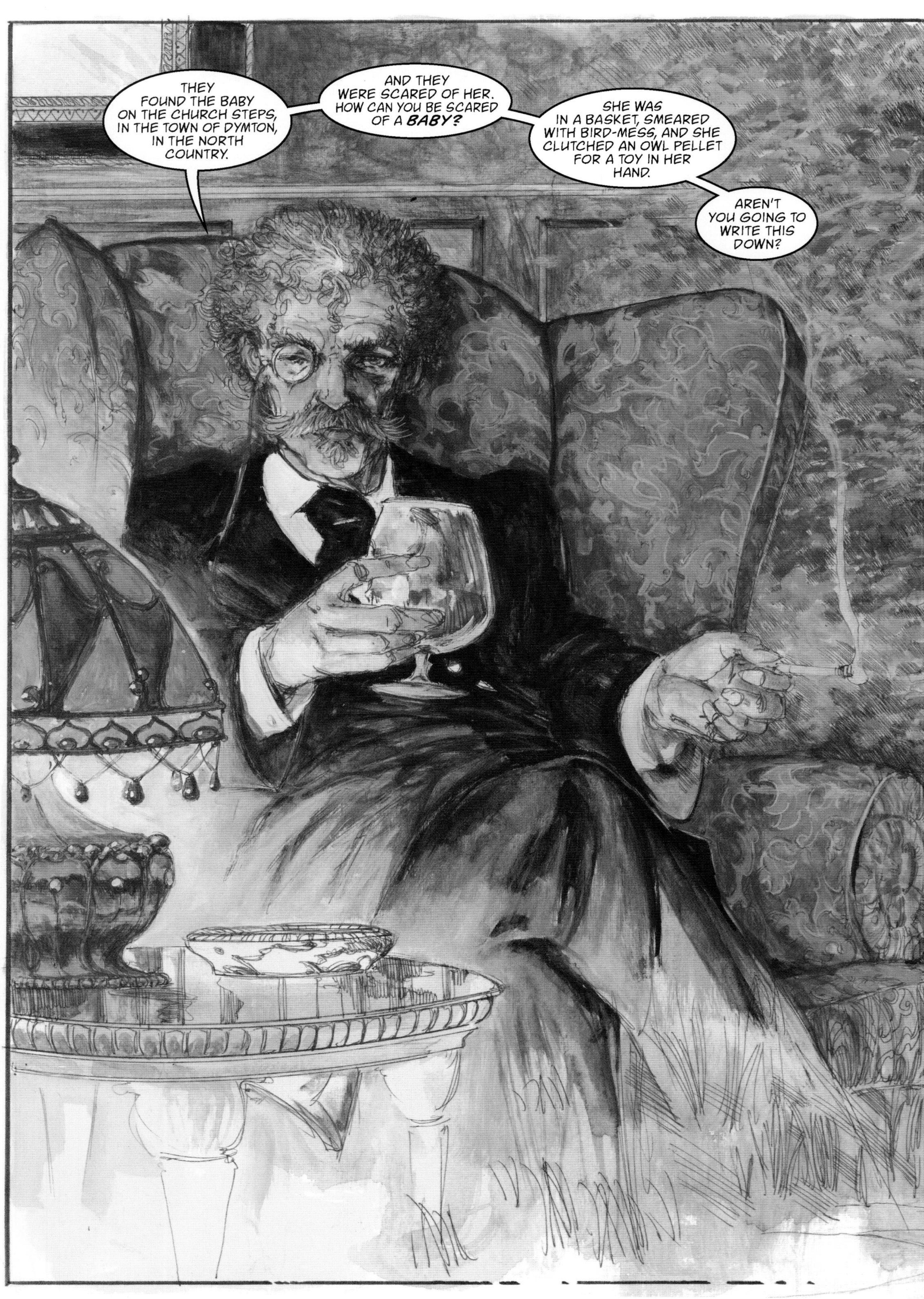
THEY FOUND THE BABY ON THE CHURCH STEPS, IN THE TOWN OF DYMTON, IN THE NORTH COUNTRY.
AND THEY WERE SCARED OF HER. HOW CAN YOU BE SCARED OF A *BABY?*
SHE WAS IN A BASKET, SMEARED WITH BIRD-MESS, AND SHE CLUTCHED AN OWL PELLET FOR A TOY IN HER HAND.
AREN'T YOU GOING TO WRITE THIS DOWN?

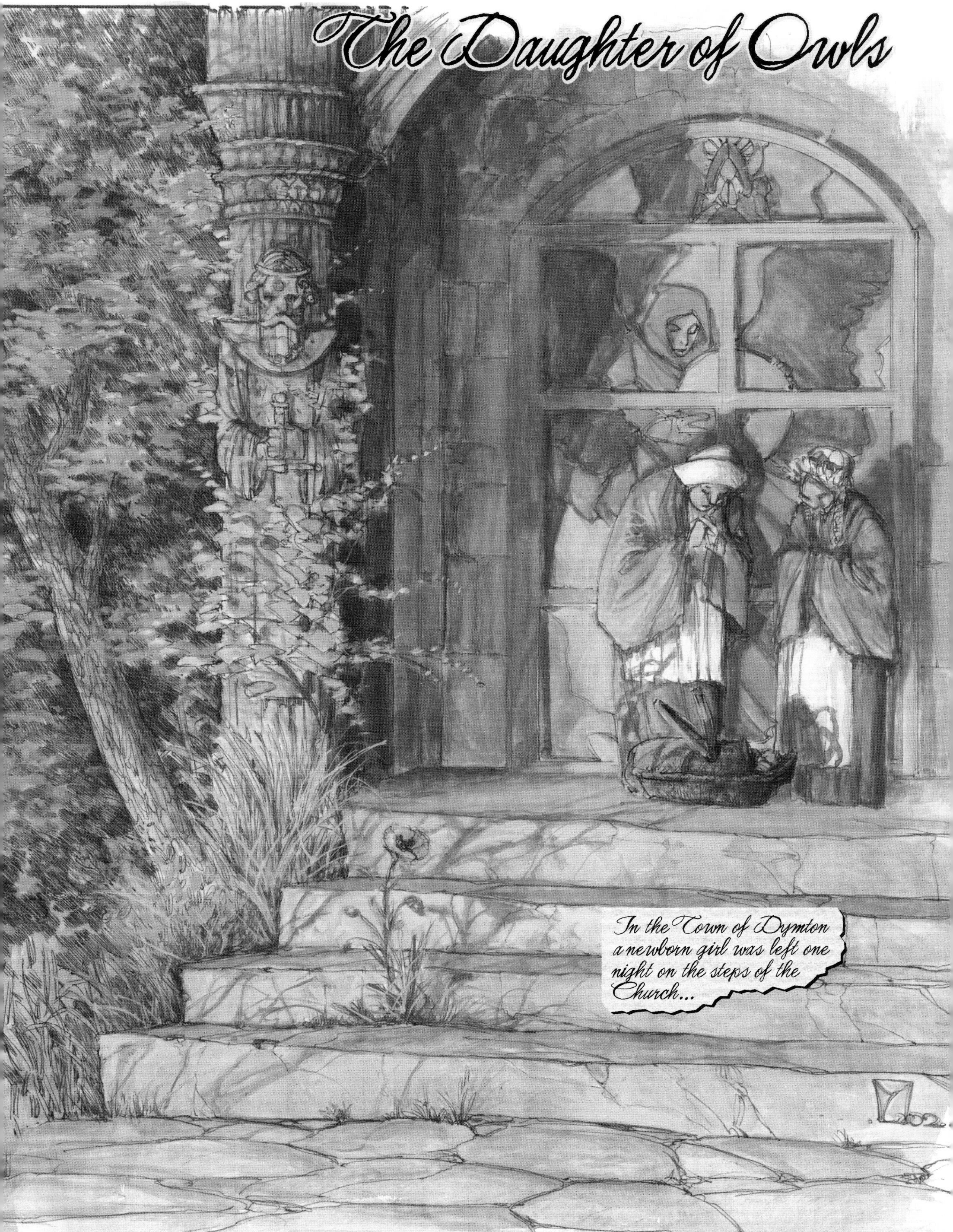
The Daughter of Owls
In the Town of Dymton a newborn girl was left one night on the steps of the Church...

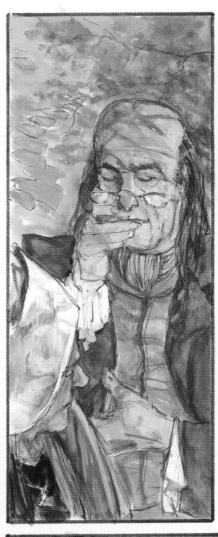

The Sexton found her there the next morning, and she had hold of a curious thing...

i.e., the pellet of an Owl, which, when crumbled, showed the usual composition of an hoot-owl's pellet:

That is to say, it contained skin and teeth and small bones.

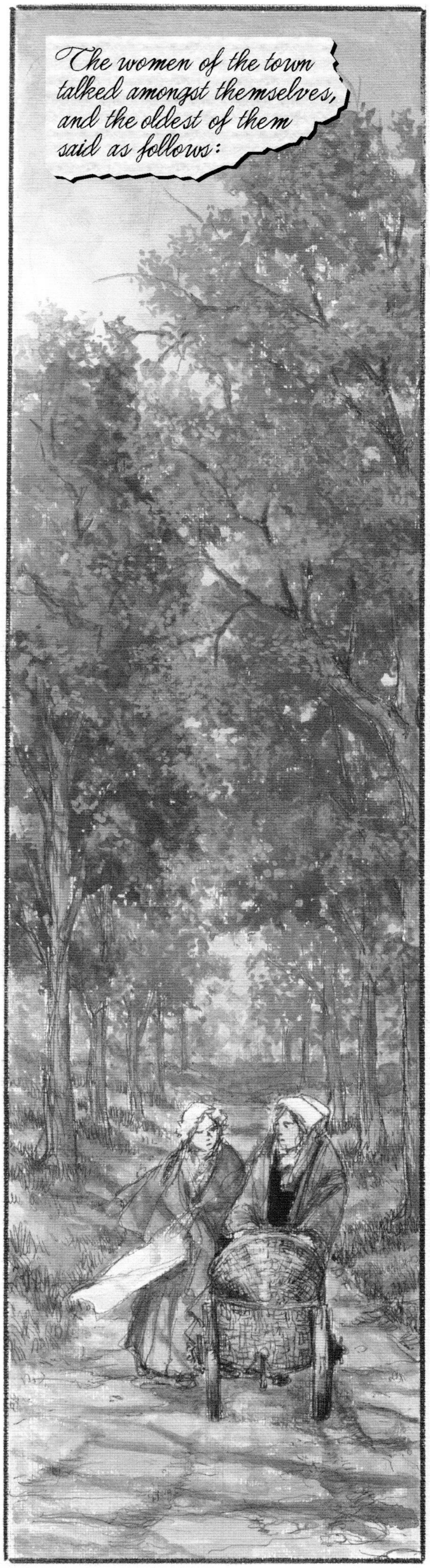
The women of the town talked amongst themselves, and the oldest of them said as follows:
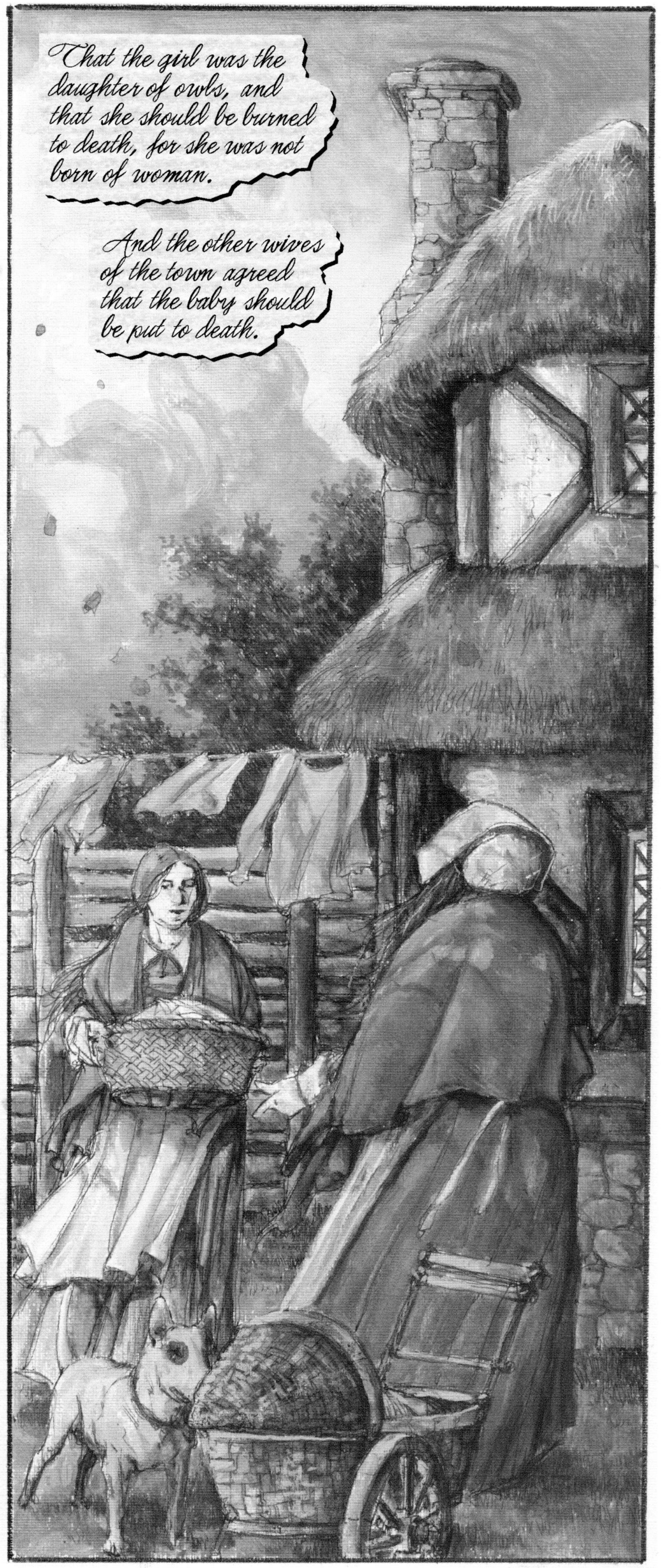
That the girl was the daughter of owls, and that she should be burned to death, for she was not born of woman.
And the other wives of the town agreed that the baby should be put to death.

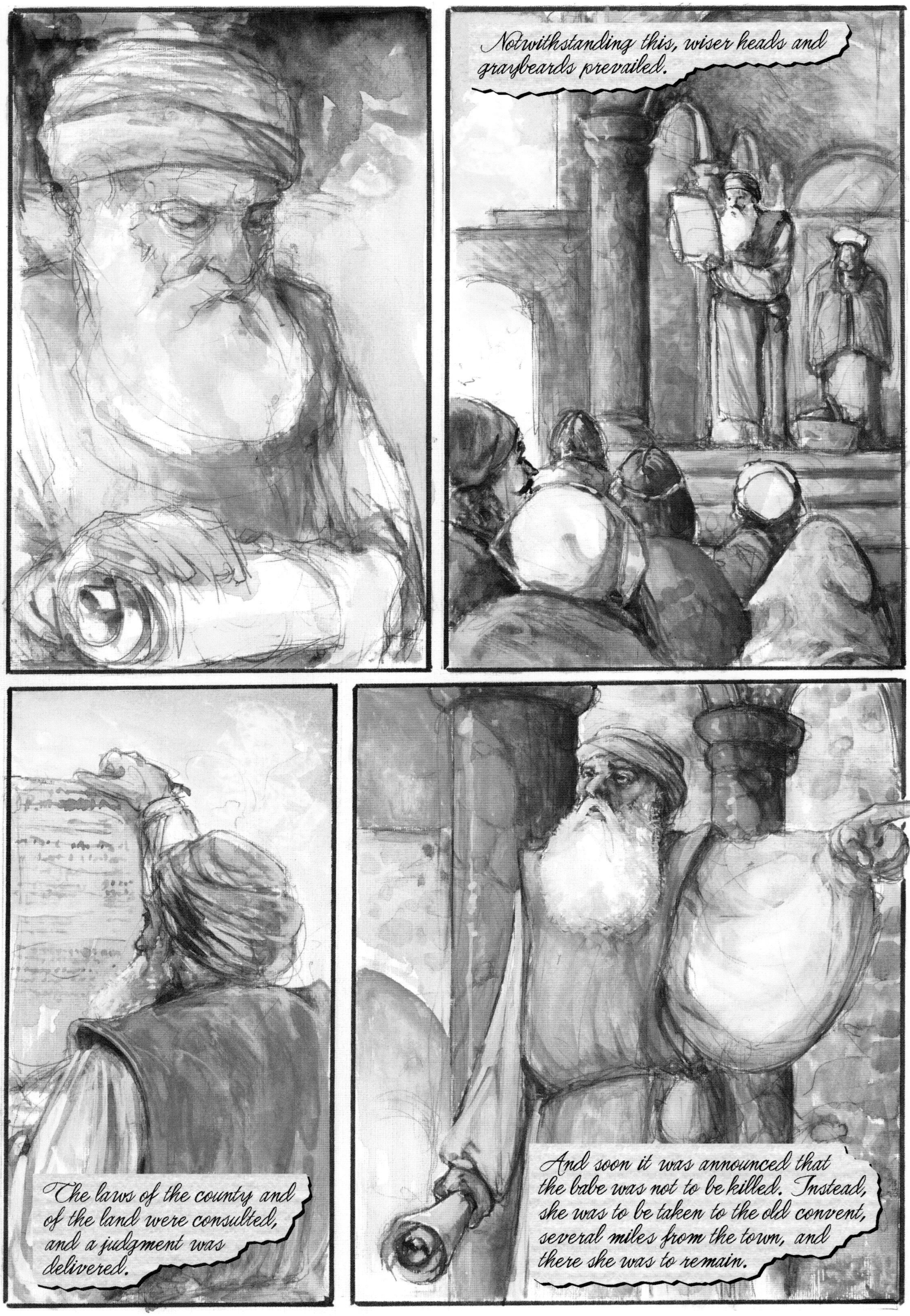
Notwithstanding this, wiser heads and graybeards prevailed.
The laws of the county and of the land were consulted, and a judgment was delivered.
And soon it was announced that the babe was not to be killed. Instead, she was to be taken to the old convent, several miles from the town, and there she was to remain.

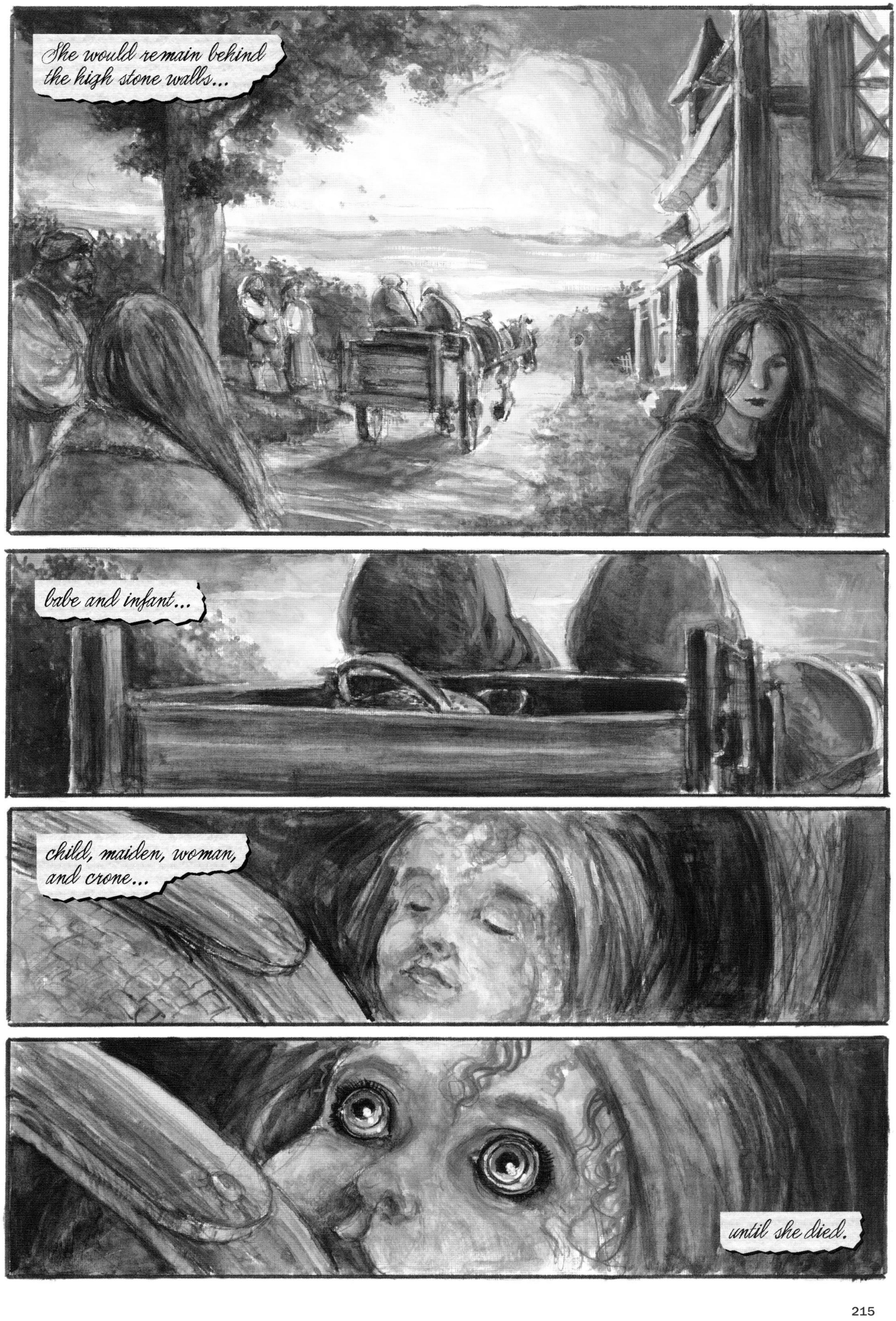
She would remain behind the high stone walls...
babe and infant...
child, maiden, woman, and crone...
until she died.

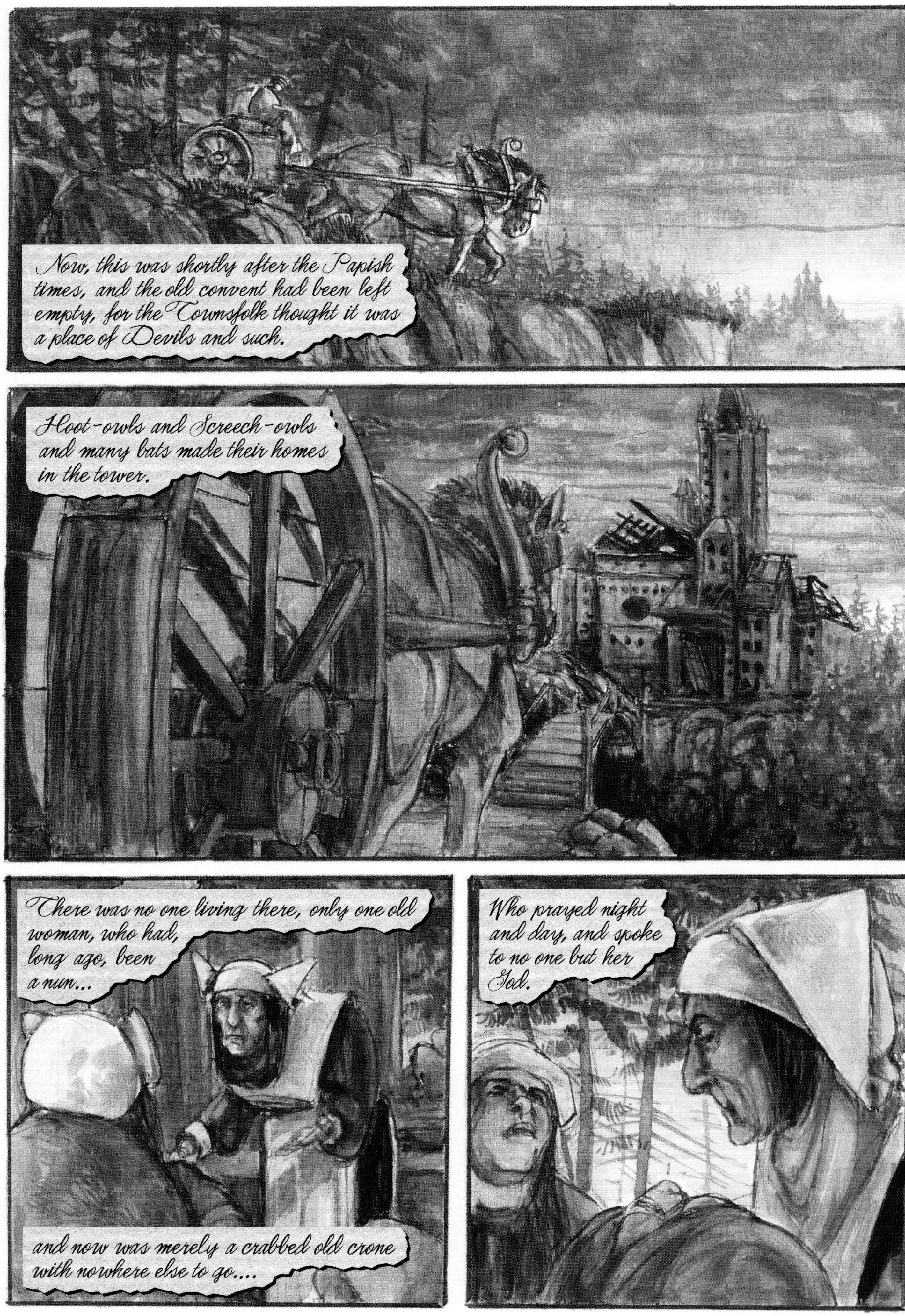
Now, this was shortly after the Papish times, and the old convent had been left empty, for the Townsfolk thought it was a place of Devils and such.
Hoot-owls and Screech-owls and many bats made their homes in the tower.
There was no one living there, only one old woman, who had, long ago, been a nun...
and now was merely a crabbed old crone with nowhere else to go....
Who prayed night and day, and spoke to no one but her God.

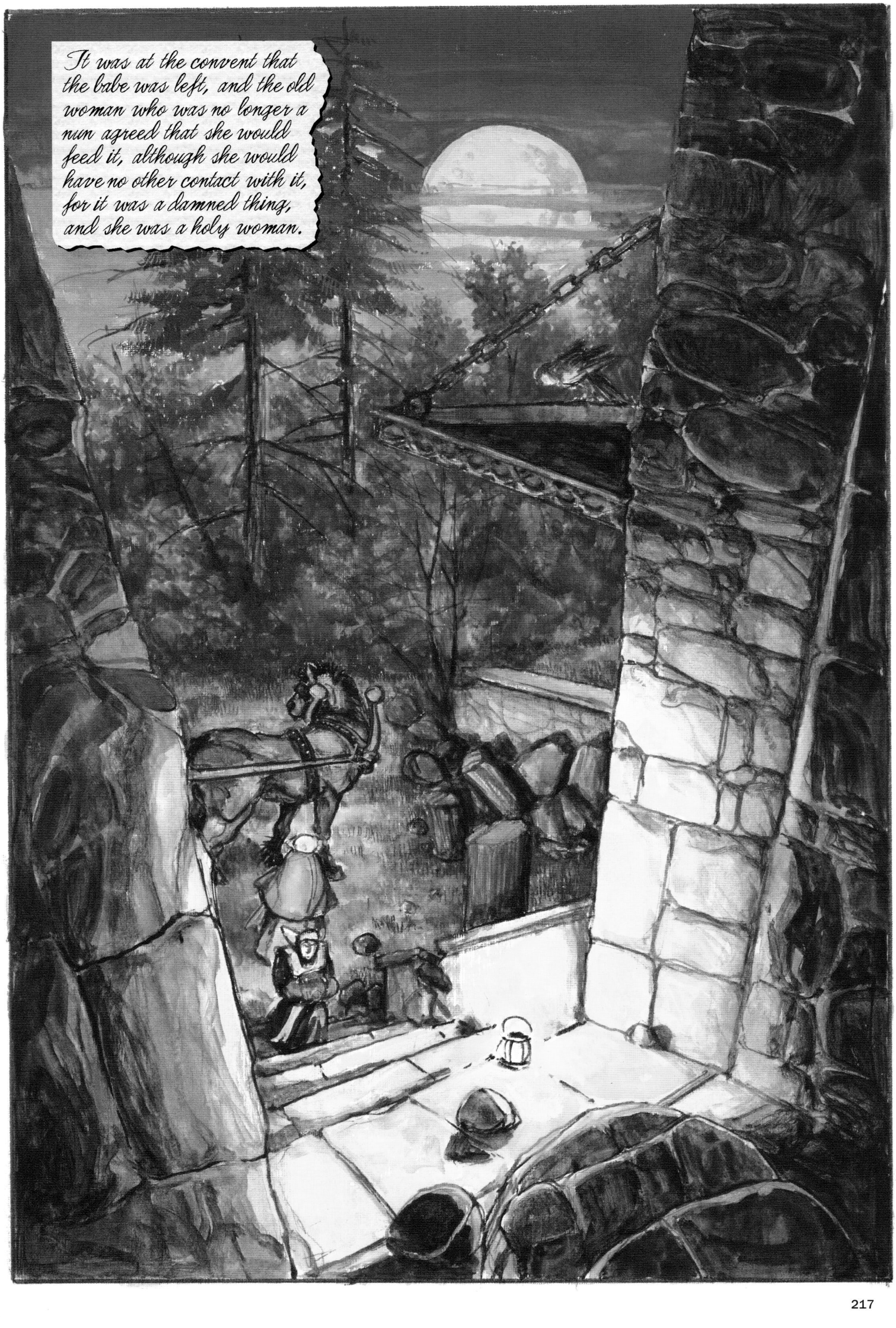
It was at the convent that the babe was left, and the old woman who was no longer a nun agreed that she would feed it, although she would have no other contact with it, for it was a damned thing, and she was a holy woman.

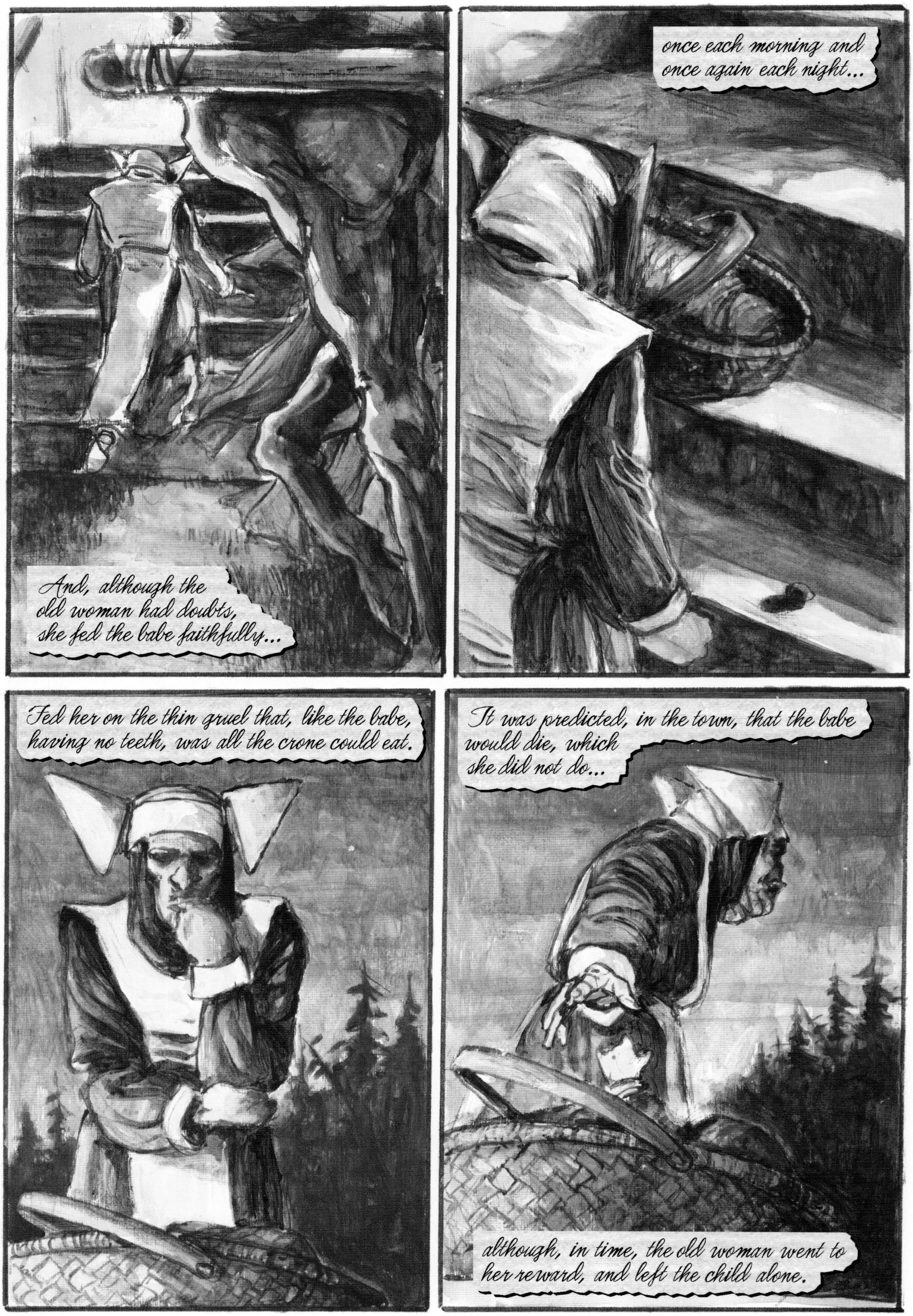
And, although the old woman had doubts, she fed the babe faithfully...
once each morning and once again each night...
Fed her on the thin gruel that, like the babe, having no teeth, was all the crone could eat.
It was predicted, in the town, that the babe would die, which she did not do...
although, in time, the old woman went to her reward, and left the child alone.

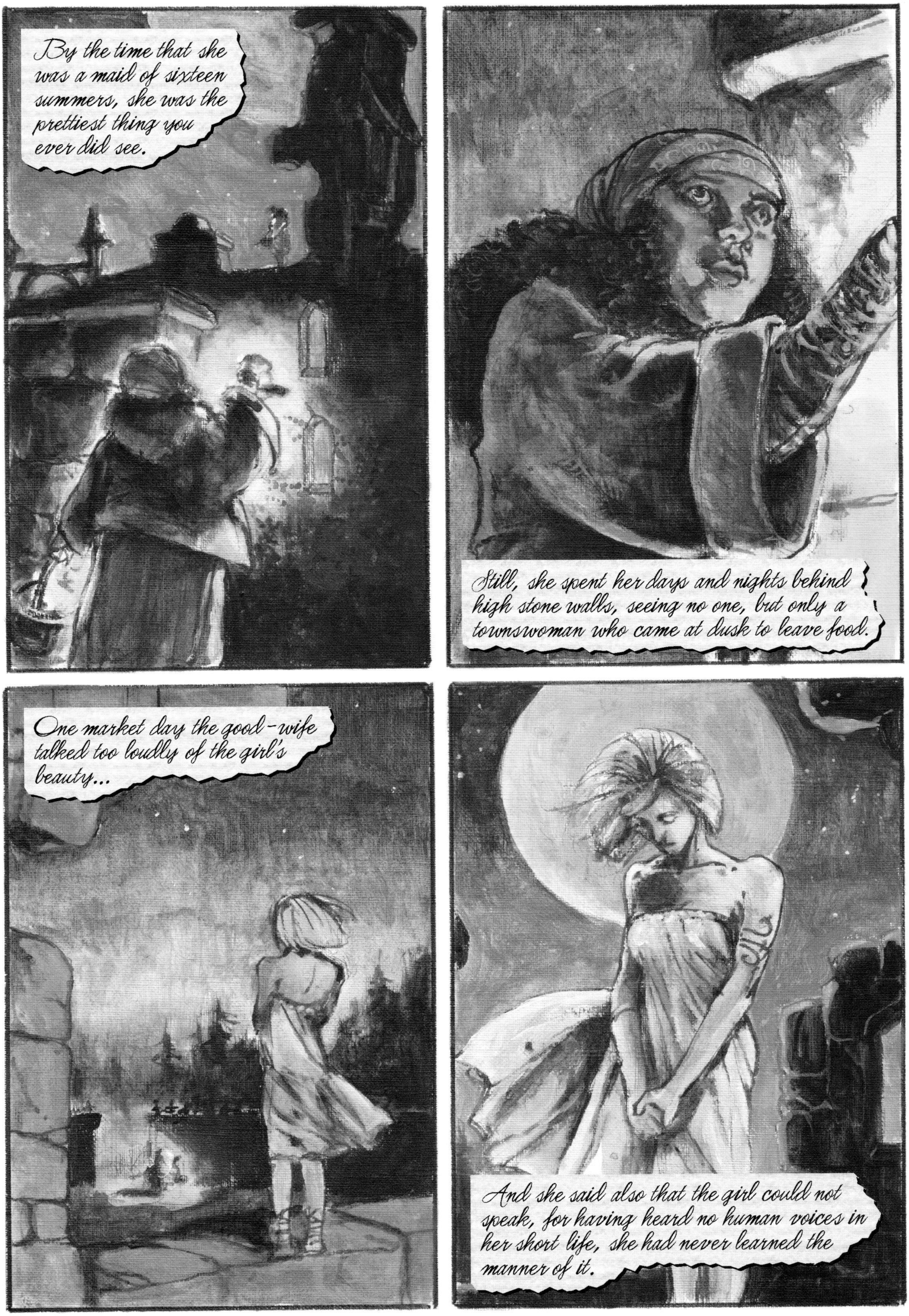
By the time that she was a maid of sixteen summers, she was the prettiest thing you ever did see.
Still, she spent her days and nights behind high stone walls, seeing no one, but only a townswoman who came at dusk to leave food.
One market day the good-wife talked too loudly of the girl's beauty...
And she said also that the girl could not speak, for having heard no human voices in her short life, she had never learned the manner of it.

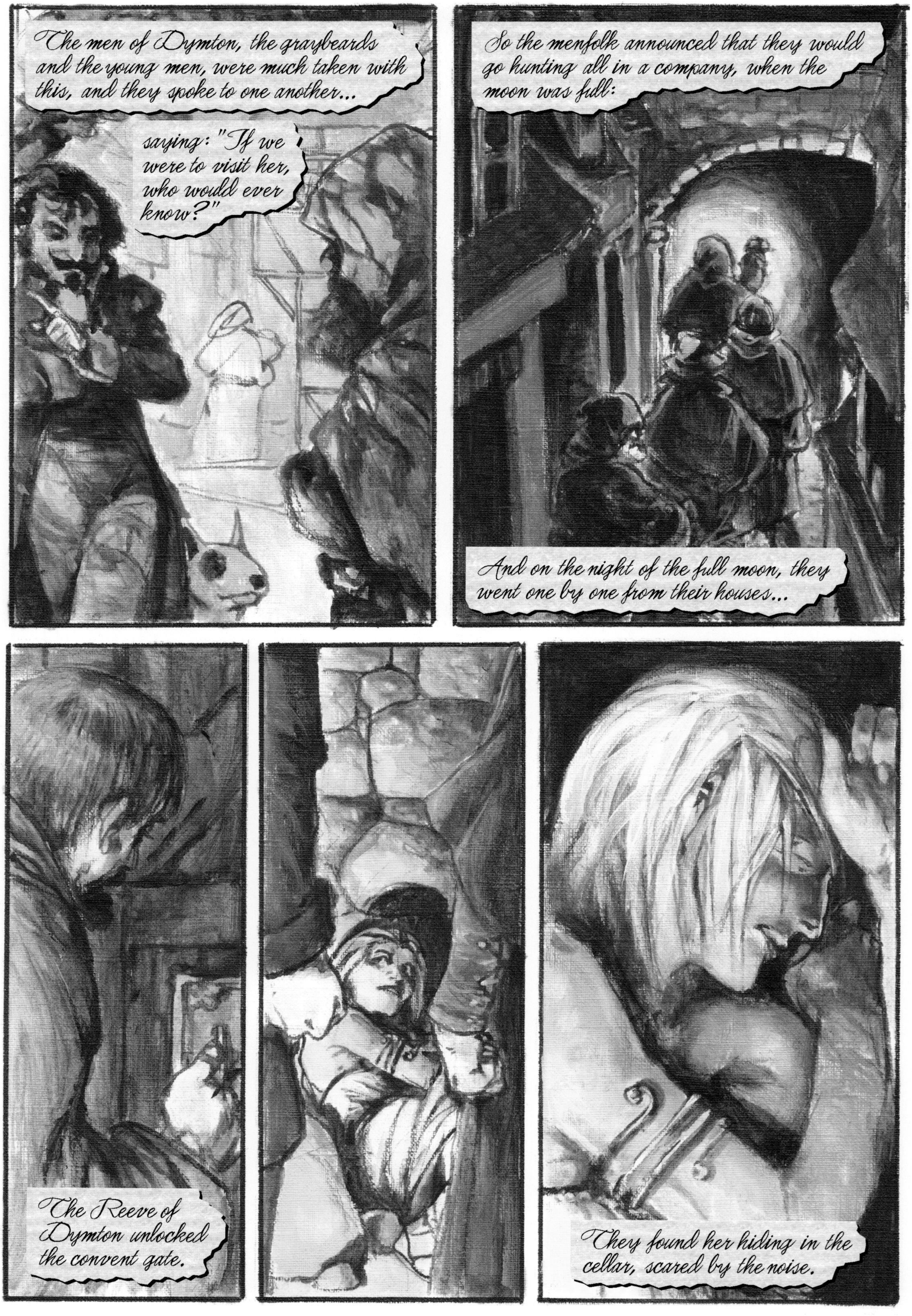

The men of Dymton, the graybeards and the young men, were much taken with this, and they spoke to one another...
saying: "If we were to visit her, who would ever know?"
So the menfolk announced that they would go hunting all in a company, when the moon was full:
And on the night of the full moon, they went one by one from their houses...
The Reeve of Dymton unlocked the convent gate.
They found her hiding in the cellar, scared by the noise.

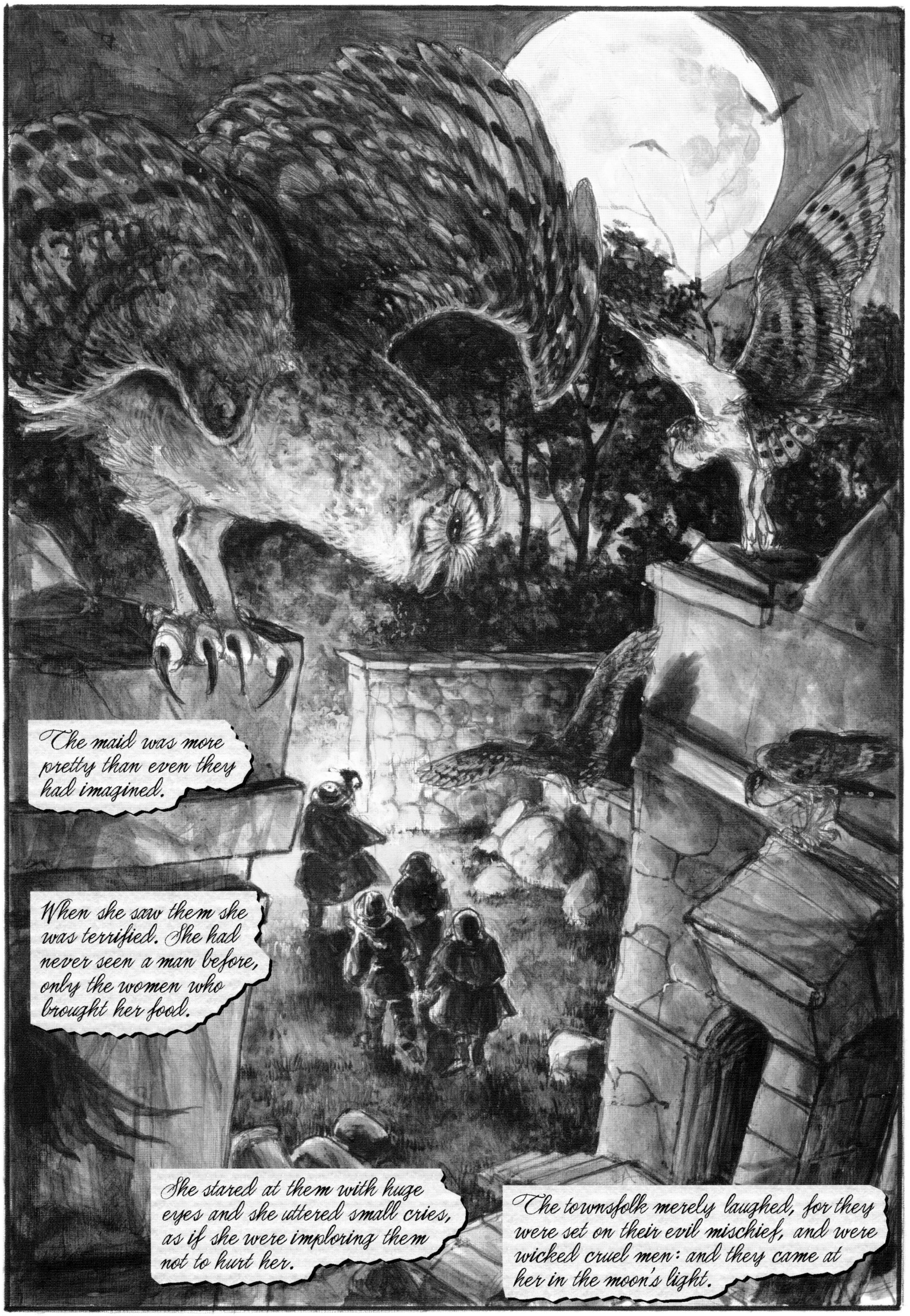
The maid was more pretty than even they had imagined.
When she saw them she was terrified. She had never seen a man before, only the women who brought her food.
She stared at them with huge eyes and she uttered small cries, as if she were imploring them not to hurt her.
The townsfolk merely laughed, for they were set on their evil mischief, and were wicked cruel men: and they came at her in the moon's light.

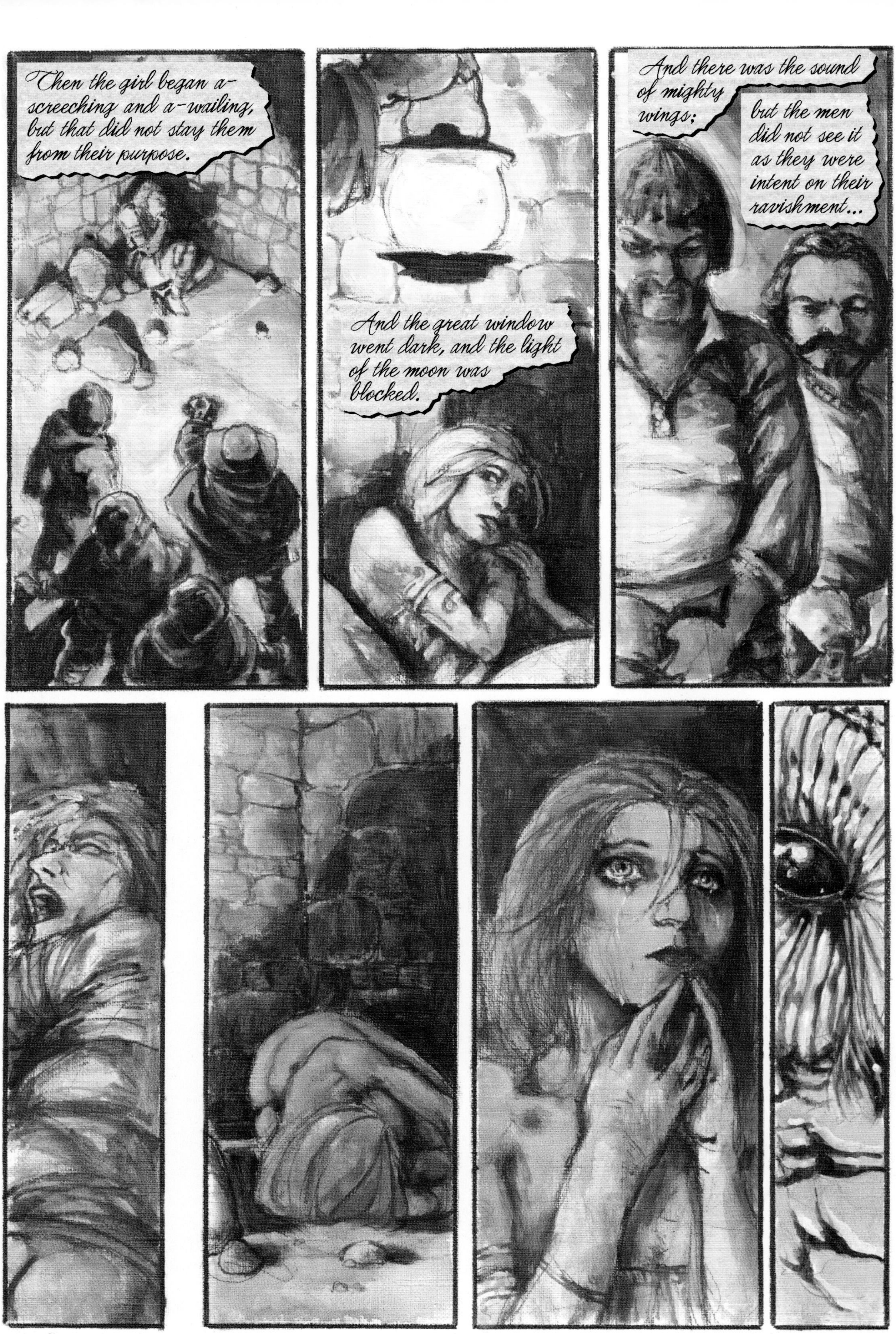
Then the girl began a-screeching and a-wailing, but that did not stay them from their purpose.
And the great window went dark, and the light of the moon was blocked.
And there was the sound of mighty wings;
but the men did not see it as they were intent on their ravishment...

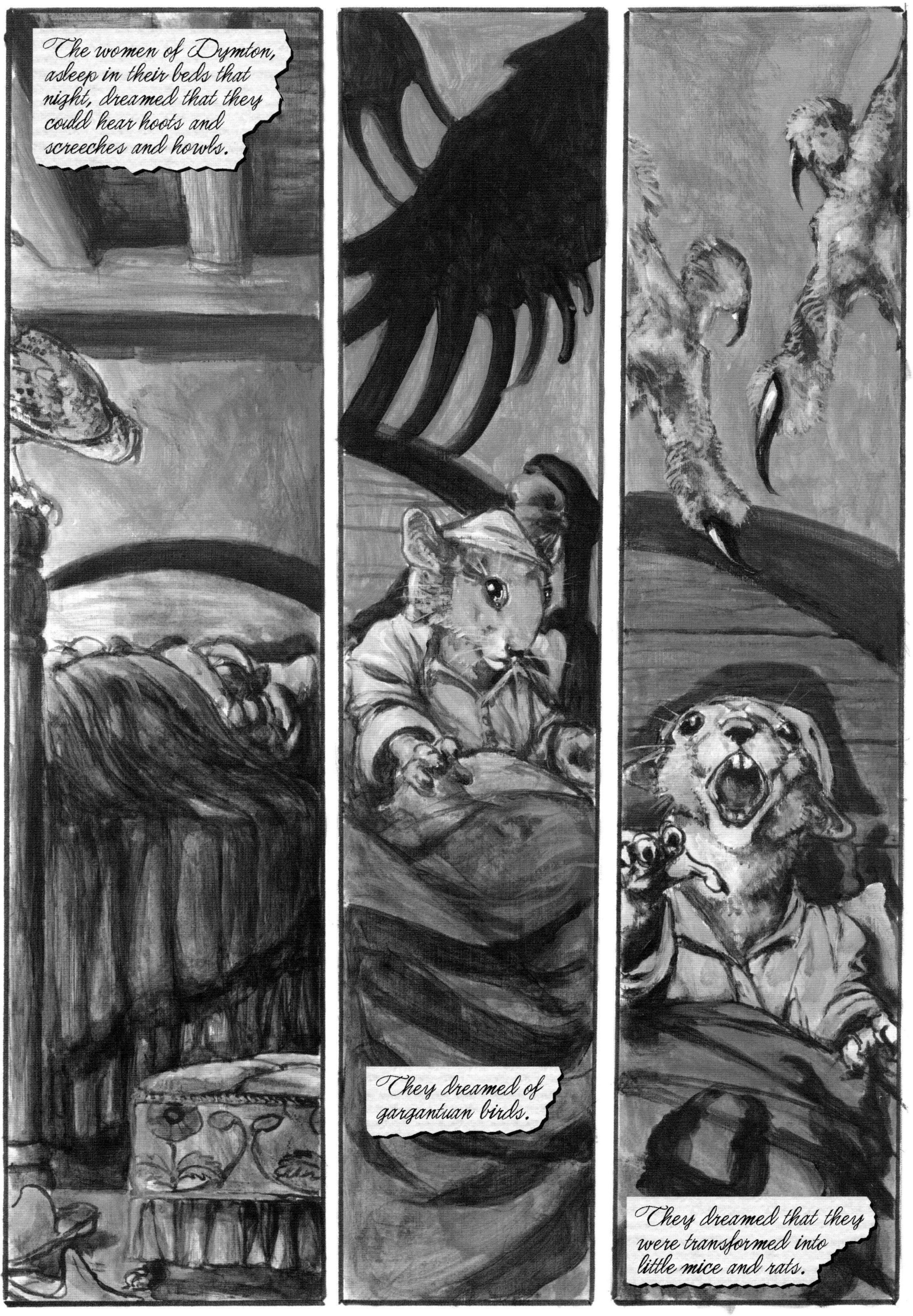
The women of Dymton, asleep in their beds that night, dreamed that they could hear hoots and screeches and howls.
They dreamed of gargantuan birds.
They dreamed that they were transformed into little mice and rats.

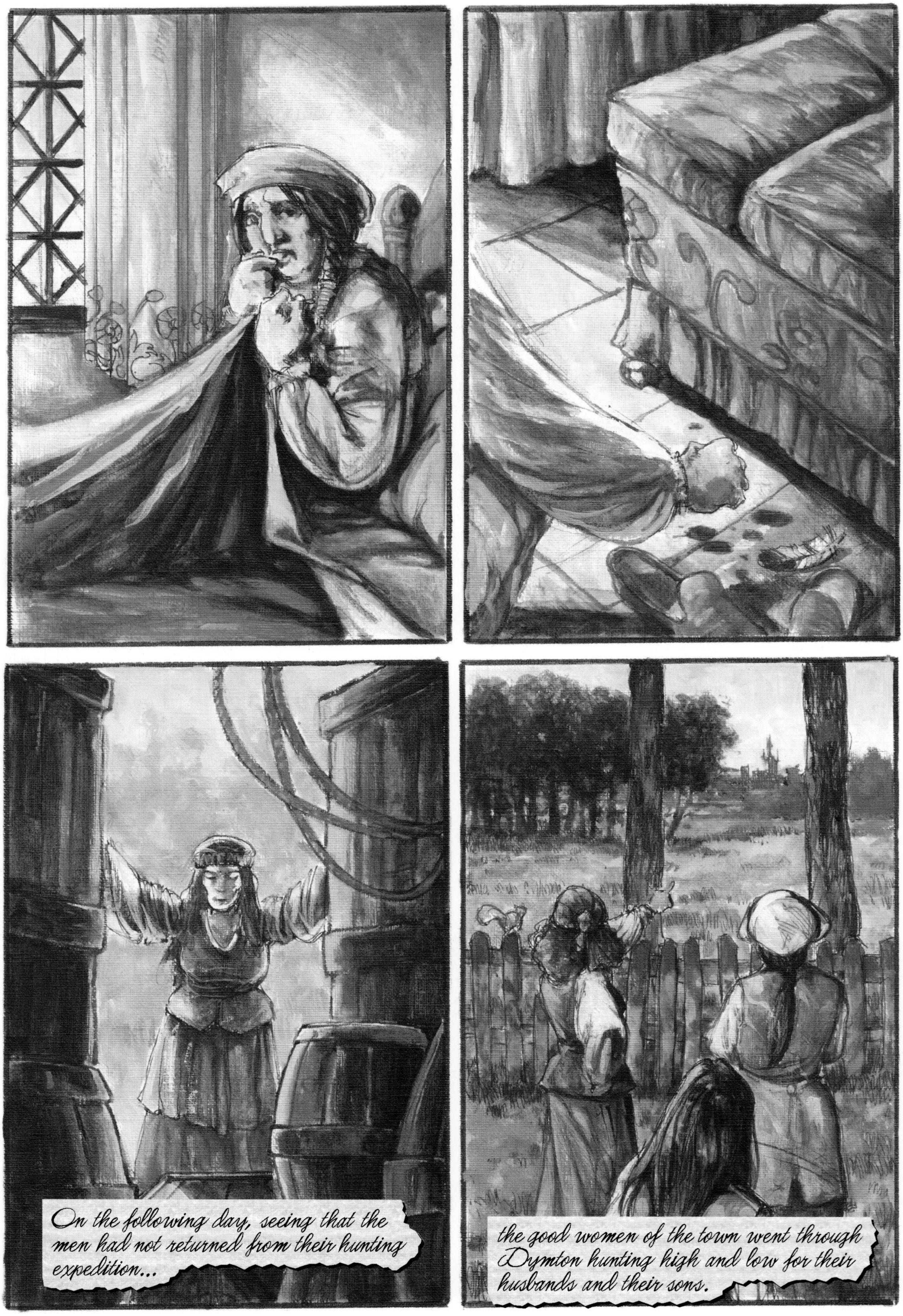
On the following day, seeing that the men had not returned from their hunting expedition...
the good women of the town went through Dymton hunting high and low for their husbands and their sons.

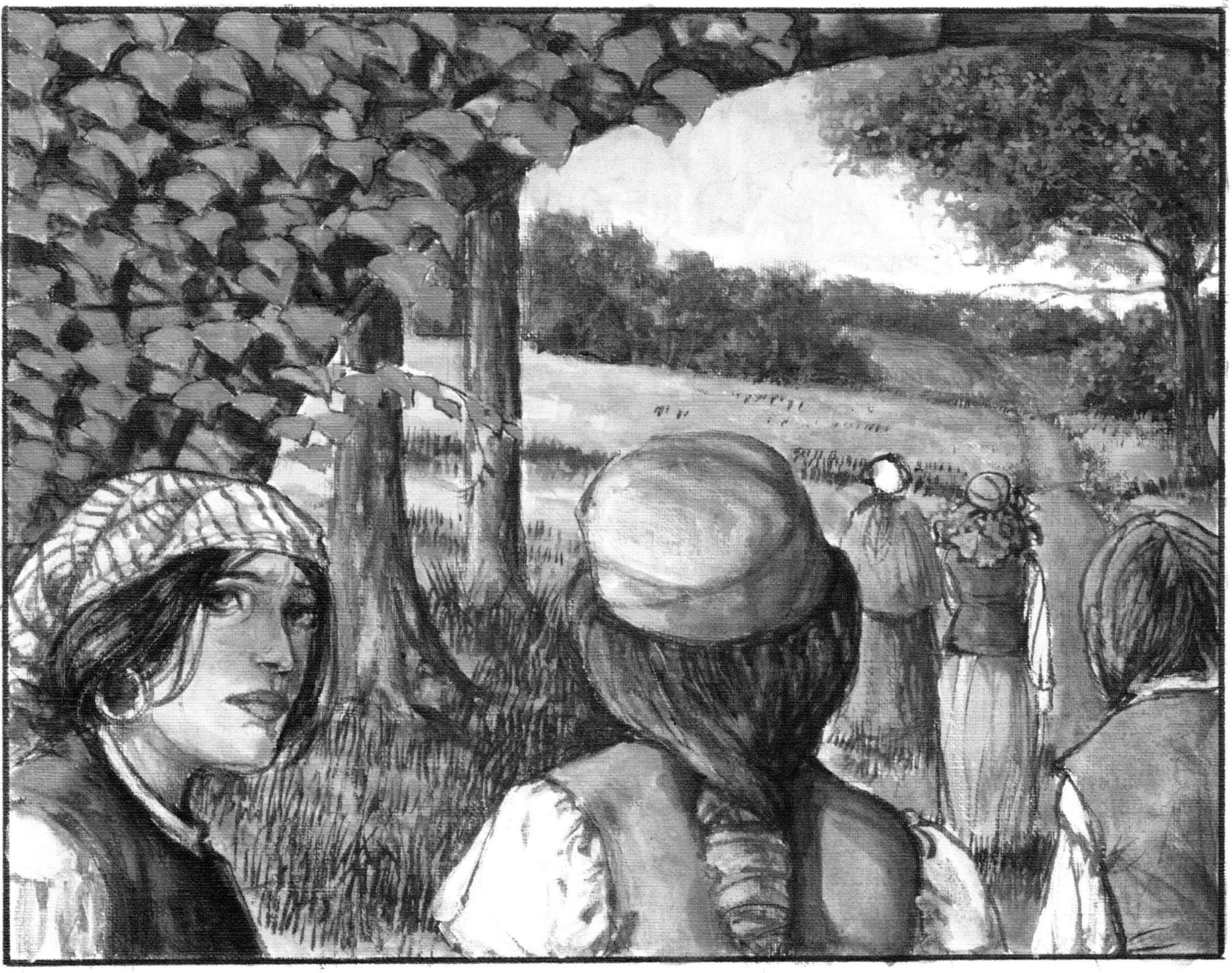

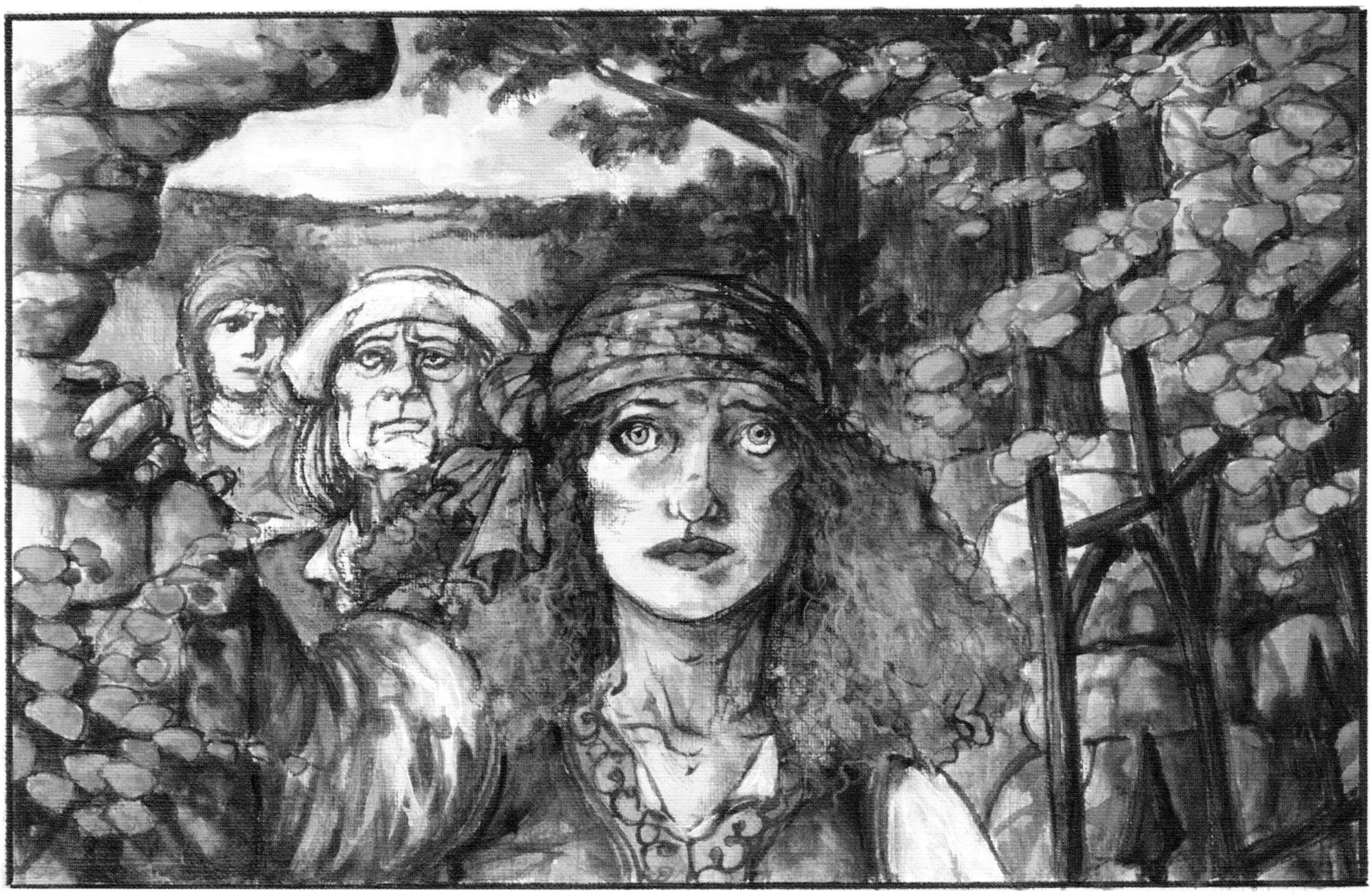

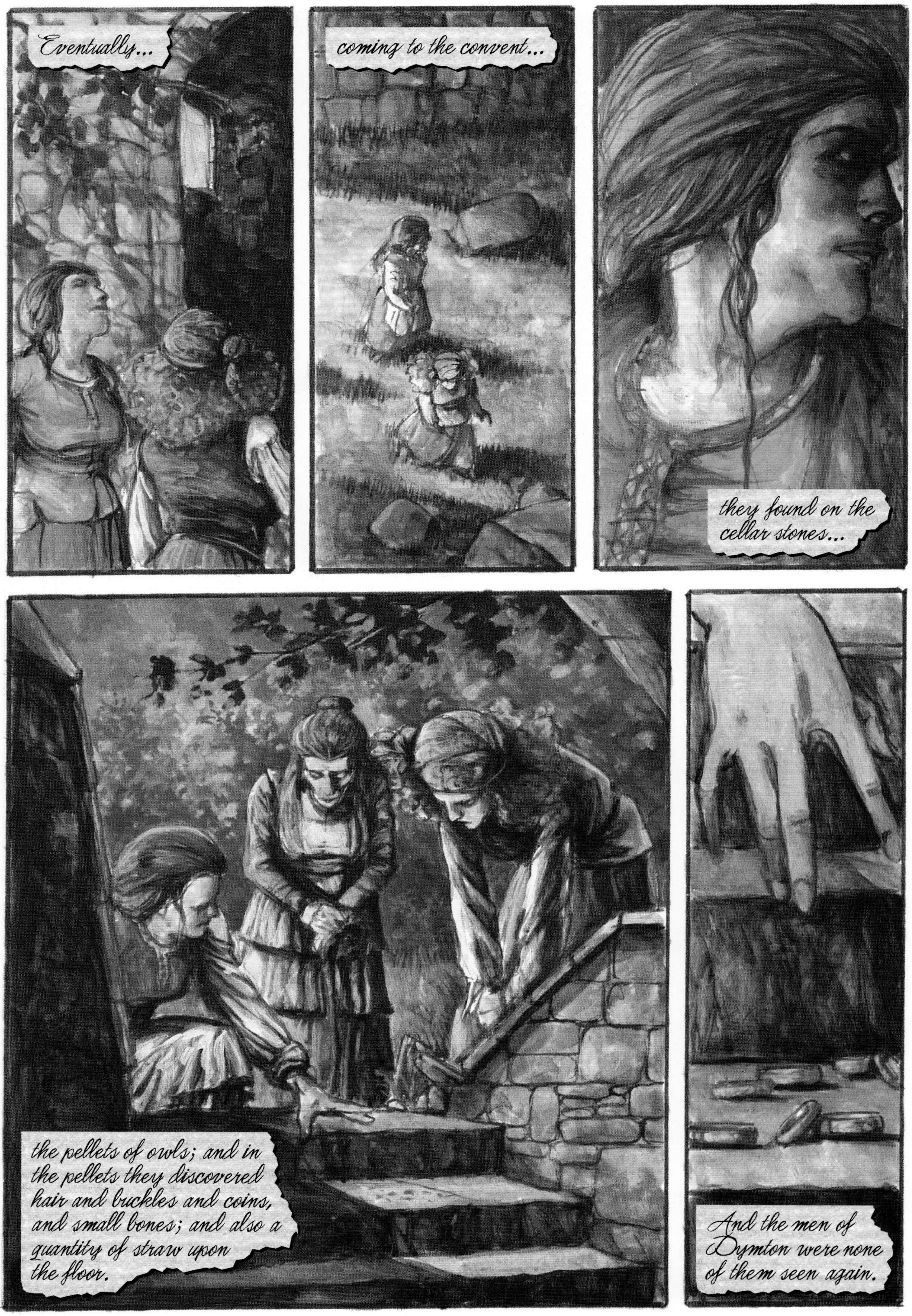
Eventually...
coming to the convent...
they found on the cellar stones...
the pellets of owls; and in the pellets they discovered hair and buckles and coins, and small bones; and also a quantity of straw upon the floor.
And the men of Dymton were none of them seen again.

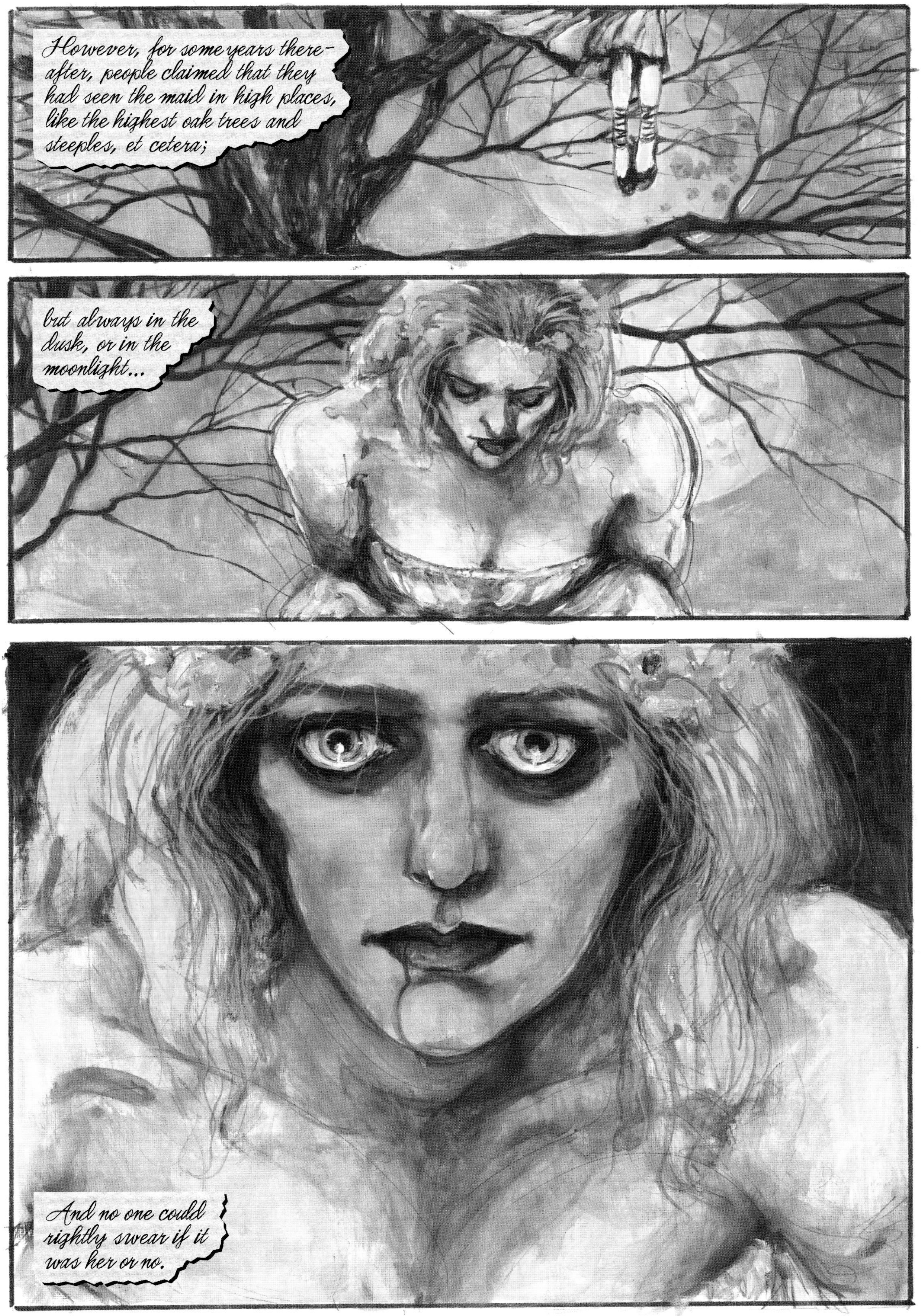
However, for some years there-after, people claimed that they had seen the maid in high places, like the highest oak trees and steeples, et cetera;
but always in the dusk, or in the moonlight...
And no one could rightly swear if it was her or no.

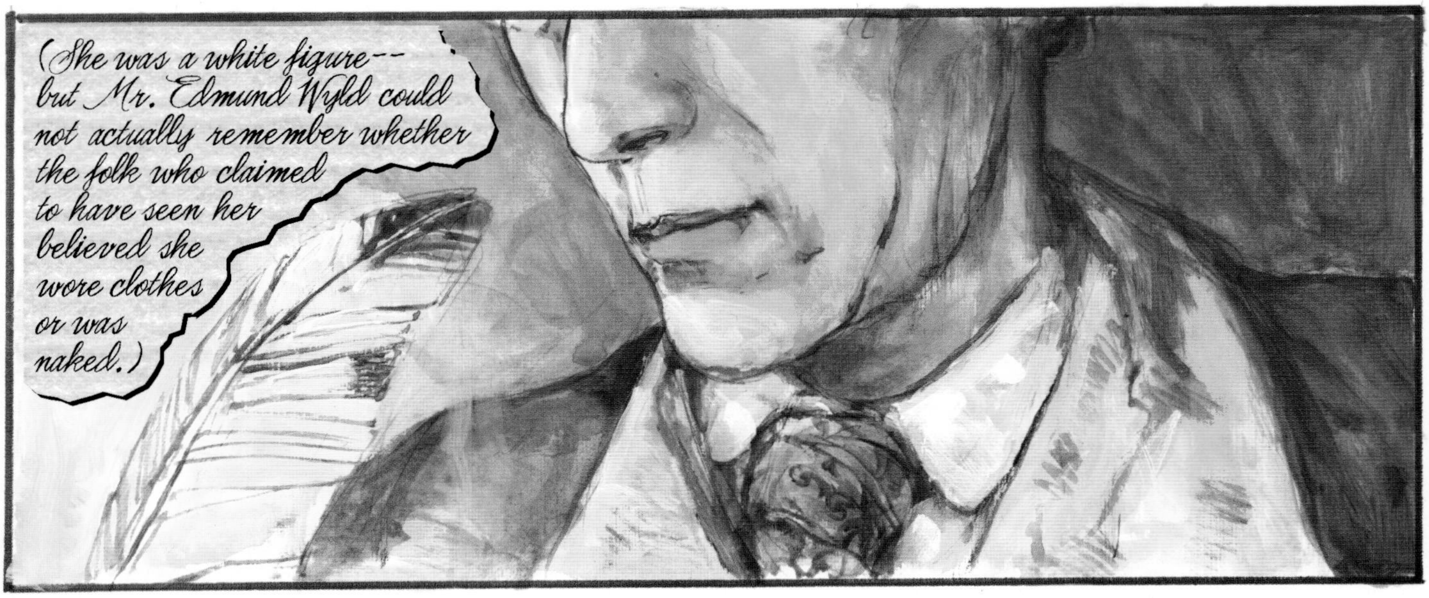
(She was a white figure-- but Mr. Edmund Wyld could not actually remember whether the folk who claimed to have seen her believed she wore clothes or was naked.)

The truth of it all is obvious, but it is a merry story and one which I write down here, to amuse my readers, and put them in mind of simpler times, when people believed such tales.

Aubrey Johns,
3rd February 1897

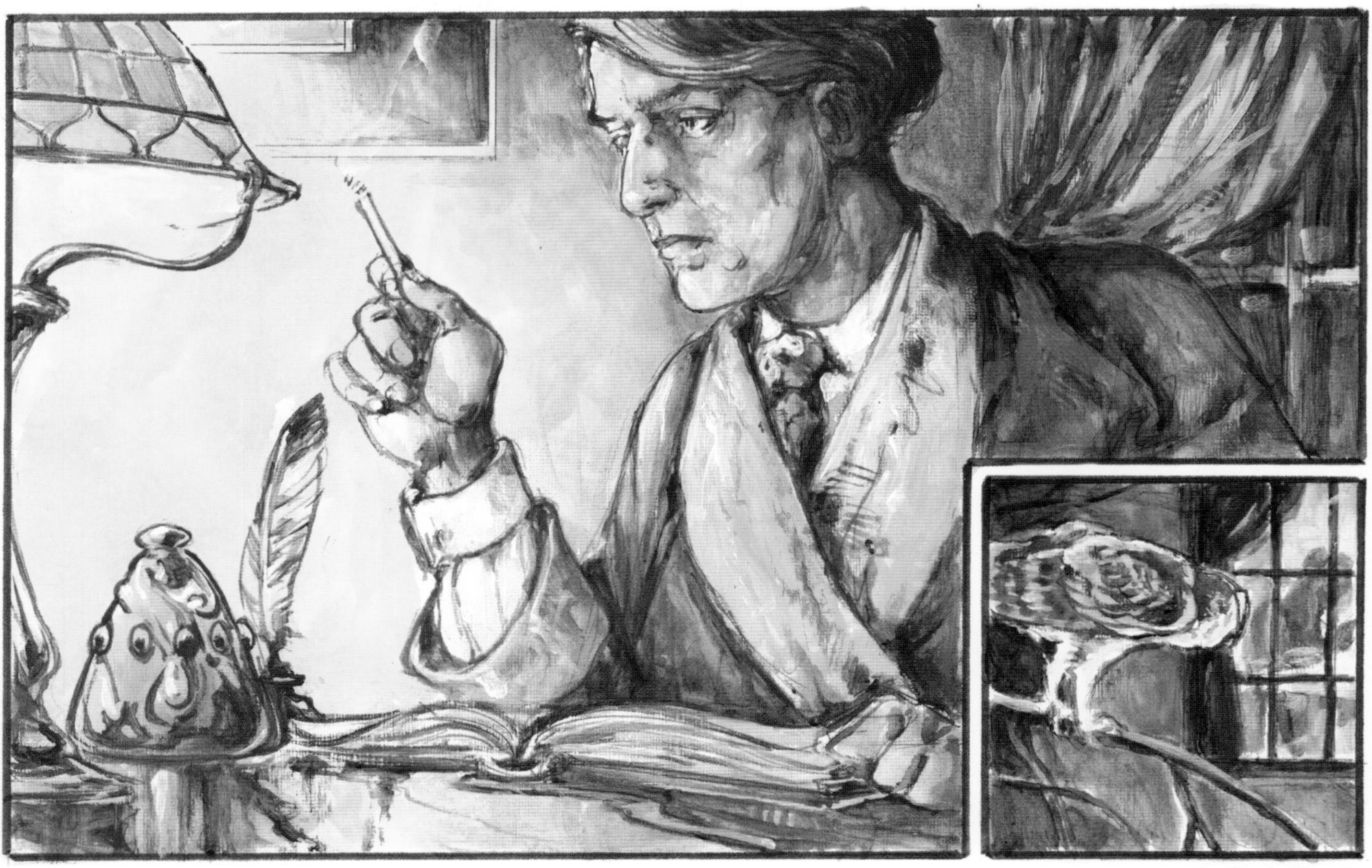

The End

BONUS
CONTENT

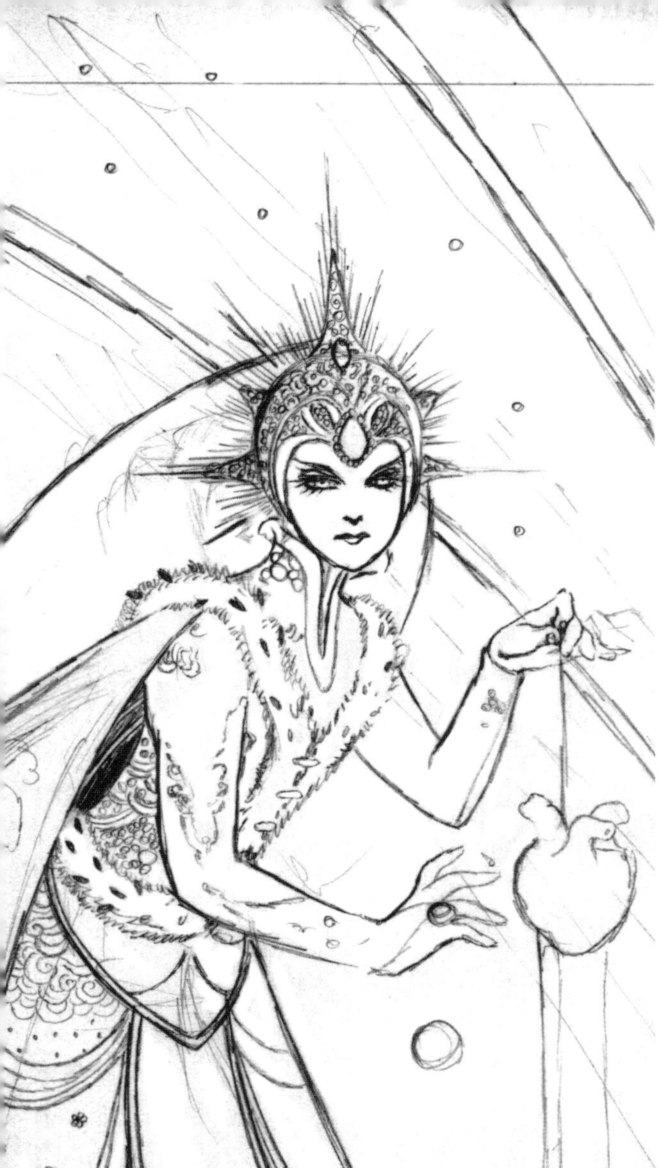

SNOW, GLASS, APPLES

SKETCHBOOK

NOTES BY
COLLEEN DORAN

I've admired Harry Clarke's work since I was a teenager. I mistook his drawing *An Angel of Peace* for art by Aubrey Beardsley, then spent years trying to track down information about his life and creations. He became a major influence on my work, but there wasn't much enthusiasm for this highly decorative style when I first got into comics, so I didn't get much opportunity to go as far as I wanted with this look.

Neil Gaiman, also a great admirer of Clarke, decided that *Snow, Glass, Apples* would be a great story for this style.

Here you see early cover designs and sketches. I wish I'd been able to complete that second sketch as well as the final! Maybe I'll finish it later, just for kicks.

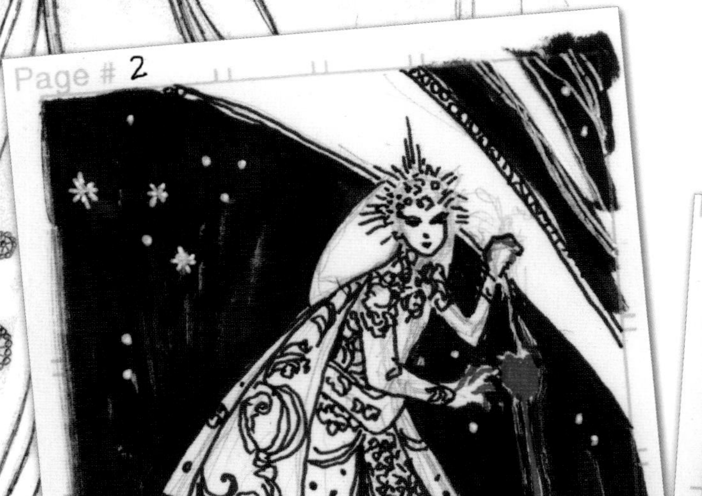
Page # 2

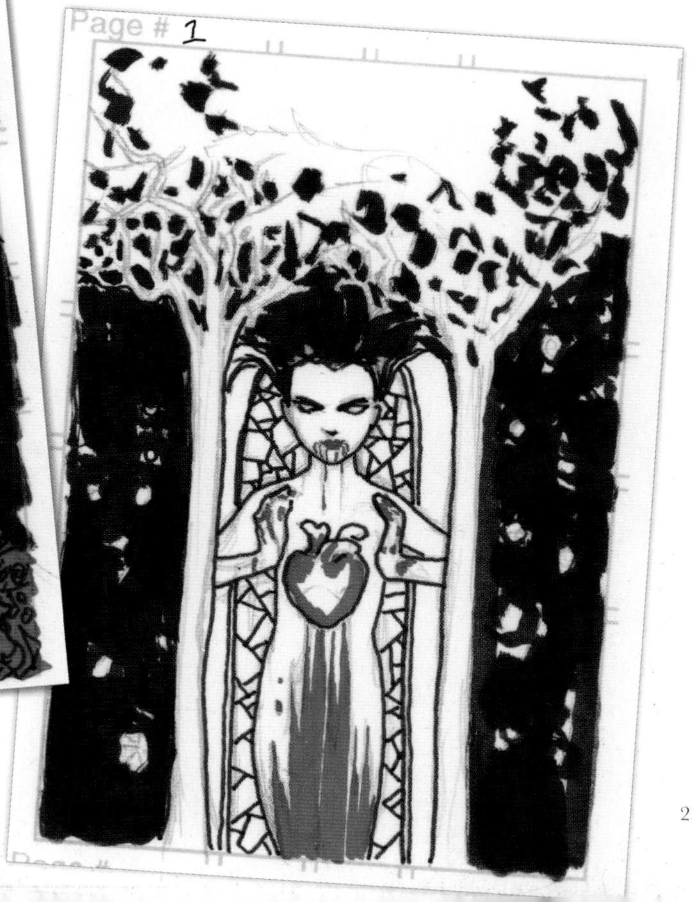
Page # 1

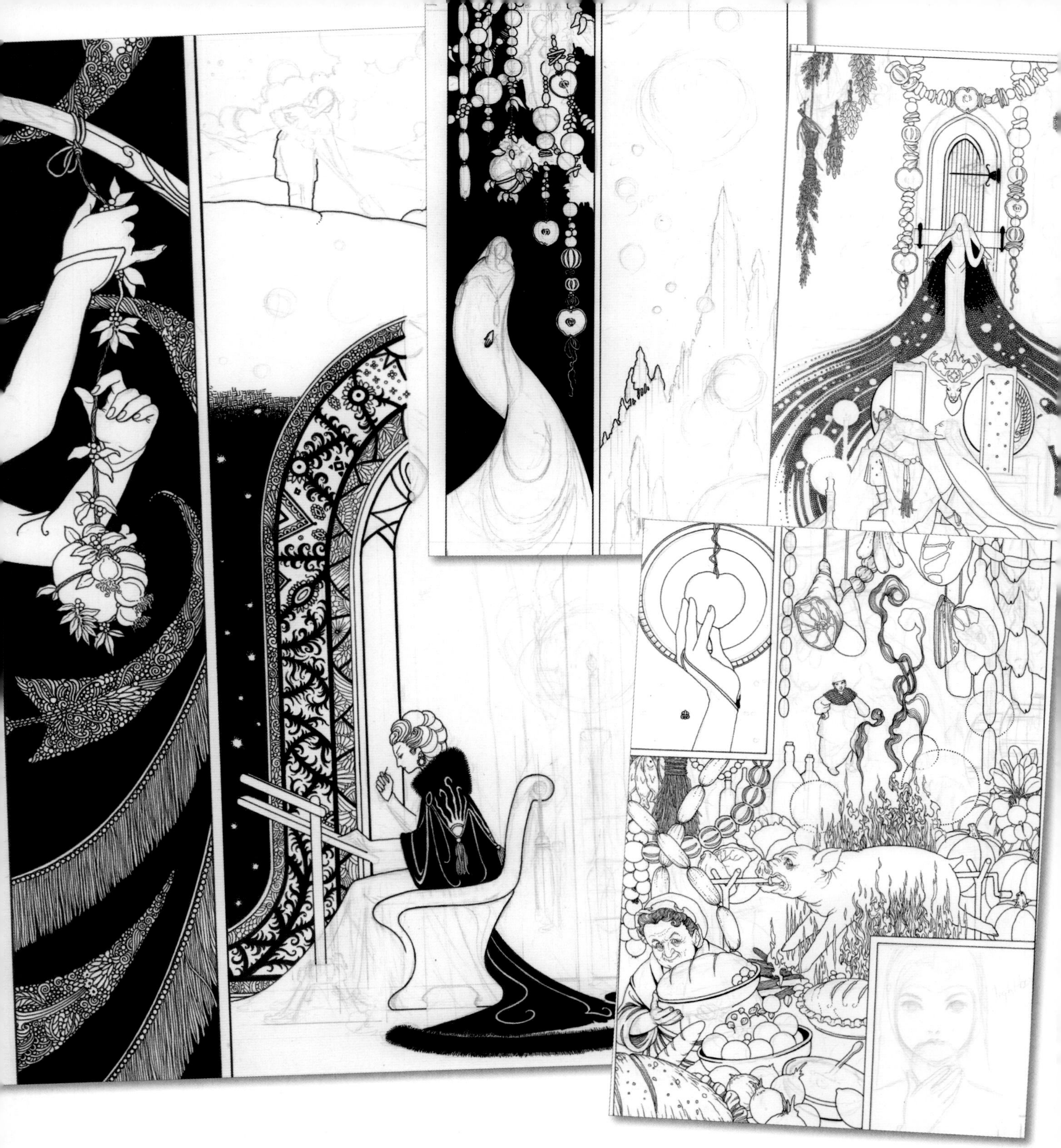

To the right, another unused cover sketch, which Neil wisely decided looked too much like a young-adult novel. We didn't want this book to appeal to kids, for obvious reasons.

On this page, scans of the art in progress. Most of the art on this book was done entirely by hand, including all the niggling little details and heavy blacks. As you may imagine, this is an exceptionally labor-intensive approach.

The kitchen scene was one of my favorites to draw. My coloring assistant Val Trullinger, with whom I worked on *Amazing Fantastic Incredible Stan Lee*, ended up doing much of the color on this page. However, I decided it would be safest to have Val help out with flats but do the rest of the final color myself because it was too hard to match coloring styles. I ended up repainting everything, even my own flats, which I'd botched at one point. Since this is my first major project coloring line art, and I'd never worked with a flatter before, her technical assistance was a huge help.

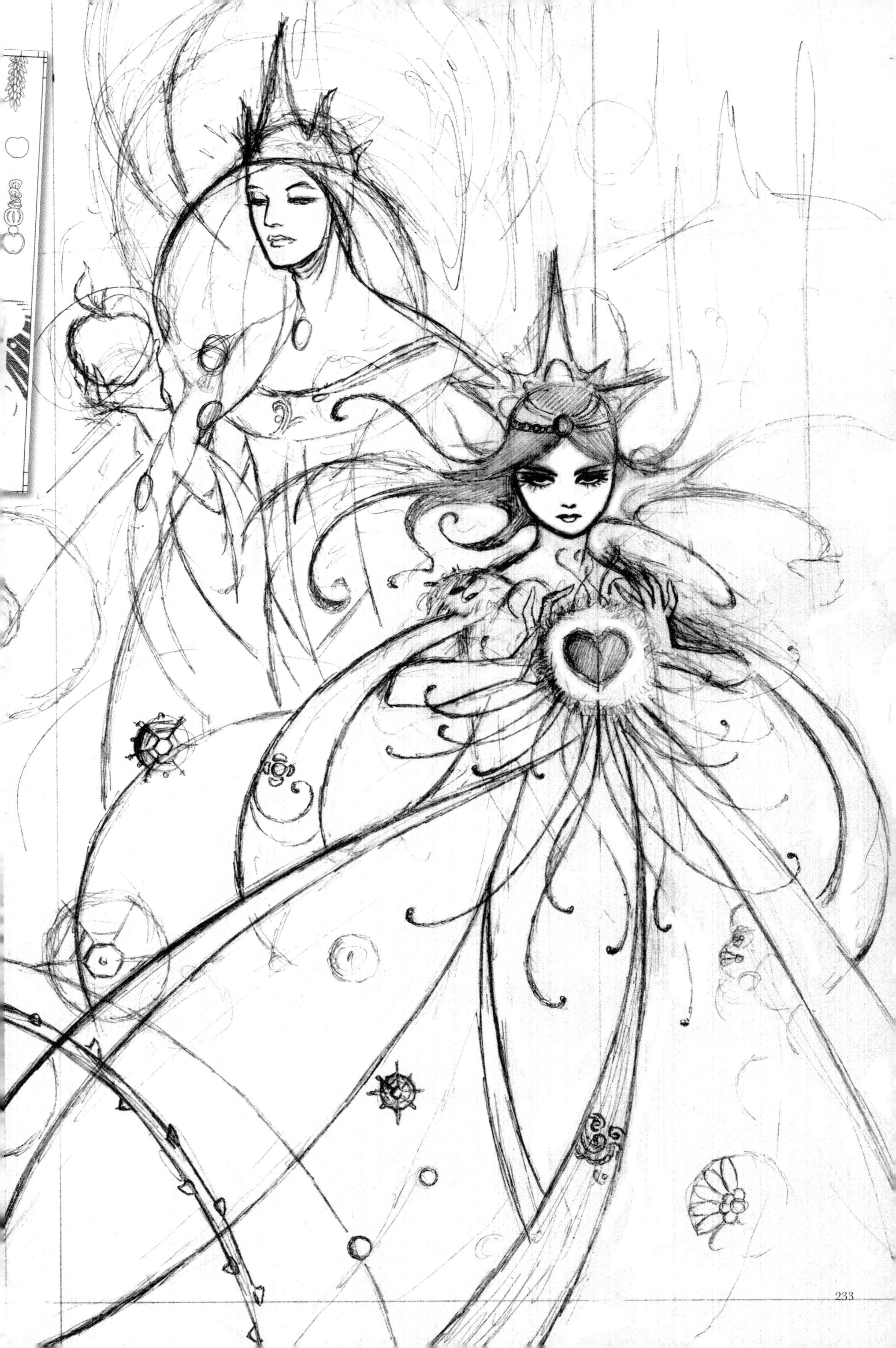

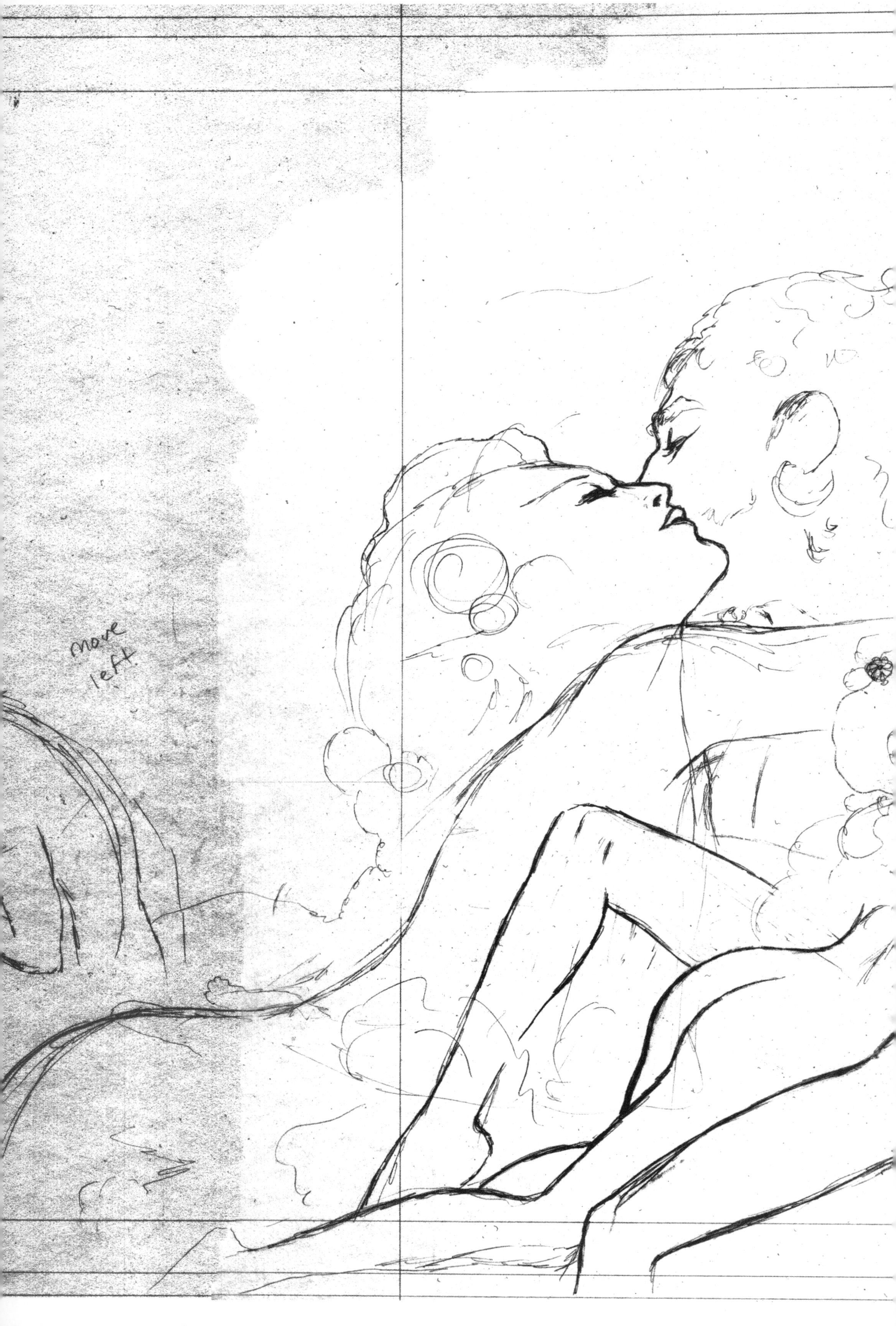
move left.

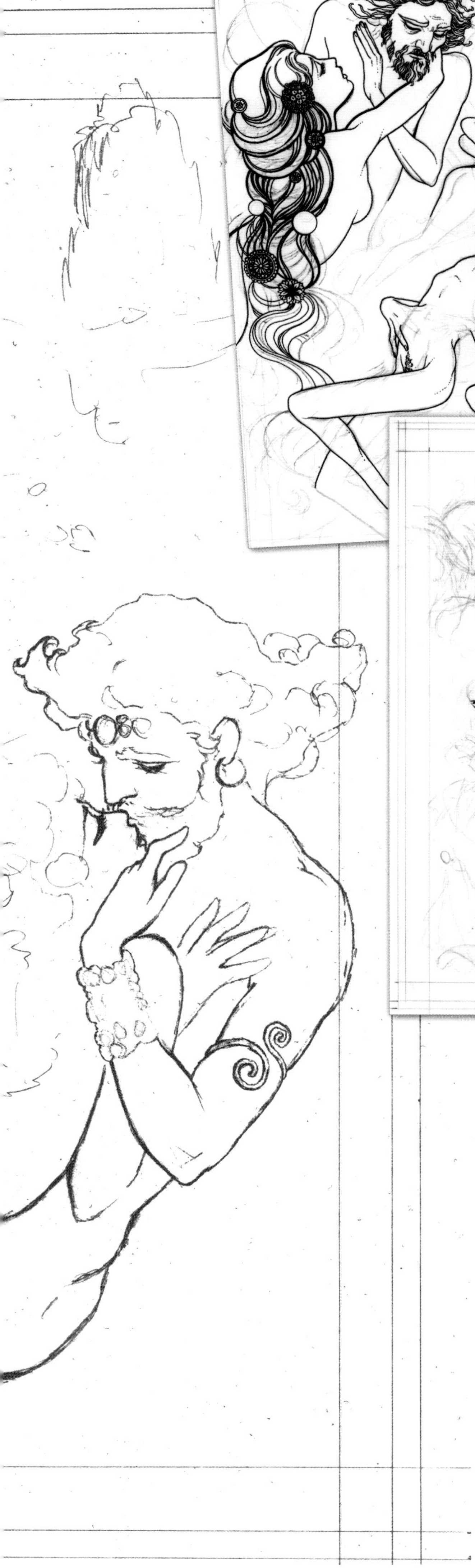

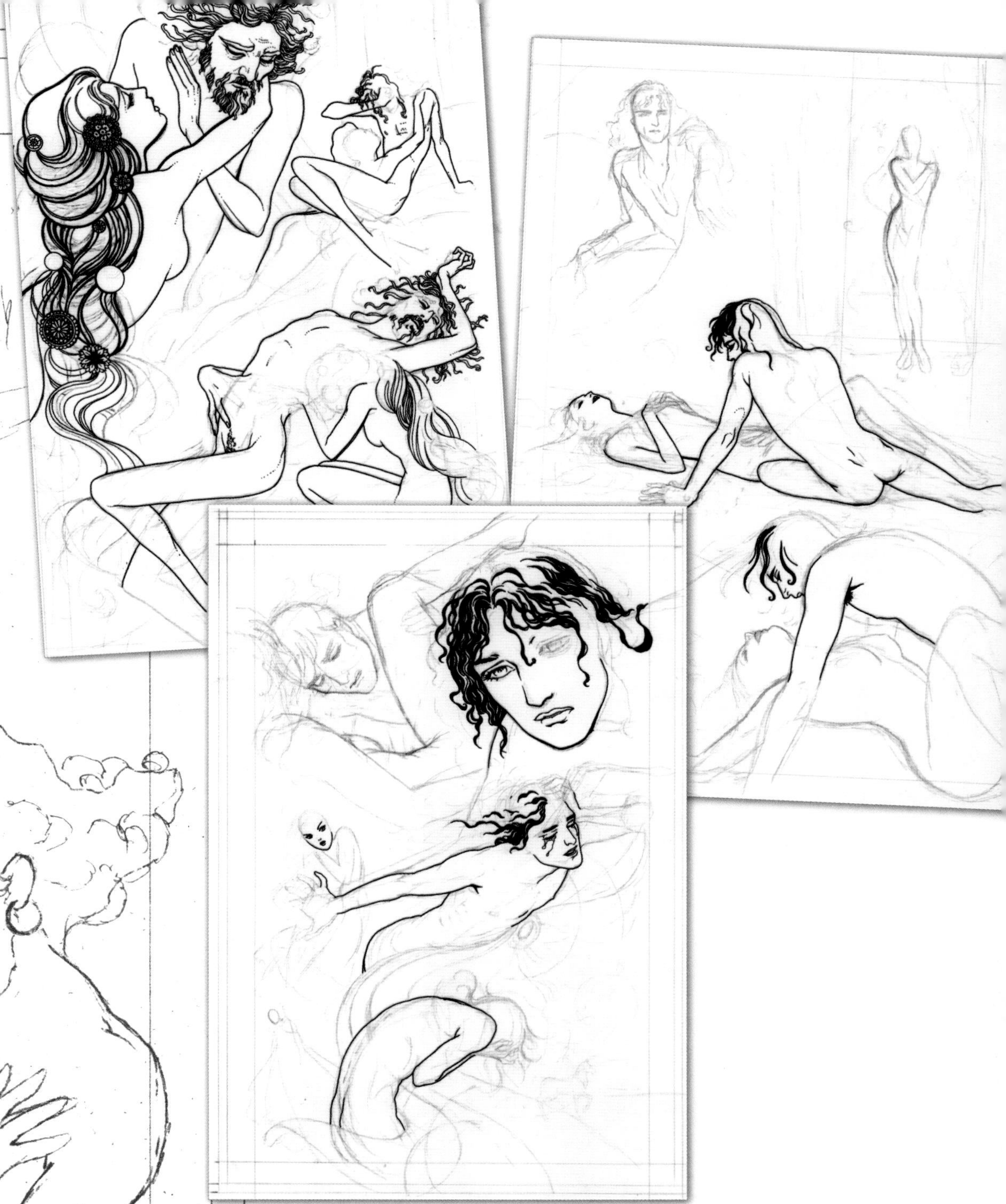

The erotic scenes were a bit of a challenge, as I struggled with how far to take the material.

I really enjoyed doing the opening double-page spread with the young queen and her king. It turned out more nouveau and less Harry Clarke than I intended, though.

I spent more time redoing art on this book than on anything I've ever drawn before, with nearly half my drawings thrown out after I began inking.

I don't do tight pencils when I ink my own work. But on this art, the final inks had to be so precise and clean that there just wasn't much wiggle room. When I made a mistake, I felt compelled to redo the whole page.

As the deadline marched on, this was a luxury I couldn't afford, as my editor can attest.

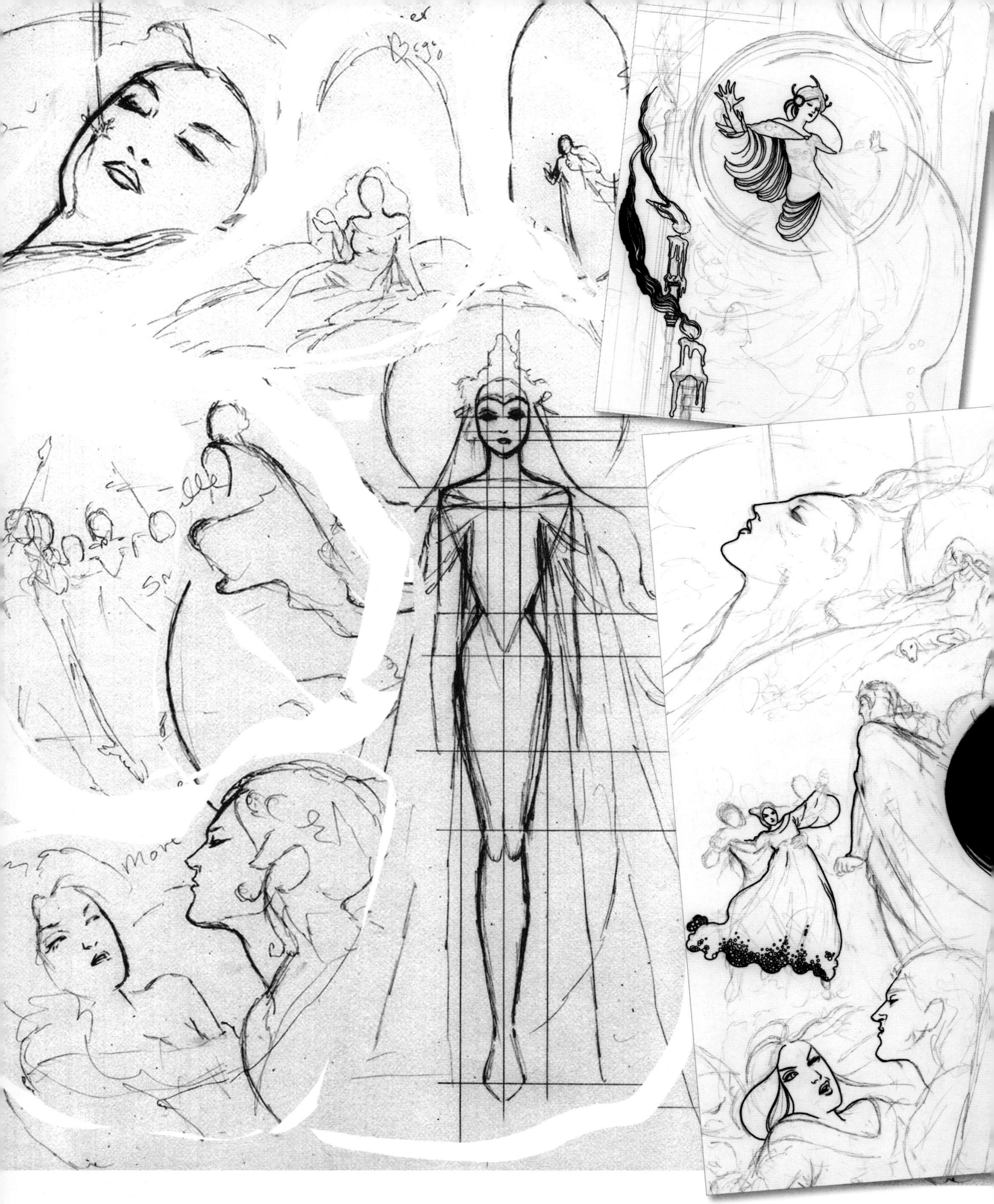

I did three versions of this page as Snow White confronts the queen. I took my original sketches, scanned them, then cut and pasted elements on the computer to work out the final composition.

The manga-looking eyes you see here are based on Clarke's style.

Over the years people assume I adopted this look into my comic art from manga, but the *fin de siècle*–era artists, creators like Beardsley and Clarke, were my early influences long before I'd ever seen manga. Clarke's work

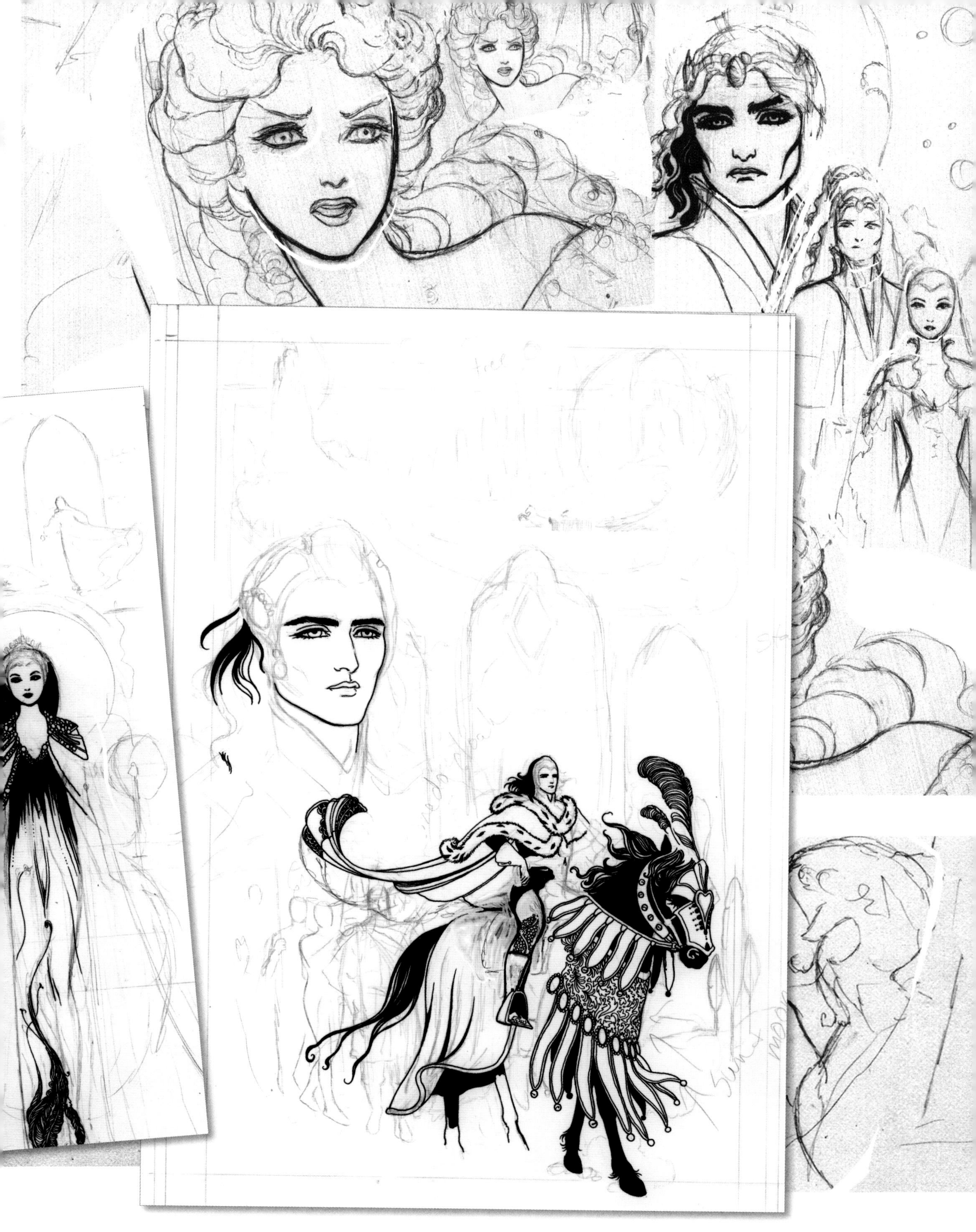

predates the manga big-eye affectation, though I'm sure I was predisposed to liking manga art because of my exposure to Beardsley and Clarke.

Clarke's approach to the human figure is very attenuated and affected, and I didn't want it to dominate the feel of the book. Still, I went with a more stylized look than I usually do.

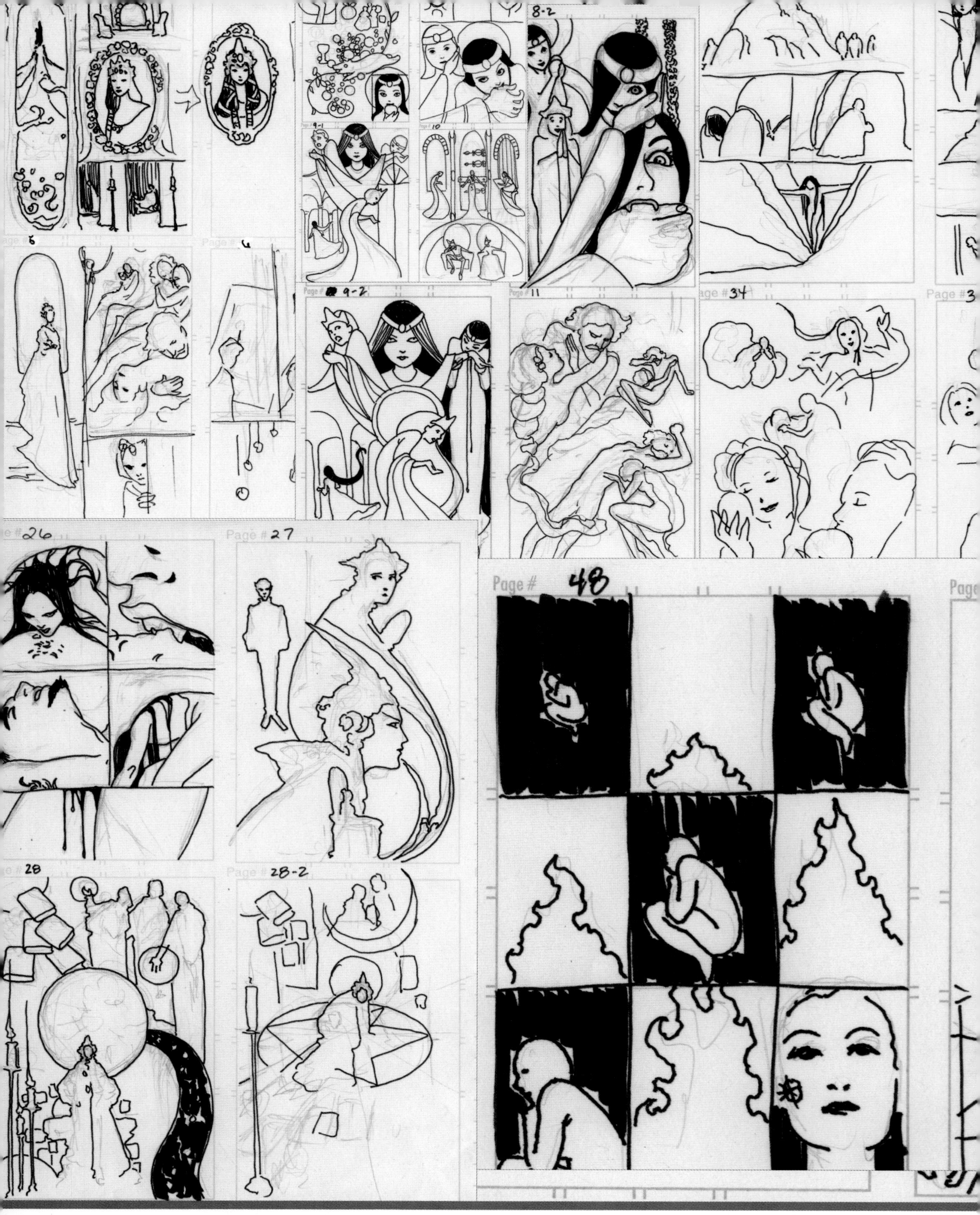
8-2
9-1
10
Page # 9-2
Page # 11
Page # 34
Page # 26
Page # 27
28
Page # 28-2
Page # 48

I strictly limited panel borders and used page flow to indicate the passage of time, mood, and feeling. For moments that require time beats, as on page 48, I used panel borders.

Most of the story is told from inside the queen's head, so I wanted a free-flowing sensibility. The challenge is to keep the narrative moving without confusing the reader or the poor letterer, who needs to be very careful with his word balloon placement.

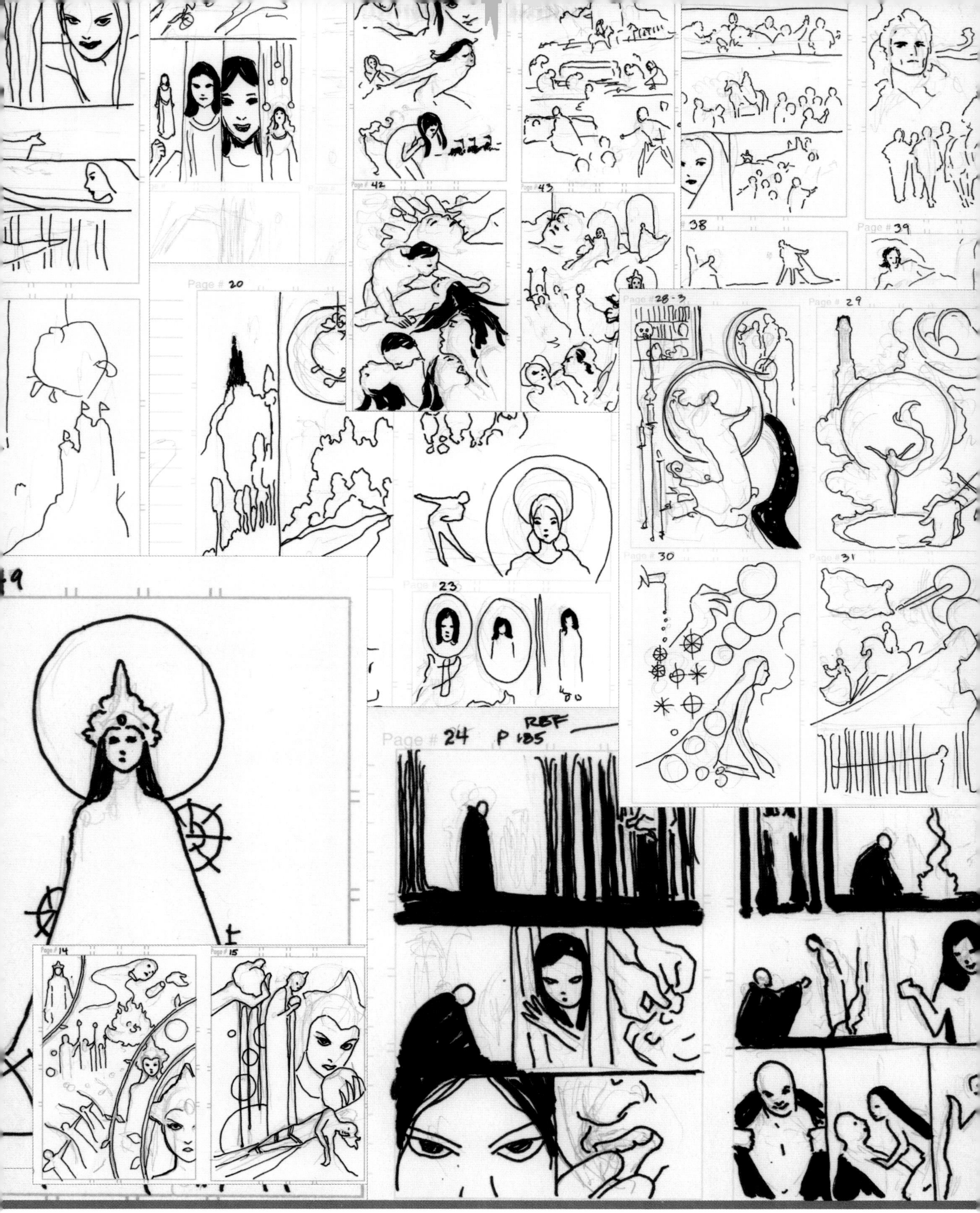
Page # 42
Page # 43
38
Page # 39
Page # 20
Page # 28-3
Page # 29
Page # 30
Page # 31
23
REF
Page # 24 P 185
Page # 14
Page # 15

For final pencils, I scanned the thumbnails, which are only about two inches high, blew them up to the final page size of about 9"x 13", and using a lightbox, traced the thumbnails onto a sheet of Bristol board. This helps to preserve the energy of the original sketch.

I love being able to work out composition problems on the computer, which can save hours of drawing and redrawing. However, all of my final art is entirely by hand, and I don't do "blue-line pencils" as many artists do.

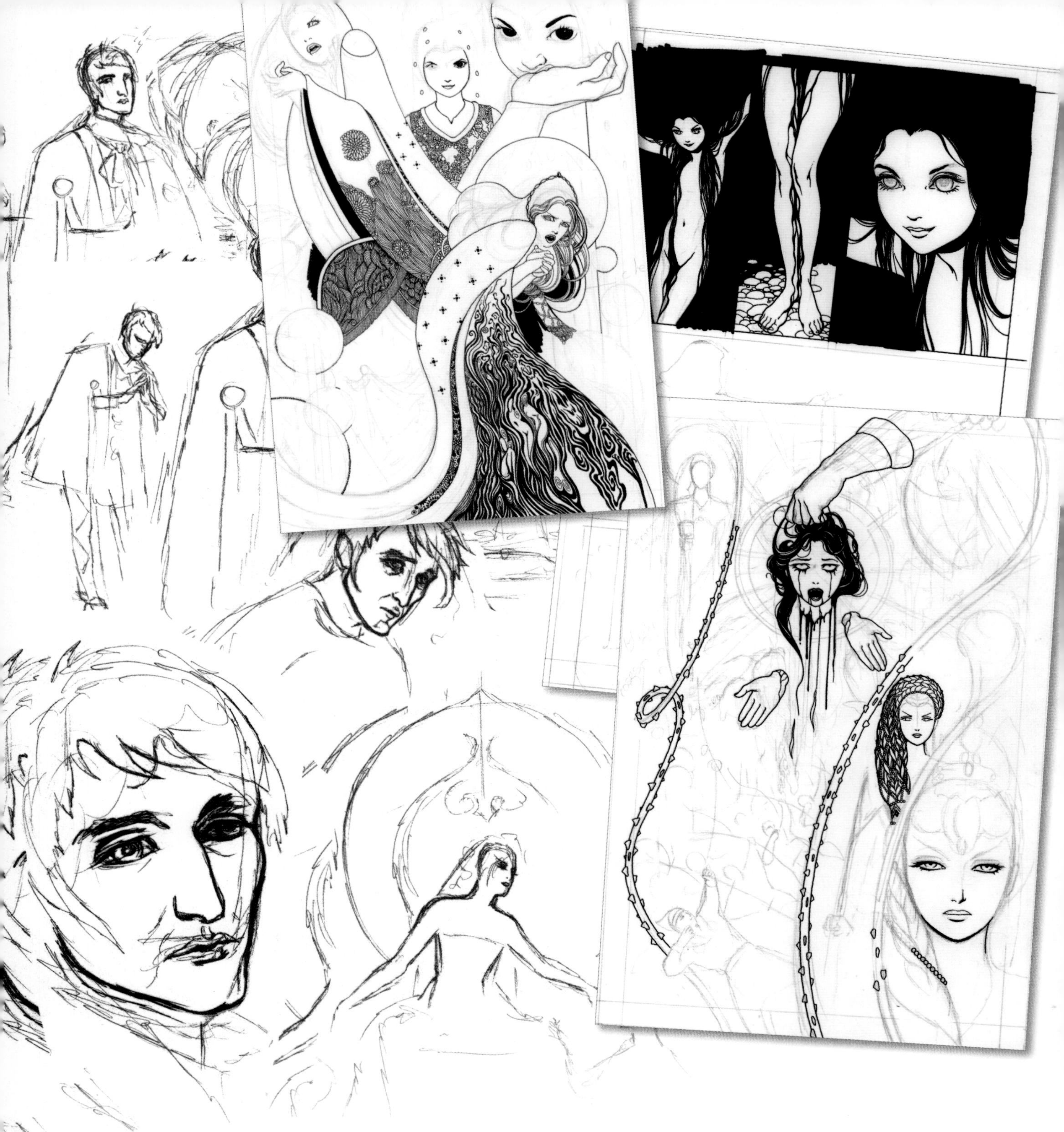

The Fair Lord is based on two works by Clarke: the main figure in *The Mad Mulrannies*, Clarke's illustration for JM Synge's *The Playboy of the Western World*, and his stained-glass work, *The Song of the Mad Prince*. *The Mad Mulrannies* was also the basis for the art on page 18. Other references from Clarke's art include illustrations from Poe's *The Pit and the Pendulum*, and a tiny spot illustration of two stylized horses ended up being incorporated into the queen's embroidery.

Clarke was the leader of the Irish Arts and Crafts Movement, and is probably best known for his stained glass. Since I'd only ever seen old, faded reproductions of his illustrations, Neil encouraged me to seek out his dazzling color originals. I went to Dublin, Ireland to get photos and reproductions of many of Clarke's works featuring deep, jewel-like blues, which I incorporated into my color approach, though my work is far more restrained than Clarke's.

I'm deeply grateful to Neil, our editor Daniel Chabon, and Dark Horse for giving me this great opportunity and so much creative freedom on this book.

ONLY THE END OF THE WORLD AGAIN

SKETCHBOOK

Featured in this sketchbook section are high-quality scans of the
original cover and inside front cover art followed by the complete layouts
drawn by P. Craig Russell and the complete inks by Troy Nixey scanned
from the original artwork and not digitally cleaned up to present a
side-by-side comparison of the actual, original artwork.

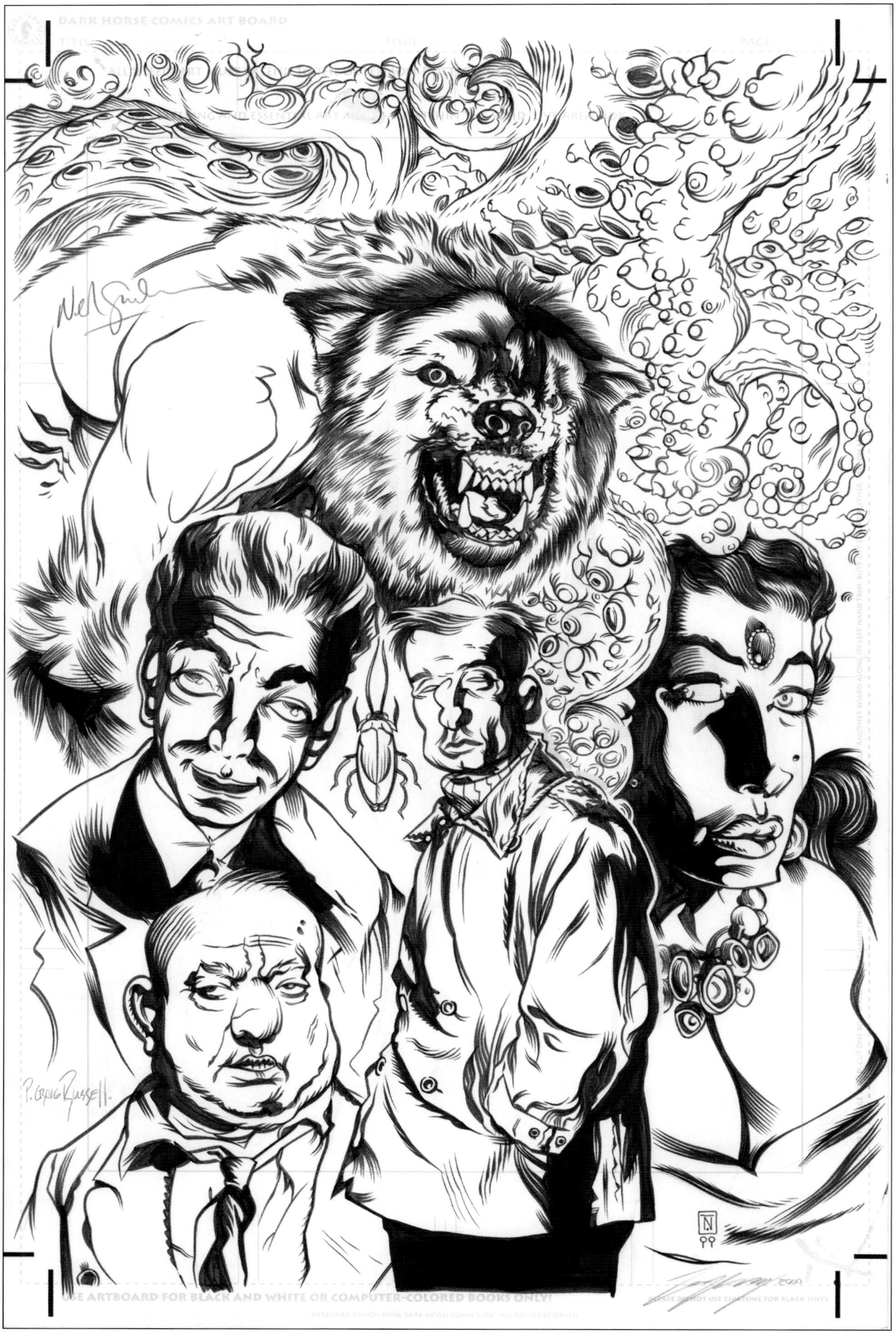
DARK HORSE COMICS ART BOARD
P. Craig Russell
USE ARTBOARD FOR BLACK AND WHITE OR COMPUTER-COLORED BOOKS ONLY!

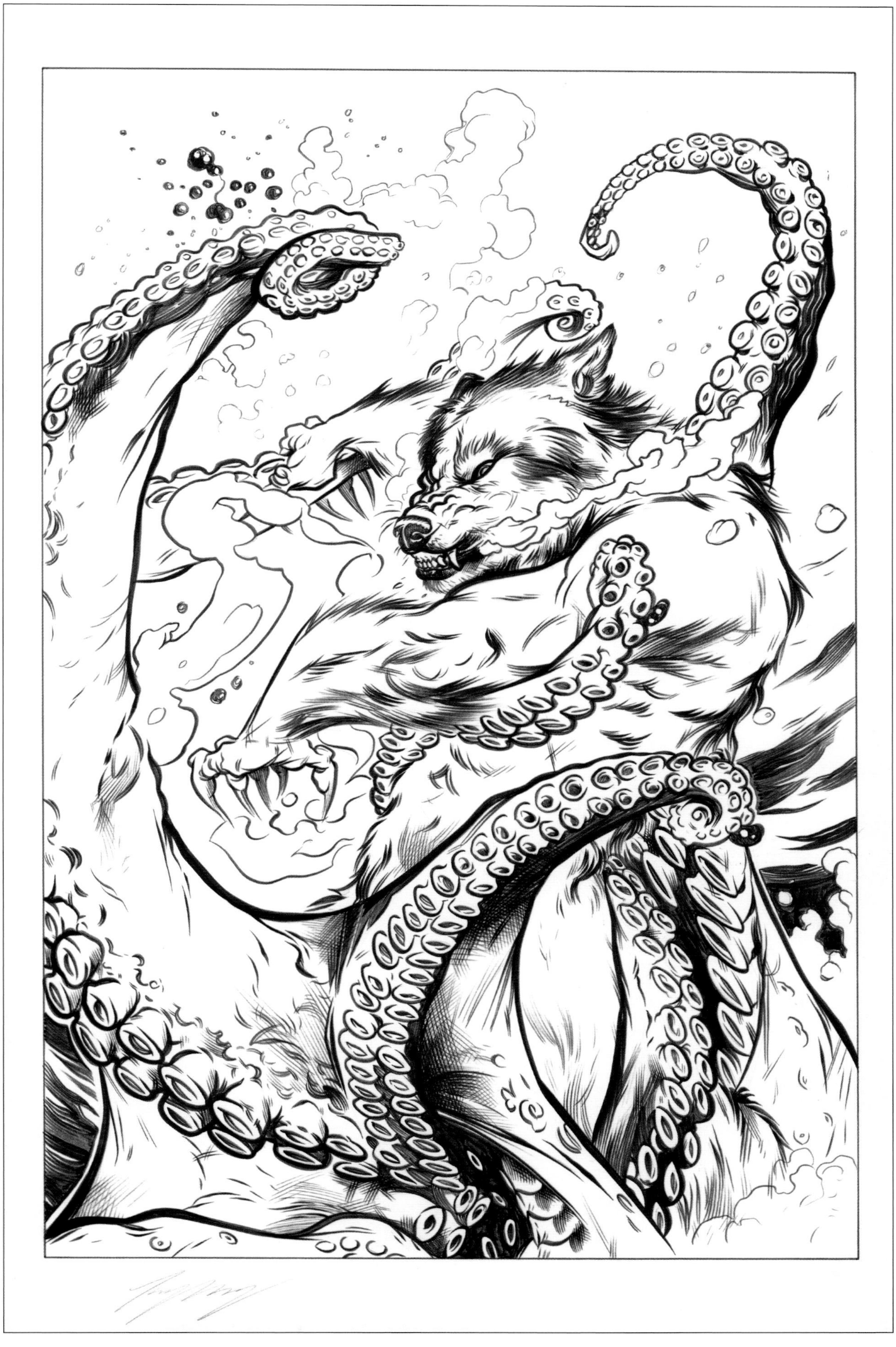

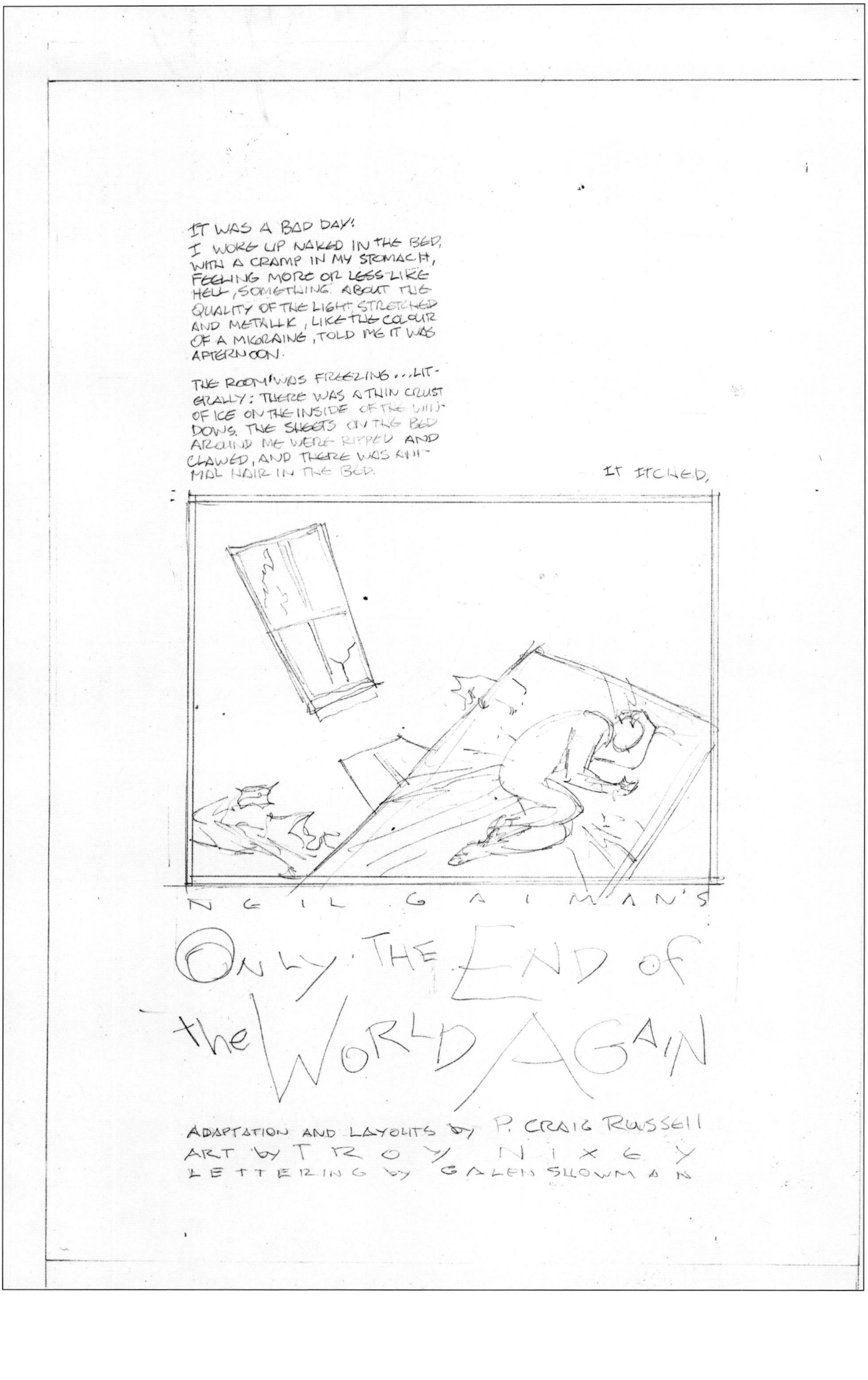
IT WAS A BAD DAY:
I WOKE UP NAKED IN THE BED, WITH A CRAMP IN MY STOMACH, FEELING MORE OR LESS LIKE HELL, SOMETHING ABOUT THE QUALITY OF THE LIGHT, STRETCHED AND METALLIC, LIKE THE COLOUR OF A MIGRAINE, TOLD ME IT WAS AFTERNOON.
THE ROOM WAS FREEZING... LIT-ERALLY: THERE WAS A THIN CRUST OF ICE ON THE INSIDE OF THE WIN-DOWS. THE SHEETS ON THE BED AROUND ME WERE RIPPED AND CLAWED, AND THERE WAS ANI-MAL HAIR IN THE BED.
IT ITCHED,
NEIL GAIMAN'S
ONLY THE END OF THE WORLD AGAIN
ADAPTATION AND LAYOUTS BY P. CRAIG RUSSELL
ART BY TROY NIXEY
LETTERING BY GALEN SHOWMAN

It was a bad day.

I woke up naked in the bed, with a cramp in my stomach, feeling more or less like hell. Something about the quality of the light, stretched and metallic, like the colour of a migraine, told me it was afternoon.

The room was freezing... literally: there was a thin crust of ice on the inside of the windows. The sheets on the bed around me were ripped and clawed, and there was animal hair in the bed.

It itched.

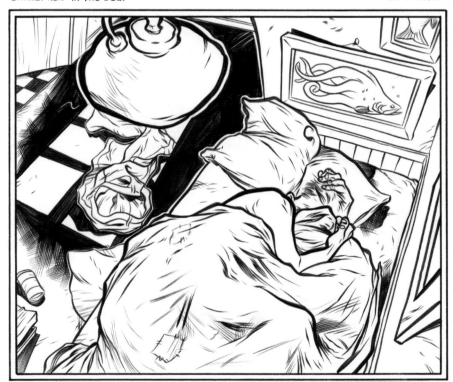

NEIL GAIMAN'S

ONLY THE END of the WORLD AGAIN

TO STEFAN,
THANKS ALOT

ADAPTATION BY P. CRAIG RUSSELL

ARTWORK & LAYOUT BY TROY NIXEY

LETTERING BY SEAN KONOT

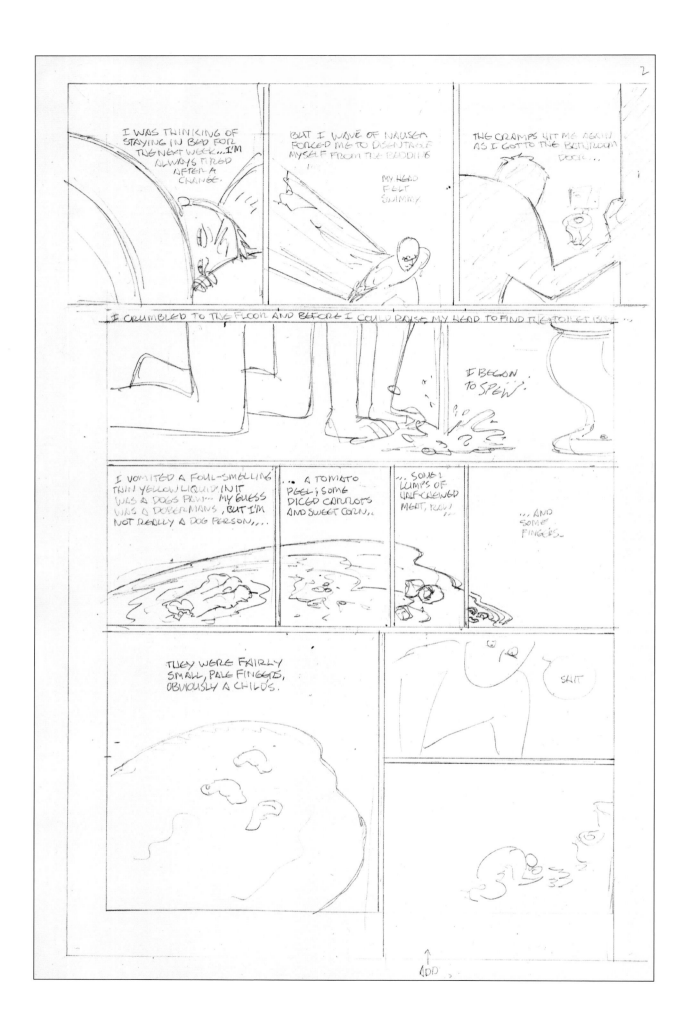

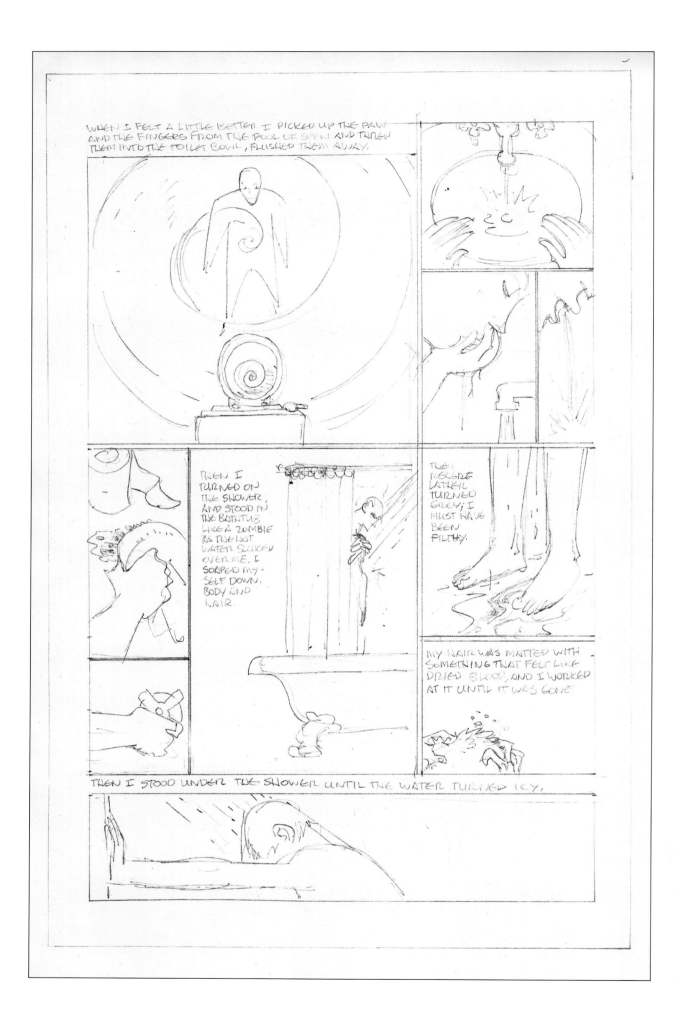

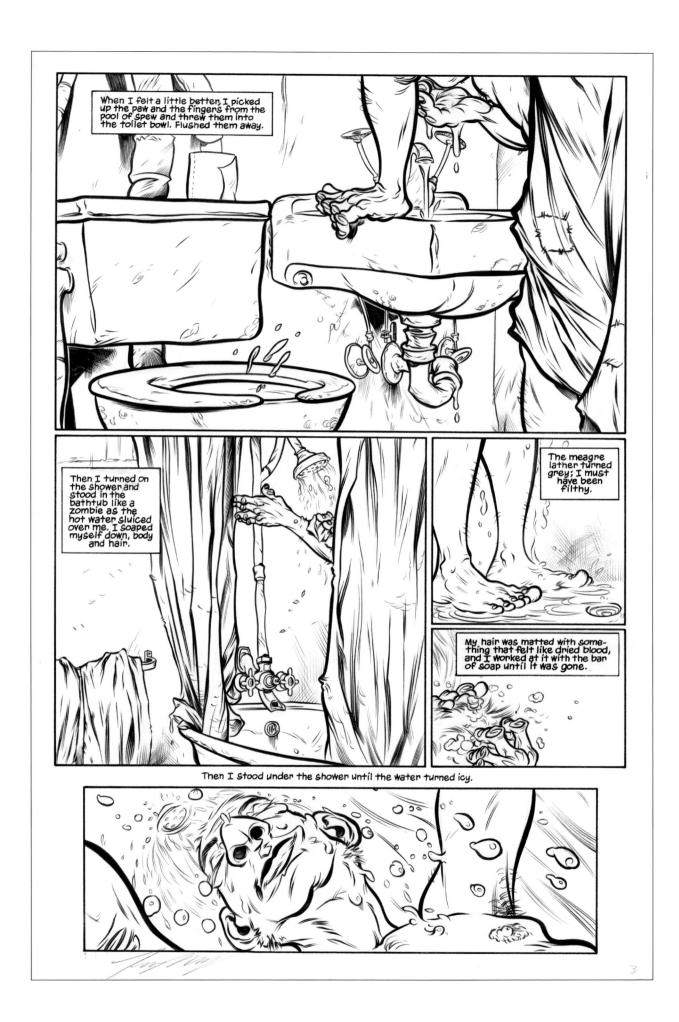

When I felt a little better, I picked up the paw and the fingers from the pool of spew and threw them into the toilet bowl. Flushed them away.

Then I turned on the shower and stood in the bathtub like a zombie as the hot water sluiced over me. I soaped myself down, body and hair.

The meagre lather turned grey; I must have been filthy.

My hair was matted with something that felt like dried blood, and I worked at it with the bar of soap until it was gone.

Then I stood under the shower until the water turned icy.

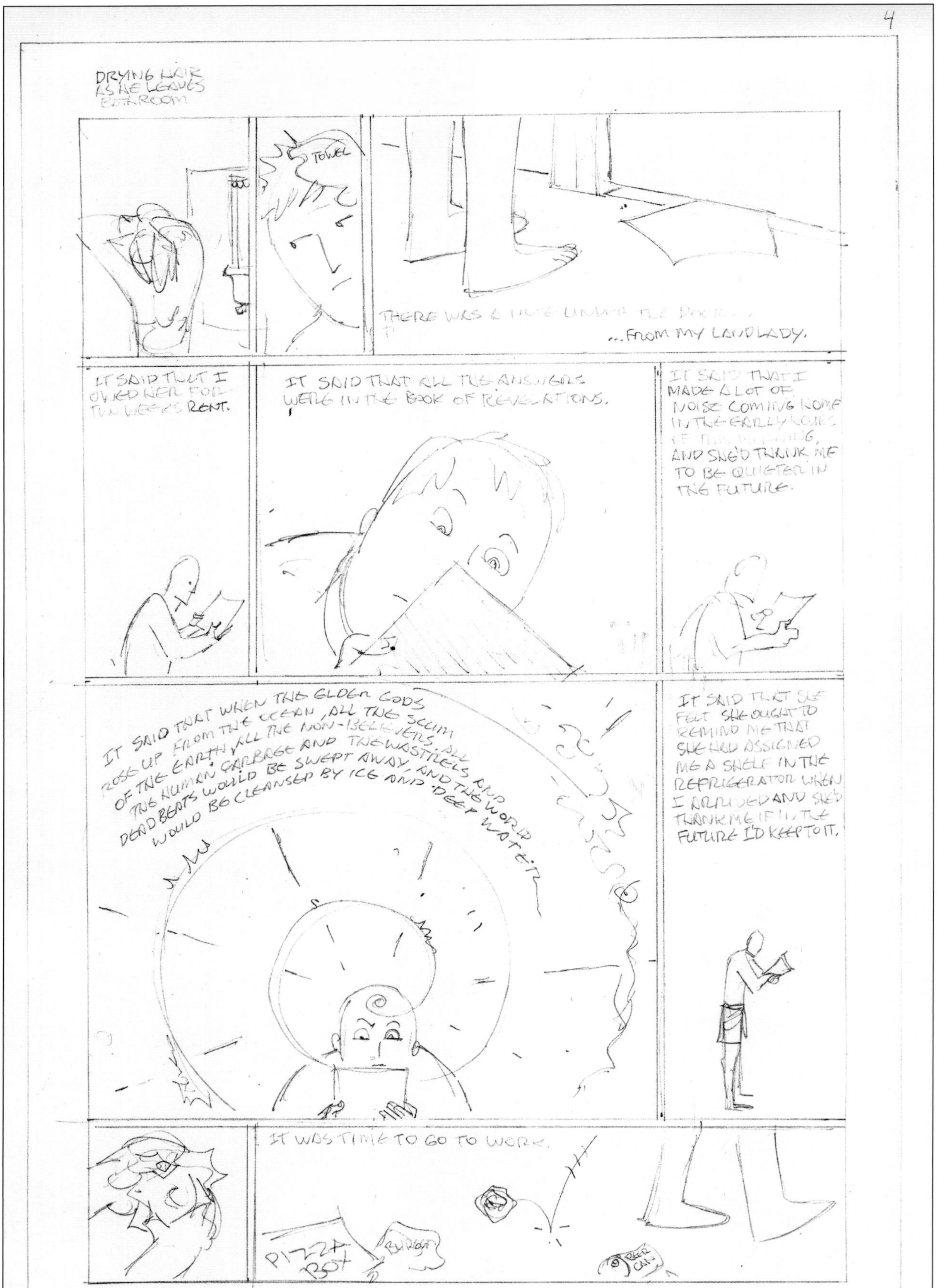
4
DRYING HAIR AS HE LEAVES BATHROOM
TOWEL
THERE WAS A NOTE UNDER THE DOOR...
...FROM MY LANDLADY.
IT SAID THAT I OWED HER FOR TWO WEEKS RENT.
IT SAID THAT ALL THE ANSWERS WERE IN THE BOOK OF REVELATIONS.
IT SAID THAT I MADE A LOT OF NOISE COMING HOME IN THE EARLY HOURS OF THIS MORNING, AND SHE'D THANK ME TO BE QUIETER IN THE FUTURE.
IT SAID THAT WHEN THE ELDER GODS ROSE UP FROM THE OCEAN, ALL THE SCUM OF THE EARTH, ALL THE NON-BELIEVERS, ALL THE HUMAN GARBAGE AND THE WASTRELS AND DEADBEATS WOULD BE SWEPT AWAY, AND THE WORLD WOULD BE CLEANSED BY ICE AND DEEP WATER.
IT SAID THAT SHE FELT SHE OUGHT TO REMIND ME THAT SHE HAD ASSIGNED ME A SHELF IN THE REFRIGERATOR WHEN I ARRIVED AND SHE'D THANK ME IF IN THE FUTURE I'D KEEP TO IT.
IT WAS TIME TO GO TO WORK.
PIZZA BOX
BURGER
BEER CAN
CRUMBLES UP NOTE

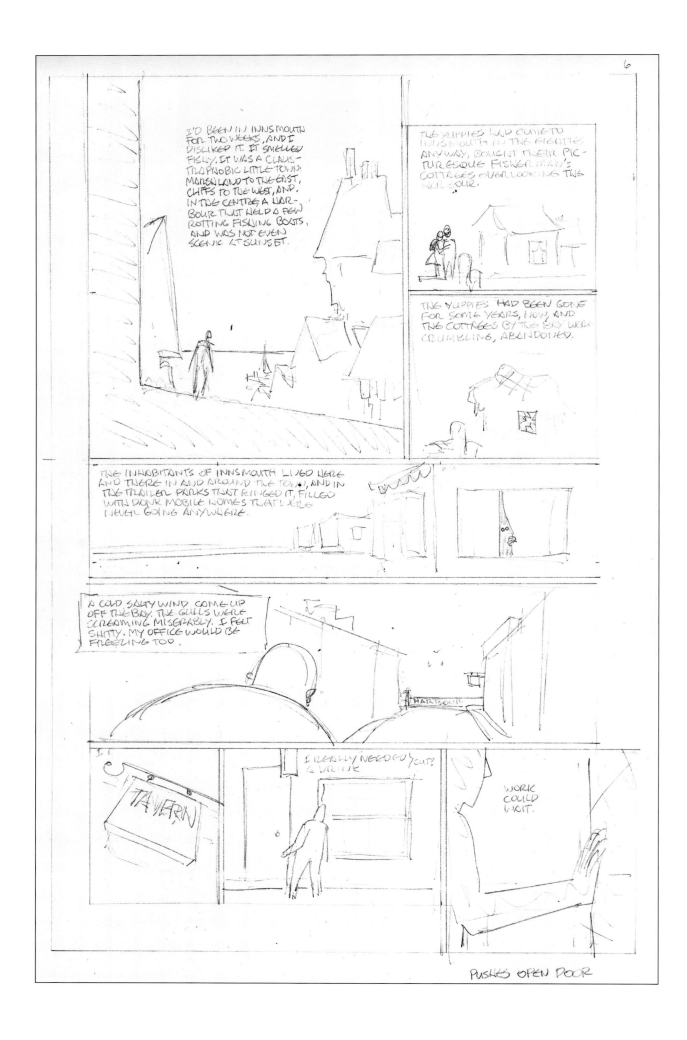

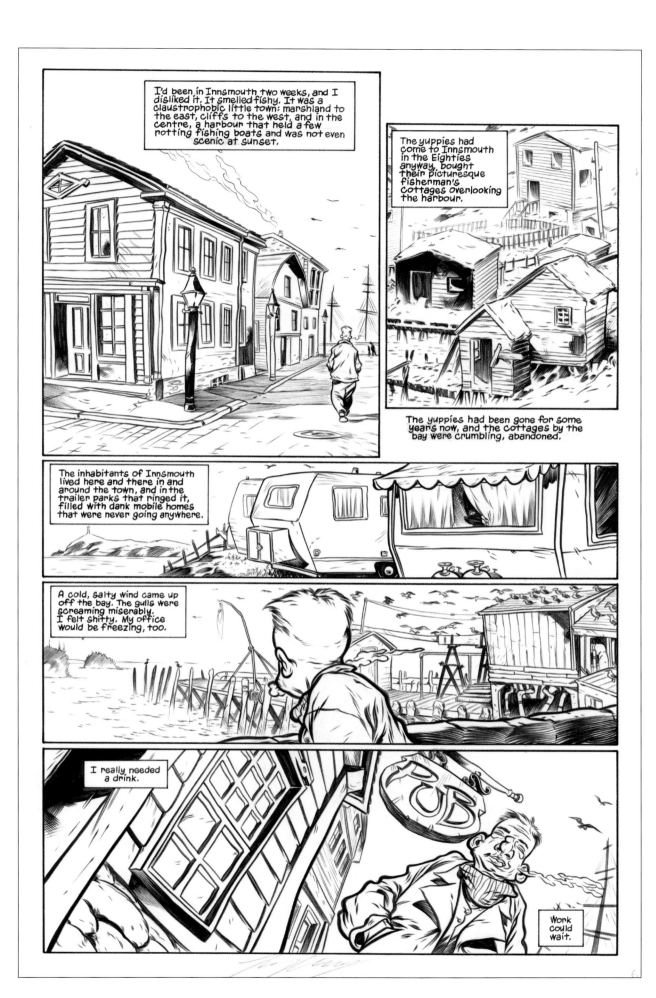

255

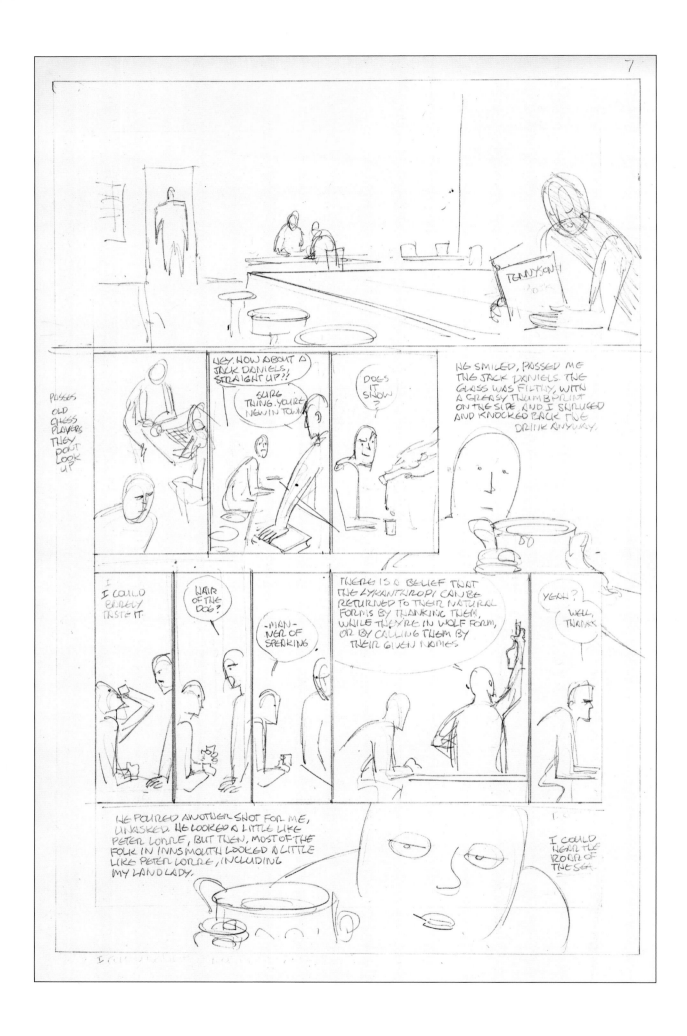

257

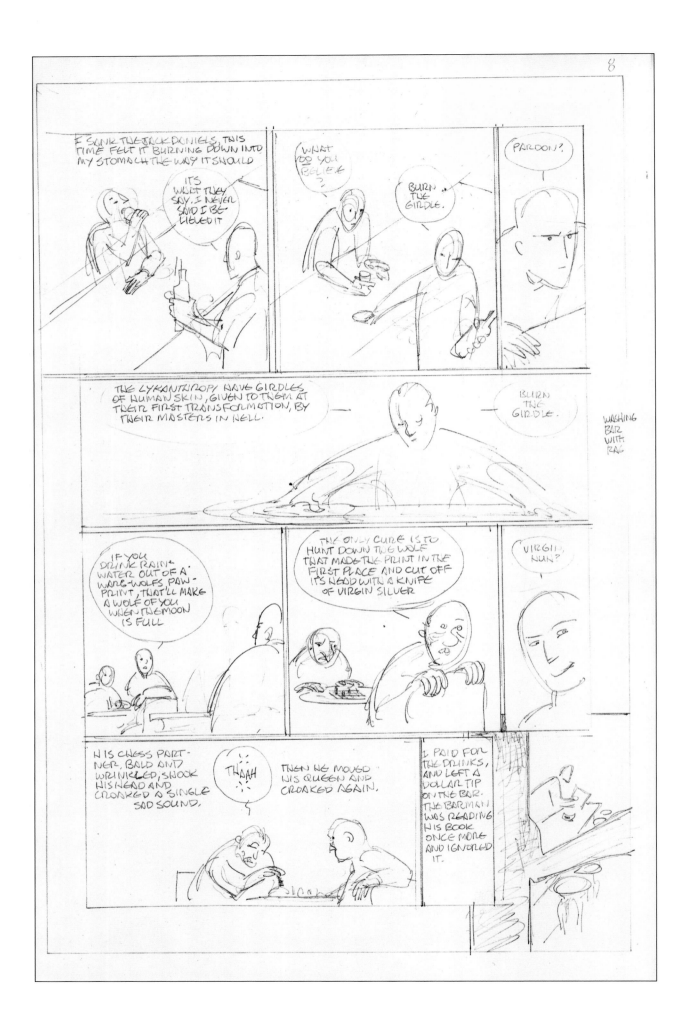

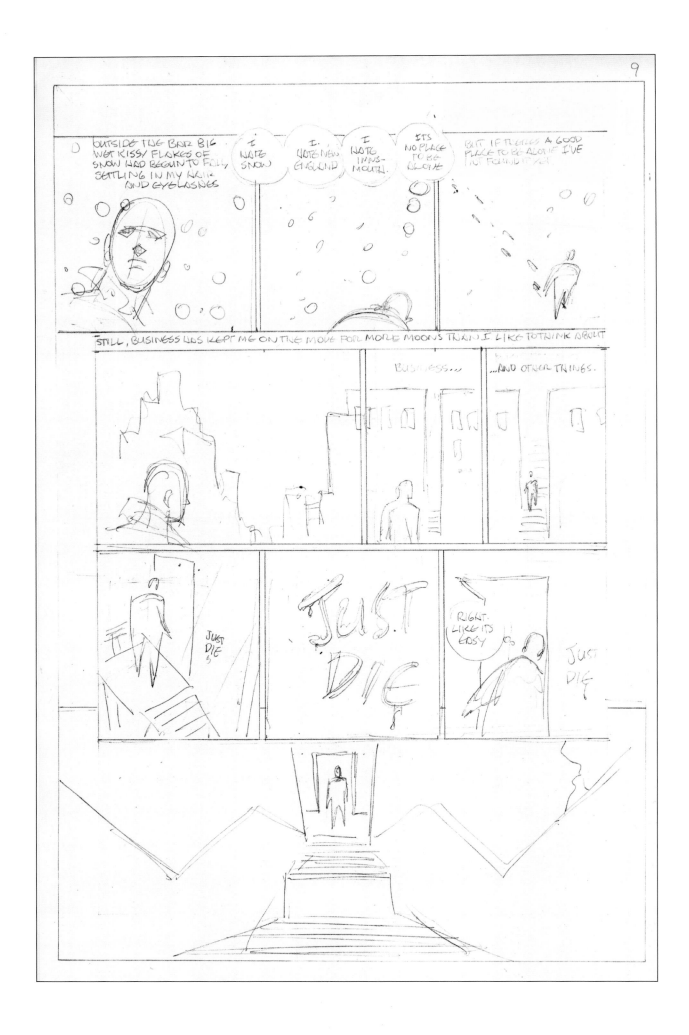

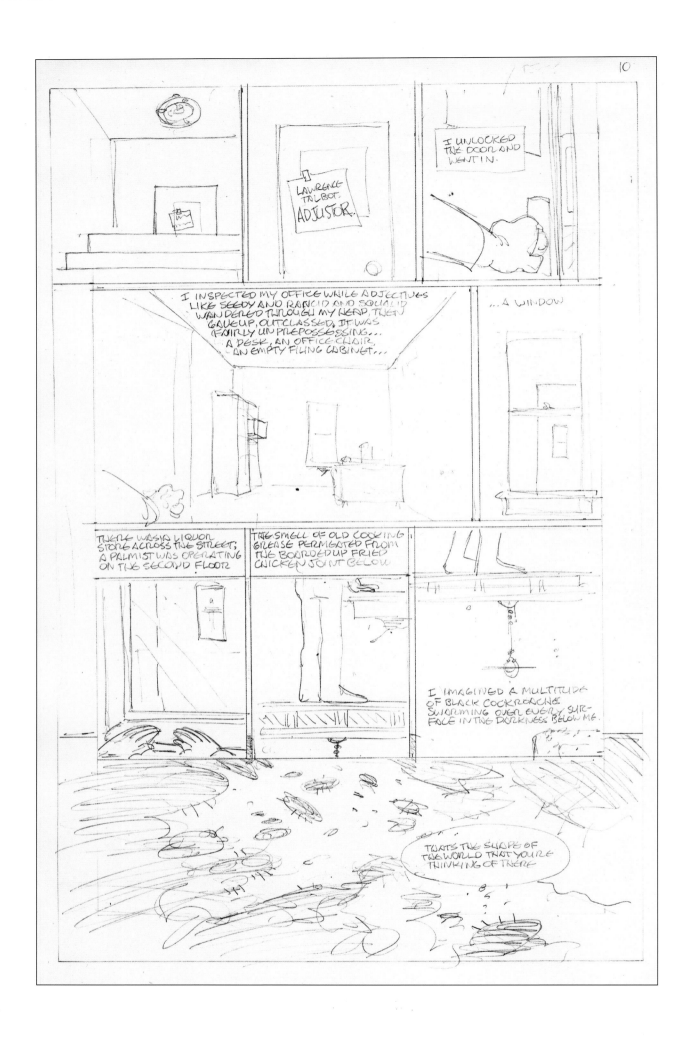

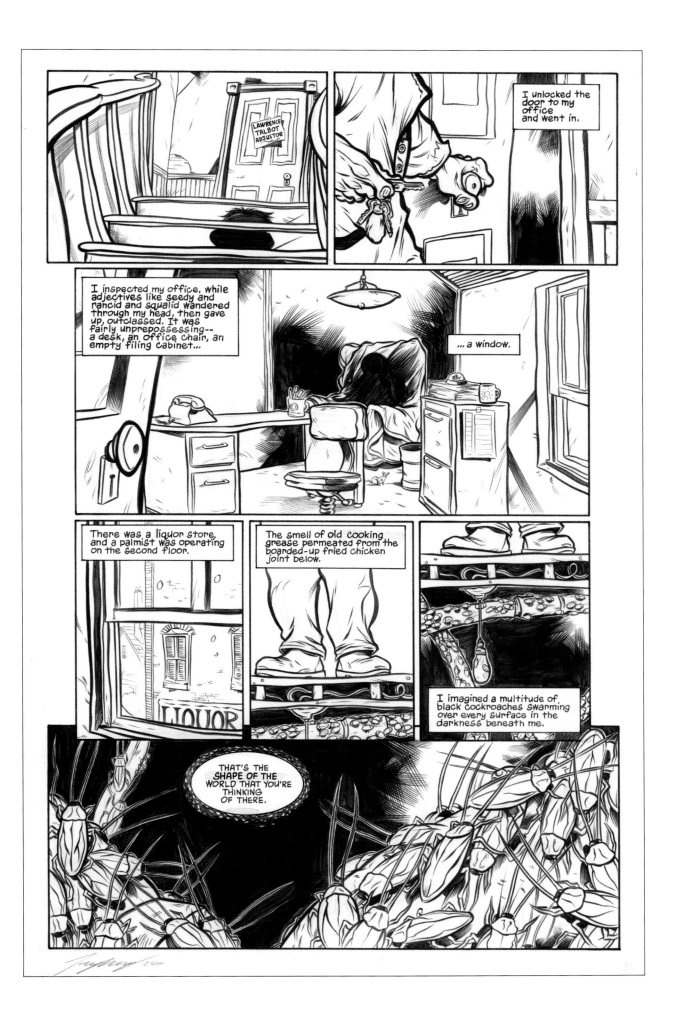

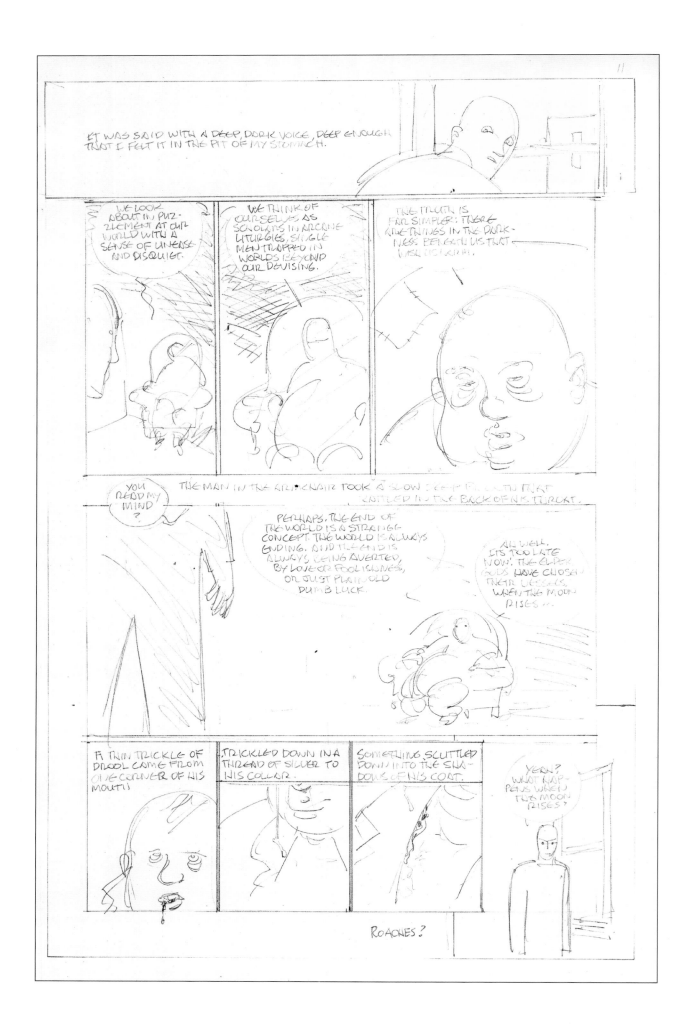

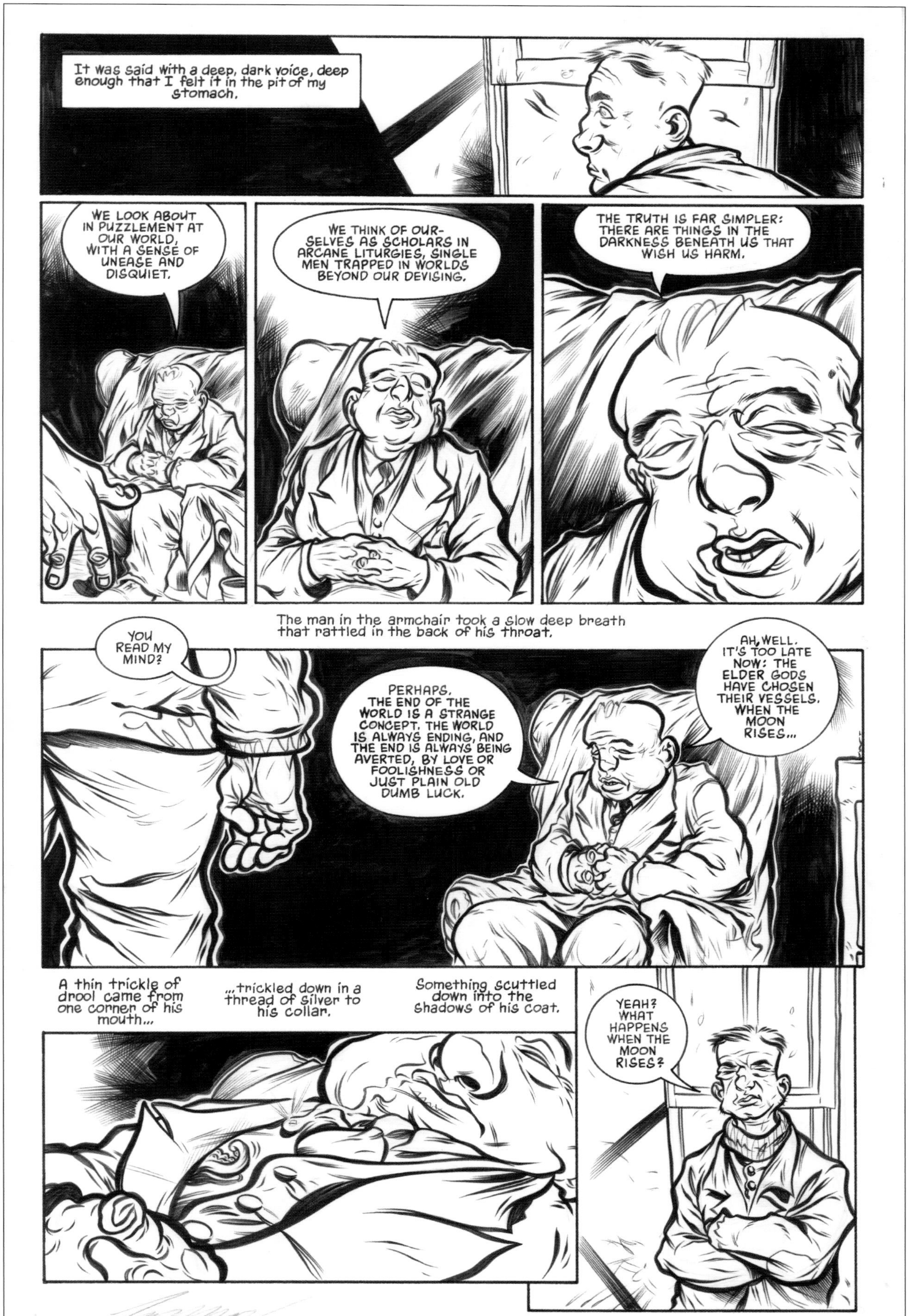

It was said with a deep, dark voice, deep enough that I felt it in the pit of my stomach.
WE LOOK ABOUT IN PUZZLEMENT AT OUR WORLD, WITH A SENSE OF UNEASE AND DISQUIET.
WE THINK OF OURSELVES AS SCHOLARS IN ARCANE LITURGIES, SINGLE MEN TRAPPED IN WORLDS BEYOND OUR DEVISING.
THE TRUTH IS FAR SIMPLER: THERE ARE THINGS IN THE DARKNESS BENEATH US THAT WISH US HARM.
The man in the armchair took a slow deep breath that rattled in the back of his throat.
YOU READ MY MIND?
PERHAPS. THE END OF THE WORLD IS A STRANGE CONCEPT. THE WORLD IS ALWAYS ENDING, AND THE END IS ALWAYS BEING AVERTED, BY LOVE OR FOOLISHNESS OR JUST PLAIN OLD DUMB LUCK.
AH, WELL. IT'S TOO LATE NOW: THE ELDER GODS HAVE CHOSEN THEIR VESSELS. WHEN THE MOON RISES...
A thin trickle of drool came from one corner of his mouth...
...trickled down in a thread of silver to his collar.
Something scuttled down into the shadows of his coat.
YEAH? WHAT HAPPENS WHEN THE MOON RISES?

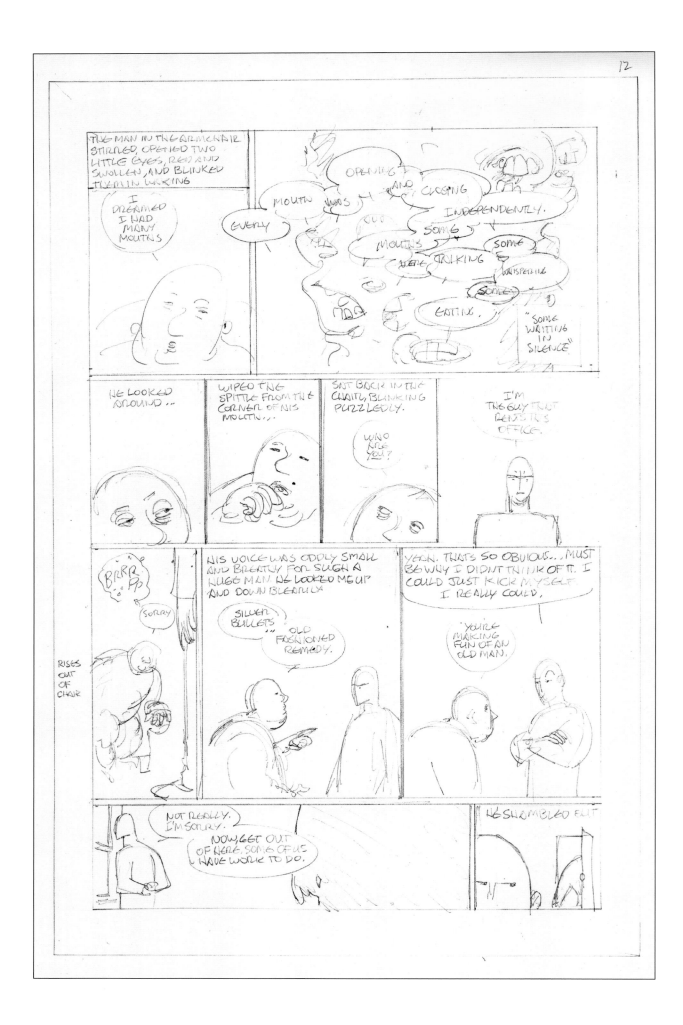

12

266

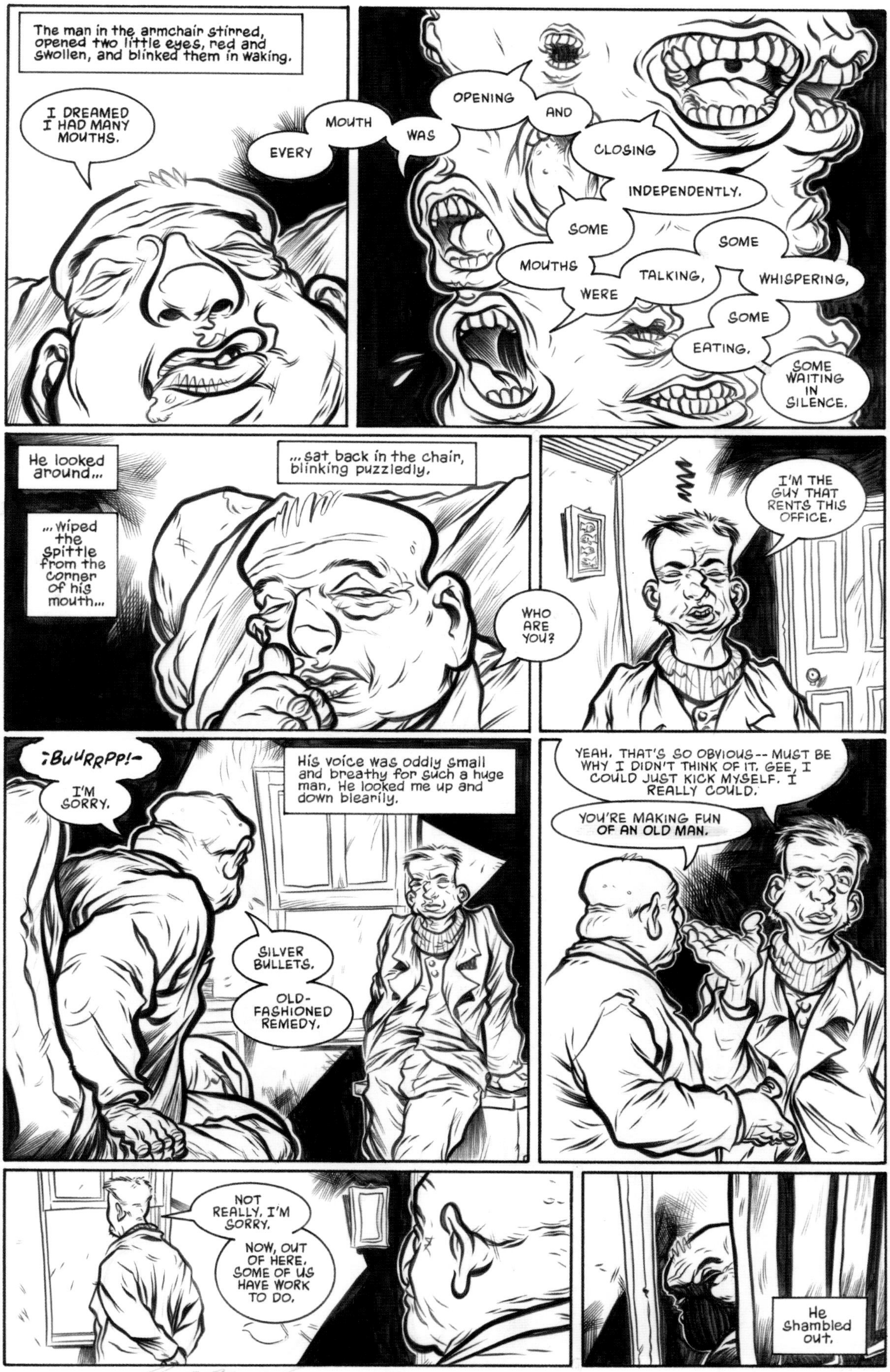

The man in the armchair stirred, opened two little eyes, red and swollen, and blinked them in waking.
I DREAMED I HAD MANY MOUTHS.
EVERY
MOUTH
WAS
OPENING
AND
CLOSING
INDEPENDENTLY.
SOME
MOUTHS
WERE
TALKING,
SOME
WHISPERING,
SOME
EATING,
SOME WAITING IN SILENCE.
He looked around...
...wiped the spittle from the corner of his mouth...
...sat back in the chair, blinking puzzledly.
WHO ARE YOU?
I'M THE GUY THAT RENTS THIS OFFICE.
;BUuRRPP!-
I'M SORRY.
His voice was oddly small and breathy for such a huge man. He looked me up and down blearily.
SILVER BULLETS.
OLD-FASHIONED REMEDY.
YEAH. THAT'S SO OBVIOUS-- MUST BE WHY I DIDN'T THINK OF IT. GEE, I COULD JUST KICK MYSELF. I REALLY COULD.
YOU'RE MAKING FUN OF AN OLD MAN.
NOT REALLY, I'M SORRY.
NOW, OUT OF HERE. SOME OF US HAVE WORK TO DO.
He shambled out.

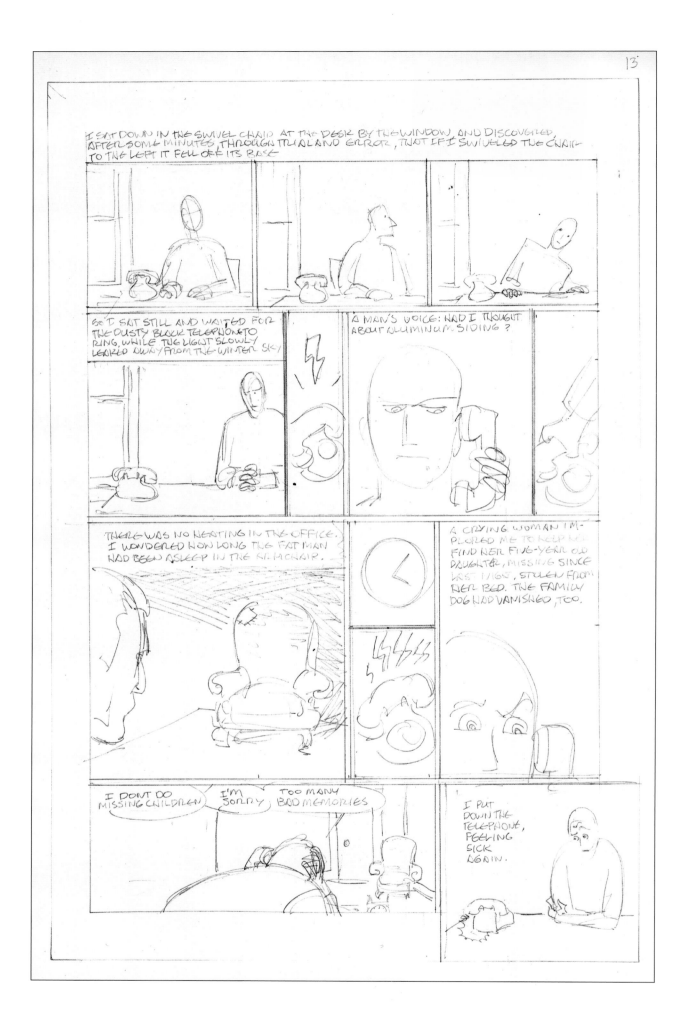

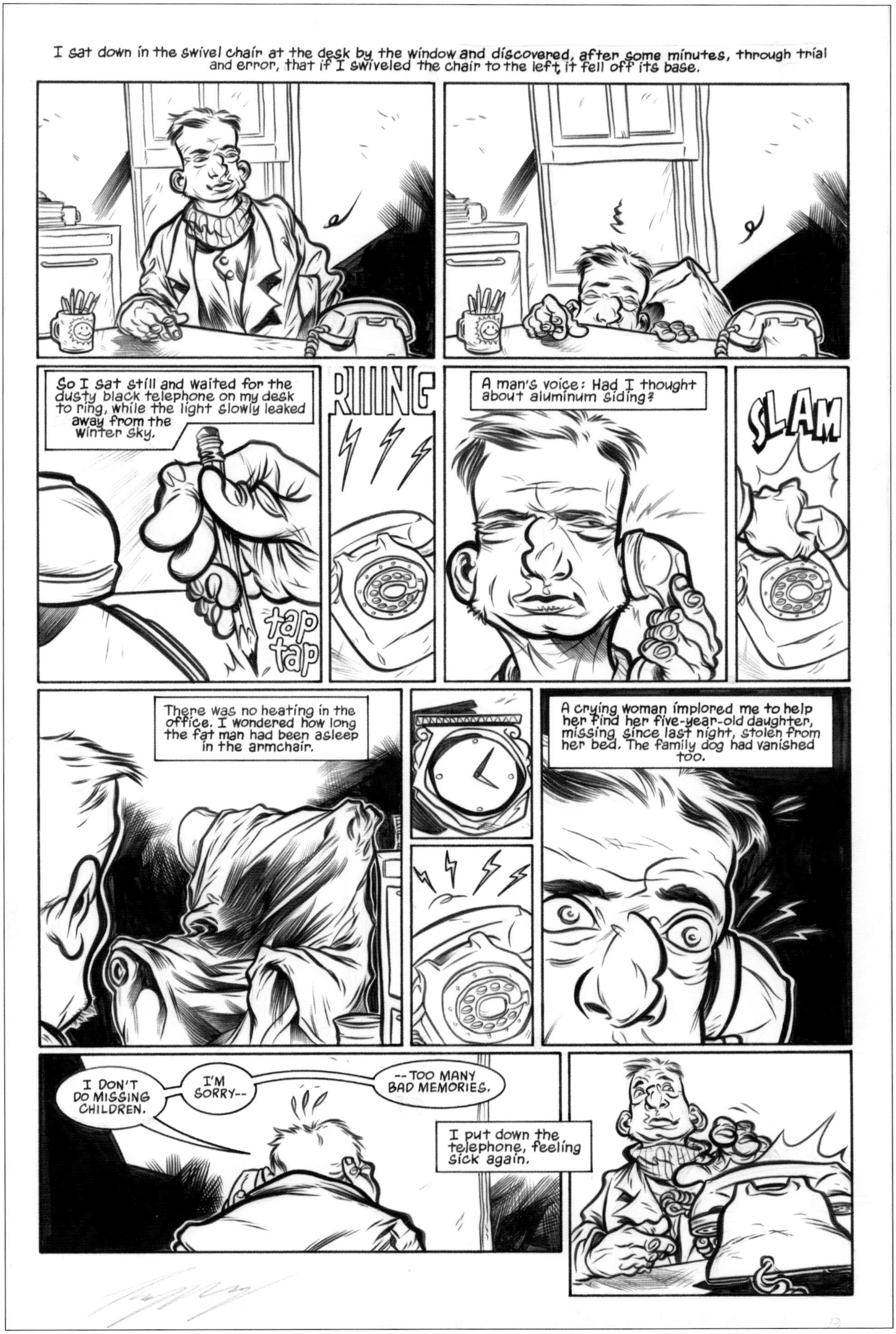
I sat down in the swivel chair at the desk by the window and discovered, after some minutes, through trial and error, that if I swiveled the chair to the left, it fell off its base.
So I sat still and waited for the dusty black telephone on my desk to ring, while the light slowly leaked away from the winter sky.
tap tap
RIIING
A man's voice: Had I thought about aluminum siding?
SLAM
There was no heating in the office. I wondered how long the fat man had been asleep in the armchair.
A crying woman implored me to help her find her five-year-old daughter, missing since last night, stolen from her bed. The family dog had vanished too.
I DON'T DO MISSING CHILDREN.
I'M SORRY--
--TOO MANY BAD MEMORIES.
I put down the telephone, feeling sick again.

271

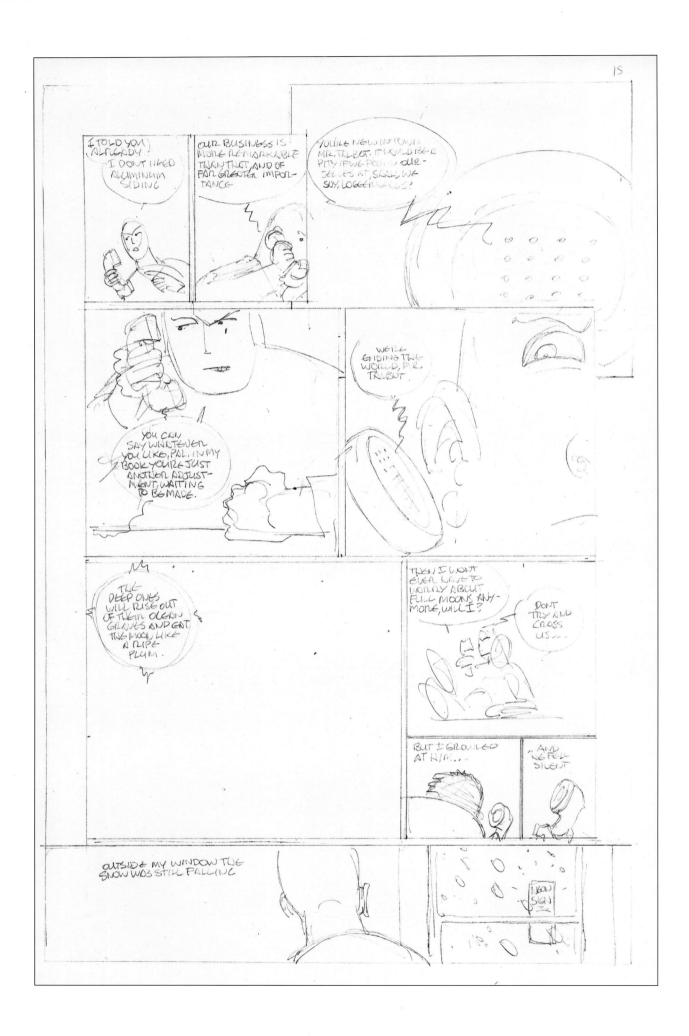

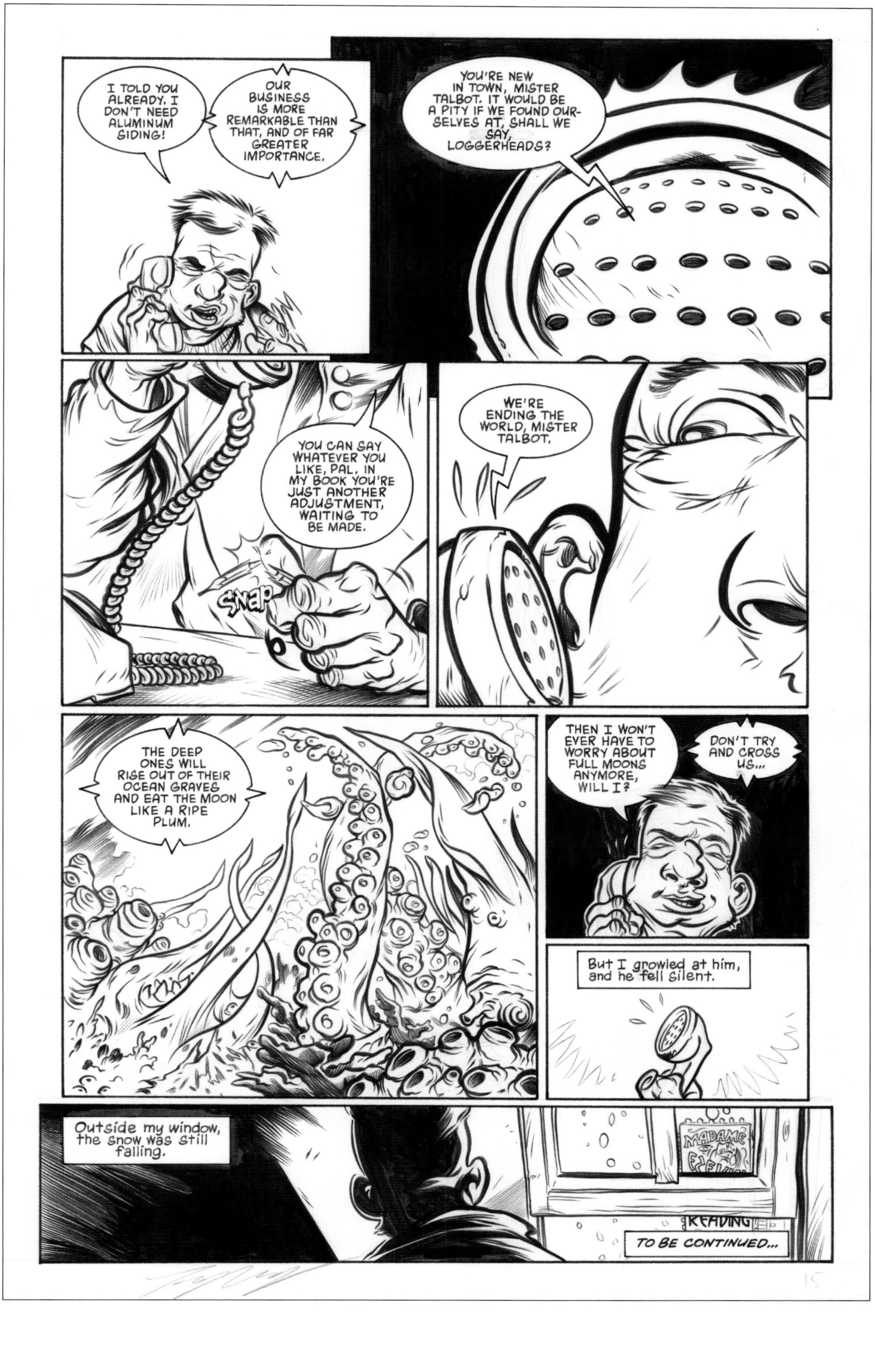
I TOLD YOU ALREADY. I DON'T NEED ALUMINUM SIDING!
OUR BUSINESS IS MORE REMARKABLE THAN THAT, AND OF FAR GREATER IMPORTANCE.
YOU'RE NEW IN TOWN, MISTER TALBOT. IT WOULD BE A PITY IF WE FOUND OUR-SELVES AT, SHALL WE SAY, LOGGERHEADS?
YOU CAN SAY WHATEVER YOU LIKE, PAL. IN MY BOOK YOU'RE JUST ANOTHER ADJUSTMENT, WAITING TO BE MADE.
SNAP
WE'RE ENDING THE WORLD, MISTER TALBOT.
THE DEEP ONES WILL RISE OUT OF THEIR OCEAN GRAVES AND EAT THE MOON LIKE A RIPE PLUM.
THEN I WON'T EVER HAVE TO WORRY ABOUT FULL MOONS ANYMORE, WILL I?
DON'T TRY AND CROSS US...
But I growled at him, and he fell silent.
Outside my window, the snow was still falling.
READING
TO BE CONTINUED...
15

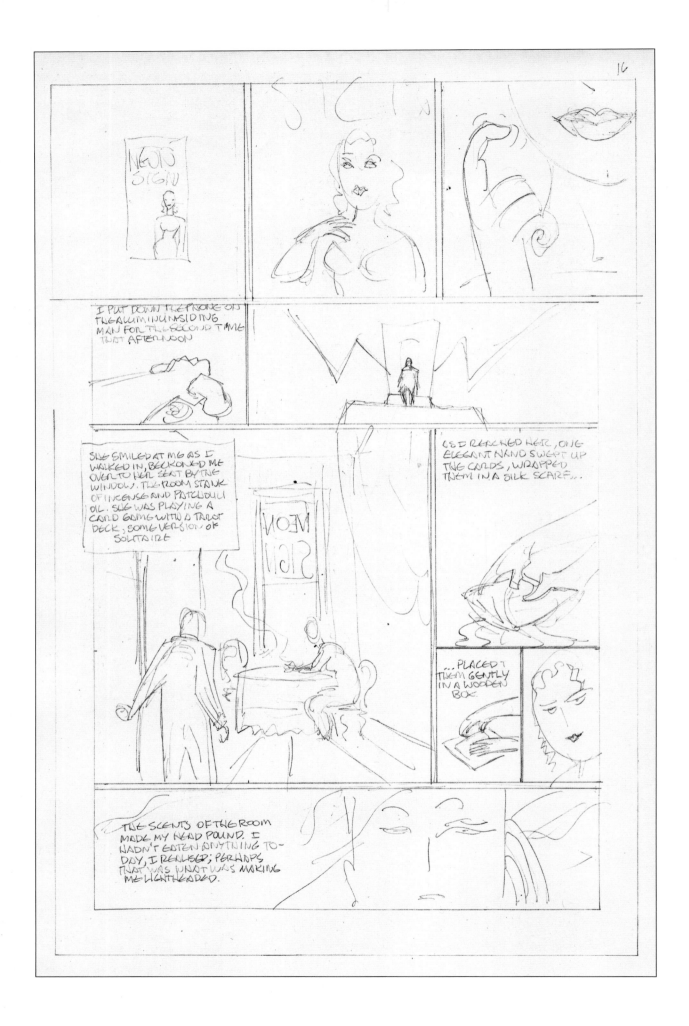

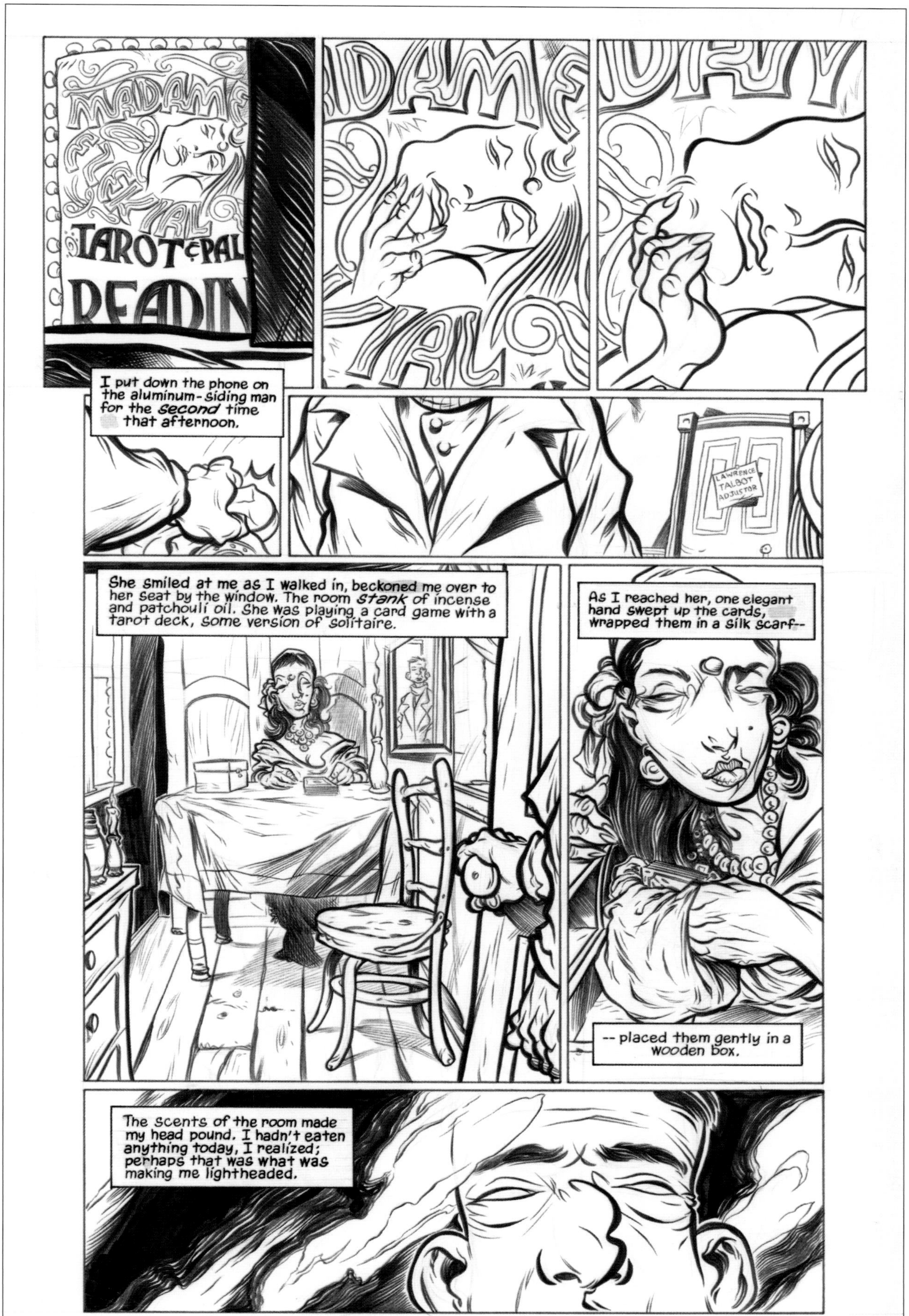
MADAME EZEKIAL
TAROT & PAL
READIN
I put down the phone on the aluminum-siding man for the *second* time that afternoon.
LAWRENCE TALBOT ADJUSTOR
She smiled at me as I walked in, beckoned me over to her seat by the window. The room *stank* of incense and patchouli oil. She was playing a card game with a tarot deck, some version of solitaire.
As I reached her, one elegant hand swept up the cards, wrapped them in a silk scarf--
-- placed them gently in a wooden box.
The scents of the room made my head pound. I hadn't eaten anything today, I realized; perhaps that was what was making me lightheaded.

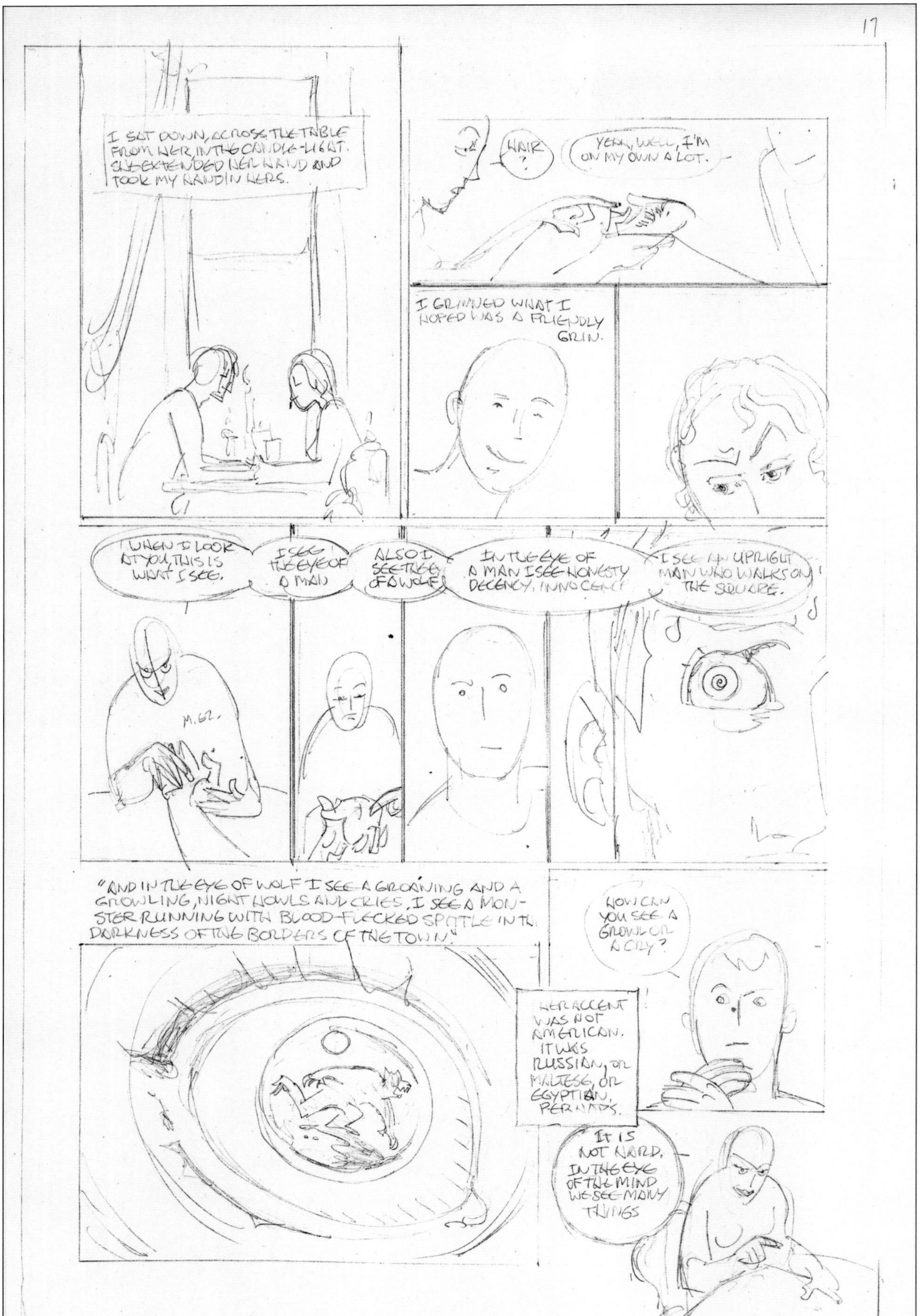
17
I SAT DOWN, ACROSS THE TABLE FROM HER, IN THE CANDLE-LIGHT. SHE EXTENDED HER HAND AND TOOK MY HAND IN HERS.
HAIR?
YEAH, WELL, I'M ON MY OWN A LOT.
I GRINNED WHAT I HOPED WAS A FRIENDLY GRIN.
WHEN I LOOK AT YOU, THIS IS WHAT I SEE.
I SEE THE EYE OF A MAN
ALSO I SEE THE EYE OF A WOLF
IN THE EYE OF A MAN I SEE HONESTY DECENCY, INNOCENCE
I SEE AN UPRIGHT MAN WHO WALKS ON THE SQUARE.
"AND IN THE EYE OF WOLF I SEE A GROANING AND A GROWLING, NIGHT HOWLS AND CRIES, I SEE A MONSTER RUNNING WITH BLOOD-FLECKED SPITTLE IN THE DARKNESS OF THE BORDERS OF THE TOWN"
HOW CAN YOU SEE A GROWL OR A CRY?
HER ACCENT WAS NOT AMERICAN. IT WAS RUSSIAN, OR MALTESE, OR EGYPTIAN, PERHAPS.
IT IS NOT HARD. IN THE EYE OF THE MIND WE SEE MANY THINGS

277

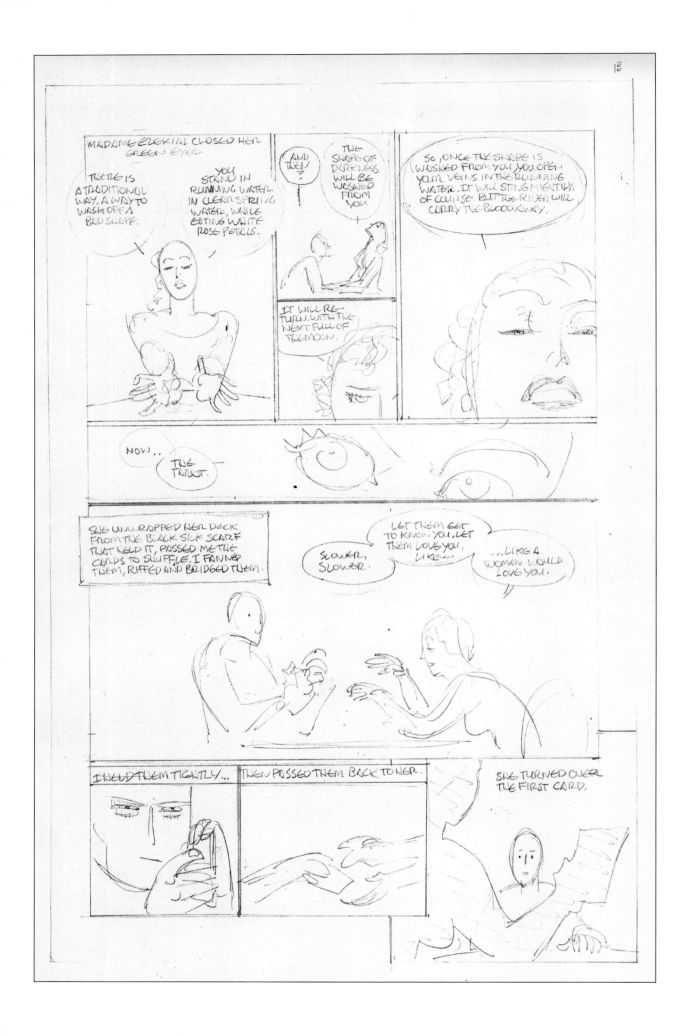

279

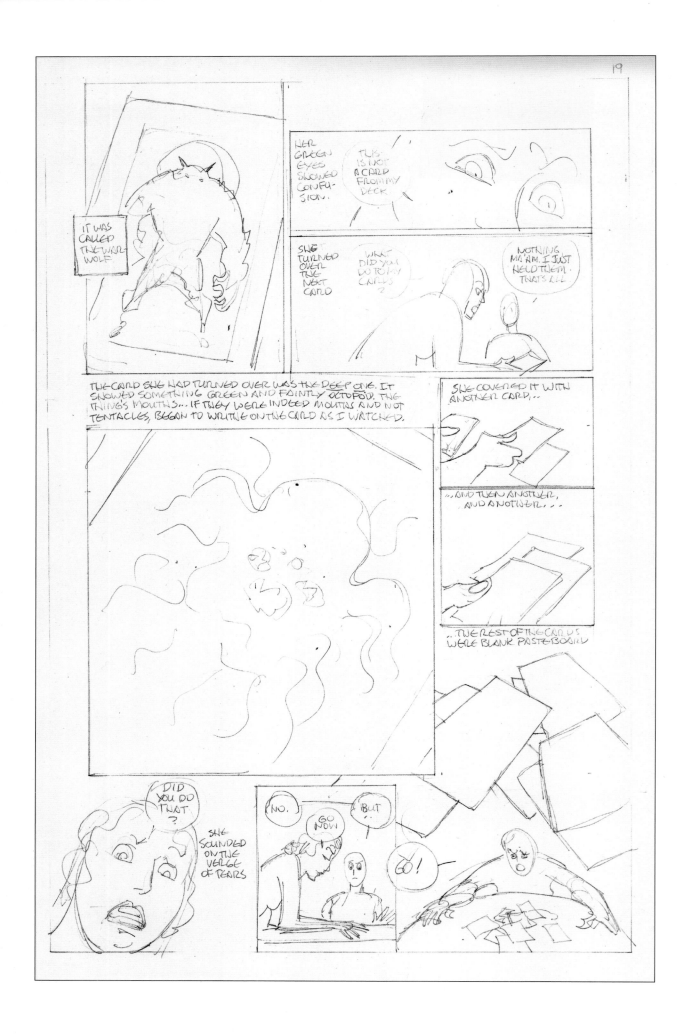

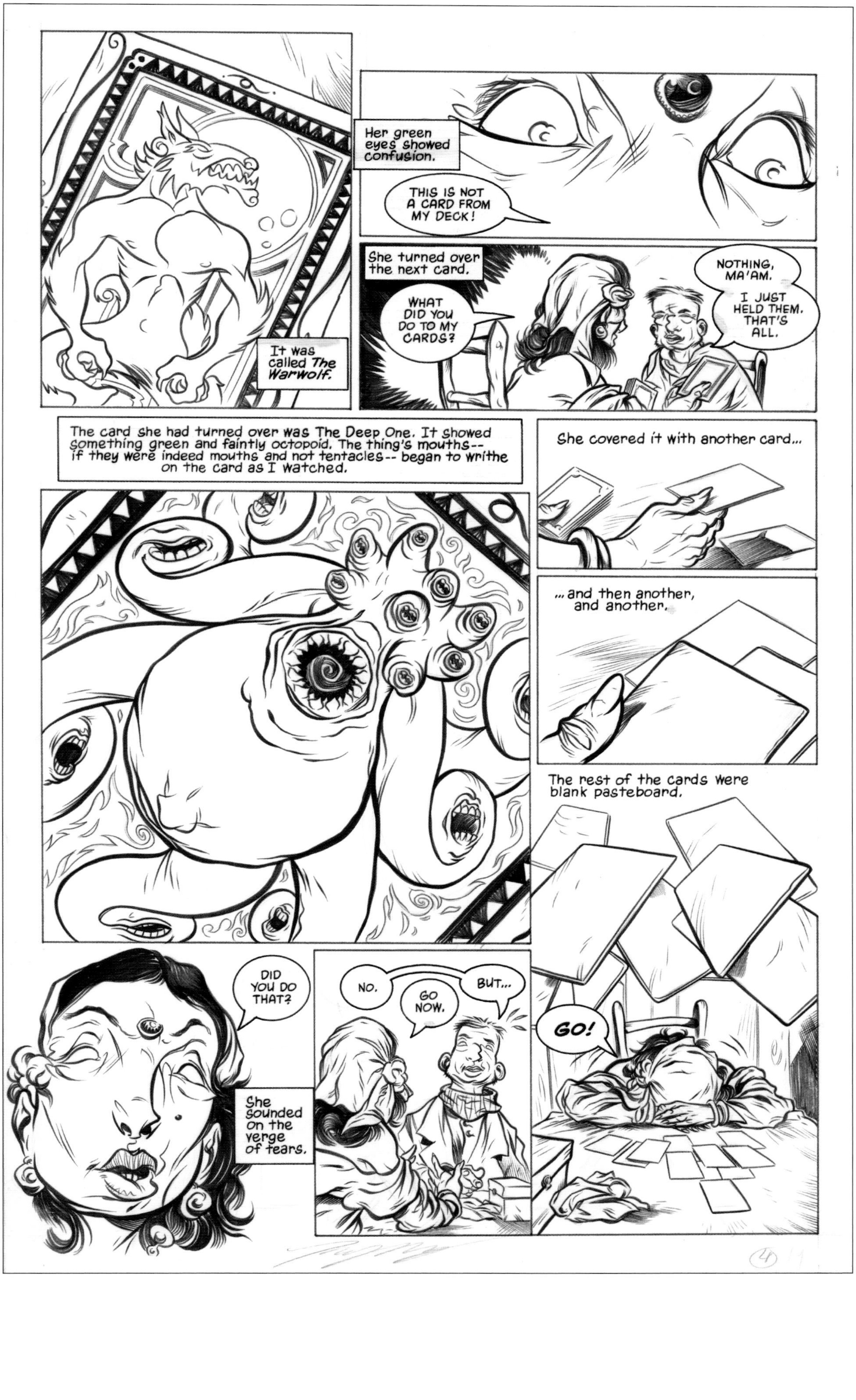
Her green eyes showed confusion.
THIS IS NOT A CARD FROM MY DECK!
It was called The Warwolf.
She turned over the next card.
WHAT DID YOU DO TO MY CARDS?
NOTHING, MA'AM.
I JUST HELD THEM. THAT'S ALL.
The card she had turned over was The Deep One. It showed something green and faintly octopoid. The thing's mouths-- if they were indeed mouths and not tentacles-- began to writhe on the card as I watched.
She covered it with another card...
...and then another, and another.
The rest of the cards were blank pasteboard.
DID YOU DO THAT?
She sounded on the verge of tears.
NO.
GO NOW.
BUT...
GO!

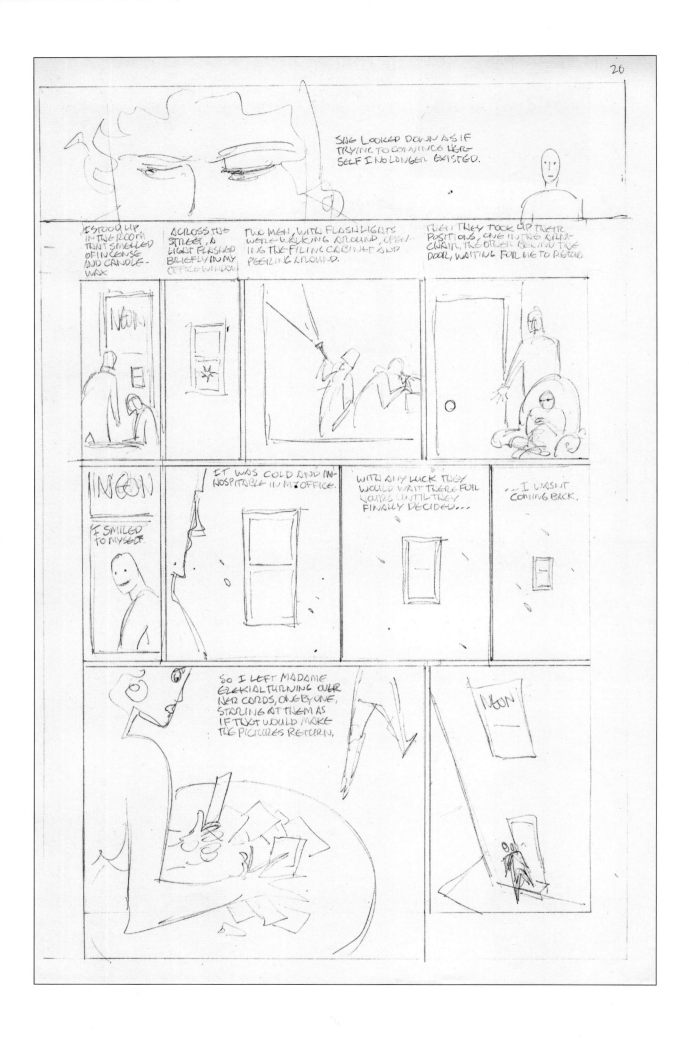

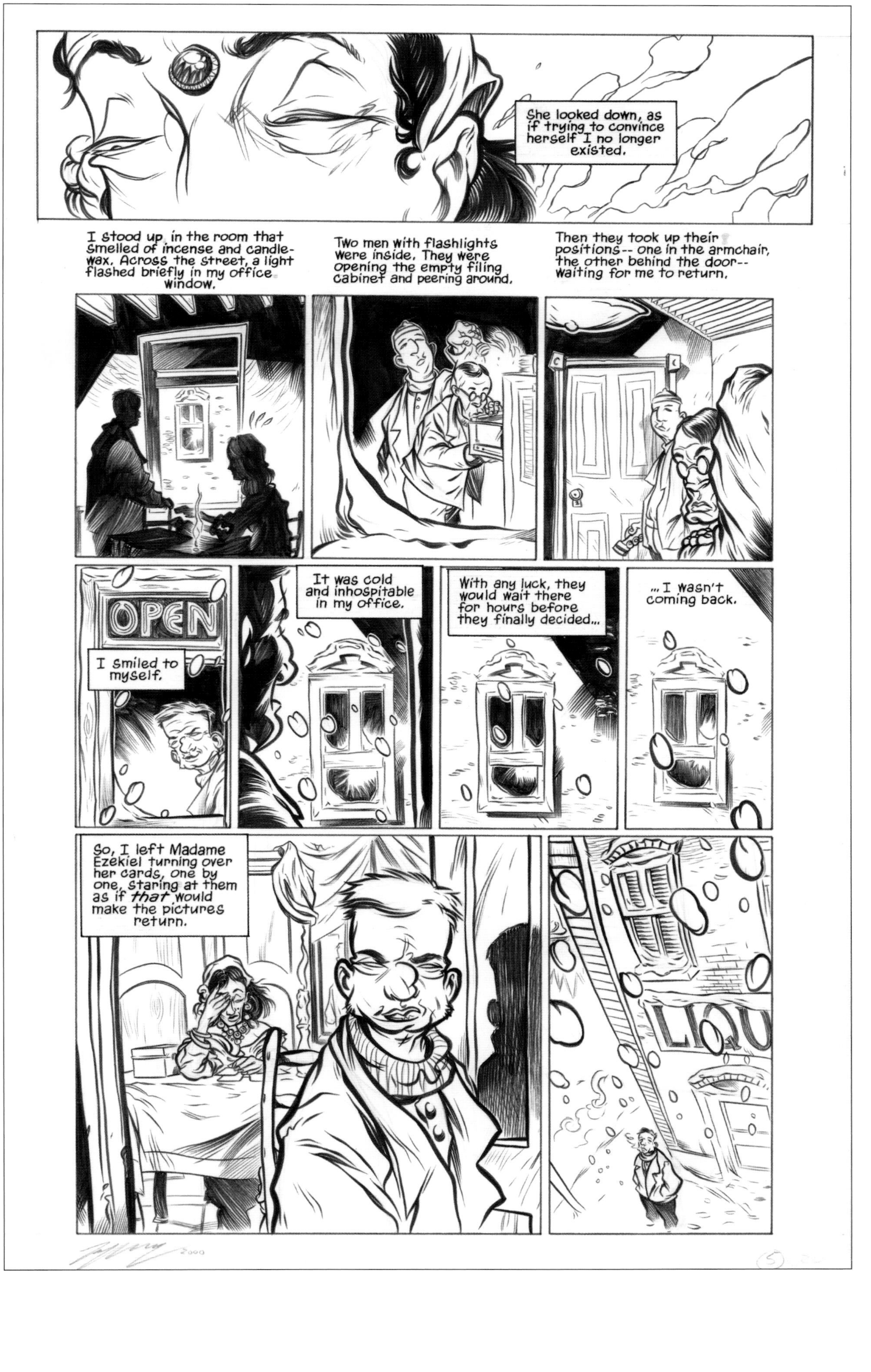

She looked down, as if trying to convince herself I no longer existed.
I stood up in the room that smelled of incense and candle-wax. Across the street, a light flashed briefly in my office window.
Two men with flashlights were inside. They were opening the empty filing cabinet and peering around.
Then they took up their positions-- one in the armchair, the other behind the door-- waiting for me to return.
OPEN
I smiled to myself.
It was cold and inhospitable in my office.
With any luck, they would wait there for hours before they finally decided...
...I wasn't coming back.
So, I left Madame Ezekiel turning over her cards, one by one, staring at them as if *that* would make the pictures return.
LIQU

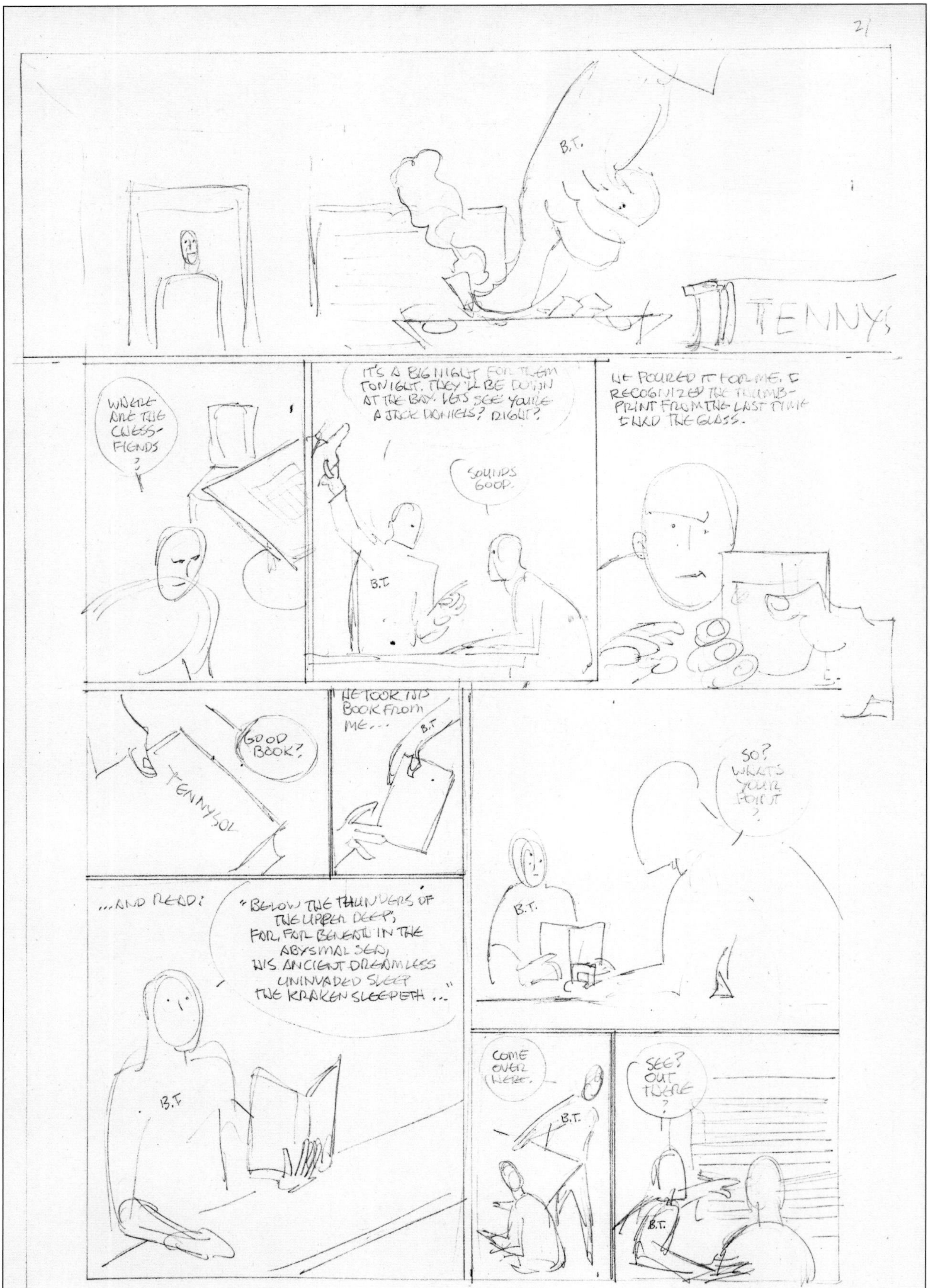
21
B.T.
TENNYS
WHERE ARE THE CHESS-FIENDS ?
IT'S A BIG NIGHT FOR THEM TONIGHT. THEY'LL BE DOWN AT THE BAY. LET'S SEE YOU'RE A JACK DANIELS? RIGHT?
SOUNDS GOOD.
B.T.
HE POURED IT FOR ME. I RECOGNIZED THE THUMB-PRINT FROM THE LAST TIME I HAD THE GLASS.
GOOD BOOK?
TENNYSON
HE TOOK HIS BOOK FROM ME...
B.T.
SO? WHAT'S YOUR POINT ?
B.T.
...AND READ:
"BELOW THE THUNDERS OF THE UPPER DEEP, FAR, FAR BENEATH IN THE ABYSMAL SEA, HIS ANCIENT DREAMLESS UNINVADED SLEEP THE KRAKEN SLEEPETH..."
B.T.
COME OVER HERE.
B.T.
SEE? OUT THERE ?
B.T.

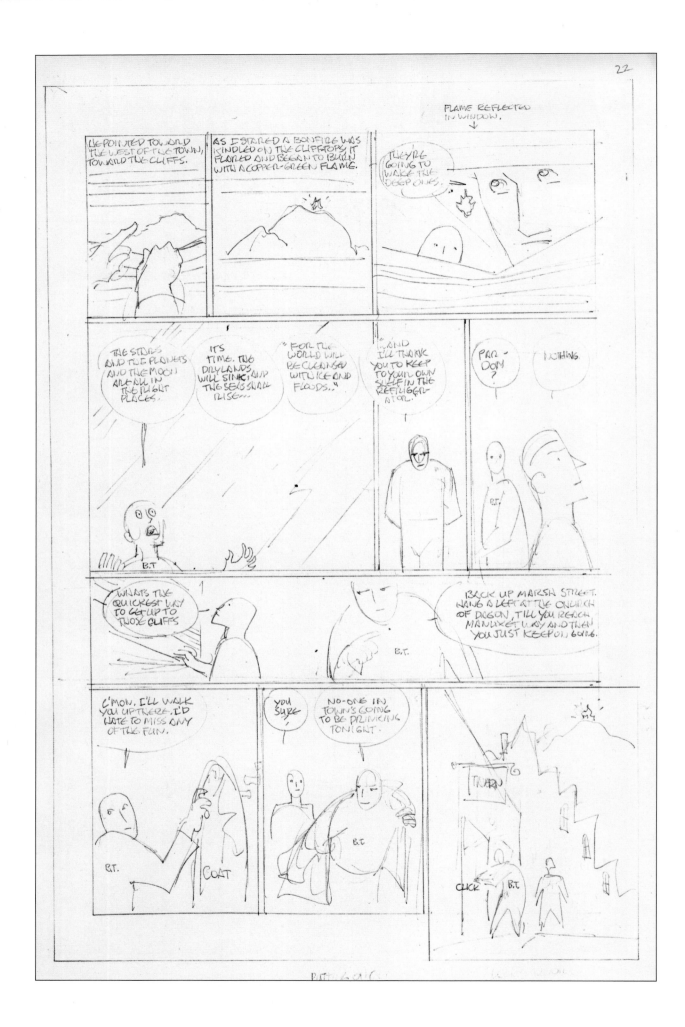

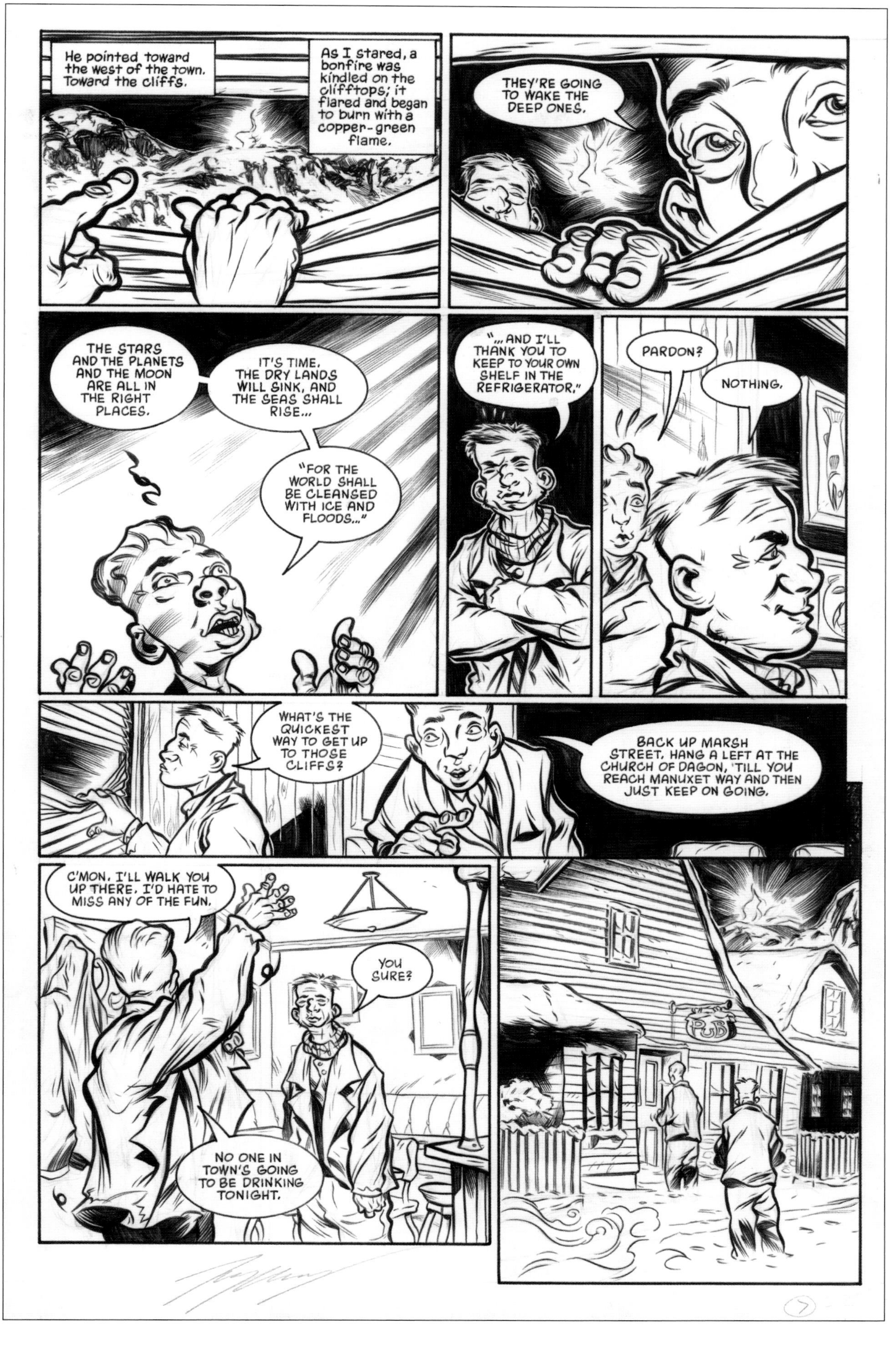
He pointed toward the west of the town. Toward the cliffs.
As I stared, a bonfire was kindled on the clifftops; it flared and began to burn with a copper-green flame.
THEY'RE GOING TO WAKE THE DEEP ONES.
THE STARS AND THE PLANETS AND THE MOON ARE ALL IN THE RIGHT PLACES.
IT'S TIME. THE DRY LANDS WILL SINK, AND THE SEAS SHALL RISE...
"FOR THE WORLD SHALL BE CLEANSED WITH ICE AND FLOODS..."
"...AND I'LL THANK YOU TO KEEP TO YOUR OWN SHELF IN THE REFRIGERATOR."
PARDON?
NOTHING.
WHAT'S THE QUICKEST WAY TO GET UP TO THOSE CLIFFS?
BACK UP MARSH STREET, HANG A LEFT AT THE CHURCH OF DAGON, 'TILL YOU REACH MANUXET WAY AND THEN JUST KEEP ON GOING.
C'MON. I'LL WALK YOU UP THERE. I'D HATE TO MISS ANY OF THE FUN.
YOU SURE?
NO ONE IN TOWN'S GOING TO BE DRINKING TONIGHT.
PUB

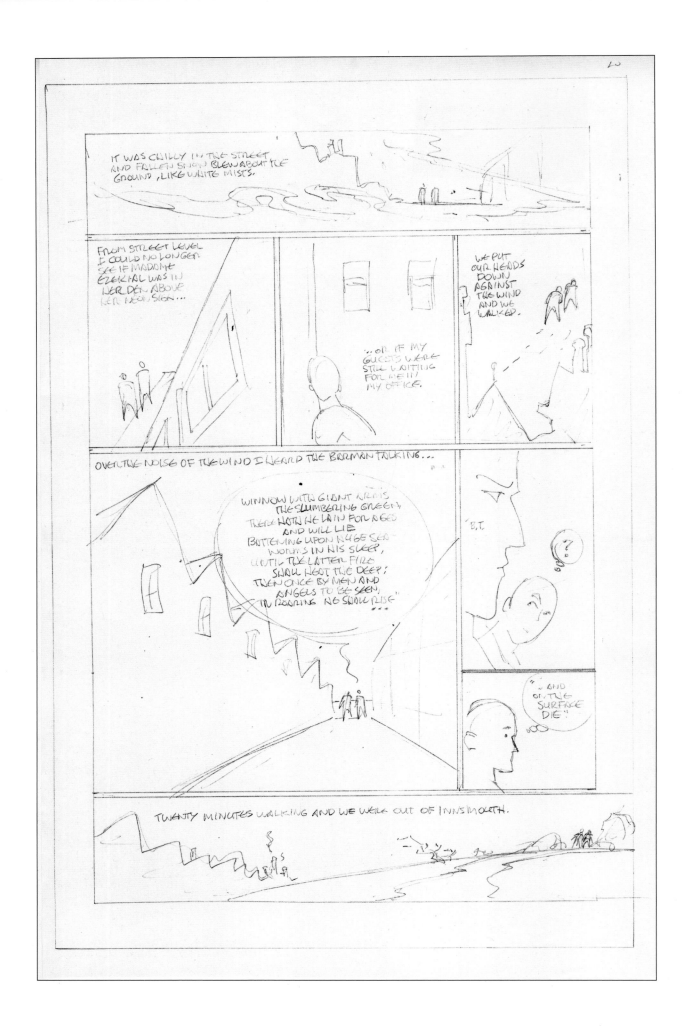

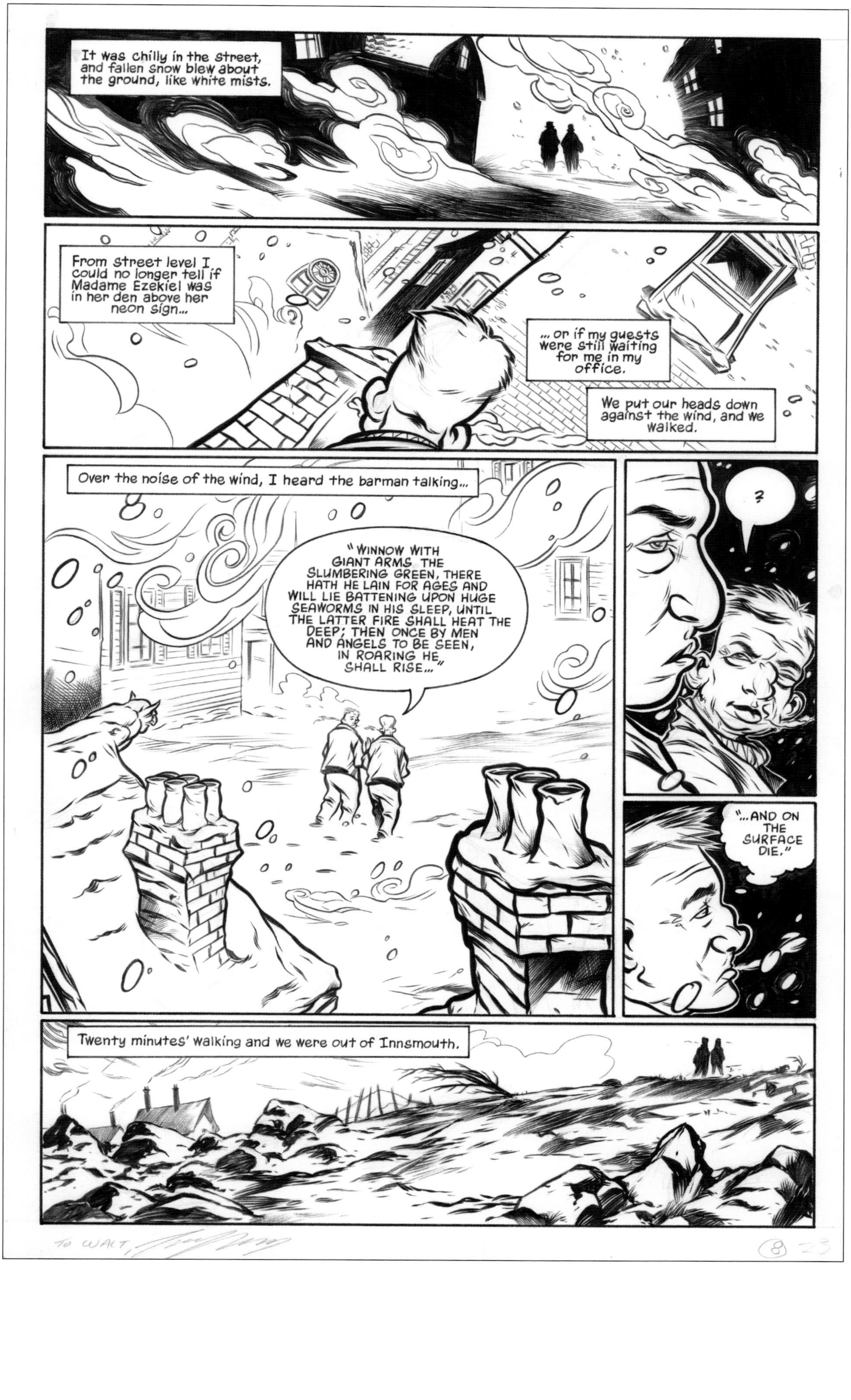
It was chilly in the street, and fallen snow blew about the ground, like white mists.
From street level I could no longer tell if Madame Ezekiel was in her den above her neon sign...
...or if my guests were still waiting for me in my office.
We put our heads down against the wind, and we walked.
Over the noise of the wind, I heard the barman talking...
"WINNOW WITH GIANT ARMS THE SLUMBERING GREEN, THERE HATH HE LAIN FOR AGES AND WILL LIE BATTENING UPON HUGE SEAWORMS IN HIS SLEEP, UNTIL THE LATTER FIRE SHALL HEAT THE DEEP; THEN ONCE BY MEN AND ANGELS TO BE SEEN, IN ROARING HE SHALL RISE..."
?
"...AND ON THE SURFACE DIE."
Twenty minutes' walking and we were out of Innsmouth.
TO WALT,

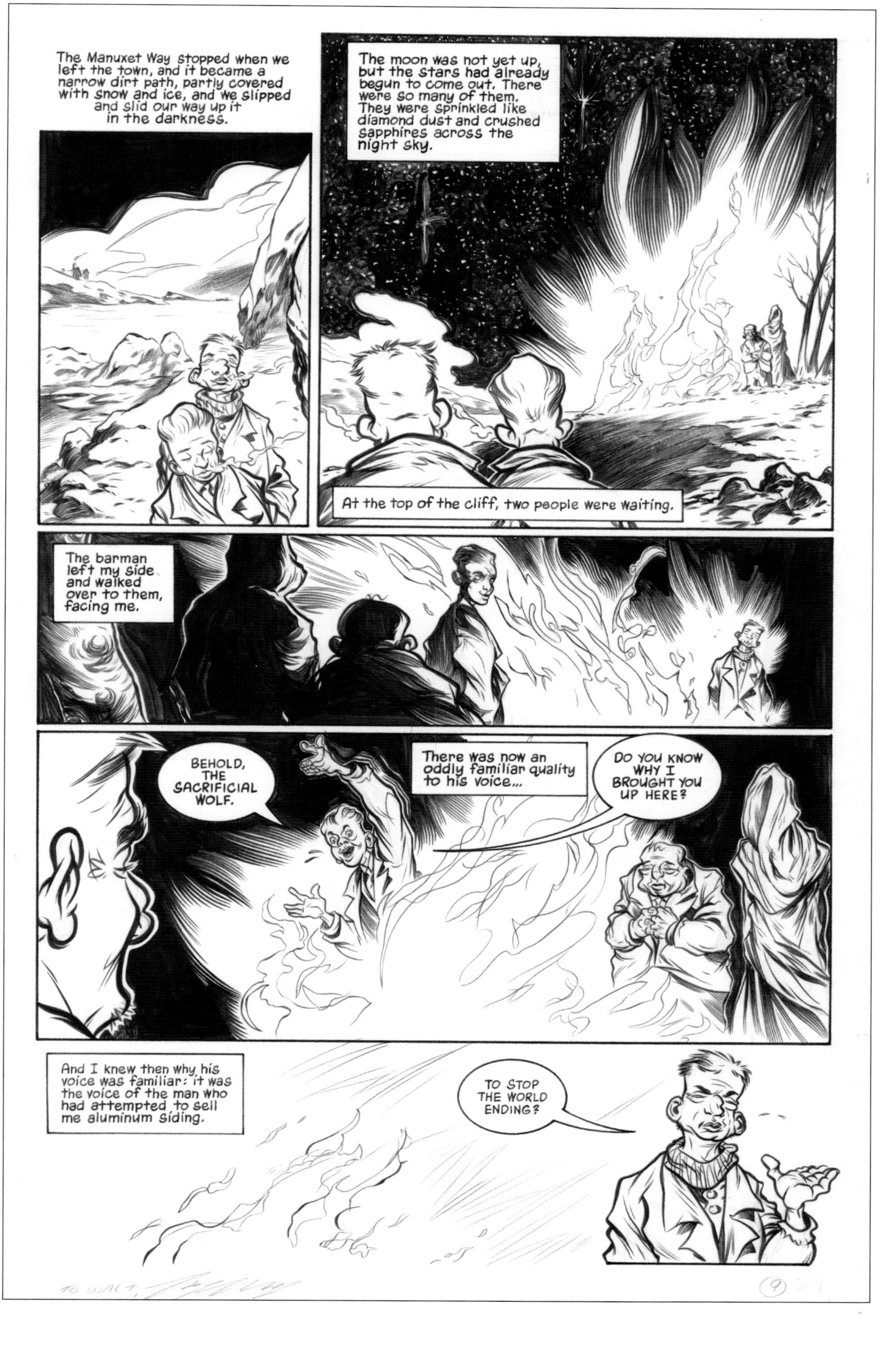
The Manuxet Way stopped when we left the town, and it became a narrow dirt path, partly covered with snow and ice, and we slipped and slid our way up it in the darkness.
The moon was not yet up, but the stars had already begun to come out. There were so many of them. They were sprinkled like diamond dust and crushed sapphires across the night sky.
At the top of the cliff, two people were waiting.
The barman left my side and walked over to them, facing me.
BEHOLD, THE SACRIFICIAL WOLF.
There was now an oddly familiar quality to his voice...
DO YOU KNOW WHY I BROUGHT YOU UP HERE?
And I knew then why his voice was familiar: it was the voice of the man who had attempted to sell me aluminum siding.
TO STOP THE WORLD ENDING?
TO WALT,
9

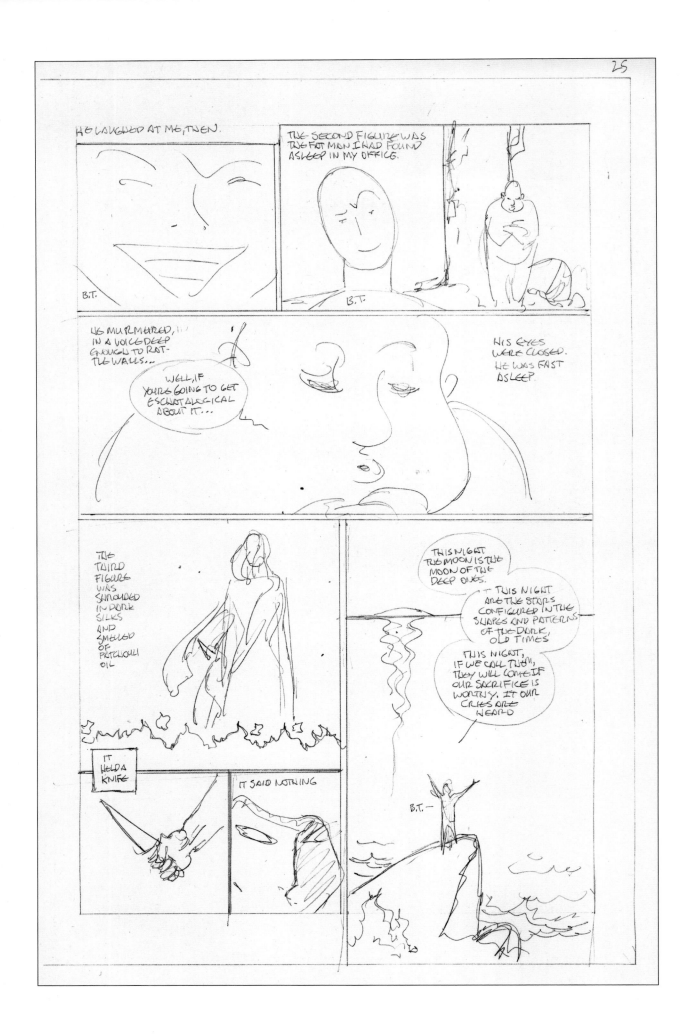

292

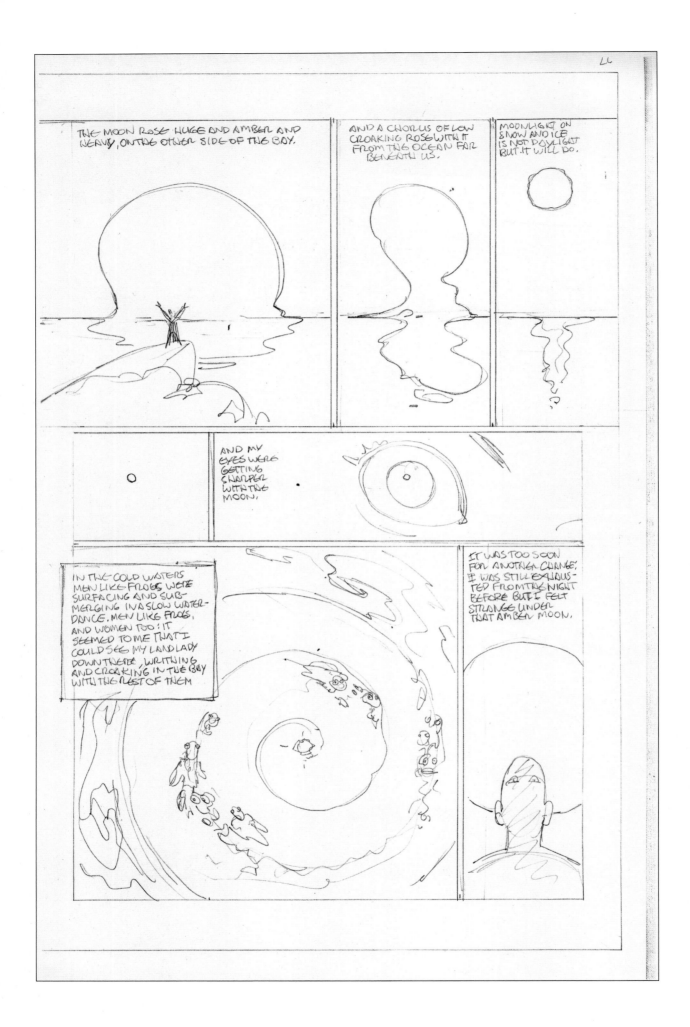

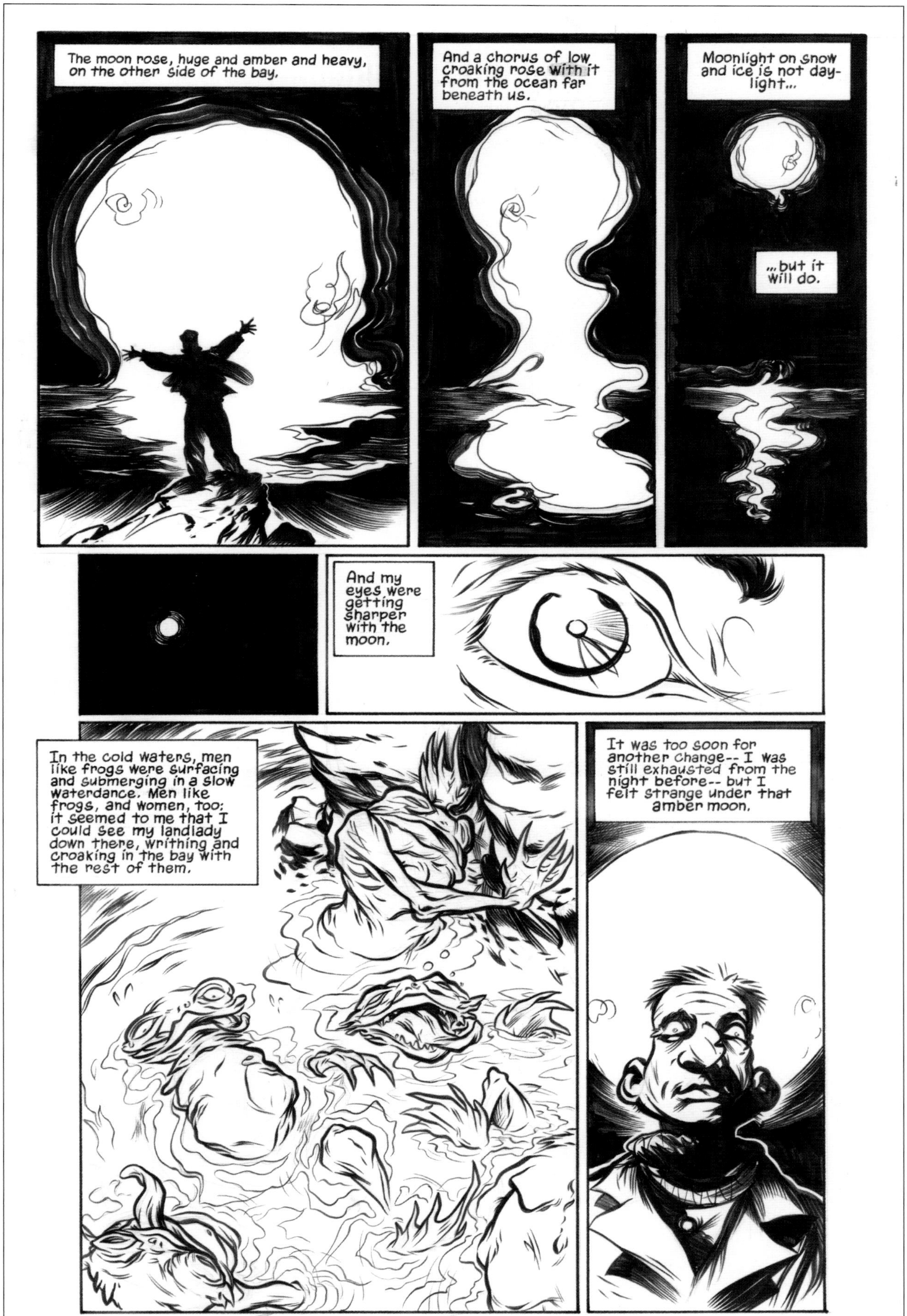
The moon rose, huge and amber and heavy, on the other side of the bay.
And a chorus of low croaking rose with it from the ocean far beneath us.
Moonlight on snow and ice is not daylight...
...but it will do.
And my eyes were getting sharper with the moon.
In the cold waters, men like frogs were surfacing and submerging in a slow waterdance. Men like frogs, and women, too; it seemed to me that I could see my landlady down there, writhing and croaking in the bay with the rest of them.
It was too soon for another change-- I was still exhausted from the night before-- but I felt strange under that amber moon.
TO WALT,
(11)

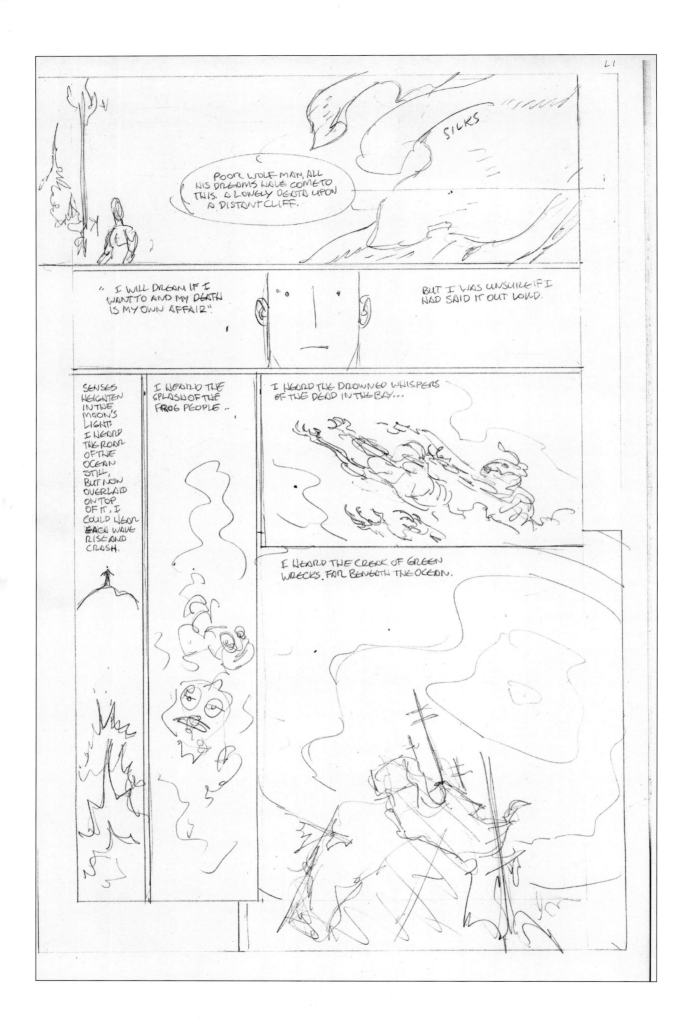

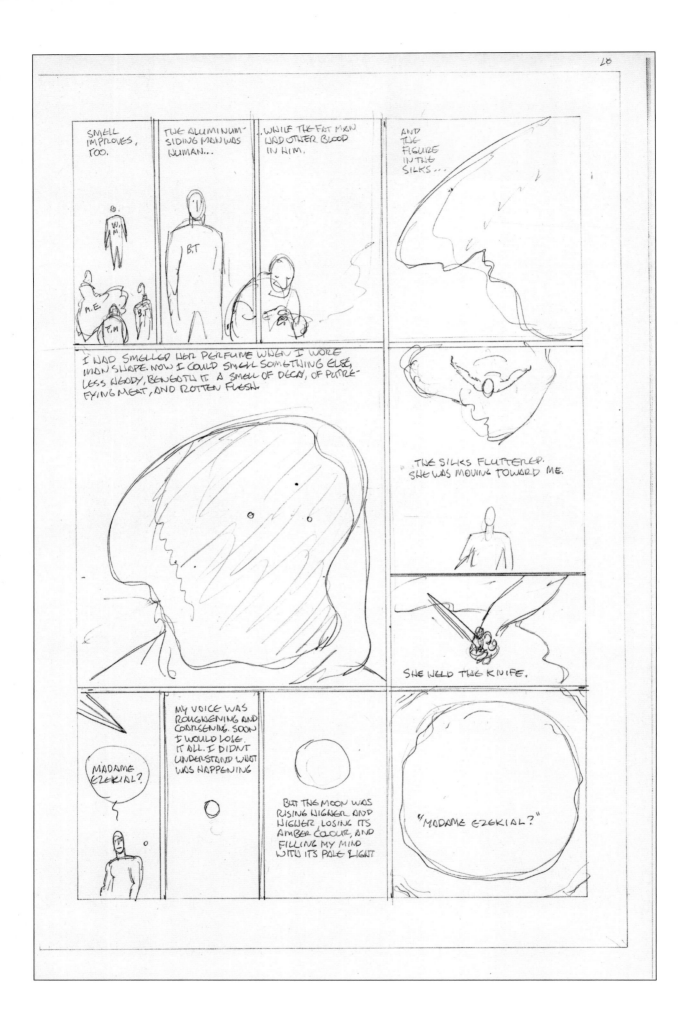

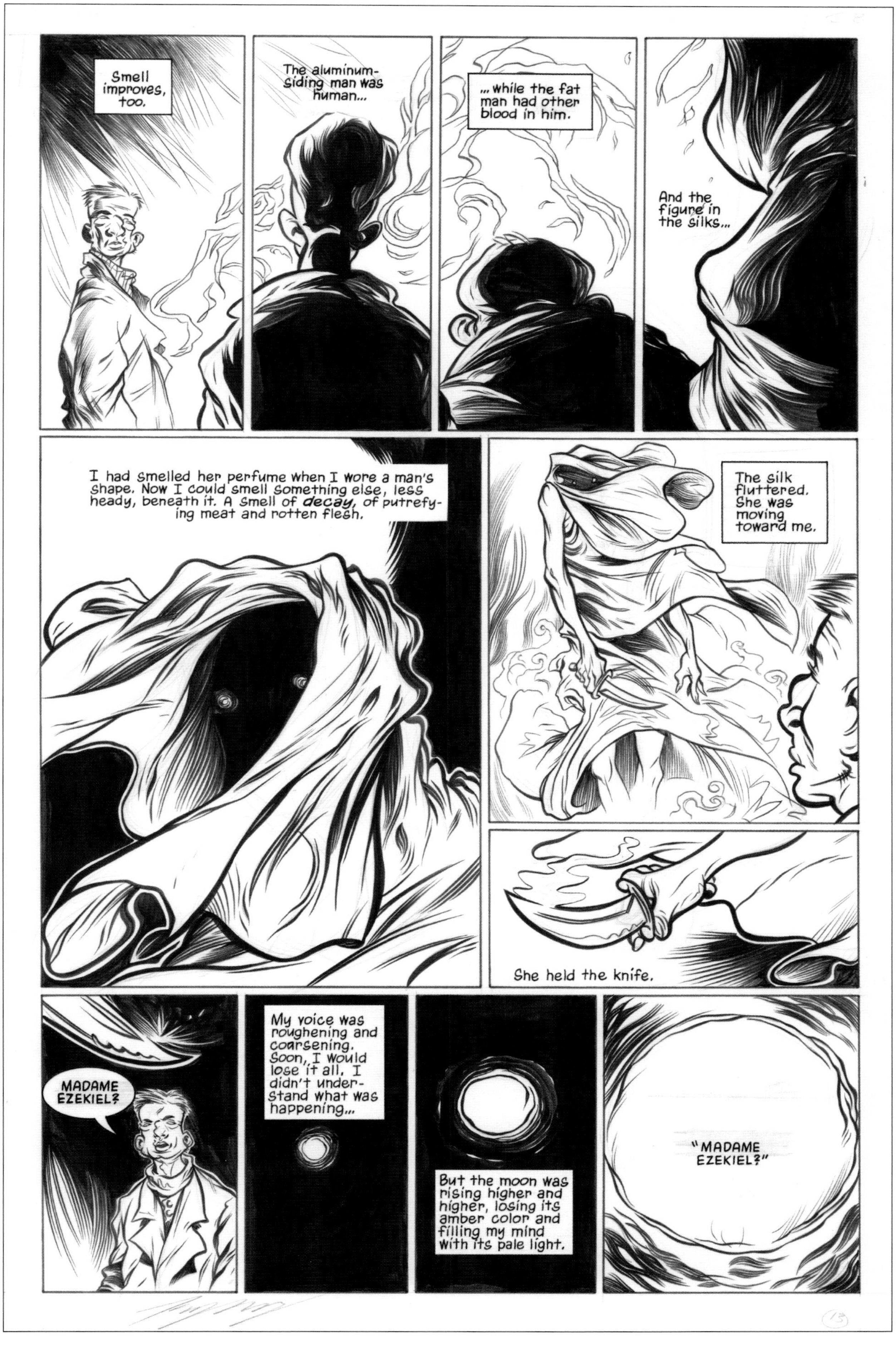
Smell improves, too.
The aluminum-siding man was human...
...while the fat man had other blood in him.
And the figure in the silks...
I had smelled her perfume when I wore a man's shape. Now I could smell something else, less heady, beneath it. A smell of *decay*, of putrefying meat and rotten flesh.
The silk fluttered. She was moving toward me.
She held the knife.
MADAME EZEKIEL?
My voice was roughening and coarsening. Soon, I would lose it all. I didn't understand what was happening...
But the moon was rising higher and higher, losing its amber color and filling my mind with its pale light.
"MADAME EZEKIEL?"

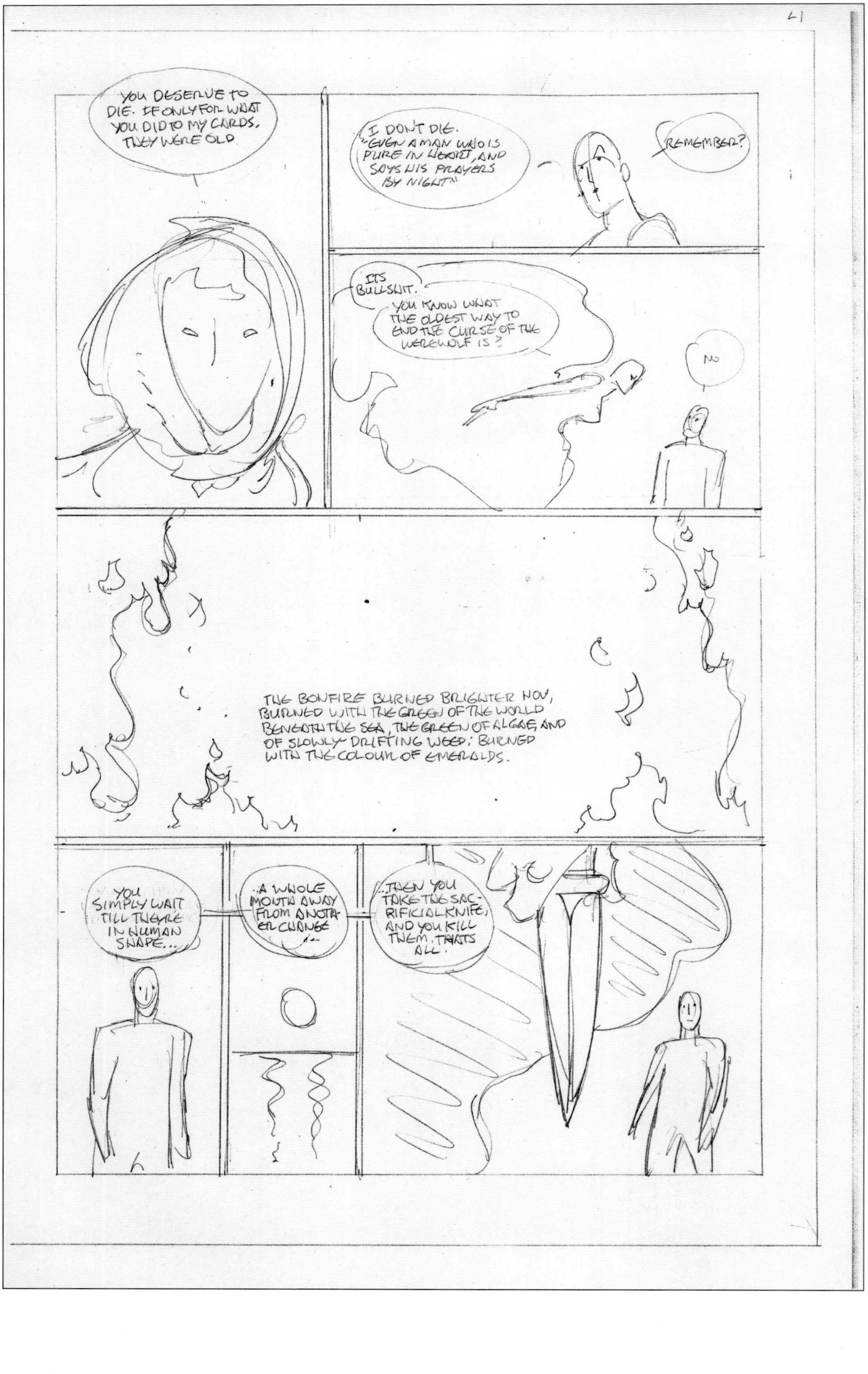
41
YOU DESERVE TO DIE. IF ONLY FOR WHAT YOU DID TO MY CARDS, THEY WERE OLD
I DON'T DIE. "EVEN A MAN WHO IS PURE IN HEART, AND SAYS HIS PRAYERS BY NIGHT"
REMEMBER?
ITS BULLSHIT.
YOU KNOW WHAT THE OLDEST WAY TO END THE CURSE OF THE WEREWOLF IS?
NO
THE BONFIRE BURNED BRIGHTER NOW, BURNED WITH THE GREEN OF THE WORLD BENEATH THE SEA, THE GREEN OF ALGAE, AND OF SLOWLY DRIFTING WEED; BURNED WITH THE COLOUR OF EMERALDS.
YOU SIMPLY WAIT TILL THEY'RE IN HUMAN SHAPE...
..A WHOLE MONTH AWAY FROM ANOTHER CHANGE
..THEN YOU TAKE THE SACRIFICIAL KNIFE, AND YOU KILL THEM. THAT'S ALL.

301

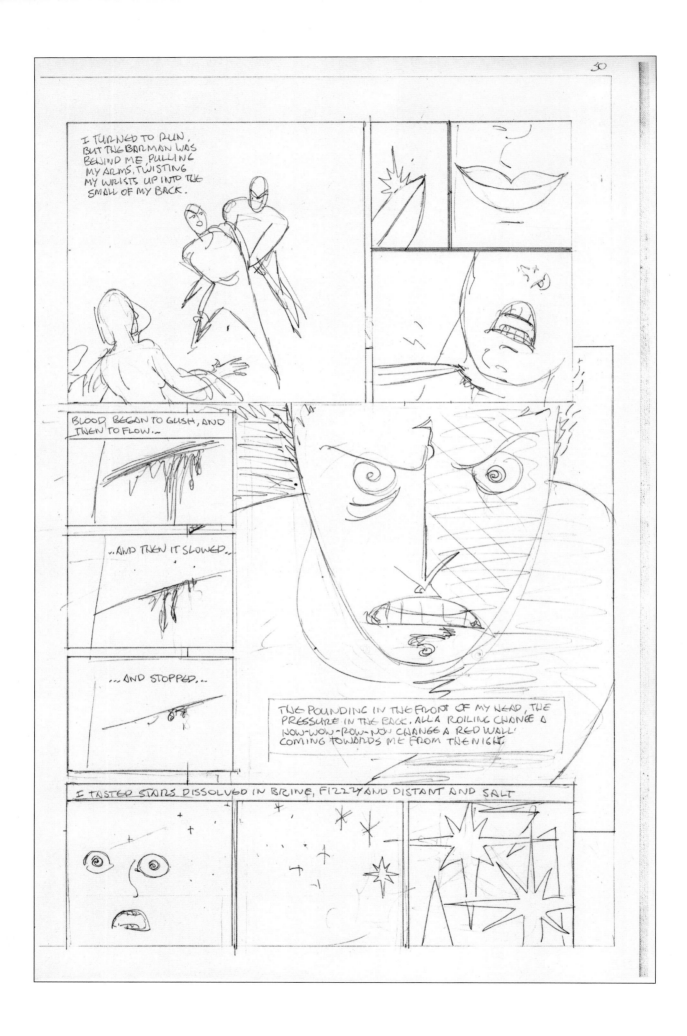

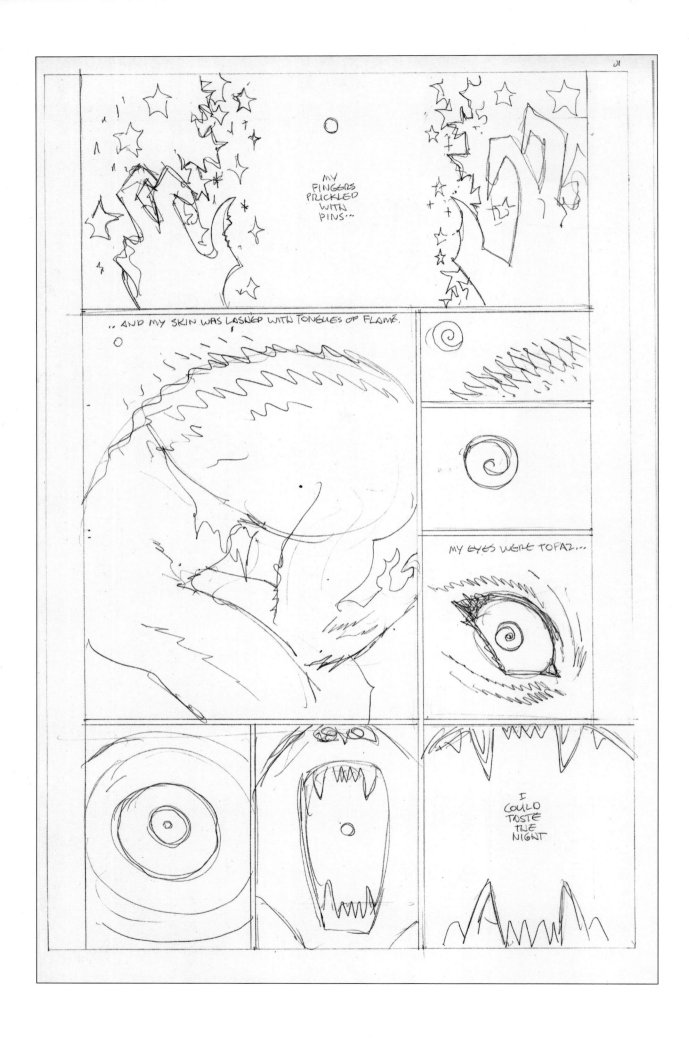

305

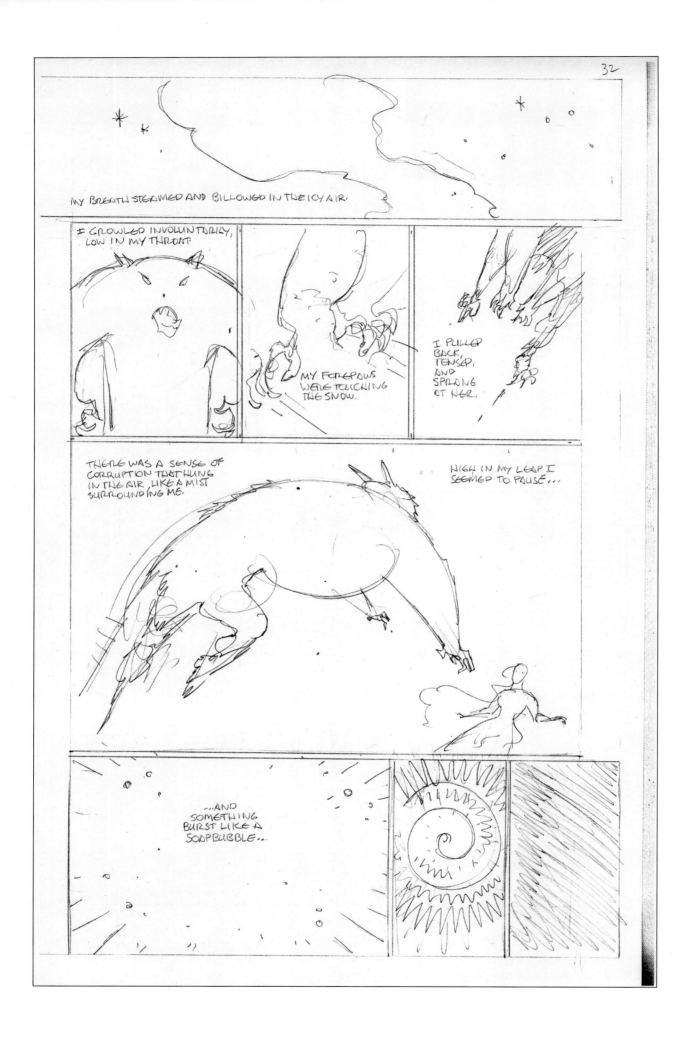

MY BREATH STEAMED AND BILLOWED IN THE ICY AIR.

I GROWLED INVOLUNTARILY, LOW IN MY THROAT.

MY FOREPAWS WERE TOUCHING THE SNOW.

I PULLED BACK, TENSED, AND SPRANG AT HER.

THERE WAS A SENSE OF CORRUPTION THAT HUNG IN THE AIR, LIKE A MIST SURROUNDING ME.

HIGH IN MY LEAP I SEEMED TO PAUSE...

...AND SOMETHING BURST LIKE A SOAP BUBBLE...

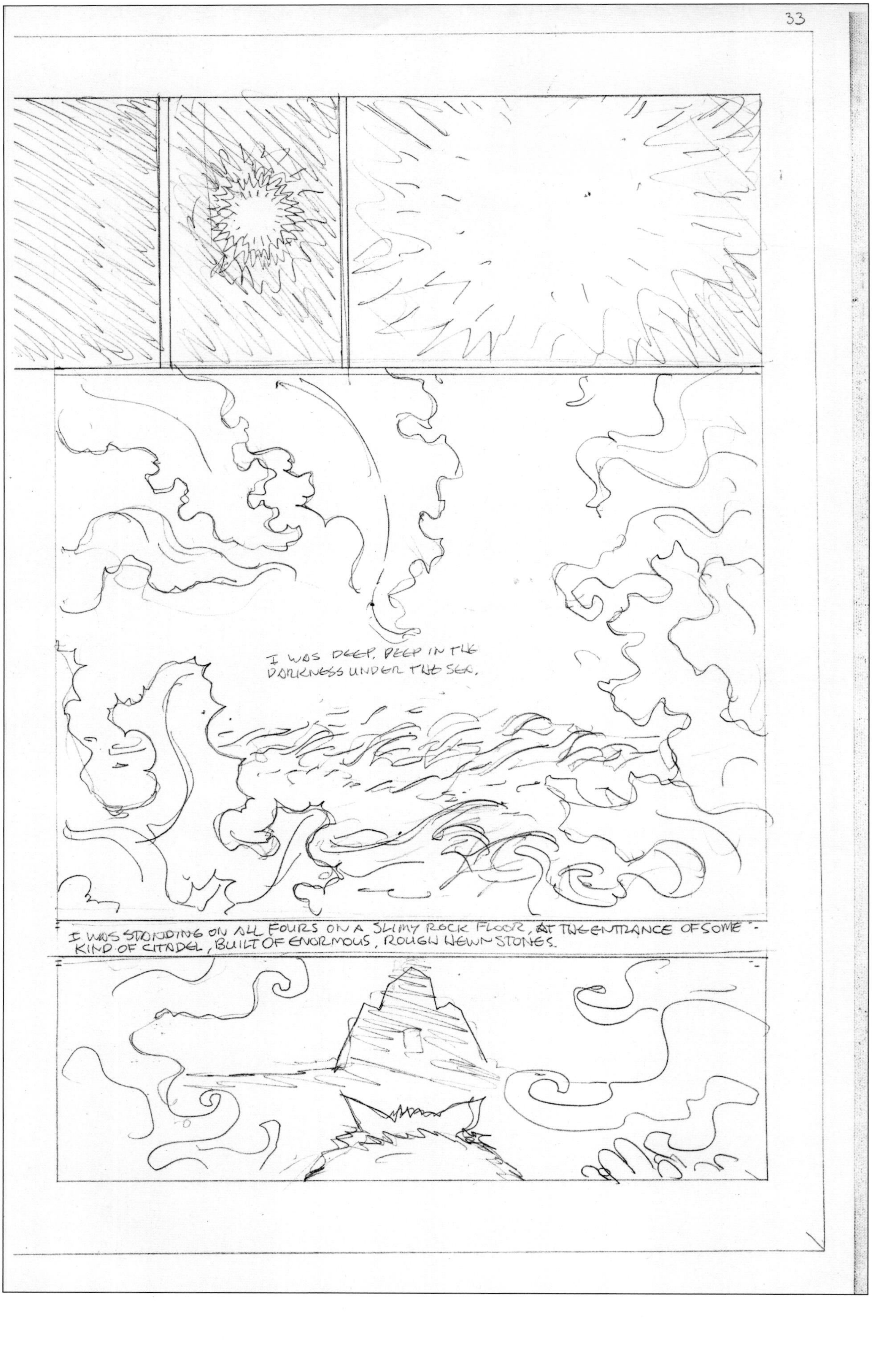
33
I WAS DEEP, DEEP IN THE DARKNESS UNDER THE SEA.
I WAS STANDING ON ALL FOURS ON A SLIMY ROCK FLOOR, AT THE ENTRANCE OF SOME KIND OF CITADEL, BUILT OF ENORMOUS, ROUGH HEWN STONES.

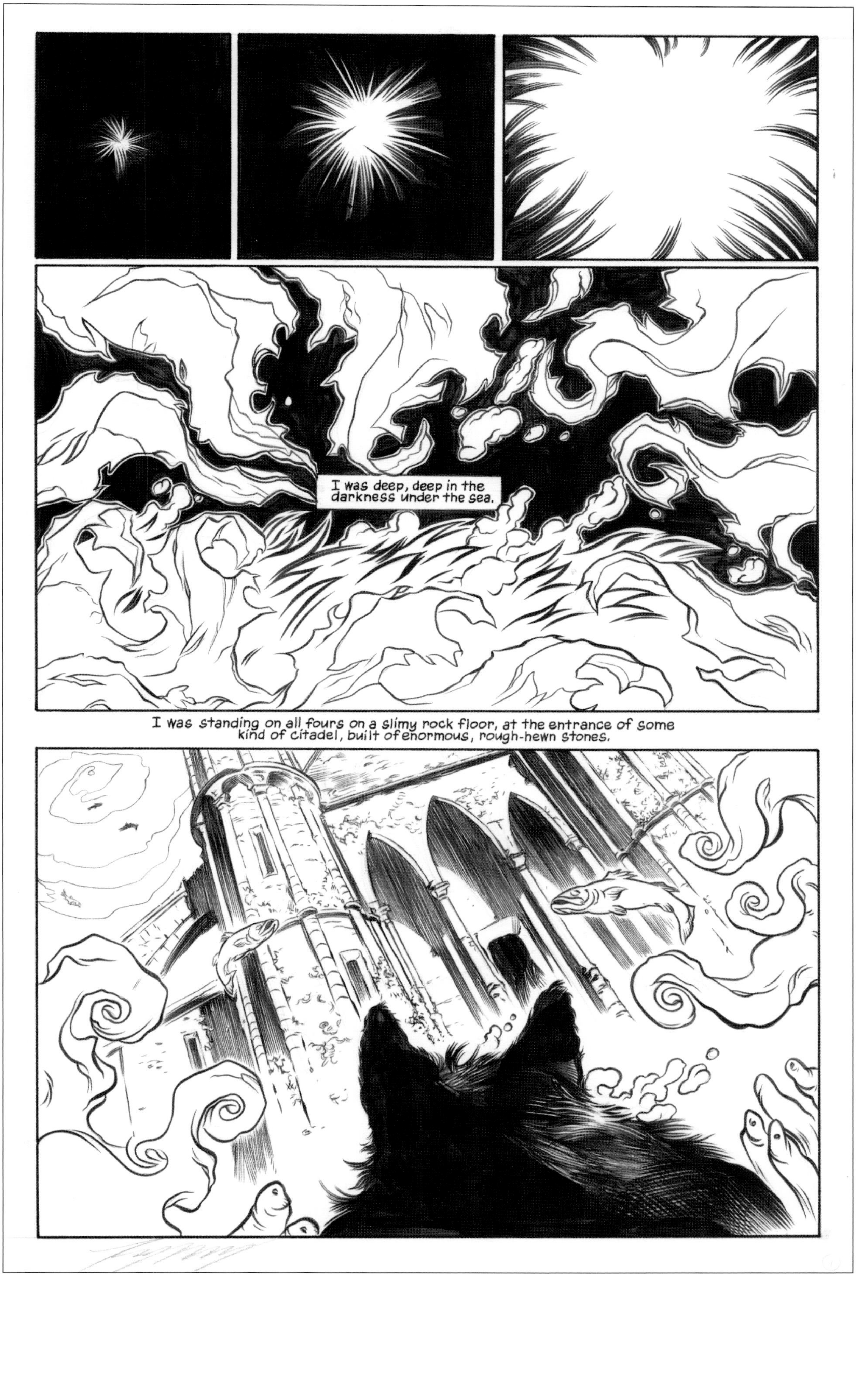
I was deep, deep in the darkness under the sea.
I was standing on all fours on a slimy rock floor, at the entrance of some kind of citadel, built of enormous, rough-hewn stones.

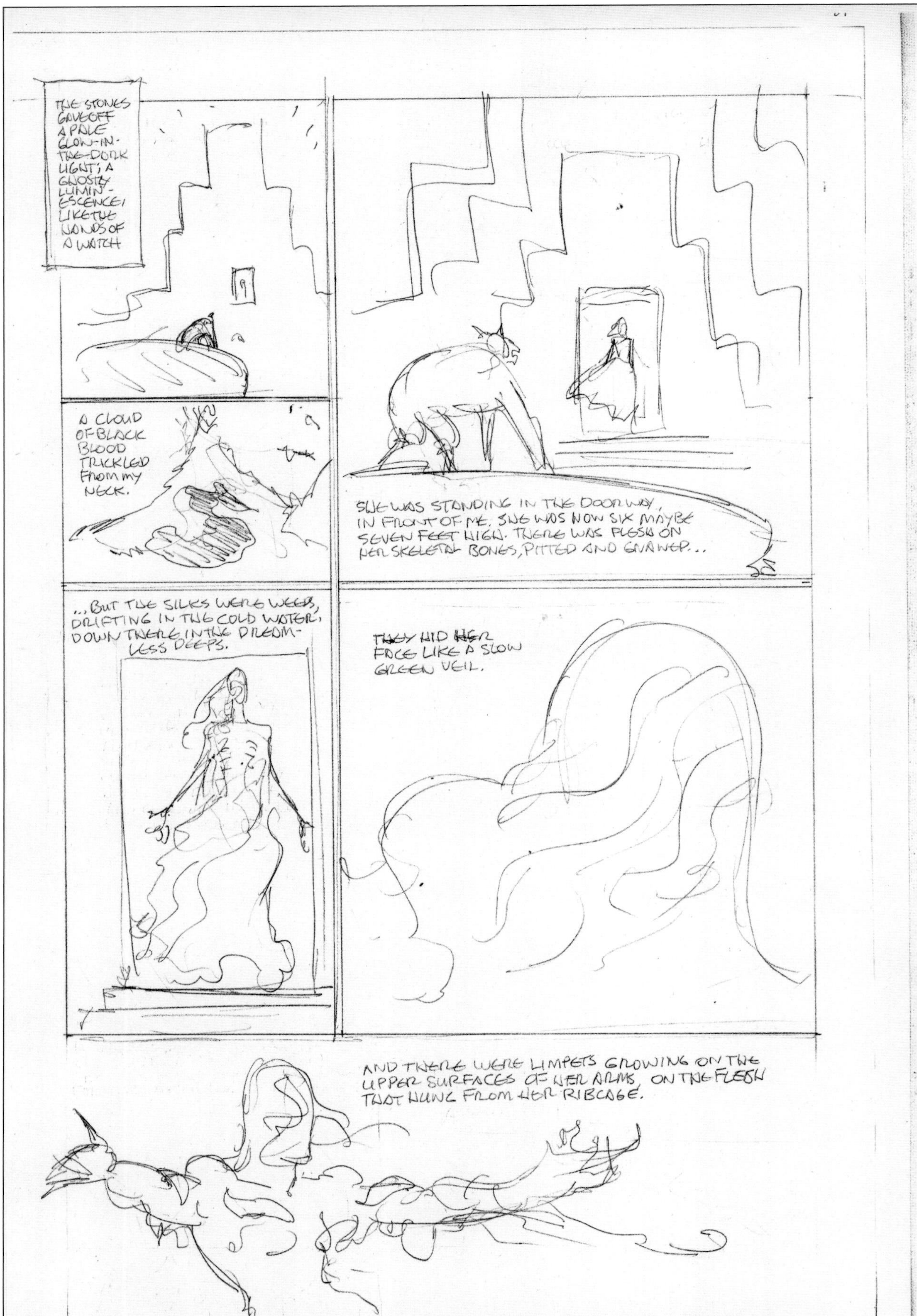
THE STONES GAVE OFF A PALE GLOW-IN-THE-DARK LIGHT; A GHOSTLY LUMIN-ESCENCE, LIKE THE HANDS OF A WATCH
A CLOUD OF BLACK BLOOD TRICKLED FROM MY NECK.
SHE WAS STANDING IN THE DOORWAY, IN FRONT OF ME. SHE WAS NOW SIX MAYBE SEVEN FEET HIGH. THERE WAS FLESH ON HER SKELETAL BONES, PITTED AND GNAWED...
...BUT THE SILKS WERE WEEDS, DRIFTING IN THE COLD WATER, DOWN THERE IN THE DREAM-LESS DEEPS.
THEY HID HER FACE LIKE A SLOW GREEN VEIL.
AND THERE WERE LIMPETS GROWING ON THE UPPER SURFACES OF HER ARMS, ON THE FLESH THAT HUNG FROM HER RIBCAGE.

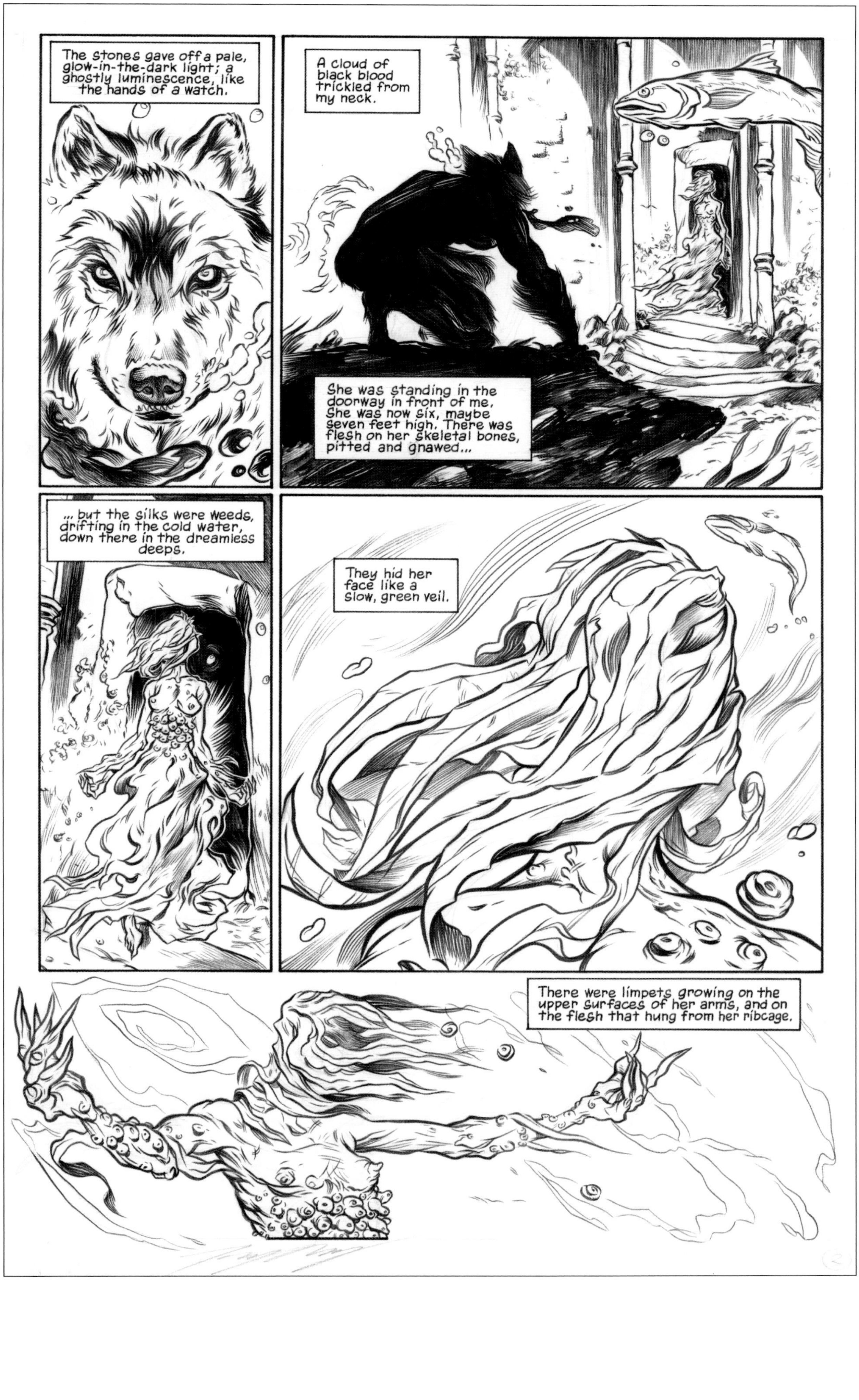
The stones gave off a pale, glow-in-the-dark light; a ghostly luminescence, like the hands of a watch.
A cloud of black blood trickled from my neck.
She was standing in the doorway in front of me, She was now six, maybe seven feet high. There was flesh on her skeletal bones, pitted and gnawed...
... but the silks were weeds, drifting in the cold water, down there in the dreamless deeps.
They hid her face like a slow, green veil.
There were limpets growing on the upper surfaces of her arms, and on the flesh that hung from her ribcage.

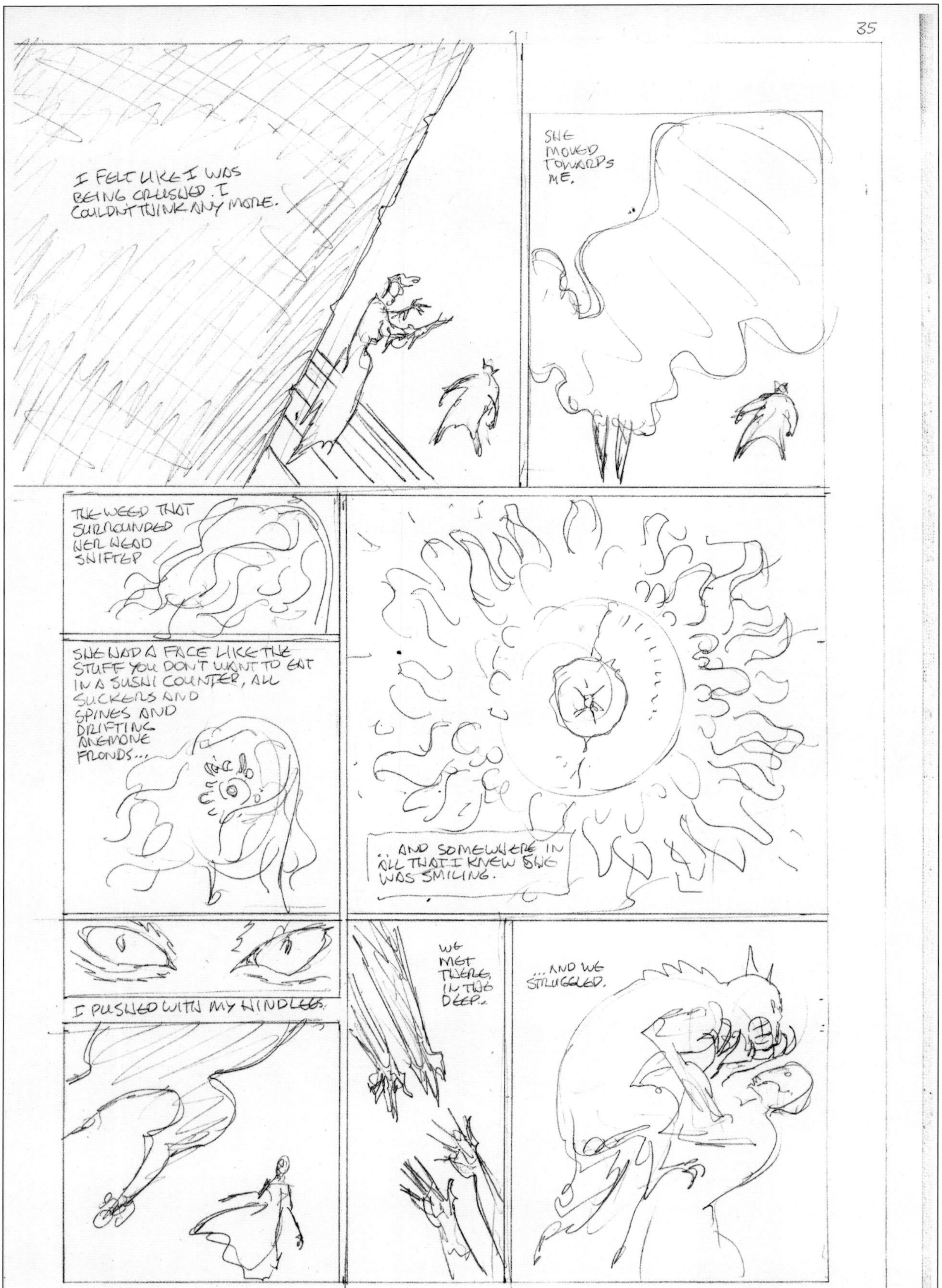
35
I FELT LIKE I WAS BEING CRUSHED. I COULDNT THINK ANY MORE.
SHE MOVED TOWARDS ME.
THE WEED THAT SURROUNDED HER HEAD SHIFTED
SHE HAD A FACE LIKE THE STUFF YOU DON'T WANT TO EAT IN A SUSHI COUNTER, ALL SUCKERS AND SPINES AND DRIFTING ANEMONE FRONDS...
...AND SOMEWHERE IN ALL THAT I KNEW SHE WAS SMILING.
I PUSHED WITH MY HINDLEGS.
WE MET THERE, IN THE DEEP...
...AND WE STRUGGLED.

313

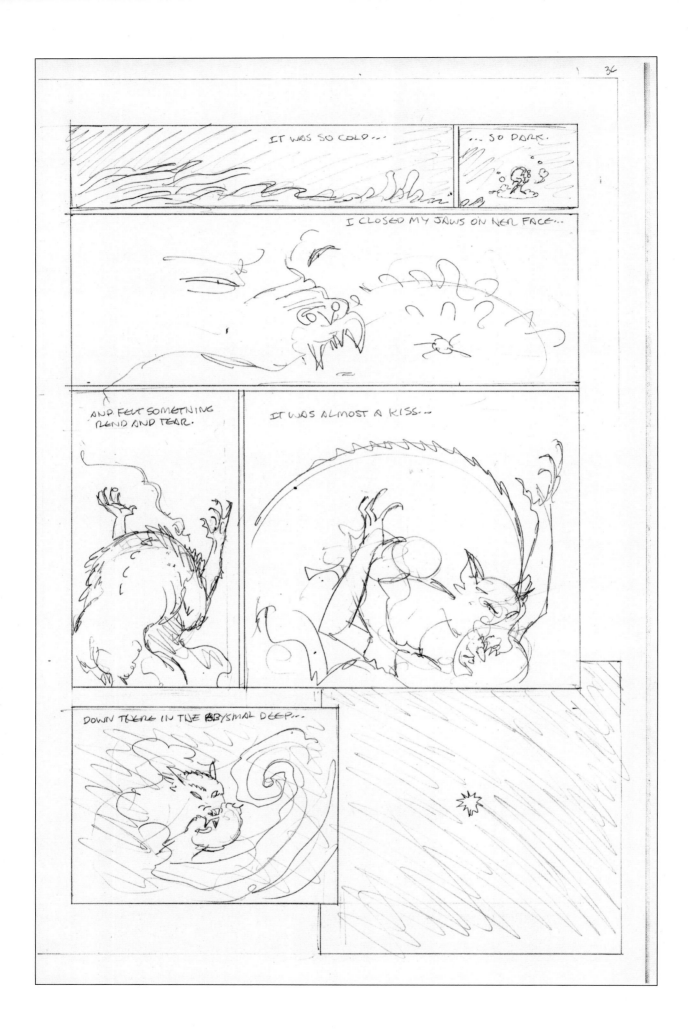

315

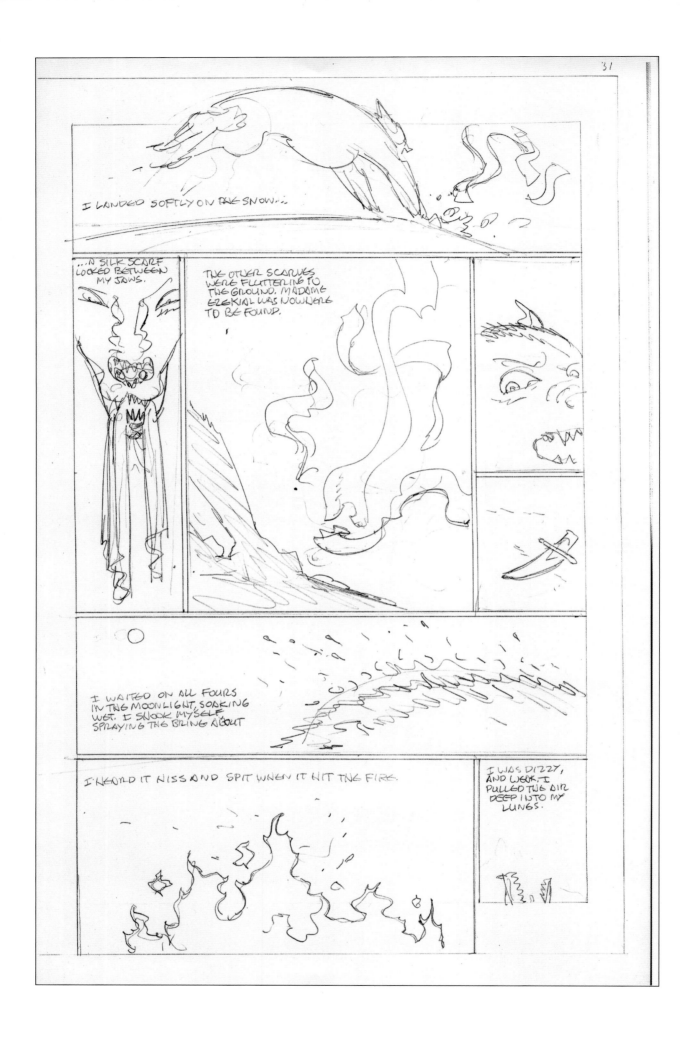

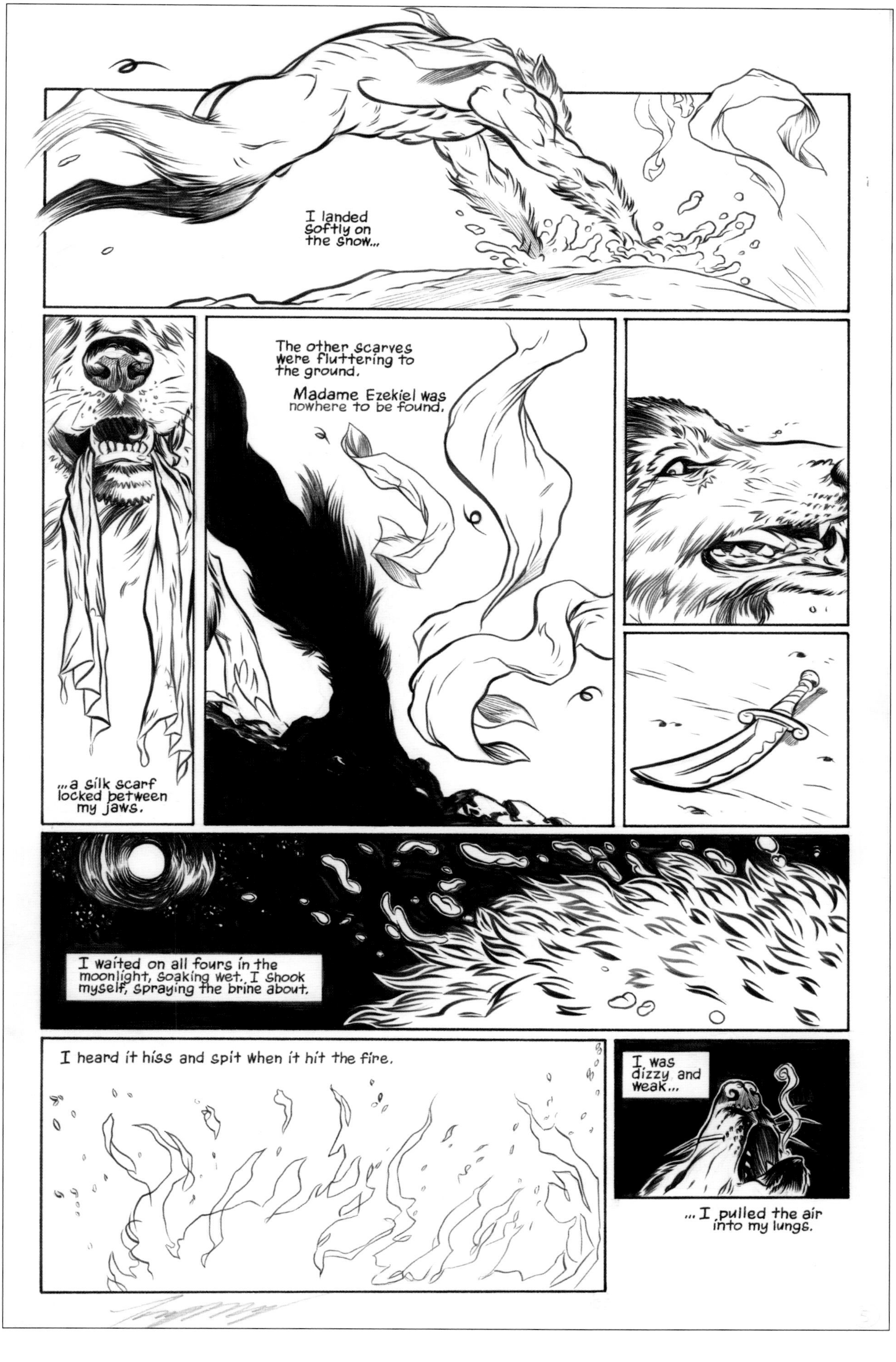
I landed softly on the snow...
...a silk scarf locked between my jaws.
The other scarves were fluttering to the ground.
Madame Ezekiel was nowhere to be found.
I waited on all fours in the moonlight, soaking wet. I shook myself, spraying the brine about.
I heard it hiss and spit when it hit the fire.
I was dizzy and weak...
...I pulled the air into my lungs.

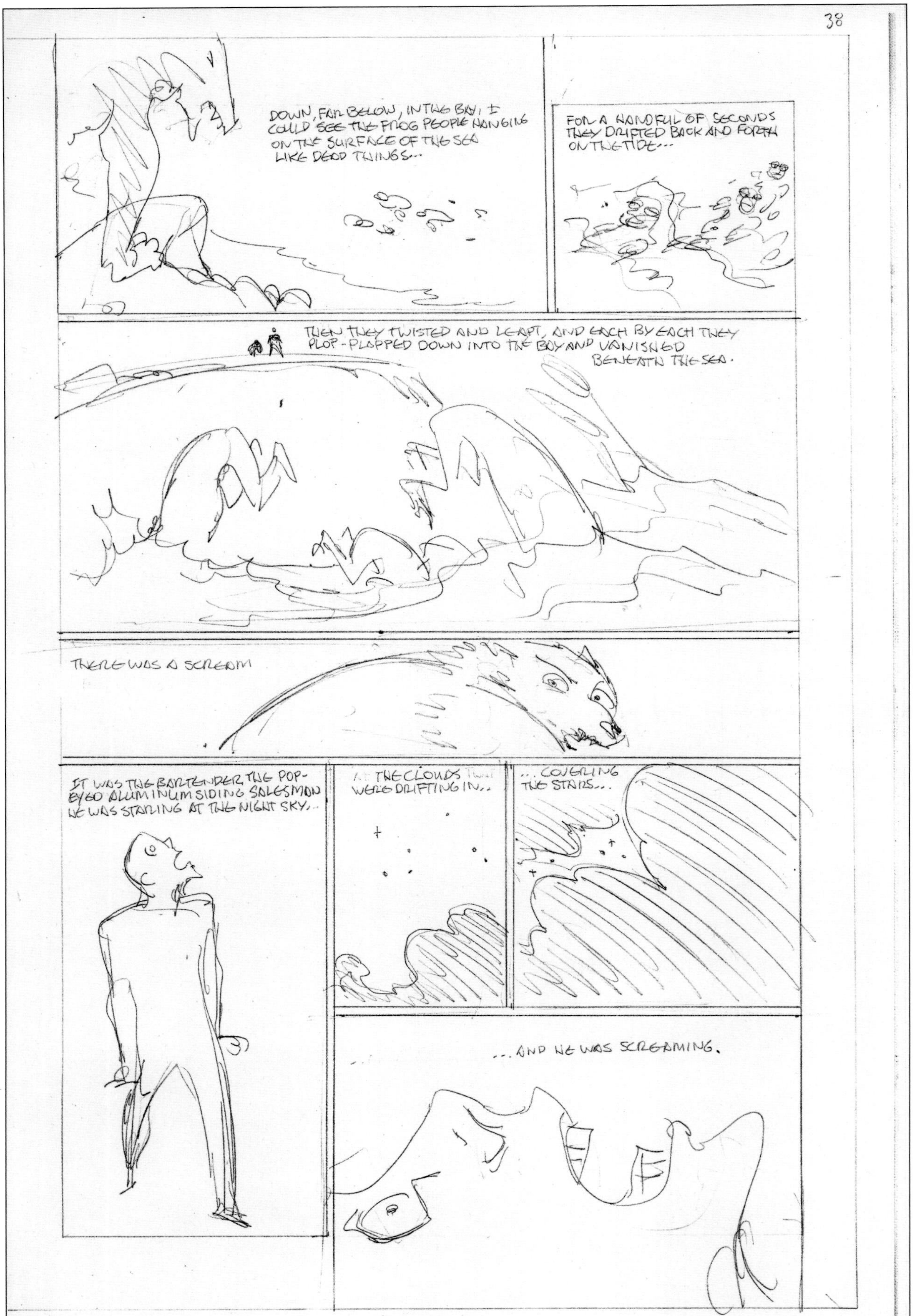
38
DOWN, FAR BELOW, IN THE BAY, I COULD SEE THE FROG PEOPLE HANGING ON THE SURFACE OF THE SEA LIKE DEAD THINGS...
FOR A HANDFUL OF SECONDS THEY DRIFTED BACK AND FORTH ON THE TIDE...
THEN THEY TWISTED AND LEAPT, AND EACH BY EACH THEY PLOP-PLOPPED DOWN INTO THE BAY AND VANISHED BENEATH THE SEA.
THERE WAS A SCREAM
IT WAS THE BARTENDER THE POP-EYED ALUMINUM SIDING SALESMAN HE WAS STARING AT THE NIGHT SKY...
AT THE CLOUDS THAT WERE DRIFTING IN..
...COVERING THE STARS...
...AND HE WAS SCREAMING.

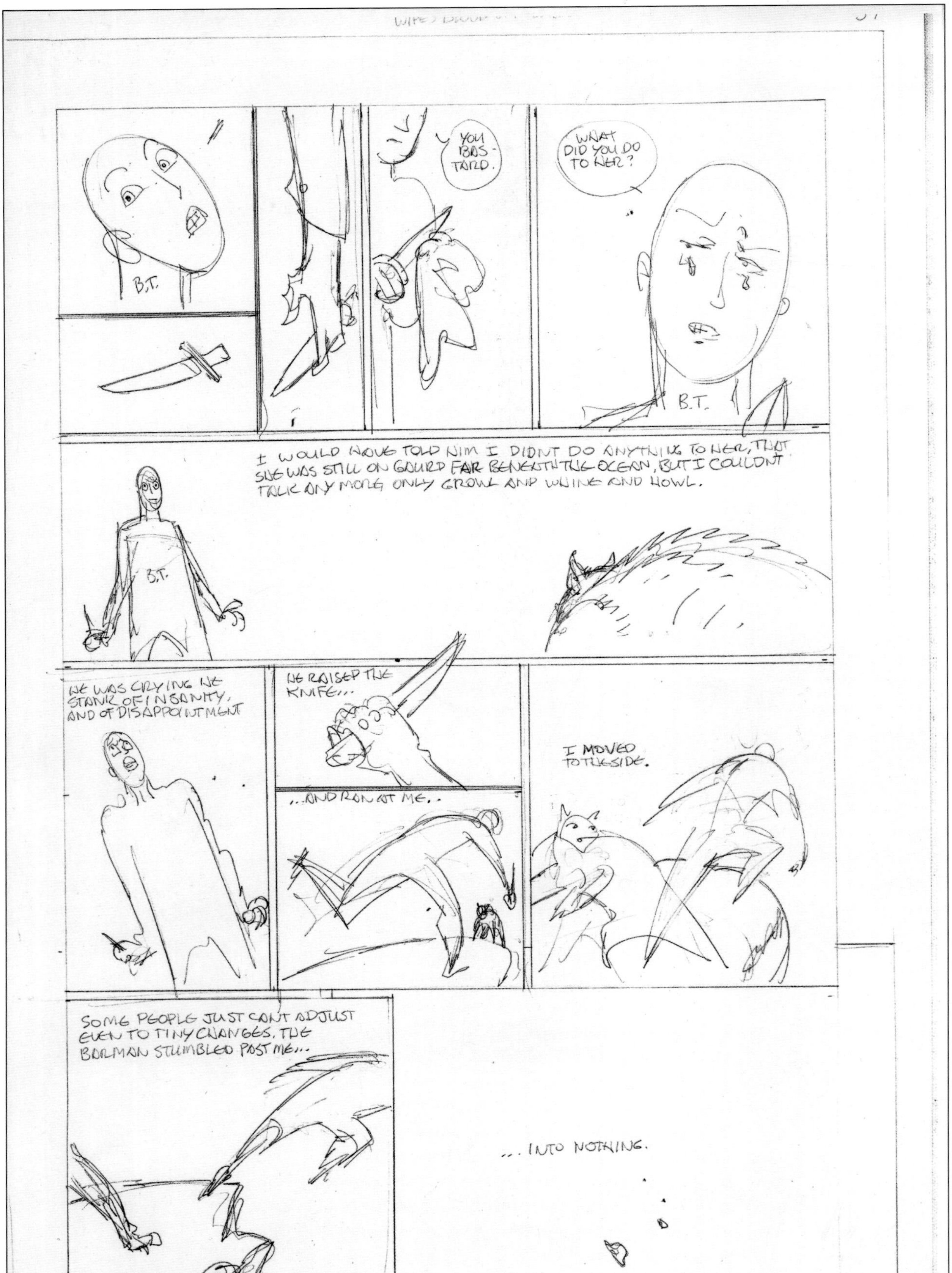

B.T.
YOU BASTARD.
WHAT DID YOU DO TO HER?
B.T.
I WOULD HAVE TOLD HIM I DIDNT DO ANYTHING TO HER, THAT SHE WAS STILL ON GOURD FAR BENEATH THE OCEAN, BUT I COULDNT TALK ANY MORE ONLY GROWL AND WHINE AND HOWL.
B.T.
HE WAS CRYING HE STANK OF INSANITY, AND OF DISAPPOINTMENT
HE RAISED THE KNIFE...
...AND RAN AT ME...
I MOVED TO THE SIDE.
SOME PEOPLE JUST CANT ADJUST EVEN TO TINY CHANGES. THE BARMAN STUMBLED PAST ME...
...INTO NOTHING.